BUSINESS WEEK BESTSELLER ▪ OVER 300,000 COPIES SOLD

START YOUR OWN BUSINESS

the *only* startup book you'll ever need

BY THE STAFF OF ENTREPRENEUR MEDIA, INC.

Ep
Entrepreneur
PRESS®

Entrepreneur Press, Publisher
Cover Design: Andrew Welyczko
Production and Composition: Eliot House Productions

Library of Congress Cataloging-in-Publication Data

Start your own business / by The Staff of Entrepreneur Media, Inc.—6th edition.
pages cm.
Revised edition of Start your own business : the only startup book you'll ever need, 5th ed., published in 2010.
ISBN-13: 978-1-59918-556-9 (alk. paper)
ISBN-10: 1-59918-556-3 (alk. paper)
1. New business enterprises—Management. 2. Small business--Management. I. Entrepreneur Media, Inc.
HD62.5.E559 2015
658'.041—dc23 2014035843

Printed in the United States of America

18 17 16 15 14 10 9 8 7 6 5 4 3 2 1

Contents

ON YOUR MARK . . .

PART 1
THINK

PART 2
PLAN

PART 3
FUND

GET SET

PART 4
PREPARE

PART 5
BUY

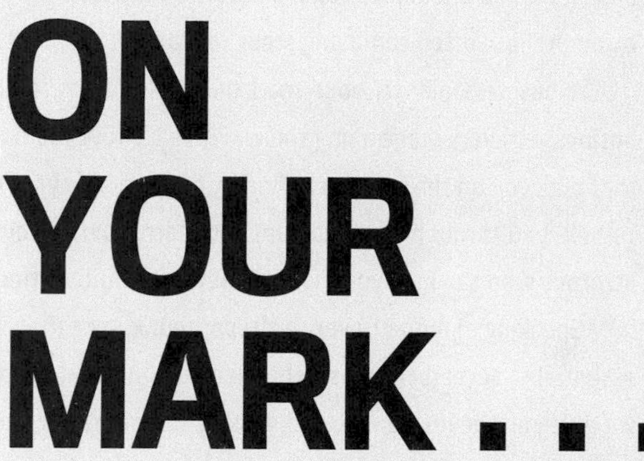

ON YOUR MARK . . .

Why did you pick up this book? Perhaps you know you want to be an entrepreneur and take charge of your own life. You've already got a great idea for a business you're sure will be a hit. Or perhaps you think, somewhere in the back of your mind, that maybe you might like to start your own business but you're not sure what venture to start, what entrepreneurship is really like, and whether it's for you.

Whichever of these categories you fall into, you've come to the right place. In Part 1, "Think," we'll show you what it means to be an entrepreneur. Use our personal goals and objectives worksheet to decide if entrepreneurship is right for you. Don't have a business idea, or not sure if your idea will fly? You'll learn the secrets to spotting trends before they happen and for coming up with dozens of surefire business ideas. We'll also discuss various ways of going into business, including part- and full-time entrepreneurship. Finally, we'll show you the different options for startup, such as starting from scratch, purchasing an existing business, or buying into a franchise or business opportunity system.

Planning is key to every thriving business. In Part 2, "Plan," you'll learn just what you need to do to lay the groundwork for success. Find out how to pinpoint your target market, plus dozens of ways to do market research—from hiring experts to money-saving do-it-yourself tips. Since the name you choose can make or break your business, we share plenty of techniques for coming up with the perfect moniker—one that will attract customers to your company in droves. And don't forget the nuts-and-bolts necessities like choosing a legal structure—corporation, partnership, sole proprietorship and more. You'll discover all the information you need to guide you through these often confusing steps to startup.

A business plan is your road map to success, guiding the growth of your business at every stage along the way. We'll show you how to craft a business plan that puts you on the fast track. Finally, find out why you need professional advisors to help you through your startup, and learn how to select an accountant and an attorney who can help you make money—without costing you a bundle.

Speaking of money, every entrepreneur knows that adequate startup capital is essential to success. But just where do you find that crucial cash? In Part 3, "Fund," we give you the inside scoop on getting the money you need, plus discover dozens of sources of capital. We will show you secrets to financing your business yourself, how to tap into the most common source of startup financing (family and friends), plus places you may never have thought of to look for money. We'll also introduce you to the idea of turning to the crowd for funding.

Do you stand a chance of getting venture capital or attracting private investors? You'll find out in this section. And if you're looking for a loan, look no further for the secrets to finding the right bank. We explain what bankers look for when evaluating a loan application—and how to make sure yours makes the grade. Seeking money from Uncle Sam? You'll learn all the details about dozens of loan programs from the government, including special assistance for women and minority entrepreneurs. Whatever your needs, you're sure to find a financing source that's right for you.

As they say, "there's no time like the present," so grab a cup of coffee, get comfortable, and let's start creating your business!

PART

1

THINK

CHAPTER

1

Introduction

With the purchase of this book, you've taken your first step on the road to entrepreneurship. It's not a step to be taken lightly, which is why buying this book may be the smartest thing you'll ever do for your business.

Start Your Own Business can have a major impact on your life. We meet people all the time who tell us how this book or *Entrepreneur* magazine changed their lives—and few are sorry they took the leap into business ownership. Whether or not they have succeeded, almost no one regrets the journey.

Start Your Own Business is designed as a road map to help you plan a course for your own journey to business ownership. We're here to show you the best routes to take, help you avoid the potholes and road closures, and navigate the curves and detours.

Some will tell you that the journey you're about to take is a hazardous one—but not with us at your side! *Start Your Own Business* prepares you every step of the way. We're here to instruct and encourage you, to show you new ways to do things and remind you of the tried and true. You wouldn't go on an adventure without the proper gear. Think of *Start Your Own Business* as part of your entrepreneurship gear kit. Refer to it every step of the way, starting with how to get an idea for a business to finally opening the doors to your new venture. Along the way, we provide lots of forms, worksheets, and checklists you can actually use in your business to make sure you're on the right track.

Since business ideas, trends, and strategies constantly change, we strive to keep *Start Your Own Business* up-to-date. For the sixth edition, we've updated and revised (or expanded) every chapter and added a lot of new ones, too. In fact, Part 7, "Engage," is updated with new sections on social media campaigns and on building an incredible web presence that will get your idea noticed.

We start by showing you how to get visitors to your website, keep them there, and make sure they return for more. Next, we move on to social media marketing and networking. If you haven't jumped on the social media bandwagon yet, your business can't afford to be left behind. We show you how to use social tools to network with potential customers, and connect and engage with your audience, because in today's marketing landscape, that's how brands are built.

We have also added chapters on running your business virtually, using the latest smartphone, tablet, and computer technology to connect seamlessly, and on funding options that were never before available, such as crowdfunding platforms.

Many business resources and tip boxes (see examples on the next page) have been updated for the sixth edition.

Finally, there's an appendix that's chock full of resources with contact information. We list business associations, federal agencies, books, magazines, and other publications in areas ranging from advertising and marketing to accounting and taxes. We even provide internet resources and equipment manufacturers.

aha!

Here you will find helpful information or ideas you may not have thought of before.

tip

This box gives you ideas on how to do something better or more efficiently, or simply how to work smarter.

warning

Heed the warnings in this box to avoid common mistakes and pitfalls.

e-fyi

This box points you to the treasures of the internet for more information.

save

Look for this box to provide valuable tips on ways you can save money during startup.

Starting your own business isn't as frightening or risky as some would have you believe. But it's a journey that shouldn't be taken alone—and that's why you bought *Start Your Own Business*. We're glad you've chosen us to take this exciting journey with you—you'll be a smarter traveler for it. Let the journey begin.

CHAPTER

2

Taking the Plunge

Get Ready to Be an Entrepreneur

Before they get started, some people worry if they have what it takes to be an entrepreneur. If this is you, stop worrying. We firmly believe anyone with the desire and the initiative can be an entrepreneur. And since you purchased this book, it's likely you have both the desire and the initiative.

But just because you can be an entrepreneur doesn't mean that now is the right time to take the plunge. This chapter will help you determine if you're ready for entrepreneurship right now or if you should hold off for a bit.

The Entrepreneurial Personality

Every year, hundreds of thousands of people start their own businesses. But while most succeed (yes, that's the truth!), many

warning

If you have a family, make sure they understand the emotional and financial sacrifices business success requires. When your family doesn't support your business—if they're always saying, "Can't you leave that alone and come to dinner?"—it's going to be tough to make your business work. If your family isn't ready for you to become an entrepreneur, this may not be the right time to do it.

do fail. Why? One of the common causes of startup failure is lack of preparation.

People come to the entrepreneurial path from different directions. Increasingly, some start fresh out of college or after a stint at home raising their kids or simply because the idea of actually retiring is abhorrent to them. Most, though, come to entrepreneurship straight out of the work force. And many of them dabble in their would-be business before they take the plunge completely, testing ideas on the side, while maintaining a day job. Quitting a full-time job to start a business isn't something to be taken lightly. You should be sure now is the right time to get started. First, you need to ask yourself some questions: Do I have enough money? If you have a family, are they ready for this? Is there a need for a product or service like mine? Parts 1, 2, and 3 of this book will help you answer those questions.

Full Steam Ahead

Many successful entrepreneurs say a sense of urgency that made starting their businesses not just a desire but a necessity was their driving force. One entrepreneur's advice: "You'll know the time is right when you can honestly say 'I'll put my house, jewelry, and other personal collateral on the line to attain the startup money I need for the long-term rewards I deserve.'" We're not recommending you put up your home (though more than a few entrepreneurs started that way). But that willingness to risk everything likely means you're ready to start now.

What motivates potential entrepreneurs to stop daydreaming about business ownership and actually do something about it? While many people think one single incident—such as getting fired or being passed over for a promotion—is the impetus for becoming your own boss, most experts agree it's usually a series of frustrations that leads to entrepreneurship.

A fundamental desire to control their own destinies ranks very high on most entrepreneurs' lists of reasons for starting their own businesses. This need is so strong that entrepreneurs will risk family, future, and careers to be their own boss. Unable to feel truly fulfilled working for someone else, these individuals cannot be happy following someone else's plan or taking orders from a boss. They're often convinced that they have a better way, or an idea that would really revolutionize their industry—or at least their little corner of it—and working within a corporate structure is simply stifling that improvement.

But opportunity comes in many guises. It might be when potential customers start calling you, or perhaps a business in your area is failing and you know you can make it work. Or maybe you feel as if you're underemployed (working below your potential salary or your skill level) or not putting your skills and talents to their best use. Perhaps there's a need for the product or service you want to provide. Or you've simply figured out a better or a new way to do something.

e-fyi

Need inspiration? Check out Ted.com/talks for inspirational talks on almost any topic, all advice and messages you can use to empower yourself to live the life you desire. While the site's subject matter covers everything from fitness to raising kids, its target audience is anybody with an entrepreneurial spirit. Speakers of all kinds—including many entrepreneurs—offer new ideas, inspiring thoughts, and powerful motivation.

Reality Check

Once you've made the decision to break away, there are several things you should do before taking the next step. Conducting thorough market research is a must. Make sure you have enough cash—not only for the business, but to sustain your life—and discuss the decision with your family. (You'll find out more about all these steps in Parts 1, 2, and 3 of this book.)

Remember, the rewards of small-business ownership are not instantaneous. You must be determined, patient, persistent, and willing to make sacrifices to ensure those rewards eventually do come.

You'll need to prepare for the responsibilities that come with business ownership. When things go wrong, the buck stops with you. You won't have the luxury of going home at 5 o'clock while the boss stays all night to fix a chaotic situation. Someone whose only desire is to get rich quick probably won't last long owning his or her own business.

Through surveys and research, we know that successful entrepreneurs share some common personality traits, the most important of which is confidence. They possess confidence not only in themselves but also in their ability to sell their ideas, set up a business, and trust their intuition along the way. Small business is fiercely competitive, and it's the business owners with confidence who survive.

Your Strengths and Weaknesses

It's rare that one person possesses all the qualities needed to be successful in business. Everyone has strong suits and weak points. What's important is to understand your strengths and weaknesses. To do this, you need to evaluate the major achievements in your personal and professional life and the skills you used to accomplish them. The following steps can help:

1. *Create a personal resume.* Compose a resume that lists your professional and personal experiences as well as your expertise. For each job, describe the duties you were responsible for and the degree of your success. Include professional skills, educational background, hobbies, and accomplishments that required expertise or special knowledge.

   When complete, this resume will give you a better idea of the kind of business that best suits your interests and experience.
2. *Analyze your personal attributes.* Are you friendly and self-motivated? Are you a hard worker? Do you have common sense? Are you well-organized? Evaluating your personal attributes reveals your likes and dislikes as well as strengths and

e-fyi

There are more than 8,000 groups with nearly 2.4 million members worldwide dedicated to entrepreneurs on Meetup.com at entrepreneur.meetup.com. Find one that suits you and you can "meet up" with individuals or for entrepreneurial events, networking, support, and even socializing.

>> From the Horse's Mouth

One of the best ways to determine if now is the best time to start a business is to meet with other entrepreneurs and see what they do and how they do it. Looking at their life and talking about entrepreneurship can help you figure out if you're ready.

Often when you talk to someone who's done it, they'll tell you all the negative things about owning a business, like the time they had to work a 24-hour day or when the power went out right as they were trying to meet a huge deadline. But those are the things you need to hear about before you get started.

In addition to meeting with successful entrepreneurs, you might want to talk to a few who weren't so successful. Find out what went wrong with their ventures so you can avoid these problems.

Many potential business owners find it useful to attend entrepreneurial seminars or classes. You can often find such courses at community colleges, continuing education programs near you, or online. Others seek assistance from consulting firms that specialize in helping small businesses get off the ground. There are associations and organizations, both private and public such as Service Corps of Retired Executives (SCORE) or the Small Business Development Centers that are eager to assist you. Don't hesitate to ask for assistance. These people want to help you succeed.

weaknesses. If you don't feel comfortable around other people, then a business that requires a lot of customer interaction might not be right for you. Or you may want to hire a "people person" to handle customer service.

3. *Analyze your professional attributes.* Small-business owners wear many different hats, but that doesn't mean you have to be a jack-of-all-trades. Just be aware of the areas where you're competent and the areas where you need help, such as sales, marketing, advertising, and administration. Next to each function, record your competency level—excellent, good, fair, or poor.

Go for the Goal

In addition to evaluating your strengths and weaknesses, it's important to define your business goals. For some people, the goal is the freedom to do what they want when they want, without anyone telling them otherwise. For others, the goal is financial security.

tip 

Once you understand your strengths and weaknesses, there are three ways to deal with them: You can either improve in the areas where you are weak (by taking a class in bookkeeping, for example), hire an employee to handle these aspects of the business (for instance, hiring a bookkeeper), or outsource the tasks (such as contracting an outside company to do your bookkeeping). Outsourcing small tasks and one-off assignments to experts at reasonable rates has become much simpler with formal work-for-hire freelancer websites like Odesk.com.

Setting goals is an integral part of choosing the business that's right for you. After all, if your business doesn't meet your personal goals, you probably won't be happy waking up each morning and trying to make the business a success. Sooner or later, you'll stop putting forth the effort needed to make the concept work. When setting goals, aim for the following qualities:

- *Specificity.* You have a better chance of achieving a goal if it is specific. "Raising capital" isn't a specific goal; "raising $10,000 by July 1" is.
- *Optimism.* Be positive when you set your goals. "Being able to pay the bills" isn't exactly an inspirational goal. "Achieving financial security" phrases your goal in a more positive manner, thus firing up your energy to attain it.
- *Realism.* If you set a goal to earn $100,000 a month when you've never earned that much in a year, that goal is unrealistic. Begin with small steps, such as increasing your monthly income by 25 percent. Once your first goal is met, you can reach for larger ones.
- *Short and long term.* Short-term goals are attainable in a period of weeks to a year. Long-term goals can be for five, ten, or even 20 years; they should be substantially greater than short-term goals but should still be realistic.

There are several factors to consider when setting goals:

- *Income.* Many entrepreneurs go into business to achieve financial security. Consider how much money you want to make during your first year of operation and each year thereafter, up to five years.
- *Lifestyle.* This includes areas such as travel, hours of work, investment of personal assets, and geographic location. Are you willing to travel extensively or to move? How many hours are you willing to work? Which assets are you willing to risk?
- *Type of work.* When setting goals for type of work, you need to determine whether you like working outdoors, in an office, with computers, on the phone, with lots of people, with children, and so on.
- *Ego gratification.* Face it: Many people go into business to satisfy their egos. Owning a business can be very ego-gratifying, especially if you're in a business that's considered glamorous or exciting. You need to decide how important ego gratification is to you and what business best fills that need.

e-fyi

The Online Women's Business Center has a lot to offer women—and men, too—from answering questions about financing businesses or becoming an international company to finding a mentor. Check it out at www.onlinewbc.gov, which is part of sba.gov.

The most important rule of self-evaluation and goal-setting is honesty. Going into business with your eyes wide open about your strengths and weaknesses, your likes and dislikes, and your ultimate goals lets you confront the decisions you'll face with greater confidence and a greater chance of success.

Personal Goals and Objectives Worksheet

Setting goals not only gives you an ongoing road map for success, but it shows you the best alternatives should you need or desire a change along the way. You should review your goals on a regular basis. Many do this daily as it helps them assess their progress and gives them the ability to make faster and more informed decisions. Take a few minutes to fill out the following worksheet. You'll find this very helpful in setting and resetting your goals.

1. The most important reason for being in business for myself is:

   ____

   ____

   ____

   ____

2. What I like best about being in business for myself is:

   ____

   ____

   ____

   ____

3. Within five years I would like my business to be:

   ____

   ____

   ____

   ____

4. When I look back over the past five years of my career I feel:

   ____

   ____

   ____

Figure 2.1. Personal Goals and Objectives Worksheet

Personal Goals and Objectives Worksheet

5. My financial condition as of today is:

____

____

____

____

6. I feel the next thing I must do about my business is:

____

____

____

____

7. The most important part of my business is (or will be):

____

____

____

____

8. The area of my business I really excel in is:

____

____

____

____

Figure 2.1. Personal Goals and Objectives Worksheet, continued

CHAPTER

3

Good Idea!

How to Get an Idea for Your Business

Many people believe starting a business is a mysterious process. They know they want to start a business, but they don't know the first steps to take. In this chapter, you're going to find out how to get an idea for a business—how you figure out exactly what it is you want to do and then how to take action on it.

But before we get started, let's clear up one point: People always wonder if this is a good time to start their business idea. The fact is, there's really never a bad time to launch a business. It's obvious why it's smart to launch in strong economic times. People have money and are looking for ways to spend it. But launching in tough or uncertain economic times can be just as smart. If you do your homework, presumably there's a need for the business you're starting. Because many people are reluctant to launch in

> *"It's not the business you're in, but the way you do business, that makes the difference. Every business has a formula for making money. You need the determination to figure out the formula for your particular business."*
>
> —Greg Brophy, founder of Shred-it America Inc.

tough times, your new business has a better chance of getting noticed. And, depending on your idea, in a down economy there is often equipment (or even entire businesses!) for sale at bargain prices.

Estimates vary, but generally more than 540,000 businesses are started each year in the United States. Yet for every American who actually starts a business, there are likely millions more who begin each year saying "OK, this is the year I am going to start a business," and then don't.

Everyone has his or her own roadblock, something that prevents them from taking that crucial first step. Most people are afraid to start; they may fear the unknown, or failure, or even success. Others find starting something overwhelming because they think they have to come up with something that no one has ever done before—a new invention, a unique service. In other words, they think they have to reinvent the wheel.

But unless you're a technological genius—another Bill Gates or Steve Jobs—trying to reinvent the wheel is a big waste of time. For most people starting a business, the issue should not be coming up with something so unique that no one has ever heard of it but instead answering the questions: "How can I improve on this?" or "Can I do this better or differently from the other guy doing it over there?" Or simply, "Is there market share not being served that makes room for another business in this category?"

Get the Juices Flowing

How do you start the idea process? First, take out a sheet of paper and across the top write "Things About Me." List five to seven things about you—things you like to do or that you're really good at, personal things (we'll get to your work life in a minute). Your list might include: "I'm really good with people, I love kids, I love to read, I love computers, I love numbers, I'm good at coming up with marketing concepts, I'm a problem solver." Just write down whatever comes to your mind; it doesn't need to make sense. Once you have your list, number the items down one side of the paper.

On the other side of the paper, list things that you don't think you're good at or you don't like to do. Maybe you're really good at marketing concepts, but you don't like to meet people or you're really not that fond of kids or you don't like to do public speaking or you don't want to travel. Don't overthink it.

When you're finished, ask yourself: "If there were three to five products or services that would make my personal life better, what would they be?" This is your personal life as a man, woman, father, husband, mother, wife, parent, grandparent—whatever your situation may be. Determine what products or services would make your life easier or happier, make you more productive or efficient, or simply give you more time.

Next, ask yourself the same question about your business life. Examine what you like and dislike about your work life as well as what traits people like and dislike about you.

Finally, ask yourself why you're seeking to start a business in the first place. Then, when you're done, look for a pattern (i.e., whether there's a need for a business doing one of the things you like or are good at). To make the process a bit easier, we've provided a "Things About Me Worksheet" for you to complete, starting on page 22.

tip

Don't overlook publications in your search for business ideas. Books, newspapers, and magazines all contain a wealth of ideas. Your reading list should include business, lifestyle, and niche publications like pets or antique tractors. Read your local newspaper, as well as major newspapers from the large trend-setting cities like Los Angeles, New York, and San Francisco, many of which you can read online for free.

They Delivered

Here's a business startup story that's a great example of seeing a need and filling it. *Entrepreneur* magazine is located in Irvine, California, a planned community. Many years ago, there weren't many fast-food restaurants in the business area. Most were across town, where the neighborhoods were.

Things About Me Worksheet

Complete the following self-assessment worksheet as honestly as you can. Just write down whatever comes to mind; don't overthink the exercise. Most likely, your first response will be your best. Once you've finished the exercise, look for patterns (i.e., is there a need for a business doing one of the things you like or are good at?).

1. List at least five things you like to do or are good at:

    ____

    ____

    ____

    ____

    ____

2. List five things you are not good at or you don't like to do:

    ____

    ____

    ____

    ____

    ____

3. List three products or services that would make your personal life better:

    ____

    ____

    ____

4. List three products or services that would make your business life better:

    ____

    ____

    ____

Figure 3.1. Things About Me Worksheet

Things About Me Worksheet

5. When people ask what you do, what's your answer? (List one occupation or whatever mainly occupies your week.)

____

____

6. List five things you enjoy about your work:

____

____

____

____

____

7. List five things you dislike about your work:

____

____

____

____

____

8. When people tell you what they like most about you, they say:

____

____

____

9. Some people dislike the fact that you:

____

____

____

Figure 3.1. Things About Me Worksheet, continued

Things About Me Worksheet

10. Other than your main occupation, list any other skills you possess, whether you excel at them or not:

    ____

    ____

    ____

11. In addition to becoming more financially independent, you would also like to be more:

    ____

    ____

12. Write down three things you want to see changed or improved in your community:

    ____

    ____

    ____

Figure 3.1. Things About Me Worksheet, continued

Two young men in Irvine found this lunch situation very frustrating. There were some affordable food courts located in strip centers, but the parking lots were really small and the wait was horrendous.

One day, as they were lamenting their lunch problem, one of them said, "Wouldn't it be great if we could get some good food delivered?" The proverbial light bulb went on! Then they did what many people don't do—they did something about their idea. Coincidentally, they purchased one of Entrepreneur Press's Step-By-Step Startup Guides and started a restaurant delivery business.

To date, their business has served more than 15 million people! It's neither a complicated business nor an original one. Their competition has gotten stiffer, and yet they're doing phenomenally well. And it all began because they listened to their own frustrations and decided to do something about them. Little did they know that research cites the shrinking lunch hour as one of the biggest complaints by American workers. Some only get 30 minutes, making it nearly impossible to get out, get lunch, and get back on time. So while these young entrepreneurs initially thought they were responding to a personal need in their local area, they actually struck a universal chord.

aha!

Your hobbies may lead you to business ideas. If gardening or antique toy collecting is what turns you on, take your passion and turn it into a real business. Sell your locally grown herbs or vegetables to restaurants or set up an online business selling your rare toy finds on eBay.

That is one way to get ideas—listening to your own (or your co-workers', family's, or neighbors') frustrations. The opportunities are all there; you just need to search them out. If your brain is always set on idea mode, then many ideas may come from just looking around or reading. For instance, if you had read an article about the shrinking lunch hour, and if you were thinking entrepreneurially, you would say, "Wow, maybe there's an opportunity there for me to do something. I should start researching it."

Inspiring Moments

Inspiration can be anywhere. Here's another classic startup story: Before the days of on-demand movies from cable providers and streaming video services, did you ever get charged a fee for returning a video late? Bet you didn't do anything about it. Well, when Reed Hastings got a whopping $40 late charge, instead of getting mad, he got inspired. Hastings wondered "How come movie rentals don't work like a health club, where, whether you use it a lot or a little, you get charged the same?" From this thought, Netflix.com was born. From its start in 1999, Netflix has grown into a big business with revenues topping $4.4 billion in 2013. And that was achieved despite some hardships for the company and a required re-invention.

> *"Drive thy business or it will drive thee."*
>
> —Benjamin Franklin

Getting an idea can be as simple as keeping your eyes peeled for the latest hot businesses; they crop up all the time. Many local entrepreneurs made tons of money bringing the Starbucks coffeehouse concept to their hometowns and then expanding from there. Take Minneapolis-based Caribou Coffee. The founders had what they describe as an "aha moment" in 1990, and two years later launched what is now the nation's second-largest corporate-owned gourmet coffeehouse chain. Other coffee entrepreneurs have chosen to stay local.

And don't overlook the tried and true. Hot businesses often go through cycles. Take gardening. For the last few years gardening products and supplies have been all the rage, but you wouldn't consider gardening a 21st century business. The same goes for shoe cobblers and seamstress businesses—with people wanting shoes and clothes to last longer or fit just-so, these businesses are in demand, and supply is short.

In other words, you can take any idea and customize it to the times and your community. Add your own creativity to any concept. In fact, customizing a concept isn't a choice; it's a necessity if you want your

>> Thinking It Through

Before you start a business, you have to examine the potential, what your product or service is, and whether the opportunity exists to make a good deal of money. It may be a "hit and run" product, where you're going to get in, make a lot of money, and then get out. That's not necessarily a bad thing; fads have made some entrepreneurs incredibly wealthy. Remember the children's bracelet fad brought on after Silly Bandz became popular? Silly Bandz and others like it are still around, but they're not all the rage (or as financially successful) that they were the first few years. But remember, once you're in the fad business, it's hard to know when it's time to get out. And if you guess wrong or try to make a classic out of a fad, you're going to lose all the money you have earned.

business to be successful. You can't just take an idea, plop it down and say, "OK, this is it." Outside of a McDonald's, Subway, or other major franchise concept, there are very few businesses that work with a one-size-fits-all approach.

> ***"Plan your hunches and use your head."***
>
> —Lillian Vernon, Founder of Lillian Vernon Corp.

One of the best ways to determine whether your idea will succeed in your community is to talk to people you know. If it's a business idea, talk to co-workers and colleagues. Run personal ideas by your family or neighbors. Don't be afraid of people stealing your idea. It's just not likely. Just discuss the general concept; you don't need to spill all the details.

Just Do It!

Hopefully by now, the process of determining what business is right for you has at least been somewhat demystified. Understand that business startup isn't rocket science. No, it isn't easy to begin a business, but it's not as complicated or as scary as many people think, either. It's a step-by-step, common-sense procedure. So take it a step at a time. First step: Figure out what you want to do. Once you have the idea, talk to people to find out what they think. Ask, "Would you buy and/or use this, and how much would you pay?"

Understand that many people around you won't encourage you (some will even discourage you) to pursue your entrepreneurial journey. Some will tell you they have your best interests at heart; they just want you to see the reality of the situation. Some will envy your courage; others will resent you for having the guts to actually do something. You can't allow these naysayers to dissuade you, to stop your journey before it even begins.

In fact, once you get an idea for a business, what's the most important trait you need as an entrepreneur? Perseverance. When you set out to launch your business, you'll be told "no" more times than you've ever been told before. You can't take it personally; you've got to get beyond the "no" and move on to the next person—because eventually, you're going to get to a "yes."

One of the most common warnings you'll hear is about the risk. Everyone will tell you it's risky to start your own business. But what in life

>> Fit to A "T"

Every December in *Entrepreneur* magazine, the hottest business trends for the coming year are profiled, representing a lot of research and a lot of homework. But that doesn't mean these businesses will work for you. After all, you may not be good at these particular businesses. Or you could live in an area where the business is already saturated or not viable. Or they simply may not suit you, and you'd end up hating your business. And chances are if you hate what you're doing, you'll fail doing it.

aha!

Is there a household chore or annoyance that drives you up the wall? Common sources of frustration or irritation are great idea generators. The woman who invented the now-ubiquitous spill-proof Snack Trap for small children (they can reach their little hands in to grab a treat, but no matter how much they shake or drop the snack cup, nothing falls out—usually) was simply tired of cleaning up Cheerios from the floor, amid the couch cushions, and in the crevices of her toddler's car seat.

isn't? Plus, there's a difference between foolish risks and calculated ones. You can mitigate your risk if you carefully consider what you're doing, get help when you need it, and never stop asking questions.

You can't allow the specter of risk to stop you from going forward. Ask yourself, "What am I really risking?" And assess the risk. What are you giving up? What will you lose if things don't work out? Don't risk what you can't afford. Don't risk your home, your family, or your health. Ask yourself, "If this doesn't work, will I be worse off than I am now?" If all you have to lose is some time, energy, and money, then the risk is likely worth it.

Determining what you want to do is only the first step. You've still got a lot of homework to do, a lot of research in front of you. Buying this book is a smart first step. Most important: Do something. Don't sit back year after year and say, "This is the year I'm going to start my business." Make this the year you really do it!

CHAPTER

4

Good Timing
Should You Launch Your Business Part or Full Time?

Should you start your business part time or full time? Even if you ultimately plan to go full time, many entrepreneurs and experts say starting part time can be a good idea.

Starting part time offers several advantages. It reduces your risk because you can rely on income and benefits from your full-time job. Starting part time also allows your business to grow gradually.

"Starting part time is simply the best way," contends Philip Holland, author of *How to Start a Business Without Quitting Your Job*. "You find out what running a business requires, while limiting your liability if it fails."

Yet the part-time path is not without its own dangers and disadvantages. Starting part time leaves you with less time to market your business, strategize, and build a clientele. Since you

aha!

If you're a part-time entrepreneur seeking a full-time professional image, check out business incubators. For a small fee, business incubators provide office space, services such as answering phones, and access to equipment like copiers and fax machines. The biggest plus: Incubators also provide startup help, such as marketing and accounting assistance. Business incubators used to be less common, but now you can find them even at local community colleges. In some cases, these incubators will also offer access to successful entrepreneurs and occasionally funders looking to back new ideas. This is particularly true of incubators attached to colleges or business schools at big universities.

won't be available to answer calls or solve customers' problems for most of the day, clients may become frustrated and feel you're not offering adequate customer service or responding quickly enough to their needs.

Perhaps the biggest problem for part-time entrepreneurs is the risk of burnout. Holding down a full-time job while running a part-time business leaves you with little, if any, leisure time; as a result, your personal and family life may suffer.

"Working by day and running a business by night creates a host of potential conflicts and can add a tremendous amount of stress," cautions Arnold Sanow, co-author of *You Can Start Your Own Business*. Sanow says conflicts between a day job and a sideline business are common, as are family problems: "I've seen a lot of divorces as a result of working full time and having a business on the side."

That's not to say a part-time business can't work. It can, Sanow says—if you have excellent time management skills, strong self-discipline, and support from family and friends. Also crucial, he says, is your commitment: "Don't think that, since you already have a job, you don't really have to work hard at your business. You must have a plan of attack."

Market Matters

As with any business, your plan of attack should start with a thorough assessment of your idea's market potential. Often, this step alone will be enough to tell you whether you should start part time or full time.

You can't become so caught up in your love for what you're doing that you overlook the business realities. If you find there is a huge unmet need for your product or service, no major competition, and a ready supply of eager customers, then by all means go ahead and start full time. If, on the other hand, you find that the market won't support a full-time business, but might someday with proper marketing and business development, then it is probably best to start part time at first.

Investigate factors such as the competition in your industry, the economy in your area, the demographic breakdown of your client base, and the availability of potential customers. If you are thinking of opening an upscale beauty salon, for example, evaluate the number of similar shops in operation, as well as the number of affluent women in the area and the fees they are willing to pay.

Once you have determined there is a need for your business, outline your goals and strategies in a comprehensive business plan. You should always conduct extensive research, make market projections for your business, and set goals for yourself based on these findings. It gives you a tremendous view of the long-range possibilities and keeps the business on the right track. Don't neglect writing a business plan even if you're starting part time: A well-written business plan will help you take your business full time later on.

Certain businesses lend themselves well to part-time operation: Holland cites ecommerce, food products, direct marketing, and service businesses as examples. Doing your market research and business plan will give you a more realistic idea of whether your business can work part time. (For specifics on conducting market research and writing a business plan, see Chapters 6, 7, and 10).

warning

Don't bite the hand that feeds you. Starting a business that competes with your current employer may get you in legal hot water by violating noncompete clauses in your employment contract.

If you've got your heart set on a business that traditionally requires a full-time commitment, think creatively: There may be ways to make it work on a part-time basis. For instance, instead of a restaurant, consider a catering business. You'll still get to create menus and interact with customers, but your work can all be done during evenings and weekends.

Financial Plan

One major factor in the decision to start part time or full time is your financial situation. Before launching a full-time business, most experts recommend putting aside enough to live on for at least six months to a year. (That amount may vary; completing your business plan will show you in detail how long you can expect to wait before your business begins earning a profit.)

Basic factors you should consider include the amount of your existing savings, whether you have assets that could be sold for cash, whether friends or family members might offer you financing or loans, and whether your spouse or other family members' salaries could be enough to support your family while you launch a business full time.

If, like many people, you lack the financial resources to start full time, beginning part time is often a good alternative. However, even if you do start part time, you'll want to keep some figures in mind: Specifically, how do you know when your business is making enough money that you can say goodbye to your day job?

A good rule of thumb, according to Sanow, is to wait until your part-time business is bringing in income equivalent to at least 30 percent of your current salary from your full-time job. "With 30 percent of their income, plus all the extra time during the day to promote their business, [entrepreneurs] should be able to make [the transition at that point]," he says. Another good idea: Start putting more money aside while you still have your day job. That way, when you take the full-time plunge, you'll have a financial cushion to supplement the income from your business.

aha!

If keeping a full-time job and a part-time business going at the same time sounds too difficult, and taking the full-time plunge sounds too scary, consider taking a part-time or temporary job while you start a full-time business. This can be a way to ensure you have some salary coming in, while giving you time to work on your business. Part-time jobs often offer evening or weekend hours—a big plus if you need to be accessible to clients during regular business hours.

Family Affairs

The emotional and psychological side of starting a business is less cut-and-dried than financial and market aspects, but it's just as important in your decision to start part time or full time.

Begin by discussing the situation with your spouse, significant other, or family members. Do they support your decision to start a business? Do they understand the sacrifices both full-time and part-time businesses will require—from you, from them, and from the whole family? Make sure your loved ones feel free to bring any objections or worries out in the open. The time to do this is now—not three months after you have committed to your business and it is too late to back out.

Then, work together to come up with practical solutions to the problems you foresee (could your spouse take over some of the household chores you currently handle, for example?). Lay some ground rules for the part-time business—for instance, no work on Sunday afternoons, or no discussing business at the dinner table.

To make your part-time business a success and keep your family happy, time management is key. Balance the hours you have available. Get

>> Take It Easy

Does all work and no play make entrepreneurship no fun? Some entrepreneurs who run part-time businesses based on hobbies, such as crafts or cooking, find that going full time takes all the fun out of the venture. "Going full time turns an adventure into a job," as business expert Arnold Sanow puts it.

Some entrepreneurs have trouble grasping the fact that their businesses aren't just pastimes anymore. They can't work at their leisure any longer, and their ventures may require them to develop talents they didn't know they had and perform tasks they'd rather leave to someone else.

Don't get so caught up in the creative aspects of the venture that you lose sight of the business responsibilities you must assume to make your startup succeed. Take a realistic look at what going full time will require. Consider hiring people to handle the business aspects you dislike, such as sales or operations.

> **tip**
>
> 
>
> What do you do if you can't afford to start your business full time but need to be available full time to answer client and customer calls? Consider teaming up with a partner whose available hours complement yours. Or hire a freelancer to take incoming calls, answer simple questions, and bring important ones to your attention. You could arrange to pay a flat fee or a fee plus a little extra bonus for handling customer issues successfully.

up early, and don't spend valuable time on frivolous phone calls and other time wasters.

Getting Personal

Besides the effect business ownership will have on your family, equally important to consider is the toll it might take on you. If the idea of taking the full-time business plunge and giving up your comfy salary and cushy benefits keeps you awake at night biting your nails, then perhaps a part-time business is best. On the other hand, if you need to work long hours at your current full-time job, you commute 60 miles round-trip, and you have two-year-old triplets, piling a part-time business on top of all those commitments could be the straw that breaks the camel's back.

Of course, a full-time business does require long, long hours, but a part-time business combined with a full-time job can be even more stressful. If this is the route you're considering, carefully assess the effects on your life. You'll be using evenings, weekends, and lunch hours—and, most likely, your holidays, sick days, and vacation time—to take care of business. You'll probably have to give up leisure activities such as going to the movies, watching TV, reading, or going to the gym. How will you feel the next time you drag yourself home, exhausted after a late night at the office . . . then have to sit right down and spend four hours working on a project that a client needs the next morning? Carefully consider whether you have the mental and physical stamina to give your best effort to both your job and your business.

Decisions, Decisions

Whether to start part time or full time is a decision only you can make. Whichever route you take, the secret to success is an honest assessment of your resources, your commitment level, and the support systems you have in place. With those factors firmly in mind, you will be able to make the right choice.

>> Part-Time Pointers

Balancing a full-time job with a part-time business isn't easy—but it can be done. Arnold Sanow, co-author of *You Can Start Your Own Business*, suggests these tips to help make your part-time business a success:

- *Give your family the chance to help out*. Answering the phone, stuffing envelopes, or putting together orders are all great ways to get more accomplished in less time, while also making your family feel like they're part of your business.
- *Be ready to give up personal time*. You won't have much time for TV, reading, or hobbies you used to enjoy. Be sure the sacrifice is worth it, or both your job and your business will suffer.
- *Focus on the task in front of you*. When you're at work, focus on work; don't let thoughts of your business distract you.
- *Make the most of every minute*. Use lunch hours or early morning to make phone calls; use commuting time on the train to catch up on paperwork.
- *Take advantage of time zone differences and technology*. If you do business with people in other states or countries, make time differences work to your advantage by calling early in the morning or after work. Use email to communicate with clients at any time of day or night.
- *Don't overstep your boundaries*. Making business calls on company time or using your employer's supplies or equipment for business purposes is a big no-no.
- *Be honest*. Only you can assess your situation, but in many cases it's best to be upfront with your boss about your sideline business. As long as it doesn't interfere with your job, many bosses won't mind—and you'll gain by being honest rather than making them feel you have something to hide.

CHAPTER

5

Build It or Buy It?

Starting a Business vs. Buying One

When most people think of starting a business, they think of beginning from scratch—developing your own idea and building the company from the ground up. But starting from scratch presents some distinct disadvantages, including the difficulty of building a customer base, marketing the new business, hiring employees and establishing cash flow . . . all without a track record or reputation to go on.

Some people know they want to own their own businesses but aren't sure exactly what type of business to choose. If you fall into this category, or if you are worried about the difficulties involved in starting a business from the ground up, the good news is that there are other options: buying an existing business, buying a franchise, or buying a business opportunity. Depending on your personality, skills, and resources, these three methods of getting into business may offer significant advantages over starting from scratch.

e-fyi

If you're looking for a business to buy or a broker to help you in your purchase, stop by BizBuySell.com. In addition to searching 45,000 businesses for sale and broker listings, you can order business valuation reports or research franchises. There are also forums and member Q&As about buying and selling a business. You might find many of your questions already asked by other would-be entrepreneurs and answered by those already in the know.

Buying an Existing Business

In most cases, buying an existing business is less risky than starting from scratch. When you buy a business, you take over an operation that's already generating cash flow and profits. You have an established customer base and reputation as well as employees who are familiar with all aspects of the business. And you do not have to reinvent the wheel—setting up new procedures, systems, and policies—since a successful formula for running the business has already been put in place.

On the downside, buying a business is often more costly than starting from scratch. However, it's often easier to get financing to buy an existing business than to start a new one. Bankers and investors generally feel more comfortable dealing with a business that already has a proven track record. In addition, buying a business may give you valuable legal rights, such as patents or copyrights, which can prove very profitable.

Of course, there's no such thing as a sure thing—and buying an existing business is no exception. If you're not careful, you could get stuck with obsolete inventory, uncooperative employees, or outdated distribution methods. To make sure you get the best deal when buying an existing business, take the following steps.

The Right Choice

Buying the perfect business starts with choosing the right type of business for you. The best place to start is by looking in an industry you are familiar with and understand. Think long and hard about the types of businesses you are interested in and which are the best matches with your skills and experience. Also consider the size of business you are looking for, in terms of employees, number of locations, and sales.

> ***"Play by the rules. But be ferocious."***
>
> —Philip Knight, co-founder of Nike

Next, pinpoint the geographical area where you want to own a business. Assess the labor pool and costs of doing business in that area, including wages and taxes, to make sure they're acceptable to you. Once you've chosen a region and an industry to focus on, investigate every business in the area that meets your requirements. Start by looking in the local newspaper's classified ad section under "Business Opportunities" or "Businesses for Sale."

You can also run your own "Wanted to Buy" ad describing what you are looking for.

Remember, just because a business isn't listed doesn't mean it isn't for sale. Talk to business owners in the industry; many of them might not have their businesses up for sale but would consider selling if you made them an offer. Put your networking abilities and business contacts to use, and you're likely to hear of other businesses that might be good prospects.

>> Taxing Matters

You are investigating a business you like, and the seller hands you income tax returns that show a $50,000 profit. "Of course," he says with a wink and a nudge, "I really made $150,000." What do you do?

There may be perfectly legal reasons for the lower reported income. For instance, if the seller gave his nephew a nonessential job for $25,000 a year, you can just eliminate the job and keep the cash. Same goes for a fancy leased car. One-time costs of construction or equipment may have legitimately lowered net profits, too.

What to watch for: a situation where a seller claims he or she made money but just didn't report it to the IRS. If this happens, either walk away from the deal, or make an offer based on the proven income, and then expect to clean up the balance sheet going forward when you take over.

Contacting a business broker is another way to find businesses for sale. Most brokers are hired by sellers to find buyers and help negotiate deals. If you hire a broker, he or she will charge you a commission—typically 5 to 10 percent of the purchase price. The assistance brokers can offer, especially for first-time buyers, is often worth the cost. However, if you are really trying to save money, consider hiring a broker only when you are near the final negotiating phase. Brokers can offer assistance in several ways:

- *Prescreening businesses for you.* Good brokers turn down many of the businesses they are asked to sell, either because the seller won't provide full financial disclosure or because the business is overpriced. Going through a broker helps you avoid these bad risks.
- *Helping you pinpoint your interests.* A good broker starts by finding out about your skills and interests, then helps you select the right business for you. With the help of a broker, you may discover that an industry you had never considered is the ideal one for you.
- *Negotiating.* During the negotiating process is when brokers really earn their keep. They help both parties stay focused on the ultimate goal and smooth over problems.
- *Assisting with paperwork.* Brokers know the latest laws and regulations affecting everything from licenses and permits to financing and escrow. They also know the most efficient ways to cut through red tape, which can slash months off the purchase process. Working with a broker reduces the risk that you'll neglect some crucial form, fee, or step in the process.

> ***"Pretend that every single person you meet has a sign around his or her neck that says 'Make Me Feel Important.' Not only will you succeed in business, but you will succeed in life."***
>
> —Mary Kay Ash, founder of Mary Kay Cosmetics

A Closer Look

Whether you use a broker or go it alone, you will definitely want to put together an "acquisition team"—your banker, accountant, and attorney—

to help you. (For more on choosing these advisors, see Chapter 11.) These advisors are essential to what is called "due diligence," which means reviewing and verifying all the relevant information about the business you are considering. When due diligence is done, you will know just what you are buying and from whom.

The preliminary analysis starts with some basic questions. Why is this business for sale? What is the general perception of the industry and the particular business, and what is the outlook for the future? Does—or can—the business control enough market share to stay profitable? Are the raw materials needed in abundant supply? How have the company's product or service lines changed over time?

You also need to assess the company's reputation and the strength of its business relationships. Talk to existing customers, suppliers, and vendors about their relationships with the business. Contact the Better Business Bureau, industry associations, and licensing and credit-reporting agencies to make sure there are no complaints against the business. (For more questions to ask before purchasing an existing business, refer to the "Business Evaluation Checklist" starting on page 42.)

If the business still looks promising after your preliminary analysis, your acquisition team should start examining the business's potential returns and its asking price. Whatever method you use to determine the fair market price of the business, your assessment of the business's value should take into account such issues as the business's financial health, earnings history, growth potential, and intangible assets (for example, brand name and market position).

To get an idea of the company's anticipated returns and future financial needs, ask the business owner and/or accountant to show you projected financial statements. Balance sheets, income statements, cash flow statements, footnotes, and tax returns for the past three years are all key indicators of a business's health. These documents will help you do some financial analyses that will spotlight any underlying problems and also provide a closer look at a wide range of less tangible information.

Among other issues, you should focus on the following:

- *Excessive or insufficient inventory.* If the business is based on a product rather than a service, take careful stock of its inventory.

Business Evaluation Checklist

If you find a business that you would like to buy, you will need to consider a number of points before you decide whether to purchase it. Take a good, close look at the business and answer the following questions. They will help you determine whether the business is a sound investment.

- ❑ Why does the current owner want to sell the business?
- ❑ Does the business have potential for future growth, or will its sales decline?
- ❑ If the business is in decline, can you save it and make it successful?
- ❑ Is the business in sound financial condition? Have you seen audited year-end financial statements for the business? Have you reviewed the most recent statements? Have you reviewed the tax returns for the past five years?
- ❑ Have you seen copies of all the business's current contracts?
- ❑ Is the business now, or has it ever been, under investigation by any governmental agency? If so, what is the status of any current investigation? What were the results of any past investigation?
- ❑ Is the business currently involved in a lawsuit, or has it ever been involved in one? If so, what is the status or result?
- ❑ Does the business have any debts or liens against it? If so, what are they for and in what amounts?
- ❑ What percentage of the business's accounts are past due? How much does the business write off each year for bad debts?
- ❑ How many customers does the business serve on a regular basis?
- ❑ Who makes up the market for this business? Where are your customers located? (Do they all come from your community or from across the state or are they spread across the globe?)
- ❑ Does the amount of business vary from season to season?

Figure 5.1. Business Evaluation Checklist

Business Evaluation Checklist

- ❑ Does any single customer account for a large portion of the sales volume? If so, would the business be able to survive without this customer? (The larger your customer base is, the more easily you will be able to survive the loss of any customers. If, on the other hand, you exist mainly to serve a single client, the loss of that client could finish your business.)
- ❑ How does the business market its products or services? Does its competition use the same methods? If not, what methods does the competition use? How successful are they?
- ❑ Does the business have exclusive rights to market any particular products or services? If so, how has it obtained this exclusivity? Do you have written proof that the current business owner can transfer this exclusivity to you?
- ❑ Does the business hold patents for any of its products? Which ones? What percentage of gross sales do they represent? Would the sale of the business include the sale of any patents?
- ❑ Are the business's supplies, merchandise, and other materials available from many suppliers, or are there only a handful who can meet your needs? If you lost the business's current supplier, what impact would that loss have on your business? Would you be able to find substitute goods of the appropriate quality and price?
- ❑ Are any of the business's products in danger of becoming obsolete or of going out of style? Is this a "fad" business?
- ❑ What is the business's market share?
- ❑ What competition does the business face? How can the business compete successfully? Have the business's competitors changed recently? Have any of them gone out of business, for instance?
- ❑ Does the business have all the equipment you think is necessary? Will you need to add or update any equipment?
- ❑ What is the business's current inventory worth? Will you be able to use any of this inventory, or is it inconsistent with your intended product line?

Figure 5.1. Business Evaluation Checklist, continued

Business Evaluation Checklist

- ❑ How many employees does the business have? What positions do they hold?
- ❑ Does the business pay its employees high wages, or are the wages average or low?
- ❑ Does the business experience high employee turnover? If so, why?
- ❑ What benefits does the business offer its employees?
- ❑ How long have the company's top managers been with the company?
- ❑ Will the change of ownership cause any changes in personnel?
- ❑ Which employees are the most important to the company?
- ❑ Do any of the business's employees belong to any unions?

Figure 5.1. Business Evaluation Checklist, continued

First-time business buyers are often seduced by inventory, but it can be a trap. Excessive inventory may be obsolete or may soon become so; it also costs money to store and insure. Excess inventory can mean there are a lot of dissatisfied customers who are experiencing lags between their orders and final delivery or are returning items they aren't happy with.

- *The lowest level of inventory the business can carry*. Determine this, then have the seller agree to reduce stock to that level by the date you take over the company. Also add a clause to the purchase agreement specifying that you are buying only the inventory that is current and saleable.
- *Accounts receivable.* Uncollected receivables stunt a business's growth and could require unanticipated bank loans. Look carefully at

tip

Study the financial records provided by the current business owner, but don't rely on them exclusively. Insist on seeing the tax returns for at least the past three years. Also, where applicable, ask for sales records.

>> Let's Make A Deal

Short on cash? Try these alternatives for financing your purchase of an existing business:

> *Use the seller's assets*. As soon as you buy the business, you'll own the assets—so why not use them to get financing now? Make a list of all the assets you're buying (along with any attached liabilities), and use it to approach banks, finance companies, and factors (companies that buy your accounts receivable).

> *Bank on purchase orders*. Factors, finance companies, and banks will lend money on receivables. Finance companies and banks will lend money on inventory. Equipment can also be sold, then leased back from equipment leasing companies.

> *Ask the seller for financing*. Motivated sellers will often provide more lenient terms and a less rigorous credit review than a bank. And unlike a conventional lender, they may take only the business's assets as collateral. Seller financing is also flexible: The parties involved can structure the deal however they want, negotiating a payback schedule and other terms to meet their needs.

> *Use an employee stock ownership plan (ESOP)*. ESOPs offer you a way to get capital immediately by selling stock in the business to employees. By offering to set up an ESOP plan, you may be able to lower the sales price.

> *Lease with an option to buy*. Some sellers will let you lease a business with an option to buy. You make a down payment, become a minority stockholder, and operate the business as if it were your own.

> *Assume liabilities or decline receivables*. Reduce the sales price by either assuming the business's liabilities or having the seller keep the receivables.

indicators such as accounts receivable turnover, credit policies, cash collection schedules, and the aging of receivables.

- *Net income*. Use a series of net income ratios to gain a better look at a business's bottom line. For instance, the ratio of gross profit to net sales can be used to determine whether the company's profit margin is in line with that of similar businesses. Likewise, the ratio of net income to net worth, when considered together with projected increases in interest costs, total purchase price, and similar factors, can show whether you would earn a reasonable return. Finally, the ratio of net income to total assets is a strong indicator of whether the company is getting a favorable rate of return on assets. Your accountant can help you assess all these ratios. As he or she does so, be sure to determine whether the profit figures have been disclosed before or after taxes and the amount of returns the current owner is getting from the business. Also assess how much of the expenses would stay the same, increase, or decrease under your management.

warning

Who are the business's employees? Beware, if it's a family-run operation: Salaries may be unrealistically low, resulting in a bottom line that's unrealistically high.

- *Working capital.* Working capital is defined as current assets less current liabilities. Without sufficient working capital, a business can't stay afloat—so one key computation is the ratio of net sales to net working capital. This measures how efficiently the working capital is being used to achieve business objectives.
- *Sales activity.* Sales figures may appear rosier than they really are. When studying the rate of growth in sales and earnings, read between the lines to tell if the growth rate is due to increased sales volume or higher prices. Also examine the overall marketplace. If the market seems to be mature, sales may be static—and that might be why the seller is trying to unload the company.
- *Fixed assets.* If your analysis suggests the business has invested too much money in fixed assets, such as the plant property and equipment, make sure you know why. Unused equipment could indicate that demand is declining or that the business owner miscalculated manufacturing requirements.
- *Operating environment.* Take the time to understand the business's operating environment and corporate culture. If the

business depends on overseas clients or suppliers, for example, examine the short- and long-term political environment of the countries involved. Look at the business in light of consumer or economic trends; for example, if you are considering a store that sells products based on a fad like Crocs, will that client base still be intact five or ten years later? Or if the company relies on just a few major clients, can you be sure they will stay with you after the deal is closed?

Law and Order

While you and your accountant review key financial ratios and performance figures, you and your attorney should investigate the business's legal status. Look for liens against the property, pending lawsuits, guarantees, labor disputes, potential zoning changes, new or proposed industry regulations or restrictions, and new or pending patents; all these factors can seriously affect your business. Be sure to:

- Conduct a uniform commercial code search to uncover any recorded liens (start with city hall and check with the department of public records).
- Ask the business's attorneys for a legal history of the company, and read all old and new contracts.
- Review related pending state and federal legislation, local zoning regulations and patent histories.

Legal liabilities in business take many forms and may be hidden so deeply that even the seller honestly doesn't know they exist. How do you protect yourself? First, have your lawyer add a "hold harmless and indemnify" clause to the contract. This assures you're protected from the consequences of the seller's previous actions as owner.

Second, make sure your deal allows you to take over the seller's existing insurance policies on an interim basis. This gives you time to review your insurance needs at greater leisure while still making sure you have basic coverage from the minute you take over. The cost of having a lawyer evaluate a business depends on your relationship with the lawyer, the complexity of the business, and the stage at which the lawyer gets involved. Generally, costs range from $3,000 to as much as $35,000 for a comprehensive appraisal.

If you're considering buying a business that has valuable intellectual property, such as a patent, trade secret, or brand name, you may want an intellectual property attorney to evaluate it. Generally, this will cost from 0.5 to 3 percent of the business's total selling cost.

warning

Make sure you're in love with the profit, not the product. Many people get emotional about buying a business, which clouds their judgment. It's important to be objective.

The Art of the Deal

If your financial and legal assessments show that the business is a good buy, don't be the first person to bring up the subject of price. Let the seller name the figure first, and then proceed from there.

Deciding on a price, however, is just the first step in negotiating the sale. More important is how the deal is structured. David H. Troob, founder of D.H. Troob & Co., a New York brokerage and investment firm, suggests you should be ready to pay 20 to 50 percent of the price in cash and finance the remaining amount.

You can finance through a traditional lender, or sellers may agree to "hold a note," which means they accept payments over a period of time, just as a lender would. Many sellers like this method because it assures them of future income. Other sellers may agree to different terms—for example, accepting benefits such as a company car for a period of time after the deal is completed. These methods can cut down the amount of upfront cash you need; however, you should always have an attorney review any arrangements for legality and liability issues. (For more ideas on financing your purchase, see "Let's Make a Deal" on page 45.)

An individual purchasing a business has two options for structuring the deal (assuming the transaction is not a merger). The first is asset acquisition, in which you purchase only those assets you want. On the plus side, asset acquisition protects you from unwanted legal liabilities since instead of buying the corporation (and all its legal risks), you are buying only its assets.

On the downside, an asset acquisition can be very expensive. The asset-by-asset purchasing process is complicated and also opens the possibility that the seller may raise the price of desirable assets to offset losses from undesirable ones.

The other option is stock acquisition, in which you purchase stock. Among other things, this means you must be willing to purchase all the business's assets—and assume all its liabilities.

The final purchase contract should be structured with the help of your acquisition team to reflect very precisely your understanding and intentions regarding the purchase from a financial, tax, and legal standpoint. The contract must be all-inclusive and should allow you to rescind the deal if you find at any time that the owner intentionally misrepresented the company or failed to report essential information. It's also a good idea to include a noncompete clause in the contract to ensure the seller doesn't open a competing operation down the street.

> ***"You don't have to be a genius or a visionary or even a college graduate to be successful. You just need a framework and a dream."***
>
> —Michael Dell, founder of Dell Computer

Remember, you have the option to walk away from a negotiation at any point in the process if you don't like the way things are going. If you don't like the deal, don't buy. Just because you spent a month looking at something doesn't mean you have to buy it. You have no obligation.

Transition Time

The transition to new ownership is a big change for employees of a small business. To ensure a smooth transition, start the process before the deal is done. Make sure the owner feels good about what is going to happen to the business after he or she leaves. Spend some time talking to the key employees, customers, and suppliers before you take over; tell them about your plans and ideas for the business's future. Getting these key players involved and on your side makes running the business a lot easier.

Most sellers will help you in a transition period during which they train you in operating the business. This period can range from a few

tip

For more information when investigating a franchise or business opportunity, check out this helpful resource: The FTC provides a free package of information about the FTC Franchise and Business Opportunity Rule. Write to: Federal Trade Commission, 600 Pennsylvania Ave., Washington, DC 20580, or visit ftc.gov.

weeks to six months or longer. After the one-on-one training period, many sellers will agree to be available for phone consultation for another period of time. Make sure you and the seller agree on how this training will be handled, and write it into your contract.

If you buy the business lock, stock, and barrel, simply putting your name on the door and running it as before, your transition is likely to be fairly smooth. On the other hand, if you buy only part of the business's assets, such as its client list or employees, and then make a lot of changes in how things are done, you'll probably face a more difficult transition period.

Many new business owners have unrealistically high expectations that they can immediately make a business more profitable. Of course, you need a positive attitude to run a successful business, but if your attitude is "I'm better than you," you'll soon face resentment from the employees you've acquired.

Instead, look at the employees as valuable assets. Initially, they'll know far more about the business than you will; use that knowledge to get yourself up to speed, and treat them with respect and appreciation. Employees inevitably feel worried about job security when a new owner takes over. That uncertainty is multiplied if you don't tell them what your plans are. Many new bosses are so eager to start running the show, they slash staff, change prices, or make other radical changes without giving employees any warning. Involve the staff in your planning, and keep communication open so they know what is happening at all times. Taking on an existing business isn't easy, but with a little patience, honesty, and hard work, you'll soon be running things like a pro.

Buying a Franchise

If buying an existing business doesn't sound right for you but starting from scratch sounds a bit intimidating, you could be suited for franchise ownership. What is a franchise—and how do you know if you're right for one? Essentially, a franchisee pays an initial fee and ongoing royalties to a franchisor. In return, the franchisee gains the use of a trademark, ongoing support from the franchisor, and the right to use the franchisor's system of doing business and sell its products or services.

McDonald's, perhaps the most well-known franchise company in the world, illustrates the benefits of franchising: Customers know they will get the same type of food, prepared the same way, whether they visit a McDonald's in Moscow or Minneapolis. Customers feel confident in McDonald's, and as a result, a new McDonald's location has a head start on success compared to an independent hamburger stand.

> **warning**
>
> 
>
> Is a franchise or business opportunity seller doing the hustle? Watch out for a salesperson who says things like "Territories are going fast," "Act now or you'll be shut out," or "I'm leaving town on Monday, so make your decision now." Legitimate sellers will not pressure you to rush into such a big decision. If someone gives you the hustle, give that opportunity the thumbs-down.

In addition to a well-known brand name, buying a franchise offers many other advantages that are not available to the entrepreneur starting a business from scratch. Perhaps the most significant is that you get a proven system of operation and training in how to use it. New franchisees can avoid a lot of the mistakes startup entrepreneurs typically make because the franchisor has already perfected daily routine operations through trial and error.

Reputable franchisors conduct market research before selling a new outlet, so you can feel greater confidence that there is a demand for the product or service. Failing to do adequate market research is one of the biggest mistakes independent entrepreneurs make; as a franchisee, it's done for you. The franchisor also provides you with a clear picture of the competition and how to differentiate yourself from them.

Finally, franchisees enjoy the benefit of strength in numbers. You gain from economies of scale in buying materials, supplies, and services, such as advertising, as well as in negotiating for locations and lease terms. By comparison, independent operators have to negotiate on their own, usually getting less favorable terms. Some suppliers won't deal with new businesses or will reject your business because your account isn't big enough.

Is Franchising Right for You?

An oft-quoted saying about franchising is that it puts you in business "for yourself, but not by yourself." While that support can be helpful, for some entrepreneurs it can be too restricting. Most franchisors impose strict rules on franchisees, specifying everything from how you should greet customers to how to prepare the product or service.

> **tip**
>
> Call the appropriate agencies to see how franchising is regulated in your state. Then keep the addresses and phone numbers for key state officials on file so you can contact them later if you have specific questions.

That's not to say you will be a mindless drone—many franchisors welcome franchisees' ideas and suggestions on how to improve the way business is done—but, for the most part, you will need to adhere to the basic systems and rules set by the franchisor. If you are fiercely independent, hate interference, and want to design every aspect of your new business, you may be better off starting your own company or buying a business opportunity (see the "Buying a Business Opportunity" section starting on page 61 for more details).

More and more former executives are buying franchises these days. For many of them, a franchise is an excellent way to make the transition to business ownership. As an executive, you were probably used to delegating tasks like ordering supplies, answering phones, and handling word-processing tasks. The transition to being an entrepreneur and doing everything for yourself can be jarring. Buying a franchise could offer the support you need in making the switch to entrepreneurship.

Do Your Homework

Once you've decided a franchise is the right route for you, how do you choose the right one? With so many franchise systems to choose from, the options can be dizzying. Start by investigating various industries that interest you to find those with growth potential. Narrow the choices down to a few industries you are most interested in; then analyze your geographic area to see if there is a market for that type of business. If so, contact all the franchise companies in those fields and ask them for information. Any reputable company will be happy to send you information at no cost.

Of course, don't rely solely on these promotional materials to make your decision. You also need to do your own detective work. Start by going online to look up all the magazine and newspaper articles you can find about the companies you are considering as well as checking out Entreprenuer.com's franchise listings (entrepreneur.com/franchise). Is the company depicted favorably? Does it seem to be well-managed and growing?

Check with the consumer or franchise regulators in your state to see if there are any serious problems with the company you are considering. If the company or its principals have been involved in lawsuits or bankruptcies, try to determine the nature of the lawsuits: Did they involve fraud or violations of FTC regulatory laws? To find out, call the court that handled the case and request a copy of the petition or judgment.

If you live in one of the 15 states that regulate the sale of franchises (California, Hawaii, Illinois, Indiana, Maryland, Michigan, Minnesota, New York, North Dakota, Oregon, Rhode Island, South Dakota, Virginia, Washington, and Wisconsin), contact the state franchise authority, which can tell you if the company has complied with state registration requirements. If the company is registered with Dun & Bradstreet (D&B), request a D&B Report, which will give you details on the company's financial standing, payment promptness, and other information. And, of course, it never hurts to check with your local office of the Better Business Bureau for complaints against the company.

Does the company still sound good? That means your investigation is just beginning. If you have not already received one, contact the franchisor again and ask for a copy of its Franchise Disclosure Document, or FDD (previously known as a Uniform Franchise Offering Circular, or UFOC). This disclosure document must, by law, be given to all prospective franchisees ten business days before any agreement is signed. If changes are made to the FDD, an additional five days are added to the ten-day

Franchise Evaluation Worksheet

This will help you determine the attractiveness of each franchise you're considering. Assign each franchise a column letter. Answer each question along the left-hand side by assigning a rating of 1 to 3, with 3 being the strongest. Total each column after you've finished. The franchise with the highest score is the most attractive.

	Franchise			
	A	B	C	D
The Franchise Organization				
Does the franchisor have a good track record?				
Do the principals of the franchise have expertise in the industry?				
Rate the franchisor's financial condition.				
How thoroughly does the franchisor check out its prospective franchisees?				
Rate the profitability of the franchisor and its franchisees.				
The Product or Service				
Is there demand for the product or service?				
Can the product or service be sold year-round?				
Are industry sales strong?				
Rate the product or service in comparison with the competition.				
Is the product or service competitively priced?				
What is the potential for industry growth?				
The Market Area				
Are exclusive territories offered?				
Rate the sales potential of the territory you are considering.				
How successful are franchises in close proximity to this area?				

Figure 5.2. Franchise Evaluation Worksheet

Franchise Evaluation Worksheet

	Franchise			
	A	B	C	D
The Contract				
Are the fees and royalties associated with the franchise reasonable?				
How attractive are the renewal, termination, and transfer conditions?				
Franchisor Support				
If the franchisor requires you to purchase proprietary inventory, how useful is it?				
If the franchisor requires you to meet annual sales quotas, are they reasonable?				
Does the franchisor help with site selection, lease negotiations, and store layout?				
Does the franchisor provide ongoing training?				
Does the franchisor provide financing to qualified individuals?				
Are manuals, sales kits, accounting systems, and purchasing guides supplied?				
How strong are the franchisor's advertising and promotion programs?				
Does the franchisor have favorable national supplier contracts?				
Totals				

Figure 5.2. Franchise Evaluation Worksheet, continued

"cooling off" period. If a company says it is a franchise but will not give you an FDD, then contact the FTC—and take your business elsewhere.

The FDD is a treasure trove of information for those who are serious about franchising. It contains an extensive written description of the company, the investment amount and fees required, any litigation and/

warning

Exaggerated profit claims are common in franchise and business opportunity sales. Is a company promising you will make $10,000 a month in your spare time? If it is a franchise, any statement about earnings (regarding others in the system or your potential earnings) must appear in the Franchise Disclosure Document (FDD). Read the FDD and talk to five franchise owners who have attained the earnings claimed.

or bankruptcy history of the franchisor and its officers, the trademark you will be licensed to use, the products you are required to purchase, the advertising program, and the contractual obligations of both franchisor and franchisee. It specifies how much working capital is required, equipment needs, and ongoing royalties. It also contains a sample copy of the franchise agreement you will be asked to sign should you buy into the system, as well as three years' worth of the franchisor's audited financial statements.

The FDD has been revamped to make it less "legalistic" and more readable, so there is no excuse for failing to read yours very carefully. Before you make any decisions about purchasing the franchise, your attorney and accountant should read it as well.

>> It's Show Time

Franchise and business opportunity trade shows can be a great opportunity to explore business investment packages. Attending one is exciting—and overwhelming—so you need to prepare carefully.

Before the Show

> *Consider what you are seeking from a business investment*. Part time or full time? What type of business do you think you would enjoy? Consider your hobbies and passions.

> *Figure out your financial resources*. What is liquid, what can you borrow from family and friends, and how much do you need to live on while initially running the business? What are your financial goals for the business?

>> It's Show Time, continued

> *Get serious.* Dress conservatively, carry a briefcase, leave the kids at home, and take business cards if you have them. Show the representatives you meet that you are a serious prospect.

At the Show

> *Take a moment to study the floor plan of the exhibitors listed.* Circle the businesses you recognize or that look interesting. Make sure you stop by these booths during your visit.

> *Don't waste time.* Pass by the sellers who are out of your price range or do not meet your personal goals. Have a short list of questions ready to ask the others:

1. What is the total investment?
2. Tell me about a franchisee's typical day.
3. What arrangements are made for product supply?
4. Is financing available from the franchisor?
5. Ask for a copy of the company's FDD. Not all franchisors will give you one at the show. This is acceptable, but if you are serious about an opportunity, insist on a copy as soon as possible.

> *Collect handout information and business cards from the companies that interest you.*

After the Show

> *Organize the materials you collected into file folders.* Then read through the information more closely.

> *Follow up.* Call the representatives you met to show them you are interested.

Calling All Franchisees

One of the most important parts of the FDD is a listing of existing franchisees as well as franchisees who've been terminated or have chosen not to renew. Both lists will include addresses and phone numbers. If the list of terminated franchisees seems unusually long, it could be an indication that there's some trouble with the franchisor. Call the former franchisees, and ask them why the agreement was terminated, whether the franchisee wasn't making the grade, or whether he or she had some type of grievance with the franchisor.

Next, choose a random sample of current franchisees to interview in person. This is perhaps the most important step in your research. Don't rely on a few carefully selected names the franchisor gives you; pick your own candidates to talk to.

Visit current franchisees at their locations. Talking to existing franchisees is often the best way to find out how much money individual stores actually make. You'll also find out what their typical day is like, whether they enjoy what they do and whether the business is challenging enough. Most will be open about revealing their earnings and their satisfaction with the franchisor; however, the key to getting all the information you need before buying is asking the right questions. Here are some ideas to help get you started:

- Was the training the franchisor offered helpful in getting the business off the ground?
- Is the franchisor responsive to your needs?
- Tell me about a typical day for you.
- Have there been problems you did not anticipate?
- Has your experience proved that the investment and cost information in the FDD were realistic?
- Is the business seasonal? If so, what do you do to make ends meet in the off-season?
- Have sales and profits met your expectations? Tell me about the numbers in the business.
- Are there expansion opportunities for additional franchise ownership in this system?
- If you knew what you know now, would you make this investment again?

Since running a franchise involves an ongoing relationship with the franchisor, be sure to get the details on the purchasing process—everything that happened from the day the franchisee signed the agreement to the end of the first year in business. Did the parent company follow through on its promises?

> ***"Starting a company is the best stage of a startup. There's the creative aspect. You also have to articulate your idea. There are a million things going on."***
>
> —Katrina Garnett, founder of Crossroads Software

Talk to as many franchisees as you can—a broader perspective will give you a more accurate picture of the company. Take careful notes of the conversations so you can refer to them later. Don't hesitate to ask about sensitive topics. One of the most important questions a prospective franchisee should ask, but rarely does, is "What conflicts do you have with the franchisor?" Even established, successful companies have conflicts. What you need to find out is how widespread and common those conflicts are.

Talking to franchisees can also give you something you won't get anywhere else: a feeling for what it's like to run this business day to day. Thinking solely in economic terms is a mistake if you end up with a franchise that doesn't suit your lifestyle or self-image. When you envision running a restaurant franchise, for instance, you may be thinking of all the money you're going to make. Talking to franchisees can bring you back to reality—which is a lot more likely to involve manning a fry station, disciplining employees, and working late than cruising around in your Ferrari. Talking to franchisees in a variety of industries can help you make a choice that fits your lifestyle.

warning

If your visits with current franchisees result in each one telling you they are unhappy or would not make the investment in this franchise again, think long and hard about your own decision. If they feel the franchisor has let them down or has a flawed program, you should look more carefully before taking the plunge.

Many franchisees and franchising experts say there's no better way to cap off your research than by spending time in a franchisee location to see what your life will be like. Buyers should spend at least one week working in a unit. This is the best way for the franchisor and franchisee to evaluate each other. Offer to work for free. If the franchisor doesn't want you to, you should be skeptical about the investment.

When all your research is completed, the choice between two equally sound franchises often comes down to your gut instinct. That's why talking to franchisees and visiting locations is so important in the selection process.

Proven Purchase

Buying a franchise can be a good way to lessen the risk of business ownership. Some entrepreneurs cut that risk still further by purchasing an existing franchise—one that is already up and running. Not only does an existing franchise have a customer base, but it also has a management system already in place and ongoing revenues. In short, it already has a foundation—something that is very attractive to a lot of entrepreneurs.

Finding existing franchisees who are willing to sell is simply a matter of asking the parent company what's available. You can also check local classified ads, or visit Franchising.com, which lists thousands of businesses for sale.

Once you have found some likely candidates, the investigation process combines the same steps used in buying an existing business with those used in buying a franchise. (For a list of questions to ask before purchasing an existing business, refer to the checklist on page 42.) The good news, however, is that you'll get far more detailed financial information than you would when assessing a franchise company. Where other potential franchisees just get vague suggestions of potential earnings, you'll get hard facts.

Of course, there is a price to pay for all the advantages of buying an existing franchise: It is generally much more costly. In fact, the purchase price of an existing location can be two to four times more than what you would pay for a new franchise from the same company. Because you are investing more money, it is even more important to make sure you have audited financial statements and to review them with your CPA.

Once in a while, you'll find a franchise that isn't doing well. Perhaps the current owner isn't good at marketing, isn't putting forth enough effort, or isn't following the system correctly. In this case, you may be able to get the existing franchise for what it would cost to buy a new franchise—or even less. It's crucial, however, to make sure the problem is something you can correct and that you'll be able to get the location up to speed fast. After all, you're going to have immediate overhead expenses—for employees, royalties, and operating costs—so you need some immediate income as well.

tip 

Put yourself in the franchisor's shoes. You want to deliver a FDD only to qualified candidates who appear serious about the investment because each copy costs several dollars to reproduce. Show you are serious about their program and are genuinely interested in the information in the FDD, and you increase your chance of receiving one early in the process.

Also be aware that even if a particular franchise location is thriving, it does not necessarily mean the parent company is equally successful. In fact, sometimes franchisees who know the parent company is in trouble will try to unload their franchises before the franchisor goes under. Carefully assess the franchisor's strength, accessibility, and the level of assistance they provide. Do not settle for anything less than you would when buying a new franchise.

Buying a Business Opportunity

If a franchise sounds too restrictive for you but the idea of coming up with your own business idea, systems, and procedures sounds intimidating, there is a middle ground: business opportunities.

A business opportunity, in the simplest terms, is a packaged business investment that allows the buyer to begin a business. (Technically, all franchises are business opportunities, but not all business opportunities are franchises.)

Unlike a franchise, however, the business opportunity seller typically exercises no control over the buyer's business operations. In fact, in most business opportunity programs, there is no continuing relationship between the seller and the buyer after the sale is made.

Although business opportunities offer less support than franchises, this could be an advantage for you if you thrive on freedom. Typically, you will not be obligated to follow the strict specifications and detailed program that franchisees must follow. With most business opportunities, you would simply buy a set of equipment or materials, and then you can operate the business any way and under any name you want. There are no ongoing royalties in most cases, and no trademark rights are sold.

However, this same lack of long-term commitment is also a business opportunity's chief disadvantage. Because there is no continuing relationship, the world of business opportunities does have its share of con artists who promise buyers instant success, then take their money and run. While increased regulation of business opportunities has dramatically lessened the likelihood of rip-offs, it is still important to investigate an opportunity thoroughly before you invest any money.

Legal Matters

In general, a business opportunity refers to one of a number of ways to get into business. These include the following:

- Dealers/distributors are individuals or businesses that purchase the right to sell ABC Corp.'s products but not the right to use ABC's trade name. For example, an authorized dealer of Minolta products might have a Minolta sign in his window, but he can't call his business Minolta. Often, the words "dealers" and "distributors" are used interchangeably, but there is a difference: A distributor may sell to several dealers, while a dealer usually sells direct to retailers or consumers.
- Licensees have the right to use the seller's trade name and certain methods, equipment, technology, or product lines. If Business Opportunity XYZ has a special technique for reglazing porcelain, for instance, it will teach you the method and sell you the supplies and machinery needed to open your own business. You can call your business XYZ, but you are an independent licensee.
- Vending machines are provided by the seller, who may also help you find locations for them. You restock your own machines and collect the money.
- Cooperatives allow an existing business to affiliate with a network of similar businesses, usually for advertising and promotional purposes.
- Direct sales (see "On the Level," page 63).

>> On the Level

Direct sales is a type of business opportunity that is very popular with people looking for part-time, flexible businesses. Some of the best-known companies in America, including Avon, Mary Kay Cosmetics, and Tupperware, fall under the direct-selling umbrella.

Direct-selling programs feature a low upfront investment—usually only a few hundred dollars for the purchase of a product sample kit—and the opportunity to sell a product line directly to friends, family, and other personal contacts. Most direct-selling programs also ask participants to recruit other sales representatives. These recruits constitute a rep's "downline," and their sales generate income for those above them in the program.

Things get sticky when a direct sales network compensates participants primarily for recruiting others rather than for selling the company's products or services. A direct-selling system in which most of the revenues come from recruitment may be considered an illegal pyramid scheme.

Since direct-selling programs are usually exempt from business opportunity regulation and are not defined as franchises under state and federal franchise laws, you will need to do your own investigation before investing any money. For more information, check out the Direct Selling Association's website at dsa.org.

Legal definitions of business opportunities vary, since not all states regulate business opportunities. (The 26 that do are Alaska, California, Connecticut, Florida, Georgia, Illinois, Indiana, Iowa, Kentucky, Louisiana, Maine, Maryland, Michigan, Minnesota, Nebraska, New Hampshire, North Carolina, Ohio, Oklahoma, South Carolina, South Dakota, Texas, Utah, Virginia, Washington, and Wisconsin.) Even among these, different states have different definitions of what constitutes a business opportunity. According to franchise law counsel Joel R. Buckberg, an attorney in Nashville, Tennessee, most definitions contain the following:

- The investor enters into an oral or written agreement for the vendor—or someone recommended by the vendor—to sell goods or services to the investor that allow him or her to begin a business.

- The purchase involves a certain amount of money. In 15 states and under FTC regulations, the minimum investment is $500; in the other 11 states, that figure drops to as little as $100.
- The seller makes any one of the following statements to the investor during the course of the sale:
  1. The seller or someone the seller recommends will assist in securing locations for display racks, vending devices, outlets, or accounts;
  2. The seller will return the money and repurchase what is sold to or made by the investor if the investor is dissatisfied with the investment;
  3. The seller will buy any or all of the products assembled or produced by the buyer;
  4. The seller guarantees (or, in some states, implies) that the buyer will be able to generate revenues in excess of the amount of the investment paid to the seller; or
  5. The seller will provide a marketing plan or a sales plan for the buyer.

tip

Don't forget to ask about the franchise or business opportunity's training program. Find out how long it is, where it takes place, and the general subjects covered. Look for a well-organized plan that combines classroom time with field orientation.

If a seller meets the definition of a business opportunity in states that regulate them, it generally means he or she must register the offering with the state authorities and deliver a disclosure document to prospective buyers at least ten business days before the sale is made. (For more information on states' regulations, check with consumer protection agencies—often a part of the attorney general's office—in your state.)

Checking It Out

Researching a business is a more challenging task than investigating a franchise. And if the business opportunity you are considering does not provide buyers with a disclosure document, you get a lot less information, so you have to do a lot more legwork on your own.

Whenever possible, follow the same steps you would for investigating a franchise. Check out Entrepreneur.com's business opportunities listing (www.entrepreneur.com/bizopportunities/index.html). Contact the Better Business Bureau to see if there have been complaints against the company, and if the company is registered with D&B, a financial report will give you details on its financial standing and other information.

warning 

Watch out for promises from third-party location hunters. The sales rep may say, "We'll place those pistachio dispensers in prime locations in your town," but more likely, you'll find out that all the best locations are taken, and the next thing you know, your garage is filled with pistachio dispensers. The solution: Get in your car, and check for available locations.

Also check with the regulatory agency—either the Commission of Securities or the Commission of Financial Institutions—in the state where the business opportunity has its headquarters. This will tell you if the company is complying with all state regulations. If you discover the company or its principals have been involved in lawsuits or bankruptcies, try to find out more details. Did the suits involve fraud or violations of regulatory laws? A copy of the petition or judgment, which you can get from the court that handled the case, will give you the answers to these questions.

Finally, see if the business opportunity seller will provide you with a list of people who have purchased the opportunity in the past. Don't let the seller give you a few handpicked names; ask for a full list of buyers in your state. Try to track them down, and talk to as many as you can. Were they satisfied with the opportunity? Would they recommend it to friends?

The path to buying a business opportunity is not as clearly defined as the road leading to franchise ownership. The good news, however, is that you have more freedom to make your business opportunity work. More so than with a franchise, the success or failure of your business opportunity depends on you, your commitment to the venture and the level of effort you put into it. Put that same effort into finding the right business opportunity program, and your chances of success increase exponentially.

PART

2

PLAN

CHAPTER

6

Choose Your Target

Defining Your Market

You've come up with a great idea for a business . . . but you're not ready to roll yet. Before you go any further, the next step is figuring out who your market is.

There are two basic markets you can sell to: consumer and business. These divisions are fairly obvious. For example, if you are selling women's clothing from a retail store, your target market is consumers; if you are selling office supplies, your target market is businesses (this is referred to as "B2B" sales). In some cases—for example, if you run a printing business—you may be marketing to both businesses and individuals.

No business—particularly a small one—can be all things to all people. The more narrowly you can define your target market, the better. This process is known as creating a niche and is key to success for even the biggest companies. Walmart and Tiffany

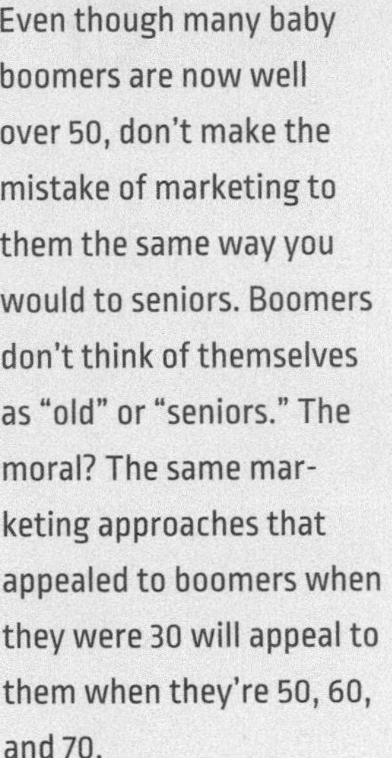

warning

Even though many baby boomers are now well over 50, don't make the mistake of marketing to them the same way you would to seniors. Boomers don't think of themselves as "old" or "seniors." The moral? The same marketing approaches that appealed to boomers when they were 30 will appeal to them when they're 50, 60, and 70.

are both retailers, but they have very different niches: Walmart caters to bargain-minded shoppers, while Tiffany appeals to upscale jewelry consumers.

"Many people talk about 'finding' a niche as if it were something under a rock or at the end of the rainbow, ready-made. That is nonsense," says Lynda Falkenstein, author of *Nichecraft: Using Your Specialness to Focus Your Business, Corner Your Market and Make Customers Seek You Out*. Good niches do not just fall into your lap; they must be very carefully crafted.

Rather than creating a niche, many entrepreneurs make the mistake of falling into the "all over the map" trap, claiming they can do many things and be good at all of them. These people quickly learn a tough lesson, Falkenstein warns: "Smaller is bigger in business, and smaller is not all over the map; it's highly focused."

Practicing Nichecraft

Creating a good niche, advises Falkenstein, involves following a seven-step process:

1. *Make a wish list.* With whom do you want to do business? Be as specific as you can: Identify the geographic range and the types of businesses or customers you want your business to target. If you don't know whom you want to do business with, you can't make contact. "You must recognize that you can't do business with everybody," cautions Falkenstein. Otherwise, you risk exhausting yourself and confusing your customers.

   These days, the trend is toward smaller niches (see "Direct Hit" on page 71). Targeting teenagers isn't specific enough; targeting male, African American teenagers with family incomes of $40,000 and up is. Aiming at companies that sell software is too broad; aiming

>> Direct Hit

Once upon a time, business owners thought it was enough to market their products or services to "18-to-49-year-olds." Those days are things of the past. According to trend experts, the consumer marketplace has become so differentiated, it's a misconception to talk about the marketplace in any kind of general, grand way. You can market to socioeconomic status or to gender or to region or to lifestyle or to technological sophistication. You can market to Millennials, a generation that shops and buys goods and services in vastly different ways than their older siblings and parents. There's no end to the number of different ways you can slice the pie.

Further complicating matters, age no longer means what it used to. Fifty-five-year-old baby boomers prefer rock 'n' roll to supper clubs; 30-year-olds may still be living with their parents. People now repeat stages and recycle their lives. Generational marketing, which defines consumers not just by age, but also by social, economic, demographic, and psychological factors, has been used since the early 1980s to give a more accurate picture of the target consumer.

A more recent twist is cohort marketing, which studies groups of people who underwent the same experiences during their formative years. This leads them to form a bond and behave differently from people in different cohorts, even when they are similar in age. For instance, people who were young adults in the Depression era behave differently from people who came of age during World War II, even though they are close in age.

To get an even narrower reading, some entrepreneurs combine cohort or generational marketing with life stages, or what people are doing at a certain time in life (getting married, having children, retiring), and physiographics, or physical conditions related to age (nearsightedness, arthritis, menopause).

Today's consumers are more marketing-savvy than ever before and don't like to be "lumped" with others—so be sure you understand your niche. While pinpointing your market so narrowly takes a little extra effort, entrepreneurs who aim at a smaller target are far more likely to make a direct hit.

at Northern California-based companies that provide internet software sales and training and have sales of $15 million or more is a better goal.

2. *Focus.* Clarify what you want to sell, remembering: a) You can't be all things to all people and b) "smaller is bigger." Your niche is not the same as the field in which you work. For example, a retail clothing business is not a niche but a field. A more specific niche may be "maternity clothes for executive women."

   To begin this focusing process, Falkenstein suggests using these techniques to help you:

   - Make a list of things you do best and the skills implicit in each of them.
   - List your achievements.
   - Identify the most important lessons you have learned in life.
   - Look for patterns that reveal your style or approach to resolving problems.

   Your niche should arise naturally from your interests and experience. For example, if you spent ten years working in a consulting firm, but also spent ten years working for a small, family-owned business, you may decide to start a consulting business that specializes in small, family-owned companies.

3. *Describe the customer's worldview.* A successful business uses what Falkenstein calls the Platinum Rule: "Do unto others as they would do unto themselves." When you look at the world from your prospective customers' perspective, you can identify their needs or wants. The best way to do this is to talk to prospective customers and identify their main concerns. (Chapter 7 will give you more ideas on ways to get inside customers' heads.)

4. *Synthesize.* At this stage, your niche should begin to take shape as your ideas and the client's needs and wants coalesce to create something new. A good niche has five qualities:

   - It takes you where you want to go—in other words, it conforms to your long-term vision.

- Somebody else wants it—namely, customers.
- It's carefully planned.
- It's one-of-a-kind, the "only game in town."
- It evolves, allowing you to develop different profit centers and still retain the core business, thus ensuring long-term success.

> ***"If you work just for the money, you'll never make it, but if you love what you're doing and you always put the customer first, success will be yours."***
>
> —Ray Kroc, founder of McDonald's Corporation

5. *Evaluate.* Now it's time to evaluate your proposed product or service against the five criteria in Step 4. Perhaps you'll find that the niche you had in mind requires more business travel than you're ready for. That means it doesn't fulfill one of the above criteria—it won't take you where you want to go. So scrap it, and move on to the next idea.
6. *Test.* Once you have a match between niche and product, test-market it. "Give people an opportunity to buy your product or service—not just theoretically but actually putting it out there," suggests Falkenstein. This can be done by offering samples, such as a free miniseminar or a sample copy of your newsletter. The test shouldn't cost you a lot of money: "If you spend huge amounts of money on the initial market test, you are probably doing it wrong," she says.
7. *Go for it!* It's time to implement your idea. For many entrepreneurs, this is the most difficult stage. But fear not: If you did your homework, entering the market will be a calculated risk, not just a gamble.

Keep It Fresh

Once your niche is established and well-received by your market, you may be tempted to rest on your laurels. Not a good idea, says Falkenstein. "[You must] keep growing by re-niching. This doesn't mean totally changing your focus, but rather further adapting it to the environment around you."

Target Market Worksheet

Use the following exercise to identify where and who your target market is. Once you're done, you'll have an audience to aim for and hone in on rather than using a shotgun approach, which is a time- and money-waster.

1. Describe the idea:

    ____

    ____

    ____

2. What will the concept be used for?

    ____

    ____

    ____

3. Where are similar concepts used and sold?

    ____

    ____

    ____

4. What places do my prospects go to for recreation?

    ____

    ____

    ____

5. Where do my prospects go for education?

    ____

    ____

    ____

Figure 6.1. Target Market Worksheet

Target Market Worksheet

6. Where do my prospects do their shopping?

____

____

____

7. What types of newspapers, magazines, and newsletters do my prospects read?

____

____

____

8. What TV and radio stations do my prospects watch and listen to?

____

____

____

Figure 6.1. Target Market Worksheet, continued

Ask yourself the following questions when you think you have found your niche—and ask them again every six months or so to make sure your niche is still on target:

- Who are your target clients?
- Who aren't your target clients?
- Do you refuse certain kinds of business if it falls outside your niche?
- What do clients think you stand for?
- Is your niche in a constant state of evolution?
- Does your niche offer what prospective customers want?
- Do you have a plan and delivery system that effectively conveys the need for your niche to the right market?

- Can you confidently predict the life cycle of your niche?
- How can your niche be expanded into a variety of products or services that act as profit centers?
- Do you have a sense of passion and focused energy with respect to your niche?
- Does your niche feel comfortable and natural?
- How will pursuing your niche contribute to achieving the goals you have set for your business?

According to Falkenstein, "Creating a niche is the difference between being in business and not being in business. It's the difference between surviving and thriving, between simply liking what you do and the joy of success."

On a Mission

Once you have designed a niche for your business, you're ready to create a mission statement. A key tool that can be as important as your business plan, a mission statement captures, in a few succinct sentences, the essence of your business's goals and the philosophies underlying them. Equally important, the mission statement signals what your business is all about to your customers, employees, suppliers, and the community.

The mission statement reflects every facet of your business: the range and nature of the products you offer, pricing, quality, service, marketplace position, growth potential, use of technology, and your relationships with your customers, employees, suppliers, competitors, and the community.

"Mission statements help clarify what business you are in, your goals and your objectives," says Rhonda Abrams, author of *The Successful Business Plan: Secrets and Strategies.*

Your mission statement should reflect your business's special niche. Studying other companies' statements can fuel your creativity. One sample mission statement Abrams developed:

> AAA Inc. is a spunky, imaginative food products and service company aimed at offering high-quality, moderately priced, occasionally unusual foods using only natural ingredients. We view ourselves as partners with our customers, our employees, our

community, and our environment. We aim to become a regionally recognized brand name, capitalizing on the sustained interest in Southwestern and Mexican food. Our goal is moderate growth, annual profitability, and maintaining our sense of humor.

Or consider the statement one entrepreneur developed for her consulting business: "ABC Enterprises is a company devoted to developing human potential. Our mission is to help people create innovative solutions and make informed choices to improve their lives. We motivate and encourage others to achieve personal and professional fulfillment. Our motto is: Together, we believe that the best in each of us enriches all of us."

tip

Doing business with the government can seem intimidating because of all the paperwork. To make it easier, many government agencies are reaching out to teach small firms how to bid—and win. Every state provides some kind of training, usually sponsored through community colleges for a small fee. Check with your local community college or SBA district office for details.

The Write Words

To come up with a statement that encompasses all the major elements of your business, start with the right questions. Business plan consultants say the most important question is, "What business are you in?" Since you

>> Profiting from Procurement

Looking for a niche? One market many entrepreneurs ignore is the lucrative procurement pie. Although the federal government is by far the biggest customer in this arena, local governments, colleges and universities, school districts, nonprofit organizations, public utilities, and corporations also have plenty of procurement opportunities available. The federal government's civilian agencies alone buy products in more than 4,000 categories, ranging from air brakes to zippers.

>> Profiting from Procurement, continued

Small businesses often have an edge in competing for procurement dollars. Government agencies and large contractors are often required by law to give a certain amount of business to small, disadvantaged, women-owned or minority-owned businesses.

How to Get Started

> Check out the SBA's subcontracting opportunities at web.sba.gov/subnet.

> Agencies like the U.S. Postal Service, Department of Interior, and the Army, as well as many others, send out solicitations to businesses that are on their mailing lists. To find out how to get on the lists, contact the agency you're interested in.

> Regularly check "Federal Business Opportunities" online for daily updates (fedbizopps.gov). At any given time, there can be more than 25,000 opportunities listed.

If you are a woman or a member of a minority group, you will need to be certified as a woman- or minority-owned business to work with government agencies and many large contractors. This can be done in several ways. Many cities have their own certification programs or can direct you to the certification programs that they accept. A good general place to start is with the SBA; you can reach them at 409 Third St. SW, Washington, DC 20416, or call (800) U-ASK-SBA or answerdesk@sba.gov. There is also a website devoted to helping women-owned small businesses navigate certification and procurement opportunities: www.sba.gov/content/contracting-opportunities-women-owned-small-businesses. And for minority businesses: www.sba.gov/content/minority-owned-businesses.

have already gone through the steps of creating your niche, answering this question should be easy for you.

Answering the following ten questions will help you to create a verbal picture of your business's mission:

1. *Why are you in business?* What do you want for yourself, your family, and your customers?

Think about the spark that ignited your decision to start a business. What will keep it burning?

2. *Who are your customers?* What can you do for them that will enrich their lives and contribute to their success—now and in the future?
3. *What image of your business do you want to convey?* Customers, suppliers, employees, and the public will all have perceptions of your company. How will you create the desired picture?
4. *What is the nature of your products and services?* What factors determine pricing and quality? Consider how these relate to the reasons for your business's existence. How will all this change over time?
5. *What level of service do you provide?* Most companies believe they offer "the best service available," but do your customers agree? Don't be vague; define what makes your service so extraordinary.
6. *What roles do you and your employees play?* Wise captains develop a leadership style that organizes, challenges, and recognizes employees.
7. *What kind of relationships will you maintain with suppliers?* Every business is in partnership with its suppliers. When you succeed, so do they.
8. *How do you differ from competitors?* Many entrepreneurs forget they are pursuing the same dollars as their competitors. What do you do better, cheaper, or faster than competitors? How can you use competitors' weaknesses to your advantage?
9. *How will you use technology, capital, processes, products, and services to reach your goals?* A description of your strategy will keep your energies focused on your goals.
10. *What underlying philosophies or values guided your responses to the previous*

tip

When it comes to mission statements, employees are number one. It's more important to communicate your mission statement to employees than to your customers. The most effective mission statements are developed strictly for internal communication and discussion. In other words, your mission statement doesn't have to be clever or catchy—just accurate.

questions? Some businesses choose to list these separately. Writing them down clarifies the "why" behind your mission.

Putting It All Together

Crafting a mission statement requires time, thought, and planning. However, the effort is well worth it. In fact, most startup entrepreneurs discover that the process of crafting the mission statement is as beneficial as the final statement itself. Going through the process will help you solidify the reasons for what you are doing and clarify the motivations behind your business.

Here are some tips to make your mission statement the best it can be:

- *Involve those connected to your business.* Even if you are a sole proprietor, it helps to get at least one other person's ideas for your mission statement. Other people can help you see strengths, weaknesses, and voids you might miss. If you have no partners or investors to include, consider knowledgeable family members and close friends, employees, or accountants. Choose supportive people who truly want you to succeed.
- *Set aside several hours*—a full day, if possible—to work on your statement. Mission statements are short—typically more than one sentence but rarely exceeding a page. Still, writing one is not a short process. It takes time to come up with language that simultaneously describes an organization's heart and soul and serves as an inspirational beacon to everyone involved in the business. Large corporations often spend an entire weekend crafting a statement.
- *Plan a date.* Set aside time to meet with the people who'll be helping you. Write a list of topics to discuss or think about. Find a quiet, comfortable place away from phones and interruptions.
- *Be prepared.* If you have several people involved, be equipped with refreshments, extra lists of topics, paper, and pencils. Explain the meaning and purpose of a mission statement before you begin—not everyone will automatically know what they're all about.
- *Brainstorm.* Consider every idea, no matter how silly it sounds. Stimulate ideas by looking at sample mission statements and

thinking about or discussing the ten questions starting on page 77 ("The Write Words"). If you're working with a group, use a flip chart to record responses so everyone can see them. Once you've finished brainstorming, ask everyone to write individual mission statements for your business. Read the statements, select the best pieces, and fit them together.

- *Use "radiant words."* Once you have the basic idea in writing, polish the language of your mission statement. "Every word counts," says Abrams. The statement should create dynamic mental visuals and inspire action. Use offbeat, colorful verbs and adjectives to spice up your statement. Don't hesitate to drop in words like "kaleidoscope," "sizzle," "cheer," "outrageous," and "marvel" to add zest. If you want customers to "boast" about your goods and services, say so—along with the reasons why.

tip

Once you've drafted your mission statement, you should periodically review and possibly revise it to make sure it accurately reflects your goals as your company and the business and economic climates evolve. To do this, simply ask yourself if the statement still correctly describes what you're doing.

Once your mission statement is complete, start spreading the word! You need to convey your mission statement to others inside and outside the business to tell everyone you know where you are going and why. Post it in your office, where you, employees, and visitors can see it every day. Print it on company materials, such as your brochures and your business plan, or even on the back of your business cards.

When you're launching a new business, you can't afford to lose sight of your objectives. By always keeping your mission statement in front of you, you'll keep your goals in mind—and ensure smooth sailing.

CHAPTER

7

If You Build It, Will They Come?

Conducting Market Research

So you have a great idea for a product—something that's bound to capture the hearts and minds (and wallets) of consumers everywhere. Or perhaps you have stumbled on a service that isn't being offered by anyone else—one that is desperately needed. This is your opportunity! Don't hesitate . . . don't look back . . . jump right into it and . . .

Wait! Before you shift into high gear, you must determine whether there really is a market for your product or service. Not only that, you need to ascertain what—if any—fine-tuning is needed. Quite simply, you must conduct market research.

Many business owners neglect this crucial step in product development for the sole reason that they don't want to hear any negative feedback. They are convinced their product or service is perfect just the way it is, and they don't want to risk tampering with it.

> *"There's only one boss—the customer."*
>
> —Sam Walton, founder of Walmart

Other entrepreneurs bypass market research because they fear it will be too expensive. With all the other startup costs you're facing, it's not easy to justify spending money on research that will only prove what you knew all along: Your product is a winner.

Regardless of the reason, failing to do market research can amount to a death sentence for your product. "A lot of companies skim over the important background information because they're so interested in getting their product to market," says Donna Barson, president and owner of Barson Marketing Inc., a marketing, advertising, and public relations consulting firm. "But the companies that do the best are the ones that do their homework."

Consider market research an investment in your future. If you make the necessary adjustments to your product or service now, you'll save money in the long run.

>> Good Question

Whether you hire a professional market research firm or take on the task yourself, your market research should clearly answer the following questions:

- Who will buy my product or service?
- Why will they buy it?
- Where will they buy it—specialty shops, department stores, mail order?
- What do I need to charge to make a healthy profit?
- What products or services will mine be competing with?
- Am I positioning my product or service correctly? (In other words, if there's a lot of competition, look for a specialized market niche.)
- What government regulations will my product or service be subject to?

What It Is, What It Does

What exactly is market research? Simply put, it's a way of collecting information you can use to solve or avoid marketing problems. Good market research gives you the data you need to develop a marketing plan that really works for you. It enables you to identify the specific segments within a market that you want to target and to create an identity for your product or service that separates it from your competitors. Market research can also help you choose the best geographic location in which to launch your new business.

tip 

When doing any type of survey, whether it is a focus group, a questionnaire, or a phone survey, pay attention to customers who complain or give you negative feedback. You don't need to worry about the customers who love your product or service, but the ones who tell you where you're going wrong provide valuable information to help you improve.

Before you start your market research, it's a good idea to meet with a consultant, talk to a business or marketing professor at a local college or university, or contact your local SBA district office. These sources can offer guidance and help you with the first step in market research: deciding exactly what information you need to gather.

As a rule of thumb, market research should provide you with information about three critical areas: the industry, the consumer, and the competition.

1. *Industry information.* In researching the industry, look for the latest trends. Compare the statistics and growth in the industry. What areas of the industry appear to be expanding, and what areas are declining? Is the industry catering to new types of customers? What technological developments are affecting the industry? How can you use them to your advantage? A thriving, stable industry is key; you don't want to start a new business in a field that is on the decline.
2. *Consumer close-up.* On the consumer side, your market research should begin with a market survey. A thorough market survey will help you make a reasonable sales forecast for your new business. To do a market survey, you first need to determine the market limits or

physical boundaries of the area to which your business sells. Next, study the spending characteristics of the population within this location.

Estimate the location's purchasing power, based on its per-capita income, its median income level, the unemployment rate, population, and other demographic factors. Determine the current sales volume in the area for the type of product or service you will sell.

Finally, estimate how much of the total sales volume you can reasonably obtain. (This last step is extremely important. Opening your new business in a given community won't necessarily generate additional business volume; it may simply redistribute the business that's already there.)

3. *Competition close-up.* Based on a combination of industry research and consumer research, a clearer picture of your competition will emerge. Do not underestimate the number of competitors out there. Keep an eye out for potential future competitors as well as current ones.

   Examine the number of competitors on a local and, if relevant, national scale. Study their strategies and operations. Your analysis should supply a clear picture of potential threats, opportunities, and the weaknesses and strengths of the competition facing your new business.

When looking at the competition, try to see what trends have been established in the industry and whether there's an opportunity or advantage for your business. Use the library, the internet, and other secondary research sources described later in this chapter to research competitors. Read as many articles as you can on the companies you will be competing with. If you are researching publicly owned companies, contact them and obtain copies of their annual reports. These often show not only how successful a company is, but also what products or services it plans to emphasize in the future.

One of the best websites for researching the competition is Hoover's Online (hoovers.com), which, for a fee, provides in-depth profiles of more than 85 million companies. However, there is also free content available,

>> Know Thy Enemy

There are two ways to define competitors. One is by strategic groups—competitors who use similar marketing strategies, sell similar products, or have similar skills. Under this definition, you might group Toyota and Nissan as competitors within the car industry.

The second, less obvious way to group competitors is by customer—how strongly do they compete for the same customers' dollar? Using this method gives you a wider view of your competitors and the challenges they could pose to your new business.

Suppose you're considering opening a family entertainment center. If there are no other family entertainment centers in the area, you might think you have no competitors. Wrong! Any type of business that competes for customers' leisure time and entertainment dollars is a competitor. That means children's play centers, amusement parks, and arcades are all your competitors. So are businesses that, on the surface, don't appear similar, like movie theaters, bookstores, and shopping malls. You could even face competition from nonprofit entities, like public parks, libraries, and beaches. In short, anything that families might do in their leisure time is your "competition."

A study by professors at UCLA and Stanford University showed most business owners are clueless about the competition. Almost 80 percent were blind to their opponents' actions, which can lead to lost customers and market share.

The answer? Role-play. Put yourself in the competitors' shoes and analyze their strategies. Visit their stores. Use the internet to dig up as much information as you can about them, their tactics, and their goals.

plus you can sign up for a free trial subscription. You can also gather information on competing businesses by visiting them in person. Take along a questionnaire like the "Sample Market Research Competition Questionnaire" on page 88. This one is for a bar/club, but you can customize it for your particular business.

Sample Market Research Competition Questionnaire

When you visit the competing bars in your area, you want to use the information you gather to develop a competitive strategy for your own establishment. Improve on their strengths and capitalize on their weaknesses. Fill out this questionnaire for each of the bars you visit to help you assess your competition and your customers.

1. What type of bar is it? ____________________
2. What is the concept/theme? ____________________
3. Does the bar offer a full bar, beer and wine, or just beer? ____________________
4. Did you have to wait to be seated? How long? ____________________
5. How long did it take to get served? ____________________
6. What kind of décor does the bar have? ____________________
7. Is the bar clean? ____________________
8. Is the layout of the bar and tables efficient? ____________________
9. Does the bar serve food? ____________________
10. If so, what types of food does it have on the menu? ____________________
11. Does the menu offer enough variety? ____________________

Figure 7.1. Sample Market Research Competition Questionnaire

Market Research Competition Questionnaire

12. How would you rate the quality of the drinks? ____________________

____

13. How would you rate the quality of the food? ____________________

____

14. Does the cost match the quality/quantity of the food and drinks served?

____

15. How do you feel about the bar's atmosphere? ____________________

____

16. How is the service? ____

____

17. What promotions and sales techniques do you notice? ____________

____

____

18. What feedback did you receive from the bartender/wait staff? ______

____

____

19. What information did you get from the customers? ______________

____

____

20. List three ways you would improve the bar.

    1. ____

    2. ____

    3. ____

Figure 7.1. Sample Market Research Competition Questionnaire, continued

>> The ABCs of Market Research

Matthew Toren, serial entrepreneur and cofounder of YoungEntrepreneur.com, offered the simple explanations of what your market research should be:

> *A is for approach.* What's your approach to research going to be? Primary research involves actual humans. Have you ever been asked to be part of a research study? Approached on the street by people in bright T-shirts wanting to ask you questions? That's an attempt to get people for primary market research—people to pose questions to, to test your market theories on real, live potential consumers in your intended demographic.

> *B is for beware.* There are some common mistakes to know about. The first big mistake is relying on only one kind of research. Most people do this by leaning only on secondary sources to save money. While it's relevant, it can be dated, whereas primary research gives you more recent and often more authentic individual data. Second, don't poll your friends and family for primary data. They have an emotional connection and reason to provide whatever answers you might want. On that same note, don't rely only on social-media polls or online surveys as primary research.

> *C is for collected data.* When you consider your collected data, analyze it in two different buckets: quantitative and qualitative. Quantitative data is the kind you can put numbers around. For instance, if you ask questions about being for or against an issue, you'll be able to quantify after the survey how many people fall on either side. Adding questions that will help you qualitatively understand your market are equally insightful as they help you develop and explain your quantitative data—and more carefully define what your market wants and needs.

Market Research Methods

In conducting your market research, you will gather two types of data: primary and secondary. Primary research is information that comes directly from the source—that is, potential customers. You can compile this information yourself or hire someone else to gather it for you via surveys, focus groups, and other methods. Secondary research involves gathering statistics, reports, studies, and other data from organizations such as government agencies, trade associations, and your local chamber of commerce.

Secondary Research

The vast majority of research you can find will be secondary research. While large companies spend huge amounts of money on market research, the good news is that plenty of information is available for free to entrepreneurs on a tight budget. The best places to start? Your local library and the internet.

Reference librarians at public and university libraries will be happy to point you in the right direction. Become familiar with the business reference section—you'll be spending a lot of time there. Two good sources to look for: ThomasNet (thomasnet.com), an online resource that connects industrial buyers and sellers, and the Hoovers Industry Reports (www.hoovers.com/industry-analysis/industry-reports.html). Both sources can be found at most libraries, as well as online, and can help you target businesses in a particular industry, read up on competitors, or find manufacturers for your product.

To get insights into consumer markets, check out the *Statistical Abstract of the United States*, which you can find at most libraries. It contains a wealth of social, political, and economic data. Ask reference librarians for other resources targeted at your specific business.

e-fyi

In the business of ecommerce? ComScore (comscore.com) is a market research company that will evaluate your ecommerce site. They offer a variety of options, from web-based marketing strategies to custom research. Even if you're not ready for professional advice, exploring the site will give you an idea of the questions you should be asking in your own research.

Associations

Your industry trade association can offer a wealth of information such as market statistics, lists of members, and books and reference materials. Talking to others in your association can be one of the most valuable ways of gaining informal data about a region or customer base.

Look in the *Encyclopedia of Associations* (Gale Cengage Learning), found in most libraries, to find associations relevant to your industry. You may also want to investigate your customers' trade associations for information that can help you market to them. Most trade associations provide information free of charge.

Read your trade associations' publications, as well as those aimed at your target customers, to get an idea of current and future trends and buying patterns. And keep an eye out for more: New magazines and newsletters are launched every year. If you're not following all of them, you could be missing out on valuable information about new products and your competitors.

Government Guidance

Government agencies are an invaluable source of market research, most of it free. Almost every county government publishes population density and distribution figures in widely available census tracts. These publications will show you the number of people living in specific areas, such as precincts, water districts, or even ten-block neighborhoods. Some counties publish reports on population trends that show the population ten years ago, five years ago, and today. Watch out for a static, declining, or small population; ideally, you want to locate where there is an expanding population that wants your products and services. Check local employment figures for the area, too. A stagnant job market—or worse, a consistently declining one—could mean that fewer people will be able to spend money, even on necessities. But, it could mean that a product or service that is less expensive than what's available might be in demand.

The U.S. Census Bureau (census.gov) turns out reams of inexpensive or free business information, most of which is available on the internet:

- *The Census Bureau's State and Metropolitan Area Data Book* offers statistics for metropolitan areas, central cities, and counties.
- *The Census Product Update* is a monthly listing of recently released and upcoming products from the U.S. Census Bureau.

Sign up for a free email subscription at census.gov.

- *County Business Patterns* is an excellent Census product that reports the number of a given type of business in a county by ZIP code and metropolitan and micropolitan statistical area.
- For breakdowns by geographical area, look to the *Economic Census*, which is published every five years.

> ***"You must be the change you wish in this world."***
>
> —Mahatma Gandhi

Most of these products should be available online or at your local library. If not, contact your nearest Census office for a list of publications and ordering information, or write to the U.S. Census Bureau, 4600 Silver Hill Rd., Washington, DC 20233, (301) 763-INFO or (800) 923-8282. Many Census Bureau reports are also available on CD or DVD, or are free on the internet.

The U.S. Government has an official web portal that is another good source of information. For instance, at the USA.gov website (usa.gov), you'll find a section for businesses that is a one-stop link to all the information and services that the federal government provides for the business community. Tax questions? Wondering about how best to deal with all the regulations and red tape? Chances are you'll find your answers at business.gov by clicking the "About Finances" and/or "Taxes and Credits" links.

Or you might try the Commerce Department's Economic Indicators web page (www.esa.doc.gov). Curious if the world is ready to spend money on your exercise equipment for goldfish? Then the Economic Indicators site is for you. Literally every day, they're releasing key economic indicators from the Bureau of Economic Analysis and the U.S. Census Bureau.

If you're planning to get into exporting, contact the Department of Commerce's International Trade Administration (ITA). The ITA publishes several thousand reports and statistical surveys, not to mention hundreds of books on everything American entrepreneurs need to know about exporting. Many of the reports and books are available for downloading immediately from the ITA's press and publications department (trade.gov/publications). Here you'll also find information on how to order printed

>> Netting Information

If your market research budget is limited, try CenStats. A free service from the Census Bureau that's available on the internet, CenStats allows you to access the bureau's most popular databases and information.

Search by county or ZIP code under "County Business Patterns," and you'll get business profiles for an area that include payroll information and business size by industry. Click on "USA Counties" to get counties' economic and demographic information, including personal income per capita, population size, and more.

To test out CenStats, visit censtats.census.gov.

copies, including archived publications. Or if you prefer, call the Trade Information Center at (800) USA-TRADE.

Maps

Maps of trading areas in counties and states are available from chambers of commerce, trade development commissions, industrial development boards, and local newspaper offices. These maps show the major areas of commerce and can also help you judge the accessibility of various sites. Access is an important consideration in determining the limits of your market area.

Colleges and Universities

Local colleges and universities are valuable sources of information. Many college business departments have students who are eager to work in the "real world," gathering information and doing research at little or no cost.

Finally, local business schools are a great source of experts. Many business professors do consulting on the side, and some will even be happy to offer you marketing, sales, strategic planning, or financial information for free. Call professors who specialize in these areas; if they can't help, they'll be able to put you in touch with someone who can. Oftentimes, their entrepreneurship students will be required to do practical work for

>> Survey Says . . .

"A recent survey shows . . ." just might be the most overused, misused and abused phrase in modern life. Try hard enough, and you can find a survey to prove that four out of five Americans have been aboard a UFO, think they can flap their arms and fly to the moon, or believe Elvis is alive and living in their spare bedroom. With all the half-baked surveys out there, how do you know what to believe?

First, consider the source. Many surveys are conducted by trade associations, which inevitably are biased in favor of good news. This doesn't mean trade association surveys are necessarily inaccurate; just keep in mind that they are likely to play up positive results and downplay negative ones. When looking at any survey, consider what the source has to gain from the information presented. Then you'll have a better idea of whether to take the information with a grain of salt.

What's more, these days you need to consider how the survey is conducted—no matter the source. Social media surveys and online polls aren't going to be as scientific and might not be reliable.

Meaningful surveys generally share the following characteristics:

- *Short-term focus.* In general, respondents are more likely to be accurate when they make predictions about the next three to six months. When it comes to predicting the long term (a year or more ahead), they're usually guessing.
- *Adequate sample size.* What constitutes adequate size depends on the topic you're surveying. In general, the broader the topic, the larger the number of respondents should be. If the survey talks about broad manufacturing trends, for example, it should survey 1,000 companies or more. Also consider where the respondents come from. If you're starting a small regional business, a large national sample may not be relevant to your needs because the sample size from your area is probably too small to tell you anything about your region.

>> **Survey Says . . . , continued**

- *Knowledgeable respondents.* Asking entrepreneurs in the electronics business to forecast the future of the industry obviously carries more weight than asking the same question of teachers or random people on the street.
- *Continual replication.* The best surveys are repeated regularly, using the same methods, so there is a good basis for comparison from survey to survey.
- *Specific information relevant to your business.* In a nutshell, the best surveys are those where respondents answer questions that are narrowly targeted to your region and niche.

their courses—they are often eager to connect with local small-business owners (or those about to launch) to do hands-on projects and research under the watchful eye of their professors. And it's free!

Community Organizations

Your local chamber of commerce or business development agency can supply useful information. They are usually free of charge, including assistance with site selection, demographic reports, and directories of local businesses. They may also offer seminars on marketing and related topics that can help you do better research.

D&B

Financial and business services firm D&B offers a range of reference sources that can help startups. Some of the information they offer as part of their Sales & Marketing Solutions are directories for career opportunities, consultants, service companies, and regional businesses. Visit their website at dnb.com, or call (866) 503-0287 for more information.

- *D&B's Regional Business Directories* provide detailed information to help identify new business prospects and assess market potential. Besides basic information (telephone number, address, and company description), the directories also tell when the company was started, sales volume, number of employees, parent company (if any) and, if it's a public company, on which exchange it's traded.

- *D&B's Million Dollar Database* can help you develop a marketing campaign for B2B sales. The Million Dollar Database lists more than 34 million companies. It has complete information on U.S. and Canadian leading public and private companies and includes information regarding the number of employees, annual sales, and ownership type. The database now also includes information on companies in 200 other countries worldwide. The database also includes biographical information on owners and officers, giving insight into their backgrounds and business experiences. For more information, go to www.mergentmddi.com.

tip

In addition to surveys conducted by trade organizations, businesses, and D&B, universities are an excellent source of objective survey information. Another place to look for survey data: Many large newspapers and radio stations do surveys to learn about their markets. These surveys are usually easy to obtain and packed with up-to-date information about demographics and potential customers. Look in your local paper's advertiser information section online for a market research packet or fact sheet.

Going Online

These days, entrepreneurs can conduct much of their market research without ever leaving their computers, thanks to the universe of online services and information. Start with the major consumer online services, which offer access to business databases. You can find everything from headline and business news to industry trends and company-specific business information, such as a firm's address, telephone number, field of business, and the name of the CEO. This information is critical for identifying prospects, developing mailing lists, and planning sales calls. Here are a few to get you started:

- *KnowThis.com's (knowthis.com)* marketing virtual library includes a tab on the site called "Marketing Links" that contains links to a wide variety of market research web resources. You can simply type in what you want to do, and voila, results for resources.

- *MarketResearch.com (marketresearch.com)* has research reports from more than 700 sources consolidated into one accessible collection that's updated daily. No subscription fee is required, and you pay only for the parts of the report you need with its "slice-and-dice" feature called Profound. After paying, the information is delivered online to your personal library on the site. Its In a Nutshell series offers three- to four-minute videos on the highlights of various topics.

e-fyi

Zoomerang.com and SurveyMonkey.com make market research easy: You can create surveys online using a variety of templates. And if you don't know who to send your survey to, you can purchase a list off Zoomerang. Another option is to post your survey on your website. Zoomerang and SurveyMonkey will even calculate the results for you.

All the sources mentioned earlier (trade associations, government agencies) should also have websites you can visit to get information quickly. For instance, the Census Bureau offers many helpful websites:

- *The American Factfinder website (factfinder2.census.gov)* provides excellent access to census information, including a "Maps" feature.
- *The Census Bureau's International Database (census.gov/population/international/)* furnishes data on foreign countries.

If you don't have time to investigate online services yourself, consider hiring an information broker to find the information you need. Information brokers gather information quickly. They can act as a small company's research arm, identifying the most accurate and cost-effective information sources.

To find information brokers, look in the Yellow Pages or ask the research librarian at your local library. Many research librarians deal with information brokers and will be able to give you good recommendations.

Primary Research

> *"The time when you need to do something is when no one else is willing to do it, when people are saying it can't be done."*
>
> —Mary Frances Berry, Geraldine R. Segal Professor of American Social Thought at the University of Pennsylvania

The secondary research you conduct should help you focus your niche and get a better idea of the challenges facing your business. To get a complete picture of your target market, however, you'll need to do some primary research as well.

A market research firm can help you if you feel that primary research is too complicated to do on your own. These firms will charge a few thousand dollars or more, but depending on the complexity of the information you need, you may feel this is money well-spent. Your local chamber of commerce can recommend firms or individuals who can conduct market research for smaller businesses on a budget.

If you need assistance but don't want to spend that kind of cash, you can go to your SBA district office for guidance, and counselors can help you figure out what types of questions you need to ask your target market. As with secondary research, the SBA, SBDCs, colleges, and universities are good sources of help with primary research.

20 Questions

Whether you use students, get help from the SBA, use a market research firm, or go it alone, there are simple ways you can get primary research information.

- *Focus groups.* A focus group consists of 5 to 12 potential customers who are asked their opinions in a group interview. Participants should fit your target market—for example, single men ages 18 to 25, or working mothers. To find participants, just go to your local mall or college campus and ask people fitting your customer profile if they would answer a few questions. You should expect to pay between $75 and $100 per participant in focus groups. Although focus group interviews are informal, you should have a list of questions to help you direct the discussion. Start by asking whether your product or service is one the participants would buy. If so, what is the highest price they would pay? Where would they shop for such a product? Do they like or dislike the product's packaging? Your questions should center on predetermined objectives, such as determining how high you can price your product or service or what to name your business. The "Sample Focus Group Questionnaire" on page 102 is for a mail order chocolates company, but you can customize it for your business.

If you're going the do-it-yourself route, you will probably act as the focus group moderator. Encourage an open-ended flow of conversation; be sure to solicit comments from quieter members, or you may end up getting all your information from only the talkative participants.

tip

Small fries have big ideas that could help your business grow. If you are starting a child-related business, consider using children as marketing consultants. Kids think creatively—a big asset for entrepreneurs trying to reach this market. Companies like Microsoft and MTV hire kids to learn their views. But you don't need to be so formal: Just try polling the kids you know. Get their responses, and ask them for suggestions.

- *Telephone interviews.* This is an inexpensive, fast way to get information from potential customers. Prepare a script before making the calls to ensure you cover all your objectives. Most people don't like to spend a lot of time on the phone, so keep your questions simple, clearly worded, and brief. If you don't have time to make the calls yourself, hire college students or freelancers through Odesk.com or another site to do it for you.
- *Direct-mail interviews.* If you want to survey a wider audience, direct mail can be just the ticket. Your survey can be as simple as a postcard or as elaborate as a cover letter, questionnaire, and reply envelope (for an example of the letter and questionnaire, see pages 104 and 105, respectively). Keep questionnaires to a maximum of

one page, and ask no more than 20 questions. Ideally, direct-mail surveys should be simple, structured with "yes/no" or "agree/disagree" check-off boxes so respondents can answer quickly and easily. If possible, only ask for one or two write-in answers at most.

- *Email interviews.* Many of the principles used in direct-mail interviews also apply to these surveys. Give clear instructions on how to respond, and be appreciative in advance for the data you get back.

Making a List . . .

How do you get the names of potential customers to call or mail questionnaires to? You can get lists from many places, including your suppliers, trade associations, or a list-rental company. List-rental companies can give you access to a mailing list of a group of people who fit into your desired market. Refer to your local Yellow Pages for the names of list-rental companies. If none are listed, contact the Direct Marketing Association. (For more information on mailing lists, see Chapter 20.)

A less sophisticated approach to finding potential customer names is picking them at random from the phone book. If you've developed a latex glove for doctors, for example, you can get doctors' names out of the Yellow Pages. Whatever method you use to gather your information, the key to market research is using what you learn. The most sophisticated survey in the world does you no good if you ignore the information and the feedback customers provide.

Sample Focus Group Questionnaire

1. How many times a year do you purchase fine chocolates for yourself?

   ____

2. How many times a year do you purchase fine chocolates as gifts:

   - For your spouse or significant other? ______________
   - For your children? ______________
   - For other relatives? What are their relationships? ______________
   - For clients or co-workers? ______________

3. Do you prefer dark chocolate or milk chocolate? ______________

   ____

4. Do you prefer to choose your own selection (nuts, chews, creams, etc.), or would you rather purchase a pre-boxed assortment? ______________

   ____

5. How much do you usually spend for a one-pound box of chocolates?

   ____

6. Would you pay more for a box specially wrapped for a gift occasion?

   ____

7. For which special occasions do you purchase chocolates?

   ____

8. How much would you expect to pay for this half-pound box of gold foil-wrapped chocolate stars? (Here you show the product to your group.)

   ____

9. How much would you expect to pay for an eight-ounce solid chocolate Elvis Presley? (Here you show the product to your group.)

   ____

Figure 7.2. Sample Focus Group Questionnaire

Sample Focus Group Questionnaire

10. Would you buy an eight-ounce solid chocolate Elvis Presley? ________

    ____

11. How many times in the past year have you purchased something by mail order? ____

12. Were you pleased with your purchase? ____

    ____

13. If so, why? ____

    ____

    ____

14. If not, why not? ____

    ____

    ____

15. Would you feel comfortable about the freshness of chocolates you received through the mail? ____

    ____

16. What would you expect to pay for shipping and handling? ________

    ____

17. Please comment on the name Chocoholic Central (love, like, dislike, or hate, and why). ____

    ____

18. Please comment on the name For Chocolate Lovers Only (love, like, dislike, or hate, and why). ____

    ____

    ____

Figure 7.2. Sample Focus Group Questionnaire, continued

Sample Direct-Mail Cover Letter

Your Own Personal Interior Decorator
OnCall Designer for Pennies!

How would you like to have your very own interior decorator available any time you need her—to redecorate a single room or your entire home, or just to answer all those "little" questions, like what color to repaint the kitchen or how to make the kids' rooms more organized?

Sound wonderful but too expensive? Not so! With OnCall Designer, you can get professional interior design services for as little as $50 per room. And we'd like to offer you a charter membership!

But first, we need your help. In order to tailor our service to your needs and desires, we're asking you to fill out the attached questionnaire and send it back. It's a self-mailer, so it's easy! And to show our appreciation for your help, we'll enroll you as a charter member of OnCall Designer. This entitles you to:

- Monthly newsletters packed with design tips and ideas
- Fantastic discounts on designer books, kits, and products
- 10% off your first decorator request

Sound exciting? It is! When you receive your first mailing, you'll be thrilled with the quality of our products and services—everything you need to give your home that exclusive designer look. Your friends will want to know how you did it!

Ready to get started? It's as easy as 1, 2, 3:

1. Fill out the attached questionnaire.
2. Fold it and send it back in its own mailer to OnCall Designer.
3. Keep the certificate below! When you receive your first mailing, you can use the coupon for your 10% discount on the product or service of your choice.

Figure 7.3. Sample Direct-Mail Cover Letter

Sample Direct-Mail Cover Letter

OnCall Designer

This certificate entitles ______________________________,

a charter member of *OnCall Designer*, to a full 10% off any

product or service offered in Mailing No. 1.

Enjoy!

123 Décor Drive, Dept. 1A, Art Deco, FL 30000 • (305) 555-9800 • oncalldesigner.com

Figure 7.3. Sample Direct-Mail Cover Letter, continued

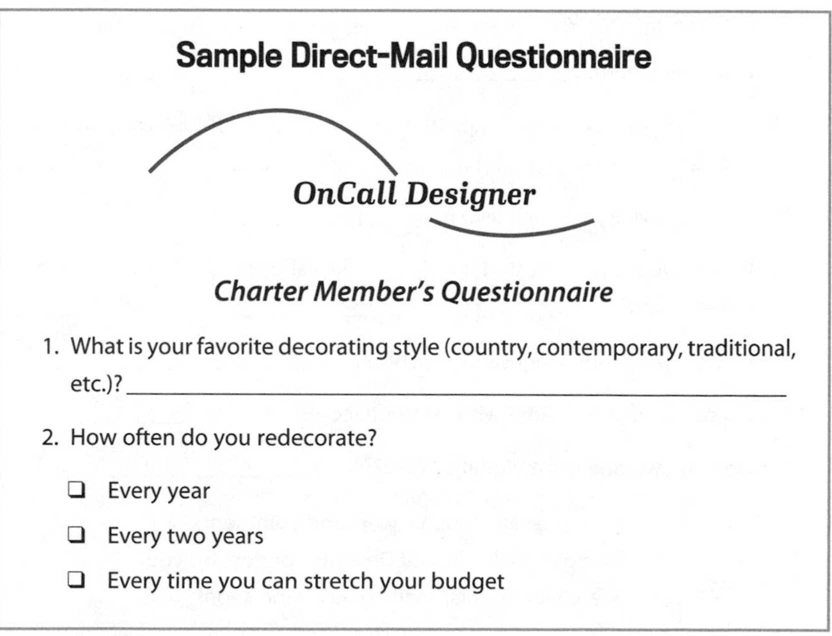

Sample Direct-Mail Questionnaire

OnCall Designer

Charter Member's Questionnaire

1. What is your favorite decorating style (country, contemporary, traditional, etc.)? ______________________________
2. How often do you redecorate?
   - ❑ Every year
   - ❑ Every two years
   - ❑ Every time you can stretch your budget

Figure 7.4. Sample Direct-Mail Questionnaire

Sample Direct-Mail Questionnaire

3. When was the last time you redecorated? ____________________
4. Which room or rooms did you do and why? ____________________

    ____

5. About how much did you spend on this project? ____________________
6. What are your biggest decorating problems or concerns? (Go ahead—tell us everything!) ____________________

    ____

7. How many people make up your household? ____________________
8. If you have kids at home, what are their ages? ____________________

    ____

9. What is the approximate square footage of your home? ____________________
10. Is it a house, a condo, or an apartment? ____________________
11. How many bedrooms? ____________________
12. How many baths? ____________________
13. Do you have a separate family room, office, or den? (Please circle all that apply.)
14. Do you have a patio or a deck? ____________________
15. Would you be interested in tips, tricks, and products for outdoor entertaining? ____________________
16. What is your annual household income? ____________________
17. Do you have a computer with internet access? ____________________
18. Do you own and use a digital camera? ____________________

We appreciate your answers and comments.
They'll help us make **OnCall Designer** perfect for you.
Watch for our first mailing—coming soon!

Figure 7.4. Sample Direct-Mail Questionnaire, continued

CHAPTER

8

The Name Game

Naming Your Business

What's in a name? A lot, when it comes to small-business success. The right name can make your company the talk of the town; the wrong one can doom it to obscurity and failure. If you're smart, you'll put just as much effort into naming your business as you did into coming up with your idea, writing your business plan, and selecting a market and location. Ideally, your name should convey the expertise, value, and uniqueness of the product or service you have developed.

Finding a good business name is more difficult than ever. Many of the best names have already been trademarked. Others might be available, but their web domain is reserved by someone else. With advertising costs and competition on the rise, the name you choose can make or break your business.

> ***"I have learned that success is to be measured not so much by the position that one has reached in life as by the obstacles overcome while trying to succeed."***
>
> —Booker T. Washington, Political Activist

There's a lot of controversy over what makes a good business name. Some experts believe that the best names are abstract, a blank slate upon which to create an image. Others think that names should be informative so customers know immediately what your business is. Some believe that coined names (names that come from made-up words) are more memorable than names that use real words. Others think most coined names are forgettable—don't tell that to the folks who dreamt up the names Google or Hulu. In reality, any name can be effective if it's backed by the appropriate marketing strategy.

Expert Assistance

Given all the considerations that go into a good company name, shouldn't you consult an expert, especially if you're in a field in which your company name will be visible and may influence the success of your business? And isn't it easier to enlist the help of a naming professional?

Yes. Just as an accountant will do a better job with your taxes and an ad agency will do a better job with your ad campaign, a naming firm will be more adept at naming your firm than you will. Naming firms have elaborate systems for creating new names, and they know their way around the trademark laws. They have the expertise to advise you against bad name choices and explain why others are good. A name consultant will take this perplexing task off your hands—and do a fabulous job for you in the process.

The downside is cost. A professional naming firm may charge from $5,000 to $80,000 to develop a name, which usually includes other identity work and graphic design as part of the package, according to Laurel Sutton, a principal with Catchword Brand Name Development. Spending the money now can save you money in the end. Professional namers may be able to find a better name—one that is so recognizable and memorable, it will pay for itself in the long run. They have the expertise to help you avoid legal hassles with trademarks and registration—problems that can cost you plenty if you end up choosing a name that already belongs to someone else. And they are familiar with design elements, such as how a potential name might work on a sign or stationery.

If you can spare the money from your startup budget, professional help could be a solid investment. After all, the name you choose now will affect your marketing plans for the duration of your business. If you're like most business owners, though, the responsibility for thinking up a name will be all your own. The good news: By following the same basic steps professional namers use, you can come up with a meaningful moniker that works without breaking the bank. There are several free services, such as Panabee (http://www.panabee.com), that can help you generate names and then check to see if they're available online and off, and you can check trademarks on Trademarkia.com and other sites like USPTO.gov.

tip

Where to get ideas for your new business's name? Get your creative juices flowing by paying attention to all the business names you run across in your daily life—whether the businesses are similar to yours or not. Which names do you like, and why? What makes them effective? Which ones don't you like, and why are they unappealing? Soon you will have a clearer idea of what makes a good (and bad) business name.

What Does It Mean?

Start by deciding what you want your name to communicate. To be most effective, your company name should reinforce the key elements of your business. Your work in developing a niche and a mission statement (see Chapter 6) will help you pinpoint the elements you want to emphasize in your name.

Consider retail as an example. In retailing, the market is so segmented that a name must convey very quickly what the customer is going after. For example, if it's a warehouse store, it has to convey that impression. If it's an upscale store selling high-quality foods, it has to convey that impression. The name combined with the logo is very important in doing that. So the

warning 

Beware of initials, says serial entrepreneur and author of *Maverick Startup* Yanik Silver. IBM and 3M have gotten away with initials, but these are multibillion-dollar corporations that have been around for decades. Initials might not represent anything to anyone but you, and that means they might not be memorable to potential customers.

first and most important step in choosing a name is deciding what your business is.

Should your name be meaningful? Most experts say yes. The more your name communicates to consumers, the less effort you must exert to explain it. According to naming experts, name developers should give priority to real words or combinations of words over fabricated words. People prefer words they can relate to and understand. That's why professional namers universally condemn strings of numbers or initials as a bad choice.

On the other hand, it is possible for a name to be too meaningful. Naming experts caution that business owners need to beware of names that are too narrowly defined. Common pitfalls are geographic names or generic names. Take the name "San Pablo Disk Drives" as a hypothetical example. What if the company wants to expand beyond the city of San Pablo, California? And what if the company diversifies beyond disk drives into software or computer instruction manuals?

Specific names make sense if you intend to stay in a narrow niche forever. If you have any ambitions of growing or expanding, however, you should find a name that is broad enough to accommodate your growth. How can a name be both meaningful and broad? There's a distinction between descriptive names (like San Pablo Disk Drives) and suggestive names. Descriptive names tell something concrete about a business—what it does, where it's located, and so on. Suggestive names are more abstract. They focus on what the business is about. Would you like to convey quality? Convenience? Novelty? These are the kinds of qualities that a suggestive name can express.

Consider the name "Italiatour," a name that was developed by one naming company to help promote package tours to Italy. Though it's not a real word, the name "Italiatour" is meaningful. Right away, you recognize what's being offered. But even better, the name "Italiatour" evokes the excitement of foreign travel. It would have been a very different name if it had been called "Italy-tour." The naming company took a foreign word, "Italia," but one that was very familiar and emotional and exciting to English speakers, and combined it with the English word "tour." The result is easy to say, it's unique, and it's unintimidating, but it still has an Italian flavor.

Before you start thinking up names for your new business, try to define the qualities that you want your business to be identified with. If you're starting a hearth-baked bread shop, you might want a name that conveys freshness, warmth and a homespun atmosphere. Immediately, you can see that names like "Kathy's Bread Shop" or "Arlington Breads" would communicate none of these qualities. But consider the name "Open Hearth Breads." The bread sounds homemade, hot and just out of the oven. Moreover, if you diversified your product line, you could alter the name to "Open Hearth Bakery." This change would enable you to hold on to your suggestive name without totally mystifying your established clientele.

Making It Up

At a time when almost every existing word in the language has been trademarked, the option of coining a name is becoming more popular. Perhaps the best coined names come from professional naming firms. Some examples are Acura, Compaq, and Aeron, names coined by NameLab.

Since its beginning, NameLab has been a champion of the coined name. According to company president Michael Barr, coined names can be more meaningful than existing words. For example, take the name "Acura": Although it has no dictionary definition, it suggests precision engineering, just as the company intended. How can that be? NameLab's team created the name "Acura" from "Acu," a word segment that means "precise" in many languages. By working with meaningful word

> ***"It's choice not chance that determines your destiny."***
>
> —Jean Nidetch, founder of Weight Watchers

segments (what linguists call morphemes) like "Acu," Barr says that the company produces new words that are both meaningful and unique.

"The naming process needs a creative approach," says Barr. He says that conventional words may not express the innovation or new ideas behind a new company or product. However, a new or "coined" word may be a better way to express that newness. Barr admits, however, that new words aren't the right solution for every situation. New words are complex and may create a perception that the product, service, or company is complex, which may not be true. Plus, naming beginners might find this sort of coining beyond their capabilities.

An easier solution is to use new forms or spellings of existing words. For instance, NameLab created the name Compaq when a new computer company came to them, touting its new portable computer. The team thought about the word "compact," but that word alone wouldn't stand out in major media like *The New York Times* or *The Wall Street Journal.* So, Barr says, the team changed the spelling to Compaq to make it more noticeable.

>> Dos and Don'ts

When choosing a business name, keep the following tips in mind:

- Choose a name that appeals not only to you, but also to the kind of customers you are trying to attract.
- To get customers to respond to your business on an emotional level, choose a comforting or familiar name that conjures up pleasant memories.
- Don't pick a name that is long or confusing. Stay away from cute puns that only you understand.
- Don't use the word "Inc." after your name unless your company is actually incorporated.
- Don't use the word "Enterprises" after your name; this term is often used by amateurs.

Namestorming

Begin brainstorming, looking in dictionaries, books, and magazines to generate ideas. Get friends and relatives to help if you like; the more minds, the merrier. Think of as many workable names as you can during this creative phase. Professional naming firms start out with a raw base of 800 to 1,000 names and work from there. You probably don't have time to think of that many, but try to come up with at least ten names that you feel good about. By the time you examine them from all angles, you'll eliminate at least half.

warning

Make sure your business name clearly conveys what you do. A flower shop named Stargazers, for example, probably won't be the first place customers think of when buying flowers, since they'll probably expect you to sell telescopes or New Age products.

The trials you put your names through will vary depending on your concerns. Some considerations are fairly universal. For instance, your name should be easy to pronounce, especially if you plan to rely heavily on print ads or signs. If people can't pronounce your name, they will avoid saying it. It's that simple. And nothing could be more counterproductive to a young company than to strangle its potential for word-of-mouth advertising.

Other considerations depend on more individual factors. For instance, if you're thinking about marketing your business globally or if you are located in a multilingual area, you should make sure that your new name has no negative connotations in other languages. On another note, if your primary means of advertising will be in the telephone directory, you might favor names that are closer to the beginning of the alphabet. Finally, make sure that your name is in no way embarrassing. Put on the mind of a child and tinker with the letters a little. If none of your doodling makes you snicker, it's probably OK.

Naming firm Interbrand advises name seekers to take a close look at their competition: The major function of a name is to distinguish your business from others. You have to weigh who's out there already, what type of branding approaches they have taken, and how you can use a name to separate yourself.

Testing, Testing

After you've narrowed the field to, say, four or five names that are memorable, expressive, and can be read by the average grade-schooler, you are ready to do a trademark search.

Must every name be trademarked? No. Many small businesses don't register their business names. As long as your state government gives you the go-ahead, you may operate under an unregistered business name for as long as you like—assuming, of course, that you aren't infringing on anyone else's trade name.

But what if you are? Imagine either of these two scenarios: You are a brand-new manufacturing business just about to ship your first orders. An obscure little company in Ogunquit, Maine, considers the name of your business an infringement on their trademark and engages you in a legal battle that bankrupts your company. Or envision your business in five years. It's a thriving, growing concern, and you are contemplating expansion. But just as you are about to launch your franchise program, you learn that a small competitor in Modesto, California, has the same name, rendering your name unusable.

tip

Google's AdWords tool is great for making sure your name will generate traffic from search online—and that it's of interest. The "find keywords" tool on AdWords will list similar search phrases, along with how many global and local monthly searches each are getting. Conduct AdWords searches with the name you are considering to ensure there isn't a slightly different name out there that might get more attention on the internet, recommends entrepreneur Yanik Silver.

To illustrate the risk you run of treading on an existing trademark with your new name, consider this: When NameLab took on the task of renaming a chain of auto parts stores, they uncovered 87,000 names already in existence for stores of this kind. That's why even the smallest businesses should at least consider having their business names screened. You never know where your corner store is going to lead. If running a corner store is all a person is going to do, then there's no need to do a trademark search. But that local business may become a big business someday if that person has any ambition.

Enlisting the help of a trademark attorney or at least a trademark search firm before you decide on a name for your business is highly advisable. After all, the extra money you spend now could save you countless hassles and expenses further down the road.

tip 

After you have thought of potential names, compile a list of your competitors' names. If some of your name ideas are too similar to your competitors', remove them from your list.

Final Analysis

If you're lucky, you'll end up with three to five names that pass all your tests. How do you make your final decision?

Recall all your initial criteria. Which name best fits your objectives? Which name most accurately describes the company you have in mind? Which name do you like the best?

Every company arrives at a final decision in its own way. Some entrepreneurs go with their gut or use personal reasons for choosing one name over another. Others are more scientific. Some companies do consumer research or testing with focus groups to see how the names are perceived. Others might decide that their name is going to be most important seen on the back of a truck, so they have a graphic designer turn the various names into logos to see which works best as a design element.

Use any or all of these criteria. You can do it informally: Ask other people's opinions. Doodle an idea of what each name will look like on a sign or on business stationery. Read each name aloud, paying attention to the way it sounds if you foresee radio advertising or telemarketing in your future.

Say It Loud

Professional naming firms devote anywhere from six weeks to six months to the naming process. You probably won't have that much time, but plan to spend at least a few weeks on selecting a name.

Once your decision is made, start building your enthusiasm for the new name immediately. Your name is your first step toward building a strong company identity, one that should last as long as you're in business.

CHAPTER

9

Make It Legal

Choosing a Business Structure

Of all the decisions you make when starting a business, probably the most important one relating to taxes is the type of legal structure you select for your company.

Not only will this decision have an impact on how much you pay in taxes, but it will affect the amount of paperwork your business is required to do, the personal liability you face, and your ability to raise money.

The most common forms of business are sole proprietorship, partnership, corporation, and S corporation. A more recent development to these forms of business is the limited liability company (LLC) and the limited liability partnership (LLP). Because each business form comes with different tax consequences, you will want to make your selection wisely and choose the structure that most closely matches your business's needs.

tip 

If you operate as a sole proprietor, be sure you keep your business income and records separate from your personal finances. It helps to establish a business checking account and get a credit card to use only for business expenses. This will be invaluable at tax time and help you keep your accounts in order.

If you decide to start your business as a sole proprietorship but later decide to take on partners, you can reorganize as a partnership or other entity. If you do this, be sure you notify the IRS as well as your state tax agency.

Sole Proprietorship

The simplest structure is the sole proprietorship, which usually involves just one individual who owns and operates the enterprise. If you intend to work alone, this structure may be the way to go.

The tax aspects of a sole proprietorship are appealing because the expenses and your income from the business are included on your personal income tax return, Form 1040. Your profits and losses are recorded on a form called Schedule C, which is filed with your 1040. The "bottom-line amount" from Schedule C is then transferred to your personal tax return. This is especially attractive because business losses you suffer may offset the income you have earned from your other sources.

As a sole proprietor, you must also file a Schedule SE with Form 1040. You use Schedule SE to calculate how much self-employment tax you owe. In addition to paying annual self-employment taxes, you must make estimated tax payments if you expect to owe at least $1,000 in federal taxes for the year after deducting your withholding and credits, and your withholding will be less than the smaller of: 1) 90 percent of the tax to be shown on your current year tax return or 2) 100 percent of your previous year's tax liability. The federal government permits you to pay estimated taxes in four equal amounts throughout the year on the 15th of April, June, September, and January. With a sole proprietorship, your business earnings are taxed only once, unlike other business structures. Another big plus is that you will have complete control over your business—you make all the decisions.

There are a few disadvantages to consider, however. Selecting the sole proprietorship business structure means you are personally responsible for your company's liabilities. As a result, you are placing your assets at risk, and they could be seized to satisfy a business debt or a legal claim filed against you.

Raising money for a sole proprietorship can also be difficult. Banks and other financing sources may be reluctant to make business loans to sole proprietorships. In most cases, you will have to depend on your financing sources, such as savings, home equity, or family loans.

> ***"Success seems to be connected to action. Successful people keep moving. They make mistakes, but they never quit."***
>
> —J. WILLARD MARRIOTT, FOUNDER OF MARRIOTT INTERNATIONAL INC.

Partnership

If your business will be owned and operated by several individuals, you'll want to take a look at structuring your business as a partnership. Partnerships come in two varieties: general partnerships and limited partnerships. In a general partnership, the partners manage the company and assume responsibility for the partnership's debts and other obligations. A limited partnership has both general and limited partners. The general partners own and operate the business and assume liability for the partnership, while the limited partners serve as investors only; they have no control over the company and are not subject to the same liabilities as the general partners.

Unless you expect to have many passive investors, limited partnerships are generally not the best choice for a new business because of all the required filings and administrative complexities. If you have two or more partners who want to be actively involved, a general partnership would be much easier to form.

One of the major advantages of a partnership is the tax treatment it enjoys. A partnership does not pay tax on its income but "passes through" any profits or losses to the individual partners. At tax time, the partnership must file a tax return (Form 1065) that reports its income and loss to the IRS. In addition, each partner reports his or her share of income and loss on Schedule K-1 of Form 1065.

Personal liability is a major concern if you use a general partnership to structure your business. Like sole proprietors, general partners are

>> Howdy, Partner!

If you decide to organize your business as a partnership, be sure you draft a partnership agreement that details how business decisions are made, how disputes are resolved, and how to handle a buyout. You'll be glad you have this agreement if for some reason you run into difficulties with one of the partners or if someone wants out of the arrangement.

The agreement should address the purpose of the business and the authority and responsibility of each partner. It's a good idea to consult an attorney experienced with small businesses for help in drafting the agreement. Here are some other issues you'll want the agreement to address:

> *How will the ownership interest be shared?* It's not necessary, for example, for two owners to equally share ownership and authority. However, if you decide to do it, make sure the proportion is stated clearly in the agreement.

> *How will decisions be made?* It's a good idea to establish voting rights in case a major disagreement arises. When just two partners own the business 50–50, there's the possibility of a deadlock. To avoid a deadlock, some businesses provide in advance for a third partner, a trusted associate who may own only one percent of the business but whose vote can break a tie.

> *When one partner withdraws, how will the purchase price be determined?* One possibility is to agree on a neutral third party, such as your banker or accountant, to find an appraiser to determine the price of the partnership interest.

> *If a partner withdraws from the partnership, when will the money be paid?* Depending on the partnership agreement, you can agree that the money be paid over three, five, or ten years, with interest. You don't want to be hit with a cash-flow crisis if the entire price has to be paid on the spot in one lump sum.

personally liable for the partnership's obligations and debts. Each general partner can act on behalf of the partnership, take out loans, and make decisions that will affect and be binding on all the partners (if the partnership agreement permits). Keep in mind that partnerships are also more expensive to establish than sole proprietorships because they require more legal and accounting services.

Corporation

The corporate structure is more complex and expensive than most other business structures. A corporation is an independent legal entity, separate from its owners, and as such, it requires complying with more regulations and tax requirements.

The biggest benefit for a business owner who decides to incorporate is the liability protection he or she receives. A corporation's debt is not considered that of its owners, so if you organize your business as a corporation, you are not putting your personal assets at risk. A corporation also can retain some of its profits without the owner paying tax on them.

Another plus is the ability of a corporation to raise money. A corporation can sell stock, either common or preferred, to raise funds. Corporations also continue indefinitely, even if one of the shareholders dies, sells the shares, or becomes disabled. The corporate structure, however, comes with a number of downsides. A major one is higher costs.

warning

Many cities require even the smallest enterprises to have a business license. Municipalities are mainly concerned with whether the area where the business is operating is zoned for its intended purpose and whether there's adequate customer parking available. You may even need a zoning variance to operate in some cities. Expect to pay a nominal license fee of around $30.

Corporations are formed under the laws of each state with its own set of regulations. You will probably need the assistance of an attorney to guide you. In addition, because a corporation must follow more complex rules and regulations than a partnership or sole proprietorship, it requires more accounting and tax preparation services.

Another drawback to forming a corporation: Owners of the corporation pay a double tax on the business's earnings. Not only are corporations subject to corporate income tax at both the federal and state levels, but any

>> The ABCs of LLC

Limited liability companies, often referred to as "Lacs," have been around since 1977, but their popularity among entrepreneurs is a relatively recent phenomenon. An LLC is a hybrid entity, bringing together some of the best features of partnerships and corporations. The advantage of an LLC over a sole proprietorship is that the owner is not personally responsible for the liabilities of the company if appropriate business formalities are followed.

Like a sole proprietorship, earnings flow to the owner, are taxed only at the personal level, and are subject to the self-employment tax. While somewhat more complex than a sole proprietorship, establishing an LLC is relatively simple. There is no limitation on the number of shareholders an LLC can have. In addition, any member or owner of the LLC is allowed a full participatory role in the business's operation; in a limited partnership, on the other hand, partners are not permitted any say in the operation.

earnings distributed to shareholders in the form of dividends are taxed at individual tax rates on their personal income tax returns.

One strategy to help soften the blow of double taxation is to pay some money out as salary to you and any other corporate shareholders who work for the company. A corporation is not required to pay tax on earnings paid as reasonable compensation, and it can deduct the payments as a business expense. However, the IRS has limits on what it believes to be reasonable compensation.

warning

Any money you've invested in a corporation is at risk. Despite the liability protection of a corporation, most banks and many suppliers require business owners to sign a personal guarantee so they know corporate owners will make good on any debt if the corporation can't.

S Corporation

The S corporation is more attractive to small-business owners than a regular (or C) corporation. That's because an S corporation has some appealing tax benefits and still provides business owners with the liability protection of a corporation. With an S corporation, income and losses are passed through to shareholders and included on their individual tax returns. As a result, there's just one level of federal tax to pay.

In addition, owners of S corporations who don't have inventory can use the cash method of accounting, which is simpler than the accrual method. Under this method, income is taxable when received and expenses are deductible when paid (see Chapter 37).

S corporations can also have up to 100 shareholders. This makes it possible to have more investors and thus attract more capital, tax experts maintain.

warning

Like an LLC, the owner of an S Corp is not personally responsible for the liabilities of the company. One note of caution is that if the formalities of setting up and running an S Corp are not followed, the owner's protection from the liabilities of the company may be forfeited.

>> Corporate Checklist

To make sure your corporation stays on the right side of the law, heed the following guidelines:

- ❑ Call the secretary of state each year to check your corporate status.
- ❑ Put the annual meetings (shareholders and directors) on tickler cards.
- ❑ Check all contracts to ensure the proper name is used in each. The signature line should read "John Doe, President, XYZ Corp.," never just "John Doe."
- ❑ Never use your name followed by "dba" (doing business as) on a contract. Renegotiate any old ones that do.
- ❑ Before undertaking any activity out of the normal course of business—like purchasing major assets—write a corporate resolution permitting it. Keep all completed forms in the corporate book.
- ❑ Never use corporate checks for personal debts and vice versa.
- ❑ Get professional advice about continued retained earnings not needed for immediate operating expenses.

warning

If you anticipate several years of losses in your business, keep in mind you cannot deduct corporate losses on your personal tax return. Business structures such as partnerships, sole proprietorships, and S corporations allow you to take those deductions.

S corporations do come with some downsides. For example, S corporations are subject to many of the same rules corporations must follow, and that means higher legal and tax service costs. They also must file articles of incorporation, hold directors and shareholders meetings, keep corporate minutes, and allow shareholders to vote on major corporate decisions. The legal and accounting costs of setting up an S corporation are also similar to those for a regular corporation.

Another major difference between a regular corporation and an S corporation is that S corporations can only issue one class of stock. Experts say this can hamper the company's ability to raise capital.

In addition, unlike in a regular corporation, S corporation stock can only be owned by individuals, estates, and certain types of trusts. In 1998, tax-exempt organizations such as qualified pension plans were added to the list. This change provides S corporations with even greater access to capital because a number of pension plans are willing to invest in closely held small-business stock.

Putting Inc. to Paper

To start the process of incorporating, contact the secretary of state or the state office that is responsible for registering corporations in your state. Ask for instructions, forms, and fee schedules on incorporating.

It is possible to file for incorporation without the help of an attorney by using books and software to guide you. Your expense will be the cost of these resources, the filing fees and other costs associated with incorporating in your state.

If you do it yourself, you will save the expense of using a lawyer, which can cost from $500 to $5,000 if you choose a firm that specializes in startup businesses. The disadvantage is that the process may take you some time to accomplish. There is also a chance you could miss some small but important detail in your state's law.

One of the first steps in the incorporation process is to prepare a certificate or articles of incorporation. Some states provide a printed form for this, which either you or your attorney can complete. The information requested includes the proposed name of the corporation, the purpose of the corporation, the names and addresses of those incorporating, and the location of the principal office of the corporation. The corporation will also need a set of bylaws that describe in greater detail than the articles how the corporation will run, including the responsibilities of the company's shareholders, directors, and officers; when stockholder meetings will be held; and other details important to running the company. Once your articles of incorporation are accepted, the secretary of state's office will send you a certificate of incorporation.

>> In Other Words

If you are starting a sole proprietorship or a partnership, you have the option of choosing a business name, or dba ("doing business as"), for your business. This is known as a fictitious business name. If you want to operate your business under a name other than your own (for instance, Carol Axelrod doing business as "Darling Donut Shoppe"), you may be required by the county, city, or state to register your fictitious name.

Procedures for doing this vary among states. In many states, all you have to do is go to the county offices and pay a registration fee to the county clerk. In other states, you also have to place a fictitious name ad in a local newspaper for a certain length of time. The cost of filing a fictitious name notice ranges from about $40 to $125. Your local bank may require a fictitious name certificate to open a business account for you; if so, a bank officer can tell you where to go to register.

In most states, corporations don't have to file fictitious business names unless the owner(s) do business under a name other than their own. In effect, incorporation documents are to corporate businesses what fictitious name filings are to sole proprietorships and partnerships.

Rules of the Road

> ***"Nobody can be a success if they don't love their work."***
>
> —David Sarnoff, Chairman of RCA

Once you are incorporated, be sure to follow the rules of incorporation. If you fail to do so, a court can pierce the corporate veil and hold you and the other business owners personally liable for the business's debts.

It is important to follow all the rules required by state law. You should keep accurate financial records for the corporation, showing a separation between the corporation's income and expenses and those of the owners.

The corporation should also issue stock, file annual reports, and hold yearly meetings to elect company officers and directors, even if they're the same people as the shareholders. Be sure to keep minutes of shareholders' and directors' meetings. On all references to your business, make certain to identify it as a corporation, using Inc. or Corp., whichever your state requires. You also want to make sure that whomever you will be dealing with, such as your banker or clients, knows that you are an officer of a corporation. (For more corporate guidelines, see "Corporate Checklist" on page 123.)

Setting up an LLC

If limited liability is not a concern for your business, you could begin as a sole proprietorship or a partnership so "passed through" losses in the early years of the company can be used to offset your other income. After the business becomes profitable, you may want to consider another type of legal structure.

To set up an LLC, you must file articles of organization with the secretary of state in the state where you intend to do business. Some states also require you to file an operating agreement, which is similar to a partnership agreement. Like partnerships, LLCs do not have perpetual life. Some state statutes stipulate that the company must dissolve after 30 years. Technically, the company dissolves when a member dies, quits, or retires.

If you plan to operate in several states, you must determine how a state will treat an LLC formed in another state. If you decide on an LLC structure, be sure to use the services of an experienced accountant who is familiar with the various rules and regulations of LLCs.

Another recent development is the limited liability partnership (LLP). With an LLP, the general partners have limited liability. For example, the partners are liable for their own malpractice and not that of their partners. This legal form works well for those involved in a professional practice, such as physicians.

The Nonprofit Option

What about organizing your venture as a nonprofit corporation? Unlike a for-profit business, a nonprofit may be eligible for certain benefits, such as sales, property, and income tax exemptions at the state level. The IRS points out that while most federal tax-exempt organizations are nonprofit

>> Laying the Foundation

When making a decision about which business structure to use, answering the following questions should help you narrow down which entity is right for you:

- How many owners will your company have, and what will their roles be?
- Are you concerned about the tax consequences of your business structure?
- Do you want to consider having employees become owners in the company?
- Can you deal with the added costs that come with selecting a complicated business structure?
- How much paperwork are you prepared to deal with?
- Do you want to make all the decisions in the company?
- Are you planning to go public?
- Do you want to protect your personal resources from debts or other claims against your company?
- Are family succession issues a concern?

organizations, organizing as a nonprofit at the state level does not automatically grant you an exemption from federal income tax.

e-fyi

To help sort through the business structure maze, you can order free IRS publications—*Partnerships* (Publication 541), *Corporations* (Publication 542), and *Taxation of Limited Liability Companies* (Publication 3402)—by downloading them from the IRS website at irs.gov.

Another major difference between a profit and nonprofit business deals with the treatment of the profits. With a for-profit business, the owners and shareholders generally receive the profits. With a nonprofit, any money that is left after the organization has paid its bills is put back into the organization. Some types of nonprofits can receive contributions that are tax deductible to the individual who contributes to the organization. Keep in mind that nonprofits are organized to provide some benefit to the public.

Nonprofits are incorporated under the laws of the state in which they are established. To receive federal tax-exempt status, the organization must apply with the IRS. First, you must have an Employer Identification Number (EIN) and then apply for recognition of exemption by filing Form 1023 (*Application for Recognition of Exemption Under Section 501(c)(3) of the Internal Revenue Code*) or Form 1024 (*Application for Recognition of Exemption under Section 501(a)*) with the necessary filing fee. Both forms are available online at irs.gov. (For information on how to apply for an EIN, see Chapter 41.)

The IRS identifies the different types of nonprofit organizations by the tax code by which they qualify for exempt status. One of the most common forms is 501(c)(3), which is set up to do charitable, educational, scientific, religious, and literary work. This includes a wide range of organizations, from continuing education centers to outpatient clinics and hospitals.

The IRS also mandates that there are certain activities tax-exempt organizations can't engage in if they want to keep their exempt status. For example, a section 50l(c)(3) organization cannot intervene in political campaigns.

Remember, nonprofits still have to pay employment taxes, but in some states they may be exempt from paying sales tax. Check with your state to make sure you understand how nonprofit status is treated in your area. In addition, nonprofits may be hit with unrelated business income tax. This is regular income from a trade or business that is not substantially related to the charitable purpose. Any exempt organization under Section 501(a) or Section 529(a) must file Form 990-T (*Exempt Organization Business Income Tax Return*) if the organization has gross income of $1,000 or more from an unrelated business, and pay tax on the income.

> ***"To be successful in business, you need friends. To be very successful, you need enemies."***
>
> —Christopher Ondaatje, Canadian Financier and Philanthropist

If your nonprofit has revenues of more than $25,000 a year, be sure to file an annual report (Form 990) with the IRS. Form 990-EZ is a shortened version of 990 and is designed for use by small exempt organizations with incomes of less than $1 million.

Form 990 asks you to provide information on the organization's income, expenses, and staff salaries. You also may have to comply with a similar state requirement. The IRS report must be made available for public review. If you use the calendar year as your accounting period (see Chapter 41), file Form 990 by May 15.

For more information on IRS tax-exempt status, download IRS Publication 557 (*Tax-Exempt Status for Your Organization*) at irs.gov.

Even after you settle on a business structure, remember that the circumstances that make one type of business organization favorable are always subject to changes in the laws. It makes sense to reassess your form of business from time to time to make sure you are using the one that provides the most benefits.

Choosing a Legal Form for Your Business

This table summarizes the characteristics of six different forms of business: sole proprietorships, general partnerships, limited partnerships, limited liability partnerships (LLPs), corporations in general, and S corporations. We list four characteristics for each legal form:

- *Control*. Who holds authority in a business operating under this form?
- *Liability*. Who is legally liable for any losses the business experiences?
- *Tax*. How will business income and expenses be reported?
- *Continuity*. If a business owner dies or wants to leave the business, does the business continue?

Sole Proprietorship			
Control	**Liability**	**Tax**	**Continuity**
Owner maintains complete control over the business.	Owner is solely liable. His or her personal assets are open to attack in any legal case.	Owner reports all income and expenses on personal tax return.	Business terminates upon the owner's death or withdrawal. Owner can sell the business but will no longer remain the proprietor.

General Partnership			
Control	**Liability**	**Tax**	**Continuity**
Each partner has the authority to enter contracts and make other business decisions, unless the partnership agreement stipulates otherwise.	Each partner is liable for all business debts.	Each partner reports partnership income on their individual tax returns. The business does not pay any taxes as its own entity.	Unless the partnership agreement makes other provisions, a partnership dissolves upon the death or withdrawal of a partner.

Figure 9.1. Choosing a Legal Form for Your Business

Choosing a Legal Form for Your Business

Limited Partnership			
Control	**Liability**	**Tax**	**Continuity**
General partners control the business.	General partners are personally responsible for partnership liabilities. Limited partners are liable for the amount of their investment.	Partnership files annual taxes. Limited and general partners report their share of partnership income or loss on their individual returns.	Death of a limited partner does not dissolve business, but death of general partner might, unless the agreement makes other provisions.

Limited Liability Partnership			
Control	**Liability**	**Tax**	**Continuity**
Owner or partners have authority.	Partners are not liable for business debts.	The partners report income and income tax on their individual tax returns.	Different states have different laws regarding the continuity of LLPs.

Corporation			
Control	**Liability**	**Tax**	**Continuity**
Shareholders appoint the board of directors, which appoints, officers, who hold the highest authority.	Shareholders generally are responsible for the amount of their investment in corporate stock.	Shareholders pay tax on their dividends. Corporation pays its own taxes.	The corporation is its own legal entity and can survive the deaths of owners, partners, and shareholders.

Figure 9.1. Choosing a Legal Form for Your Business, continued

Choosing a Legal Form for Your Business

S Corporation			
Control	Liability	Tax	Continuity
See entry for corporations.	See entry for corporations.	Shareholders report shares of corporate profit or loss on their individual tax returns.	See entry for corporations.

Figure 9.1. Choosing a Legal Form for Your Business, continued

CHAPTER

10

Plan of Attack

Creating a Winning Business Plan

Think you don't need a full-fledged business plan? Think again. According to a recent *State of Small Business* report, commissioned by Palo Alto Software, 79 percent of companies with a business plan say they are better off financially year after year, while only a third of small businesses without a business plan can say the same thing. Additionally, nearly 75 percent of established companies that have a business plan in place expect to grow, compared to only 17 percent that don't have a business plan. That's even stronger evidence than an earlier study conducted for AT&T, showing only 42 percent of small-business owners bother to develop a formal business plan; of those who do use a plan, 69 percent say it was a major contributor to their success.

Some people think you don't need a business plan unless you're trying to borrow money. Of course, it's true that you do need a good plan if you intend to approach a lender—whether a banker, a venture capitalist, or any number of other sources—for startup capital. But a business plan is more than a pitch for financing; it's a guide to help you define and meet your business goals.

> ***"My interest is in the future because I am going to spend the rest of my life there."***
>
> —Charles F. Kettering, American inventor and scientist

Just as you wouldn't start off on a cross-country drive without a road map, you should not embark on your new business without a business plan to guide you. A business plan won't automatically make you a success, but it will help you avoid some common causes of business failure, such as undercapitalization or lack of an adequate market.

As you research and prepare your business plan, you'll find weak spots in your business idea that you'll be able to repair. You'll also discover areas with potential you may not have thought about before—and ways to profit from them. Only by putting together a business plan can you decide whether your great idea is really worth your time and investment.

What is a business plan, and how do you put one together? Simply stated, a business plan conveys your business goals and the strategies you'll use to meet them, potential problems that may confront your business and ways to solve them, the organizational structure of your business (including titles and responsibilities), and the amount of capital required to finance your venture and keep it going until it breaks even.

Sound impressive? It can be, if put together properly. A good business plan follows generally accepted guidelines for both form and content. There are three primary parts of a business plan.

1. The first is the business concept, where you discuss the industry, your business structure, your product or service, and how you plan to make your business a success.
2. The second is the marketplace section, in which you describe and analyze potential customers: who and where they are, what makes

them buy, and so on. Here, you also describe the competition and how you will position yourself to beat it.

3. Finally, the financial section contains your income and cash-flow statements, balance sheet, and other financial ratios, such as break-even analyses. This part may require help from your accountant and a good spreadsheet software program.

Breaking these three major sections down further, a business plan consists of seven major components:

1. Executive summary
2. Business description
3. Market strategies
4. Competitive analysis
5. Design and development plan
6. Operations and management plan
7. Financial factors

In addition to these sections, a business plan should also have a cover, title page, and table of contents.

tip 

Although it's the first part of the plan to be read, the executive summary is most effective if it's the last part you write. By waiting until you have finished the rest of your business plan, you ensure you have all the relevant information in front of you. This allows you to create an executive summary that hits all the crucial points of your plan.

Executive Summary

Anyone looking at your business plan will first want to know what kind of business you are starting. So the business concept section should start with an executive summary, which outlines and describes the product or service you will sell.

The executive summary is the first thing the reader sees. Therefore, it must make an immediate impact by clearly stating the nature of the business and, if you are seeking capital, the type of financing you want. The executive summary describes the business, its legal form of operation (sole proprietorship, partnership, corporation, or limited liability company), the amount and purpose of the loan requested, the repayment schedule, the borrower's equity share, and the debt-to-equity ratio after the loan, security, or collateral is offered. Also listed are the market value, estimated value, or price quotes for any equipment you plan to purchase with the loan proceeds.

Your executive summary should be short and businesslike—generally between half a page and one page, depending on how complicated the use of funds is.

Business Description

This section expands on the executive summary, describing your business in much greater detail. It usually starts with a description of your industry. Is the business retail, wholesale, food service, manufacturing, or service-oriented? How big is the industry? Why has it become so popular? What kind of trends are responsible for the industry's growth? Prove, with statistics and anecdotal information, how much opportunity there is in the industry.

Explain the target market for your product or service, how the product will be distributed, and the business' support systems—that is, its advertising, promotions, and customer service strategies.

Next, describe your product or service. Discuss the product's applications and end users. Emphasize any unique features or variations that set your product or service apart from others in your industry.

If you're using your business plan for financing purposes, explain why the money you seek will make your business more profitable. Will you use the money to expand, to create a new product, or to buy new equipment?

Market Strategies

Here's where you define your market—its size, structure, growth prospects, trends, and sales potential. Based on research, interviews, and sales analysis, the marketplace section should focus on your customers and your competition. How much of the market will your product or service be able to capture?

The answer is tricky since so many variables influence it. Think of it as a combination of words and numbers. Write down the who, what,

>> Sample Executive Summary

The business will provide ecology-minded consumers with an environmentally safe disposable diaper that will feature all the elements that are popular among users of disposable diapers but will include the added benefit of biodegradability. The product, which is patent pending, will target current users of disposable diapers who are deeply concerned about the environment as well as those consumers using cloth diapers and diaper services. The product will be distributed to wholesalers who will, in turn, sell to major supermarkets, specialty stores, department stores, and major toy stores.

The company was incorporated in 1989 in the state of California under the name of Softie Baby Care. The company's CEO, president, and vice president have more than 30 years of combined experience in the diaper industry.

With projected net sales of $871 million in its third year, the business will generate pretax net profits of 8 percent. Given this return, investment in the company is very attractive. Softie Baby Care Inc. will require a total amount of $26 million over three stages to start the business.

1. The first stage will require $8 million for product and market development.
2. The second stage of financing will demand $12 million for implementation.
3. The third stage will require $6 million for working capital until break-even is reached.

First-stage capital will be used to purchase needed equipment and materials to develop the product and market it initially. To obtain its capital requirements, the company is willing to relinquish 25 percent equity to first-stage investors.

The company has applied for a patent on the primary technology that the business is built around, which allows the plastic within a disposable diaper to break down upon extended exposure to sunlight. Lease agreements are also in place for a 20,000-square-foot facility in a light industrial area of Los Angeles, as well as for major equipment needed to begin production. Currently, the company has funding of $3 million from the three principals, with purchase orders for 500,000 units already in hand.

when, where, and why of your customers. (You know all this because you researched it in Chapter 7.) The answer is critical to determining how you will develop pricing strategies and distribution channels.

Be sure to document how and from what sources you compiled your market information. Describe how your business fits into the overall market picture. Emphasize your unique selling proposition (USP)—in other words, what makes you different? Explain why your approach is ideal for your market.

Once you've clearly defined your market and established your sales goals, present the strategies you'll use to meet those goals.

- *Price.* Thoroughly explain your pricing strategy and how it will affect the success of your product or service. Describe your projected costs and then determine pricing based on the profit percentage you expect. Costs include materials, distribution, advertising, and overhead. Many experts recommend adding 25 to 50 percent to each cost estimate, especially overhead, to ensure you don't underestimate.
- *Distribution.* This includes the entire process of moving the product from the factory to the end user. The type of distribution network you choose depends on your industry and the size of the market. How much will it cost to reach your target market? Does that market consist of upscale customers who will pay extra for a premium product or service, or budget-conscious consumers looking for a

e-fyi

Looking for inspiration? Visit Uncle Sam: The SBA (www.sba.gov/writing-business-plan) offers clear, concise business plan outlines and tutorials. When you're done, if you feel like your business plan has the right stuff, consider submitting it to a business plan competition. Universities, such as Wharton and Harvard Business School, and corporations often sponsor such competitions, offering grants and other cash prizes that can really help offset your startup costs. To find a competition, Google "business plan competition" and see what turns up.

good deal? Study your competitors to see what channels they use. Will you use the same channels or a different method that may give you a strategic advantage?

- *Sales.* Explain how your sales force (if you have one) will meet its goals, including elements such as pricing flexibility, sales presentations, lead generation, and compensation policies.

Competitive Analysis

How does your business relate to the competition? The competitive analysis section answers this question. Using what you've learned from your market research, detail the strengths and weaknesses of your competitors, the strategies that give you a distinct advantage, any barriers you can develop to prevent new competition from entering the market, and any weaknesses in your competitors' service or product development cycle that you can take advantage of.

The competitive analysis is an important part of your business plan. Often, startup entrepreneurs mistakenly believe their product or service is the first of its kind and fail to recognize that competition exists. In reality, every business has competition, whether direct or indirect. Your plan must show that you recognize this and have a strategy for dealing with the competition.

>> Write Your Plan in Pencil

Bob Reiss, author of *Bootstrapping 101: Tips to Build Your Business with Limited Cash and Free Outside Help*, has been involved in 16 startups. His recommendation: Have a business plan, but write it in pencil. Why? You will likely have to change, amend, modify, scrap, or abandon your original business plan altogether. One of the attributes of successful entrepreneurs is flexibility, Reiss says. Writing your business plan in pencil forces you to look at change as the only constant. Make change your friend, embrace it, and work it to your benefit.

Design and Development Plan

This section describes a product's design and charts its development within the context of production, marketing, and the company itself. If you have an idea but have not yet developed the product or service, if you plan to improve an existing product or service, or if you own an existing company and plan to introduce a new product or service, this section is extremely important. (If your product is already completely designed and developed, you don't need to complete this section. If you are offering a service, you will need to concentrate only on the development half of the section.)

The design section should thoroughly describe the product's design and the materials used; include any diagrams if applicable. The development plan generally covers these three areas: 1) product development, 2) market development, and 3) organizational development. If you're offering a service, cover only the last two.

Create a schedule that shows how the product, marketing strategies, and organization will develop over time. The schedule should be tied to a development budget so expenses can be tracked throughout the design and development process.

Operations and Management Plan

Here, you describe how your business will function on a daily basis. This section explains logistics such as the responsibilities of each member of the management team, the tasks assigned to each division of the company (if applicable), and the capital and expense requirements for operating the business.

Describe the business's managers and their qualifications, and specify what type of support staff will be needed for the business to run efficiently. Any potential benefits or pitfalls to the community should also be presented, such as new job creation, economic growth, and possible effects on the environment from manufacturing and how they will be handled to comply with local, state, and federal regulations.

Financial Factors

The financial statements are the backbone of your business plan. They show how profitable your business will be in the short and long term, and should include the following:

- The income statement details the business's cash-generating ability. It projects such items as revenue, expenses, capital (in the form of depreciation), and cost of goods. You should generate a monthly income statement for the business's first year, quarterly statements for the second year, and annual statements for each year thereafter (usually for three, five, or ten years, with five being the most common).
- The cash-flow statement details the amount of money coming into and going out of the business—monthly for the first year and quarterly for each year thereafter. The result is a profit or loss at the end of the period represented by each column. Both profits and losses carry over to the last column to show a cumulative amount. If your cash-flow statement shows you consistently operating at a loss, you will probably need additional cash to meet expenses. Most businesses have some seasonal variations in their budgets, so re-examine your cash-flow calculations if they look identical every month.
- The balance sheet paints a picture of the business's financial strength in terms of assets, liabilities, and equity over a set period. You should generate a balance sheet for each year profiled in the development of your business.

After these essential financial documents, include any relevant summary information that's not included elsewhere in the plan but will significantly affect the business. This could include ratios such as return on investment, break-even point, or return on assets. Your accountant can help you decide what information is best to include.

Many people consider the financial section of a business plan the most difficult to write. If you haven't started your business yet, how do you know what your income will be? You have a few options. The first is to enlist your accountant's help. An accountant can take your raw data and organize it into categories that will satisfy all the requirements of a financial section, including monthly and yearly sales projections. Or, if you are familiar with accounting procedures, you can do it yourself with the help of a good spreadsheet program. (For more information on developing financial statements, see Chapter 38.)

>> Finding Funding

One of the primary purposes of a business plan is to help you obtain financing for your business. When writing your plan, it's important to remember who those financing sources are likely to be.

Bankers, investors, venture capitalists, and investment advisors are sophisticated in business and financial matters. How can you ensure your plan makes the right impression? Three tips are key:

1. *Avoid hype*. While many entrepreneurs tend to be gamblers who believe in relying on their gut feelings, financial types are likely to go "by the book." If your business plan praises your idea with superlatives like "one of a kind," "unique," or "unprecedented," your readers are likely to be turned off. Wild, unsubstantiated promises or unfounded conclusions tell financial sources you are inexperienced, naïve, and reckless.
2. *Polish the executive summary*. Potential investors receive so many business plans, they cannot afford to spend more than a few minutes evaluating each one. If at first glance your proposal looks dull, poorly written, or confusing, investors will toss it aside without a second thought. In other words, if your executive summary doesn't grab them, you won't get a second chance.
3. *Make sure your plan is complete*. Even if your executive summary sparkles, you need to make sure the rest of your plan is just as good and that all the necessary information is included. Some entrepreneurs are in such a hurry to get financing, they submit a condensed or preliminary business plan, promising to provide more information if the recipient is interested. This approach usually backfires for two reasons: First, if you don't provide information upfront, investors will assume the information doesn't exist yet and that you are stalling for time. Second, even if investors are interested in your preliminary plan, their interest may cool in the time it takes you to compile the rest of the information.

>> Finding Funding, continued

When presenting a business plan, you are starting from a position of weakness. And if potential investors find any flaws in your plan, they gain an even greater bargaining advantage. A well-written and complete plan gives you greater negotiating power and boosts your chances of getting financing on your own terms.

A Living Document

You've put a lot of time and effort into your business plan. What happens when it's finished? A good business plan should not gather dust in a drawer. Think of it as a living document, and refer to it often. A well-written plan will help you define activities and responsibilities within your business as well as identify and achieve your goals.

To ensure your business plan continues to serve you well, make it a habit to update yours annually. Set aside a block of time near the beginning of the calendar year, fiscal year, or whenever is convenient for you. Meet with your accountant or financial advisor, if necessary, to go over and update financial figures. Is your business heading in the right direction . . . or has it wandered off course?

Making it a practice to review your business plan annually is a great way to start the year fresh and reinvigorated. It lets you catch any problems before they become too large to solve. It also ensures that if the possibility of getting financing, participating in a joint venture, or other such occasion arises, you'll have an updated plan ready to go so you don't miss out on a good opportunity.

Whether you're writing it for the first time or updating it for the 15th, creating a good business plan doesn't mean penning a 200-page novel or adding lots of fancy

aha!

Still need another reason to write a business plan? Consider this: If you decide to sell your business in the future, or if you become disabled or die and someone else takes over, a written business plan will help make the transition a smooth one.

clip art and footnotes. It means proving to yourself and others that you understand your business, and that you know what's required to make it grow and prosper.

CHAPTER

11

Call in the Pros

Hiring a Lawyer and an Accountant

As you start off on your business journey, there are two professionals you will soon come to rely on to guide you along the path: your lawyer and your accountant. It's hard to navigate the maze of tax and legal issues facing entrepreneurs these days unless these professionals are an integral part of your team.

Hiring a Lawyer

When do you need a lawyer? Although the answer depends on your business and your particular circumstances, it's generally worthwhile to consult one before making any decision that could have legal ramifications. These include setting up a partnership or corporation, checking for compliance with regulations, negotiating

tip

When a client refuses to pay, do you hand the case to a lawyer? Some entrepreneurs do, but others handle small legal matters on their own by using their attorney as a coach. Lawyers can be very effective in helping you to file lawsuits in small-claims court, draft employment manuals, and complete other legal tasks.

loans, obtaining trademarks or patents, preparing buy-sell agreements, assisting with tax planning, drawing up pension plans, reviewing business forms, negotiating and drawing up documents to buy or sell real estate, reviewing employee contracts, exporting or selling products in other states, and collecting bad debts. If something goes wrong, you may need an attorney to stand up for your trademark rights, go to court on an employee dispute, or defend you in a product liability lawsuit. Some entrepreneurs wait until something goes wrong to consult an attorney, but in today's litigious society, that isn't the smartest idea. "Almost every business, whatever its size, requires a lawyer's advice," says James Blythe Hodge formerly of the law firm Sheppard, Mullin, Richter & Hampton. "Even the smallest business has tax concerns that need to be addressed as early as the planning stages."

In a crisis situation—such as a lawsuit or trademark wrangle—you may not have time to thoroughly research different legal options. More likely, you'll end up flipping through the Yellow Pages in haste . . . and getting stuck with a second-rate lawyer. Better to start off on the right foot from the beginning by doing the proper research and choosing a good lawyer now. Many entrepreneurs say their relationship with a lawyer is like a marriage—it takes time to develop. That's why it's important to lay the groundwork for a good partnership early.

Choosing an Attorney

How do you find the right attorney? Ask for recommendations from business owners in your industry or from professionals such as bankers or accountants you trust. Don't just get names; ask them for the specific strengths and weaknesses of the attorneys they recommend. Then take the process one step further: Ask your business associates' attorneys whom they recommend and why. (Attorneys are more likely to be helpful if you phrase the request as "If for some reason I couldn't use you, who would you recommend and why?") If you still need more prospects, contact your local Bar Association; many of them have referral services.

Next, set up an interview with the top five attorneys you're considering. Tell them you're interested in building a long-term relationship, and find out which ones are willing to meet with you for an initial consultation without charging a fee.

At this initial conference, be ready to describe your business and its legal needs. Take note of what the attorney says and does, and look for the following qualities:

save

When you are starting a business, you are short of money for just about everything—including legal services. Realizing this, many law firms offer a "startup package" of legal services for a set fee. This typically includes drawing up initial documents, attending corporate board meetings, preparing minutes, drafting ownership agreements and stock certificates, and offering routine legal advice.

- *Experience.* Although it's not essential to find an expert in your particular field, it makes sense to look for someone who specializes in small-business problems as opposed to, say, maritime law. "Find someone who understands the different business structures and their tax implications," says Hodge. Make sure the lawyer is willing to take on small problems; if you're trying to collect on a small invoice, will the lawyer think it's worth his or her time?
- *Understanding.* Be sure the attorney is willing to learn about your business's goals. You're looking for someone who will be a long-term partner in your business's growth. Sure, you're a startup today, but does the lawyer understand where you want to be tomorrow and share your vision for the future?
- *Ability to communicate.* If the lawyer speaks in legalese and doesn't bother to explain the terms he or she uses, you should look for someone else.
- *Availability.* Will the attorney be available for conferences at your convenience, not his or hers? How quickly can you expect emergency phone calls to be returned?

- *Rapport.* Is this someone you can get along with? You'll be discussing matters close to your heart, so make sure you feel comfortable doing so. Good chemistry will ensure a better relationship and more positive results for your business.
- *Reasonable fees.* Attorneys charge anywhere from $50 to $1,000 or more per hour, depending on the location, size, and prestige of the firm as well as the lawyer's reputation and experience. Shop around and get quotes from several firms before making your decision. However, beware of comparing one attorney with another on the basis of fees alone. The lowest hourly fees may not indicate the best value in legal work because an inexperienced attorney may take twice as long to complete a project as an experienced one will.
- *References.* Don't be afraid to ask for references. Ask what types of businesses or cases the attorney has worked with in the past. Get a list of clients or other attorneys you can contact to discuss competence, service, and fees.

Cost Cutters

For many entrepreneurs, the idea of consulting a lawyer conjures up scary visions of skyrocketing legal bills. While there's no denying that lawyers are expensive, the good news is, there are more ways than ever to keep a lid on costs. Start by learning about the various ways lawyers bill their time:

- *Hourly or per diem rate.* Most attorneys bill by the hour. If travel is involved, they may bill by the day. They might also bill hourly for travel time, so be sure to ask.
- *Flat fee.* Some attorneys suggest a flat fee for certain routine matters, such as reviewing a contract or closing a loan.
- *Monthly retainer.* If you anticipate a lot of routine questions, one option is a monthly fee that entitles you to all the routine legal advice you need.
- *Contingent fee.* For lawsuits and other complex matters, lawyers often work on a contingency basis. This means that if they succeed, they receive a percentage of the proceeds—usually between 20 and 50 percent. If they fail, they receive only out-of-pocket expenses.

- *Value billing.* Some law firms bill at a higher rate on business matters if the attorneys obtain a favorable result, such as negotiating a contract that saves the client thousands of dollars. Try to avoid lawyers who use this method, which is also sometimes called "partial contingency."

If you think one method will work better for you than another, don't hesitate to bring it up with the attorney; many will offer flexible arrangements to meet your needs.

When you hire an attorney, draw up an agreement (called an "engagement letter") detailing the billing method. If more than one attorney works on your file, make sure you specify the hourly rate for each individual so you aren't charged $200 an hour for legal work done by an associate who only charges $75 an hour.

This agreement should also specify what expenses you're expected to reimburse. Some attorneys expect to be reimbursed for meals, secretarial overtime, postage, and photocopies, which many people consider the costs of doing business. If an unexpected charge comes up, will your attorney call you for authorization? Agree to reimburse only reasonable and necessary out-of-pocket expenses. No matter what methods your attorney uses, here are steps you can take to control legal costs:

- *Have the attorney estimate the cost of each matter in writing, so you can decide whether it's worth pursuing.* If the bill comes in over the estimate, ask why. Some attorneys also offer "caps," guaranteeing in writing the maximum cost of a particular service. This helps you budget and gives you more certainty than just getting an estimate.

save

Using paralegals as part of your legal team can be a good way to cut costs. Certain legal tasks—preparing a simple document, for instance—are straightforward enough that a paralegal may be able to handle them instead of a higher-priced lawyer. Don't assume your lawyer will suggest this route; ask him or her about it. And always make sure the paralegal is supervised by a business lawyer. The same goes for legal assistants and junior attorneys. Ask your lawyer if it's possible for the most junior member qualified to do the work to handle more mundane or simple tasks. This could save you hundreds of dollars per hour.

>> Pay Now, Not Later

A new method has arisen to take charge of skyrocketing legal fees. It's called the prepaid legal plan, and more and more small businesses are using it.

Prepaid legal plans have been compared to HMOs because they offer certain basic services for a monthly fee. Prices range from as little as $10 a month to $100 or more; in return, an entrepreneur gets a package of services such as, say, unlimited phone consultation with a lawyer, review of three contracts per month, up to ten debt collection letters per month, and discounts on other legal services.

According to prepaid legal services firm Caldwell Legal, USA, 73 percent of all legal problems members bring can be resolved with a single telephone call.

Typically, prepaid legal services contract with one law firm in each state to handle routine matters. Because the service is usually that firm's biggest client, business owners using the service receive a warmer welcome than they might at a big law firm. Specialists are usually available at reduced rates.

When thinking about a prepaid legal service, here are some factors to consider:

- What is included? Check the plan to make sure it has what you need. The number of services offered at a reduced rate may be limited; what are the charges for other services?
- Consider whether you'd prefer to build a relationship with one attorney rather than talk to a different lawyer every time you call.
- Ask other entrepreneurs who have used such services about the quality of work. Also ask how the company handles conflicts of interest in case you have a dispute against a business that uses the same prepaid firm.

With these caveats in mind, a prepaid legal service firm could be just what a business on a budget needs. For more information, contact the American Prepaid Legal Services Institute at 541 N Fairbanks Ct. Chicago, IL 60611, call (312) 988-5751, or visit its website at aplsi.org or email info@aplsi.org.

- *Learn what increments of time the firm uses to calculate its bill.* Attorneys keep track of their time in increments as short as six minutes or as long as half an hour. Will a five-minute phone call cost you $50?
- *Request monthly, itemized bills.* Some lawyers wait until a bill gets large before sending an invoice. Ask for monthly invoices and review them. The most obvious red flag is excessive fees; this means that too many people—or the wrong people—are working on your file. It's also possible you may be mistakenly billed for work done for another client, so review your invoices carefully.
- *See if you can negotiate prompt-payment discounts.* Request that your bill be discounted if you pay within 30 days of your invoice date. A 5 percent discount can add thousands of dollars to your bottom line.
- *Be prepared.* Before you meet with or call your lawyer, have the necessary documents with you and know exactly what you want to discuss. Fax needed documents ahead of time so your attorney doesn't have to read them during the conference and can instead get right down to business. And refrain from calling your attorney 100 times a day—or even ten times.
- *Meet with your lawyer regularly.* At first glance, this may not seem like a good way to keep costs down, but you will be amazed at how much it reduces the endless rounds of phone tag that plague busy entrepreneurs and attorneys. More important, a monthly five- or ten-minute meeting (even by phone) can save you substantial sums by nipping small legal problems in the bud before they even get a chance to grow.

Making the Most of Your Lawyer

Once your relationship with your lawyer is established, keep the lines of communication open. In addition to brief regular meetings, sit down with your attorney once annually to discuss the past year's progress and your goals for the coming year. Meet at your place of business so the attorney can get to know your operation.

How can you tell if your attorney is doing a good job for you? The quickest measure is how many legal difficulties you're having. Lawyers

>> Different Strokes

When you're hit with a lawsuit, the costs can be mind-boggling—even if you win. That's why more and more small businesses are using alternative dispute resolution (ADR), a concept that includes mediation, arbitration, and other ways of resolving disputes without resorting to litigation. Both in contracts between businesses or in agreements between employers and employees, people are consenting ahead of time to submit future disputes to ADR. Here are the most common forms of ADR:

- > *Negotiation.* In the simplest form of ADR, the two parties (or their lawyers) discuss their differences and agree on a settlement.
- > *Mediation.* When the two parties need more help in working out a solution, they can hire a neutral third party (a mediator) skilled in asking questions, listening, and helping make decisions. The result is a written agreement to settle the dispute; both parties share the mediation costs.
- > *Arbitration.* An arbitrator hears a case like a judge, then issues a decision. The parties have control over who hears the case—often, an expert in their field. In nonbinding arbitration, the arbitrator makes a recommendation that parties can accept or reject. In binding arbitration, the arbitrator's decision is legally binding.
- > *Mini-trial.* Less common, this gives both parties a sense of how their disagreement might resolve in court. They watch their lawyers argue the case as if they were at trial. In most cases, the parties are better able to see the other side and end up settling the case.
- > *Summary jury trial.* Here, a jury of citizens hears a shortened trial and makes a nonbinding decision. Again, this usually helps the parties agree on a settlement.

Any time two parties enter a contract, they can include an agreement to submit any disputes to a specified type of ADR. Your attorney can help you draft a clause specifying how the situation will be handled. If you have employees sign an ADR agreement, make sure they understand that they will lose the option of a jury trial.

>> Different Strokes, continued

Even if you don't have an ADR clause in your contracts, it's still possible to suggest using ADR after a dispute arises. Once they understand how much money, time, and aggravation ADR can save, the other side may agree to use it.

should be fending off legal problems. A good attorney identifies potential problems in advance.

Like any competent professional, a good lawyer also returns phone calls promptly, meets deadlines, and follows through on promises. A good lawyer is thorough in asking for information and discerning your goals. And good lawyers either research what they do not know and explain your options, or refer you to someone who can help.

In evaluating the attorney's work on any matter, consider whether you have been able to meet your goals. If you have met your goals without undue costs, the attorney is probably doing a good job. Once you have found a lawyer who understands your business and does a good job, you have found a valuable asset.

e-fyi

Need a quick, free expert answer? Go to sba.gov and/or write to answerdesk@sba.gov, or call (800) 827-5722. The Answer Desk, according to the SBA, is the only national toll-free telephone service providing information to the public on small-business problems and concerns. They're ready to talk Monday through Friday, from 9 A.M. to 7 P.M. EST. You can access services at local district offices, too. There's a list of locations by state at www.sba.gov/tools/local-assistance/district offices.

Hiring an Accountant

Don't assume only big companies need the services of an accountant. Accountants help you keep an eye on major costs as early as the startup stage, a time when you're probably preoccupied with counting every paper clip and postage stamp. Accountants help you look at the big picture.

Even after the startup stage, many business owners may not have any idea how well they're doing financially until the end of the year, when they file their tax returns. Meanwhile, they equate their cash flow with profits, which is wrong. Every dollar counts for business owners, so if you don't know where you stand on a monthly basis, you may not be around at the end of the year.

While do-it-yourself accounting software is plentiful and easy to use, it's not the sole answer. Just as having Microsoft Word does not make you a writer, having accounting software doesn't make you an accountant. Software can only do what you tell it to do—and a good accountant's skills go far beyond crunching numbers.

In fact, perhaps no other business relationship has such potential to pay off. Nowadays, accountants are more than just bean counters. A good accountant can be your company's financial partner for life—with intimate knowledge of everything from how you're going to finance your

>> All the Right Questions

Here are ten questions to ask when interviewing a potential accountant:

1. Are you a CPA? (Don't assume every accountant is.)
2. Are you licensed to practice in your state?
3. When and where did you receive a license to practice?
4. Where did you go to school, and what degrees did you earn?
5. Who are some of your clients? (Call them and get references.)
6. In what area do you specialize?
7. How big or small are your clients, and what size were they when you began your relationship with them?
8. How accessible are you? (Some accountants are only available during business hours; others will give you their home or pager number.)
9. To what professional organizations do you belong? How active are you in those groups?
10. What are your fees? (Ask to see some current invoices.)

next forklift to how you're going to finance your daughter's college education.

While many people think of accountants strictly as tax preparers, in reality, accountants have a wide knowledge base that can be an invaluable asset to a business. A general accounting practice covers four basic areas of expertise:

1. Business advisory services
2. Accounting and record-keeping
3. Tax advice
4. Auditing

e-fyi

The American Institute of Certified Public Accountants has a website that provides news updates, information about legislative activities, and general consumer information, as well as links to state CPA societies, where you can get CPA referrals. Visit aicpa.org.

These four disciplines often overlap. For instance, if your accountant is helping you prepare the financial statements you need for a loan, and he or she gives you some insights into how certain estimates could be recalculated to get a more favorable review, the accountant is crossing the line from auditing into business advisory services. And perhaps, after preparing your midyear financial statements, he or she might suggest how your performance year-to-date will influence your year-end tax liability. Here's a closer look at the four areas:

1. *Business advisory services.* This is where accountants can really earn their keep. Since the accountant is knowledgeable about your business environment, your tax situation, and your financial statements, it makes sense to ask him or her to pull all the pieces together and help you come up with a business plan and personal financial plan you can really achieve. Accountants can offer advice on everything from insurance (do you really need business interruption insurance, or would it be cheaper to lease a second site?) to expansion (how will additional capacity affect operating costs?). Accountants can bring a new level of insight to the picture, simply by virtue of their perspective.
2. *Accounting and record-keeping.* Accounting and record-keeping are perhaps the most basic accounting discipline. However, most busi-

ness owners keep their own books and records instead of having their accountant do it. The reason is simple: If these records are examined by lenders or the IRS, the business owner is responsible for their accuracy; therefore, it makes more sense for the owner to maintain them.

Where accountants can offer help is in initially setting up bookkeeping and accounting systems and showing the business owner how to use them. A good system allows you to evaluate your profitability at any given point in time and modify prices accordingly. It also lets you track expenses to see if any particular areas are getting out of hand. It lets you establish and track a budget, spot trends in sales and expenses, and reduce accounting fees required to produce financial statements and tax returns.

aha!

If you're looking to master accounting for your new business—or simply don't want to be left in the dark when talking to your accountant—check out *Small Business Accounting Simplified* by Daniel Sitarz (Nova Publishing). This useful reference book features easy techniques you can use, simple solutions to common problems, and everything you need to gain an overall understanding of the accounting process. It also includes a CD with commonly used forms.

3. *Tax advice.* Tax help from accountants comes in two forms: tax compliance and tax planning. Planning refers to reducing your overall tax burden; compliance refers to obeying the tax laws.
4. *Auditing.* Auditing services are required for many different purposes, most commonly by banks as a condition of a loan. There are many levels of auditing, ranging from simply preparing financial statements from figures that the entrepreneur supplies all the way up to an actual audit, where the accountant or other third party gives assurance that a company's financial information is accurate.

Choosing an Accountant

The best way to find a good accountant is to get a referral from your attorney, your banker, or a business colleague in the same industry. If you need more possibilities, almost every state has a Society of Certified Public Accountants that will make a referral. Don't underestimate the importance of a CPA. This title is only awarded to people who have passed a rigorous two-day, nationally standardized test. Most states require CPAs to have at least a college degree or its equivalent, and several states also require post-graduate work.

>> A Little Help from Your Friends

Mentors can be valuable sources of information at any stage of your company's growth. It is always in your best interest to reach out to a variety of sources of information when you make decisions, advises SCORE. An SBA partner, SCORE offers 11,000 volunteer members and 320-plus chapters throughout the United States.

Mentors can often give you a fresh perspective on problems or challenges because they're not personally involved with your business like other advisors, including attorneys, accountants, and friends. For this reason, it's important to find not only a mentor who has experience and knowledge, but also someone you can trust and feel at ease with.

Building a relationship takes work on your part, too.

To get matched with a mentor, your first step should be locating your local SCORE chapter. Call (800) 634-0245, or visit score.org. If there's not a chapter near you, no problem. SCORE also offers free email counseling provided by its 11,000 volunteers.

Other mentoring resources can be found through networking in your community. Join the local chamber of commerce, Rotary Club, or Toastmasters. Attend luncheons, seminars, and conferences related to your business and talk to guest speakers. Find out what types of business organizations closely match your company so you can team up with other individuals with similar interests and concerns. Developing these types of personal and business relationships can put you in touch with successful people who may be potential mentors.

Accountants usually work for large companies; CPAs, on the other hand, work for a variety of large and small businesses. When dealing with an accountant, you can only hope he or she is well-educated and well-versed in your business's needs. Passing the CPA exam, however, is a guarantee of a certain level of ability. Once you have come up with some good candidates, a little preparation is in order before you interview them. The first step in setting the stage for a successful search is to take an inventory of what you will need. It is important to determine beforehand just how much of the work your company will do and how much of it will be done by the accountant.

Accounting services can be broken down into three broad categories: recording transactions, assembling them, and generating returns and financial statements. Typically, the latter part—that is, the generation of returns and financial statements—requires the highest level of expertise. But though the other activities require a lower skill level, many firms still charge the same hourly rate for them. Given the level of fees you are prepared to pay, you must decide where your responsibility stops and where the accountant's begins.

Once you have compiled your documentation and given some thought to your expectations, you're ready to interview your referrals. Five candidates is a good number to start with. For each candidate, plan on two meetings before making your decision. One of these meetings should be at your site; one should be at theirs. Both parties need to know the environment the other works in. Your principal goal is to find out about three things: services, personality, and fees.

1. *Services.* Most accounting firms offer tax and auditing services. But what about bookkeeping? Management consulting? Pension fund accounting? Estate planning? Will the accountant help you design and implement financial information systems? Other services a CPA may offer include analyzing transactions for loans and financing; preparing, auditing, reviewing and compiling financial statements; managing investments; and representing you before tax authorities.

   Although smaller accounting firms are generally a better bet for entrepreneurs (see "The Size of It" on page 159), they may not offer all these services. Make sure the firm has what you need. If it can't offer specialized services, such as estate planning, it may have relationships with other firms to which it can refer you to handle these matters. In addition to services, make sure the firm has experience with small business and with your industry. Someone who is already familiar with the financial issues facing your field of business won't have to waste time getting up to speed.

2. *Personality.* Is the accountant's style compatible with yours? Be sure the people you are meeting with are the same ones who will be handling your business. At many accounting firms, some partners handle sales and new business, then pass the actual account work on to others.

>> The Size of It

Are you debating over the choice between that large, fancy law or accounting firm with offices in every corner of the globe, or that humble, one-person legal or accounting office down the street? Before you bust your budget to retain Squelch, Withers & Ream, know this: When it comes to professional service firms, bigger isn't always better.

A big law or accounting firm may boast impressive credentials on your first meeting with them. The problem is that they usually boast an impressive price to match. What's more, the hotshot you meet with on your initial conference may not be the person who will actually work on your legal cases or taxes. That task is likely to fall to a less experienced junior partner with limited know-how. This isn't necessarily bad, but make sure you know who will be working on your file and what their experience is. Also be sure you're billed correctly and don't get charged $300 an hour for something a paralegal did.

Only you can decide what is right for you, but make sure you're not being swayed by a big name or a fancy office. While a big law or accounting firm may be right for some small businesses' needs, the reality is that your company will make up a much smaller share of such a firm's client list. As such, you may not get the attention they're devoting to bigger clients.

When evaluating competency and compatibility, ask candidates how they would handle situations relevant to you. For example: How would you handle a change in corporation status from S to C? How would you handle an IRS office audit seeking verification of automobile expenses? Listen to the answers, and decide if that's how you would like your affairs to be handled.

> **tip**
>
> 
>
> Find out how well-connected the CPA and his/her firm are before making a final decision. CPAs are often valuable resources for small businesses needing to borrow money or to raise capital from other sources. A well-connected CPA might help you get a foot in the door with a bank or investor.

Realize, too, that having an accountant who takes a different approach can be a good thing. If you are super conservative, it's not a bad thing to have an accountant who exposes you to the aggressive side of life. Likewise, if you are aggressive, it's often helpful to have someone who can show you the conservative approach. Be sure that the accountant won't pressure you into doing things you aren't comfortable with. You need to be able to sleep at night.

3. *Fees.* Ask about fees upfront. Most accounting firms charge by the hour; fees can range from $100 to $275 per hour. However, there are some accountants who work on a monthly retainer. Figure out what services you are likely to need and which option will be more cost-effective for you.

   Get a range of quotes from different accountants. Also try to get an estimate of the total annual charges based on the services you have discussed. Don't base your decision solely on cost, however; an accountant who charges more by the hour is likely to be more experienced and thus able to work faster than a novice who charges less.

   At the end of the interview, ask for references—particularly from clients in the same industry as you. A good accountant should be happy to provide you with references; call and ask how satisfied they were with the accountant's services, fees, and availability.

Good Relations

After you have made your choice, spell out the terms of the agreement in an "engagement letter" that details the returns and statements to be prepared and the fees to be charged. This ensures you and your accountant have the same expectations and helps prevent misunderstandings and hard feelings.

Make the most of the accounting relationship by doing your part. Don't hand your accountant a shoebox full of receipts. Write down details of all the checks in your check register—whether they are for utilities, supplies, and so on. Likewise, identify sources of income on your bank deposit slips. The better you maintain your records, the less time your accountant has to spend—and the lower your fees will be.

tip 

If you are starting a retail or service business involving a lot of cash, make sure the CPA has expertise in providing input on controlling your cash. As you grow, this becomes an increasingly vital issue, and a good CPA should be able to advise you in this area.

It's a good idea to meet with your accountant every month. Review financial statements and go over any problems so you know where your money is going. This is where your accountant should go beyond number-crunching to suggest alternative ways of cutting costs and act as a sounding board.

A good accountant can help your business in ways you never dreamed possible. Spending the time to find the right accountant—and taking advantage of the advice he or she has to offer—is one of the best things you can do to help your business soar.

PART

3

FUND

CHAPTER

12

All in the Family

Financing Starts with Yourself and Friends and Relatives

Once you have decided on the type of venture you want to start, the next step on the road to business success is figuring out where the money will come from to fund it. Where do you start?

The best place to begin is by looking in the mirror. Self-financing is the number-one form of financing used by most business startups. In addition, when you approach other financing sources such as bankers, venture capitalists, or the government, they will want to know exactly how much of your own money you are putting into the venture. After all, if you don't have enough faith in your business to risk your own money, why should anyone else risk theirs?

Do It Yourself

Begin by doing a thorough inventory of your assets (the "Personal Balance Sheet" on page 167 can help with this). You are likely to uncover resources you didn't know you had. Assets include savings accounts, equity in real estate, retirement accounts, vehicles, recreational equipment, and collections. You may decide to sell some assets for cash or to use them as collateral for a loan.

If you have investments, you may be able to use them as a resource. Low-interest-margin loans against stocks and securities can be arranged through your brokerage accounts.

The downside here is that if the market should fall and your securities are your loan collateral, you'll get a margin call from your broker, requesting you to supply more collateral. If you can't do that within a certain time, you'll be asked to sell some of your securities to shore up the collateral. Also take a look at your personal line of credit. Some businesses have successfully been started on credit cards, although this is one of the most expensive ways to finance yourself (see Chapter 14 for more on credit card financing).

If you own a home, consider getting a home equity loan on the part of the mortgage that you have already paid off. The bank will either provide a lump-sum loan payment or extend a line of credit based on the equity in your home. Depending on the value of your home, a home-equity loan could become a substantial line of credit. If you have $50,000 in equity, you could possibly set up a line of credit of up to $40,000. Home-equity loans carry relatively low interest rates, and all interest paid on a loan of up to $100,000 is tax-deductible. But be sure you can repay the loan—you can lose your home if you do not.

Consider borrowing against cash-value life insurance. You can use the value built up in a cash-value life insurance policy as a ready source of cash. The interest rates are reasonable because the insurance companies always get their money back. You don't even have to make payments if you do not want to. Neither the amount you borrow nor the interest that accrues has to be repaid. The only loss is that if you die and the debt hasn't been repaid, that money is deducted from the amount your beneficiary will receive.

If you have a 401(k) retirement plan through your employer and are starting a part-time business while you keep your full-time job, consider

Personal Balance Sheet

By filling out a personal balance sheet, you will be able to determine your net worth. Finding out your net worth is an important early step in the process of becoming a business owner because you need to find out what assets are available to you for investment in your business.

Assets		**Totals**
Cash and Checking		
Savings Accounts		
Real Estate/Home		
Automobiles		
Bonds		
Securities		
Insurance Cash Values		
Other		
Total Assets	**A**	**$**

Liabilities		**Totals**
Current Monthly Bills		
Credit Card/Charge Account Bills		
Mortgage		
Auto Loans		
Finance Company Loans		
Personal Debts		
Other		
Total Liabilities	**B**	**$**
Net Worth (A–B=C)	**C**	**$**

Degree of Indebtedness		
Total Liabilities	**B**	**$**
Total Assets	**A**	**$**
Degree of Indebtedness (B–A=D)	**D**	**$**

Note: If total liabilities exceed total assets, subtract assets from liabilities to determine degree of indebtedness (B–A=D).

Figure 12.1. Personal Balance Sheet

> *"If you think you can, you can. And if you think you can't, you're right."*
>
> —Mary Kay Ash, founder of Mary Kay Cosmetics

borrowing against the plan. It's very common for such plans to allow you to borrow up to 50 percent of your vested account balance up to a maximum of $50,000. The interest rate is usually 1 to 2 percent above prime rate with a specified repayment schedule. The downside of borrowing from your 401(k) is that if you lose your job, the loan has to be repaid in a short period of time—often 60 days (but occasionally as long as six months) or it is taxed heavily, as if you've taken an early withdrawal from the plan. Consult the plan's documentation to see if this is an option for you.

Another option is to use the funds in your individual retirement account (IRA). Within the laws governing IRAs, you can actually withdraw money from an IRA as long as you replace it within 60 days. This is not a loan, so you don't pay interest. This is a withdrawal that you're allowed to keep for 60 days. It's possible for a highly organized entrepreneur to juggle funds among several IRAs. But if you're one day late—for any reason—you'll be hit with a 10 percent premature-withdrawal fee, and the money you haven't returned becomes taxable.

>> Good Benefits

If you have been laid off or lost your job, another source of startup capital may be available to you. Some states have instituted self-employment programs as part of their unemployment insurance systems.

People who are receiving unemployment benefits and meet certain requirements are recruited into entrepreneurial training programs that show them how to start businesses. This gives them an opportunity to use their unemployment funds for startup, while boosting their chances of success.

Contact the department in your state that handles unemployment benefits to see if such a program is available to you.

If you have a Roth IRA, you're entitled to withdrawals tax and penalty-free, so long as the funds were in the account for at least five years. That's because a Roth is taxed at the time you put funds into the IRA account—not when you retire and withdraw it. Consider switching your regular IRA to a Roth over a couple of years if you know you plan to finance a business this way. You'll have to pay the taxes in the year you make the conversion, but the money will then be free to withdraw when you need it, without the big penalties. Make the conversions well before you need the cash.

If you are employed, another way to finance your business is by squirreling away money from your current salary until you have enough to launch the business. If you don't want to wait, consider moonlighting or cutting your full-time job back to part time. This ensures you'll have some steady funds rolling in until your business starts to soar.

People generally have more assets than they realize. Use as much of your own money as possible to get started; remember, the larger your own investment, the easier it will be for you to acquire capital from other sources.

> **warning**
>
> Watch out for the relative or friend who agrees to lend you money even though he or she can't really afford to. "There will always be people who want to do anything they can to help you, who will give you funds that are critical to their future just because you ask for it," says Mike McKeever, author of *How to Write a Business Plan*. "These relatives will not tell you they really can't afford it, so you must be extra perceptive."

Friends and Family

Your own resources may not be enough to give you the capital you need. "Most businesses are started with money from four or five different sources," says Mike McKeever, author of *How to Write a Business Plan*. After self-financing, the second most popular source for startup money is composed of friends, relatives, and business associates.

"Family and friends are great sources of financing," says Tonia Papke, president and founder of MDI Consulting. "These people know you have integrity and will grant you a loan based on the strength of your character."

It makes sense. People with whom you have close relationships know you are reliable and competent, so there should be no problem in asking for a loan, right? Keep in mind, however, that asking for financial help isn't the same as borrowing the car. While squeezing money out of family and friends may seem an easy alternative to dealing with bankers, it can actually be a much more delicate situation. Papke warns that your family members or friends may think lending you money gives them license to meddle. "And if the business fails," she says, "the issue of paying the money back can be a problem, putting the whole relationship in jeopardy."

The bottom line, says McKeever, is that "whenever you put money into a relationship that involves either friendship or love, it gets very complicated." Fortunately, there are ways to work out the details and make the business relationship advantageous for all parties involved. If you handle the situation correctly and tactfully, you may gain more than finances for your business—you may end up strengthening the personal relationship as well.

The Right Source

The first step in getting financing from friends or family is finding the right person to borrow money from. As you search for potential lenders or investors, don't enlist people with ulterior motives. "It's not a good idea to take money from a person if it's given with emotional strings," says McKeever. "For example, avoid borrowing from relatives or friends who have the attitude of 'I'll give you the money, but I want you to pay extra attention to me.'"

Once you determine whom you'd like to borrow money from, approach the person initially in an informal situation. Let the person know a little about your business, and gauge his or her interest. If the person seems interested and says he or she would like more information about the business,

tip

A business plan sets out in writing the expectations for the company. It shows family members who are putting up the money what they can expect for their contribution. And it helps keep the entrepreneur—you—mindful of responsibilities to family members who backed you and keeps you on track to fulfill your obligations.

make an appointment to meet with them in a professional atmosphere. "This makes it clear that the subject of discussion will be your business and their interest in it," says McKeever. "You may secure their initial interest in a casual setting, but to go beyond that, you have to make an extra effort. You should do a formal sales presentation and make sure the person has all the facts."

A large part of informing this person is compiling a business plan, which you should bring to your meeting. Explain the plan in detail, and do the presentation just as you would in front of a banker or other investor. Your goal is to get the other person on your side and make him or her as excited as you are about the possibilities of your business.

During your meeting—and, in fact, whenever you discuss a loan—try to separate the personal from the business as much as possible. Difficult as this may sound, it's critical to the health of your relationship. "It's important to treat the lender formally, explaining your business plan in detail rather than casually passing it off with an 'if you love me, you'll give me the money' attitude," says McKeever.

Be prepared to accept rejection gracefully. "Don't pile on the emotional pressure—emphasize that you'd like this to be strictly a business decision for them," says McKeever. "If relatives or friends feel they can turn you down without offending you, they're more likely to invest. Give them an out."

Putting It on Paper

Now it's time to put the loan in motion. First, you must state how much money you need, what you'll use it for, and how you'll pay it back. Next, draw up the legal papers—an agreement stating that the person will indeed put money into the business.

Too frequently, business owners fail to take the time to figure out exactly what kind of paperwork should be completed when they borrow from family or friends. "Often small-business owners put more thought into figuring out what type of car to buy than how to structure this type of lending arrangement," says Steven I. Levey of accounting firm GHP Financial Group. Unfortunately, once you've made an error in this area, it's difficult to correct it.

Startup Costs Worksheet

The following two worksheets will help you to compute your initial cash requirements for your business. They list the things you need to consider when determining your startup costs and include both the one-time initial expenses to open your doors and the ongoing costs you'll face during the first 90 days.

Startup Capital Requirements

One-time Startup Expenses

Startup Expenses	Description	Amount
Advertising	Promotion for opening the business	
Starting inventory	Amount of inventory required to open	
Building construction	Amount per contractor bid and other costs	
Cash	Amount needed for the cash register	
Decorating	Estimate based on bid, if appropriate	
Deposits	Check with utility companies	
Fixtures and equipment	Use actual bids	
Insurance	Bid from insurance agent	
Lease payments	Fees to be paid before opening	
Licenses and permits	Check with city or state offices	
Miscellaneous	All other costs	
Professional fees	Include CPA, attorney, etc.	
Remodeling	Use contractor bids	
Rent	Fee to be paid before opening	
Services	Cleaning, accounting, etc.	
Signs	Use contractor bids	
Supplies	Office, cleaning, etc.	
Unanticipated expenses	Include an amount for the unexpected	
Other		
Other		
Total Startup Costs		$

Figure 12.2. Startup Costs Worksheet

Startup Costs Worksheet

Startup Capital Requirements

Ongoing Monthly Expenses*

Startup Expenses	Description	Amount
Advertising		
Bank service fees		
Credit card charges		
Delivery fees		
Dues and subscriptions		
Insurance	Exclude amount on preceding page	
Interest		
Inventory	See ** below	
Lease payments	Exclude amount on preceding page	
Loan payments	Principal and interest payments	
Office expenses		
Payroll other than owner		
Payroll taxes		
Professional fees		
Rent	Exclude amount on preceding page	
Repairs and maintenance		
Sales tax		
Supplies		
Telephone		
Utilities		
Your salary	Only if applicable during the first three months	
Other		
Total Ongoing Costs		$
Total Startup Costs	Amount from preceding page	$
Total Cash Needed		$

*Include the first three months' cash needs unless otherwise noted.

**Include amount required for inventory expansion. If inventory is to be replaced from cash sales, do not include here. Assume sales will generate enough cash for replacements.

Figure 12.2. Startup Costs Worksheet, continued

Your loan agreement needs to specify whether the loan is secured (that is, the lender holds title to part of your property) or unsecured, what the payments will be, when they're due, and what the interest is. If the money is in the form of an investment, you have to establish whether the business is a partnership or corporation, and what role, if any, the investor will play. To be sure you and your family and friends have a clear idea of what financial obligations are being created, you have a mutual responsibility to make sure everyone is informed about the process and decide together how best to proceed.

Most important, says McKeever, "Outline the legal responsibilities of both parties and when and how the money should be paid back." If your loan agreement is complex, it's a good idea to consult your accountant about the best ways to structure the loan (see the "Taxing Matters" section below).

Whichever route you take, make sure the agreement is in writing if you expect it to be binding. "Any time you take money into a business, the law is very explicit: You must have all agreements written down and documented," says McKeever. If you don't, emotional and legal difficulties could result that end up in court. And if the loan isn't documented, you may find yourself with no legal recourse.

Taxing Matters

Putting the agreement on paper also protects both you and your lender come tax time. Relying on informal and verbal agreements results in tax quagmires. "In these cases, you have a burden of proof to show the IRS that [the money] was not a gift," says Tom Ochsenschlager, vice president of taxation for the American Institute of Certified Public Accountants. If the IRS views it as a gift because there was no intention to repay it, then the lender becomes subject to the federal gift tax rules and will have to pay taxes on the money if it is more than $14,000 as of 2014. Also make sure the person providing the money charges an interest rate that reflects a fair market value.

If your friend or family member wants to give you a no-interest loan, make sure the loan is not more than $100,000. If you borrow more, the IRS will slap on what it considers to be market-rate interest, better known as "imputed interest," on the lender. That means that while your friend or relative may not be receiving any interest on the money you borrowed, the IRS will tax them as if they were.

No interest is imputed if the aggregate loans are less than $10,000. Between $10,000 and $100,000, the imputed amount is limited to your net investment income, such as interest, dividends, and, in some cases, capital gains. Taxable imputed interest income to you is zero as long as the borrower's net investment income for the year is no more than $1,000. To determine the interest rate on these transactions, the IRS uses what it calls the applicable federal rate, which changes monthly. Keep in mind that if you don't put all the details of the loan in writing, it will be very difficult for you to deduct the interest you pay on it. Additionally, the relative who lent the money won't be able to take a tax deduction on the loss if you find you can't repay and the money could be considered a gift in an audit if the paperwork isn't in order.

To be absolutely safe, Ochsenschlager recommends that you make the friend or relative who is providing the money one of the business' shareholders. This effectively makes the transaction an investment in your company and also makes it easier from a tax standpoint for your friend or relative to write off the transaction as an ordinary loss if the business fails. (This applies only if the total amount your company received for its stock, including the relative's investment, does not exceed $1 million.)

In addition, "if your company is wildly successful, your relative will have an equity interest in the business, and his or her original investment will be worth quite a bit more," Ochsenschlager says. In contrast, if a relative gives you a loan and your company goes under, the relative's loss would generally be considered a personal bad debt. This creates more of a tax disadvantage because personal

save

You don't necessarily need a lawyer to write your loan agreement. You can find examples of loan agreements in many business books; just write up the same information, complete it, and sign it. If you do decide to get legal advice, you can save money by drawing up the loan agreement yourself and then giving it to an attorney to redraft.

bad debts can be claimed as capital losses only to offset capital gains. If the capital loss exceeds the capital gains, only $3,000 of the loss can be used against ordinary income in any given year. Thus, an individual making a large loan that isn't repaid may have to wait several years to realize the tax benefits from the loss.

If the loan that can't be repaid is a business loan, however, the lender receives a deduction against ordinary income and can take deductions even before the loan becomes totally worthless. (One catch: The IRS takes a very narrow view of what qualifies as a business loan. To qualify as a business loan, the loan would have to be connected to the lender's business.) This will be difficult, so consult an accountant about the best way to structure the loan for maximum tax benefits to both parties.

Making your relative a shareholder doesn't mean you'll have to put up with Mom or Pop in the business. Depending on your company's organizational structure, your friend or relative can be a silent partner if your company is set up as a partnership, or a silent shareholder if you are organized as an S corporation or limited liability company.

Keep 'Em Happy

Even with every detail documented, your responsibilities are far from over. Don't make assumptions or take people for granted just because they are friends or family members. Communication is key.

If your relative or friend is not actively involved in the business, make sure you contact him or her once every month or two to explain how the business is going. "When people invest in small businesses, it often becomes sort of their pet project," says McKeever. "It's important to take the time to keep them informed."

And, of course, there are the payments. Though friends or relatives who invest in your business understand the risks, you must never take the loan for granted. "Don't be cavalier about paying the money back," McKeever says. "That kind of attitude could ruin the relationship."

How Much Is Enough?

Before you begin planning for the cash needs of your business, you must figure out how much money you will need to live on for the first six to

>> Go to the Crowd

Did you hear the story about the bakery owner who turned to strangers to get new ovens for her shop? Or perhaps you've heard talk about lending clubs? Strangers giving money outright or lending through an organized platform have become legitimate, albeit, small, sources for funding. There are two ways to finance your business using the crowd:

1. *Peer-to-peer lending.* Borrowers—that's you—open an account on a P2P site such as Lending Club (www.lendingclub.com) or Zopa (www.zopa.com) and fill out a funding request, detailing how much you need and what it will be used for. You'll receive an interest rate based on your credit rating. Investors—mostly, regular people looking to earn more on their savings than a typical bank savings account might offer—choose what they'd like to fund and earn money off the interest you're charged. In 2013, according to LendingClub data, the company facilitated nearly $2.1 billion in consumer loans with terms of three to five years.
2. *Crowdfunding.* Websites such as Kickstarter (www.kickstarter.com) or Indiegogo (www.indiegogo.com) serve as a platform for your ideas to get free money. That is, if strangers like what you're trying to do. It's a simple concept: An individual or group posts an idea or cause and then markets it heavily on the site. On the other side, funders (people just like you) search for new products or initiatives to support. It's not a loan or investment. People who give money to crowdfunding projects don't receive shares or interest in return, although most will offer something small as a token. For instance, the bakery owner who raised $26,000 for a new oven offered a batch of cookies to every funder.

12 months of your business's operation. The best way to accomplish this is to create a budget that shows where you spent your money in the past 12 months. Make sure you look over the whole 12-month period, because expenses often change a lot from month to month. When creating the schedule, be on the lookout for expenses that could be reduced or eliminated if necessary. Use the form starting on page 178 to create your own budget.

Monthly Budget

	JAN	FEB	MAR	APR	MAY	JUN	JUL	AUG	SEP	OCT	NOV	DEC	TOTAL
Income													
Wages (take-home)—partner 1													
Wages (take-home)—partner 2													
Interest and dividends													
Other													
Total Income													
Expenses													
Auto expenses													
Auto insurance													
Auto payment													
Beauty shop and barber													
Cable TV													
Charity													
Child care													
Clothing													
Credit card payments													
Dues and subscriptions													
Entertainment and recreation													

Figure 12.3. Monthly Budget

Monthly Budget

	JAN	FEB	MAR	APR	MAY	JUN	JUL	AUG	SEP	OCT	NOV	DEC	TOTAL
Gifts													
Groceries and dining out													
Health insurance													
Home repairs													
Household													
Income tax (additional)													
Laundry and dry cleaning													
Life insurance													
Medical and dental													
Mortgage payment or rent													
Other debt payments													
Telephone bill													
Tuition													
Utilities													
Vacations													
Other													
Total Expenses													
Surplus/Deficit													

Figure 12.3. Monthly Budget, continued

CHAPTER

13

Nothing Ventured, Nothing Gained

How to Find and Attract Investors

No matter what type of financing source you approach—a bank, a venture capitalist, or your cousin Lenny—there are two basic ways to finance a business: equity financing and debt financing. In equity financing, you receive capital in exchange for part ownership of the company. In debt financing, you receive capital in the form of a loan, which must be paid back. This chapter explains various types of equity financing; Chapter 14 explains debt financing.

Equity Basics

Equity financing can come from various sources, including venture capital firms and private investors. Whichever source you choose, there are some basics you should understand before

aha!

One entrepreneur who wanted to open a restaurant got a list of potential investors by attending all the grand openings of restaurants in the area where he wanted to locate. By asking for the names of people who invested in those restaurants, he soon had enough contact names to finance his own business.

you try to get equity capital. An investor's "share in your company" comes in various forms. If your company is incorporated, the investor might bargain for shares of stock. Or an investor who wants to be involved in the management of the company could come in as a partner.

Keeping control of your company can be more difficult when you are working with outside investors who provide equity financing. Before seeking outside investment, make the most of your own resources to build the company. The more value you can add before you go to the well, the better. If all you bring to the table is a good idea and some talent, an investor may not be willing to provide a large chunk of capital without receiving a controlling share of the ownership in return. As a result, you could end up losing control of the business you started.

Don't assume the first investor to express interest in your business is a godsend. Even someone who seems to share your vision for the company may be bad news. It pays to know your investor. An investor who doesn't understand your business may pull the plug at the wrong time—and destroy the company.

How It Works

Because equity financing involves trading partial ownership interest for capital, the more capital a company takes in from equity investors, the more diluted the founder's control. The question is: How much management are you willing to give up?

Don't overlook the importance of voting control in the company. Investors may be willing to accept a majority of the preferred (nonvoting) stock rather than common (voting) stock. Another possibility is to give the investor a majority of the profits by granting dividends to the preferred stockholders first. Or, holders of nonvoting stock can get liquidation preference, meaning they're first in line to recover their investment if the company goes under.

Even if they're willing to accept a minority position, financiers generally insist on contract provisions that permit them to make management changes under certain conditions. These might include covenants permitting the investor to take control of the company if the corporation fails to meet a certain income level or makes changes without the investor's permission.

Investors may ask that their preferred stock be redeemable either for common stock or for cash a specified number of years later. That gives the entrepreneur a chance to buy the company back if possible but also may allow the investor to convert to common stock and gain control of the company.

Some experts contend that retaining voting control is not important. In a typical high-growth company, the founder only owns 10 percent of the business by the time it goes public. That's not necessarily bad, because 10 percent of $100 million is better than 100 percent of nothing. The key is how valuable the founder is to the success of the company. If you can't easily be replaced, then you have a lot of leverage even though you may not control the business. But keep in mind, you might think you're really valuable—but you might not be in the eyes of your investors.

If the entrepreneur is good enough, the investors may find their best alternative is to let the entrepreneur run the company. Try not to get hung up on the precise percentage of ownership: If it's a successful business, most people will leave you alone even if they own 80 percent. To protect yourself, however, you should always seek financial and legal advice before involving outside investors in your business.

tip

When it comes to pitching to investors, it's not what you say, but how you say it. Breathe. Enunciate. Pace yourself, speaking neither too quickly nor too slowly. Nervous? Fess up—admitting your insecurity puts the listeners on your side. Finally, remember—practice makes perfect.

Venture Capital

When most people think of equity financing, they think of venture capital. Once seen as

tip

Keep this in mind when crafting your pitch to investor angels: When angels reject a potential investment, it's typically because: 1) They don't know the key people well enough or 2) they don't believe the owner and management have the experience and talent to succeed.

a plentiful source of financing for startup businesses, venture capital—like most kinds of capital—is no longer so easy to come by. Yes, there are venture capital firms out there. Quite a few, actually. There are websites you can go to, like Entrepreneur.com's Top 100 Venture Capital Firms (entrepreneur.com/vc100)—a directory of venture capital firms—and you may find some luck. And luck is exactly what you need to convince venture capitalists to invest in your business. If you think we're trying to discourage you, we are. Money can be found for investing in your company, but the era of the venture capitalist happily handing out forklifts of money is over—especially for startups.

Venture capital is most likely to be given to an established company with an already proven track record. If you are a startup, your product or service must be better than the wheel, sliced bread, and the PC—with an extremely convincing plan that will make the investor a lot of money. And even that might not be good enough.

Earth Angels

The unpleasant reality is that getting financing from venture capital firms is an extreme long shot. The pleasant reality is that there are plenty of other sources you can tap for equity financing—typically with far fewer strings attached than an institutional venture capital deal. One source of private capital is an investment angel.

Originally a term used to describe investors in Broadway shows, "angel" now refers to anyone who invests his or her money in an entrepreneurial company (unlike institutional venture capitalists, who invest other people's money). Angel investing has soared in recent years as a growing number of individuals seek better returns on their money than they can get from traditional investment vehicles. Contrary to popular belief, most angels are not millionaires. Typically, they earn between $60,000 and $200,000 a year—which means there are likely to be plenty of them right in your backyard.

Where Angels Fly

> ***"It is only as we develop others that we permanently succeed."***
>
> —Harvey Samuel Firestone, founder of The Firestone Tire and Rubber Co.

Angels can be classified into two groups: affiliated and nonaffiliated. An affiliated angel is someone who has some sort of contact with you or your business but is not necessarily related to or acquainted with you. A nonaffiliated angel has no connection with either you or your business.

It makes sense to start your investor search by seeking an affiliated angel since he or she is already familiar with you or your business and has a vested interest in the relationship. Begin by jotting down names of people who might fit the category of affiliated angel.

- *Professionals.* These include professional providers of services you now use—doctors, dentists, lawyers, accountants, and so on. You know these people, so an appointment should be easy to arrange. Professionals usually have discretionary income available to invest in outside projects, and if they're not interested, they may be able to recommend a colleague who is.
- *Business associates.* These are people you come in contact with during the normal course of your business day. They can be divided into four subgroups:
  1. *Suppliers/vendors.* The owners of companies who supply your inventory and other needs have a vital interest in your company's success and make excellent angels. A supplier's investment may not come in the form of cash but in the form of better payment terms or cheaper prices. Suppliers might even use their credit to help you get a loan.
  2. *Customers.* These are especially good contacts if they use your product or service to make or sell their own goods. List all the customers with whom you have this sort of business relationship.
  3. *Employees.* Some of your key employees might be sitting on unused equity in their homes that would make excellent collateral for a business loan to your business. There is no greater incentive to an employee than to share ownership in the company for which he or she works.

>> Netting Angels

Looking for angels? Now there's a simple way to find them—online. Go4Funding, an angel investor directory, lists dozens of angels and investment networks on its site at go4funding.com. The site also has links to articles that run the gamut from the pros and cons of angel investing to tips for how the angel/investor relationship should work. You can also put your own requests for funding on the site, find experts to consult, and get business ideas.

Another user-friendly site for more in-depth information about angels is the Angel Capital Association (ACA). Although ACA is not a source of capital, this membership organization does provide plenty of information for entrepreneurs who are interested in raising angel capital. It also has an online directory of North American angel organizations sorted by region. It's a great resource for leads, news, and information about angels who are willing and able to support your venture. Visit ACA at angelcapitalassociation.org. Other websites to check out include AngelList (https://angel.co/) and MicroVentures (https://microventures.com).

- *Competitors.* These include owners of similar companies you don't directly compete with. If a competitor is doing business in another part of the country and does not infringe on your territory, he or she may be an empathetic investor and may share not only capital, but information as well.

The nonaffiliated angels category includes:

1. *Professionals.* This group can include lawyers, accountants, consultants, and brokers whom you don't know personally or do business with.
2. *Middle managers.* Angels in middle management positions start investing in small businesses for two major reasons—either they're bored with their jobs and are looking for outside interests, or they are nearing retirement, or fear they are being phased out.
3. *Entrepreneurs.* These angels are (or have been) successful in their own businesses and like investing in other entrepreneurial

ventures. Entrepreneurs who are familiar with your industry make excellent investors.

> ***"Quality, quality, quality: Never waver from it, even when you don't see how you can afford to keep it up. When you compromise, you become a commodity and then you die."***
>
> —Gary Hirshberg, founder of Stonyfield Farm Yogurt

Make the Connection

Approaching affiliated angels is simply a matter of calling to make an appointment. To look for nonaffiliated angels, try these proven methods:

- *Advertising.* The business opportunity section of your local newspaper or *The Wall Street Journal* is an excellent place to advertise for investors. Classified advertising is inexpensive, simple, quick, and effective.
- *Business brokers.* Business brokers know hundreds of people with money who are interested in buying businesses. Even though you don't want to sell your business, you might be willing to sell part of it. Since many brokers are not open to the idea of their clients buying just part of a business, you might have to use some persuasion to get the broker to give you contact names. You'll find a list of local business brokers in the Yellow Pages under "Business Brokers."
- *Telemarketing.* This approach has been called "dialing for dollars." First you get a list of wealthy individuals in your area. Then you begin calling them. Obviously, you have to be highly motivated to try this approach, and a good list is your most important tool. Look up mailing-list brokers in the Yellow Pages. If you don't feel comfortable making cold calls yourself, you can always hire someone to do it for you.
- *Networking.* Attending local venture capital group meetings and other business associations to make contacts is a time-consuming approach but can be effective. Most newspapers contain an events calendar that lists when and where these types of meetings take place.
- *Intermediaries.* These are firms that find angels for entrepreneurial companies. They are usually called "boutique investment bankers."

This means they are small firms that focus primarily on small financing deals. These firms typically charge a percentage of the amount of money they raise for you. Ask your lawyer or accountant for the name of a reputable firm in your area.

- *Matchmaking services.* Matchmakers run the gamut from services that offer face time with investors to websites that post business plans for companies seeking investments. Fundraising success often hinges on the matchmaker's screening process. In other words: Does the matchmaker have a rigorous selection process, or does it take money from anyone regardless of funding prospects? While rates vary, a matchmaking service may charge as much as $25,000 to locate investors, in addition to a percentage of funds raised. Before using any matchmaker, obtain a list of clients to assess recent successes and failures. A good place to start is Angel List at Angel.com or Google "investor matchmaking."

warning

Looking for an investor through classified ads? Be aware there are legal implications when you solicit money through the newspaper. Always get legal advice before placing an ad.

Angels tend to find most of their investment opportunities through friends and business associates, so whatever method you use to search for angels, it is also important to spread the word. Tell your professional advisors and people you meet at networking events, or anyone who could be a good source of referrals, that you are looking for investment capital. You never know what kind of people they know.

Getting the Money

Once you've found potential angels, how do you win them over? Angels look for many of the same things professional venture capitalists look for:

- *Strong management.* Does your management team have a track record of success and experience?
- *Proprietary strength.* Proprietary does not necessarily mean you must have patents, copyrights, or trademarks on all your products. It just

means that your product or service should be unusual enough to grab consumers' attention.

- *Window of opportunity.* Investors look for a window of opportunity when your company can be the first in a market and grab the lion's share of business before others.
- *Market potential.* Investors prefer businesses with strong market potential. That means a restaurateur with plans to franchise stands a better chance than one who simply wants to open one local site.
- *Return on investment.* Most angels will expect a return of 20 to 25 percent over five years. However, they may accept a lower rate of return if your business has a lower risk.

aha! 

Angels invest in companies for reasons that often go beyond just dollars and cents. As a result, your appeal must not only be financial but also emotional. For example: "We need more than just dollars. We need you to bring your incredible wealth of experience to the table as well." In the long run, that may be even more important than capital.

If angels consider the same factors as venture capital companies, what is the difference between them? You have an edge with angels because many are not motivated solely by profit.

Particularly if your angel is a current or former entrepreneur, he or she may be motivated as much by the enjoyment of helping a young business succeed as by the money he or she stands to gain. Angels are more likely than venture capitalists to be persuaded by an entrepreneur's drive to succeed, persistence, and mental discipline.

That is why it is important that your business plan convey a good sense of your background, experience, and drive. Your business plan should also address the concerns above and spell out the financing you expect to need from startup to maturity.

What if your plan is rejected? Ask the angel if he or she knows someone else your business might appeal to. If your plan is accepted, you have some negotiating to do. Be sure to spell out all the terms of the investment in a written agreement; get your lawyer's assistance here. How long will the investment last? How will return be calculated? How will the investment be cashed out? Detail the amount of involvement each angel will have in the business and how the investment will be legalized.

Examine the deal carefully for the possibility of the investor parlaying current equity or future loans to your business into controlling interest. Such a deal is not made in heaven and could indicate you are working with a devil in angel's garb.

CHAPTER

14

Looking for Loans

The Ins and Outs of Debt Financing

Unlike equity financing, where you sell part of your business to an investor, debt financing simply means receiving money in the form of a loan that you will have to repay. There are many sources you can turn to for debt financing, including banks, commercial lenders, and even your personal credit cards.

Types of Loans

You don't need to pinpoint the exact type of loan you need before you approach a lender; he or she will help you decide what type of financing is best for your needs. However, you should have some general idea of the different types of loans available so you will understand what your lender is offering.

There is a mind-boggling variety of loans available, complicated by the fact that the same type of loan may have different terms at different banks. For instance, a commercial loan at one bank might be written with equal installments of principal and interest, while at another bank the loan is written with monthly interest payments and a balloon payment of the principal.

Here is a look at how lenders generally structure loans, with common variations.

Line-of-Credit Loans

The most useful type of loan for the small business is the line-of-credit loan. In fact, it's probably the one permanent loan arrangement every business owner should have with his or her banker since it protects the business from emergencies and stalled cash flow. Line-of-credit loans are intended for purchases of inventory and payment of operating costs for working capital and business cycle needs. They are not intended for purchases of equipment or real estate.

tip

HUD (the federal Department of Housing and Urban Development) provides job and other grants to startups and small businesses for job creation (for example, $10,000 per job created) in the form of low-interest loans, often in conjunction with the SBA. HUD can provide the names and phone numbers of city, county, and state organizations in your area that represent HUD for development of targeted geographic urban areas.

A line-of-credit loan is a short-term loan that extends the cash available in your business's checking account to the upper limit of the loan contract. Every bank has its own method of funding, but, essentially, an amount is transferred to the business's checking account to cover checks. The business pays interest on the actual amount advanced, from the time it is advanced until it is paid back.

Line-of-credit loans usually carry the lowest interest rate a bank offers since they are seen as fairly low-risk. Some banks even include a clause that gives them the right to cancel the loan if they think your business is in jeopardy. Interest payments are made monthly, and the principal is paid off at your convenience. It is wise to make payments on the principal often. Bankers may also call this a revolving line of credit, and they see it as an indication that your business is earning enough income.

Most line-of-credit loans are written for periods of one year and may be renewed almost automatically for an annual fee. Some banks require that your credit line be fully paid off for seven to 30 days each contract year. This period is probably the best time to negotiate.

Even if you don't need a line-of-credit loan now, talk to your banker about how to get one. To negotiate a credit line, your banker will want to see current financial statements, the latest tax returns, and a projected cash-flow statement.

e-fyi

Want to apply for a loan from the comfort of home? C-Loans.com analyzes your loan application against a database of 750 commercial mortgage lenders and comes up with offers from the top 30 or so lenders who want your business. It may also be a good trial run to help you determine whether you're ready to get a loan for your business.

Installment Loans

These loans are paid back with equal monthly payments covering both principal and interest. Installment loans may be written to meet all types of business needs. You receive the full amount when the contract is signed, and interest is calculated from that date to the final day of the loan. If you repay an installment loan before its final date, there will be no penalty and an appropriate adjustment of interest.

The term of an installment loan will always be correlated to its use. A business cycle loan may be written as a four-month installment loan from, say, September 1 until December 31, and would carry the low interest rate since the risk to the lender is under one year. Business cycle loans may be written from one to seven years, while real estate and renovation loans may be written for up to 21 years. An installment loan is occasionally written with quarterly, half-yearly, or annual payments when monthly payments are inappropriate.

Balloon Loans

Though these loans are usually written under another name, you can identify them by the fact that the full amount is received when the contract is signed, but only the interest is paid off during the life of the loan, with a "balloon" payment of the principal due on the final day.

Occasionally, a lender will offer a loan in which both interest and principal are paid with a single "balloon" payment. Balloon loans are usually reserved for situations when a business has to wait until a specific date before receiving payment from a client for its product or services. In all other ways, they are the same as installment loans.

Interim Loans

When considering interim loans, bankers are concerned with who will be paying off the loan and whether that commitment is reliable. Interim loans are used to make periodic payments to the contractors building new facilities when a mortgage on the building will be used to pay off the interim loan.

Secured and Unsecured Loans

Loans can come in one of two forms: secured or unsecured. When your lender knows you well and is convinced that your business is sound and that the loan will be repaid on time, he or she may be willing to write an unsecured loan. Such a loan, in any of the aforementioned forms, has no collateral pledged as a secondary payment source should you default on the loan. The lender provides you with an unsecured loan because it considers you a low risk. As a new business, you are highly unlikely to qualify for an unsecured loan; it generally requires a track record of profitability and success.

A secured loan, on the other hand, requires some kind of collateral but

tip

Almost every loan has covenants. These are promises that borrowers make to lenders about their actions and responsibilities. A typical covenant specifies the amount of debt the borrower is allowed to take on in the future. If you want to see just how restrictive your loan will be, look at the covenants section of the loan agreement.

generally has a lower interest rate than an unsecured loan. When a loan is written for more than 12 months, is used to purchase equipment, or does not seem risk-free, the lender will ask that the loan be secured by collateral. The collateral used, whether real estate or inventory, is expected to outlast the loan and is usually related to the purpose of the loan.

Since lenders expect to use the collateral to pay off the loan if the borrower defaults, they will value it appropriately. A $20,000 piece of new equipment will probably secure a loan of up to $15,000; receivables are valued for loans up to 75 percent of the amount due; and inventory is usually valued at up to 50 percent of its sale price.

Letter of Credit

Typically used in international trade, this document allows entrepreneurs to guarantee payment to suppliers in other countries. The document substitutes the bank's credit for the entrepreneur's up to a set amount for a specified period of time.

Other Loans

Banks all over the country write loans, especially installment and balloon loans, under a myriad of names. They include:

- Term loans, both short- and long-term, according to the number of years they are written for
- Second mortgages where real estate is used to secure a loan; usually long-term, they're also known as equity loans
- Inventory loans and equipment loans for the purchase of, and secured by, either equipment or inventory
- Accounts receivable loans secured by your outstanding accounts
- Personal loans where your signature and personal collateral guarantee the loan, which you, in turn, lend to your business
- Guaranteed loans in which a third party—an investor, spouse, or the SBA—guarantees repayment (for more on SBA-guaranteed loans, see Chapter 15)
- Commercial loans in which the bank offers its standard loan for small businesses

Once you have an understanding of the different types of loans available, you are better equipped for the next step: "selling" a lender on your business.

Sources of Financing

When seeking debt financing, where do you begin? Carefully choosing the lenders you target can increase your odds of success. Here is a look at various loan sources and what you should know about each.

Bank On It

Traditionally, the paperwork and processing costs involved in making and servicing loans have made the small loans most entrepreneurs seek too costly for big banks to administer. Put plainly, a loan under $25,000—the type many startups are looking for—may not be worth a big bank's time.

In recent years, however, the relationship between banks and small businesses has been improving as more and more banks realize the strength and importance of this growing market. With corporations and real estate developers no longer spurring so much of banks' business, lenders are looking to entrepreneurs to take up the slack.

Many major banks have added special services and programs for small businesses; others are streamlining their loan paperwork and approval process to get loans to entrepreneurs faster. On the plus side, banks are marketing to small businesses like never before. On the downside, however, the "streamlining" process often means that, more than ever, loan approval is based solely on numbers and scores on standardized rating systems rather than on an entrepreneur's character or drive.

Given the challenges of working with a big bank, many entrepreneurs are taking a different tack. Instead of wooing the big

aha!

Federal, state, and local governments all offer their own financing programs designed especially for small-business owners. These programs include low-interest loans, venture capital, and economic and scientific development grants. You can find reliable information on how and where to find these programs on the Business.gov website, which is affiliated with the U.S. government.

commercial institutions, they are courting community banks, where "relationship banking" is the rule, not the exception. It is easier to get a startup loan from community banks, according to the Independent Community Bankers of America. They can be a little more flexible, don't have a bureaucracy to deal with, and are more apt to make character loans.

aha!

You don't have to do business in your own town. Lots of banks are scouring the country looking for small-business customers. Many of the top names in banking show up in your mailbox with loan offers. These loans can be a ready source of capital. So don't toss that junk mail.

You'll still have to meet credit and collateral requirements just as you would at a larger institution. The difference: Smaller banks tend to give more weight to personal attributes. If the business is located in town, the banker likely already knows the entrepreneur, and the family has lived in the area for years; these things count more in a community bank.

Whether the bank you target is big or small, perhaps what matters most is developing relationships. If you have done your personal banking at the same place for 20 years and know the people with authority there, it makes sense to target that bank as a potential lender. If you do not have that kind of relationship at your bank, start to get to know bankers now. Visit chamber of commerce meetings; go to networking events; take part in community functions that local bankers or other movers and shakers are part of. A banker with a personal interest in you is more likely to look favorably on your loan application.

Boost your chances of getting a loan by finding a lender whose experience matches your needs. Talk to friends, lawyers, or accountants and other entrepreneurs in the same industry for leads on banks that have helped people in your business. Pound the pavement and talk to banks about the type and size of loans they specialize in. Put in the work to find the right lender, and you'll find it pays off.

Commercial Finance Companies

Banks aren't your only option when seeking a loan. Nonbank commercial lenders, or commercial finance companies, have expanded their focus on small business in recent years as more and more small banks, which traditionally made loans to entrepreneurs, have been swallowed up in mergers. The advantage of approaching commercial finance companies is that, like community banks, they may be more willing to look beyond numbers and assets. Commercial finance companies give opportunities to startups and a lot of other companies banks will not lend to. Here are some commercial finance companies to get you started:

- FundingUniverse offers business loans of $10,000 to $200,000 for any purpose and up to $1million with full income and asset

>> Franchise Focus

Financing is any startup entrepreneur's biggest challenge—and it's no different for franchisees. The good news is, franchisors may offer a little extra help in getting the capital you need.

Some franchisors offer direct financing to help franchisees with all or part of the costs of startup. This may take the form of equipment, real estate, or inventory financing. The goal is to free up money so franchisees have more working capital.

Many franchisors are not directly involved in lending but have established relationships with banks and commercial finance companies. Because these lenders have processed loans for other franchisees, they are more familiar with new franchisees' needs.

The franchisor you're interested in can tell you about any direct financing or preferred lender programs available. The Franchise Disclosure Document should also include this information.

If your franchisor doesn't have a preferred lender, you can often find financing by approaching banks that have made loans to other franchisees in the system. Talk to franchisees and see how they financed their businesses.

Once you've found a lender to target, you'll need to provide the same information and follow the same steps as you would with any type of business loan.

documentation. Upon application, the company analyzes your funding situation and may recommend anything from an unsecured line of credit to venture capital investment. According to its website (fundinguniverse.com), the company has facilitated more than $240 million in loans to small businesses. It launched a subsidiary called Lendio that is geared specifically toward small businesses seeking loans.

- Privately held Commercial Finance Group (cfgroup.net) specializes in providing finance solutions to small and mid-sized companies in a wide range of industries that are unable to qualify for bank financing.
- At Hartford, Connecticut-based Business Lenders, loan evaluators look beyond traditional lending criteria to consider management ability and character. "Somebody who has bad credit could still be a good credit risk," says founder Penn Ritter. "It depends on why they had the credit problem."

Commercial lenders require a business plan, personal financial statements, and cash-flow projections and will usually expect you to come up with 20 to 25 percent of the needed capital yourself. For more information about commercial finance companies, call the Commercial Finance Association at (212) 792-9390, email info@cfa.com, or visit cfa.com.

Give Yourself Credit

One potentially risky way to finance your business is to use your personal credit cards. The obvious drawback is the high interest rates; if you use the cards for cash advances rather than to buy equipment, the rates are even higher.

Some entrepreneurs take advantage of low-interest credit card offers they receive in the mail, transferring balances from one card to another as soon as interest rates rise (typically after six months). If you use this strategy, keep a close eye on when the rate will increase. Sometimes, you can get the bank to extend the low introductory rate over the phone.

Experts advise using credit card financing as a last resort because interest rates are higher than any other type of financing. However, if you are good at juggling payments, your startup needs are low, and you are confident you'll be able to pay the money back fairly quickly, this could be the route to take.

aha!

Looking for financing? Consider an unexpected source—your vendors. Vendors may be willing to give you the capital you need, either through a delayed financing agreement or a leasing program. Vendors have a vested interest in your success and a belief in your stability, or they wouldn't be doing business with you. Before entering any agreement, however, compare long-term leasing costs with short-term loan costs; leasing could be more costly.

Applying for a Loan

The next step is applying for the loan. It's important to know what you'll need to provide and what lenders are looking for.

The Loan Application

Think of your loan application as a sales tool, just like your brochures or ads. When you put together the right combination of facts and figures, your application will sell your lender on the short- and long-term profit potential of lending money to your business. To do that, the application must convince your lender that you will pay back the loan as promised and that your managerial ability (and future loans) will result in a profit-making partnership.

Banks are in the money-lending business. To lend money, they need evidence of security and stability. It's that simple.

How can you provide this evidence when your business hasn't even gotten off the ground? Begin by making sure your loan application is both realistic and optimistic. If you predict an increase in sales of between 8 and 12 percent, base your income projections on an increase of 10 percent, and then specify what you intend to do to ensure the additional sales.

Also make sure your application is complete. When a piece of an application is missing, bankers instantly suspect that either something is being hidden or the applicant doesn't know his or her business well enough to pull the information together.

There are 12 separate items that should be included in every loan application. The importance of each one varies with the size of your business, your industry, and the amount you are requesting.

1. Cover sheet
2. Cover letter
3. Table of contents
4. Amount and use of the loan
5. History and description of your business
6. Functions and background of your management team
7. Market information on your product or service
8. Financial history and current status
9. Financial projections to demonstrate that the loan will be repaid
10. A list of possible collateral
11. Personal financial statements
12. Additional documents to support the projections

> ***"You fail if you don't try. If you try and you fail, yes, you'll have a few articles saying you've failed at something. But if you look at the history of American entrepreneurs, one thing I do know about them: An awful lot of them have tried and failed in the past and gone on to great things."***
>
> —RICHARD BRANSON, FOUNDER OF THE VIRGIN GROUP

Many of these items are part of your business plan; a few of them will have to be added. Here's a closer look at each section:

1. *Cover sheet.* This is the title page to your "book." All it needs to say is "Loan application submitted by John Smith, Sunday's Ice Cream Parlor, to Big Bucks Bank, Main Street, Anytown." It should also include the date and your business telephone number.
2. *Cover letter.* The cover letter is a personal business letter to your banker requesting consideration of your application for a line of credit or an installment loan. The second paragraph should describe your business: "Our company is a [sole proprietorship, partnership, or corporation] in manufacturing, distributing, and retailing X type of goods." The third paragraph is best kept to just one or two sentences that "sell" your application by indicating what your future plans are for your business.

3. *Table of contents.* This page makes it easy for your banker to see that all the documents are included.
4. *Amount and use of the loan.* This page documents how much you want to borrow and how you will use the loan. If you are buying a new piece of equipment, for instance, it should show the contract price, add the cost of freight and installation, deduct the amount you will be contributing, and show the balance to be borrowed.

tip

Loan officers at your bank may be a valuable resource in identifying state, local, and agency assistance. They may have gone through the steps with other new business owners in your area.

5. *History and description of your business.* This is often the most difficult to write. The key is to stay with the facts and assume the reader knows nothing about your business. Describe, more fully than in the cover letter, the legal form of your business and its location. Tell why you believe the business is going to succeed. Conclude with a paragraph on your future plans.
6. *Management team.* Bankers know that it's people who make things happen. Your management team might consist of every employee, if they oversee an important part of your operation, or it might be just you and one key person. It also includes any outside consultants you plan to use regularly, such as your accountant or banker. In one or two pages, list each person's name and responsibilities. Where appropriate, describe the background that makes this person the right choice for that job.
7. *Market information.* You should begin these pages with a complete description of your product line or service, and the market it is directed toward. Next, describe how you have targeted your market niche and how successful you have been. Finally, detail your future plans to add new products or services.
8. *Financial history.* Most bankers want to see balance sheets and income (profit and loss) statements. As a startup, you will need to use projections. Bankers will compare these to norms in your industry.

9. *Financial projections.* This set of three documents—a projected income statement, balance sheet, and cash-flow statement—should show how the business, with the use of the loan, will generate sufficient profits to pay off the loan. Your accountant can help you prepare these documents.
10. *Collateral.* Listing your available collateral—cash reserves, stocks and bonds, equipment, home equity, inventory, and receivables—demonstrates your understanding that your banker will normally look for a backup repayment source. Each piece of collateral listed should be described with its cost and current fair market value. You might need to provide documentation of value—so be prepared to get appraisals or get your paperwork in order.
11. *Personal financial statements.* As a startup, you will need to add your personal guarantee to any loan the bank makes. The banker will want to see your tax return and balance sheets showing personal net worth. Most banks have preprinted forms that make pulling these figures together relatively easy.
12. *Additional documents.* In this section, you can include whatever documents you feel will enhance your loan package. This might include a copy of the sales contract on a new piece of equipment, a lease and photograph of a new location, blueprints, or legal documents. If you are introducing a new product or service, include a product brochure and additional market research information.

    This section can help a new business overcome the lack of a track record. While glowing letters won't make a banker overlook weak finances, an assurance from your largest customer that your services are valued can help your banker see your full potential.

aha!

If you are a woman or a member of a minority group looking to purchase a franchise, you may be eligible for special financial incentives or assistance from the franchisor. Ask franchisors you are considering whether they have such programs and what the requirements are.

What Lenders Look For

Your application is complete, with every "i" dotted and every "t" crossed. But is it enough to get you the cold, hard cash? What are lenders really looking for when they pore over your application? Lenders typically base their decisions on four criteria, often called the "Four C's of Credit":

1. *Credit.* The lender will examine your personal credit history to see how well you've managed your past obligations. If you have some black marks on your credit, the banker will want to hear the details and see proof that you repaid what you owed. A couple of late payments are not a big deal, but two or more consecutive missed payments are. Get a copy of your credit history before you turn in your application. This way, you can find out about any problems and explain them before your banker brings them up.
2. *Character.* Character is hard to measure, but lenders will use your credit history to assess this as well. They take lawsuits, bankruptcies, and tax liens particularly seriously in evaluating your character. They will also do a background check and evaluate your previous work experience. They might ask for personal references.
3. *Capacity.* What happens if your business slumps? Do you have the capacity to convert other assets to cash, either by selling or borrowing against them? Your secondary repayment sources may include real estate, stocks, and other savings. The lender will look at your business balance sheet and financial statement to determine your capacity.
4. *Collateral.* As a startup, you will most likely be seeking a secured loan. This means you must put up collateral—either personal assets, such as stocks or certificates of deposit, or business assets like inventory, equipment, or real estate.

A Loan at Last

A good relationship with your banker is just as important after you get that loan as it is in getting one in the first place. The key word is "communication." The bank wants to be told all the good news—and bad news—about your business as soon as it occurs. Most business owners

>> Read the Fine Print

Hallelujah and yippee! You can almost hear the choirs of angels singing as your banker smiles and hands you the loan documents. You got the loan!

Not so fast. Before you sign that piece of paper, take a good look at what you're getting into. Many entrepreneurs are so excited about having their loans approved, they fail to read the fine print on their loan agreements. That can lead to trouble later on.

It's a good idea to get the loan documents ahead of time so you have a chance to review them for a couple of days before you sign, according to the American Bankers Association. Bankers won't have a problem sending advance copies of the documents but will generally do so only if they're specifically asked.

Most bankers will be happy to help you understand the fine print, but it's also a good idea to have your accountant and lawyer review the documents, too.

Although it varies slightly from bank to bank, a small-business loan package usually consists of several documents, typically including a loan agreement, a promissory note, and some form of guarantee and surety agreement.

> *Loan agreement.* This specifies, in essence, the promises you are making to the bank and asks you to affirm that you are authorized to bind your business to the terms of the loan. Most banks require you to verify that all the information on your loan application is still true before they disburse the loan.

> *Promissory note.* This details the principal and interest owed and when payments are due. It outlines the events that would allow the bank to declare your loan in default. Knowing these events ahead of time can help you protect your credit record. Look for "cure" language in the default section. A cure provision allows you a certain amount of time (usually ten days) to remedy the default after you've been notified by the bank. If such a provision isn't included, ask if it can be added to prevent you from defaulting accidentally (in case a payment is lost in

>> Read the Fine Print, continued

the mail, for example]. Also make sure you understand what the bank can and can't do after declaring default.

> *Guarantee and surety agreement*. Because startups generally have insufficient operating history or assets on which to base a loan, banks usually require the loan to be guaranteed with your personal assets. The bank may ask you to secure the loan with the equity in your home, for example.

fear telling bankers bad news, but keeping problems hidden would be a mistake. Like any relationship, yours with your banker is built on trust. Keep him or her apprised of your business's progress. Invite your banker to visit your business and see how the proceeds of the loan are being put to good use.

Once you've established a relationship with a banker, it is simple to expand your circle of friends at the bank. Every time you visit, spend some time meeting and talking to people, especially those further up the ladder. Often, the bankers will be the ones to initiate contact. Take advantage of this opportunity. The more people you know at the bank, the easier it will be to get the next round of financing.

CHAPTER

15

Fed Funds

How to Get Government Loans

Where can you go when private financing sources turn you down? For many startup entrepreneurs, the answer is the U.S. Small Business Administration (SBA). The federal government has a vested interest in encouraging the growth of small business. As a result, some SBA loans have less stringent requirements for owner's equity and collateral than do commercial loans, making the SBA an excellent financing source for startups. In addition, many SBA loans are for smaller sums than most banks are willing to lend.

Of course, that doesn't mean the SBA is giving money away. In fact, the SBA does not actually make direct loans; instead, it provides loan guarantees to entrepreneurs, promising the bank to pay back a certain percentage of your loan if you are unable to.

tip

When seeking an SBA loan, choose your bank carefully. Not all banks are versed in SBA loans, so look for one that is experienced. It could be the difference between terms you can live with and mistakes that could haunt your finances.

Banks participate in the SBA program as regular, certified, or preferred lenders. The SBA can help you prepare your loan package, which you then submit to banks. If the bank approves you, it submits your loan package to the SBA. Applications submitted by regular lenders are reviewed by the SBA in an average of two weeks, certified lender applications are reviewed in three days, and approval through preferred lenders is even faster.

The most basic eligibility requirement for SBA loans is the ability to repay the loan from cash flow, but the SBA also looks at personal credit history, industry experience or other evidence of management ability, collateral, and owner's equity contributions. If you own 20 percent or more equity in the business, the SBA asks that you personally guarantee the loan. After all, you can't ask the government to back you if you're not willing to back yourself. The SBA offers a wide variety of loan programs for businesses at various stages of development. Here's a closer look.

7(a) Loan Program

The primary and the most flexible SBA loan program is the 7(a) Loan Program. The SBA does not lend money itself, but provides maximum

>> For Women Only

Women business owners have a friend in Washington: the Office of Women's Business Ownership (OWBO), part of the SBA. The OWBO coordinates federal efforts that support women entrepreneurs through business training and technical assistance, and by providing access to financing, federal contracts, and international trade opportunities.

In addition, the office directs Women's Business Centers in all 50 states. Women's Business Centers provide assistance, training, and business counseling through the SBA. For information about OWBO services, call (800) U-ASK-SBA or visit sba.gov.

loan guarantees of up to $5 million or 75 percent of the total loan amount, whichever is less. The average loan in 2012 was $337,730. For loans that are less than $150,000, the maximum guarantee is 85 percent of the total loan amount. SBA policy prohibits lenders from charging many of the usual fees associated with commercial loans. Still, you can expect to pay a one-time guaranty fee, which the agency charges the lender and allows the lender to pass on to you. Fees for smaller loans can be as little as zero percent.

A 7(a) loan can be used for many business purposes, including real estate, expansion, equipment, working capital, and inventory. The money can be paid back over as long as 25 years for real estate and equipment, and ten years for working capital. Interest rates vary with the type of loan you apply for.

SBA Express Program

A general 7(a) loan may suit your business's needs best, but the 7(a) Program also offers several specialized loans. One of them, the SBA

>> Business 101

Worried your business acumen isn't as sharp is it could be? Wishing you had taken an accounting class instead of that film history course on John Wayne? Then the Small Business Training Network might be for you.

The Small Business Training Network is an internet-based learning environment—functioning like a virtual campus. As its website says, it offers online courses, workshops, information resources, learning tools, and direct access to electronic counseling and other forms of technical assistance.

The classes run the gamut from how to start your own business—with titles like "Franchising Basics" and "Technology 101"—to how to prepare a loan package, develop employees, and plan for retirement. The workshops are self-paced and usually extremely topical. Some classes were developed within the SBA, while others have been developed by academic institutions. For more information, log on to sba.gov/training.

Express Program, promises quick processing for amounts less than $350,000. SBA Express can get you an answer quickly because approved SBA Express lenders can use their own documentation and procedures to attach an SBA guarantee to an approved loan without having to wait for SBA approval. The SBA guarantees up to 50 percent of SBA Express loans.

CAPLines

For businesses that need working capital on a short-term or cyclical basis, the SBA has a collection of revolving and nonrevolving lines of credit called CAPLines. A revolving loan is similar to a credit card, with which you carry a balance that goes up or down, depending on the payments and amounts you borrow. With nonrevolving lines of credit, you borrow a flat amount and pay it off over a set period of time.

CAPLine loans provide business owners short-term credit, with loans that are guaranteed up to $5 million. There are four loan and line-of-credit programs that operate under the CAPLines umbrella:

1. *Seasonal line of credit*: designed to help businesses during peak seasons, when they face increases in inventory, accounts receivable, and labor costs.
2. *Contract line of credit*: used to finance labor and material costs involved in carrying out contracts.
3. *Builders line program*: provides financing for small contractors or developers to construct or rehabilitate residential or commercial property that will be sold to a third party. Loan maturity is generally three years, but can be extended up to five years, if necessary, to facilitate the sale of the property.
4. *Working capital line of credit*: a revolving line of credit (up to $5 million) that provides short-term working capital. Businesses that generally use these lines provide credit to their customers or have inventory as their major asset.

Each of the four credit lines has a maturity of up to five years, although the contract loan program has a limit of ten years, and all can be tailored to the borrower's needs.

SBA Loan Document Checklist

Documents to Prepare for a New Business

- ❑ Your SBA loan application form
- ❑ Your personal history statement with your resume and accomplishments and the resumes of key managers you plan to employ
- ❑ Statement of your investment capabilities
- ❑ Current financial statement of all personal liabilities and assets
- ❑ Projection of revenue statement
- ❑ Collateral list

Documents to Prepare for an Existing Business

- ❑ Balance sheet
- ❑ Profit and loss statements
- ❑ Income statement of previous and current year-to-date incomes, including business tax returns
- ❑ Personal financial statement with each owner itemized, including personal tax returns for each owner
- ❑ Collateral list
- ❑ Your dba or incorporation paperwork
- ❑ Copy of your business lease
- ❑ Loan request statement describing business history, loan amount, and purpose

Figure 15.1. SBA Loan Document Checklist

Pre-Qualification Program

The SBA's Pre-Qualification Loan Program helps pre-qualify borrowers in underserved markets, including women business owners. Under the

>> Export Expertise

If exporting is part of your business game plan, the Export-Import Bank of the United States (Ex-Im Bank) can be your biggest ally. The Ex-Im Bank is committed to supporting small exporters and provides many financing tools targeted to small businesses, such as working capital guarantees and export credit insurance.

With a working capital guarantee and credit insurance, small businesses can increase sales by entering new markets, expanding their borrowing base, and offering buyers financing while carrying less risk. Often, small exporters do not have adequate cash flow or cannot get a loan to fulfill an export sales order. The Ex-Im Bank working capital guarantee assumes 95 percent of the lender's risk so exporters can access the necessary funds to purchase raw materials or supplies to fulfill an export order.

The export credit insurance protects an exporter from buyer payment default and also allows exporters to extend credit to their international buyers.

To be eligible for the Ex-Im Bank's programs, U.S. exporters must simply meet the Small Business Administration's definition of a small business, export goods or services produced with more than 50 percent U.S. parts and labor (usually excluding those military in nature), and have export credit sales of less than $7.5 million. Business owners can contact the Ex-Im Bank directly at (800) 565-3946 or through any commercial lender that works with the agency (see the Lender Locator at exim.gov). Based in Washington, DC, the Ex-Im Bank also has regional offices in Chicago, Dallas, Detroit, Houston, Miami, Minneapolis, New York City, Orange County (California), San Diego, San Francisco, and Seattle.

program, with the aid of private intermediary organizations chosen by the SBA, eligible entrepreneurs prepare a business plan and complete a loan application. The intermediary submits the application to the SBA.

If the application is approved, the SBA issues you a pre-qualification letter, which you can then take, along with your loan package, to a commercial bank. With the SBA's guarantee attached, the bank is more likely to approve the loan.

MicroLoan Program

SBA financing isn't limited to the 7(a) group of loans. The MicroLoan Program helps entrepreneurs get very small loans, up to $50,000. The average loan in 2012 was for $13,000. The loans can be used for machinery and equipment, furniture and fixtures, inventory, supplies, and working capital, but they cannot be used to pay existing debts or to purchase real estate. This program is unique because it assists borrowers who generally do not meet traditional lenders' credit standards.

MicroLoans are administered through nonprofit intermediaries. These organizations receive loans from the SBA and then turn around and make loans to entrepreneurs. Small businesses applying for MicroLoan financing may be required to complete some business-skills training before a loan application is considered.

> **aha!**
>
> 
>
> Check out the SBA's Women's Business Center, a website for women who want to start or expand their businesses. There are free online courses and a world of information about marketing, government contracting, technology training, international trade, and SBA services, plus success stories to inspire you. Visit the site at onlinewbc.gov.

The maximum term for MicroLoans is six years, and the interest rates vary.

CDC/504 Loan Program

On the opposite end of the loan size spectrum is the 504 Loan, which provides long-term, fixed-rate loans for financing fixed assets, usually real estate and equipment. Loans are most often used for growth and expansion.

504 Loans are made through Certified Development Companies (CDCs)—nonprofit intermediaries that work with the SBA, banks, and businesses looking for financing. There are CDCs throughout the country, each covering an assigned region.

If you are seeking funds up to $1.5 million to buy or renovate a building or put in some major equipment, consider bringing your business plan and financial statements to a CDC. Typical percentages for this type of package are 50 percent financed by the bank, 40 percent by the CDC, and 10 percent by the business.

In exchange for this below-market, fixed-rate financing, the SBA expects the small business to create or retain jobs or to meet certain public policy goals. Businesses that meet these public policy goals are those whose expansion will contribute to a business district revitalization, such as an empowerment zone; a minority-owned business; an export or manufacturing company; or a company whose expansion will contribute to rural development.

aha!

Looking into exporting? Look into the U.S. Export Assistance Centers. These one-stop shops combine the trade promotion and export finance resources of the SBA, the U.S. Department of Commerce, and the Export-Import Bank. Locate a center at export.gov/eac/index.asp.

If your business has the goal of job creation, the SBA program will lend up to $5 million for meeting the job creation criteria or a community development goal. Generally, your business must create or retain one job for every $65,000 provided by the SBA, except for small manufacturers, which have a $100,000 job creation or retention goal, according to the guidelines for the program.

Empowerment Zones/Renewal Communities

Since 1980, 40 states have established programs to designate enterprise zones, offering tax breaks and other incentives to businesses that locate in certain economically disadvantaged areas. States vary widely in the number of zones designated, incentives offered, and success of the programs. In some areas, businesses may also qualify for lower utility rates or low-interest financing from eligible government jurisdictions. To be eligible for any of these incentives, businesses must generally meet certain criteria, such as creating new jobs in a community. There are about 30 renewal communities under the Department of Housing and Urban Development, including many major cities in the U.S.

The Empowerment Zone/Renewal Communities initiative was set up to provide tax incentives and stimulate community investment and development. Specified urban and rural communities will receive grants and tax breaks for businesses in the area. The federal government's involvement means entrepreneurs in those areas can get federal tax breaks, not just state.

> ***"Customers aren't just buying our software, they're buying a relationship."***
>
> —Katrina Garnett, founder of Crossroads Software Inc.

If you choose to locate in an enterprise or empowerment zone, look beyond the tax breaks to consider long-term concerns such as availability of a work force and accessibility of your target market. Make sure the zone offers other support services, such as streamlined licensing and permitting procedures. Most zones that succeed have high development potential to begin with, with good highway access, a solid infrastructure, and a trainable labor force.

For more information on enterprise zones, contact your state's economic development department or call HUD's Office of Community Renewal at (202) 708-6339 or email OCRTaxCredit@hud.gov.

8(a) Business Development Program

The SBA's 8(a) Program is a small-business set-aside program that allows certified socially and economically disadvantaged companies to enter the federal procurement market as well as the economic mainstream. The 8(a) Program is envisioned as a starter program for minority businesses, which must leave the program after nine years.

Entrepreneurs who participate in the 8(a) Program are eligible for the 7(a) Guaranty Loan and the Pre-Qualification Programs. Businesses must be owned by a socially and economically disadvantaged individual. Socially disadvantaged categories include race and ethnicity. Participants can receive sole-source contracts, up to a ceiling of $4 million for goods and services and $6.5 million for manufacturing, according to the SBA. To qualify as economically disadvantaged, the person must have a net worth of less than $250,000, assets under $4 million, as well as two years' worth of tax returns. There are other qualifications, including that the firm must be at least 51 percent owned by the program applicant and owners must show good character.

>> Information, Please

Dealing with the federal government has gotten easier, thanks to the U.S. Business Advisor, an online clearinghouse for small business. Instead of contacting dozens of agencies and departments for information on laws and regulations, you can use this one-stop shop to find information on business development, taxes and laws, a variety of workplace concerns, as well as government procurement loans. You can find the U.S. Business Advisor at business.gov.

Export Working Capital Program

If you are planning to export, you should investigate the Export Working Capital Program. This allows a 90 percent guarantee on loans up to $5 million. Loan maturity is one year, and funds can be used for transaction financing. The exports financed must be shipped and titled from the United States. The loans are typically processed quickly.

Special Purpose Loans

If you believe you have a special case that requires extra help, you may be in luck. Of course, keep in mind that everybody believes they deserve extra help with financing, but in many situations, the SBA has a loan program tailor-made for your situation. If you're starting a business, for instance, that pollutes the environment, but you plan to spend additional money to reduce the toxins you're putting into the air, soil, or water, you may be eligible for a Pollution Control Loan, which is basically a 7(a) loan earmarked for businesses that are planning, designing, or installing a pollution control

aha!

Buying a franchise? Many municipalities and states have financing programs that can underwrite the cost of a franchise. Be aware, however, that the focus of these programs is job creation. To find programs in your area, call the nearest Small Business Development Center or economic development program. It takes a bit of investigating to find the programs, but the results could be well worth the effort.

facility. The facility must prevent, reduce, abate, or control any form of pollution, including recycling.

If your business plans to be active in international trade or your top competition is cheap imports, the International Trade (IT) Loan Program is something you should look into. The SBA can guarantee up to $5 million for fixed-asset financing (facilities and equipment) or refinancing of an existing loan for the same purposes. Working capital cannot be a part of an IT loan.

Numerous variations of the SBA's basic loan programs are made available to support special needs. So if you believe your business might fall into a category in which the SBA can funnel additional loans to you, it's definitely an avenue worth checking out.

Making the Most of the SBA

The SBA is more than a source of financing. It can help with many aspects of business startup and growth. The SBA is an excellent place to "get your ducks in a row" before seeking financing. SBA services include free resources to help you with such tasks as writing a business plan and improving your presentation skills—all of which boost your chances of getting a loan.

For more information on other SBA programs, visit the SBA's website at sba.gov, call the SBA's Answer Desk at (800) U-ASK-SBA, or contact your local SBA district office by visiting sba.gov/localresources/index.html. Your SBA district office can mail you a startup booklet and a list of lenders, and inform you about specialized loans tailored to your industry and where to go for help with your business plan or putting together financial statements.

Granting Wishes

When most people think of grants, they think of money given free to nonprofit organizations. But for-profit companies, and frequently startups, can also win grant money. But how do you find these grants? Unfortunately, locating the right grant is a little like looking for your soul mate. The grant is out there, but you're going to have to do a lot of looking to find a good match. A good place to start is at your local bookstore. There are a lot of books about getting grants, with titles like *Grant Writing for Dummies* (Wiley) by Beverly A. Browning, *Grantseeker's Toolkit* (Wiley) by Cheryl Carter New and James Quick, and *Demystifying Grant Seeking* (Wiley) by Larissa Golden Brown and Martin John Brown. And then there's the Bible of grant books—the annual *The Grants Register* (Palgrave Macmillan), which lists more than 4,200 grants.

There are other places to look, of course. The most logical place to get an infusion of cash is from Uncle Sam, but you can also win grants from foundations and even some corporations.

aha!

If you believe your future business could contribute to community development or empower a group of economically disadvantaged people, visit your state economic development office to find out what types of community development grants may be available.

Even in the most economically challenged of times, the government is one of the best sources for grants. For instance, the National Institute of Standards and Technology's Advanced Technology Program offers grants to co-fund "high-risk, high-payoff projects" in order to provide Americans with a higher standard of living. Whatever the project is, you can bet it will be scrutinized by a board of qualified experts and academia.

The Small Business Innovation Research (SBIR) Program is another government program that gives grants. The SBIR Program specializes in small businesses looking for funding for high-risk technologies. Founded in 1982, the SBIR recently awarded funds for research in advanced metals and chemicals, biotechnology, information technology, and manufacturing. So if you're planning on opening a pizzeria, you might have trouble with this one.

e-fyi

Check out grants.gov, the website that lists all the federal government's grant programs. You can find opportunities in categories ranging from arts and humanities to science and technology.

But there are federal grants awarded to food and nutrition companies. For instance, a pizzeria that caters to children and specializes in serving nutritious, healthy pizzas may be able to win a grant. You can also check with your state or local government—start with your local or state chamber of commerce.

Of course, finding the grant is the easy part; the hard part is getting the grant. It's a lot like applying to college. You have to jump through the hoops of each organization, which usually involves writing an extensive essay on why you need the money. There are grant-writing businesses out there as well as grant brokers—people who try to find the right grant for you. You pay them regardless of whether they find you a grant; on the other hand, if they land you a $750,000 grant, you still pay them the flat fee, which is generally from $25 to $100 an hour, depending on their level of success. But if you don't have the funds to pay for a grant-writer or a broker, and you're a decent writer and have a passion for your business, then start researching, and fill out the forms and compose the essay yourself. There's no rule that says you can't try to get a grant on your own. And who knows—you might be successful!

GET SET . . .

You have a great idea, a perfect plan, and the money to make it all happen. What's the next step? Get set for business with Part 4, "Prepare." First, we'll show you how to get what you want out of every deal, with negotiating tips that will put you in the driver's seat in any situation. Learn how to select a prime location that will get customers to come in and come back. We'll show you retail operating options, such as kiosks and carts, plus how to negotiate the lease you want.

Or maybe your plan is to start your business from home. If so, you'll learn the steps to setting up a home office. Or perhaps you're looking for a flexible, shared space to call home. You'll learn about the options—and support—available in your own backyard. Whether it's at home or away, once you've found the right site, we share secrets for giving your business a professional image with furniture, business cards, and stationery that all spell success. Next, stock your shelves—virtual and otherwise—with inventory: You'll learn how to choose, track, and maintain your product supply and discover the best sources for getting what you need.

Once you have the inventory, you have to sell it. That's why in the next section, we discuss setting up mailing systems, credit, including the most important part of business ownership—getting paid. We'll reveal how to give your customers credit without getting taken, plus tips for accepting credit cards, debit cards, and checks and collecting on slow-paying accounts. Discover how to choose the right mailing equipment as well as the most efficient, convenient, and economical ways to send mail.

Protect the business you've worked so hard to start by checking out our chapter on insurance. We show you the basic insurance no business owner should be without, plus how to put together the perfect insurance package for your needs. Finally, if employees are part of your game plan, you'll find all the information you need to hire smart. Learn the secrets of a good job interview, low-cost hiring options, and the laws you must know to stay out of hot water.

Now, get geared up for business! Part 5, "Buy," takes you step by step through setting up your office. Office machines are more affordable than ever these days, so it's simple to get set up on a budget; we'll show you the options, from superstores and mail order to leasing and more.

Today's technology can boost your business productivity like never before. Whether you're in the office, at home, or on the road, we'll explain the hardware and software tools you need to make the most out of every working moment. We'll show you how to set up your business's website, including choosing a web designer, getting set for ecommerce, and more. And finally, we'll give you the latest on how smartphones, tablets, instant messaging, and more can keep you connected 24/7.

PART

4

PREPARE

CHAPTER

16

What's Your Deal?

Negotiating Successfully

By Cliff Ennico, Author, Business Consultant, and Former Host of the PBS TV series *Money Hunt*

If you're in business, you're a negotiator. You have no choice. Business doesn't happen unless two or more people enter into a transaction. This can be as simple as buying inventory or as complicated as a merger of two public companies. Without transactions, business doesn't happen, and every transaction involves a certain amount of negotiation.

If I had to pick one of the scariest challenges facing every first-time entrepreneur, it would be learning how to negotiate. Nobody (except perhaps a lawyer) likes to negotiate—it's confrontational, it involves a certain amount of "play acting," and it may put you in the position of thinking you're "putting something over" on another human being. In a big company, you had the luxury of hiring people to do this for you. Not anymore.

When you're in business, negotiating the best possible deals is a high, if not the highest, priority. As a business owner, you can't know enough about negotiating.

> ***"I don't know the key to success, but the key to failure is trying to please everybody."***
>
> —BILL COSBY

What Is Negotiation?

It's a lot easier to describe what negotiation "isn't" than what it is. Let's get some things straight upfront. Negotiation is not:

- A search for truth, justice, and the American way
- A friendly discussion at the corner Starbucks
- A quest for the perfect solution to a business problem

Make no mistake: Negotiation is a game. Whether sellers have paid good money for something or are emotionally attached to it, they'll want to get the most money they can from its sale. Buyers are worried about losing money and want to pay as little as possible for something so the chances of making a profit on resale are as high as possible. Somewhere between these two goals, there's a deal waiting to happen.

The goal in negotiating is to win—to get the best deal you can. Period.

Preparing for Negotiation

To get ready for any negotiation, you must do three things:

1. *Know your bargaining position.* In every negotiation, someone is in a stronger position and someone is in a weaker position. Where are you?

   Let's say you're looking to lease 1,000 square feet of retail space in a shopping center. The landlord is a large commercial real estate developer with two million square feet of space in five major shopping malls in your town. How flexible do you think this landlord will be in the negotiation? Not very. One thousand square feet is a drop in the bucket to this landlord, so you'll be the one making all the concessions.

   Now, let's say you're looking to lease 1,000 square feet of retail space in a strip mall. The landlord is a local widow whose husband

>> Never Let 'Em See You Sweat

Are you serious about wanting to be a better negotiator? Then learn to play poker. A good poker player is almost always a good negotiator. Consider the lessons poker teaches you:

> Use a "poker face" to conceal your emotions from the other side.

> It isn't so much the hand you're dealt, as what the other players think you've got. If you get a great hand and show too much enthusiasm, the other players will fold early and leave you with a small pot, but if the other players think you have only a mediocre hand, they'll stay in the game and leave a lot more money on the table.

> Likewise, if you truly have a mediocre hand, by making the other players think you've got something better, they'll yield to their insecurity and fold early. This leaves you with money you wouldn't have gotten if you'd shown your cards too soon.

Bluffing and posturing are part of the game of negotiation. If you master these techniques early, you stand a much better chance of winning negotiations on a regular basis.

died several years ago. The strip mall is the only property she owns, the 1,000 square feet is the largest tenant space in the mall, and it's been vacant for the last six months. Who's in the stronger position now?

You—and you're crazy if you don't take advantage of it. (See "The Golden Rule" on page 229.)

2. *Know how the other side perceives its position.* It isn't enough to know what your real bargaining position is. You also have to consider how each side perceives its position. As any poker player knows, sometimes a mediocre hand can be a winning hand if it's played properly. If the person with the mediocre hand can convince the other players that he or she has a much better hand than he or she actually has, and the other players (with better hands) buy into that, they're likely to fold early to cut their losses, leaving the pot to the bluffer.

If your negotiating position isn't great but you see the other side is worried about losing the deal, you can't go wrong by coming on strong and playing to the other side's fears.

3. *Assess your bargaining style.* Are you aggressive or passive by nature? I hate to say it, but in 25 years of studying lawyers, I've found that those who are naturally aggressive, fearless, and downright ornery tend to make the best negotiators. People are afraid of them, want to avoid their nasty behaviors, and give them what they want. To truly succeed at negotiating, it helps if you can find your inner Rottweiler. Remember, it's a game.

   I'm not saying you should yell, scream, or threaten violence during a negotiation (although some negotiators use these techniques to great effect). You can be pleasant and communicate your willingness to get the deal done as quickly and efficiently as possible. Just make sure the other side doesn't misinterpret your nice behavior as a sign of weakness, or you'll lose the negotiation.

tip

Sometimes silence is the best weapon. By quietly pondering for several moments what the other side has just said, you raise their anxiety about your willingness to do the deal. Your body language should send the signal that you have all the time in the world and don't need the deal. This often makes the other side uncomfortable and more willing to negotiate. Just don't do this too often; you'll appear indecisive.

What Do You Want?

Now that you're psychologically ready to sit down at the bargaining table, it's time to figure out what you need to get out of the deal.

Sit down with a sheet of paper, fold it down the middle, and label each half "deal points" and "trading points." Then list all the points you need to reach agreement on. Deal points are those you must win—if you can't get those, you walk from the table and look for another deal. For example, if you paid $1,000 for a painting and need to get a 20 percent return on your

>> The Golden Rule

"You can never get a bargain on something you really, really want."

In any negotiation, the side that needs the deal more is the side that gives up the most—precisely because they need the deal and can't afford to have the other side walk away.

Winning the most points in a negotiation is almost always a function of: 1) not needing the deal as much as the other side does, 2) convincing the other side they need the deal more than you do, or 3) a combination of 1 and 2.

Nervous about negotiating? Here's a great way to practice. Go to collectibles shows and look for items you don't feel strongly about—you can take them or leave them. When you find one, approach the dealer and offer him 50 percent of the asking price. He'll almost certainly refuse your offer—sometimes nicely, sometimes by pretending to be offended—but don't worry about it. You don't really want the item, and you know he paid less than 50 percent of the tag price. Thank him politely, tell him you really couldn't justify paying more than 60 percent of the price, and move to the next booth.

Then, return to the dealer in the late afternoon and ask politely if he has reconsidered your offer. If the item hasn't sold by then, the dealer is concerned about having to lug the thing back to his showroom and will be in a better bargaining mood. Stay firm. Remember the goal isn't to add to your antiques collection, but to practice your negotiating skills. Make it a point to say no to whatever counteroffer he proposes, and walk away.

Do not try this if you see an item you really want—your body language will inevitably tip your hand to "the dealer," and he will turn the tables on you by saying something like "I'm sorry, but I'm only making a 10 percent profit at this price." At this point the negotiation is over—you're reaching for your wallet, and you'll pay the dealer's price.

inventory to stay afloat, getting a purchase price of at least $1,200 is one of your deal points.

Any point that isn't a deal point is a trading point—nice if you can get it, but you can live without it if you sense it's a deal point for the other person. In a negotiation, your goal is to get all your deal points and as many of your trading points as possible, recognizing that often you'll have to yield one or more trading points to get your deal points.

Be realistic when identifying your deal points. A lot of things you negotiate for aren't really life or death for your business. If you aren't sure if you really need something or not, it's a trading point.

warning 

Don't agree to give up something without asking for anything in return—a "gratuitous concession." You may think you're being generous, nice, or respectful to the other party. But the other side sees it as a sign of weakness and an invitation to press for bigger, more damaging concessions.

The Negotiation Process

There are three basic steps in any negotiation—sometimes they happen in order, sometimes not.

1. *Step one*: State your position. At the beginning of a negotiation, each side lays out its position and tells the other side what it needs. As soon as it's apparent the two sides agree on something, that point is taken off the table so the parties can focus on the issues where they disagree.
2. *Step two*: Search for win-win compromises. Sometimes when a negotiator asks for something, what he or she really needs is a lot narrower. By probing the other side, you can often find a way to give them what they really need without giving them everything they're asking for. Here's an example: The other side wants you to promise you won't compete with them anywhere in the State of X for five years. By asking probing questions, you learn that the other side doesn't plan to do business outside of Town Y. You agree not to compete with the other side in Town Y for five years, and keep your options open for the rest of the state.
3. *Step three*: Do a little "horse trading." Sooner or later, in every negotiation you get to a point where further compromise is impossible. For a deal to happen at this point, both sides have to engage in a little "horse trading." You look at the list of three open points, realize

that only one of them is a deal point, and offer to give on the other two points to get the one you need. If the other side agrees (one or both of the two points you gave them were deal points for them), you make the deal. If the other side refuses (your deal point was also their deal point), the negotiation's over—and so is the deal.

Everything Is Negotiable

When you first start negotiating, it's hard to separate deal points from trading points—everything seems important. Experienced negotiators know something you don't—everything is a trading point. Nothing is non-negotiable. If you need the deal badly enough, you can give up some deal points and still survive to negotiate another day. As any lawyer will tell you, you know a deal's been well-negotiated when both sides walk away from the table feeling at least somewhat disappointed in the outcome.

Sales Contract Negotiating Points

Do you think the only thing to negotiate in a sales contract is the purchase price? Think again. Here are some noncash terms you can negotiate.

- ❑ The number of goods to be sold
- ❑ The condition of the goods at the time of delivery
- ❑ Return privileges and/or credits for goods delivered in defective condition
- ❑ Rebates for goods that aren't sold within a specified time period
- ❑ Shipping and delivery dates
- ❑ Method of shipping (UPS vs. FedEx, for example)
- ❑ Method of payment (money order vs. credit card, for example)
- ❑ Currency of payment (for international sales)
- ❑ Whether discounts will be offered for volume or bulk purchases

Figure 16.1. Sales Contract Negotiating Points

Sales Contract Negotiating Points

- ❑ The timing of payment (cash upfront vs. installment payments)
- ❑ The interest rate to be paid on any deferred portion of the purchase price
- ❑ The penalty rate of interest to be paid if any portion of the purchase price isn't paid on time
- ❑ Whether the seller will have a lien on the goods until the purchase price is paid
- ❑ Whether the buyer's principals will guarantee payment of the purchase price if the buyer defaults
- ❑ Whether the seller or buyer will pay sales and/or transfer taxes
- ❑ Whether the seller or buyer will insure the goods while in transit
- ❑ When title to the goods transfers from seller to buyer
- ❑ Whether or not the seller will "warrant" title or condition to the goods
- ❑ The sale closing date
- ❑ Whether the seller will assume responsibility for the products' liability and other legal claims if the goods turn out to be defective
- ❑ Whether the seller will provide the buyer with advertising and promotional materials to assist in the resale of goods
- ❑ If a broker was involved, who will pay his/her commission?

Figure 16.1. Sales Contract Negotiating Points, continued

CHAPTER

17

Site Seeking

Choosing a Location for Your Business

Where should you locate your business? One expert will tell you location is absolutely vital to your company's success; another will argue that it really doesn't matter where you are—and they're both right. How important location is for your new company depends on the type of business and the facilities and other resources you need, and where your customers are.

If you're in retailing, or if you manufacture a product and distribution is a critical element of your overall operation, then geographic location is extremely important. If your business is information- or service-related, the actual location takes a back seat to whether the facility itself can meet your needs.

Regardless of the nature of your business, before you start shopping for space, you need to have a clear picture of what you must have, what you'd like to have, what you absolutely won't tolerate and how much you're able to pay. Developing that picture can be a time-consuming process that is both exciting and tedious, but it's essential that you give it the attention it deserves. While many startup mistakes can be corrected later on, a poor choice of location is difficult—and sometimes impossible—to repair.

aha!

If you're in a technology-related business, choose a location near a university that can help you with research, provide a resource for further education for your staff, and serve as a breeding ground for future employees. Some universities even offer space to entrepreneurs, at a low cost—or even free.

Types of Locations

The type of location you choose depends largely on the type of business you're in, but there are enough mixed-use areas and creative applications of space that you should give some thought to each type before making a final decision. For example, business parks and office buildings typically have retail space so they can attract the restaurants and stores that business tenants want nearby. Shopping centers are often home to an assortment of professional services—accounting, insurance, medical, legal, etc.—as well as retailers. It's entirely possible some version of nontraditional space will work for you, so use your imagination.

- *Homebased.* This is probably the trendiest location for a business these days, and many entrepreneurs start at home and then move into commercial space as their business grows. Others start at home with no thought or intention of ever moving. You can run a home-based business from an office in a spare bedroom, the basement, the attic—even the kitchen table. On the plus side, you do not need to worry about negotiating leases, coming up with substantial deposits, or commuting. On the downside, your room for physical growth is limited, and you may find accommodating employees or meetings with clients a challenge.
- *Retail.* Retail space comes in a variety of shapes and sizes and may be located in free-standing buildings, enclosed malls, strip shopping

centers, downtown shopping districts, or mixed-use facilities. You will also find retail space in airports and other transportation facilities, hotel lobbies, sports stadiums, and temporary or special-event venues.

- *Mobile.* Whether you're selling to the public or to other businesses, if you have a product or service that you take to your customers, your ideal "location" may be a car, van, or truck. With so many options for wireless connectivity, laptop and tablet computing and smartphones that can practically mimic a low-powered computer, a mobile office isn't so hard to fathom.
- *Commercial.* Commercial space includes even more options than retail. Commercial office buildings and business parks offer traditional office space geared to businesses that do not require a significant amount of pedestrian or automobile traffic for sales. You'll find commercial office space in downtown business districts, business parks, and sometimes interspersed among suburban retail facilities. One office option to consider is an executive suite, where the landlord provides receptionist and secretarial services, faxing, photocopying, conference rooms, and other support services as part of the package. Executive suites help you project the image of a professional operation at a more affordable cost and can be found in most commercial office areas. Some executive suites even rent their facilities by the hour to homebased businesses or out-of-towners who need temporary office space.
- *Hot-desking spaces.* Companies like Regus offer thousands of spaces across the globe for day rates, regular rentals, or occasional use. There are private spaces, shared spaces, and open-plan office spaces to choose from and many

warning

Be wary of incentives. Often incentives—such as free rent or tax breaks—may mask problems. There's usually a good reason why any location offers incentives, and you need to be sure what it is before you sign up. You should be able to start a profitable business in that location without any incentives—and then let the incentives be a bonus.

offerings are fully equipped with computers and video conferencing, along with meeting spaces. Check out Regus.com or other companies like DavinciVirtual.com for locations, or Google "shared office

>> Bring It Home

Looking for a way to launch your business with the minimum investment possible? Then consider setting up shop in a home office rather than in a commercial space.

Working from home makes a lot of sense when you're launching a business and have limited startup funds. In addition to saving beaucoup bucks on operating expenses like rent and utilities, you'll save on commuting costs and wardrobe expenses. You may even be able to take a tax deduction equal to the percentage of your home that's used as Business Central.

But there are some disadvantages to working from home. Clients may not find your cozy home office very professional. You personally may find it difficult to concentrate on work when the sun is shining, or when the mall, golf course, or your children are chanting your name. Friends and family also may drop in unannounced because you're at home. And the list of distractions goes on.

Minimize those distractions by establishing your office in a spare room or quiet corner that can be dedicated strictly to the business. Furnish it with office furniture (even if second-hand) and invest in a business computer. Install a separate business phone line with voice mail. Then make it very clear to well-meaning visitors that you maintain regular business hours and that the computer is off-limits to the kids. If necessary, arrange to meet clients offsite if your home office doesn't reflect your image as a savvy professional.

Finally, before you hang out that shingle, make sure your municipality doesn't have any zoning ordinances that prohibit homebased businesses. Some communities ban certain types of businesses, including those that will generate a lot of traffic or have employees working onsite. Make sure you know the rules before you hang out your shingle.

space" and your location. There are also more local companies like ShareDesk.net, Pivotdesk.com, and ShareYourOffice.com, which create formal shared office spaces among various buildings and office leases in an area.

- *Industrial.* If your business involves manufacturing or heavy distribution, you will need a plant or a warehouse facility. Light industrial parks typically attract smaller manufacturers in non-polluting industries as well as companies that need showrooms in addition to manufacturing facilities. Heavy industrial areas tend to be older and poorly planned and usually offer rail and/or water port access. Though industrial parks are generally newer and often have better infrastructures, you may want to consider a free-standing commercial building that meets your needs and is adequately zoned.

Issues to Consider

With an overview of what's available, you now need to decide what's most appropriate for your business. Julien J. Studley, founder of Julien J. Studley Inc., a real estate firm that represents commercial tenants nationwide, says the major things tenants are looking for are the best possible deal on the space and an available work force. Be systematic and realistic as you consider the following points.

aha!

Consider stockpiling space. If you're reasonably sure you're going to need additional space within a few years, it might be wise to lease a facility of that size now and sublease the extra space until you need it. That way, you'll know the space will be available later on, and you won't be faced with moving.

Style of Operation

Is your operation going to be formal and elegant? Or kicked-back and casual? Your location should be consistent with your particular style and image. If your business is retailing, do you want a traditional store, or would you like to try operating from a kiosk (or booth) in a mall or a cart that you can move to various locations? If you're in a traditional mall or shopping center, will the property permit you to have a sidewalk sale if you want to? Can you decorate your windows the way you want to?

And here's another option: Consider opening a pop-up retail location (see "Cart Blanche" on page 239). Pop-up retail operations suddenly "pop up" unannounced in highly visible locations, (hopefully) draw in big crowds, then vanish or transform themselves into another type of retail location once they've raked in the cash. In some cases, these stores are in business for a ridiculously short period of time—from just a few days to just a few weeks. But they're a great way to determine the local interest in your product, move product fast, and generate new excitement and interest in whatever you sell. Halloween and Christmas stores have been using the concept successfully for years, and some of the biggest mainstream retailers like Target, Toys 'R Us, and the Gap have adopted the concept as well. Pop-up spaces are usually leased temporarily for a flat fee, so you won't be locked into a typical retail lease of about five years. Since landlords are always desperate to lease space, all you generally have to do is ask to land a great pop-up location.

Demographics

There are two important angles to the issue of demographics. One is your customers; the other is your employees. First, consider who your customers are and how important their proximity to your location is. For a retailer and some service providers, this is critical; for other types of businesses, it might not be as important. The demographic profile you've developed of your target market will help you make this decision (see Chapter 7 for more on developing your target market).

Then, take a look at the community. If your customer base is local, is the population large enough, or does a sufficient percentage of that population match your customer profile to support your business? Does the community have a stable economic base that will provide a healthy environment for your business? Be cautious when considering communities that are largely dependent on a particular industry for their economy; a downturn could be a death knell for your company.

Now think about your work force. What skills do you need, and are people with those talents available? Does the community have the resources

>> Cart Blanche

Carts and kiosks have become familiar sights in American malls and in public spaces in big cities around the country. They sell everything from inexpensive gift items to pricey jewelry and artwork. They make mall and other prime space affordable for the business owner, and the mall operators benefit from extra rent and a wider variety of merchandise. For business owners, leases can also be shorter and lease terms more favorable to someone just starting out.

Consider using carts and kiosks to test your product in a retail setting before making the larger investment in a traditional store. Styles range from simple to elaborate; whatever you choose, be sure it's attractive, well-lighted, functional, and situated in a good spot for foot traffic.

to serve their needs? Is there sufficient housing in the appropriate price range? Will your employees find the schools, recreational opportunities, culture, and other aspects of the community satisfactory?

Especially when the economy is strong and unemployment figures are low, you may be concerned about the availability of good workers. Keep in mind that in many areas, few people may be unemployed, but many may be underemployed. If you are offering attractive jobs at competitive wages, you may find staffing your company easier than you thought.

Look beyond the basic employment statistics to find out what the job market is really like. Think about placing a blind test ad (the local economic development agency may do this for you) to see what type of response you will get in the way of applicants before making a final location decision.

Demographic information is available to you through a variety of resources. You could do the research yourself by visiting the library or calling the U.S. Census Bureau and gathering a bunch of statistics, then trying to figure out what they mean, but chances are you probably do not have the time or statistical expertise to do that. So why not let other people do it for you—people who know how to gather the data and translate it into information you can understand and use. Contact your state, regional, or local economic development agency (see "To the Rescue" on page 241) or commercial real estate companies and use the data they've already collected, analyzed, and processed.

Foot Traffic

For most retail businesses, foot traffic is extremely important. You don't want to be tucked away in a corner where shoppers are likely to bypass you, and even the best retail areas have dead spots. By contrast, if your business requires confidentiality, you may not want to be located in a high-traffic area. Monitor the traffic outside a potential location at different times of the day and on different days of the week to make sure the volume of pedestrian traffic meets your needs.

Accessibility and Parking

Consider how accessible the facility will be for everyone who will be using it—customers, employees, and suppliers. If you're on a busy street, how easy is it for cars to get in and out of your parking lot? Is the facility accessible to people with disabilities? What sort of deliveries are you likely to receive, and will your suppliers be able to easily and efficiently get materials to your business? Small-package couriers need to get in and out quickly; trucking companies need adequate roads and loading docks if you're going to be receiving freight on pallets.

Find out about the days and hours of service and access to locations you're considering. Are the heating and cooling systems left on or turned off at night and on weekends? If you're inside an office building, are there periods when exterior doors are locked and, if so, can you have keys? A beautiful office building at a great price is a lousy deal if you plan to work weekends but the building is closed on weekends—or they allow you access, but the air conditioning and heat are turned off so you roast in the summer and freeze in the winter.

tip

If you are buying an existing business, look at the location as if you were starting from scratch. Ask questions like: Does the site meet your present and future needs? Have there been any changes regarding the location in recent years that could have a positive or negative impact? Will you be taking over the seller's lease, and can it be renegotiated?

Be sure, too, that there's ample convenient parking for both customers and employees. As with foot traffic, take the time to monitor the facility at various times and days to see how the demand for parking fluctuates. Also, consider safety issues: The parking lot should be well-maintained and adequately lighted.

Competition

Are competing companies located nearby? Sometimes that's good, such as in industries where comparison shopping is popular. (That's why competing retail businesses, such as fast-food restaurants, antique shops,

>> To the Rescue

One of the best sources of information and assistance for startup and expanding businesses is state, regional, and local economic development agencies. According to Ted M. Levine, founder and chairman of Development Counsellors International, a consulting firm specializing in economic development and travel marketing, there are nearly 20,000 economic development groups worldwide. Their purpose is to promote economic growth and development in the areas they serve. They accomplish that by encouraging new businesses to locate in their area, and to do that, they've gathered all the statistics and information you'll need to make a decision.

Levine says economic development agencies will help any new business, regardless of size, in four primary ways:

1. Market demographics
2. Real estate costs and availability; zoning and regulatory issues
3. Work-force demographics
4. Referrals to similar companies and other resources

For the best overview, start with your state agency. The state agency can then guide you to regional and local groups for expanded information. Also consider looking into resources and incentives available through local Business Improvement Districts.

and clothing stores, tend to cluster together.) You may also catch the overflow from existing businesses, particularly if you're located in a restaurant and entertainment area. But if a nearby competitor is only going to make your marketing job tougher, look elsewhere.

Proximity to Other Businesses and Services

Take a look at what other businesses and services are in the vicinity from two key perspectives. First, see if you can benefit from nearby businesses—by the customer traffic they generate—because those companies and their employees could become your customers, or because it may be convenient and efficient for you to be their customer.

Second, look at how they will enrich the quality of your company as a workplace. Does the vicinity have an adequate selection of restaurants so your employees have places to go for lunch? Is there a nearby day-care center for employees with children? Are other shops and services you and your employees might want conveniently located?

Image and History of the Site

What does this address say about your company? Particularly if you're targeting a local market, be sure your location accurately reflects the image you want to project. It's also a good idea to check out the history of the site. Consider how it has changed and evolved over the years.

Ask about previous tenants. If you're opening a restaurant where five restaurants have failed, you may be starting off with an insurmountable handicap—either because there's something wrong with the location or because the public will assume that your business will go the way of the previous tenants. If several types of businesses have been there and failed, do some research to find out why—you need to confirm whether the problem was with the businesses or the location. That previous occupants have been wildly successful is certainly a good sign, but temper that with information on what type of businesses they were compared to yours.

> ***"There is nothing so useless as doing efficiently that which should not be done at all."***
>
> —Peter Drucker, Management Guru

Another historical point you'll want to know is whether a serious crime, tragedy, or other notable event occurred on the property. If so, will the public's memory reflect on your operation, and is that reflection likely to be positive or negative?

Ordinances

Find out if any ordinances or zoning restrictions could affect your business in any way. Check for the specific location you're considering as well as neighboring properties—you probably don't want a liquor store opening up next to your day-care center.

The Building's Infrastructure

Many older buildings do not have the necessary infrastructure to support the high-tech needs of contemporary operations. Make sure the building you choose has adequate electrical, air conditioning, and telecommunications

>> Growing Places

Incubators are organizations sponsored by public and private investors that assist startup and young companies in their critical early days with a variety of well-orchestrated business assistance programs. Incubators provide hands-on management assistance, access to financing, shared office services, access to equipment, flexible leases, expandable space and more—all under one roof.

The time your business can spend in an incubator is limited—typically two years—but it can vary. The idea is to get a fledgling business off the ground, turn it into a sound operation, then let it "leave the nest" to run on its own, making room for another startup venture in the incubator.

Incubators generally fall into the following categories: technology, industrial, mixed-use, economic empowerment, and industry-specific. For more information about incubators and for help finding one appropriate for your business, contact the National Business Incubation Association (NBIA) at (740) 593-4331. For a list of incubators in your state, visit nbia.org and click on the link that says "Find a Business Incubator."

service to meet your present and future needs. It is a good idea to hire an independent engineer to check this out for you so you are sure to have an objective evaluation.

Utilities and Other Costs

Rent composes the major portion of your ongoing facilities expense, but it's not the only thing that'll eat up your money. Consider extras such as utilities—they're included in some leases but not in others. If they're not included, ask the utility company for a summary of the previous year's usage and billing for the site. Also, find out what kind of security deposits the various utility providers require so you can develop an accurate move-in budget; however, you may not need a deposit if you have an established payment record with the company.

If you have to provide your own janitorial service, what will it cost? What are insurance rates for the area? Do you have to pay extra for parking? Consider all your location-related expenses, and factor them into your decision.

Room for Growth

Look at the facility with an eye to the future. If you anticipate growth, be sure the facility you choose can accommodate you. Keep your long-range plan in mind, even when short-term advantages make a location look attractive. A great deal on a place you're likely to outgrow in a few years probably is not that great of a deal. Similarly, if there is evidence of pending decline in the vicinity, you should consider whether you want to be located there in five years.

save

To keep costs down, consider sharing space with another company that does not compete with your business—one that might even complement yours. This is known as co-branding, such as when a sandwich chain places a unit in a convenience store. Put your space-sharing agreement in writing, detailing each party's rights and responsibilities, and give yourself an out if you need it.

What Can You Expect to Pay?

Real estate costs vary tremendously based on the type of facility, the region, the specific

Location Worksheet

Answer the following questions by indicating whether it is a strength (S) or weakness (W) of the potential site as it relates to your business. Once you have completed a worksheet for each prospective location, compare the relative strengths and weaknesses of each site to help you choose the best one for your business.

	S	W
Is the facility large enough for your business?		
Does it meet your layout requirements well?		
Does the building need any repairs?		
Will you have to make any leasehold improvements?		
Do the existing utilities meet your needs, or will you have to do any rewiring or plumbing work? Is ventilation adequate?		
Is the facility easily accessible to your potential clients or customers?		
Can you find a number of qualified employees in the area in which the facility is located?		
Is the facility consistent with the image you would like to maintain?		
Is the facility located in a safe neighborhood with a low crime rate?		
Are neighboring businesses likely to attract customers who will also patronize your business?		
Are there any competitors located close to the facility? If so, can you compete with them successfully?		
Can suppliers make deliveries conveniently at this location?		
If your business expands in the future, will the facility be able to accommodate this growth?		
Are the lease terms and rent favorable?		
Is the facility located in an area zoned for your type of business?		

Figure 17.1. Location Worksheet

location, and the market. A commercial real estate broker will be able to give you an overview of costs in your area. You may want to look at historical data—how has the rate for your type of facility fluctuated over the years? Also ask for forecasts so you know what to expect in the future. Understanding the overall market will be a tremendous help when you begin negotiating your lease.

Commercial Leases

If you've never been involved in renting commercial space, your first glimpse of a commercial lease may be overwhelming. They are lengthy, full of jargon and unfamiliar terms, and always written to the landlord's advantage. But they are negotiable. Whether you're working on the deal yourself or using an agent, the key to successful lease negotiations is knowing what you want, understanding what the lease document says, and being reasonable in your demands.

Especially for retail space, be sure your lease includes a bail-out clause, which lets you out of the lease if your sales don't reach an agreed-on amount, and a co-tenancy clause so you can break the lease if an anchor store closes or moves. If you have to do a lot of work to get the space ready for occupancy, consider negotiating a construction allowance—generally $10 to $25 per square foot—to help offset the costs.

Be sure you clearly understand the difference between rentable and usable space. Rentable space is what you pay for; usable is what you can use and typically does not include hallways, restrooms, lobbies, elevator shafts, stairwells, and so forth. You may be expected to pay a prorated portion of common area maintenance costs. This is not unusual, but be sure the fees are reasonable and that the landlord is not making a profit on them. Also, check for clauses that allow the landlord the right to remodel at the tenant's expense without approval, and insist on language that limits your financial liability.

Leasehold Improvements

Leasehold improvements are the nonremovable installations—either original or the results of remodeling—that you make to the facility to accommodate your needs. Such improvements are typically more

>> Agent Avenues

Unless you have a significant amount of experience in shopping for commercial real estate, it's a good idea to use a qualified real estate agent. Whether you are buying or leasing, an agent can help by prescreening properties, which saves you time, and by negotiating on your behalf, which can save you money.

Typically the seller or landlord pays the agent's commission, which may raise some questions in your mind about loyalty of the agent. However, keep in mind that the agent doesn't get paid until a deal that satisfies you both is negotiated.

You may opt to use a tenant's or buyer's agent whom you pay yourself. In the real estate world, that's called tenant (or buyer) representation. Especially in tight market situations, it may be to your advantage to invest in an advocate who will negotiate on your behalf. For more information about tenant representation and for help finding someone to assist you, contact the Society of Industrial and Office Realtors in Washington, DC, at (202) 449-8200, email admin@sior.com, or visit sior.com.

Shop for a real estate agent as you would any professional service provider: Ask for referrals from friends and associates; interview several agents; be sure the agent you choose has expertise in the type of property or facility you need; check out the agent's track record, professional history, and reputation; clarify how the agent will be compensated and by whom; and draw up a written agreement that outlines your mutual expectations.

substantial when renting new space, which may consist of only walls and flooring. Often existing space will include at least some fixtures. Get estimates on the improvements you'll need to make before signing the lease so you'll know the total move-in costs and can make a fair construction allowance request.

Negotiating the Lease

The first lease the landlord presents is usually just the starting point. You may be surprised at what you can get in the way of concessions and extras

>> Speaking the Language

Following are some of the leases you may come across:

> *Flat lease.* The oldest and simplest type of lease, the flat lease sets a single price for a definite period of time. It generally is the best deal for the tenant but is becoming increasingly harder to find. (Caution: Avoid a flat lease if the term is too short; a series of short-term flat leases could cost you more in the long run than a longer-term lease with reasonable escalation clauses.)

> *Step lease.* The step lease attempts to cover the landlord's expected increases in expenses by increasing the rent on an annual basis over the life of the agreement. The problem with step leases is that they are based on estimates rather than actual costs, and there's no way for either party to be sure in advance that the proposed increases are fair and equitable.

> *Net lease.* Like a step lease, the net lease increases the rent to cover increases in the landlord's costs but does so at the time they occur rather than on estimates. This may be more equitable than a step lease, but it's less predictable.

> *Cost-of-living lease.* Rather than tying rent increases to specific expenses, this type of lease bases increases on the rises in the cost of living. Your rent will go up with general inflation. Of course, the prices for your products and services will also likely rise with inflation, and that should cover your rent increases, so this type of lease can be very appealing.

> *Percentage lease.* This lease lets the landlord benefit from your success. The rent is based on either a minimum amount or a base amount, or a percentage of your business's gross revenue, whichever is higher. Percentages typically range from 3 to 12 percent. With this type of lease, you'll be required to periodically furnish proof of gross sales; to do this, you may allow the landlord to examine your books or sales tax records, or provide a copy of the appropriate section of your tax return. Percentage leases are common for retail space.

simply by asking. Of course, you need to be reasonable and keep your demands in line with acceptable business practices and current market conditions. A good commercial real estate agent can be invaluable in this area.

Avoid issuing ultimatums; they almost always close doors—and if you fail to follow through, your next "ultimatum" will not mean much. Consider beginning the process with something that is close to your "best and final offer." That way, your negotiations will not be lengthy and protracted, and you can either reach a mutually acceptable deal or move on to a different property. The longer negotiations take, the more potential there is for things to go wrong.

Business Lease Checklist

After you have chosen a particular site, check the following points before you sign the lease:

- ❑ Is there sufficient electrical power?
- ❑ Are there enough electrical outlets?
- ❑ Are there enough parking spaces for customers and employees?
- ❑ Is there sufficient lighting? Heating? Air conditioning?
- ❑ Do you know how large a sign and what type you can erect?
- ❑ Will your city's building and zoning departments allow your business to operate in the facility?
- ❑ Will the landlord allow the alterations that you deem necessary?
- ❑ Must you pay for returning the building to its original condition when you move?
- ❑ Is there any indication of roof leaks? (A heavy rain could damage goods.)
- ❑ Is the cost of burglary insurance high in the area? (This varies tremendously.)

Figure 17.2. Business Lease Checklist

Business Lease Checklist

- ❑ Can you secure the building at a low cost against the threat of burglary?
- ❑ Will the health department approve your business at this location?
- ❑ Will the fire department approve your business at this location?
- ❑ Have you included a written description of the property?
- ❑ Have you attached drawings of the property to the lease document?
- ❑ Do you have written guidelines for renewal terms?
- ❑ Do you know when your lease payment begins?
- ❑ Have you bargained for one to three months of free rent?
- ❑ Do you know your date of possession?
- ❑ Have you listed the owner's responsibility for improvements?
- ❑ Do you pay the taxes?
- ❑ Do you pay the insurance?
- ❑ Do you pay the maintenance fees?
- ❑ Do you pay the utilities?
- ❑ Do you pay the sewage fees?
- ❑ Have you asked your landlord for a cap of 5 percent on your rent increase?
- ❑ Have you included penalty clauses in case the project is late and you are denied occupancy?
- ❑ Have you retained the right to obtain your own bids for signage?
- ❑ Can you leave if the center is never more than 70 percent leased?
- ❑ Has a real estate attorney reviewed your contract?

Figure 17.2. Business Lease Checklist, continued

Essentially, everything in the lease is subject to negotiation, including financial terms, the starting rent, rent increases, the tenant's rights and responsibilities, options for renewal, tenant leasehold improvements, and other terms and conditions. You or your agent can negotiate the lease, but then it should be drawn up by an attorney. Typically, the landlord or his attorney will draft the lease, and an attorney you hire who specializes in real estate should review it for you before you sign.

It Still Comes Down to You

Technology and statistics are important elements of your site selection decision, but nothing beats your personal involvement in the process. Real estate brokers and economic development agencies can give you plenty of numbers, but remember that their job is to get you to choose their location. To get a balanced picture, take the time to visit the sites yourself, talk to people who own or work in nearby businesses, and verify the facts and what they really mean to the potential success of your business.

CHAPTER

18

Looking Good

Creating a Professional Image

These days, it is just not enough to create a terrific product, offer super service, and have a solid business plan to back you up. Your company image is equally important to the overall success of your business.

Every time you hand out your business card, send a letter, or welcome a client into your office or store, you are selling someone on your company. Even the look of your office helps "sell" your business by conveying an image, whether it is that of a funky, creative ad agency or a staid, respectable accounting firm.

Your logo, business card, signage, and style are all part of a cohesive image program known as corporate identity. And with the right corporate identity, your company can appear highly professional and give the impression of having been in business for years.

In this chapter, we will discuss how to create a corporate image that works.

Office Space

When you are a startup with limited capital, it may be tempting to put all your money into advertising and equipment and skimp on office furniture. How you furnish your office might not seem to matter, especially if your customers will not see it. And if your office is located at home, the dining room table might look like the most logical choice.

But a nicely furnished office is not just a matter of aesthetics. Grabbing whatever furniture is at hand and plunking it down without a thought to organization can put you at a major disadvantage in terms of productivity.

Everything in Its Place

Improving your own and your employees' performance involves a lot more than finding comfortable chairs. It involves placement of offices or cubicles within the building, proximity to equipment, lighting, desk space,

>> What's in Store?

Got a retail location? Ask yourself these questions to make sure your store has the "eye appeal" it needs to keep customers coming back:

- Are your shelves clean and neat? Is merchandise displayed so people can see it easily?
- Is the area around your cash registers or terminals clean and orderly?
- Can you find forms, packaging, and related materials quickly and easily?
- Are light fixtures clean, bright, and working properly?
- Is there plenty of room between counters and shelves so that aisles are wide and free of barriers?
- Are glass surfaces clean and floors vacuumed or swept and scrubbed regularly?

> ***"When I see a barrier, I cry and I curse, and then I get a ladder and climb over it."***
>
> —JOHN JOHNSON, FOUNDER OF JOHNSON PUBLISHING CO.

meeting areas, privacy, and more. People spend most of their waking hours at the office, so its design has a tremendous effect on morale.

How can you create a high-performance office? The first step is addressing organizational issues . . . of who sits where. The days of big "power desks" and hierarchical corner offices are over. More businesses are turning to flexible environments ideal for small companies where the business owner probably doubles as salesperson.

With today's emphasis on team-building, office design is moving away from compartmentalized offices and moving toward large spaces where teams of employees can work. When setting up your space, think about who needs to work with whom and which employees share what resources. If you group those people together, you enhance their productivity.

>> On the Outside

The inside of your office may look great, but don't stop there. What about the outside? If the first impression a potential customer has of your business is a shabby door or an unkempt parking lot, you're not sending the right message . . . and all your hard work in designing an attractive, efficient office could be going to waste.

Step outside your place of business and take a long, hard look at the parking lot, sidewalks, windows, outside lighting, landscaping, and the outside of the building itself. A well-maintained building projects an industrious, professional image. Weeds, trash, broken sidewalks, tattered awnings, dirty windows, dead plants, and overflowing trash containers send the message "We don't care."

Whether you're in a retail location or an office building, take the time to check the property from the outside, and make sure it's inviting and appealing every day.

In addition to maximizing your own and your employees' productivity, your office may also function as a marketing tool if clients or customers visit. Think about what visitors will see when they come by. Will they be bombarded with noise from one department near the entrance? Or will they see a series of closed doors with seemingly no activity taking place? Visitors should not be overwhelmed by chaos as they walk through your building, but they should see signs of life and get glimpses of the daily activities going on at your company.

Designing a Logo

Before you start designing a business card or picking colors for your letterhead, you need a logo. Featuring your company name, embellished with a little color and perhaps a few graphic touches here and there, your logo is the most important design element because it is the basis for all your other materials: stationery, packaging, promotional materials, and signage.

Through the use of color and graphics, your logo should reflect the overall image you want your company to convey, advises Interbrand, a brand identity and marketing company. It should give people a feel for what your company is all about.

For example, say your product is an organic facial cream you will be marketing to health-conscious consumers. Your logo should represent your product's best benefits—being all-natural and environmentally sound. Creating a simple, no-nonsense logo using earth tones and a plain typeface will give the impression of a product that is "back to basics," which is exactly what you want to achieve. Take that same product and give it a slick, high-tech look with neon colors, however, and people won't associate your logo with the down-to-earth product you're selling.

tip

Evaluate business card designs with these criteria in mind:

- Is the card easy to read?
- Does the design catch your eye? (A good designer can make even an all-type card appealing.)
- Is your name or the business's name immediately identifiable?

>> Secrets to Making Your Logo Stand Out

If asked, most of us could name at least a few iconic logos, whether it be Coca-Cola's cursive script or the charging bull of Merrill Lynch. That's the point—for a logo to stick in your mind.

"Other people have to be able to speak for your brand," says Jonah Berger, author of *Contagious: Why Things Catch On* (Simon & Schuster, 2013) and a marketing professor at the Wharton School of the University of Pennsylvania. "You love your company, you think your company is great, but if you're not around, what are people going to be able to remember? And what are they going to tell others?"

The best logos have several things in common. Here are Berger's five keys to a successful logo.

1. *Simplicity*. "A good way to think about simplicity is how many moving pieces are there in the logo," Berger says. For instance, the old Apple logo was rainbow-colored, while the current one is rendered in solid black or simple grayscale. That newfound simplicity makes the logo easy to look at, which customers appreciate. "The easier it is to process things, the more we like those things," Berger says. For that reason, most brands want to present a simple aesthetic that is easy for consumers to digest.
2. *Brand consistency*. Your logo will communicate things to consumers about your brand, so you need to ensure that its design fits your company's overall message. Consider the Apple logo again. A few decades ago, Berger says, "rainbow colors had a certain association [with] being free and easygoing," but not anymore. Whereas Apple's old logo connoted the free spirit of an upstart that was taking on staid tech giants, its current position as one of the most valuable corporations in the world calls for the sleek, futuristic logo it has now. "That's consistent with the message that Apple wants to suggest: We are technology, but we're friendly technology, we're easy-to-use technology." If you're starting up a new company, Berger says, you

>> Secrets to Making Your Logo Stand Out, continued

should put some serious thought into your brand's key characteristics and how you want to convey them in your logo.

3. *Memorability*. Memorability is the quality that makes your logo easy for customers to recall, which leads to repeat customers and word-of-mouth, says Berger. Your logo should "help them remember that you exist and what you stand for," he says.
4. *Remarkability*. The remarkability of a logo is what makes it "worthy of remark," cutting through the clutter of your industry to reach customers, Berger says. TalentBin's logo exemplifies this quality. The logo for the search engine that helps companies with talent acquisition consists of a cartoonish purple squirrel riding a unicorn. While it may seem ridiculous, it has a specific meaning. "In the recruiting industry, a 'purple squirrel' is a type of person who is really hard to find," Berger says. "It's a way for them to show that they're insiders, that they know the culture." The purple squirrel is not TalentBin's primary logo, but instead is used internally, at conferences and on promotional materials given to people in the recruiting industry. "If you're an established brand, you may not want a remarkable logo," Berger says. "But if you're a startup you need to take a little more risk."
5. *Market testing*. Don't just trust to your gut when designing a logo, Berger says. Do market research. One way to test various logo designs is to put out a survey on a service such as Amazon's Mechanical Turk. "We could throw up a quick study for an entrepreneur for $10, and within a day get a lot of feedback from different people about how heavy or light, fast or slow a logo would be," Berger says. The point is not to assume that a given logo is great. Get some independent feedback about whether your logo is saying everything you want it to say.

Logos come in two basic forms: abstract symbols (like the apple in Apple Computer) or logotypes, a stylized rendition of your company's name. You can also use a combination of both. Alan Siegel, former chairman of Siegel+Gale, a design firm specializing in corporate identity, warns that promoting an abstract symbol can prove very costly for a small business on a budget. In addition, he says, such logos are harder to remember. "A logotype or word mark is much easier to recall," says Siegel. "If you use an abstract symbol, always use it in connection with your business name."

Trying to create a logo on your own may seem like the best way to avoid the high costs of going to a professional design firm, which will charge thousands for a logo alone. However, be aware that there are a lot of independent designers, including many who advertise online, who charge much less. According to Stan Evenson, founder of Evenson Design Group, "Entrepreneurs on a tight budget should shop around for a designer. There are a lot of freelance designers who charge rates ranging from $35 to $150 per hour, based on their experience. But don't hire someone because of their bargain price. Find a designer who's familiar with your field . . . and your competition. If the cost still seems exorbitant, remember that a good logo should last at least ten years. If you look at the amortization of that cost over a ten-year period, it doesn't seem so bad."

Even if you have a good eye for color and a sense of what you want your logo to look like, you should still consult a professional designer. Why? They know whether or not a logo design will transfer easily into print or onto a sign, while you might come up with a beautiful design that can't be transferred or would cost too much to be printed. Your logo is the foundation for all your promotional materials, so this is one area where spending a little more now really pays off later.

Business Cards

Once you have your logo, it's time to apply it to the marketing items you will use most, such as business cards. A good business card should convey the overall image of your business—not easy, considering the card measures only two inches by three inches. How can you possibly get a message across in such a small amount of space?

You can't expect your business card to tell the whole story about your company. What

aha!

Ask owners of noncompeting but related businesses if you can display some of your business cards on their counters. A pet-sitter, for example, could leave her business cards on the counter at a pet store. Offer to do the same for them.

you should expect it to do is present a professional image people will remember. "A business card can make or break a client's first impression of your company," says Evenson. That little card makes as much of an impression as your personal appearance—the suit you wear or the briefcase you carry.

The color, wording, and texture of your business card have a lot to do with its appeal and its ability to convey your company image. Use common sense when you are designing your business card. If your business markets children's toys and games, you might try using bright, primary colors and words written in a child's script. On the other hand, if you run a financial consulting service, then you want your business card to convey professionalism and reliability, so stick to traditional looks such as black printing on a gray, beige, or white background.

Of course, professional designers claim entrepreneurs should not try to attempt designing a business card on their own, but many cash-strapped business owners have no other choice. And there are multiple inexpensive printing services that offer ideas and basic design templates. Among them: VistaPrint, whose online tools can be just the ticket for creating a card when you have an idea in mind and a logo in hand. The best course of action: Look at all the business cards you receive, and emulate the cards that you like. You have more leeway if you are in a creative business, such as party planning or retailing, but in general, keep the following tips in mind:

- *Use your logo as the basis.* Make it the largest element on the card.
- *Keep it simple.* Do not cram too much information on the card.
- *Do include the essentials*—your name, title, company name, address, phone and fax numbers, and email and website addresses.
- *Make sure the typeface is easy to read.*
- *Stick to one or two colors.*

Once you've got business cards, make the most of them:

- Always give people more than one card (so they can give it to others).
- Include your card in all correspondence.
- Carry cards with you at all times, in a card case so they're clean and neat.

>> In the Cards

Business cards don't have to be boring. If your industry allows for a little creative flair, here are some ideas to try.

> Use 4-inch-by-7-inch cards that fold over (like a mini-brochure), cards made of plastic, or cards with photos on them.

> Although they are more expensive than standard business cards, cards in nontraditional shapes get attention. Try a teddy bear shape for a day-care service, for example, or a birthday cake for a party planner.

> Textured paper can add to a card's interest (make sure it does not detract from readability, though), as can colored paper. In general, stay with lighter shades that enhance readability.

> Thermography, a process that creates raised, shiny print, adds interest to a card. Embossing and foil stamping are two other printing processes that can give your card visual appeal.

Selecting Stationery

Every time you mail a letter to a prospective client or to an existing customer, the missive leaves a long-lasting impression of your company. In a service business, your written materials are among your company's most important marketing items. And if you run a homebased business that doesn't have a commercial location or sign, introducing your company to clients through the mail can be one of your most effective marketing techniques. The paper stock you choose, as well as the colors and graphics embellishing it, plays an important role in the image your stationery presents to your customers. A neon pink stock may work well for a new suntan lotion manufacturer, but not for an

save

Creating your image can be costly, but you don't have to splurge on the whole works at once. To save money, start with the key items the public will see immediately. If you expect to attract most of your clients through sales calls, for instance, put more money into your business cards; if you expect to lure people with your sign, put the money there.

accounting service. Your stationery should tie in with your business cards, featuring the same color scheme and overall look.

Do not get so caught up in the design elements of your business stationery that you forget the obvious. You want to make it as easy as possible for your clients to respond to your offer by making all the information they need readily available. Attach your business card to each letter as well, so clients can put it in their Rolodexes or quickly add them to an Outlook contact list for future reference.

Designing Your Sign

Retailers and restaurateurs alike realize the power of a good sign. Some companies rely on drive-by or walk-by traffic for customers, and if that's the case with your company, your sign may be the most important element of your entire corporate identity.

A good sign must do more than just attract attention; it also has to be readable from a good distance. That's why your original logo is so important—one that looks great on a tiny business card may not transfer well to a huge sign above your store. Clearly, going to a professional in the first stages of developing your image is essential. If you find out your great logo can't be reproduced on a sign, you'll have to go back to square one and rethink your logo, which will end up costing you more in the long run.

In recent years, a whole host of new signage materials has emerged to provide more variety and individuality. This also means it's harder to choose among all the possibilities, which include neon, plastic, metal, wood, and more. Do some investigating before making your final decision; there is a wide range of prices for various materials. Depending on your location, sign placement can make a big difference, too. Options include a free-standing sign, a wall sign, a projecting sign, or a roof sign.

Before you head to a sign manufacturer with your design specifications, check your local zoning laws. You may find that the design you've come up with for your fried chicken restaurant—a 30-foot neon number in the shape of a chicken—isn't allowed in your area. If you are moving into a shopping center, the developer may have additional regulations governing signage that can be used in the facility.

Most entrepreneurs need professional assistance with signage since they do not have experience in this area. You probably will not know how big the letters should be to be visible from down the block, and you may not know which materials fare best in inclement weather. For this reason, you should visit a professional—either a designer or a sign fabricator. A good designer knows when fabricators are cutting corners and not using the material requested or doing a shoddy job. A designer will also be present at the time of installation to make sure the sign is properly installed.

The cost of a sign varies greatly depending on the materials, type of sign, and whether it's lighted. Buying directly from a fabricator can cost as little as $500, but you run the risk of not meeting zoning requirements. If you hire a designer, you'll pay a design fee in addition to fabrication costs, but you have a better guarantee that the finished product will work for you.

CHAPTER

19

Stock Answers

The Lowdown on Inventory

Where would an apparel company be without clothing? An auto supply store without auto parts? A computer company without computers? Nowhere, of course. Understanding and managing your inventory is one of the most critical factors in business success.

tip

Inventory control doesn't just mean counting. Take physical control of your inventory, too. Lock it up or restrict access. Remember that inventory is money.

Yet many entrepreneurs fail to answer such basic questions as "What items are the winners and losers?" and "How often does inventory turn over?" Don't make this mistake. Management education expert Ashok Rao believes that companies can increase their profitability 20 to 50 percent or more through careful inventory management.

Inventory Control

There is more to inventory control than simply buying new products. You have to know what to buy, when to buy it, and how much to buy. You also need to track your inventory—whether manually or by computer—and use that knowledge to hone your purchasing process.

Startup entrepreneurs are at a disadvantage when it comes to inventory control, says Rao. "They may not have the right kinds of systems to manage their inventory. They don't have the right kinds of skills for handling inventory. They don't know how to go about actually maintaining their inventory, and they sometimes have to purchase in larger quantities than what they want or need."

Maintaining Enough Inventory

Your business's basic stock should provide a reasonable assortment of products and should be big enough to cover the normal sales demands of your business. Since you won't have actual sales and stocking figures from previous years to guide you during startup, you must project your first year's sales based on your business plan.

When calculating basic stock, you must also factor in lead time—the length of time between reordering and receiving a product. For instance, if your lead time is four weeks and a particular product line sells 10 units a week, then you must reorder before the basic inventory level falls below 40 units. If you do not reorder until you actually need the stock, you'll have to wait four weeks without the product.

> *"The secret of success is to do the common things uncommonly well."*
>
> —John D. Rockefeller, founder of Standard Oil

Insufficient inventory means lost sales and costly, time-consuming back orders. Running out of raw materials or parts that are crucial to your production process means increased operating costs, too. Your employees will be getting paid to sit around because there's no work for them to do; when the inventory does come in, they'll be paid for working overtime to make up for lost production time. In some situations, you could even end up buying emergency inventory at high prices.

One way to protect yourself from such shortfalls is by building a safety margin into basic inventory figures. To figure out the right safety margin for your business, try to think of all the outside factors that could contribute to delays, such as suppliers who tend to be late or goods being shipped from overseas. Once you have been in business a while, you'll have a better feel for delivery times and will find it fairly easy to calculate your safety margin.

Avoiding Excess Inventory

Avoiding excess inventory is especially important for owners of companies with seasonal product lines, such as clothing, home accessories, and holiday and gift items. These products have a short "shelf life" and are hard to sell once they are no longer in fashion. Entrepreneurs who sell more timeless products, such as plumbing equipment, office supplies, or auto products, have more leeway because it takes longer for these items to become obsolete.

No matter what your business, however, excess inventory should be avoided. It costs money in extra overhead, debt service on loans

>> On with the Show

Trade shows are the primary way for new businesses to find suppliers. All major suppliers in an industry display their products at seasonal trade shows, where retailers go to buy and look at new items.

Although retailers buy from various sources year-round, trade shows are an important event in every store owner's buying cycle. Most retailers attend at least one trade show per year. Smart buyers come prepared with a shopping list and a seasonal budget calculated either in dollar amounts or in quantities of various merchandise.

Practically every major city hosts one or more trade shows relevant to specific retailers. You can contact your local chamber of commerce or convention and visitor's bureau for upcoming shows in your city or state. Your industry's trade publications should also list relevant trade shows.

> **tip**
> 
> In addition to counting inventory weekly, monthly, or annually, some experts recommend checking a few items each day to see if your actual amount is the same as what you have in your records. This is a good way to troubleshoot and nip inventory problems in the bud.

to purchase the excess inventory, additional personal property tax on unsold inventory, and increased insurance costs. One merchandise consultant estimates that it costs the average retailer from 20 to 30 percent of the original inventory investment just to maintain it. Buying excess inventory also reduces your liquidity—something to be avoided. Consider the example of an auto supply retailer who finds himself with the opportunity to buy 1,000 gallons of antifreeze at a huge discount. If he buys the antifreeze and it turns out to be a mild winter, he'll be sitting on 1,000 gallons of antifreeze. Even though he knows he can sell the antifreeze during the next cold winter, it's still taking up space in his warehouse for an entire year—space that could be devoted to more profitable products.

When you find yourself with excess inventory, your natural reaction will probably be to reduce the price and sell it quickly. Although this solves the overstocking problem, it also reduces your return on investment. All your financial projections assume that you will receive the full price for your goods. If you slash your prices by 15 to 25 percent just to get rid of the excess inventory, you're losing money you had counted on in your business plan.

Some novice entrepreneurs react to excess inventory by being overly cautious the next time they order stock. However, this puts you at risk of having an inventory shortage. To avoid accumulating excess inventory, set a realistic safety margin and order only what you're sure you can sell.

Inventory and Cash Flow

Cash-flow problems are some of the most common difficulties small businesses encounter, and they are usually the first signs of serious financial trouble ahead. According to management education expert Ashok Rao, tying up money in inventory can severely damage a small company's cash flow.

> *"What we think determines what happens to us, so if we want to change our lives, we need to stretch our minds."*
>
> —Wayne Dyer, self-help advocate

To control inventory effectively, prioritize your inventory needs. It might seem at first glance that the most expensive items in your inventory should receive the most attention. But in reality, less expensive items with higher turnover ratios have a greater effect on your business than more costly items. If you focus only on the high-dollar-value items, you run the risk of running out of the lower-priced products that contribute more to your bottom line.

Divide materials into groups A, B, and C, depending on the dollar impact they have on the company (not their actual price). You can then stock more of the vital A items while keeping the B and C items at more manageable levels. This is known as the ABC approach.

Oftentimes, as much as 80 percent of a company's revenues come from only 20 percent of the products. Companies that respect this "80-20 rule" concentrate their efforts on that key 20 percent of items. Most experts agree that it's a mistake to manage all products in the same manner.

Once you understand which items are most important, you'll be able to balance needs with costs, carrying only as much as you need of a given item. It's also a good idea to lower your inventory holding levels, keeping smaller quantities of an item in inventory for a short time rather than keeping large amounts for a long time. Consider ordering fewer items but doing so more often.

Tracking Inventory

A good inventory tracking system will tell you what merchandise is in stock, what is on order, when it will arrive, and what you've sold. With such a system, you can plan purchases intelligently and quickly recognize the fast-moving items you need to reorder and the slow-moving items you should mark down or specially promote.

You can create your own inventory tracking system or ask your accountant to set one up for you. Systems vary according to the amount of inventory displayed, the amount of backup stock required, the diversity of merchandise, and the number of items that are routinely reordered compared to new items or one-time purchases.

Some retailers track inventory using a manual tag system, which can be updated daily, weekly, or even monthly. In a manual tag system, you remove price tags from the product at the point of purchase. You then cross-check the tags against physical inventory to figure out what you have sold.

For example, a shoe-store retailer could use the tag system to produce a monthly chart showing sales according to product line, brand name,

>> Just One Look

Radio frequency identification—or RFID—is largely the domain of big companies because of its cost, but small businesses should still keep an eye on this growing tech trend. Patrick J. Sweeney II, author of *RFID for Dummies* and former president and CEO of RFID solutions firm ODIN Technologies, describes the technology as "bar codes on steroids."

Small tags affixed to individual products or to pallets of merchandise absorb and reflect radio waves that can be read by an RFID scanner, revealing such helpful facts as when and where the product was manufactured, when it was shipped, price, and other information. According to Sweeney, the applications for small businesses include asset and inventory tracking and management, loss prevention, and even automated checkout.

"Rather than scanning one product at a time, you can scan a whole cartload without any human intervention," says Sweeney. "Customers could simply walk [their carts] past an RFID scanner, and their total is read with a properly designed system."

The price of RFID technology has fallen recently, from $50,000 for an entry-level solution to around $8,000 to $10,000, and Sweeney anticipates that the prices will drop further. Large retailers like Target and Walmart, and even government agencies like the Department of Defense, require RFID-tagged merchandise from their suppliers, so it's definitely technology worth considering.

and style. At the top of the chart, he would list the various product lines (pumps, sneakers, loafers), and down the left margin, the various brand names and different styles. At the intersecting spaces down the column, he would mark how many of each brand were sold, in what style and color, whether the shoes were on sale or discounted, and any other relevant information.

Dollar-control systems show the cost and gross profit margin on individual inventory items. A basic method of dollar control begins at the cash register, with sales receipts listing the product, quantity sold, and price. You can compare sales receipts with delivery receipts to determine your gross profit margin on a given item. You can also use software programs to track inventory by type, cost, volume, and profit. A few programs to investigate include inFlow (inflowinventory.com), AdvancePro (advanceware.net), and Inventory Traker for Manufacturing/Distribution (trakersystems.com). (For more on computerized inventory tracking, see the section on "Computerized Inventory Control" below).

Unit-control systems use methods ranging from eyeballing shelves to using sophisticated bin tickets—tiny cards kept with each type of product that list a stock number, a description, maximum and minimum quantities stocked, cost (in code), selling price, and any other information you want to include. Bin tickets correspond to office file cards that list a stock number, selling price, cost, number of items to a case, supply source and alternative source, order dates, quantities, and delivery time.

Retailers make physical inventory checks daily, weekly, or as often as is practical—once a year at the minimum. Sometimes an owner will assign each employee responsibility for keeping track of a group of items or, if the store is large enough, hire stock personnel to organize and count stock.

Computerized Inventory Control

While manual methods may have their place, most entrepreneurs these days find that computerizing gives them a far wider range of information with far less effort. Inventory software programs now on the market let you track usage, monitor changes in unit dollar costs, calculate when you need to reorder, and analyze inventory levels on an item-by-item basis. You can even expand your earlier ABC analysis to include the profit margin per item.

In fact, many experts say that current computer programs are changing the rules of ABC analysis. By speeding up the process of inventory control, computers allow you to devote more time to your A products to further increase your profitability. You can even control inventory right at the cash register with point-of-sale (POS) software systems. POS software records each sale when it happens, so your inventory records are always up-to-date. Better still, you get much more information about the sale than you could gather with a manual system. By running reports based on this information, you can make better decisions about ordering and merchandising.

aha!

APICS can provide expert advice on inventory management and suggest software programs to use; you can contact the company at (800) 444-2742 or apics.org. In addition, many computer and software vendors sponsor free seminars to introduce new lines of inventory control products to prospective buyers.

With a POS system:

- You can analyze sales data, figure out how well all the items on your shelves sell, and adjust purchasing levels accordingly.
- You can maintain a sales history to help adjust your buying decisions for seasonal purchasing trends.
- You can improve pricing accuracy by integrating bar-code scanners and credit card authorization ability with the POS system.

There are plenty of popular POS software systems that enable you to use add-on devices at your checkout stations, including electronic cash drawers, bar-code scanners, credit card readers, and receipt or invoice printers. POS packages frequently come with integrated accounting modules, including general ledger, accounts receivable, accounts payable, purchasing, and inventory control systems. In essence, a POS system is an all-in-one way to keep track of your business's cash flow.

Features to consider in a POS system include the following:

- *Ease of use.* Look for software with a user-friendly graphical interface.
- *Entry of sales information.* Most systems allow you to enter inventory codes either manually or automatically via a bar-code scanner.

Once the inventory code is entered, the systems call up the standard or sales price, compute the price at multiple quantities, and provide a running total. Many systems make it easy to enter sales manually when needed by letting you search for inventory codes based on a partial merchandise number, description, manufacturing code or vendor.

> *"The definition of salesmanship is the gentle art of letting the customer have it your way."*
>
> —Ray Kroc, founder of McDonald's Corporation

- *Pricing*. POS systems generally offer a variety of ways to keep track of pricing, including add-on amounts, percentage of cost, margin percentage, and custom formulas. For example, if you provide volume discounts, you can set up multiple prices for each item.
- *Updating product information*. Once a sale is entered, these systems automatically update inventory and accounts receivable records.
- *Sales tracking options*. Different businesses get paid in different ways. For example, repair or service shops often keep invoices open until the work is completed, so they need a system that allows them to put sales on hold. If you sell expensive goods and allow installment purchases, you might appreciate a loan calculator that tabulates monthly payments. And if you offer rent-to-own items, you'll want a system that can handle rentals as well as sales.
- *Security*. In retail, it's important to keep tight control over cash receipts to prevent theft. Most of these systems provide audit trails so you can trace any problems.
- *Taxes*. Many POS systems can support numerous tax rates—useful if you run a mail order or online business and need to deal with taxes for more than one state.

Perhaps the most valuable way POS systems help you gain better control of your business is through their reporting features. You can slice and dice sales data in a variety of ways to determine what products are selling best at what time and to figure out everything from the optimal ways to arrange shelves and displays to what promotions are working best and when to change seasonal promotions.

> **tip** 
>
> As your business expands and becomes more complex, you'll need more complex inventory techniques to keep up. Tap outside sources to beef up your own and your employees' inventory management expertise. Inexpensive seminars held by banks, consultants, and management associations offer a quick but thorough introduction to inventory management techniques.

Reporting capabilities available in POS programs include sales, costs, and profits by individual inventory items, by salesperson, or by category for the day, month, and year to date. Special reports can include sales for each hour of the day for any time period. You can also create multiple formats for invoices, accounting statements, and price tags. Additional reports include day-end cash reconciliation worksheets and inventory management. Examine a variety of POS packages to see which comes closest to meeting your needs.

Every business is unique; you may find that none of the off-the-shelf systems meets your requirements. Industry-specific POS packages are available—for auto repair shops, beauty and nail salons, video rental stores, dry cleaners, and more. In addition, some POS system manufacturers will tailor their software to your needs.

Inventory Turnover

When you have replaced 100 percent of your original inventory, you have "turned over" your inventory. If you have, on the average, a 12-week supply of inventory and turn it over four times a year, the count cycle plus the order cycle plus the delivery cycle add up to your needs period. Expressed as an equation, it would read:

Count Cycle + Order Cycle + Delivery Cycle = Needs Period

For instance, suppose you decided to count inventory once every four weeks (the count cycle). Processing paperwork and placing orders with your vendors take two weeks (the order cycle). The order takes six weeks to get to you (delivery cycle). Therefore, you need 12 weeks' worth of inventory from the first day of the count cycle to stay in operation until your merchandise arrives.

You can improve your inventory turnover if you count inventory more often—every two weeks instead of every four—and work with your suppliers to improve delivery efficiency. Alternate ways of distributing goods to the store could cut the delivery cycle down to three weeks, which would cut inventory needs to six weeks. As a result, inventory turnover could increase from four times a year to eight times.

Another way to look at turnover is by measuring sales per square foot. Taking the average retail value of inventory and dividing it by the number of square feet devoted to a particular product will give you your average sales per square foot.

You should know how many sales per square foot per year you need to survive. Calculate your sales per square foot once a month to make sure they are in line with your expectations.

Inventory Accounting

If you spend a few minutes considering inventory, how you account for that inventory, and the taxes you must pay on it, you'll never again question the need for an accountant. However, it's important for every entrepreneur to have a basic understanding of inventory accounting, even if you rely on your accountant to do the actual numbers. There are two methods used for inventory valuation:

The last in, first out (LIFO) method assumes that you will sell the most recently purchased inventory first. For instance, suppose you bought ten ceiling fans a year ago at $30 each. A week ago, you purchased a second lot of ten ceiling fans, but now the price has gone up to $50 each. By using the LIFO method, you sell your customers the $50 ceiling fans first, which allows you to keep the less expensive units (in terms of your inventory cost) in inventory.

aha!

A letter of credit from a major customer can be used as a form of security in establishing relationships with suppliers. For instance, if you're starting a business manufacturing garden hoses, you could get a letter of credit from your biggest customer when the order is placed, showing that the customer has contracted to buy the finished hoses. The material to make the hoses is then purchased using the letter of credit as security . . . and you don't have to put up a penny.

>> The One and Only

For decades, conventional wisdom warned that depending on a sole supplier could sink your business. After all, such a situation could spell doom if there were any interruption in your supply of products.

However, there are some situations where relying on a sole supplier makes sense. For example, if you're a specialty clothing retailer and most of your sales come from a certain product line, you may find yourself with a sole supplier. In some cases, there is only one supplier who can deliver the raw materials you need to make a product. In other cases, a company strikes an agreement with a sole supplier in return for special pricing deals.

The key to making a sole supplier relationship work is to make sure all the right safeguards are in place. Protect yourself by asking suppliers about backup product sources. Find out how many manufacturing plants and distribution centers exist in their product pipeline. Ask what contingency plans they have to supply you in case of emergency. What are their obligations to you in the event of a shortage? Will their top one or two customers get all the products they need, while your business has to wait in line?

Keep up-to-date on alternative supply sources that could help your business survive temporary shutdowns from your sole supplier. Use your trade association directory and industry networking contacts to help expand your supplier pipeline. Above all, make sure you feel comfortable entering into a sole supplier relationship before you sign on the dotted line.

Then, when you have to calculate inventory value for tax purposes, LIFO allows you to value your remaining inventory (the $30 fans) at substantially less than the $50 fans, so you pay less in taxes.

First in, first out (FIFO) was the traditional method used by most businesses before inflation became common. Under FIFO, the goods you receive first are the goods you sell first. Under this method, you value inventory at its most recent price. FIFO is usually used during periods of relatively low inflation since high inflation and increasing replacement costs tend to skew inventory accounting figures.

LIFO establishes the value of your inventory based on the most recent quantity received, while FIFO establishes the value of your inventory based on the oldest item in it. You can use either dollar control or unit control with these methods. Match your system to your needs, based on your accountant's recommendations.

Buying Inventory

Your inventory control system will tell you when to buy replacement inventory, what to buy (and what not to buy), and how much to buy.

The open-to-buy is the amount budgeted for inventory purchases for a given period—usually one, three, or four months. Since you are a startup without past performance to guide you, you must calculate the open-to-buy by determining the gross sales you need to pay store overhead and cover your other costs.

Your business plan should give you an idea of the basic stock levels and monthly or seasonal sales volume you need to have during startup. After your business has been up and running for several months to a year, your inventory control system will provide this information.

e-fyi

Trade shows are a great place to show off your products to the public as well as potential suppliers. At the same time, you can check out the competition. They're also a great resource for networking. To find a trade show in your area, visit the Trade Show News Network (tsnn.com), an online directory of more than 25,000 trade shows and conferences.

Figure out your open-to-buy using the following formula:

planned inventory	$25,000
plus planned sales	+$25,000
equals	$50,000
less actual inventory	–$27,000
less stock on order	–$13,000
equals open-to-buy	$10,000

Most seasonal retailers calculate their open-to-buy seasonally to accommodate variations in the type of merchandise they sell and seasonal sales fluctuations. Instead of figuring open-to-buy in dollars, some retailers approach trade shows and other merchandise sources with a list of what they need to fill out their inventories and meet sales projections. But whether they work with dollars or by unit, experienced retailers recommend that the owner of a seasonal business should feel free to go beyond the budget or use less than the entire open-to-buy amount. In fact, you should leave room for unanticipated items.

Suppliers

Suppliers are essential to any retail business. Depending on your inventory selection, you may need a few or dozens of suppliers. Sometimes suppliers will contact you through their sales representatives, but more often, particularly when you are starting out, you will need to locate them yourself—either at trade shows, wholesale showrooms and conventions, or through buyers' directories, industry contacts, the business-to-business Yellow Pages and trade journals, or websites. Suppliers can be divided into four general categories.

1. *Manufacturers.* Most retailers will buy through independent representatives or company salespeople who handle the wares of different companies. Prices from these sources are usually lowest, unless the retailer's location makes shipping freight expensive.
2. *Distributors.* Also known as wholesalers, brokers or jobbers, distributors buy in quantity from several manufacturers and warehouse the goods for sale to retailers. Although their prices are higher than a manufacturer's, they can supply retailers with small orders from a variety of manufacturers. (Some manufacturers refuse to fill small orders.) A lower freight bill and quick delivery time from a nearby distributor often compensate for the higher per-item cost.
3. *Independent craftspeople.* Exclusive distribution of unique creations is frequently offered by independent craftspeople, who sell through reps or at trade shows.
4. *Import sources.* Many retailers buy foreign goods from a domestic importer, who operates much like a domestic wholesaler. Or, depending on your familiarity with overseas sources, you may want to travel abroad to buy goods.

Dealing with Suppliers

Reliability is the key factor to look for in suppliers. Good suppliers will steer you toward hot-selling items, increasing your sales. If you build a good relationship and your business is profitable for them, suppliers may be willing to bail you out when your customers make difficult demands. Remember, though, that suppliers are in business to make money. If you go to the mat with them on every bill, ask them to shave prices on everything they sell to you, or fail to pay your bills promptly, don't be surprised when they stop calling.

e-fyi

Before you go to a trade show in search of inventory suppliers, do your homework. Trade Show Signage Solutions (event-trade-show-signs provides a wealth of information, sign design tips, and checklists to help you prepare.

As a new business owner, you can't expect to receive the same kind of attention a long-standing customer gets right off the bat. Over time, however, you can develop excellent working relationships that will be profitable for both you and your suppliers. Once you have compiled a list of possible suppliers, ask for quotes or proposals, complete with prices, available discounts, delivery terms, and other important factors. Do not just consider the terms; investigate the potential of your supplier's financial condition, too. And ask them for customer references; call these customers and find out how well the supplier has performed. If there have been any problems, ask for details about how they were reconciled. Every relationship hits bumps now and then; the key is to know how the rough spots were handled. Was the supplier prompt and helpful in resolving the problem, or defensive and uncooperative?

Be open, courteous, and firm with your suppliers, and they will respond in kind. Tell them what you need and when you need it. Have a specific understanding about the total cost, and expect delivery on schedule. Keep in constant communication with your suppliers about possible delays, potential substitutions for materials or product lines, production quality, product improvements or new product introductions, and potential savings.

Suppliers often establish a minimum order for merchandise, and this minimum may be higher for first orders. Some suppliers also demand a minimum number of items per order.

Payment Plans

While most service providers bill you automatically without requiring credit references, equipment and merchandise suppliers are more cautious. Since you are just getting started, you will not be able to give them trade references, and your bank probably will not give you a credit rating if your account has just opened.

tip

While it is almost impossible to get exclusive rights to a manufacturer's goods, you can ask that a sales representative not sell identical merchandise to another store in the immediate area. However, you may be expected to buy large amounts of the product to make up for lost sales to other stores.

If your supplier is small, the manner in which you present yourself is important in establishing credit. You may find the going tougher when dealing with a large supplier. A personal visit will accelerate your acceptance.

Present your financial statements and a description of your prospects for success in your new business. Don't even think of inflating your financial statements to cover a lack of references. This is illegal and is easily detected by most credit managers.

Some suppliers will put you on a c.o.d. basis for a few months, knowing that if you are underfinanced, you will soon have problems with this payment method. Once you pass that test, they will issue you a line of credit. This creates a valid credit reference you can present to new suppliers until credit agencies accumulate enough data on your business to approve you for suppliers. Most suppliers operate on a trade credit basis when dealing with other businesses. This basically means that when you're billed for a product or service, you have a certain grace period before the payment is due (typically 30 days). During this time, the supplier will not charge interest.

Carefully consider all costs, discounts, and allowances before deciding whether to buy an item. Always take into account what the final shelf cost of any item will be. The most common discounts are given for prompt payment; many suppliers also give discounts for payment in cash. When you can, make sure you specify on all orders how the goods are to be shipped so they will be sent in the least expensive way.

Occasionally, suppliers grant customers discounts for buying in quantity, usually as a freight allowance for a specific amount of merchandise purchased. Some suppliers pay an increasing percentage of the freight bill as the retailer's orders increase; others simply cover the entire freight cost for purchases over a minimum amount.

e-fyi

One good source for finding suppliers is ThomasNet.com. This comprehensive online directory lists manufacturers by categories and geographic area.

If you order merchandise from distant suppliers, freight charges can equal more than 10 percent of your merchandise cost. Ask what a manufacturer's or supplier's freight policy is before ordering, and make sure the order is large enough to warrant the delivery charges. If the manufacturer does not pay freight on back orders, you might consider canceling a back order and adding it to the next regular shipment.

Become familiar with each of your suppliers' order-filling priorities. Some suppliers fill orders on a first-in, first-out basis; others give priority to the larger orders while customers with smaller orders wait. Consequently, most retailers specify a cancellation date on their orders. In other words, any goods shipped after that date will be returned to the suppliers. By specifying a cutoff date, you increase the chances that your orders will be shipped promptly and arrive in time.

Give careful attention to shipments when they arrive. Make sure you've received the correct amount and type of merchandise, and make sure the quality matches the samples you were shown.

CHAPTER

20

It's in the Mail

Setting Up Mailing Systems

Mail is one of the lifelines of your business, and, depending on your industry, it can also be one of your biggest costs. That's why it's so important to figure out the most efficient, convenient, and economical ways to send mail. This chapter covers everything you need to know about mailing—from postage metering and sorting to letter-opening machines.

e-fyi

The Click2Mail service offers a convenient way to create and send hard-copy mailings right from your PC. Simply place your order online at click2mail.com and have postcards, direct mail, fliers, or greeting cards delivered directly to your customers' doors.

Mailing Equipment

There are many mailing machines that you can buy on the market that can help you save valuable time—so you can spend it on more important things, like growing your business.

Postage Meters

Having your own postage meter saves a small business time and money. No more licking and sticking envelopes and stamps. With today's electronic mailing machines, you don't even have to stand in line at the post office to get your meter reset.

>> Change of Address

The Postal Service also offers online shipping setup, pre-printed labels you can simply print off your home printer, and free, pre-arranged pickups of packages and mail. The USPS can also help set up direct-mail campaigns through its small-business services. Visit https://www.usps.com/business/business-solutions.htm for more information.

At the USPS website (usps.com), you'll find dozens of time- and money-saving services, including the popular Shipping Assistant software that can be downloaded to your computer. This easy-to-use desktop application puts all the USPS online tools at your fingertips so you can quickly access shipping information, including rate calculations and delivery information.

There's also a "rate calculator" that helps you find the most cost-effective method of mailing letters and packages. Just enter the article's weight plus ZIP codes of the origin and destination, and up pops the price for shipping it by various methods.

Want shipping supplies sent to your door? Click on "Business Center," then "Order Supplies" to order Express or Priority Mail envelopes, labels, boxes, and tags after registering your business information. Print online postage by going to USPS Click-n-Ship, or use another authorized provider, such as Stamps.com or Endicia.com.

Electronic postage meters consist of a base machine through which envelopes are guided for stamping, which can be rented, leased, or bought from a mailing equipment manufacturer. The machine also has a meter, which must be leased from a U.S. Postal Service-approved mailing equipment manufacturer such as Pitney Bowes; federal regulations prohibit the ownership of the actual meter, as that is strictly controlled by the U.S. Postal Service. The faster and more automated the machine, and the more features it incorporates, the more it costs to rent, lease, or own.

Even the smallest office can benefit from a meter to determine exact postage and print out a stamp, and a scale to weigh mail. The U.S. Postal Service estimates accurate weighing can save customers up to 20 percent on mailings.

An efficient, automated mailing machine can also save hours of time if you handle direct mail or large mailings. Mail that's presorted

>> The Postage Meter Goes Online

The venerable postage meter has also gone virtual. Pitney Bowes, facing growing competition from virtual mail solutions from Stamps.com, Endicia, eBay, and even the U.S. Postal Service, beefed up its own internet-based shipping service beginning in 2011.

The company has an online mailing tool called pbSmartPostage (www.pb.com/pbsmartpostage/shipping/), with accounts starting at $15 per month. Postage and supplies are extra. The tool seeks to integrate postage, package routing, shipping management, and reporting into a web app that can be accessed from any PC with a printer.

PbSmartPostage is a web-based mailing and shipping application that puts a virtual postal service location on your desktop computer. The interface runs from a web browser and lets users fill out online forms to track company shipping, create labels, print stamps, manage a sophisticated address book, and generate shipping reports. A scale is not required, but experts recommend it. You can try it for your business and see if the option works alone, or if you still need a combination of mailing options.

and barcoded bypasses many of the post office handling steps and is delivered 24 hours sooner than mail lacking automated preparation, according to the USPS. That's key these days when big online companies can offer free or cheap overnight shipping and some services even deliver same-day.

The latest mailing systems are multifunctional, handling everything from printing, folding, stapling, inserting, sealing, labeling, weighing, and stamping to sorting, stacking, and putting on a wrapper or binder. Many interact with a computer so you can track exactly how, when, and to whom orders are sent out and are able to handle different-sized paper—checks, invoices, brochures—without stopping the machine to reset the equipment.

Postal Scales

Besides postage meters, the second crucial piece of mailing equipment most businesses need is a postal scale. Scales are sold in 5-, 10-, 30-, 100-, 200-, and 250-pound capacities and can be purchased as stand-alone units or combined with a postage meter. A postal scale ensures that you're not paying more than you need to for your outgoing mail. What to look for when buying? Both electronic and manual versions are available. Because manual scales require you to read the postage amount, they increase the chance of human error. Electronic scales are more expensive, but their digital readouts reduce errors and ensure you get the most value from your scale.

aha!

Presorting bulk mail saves money but takes time. Speed up the process by using mail consolidation companies—firms that presort mail and deliver it to bulk-mail centers around the country. To find such companies, look in the Yellow Pages or Google "Mailing Services."

If you need your scale to interface with a postage meter, you'll want to be sure the model you choose is compatible with your metering equipment.

Questions to ask the dealer:

- What adjustments will need to be made to the scale if postage rates change? What charges are involved?

- Does the scale offer alternative pricing options based on various postal classifications?
- Does the scale have a password feature to help guard against unauthorized use?
- What are its size and weight limitations?

>> Pushing the Envelope

Looking for ways to prune postal bloat? The Direct Marketing Association offers this checklist of cost-cutting ideas:

1. Fine-tune your mailing list.
    - > Stop mailing to duplicate names.
    - > Eliminate nonresponders and marginal prospects. There are many mailing list software programs that can help you keep your mailing lists current.
2. Be sure you're using accurate addresses.
    - > Check for correct ZIP codes, especially when using addresses supplied by customers.
    - > Watch for mail shipped to wrong suite or apartment numbers.
    - > Check for missing directionals, such as "N." for "North."
3. Take advantage of postal discounts and services.
    - > Use the USPS' National Change of Address list to keep your mailing list current.
    - > Print "Address Correction Requested" on the face of your mail. The Postal Service will tell you if the recipient files a change of address.
    - > Investigate commingling your mail with that of other small mailers to take advantage of discounts available to large mailers. Contact your local mailing service for more information.
    - > Print your bar-coded ZIP+4 on business reply mail. The Postal Service charges much less for cards using the nine-digit ZIPs.
    - > Stockpile mail to build up larger volumes.

- How should the machine be maintained?
- What type of maintenance agreement is offered?
- Does the scale offer rates for foreign mailings?
- Does the scale offer rates for FedEx and UPS?

Letter-Folding Machines

When you are preparing for a promotional mailing, you may find yourself dealing with hundreds or thousands of letters or brochures. Folding letters yourself can be very time-consuming; it's also unnecessary, thanks to today's letter-folding machines.

> ***"In the realm of ideas, everything depends on enthusiasm . . . in the real world all rests on perseverance."***
>
> —Johann Wolfgang Von Goethe, author

When buying a letter-folding machine, consider the volume the machine is capable of processing. Low-end equipment processes a few hundred pieces per hour; high-end equipment is capable of operating at speeds from 1,500 to 18,000 sheets per hour. Also, consider the types of fold the equipment can provide. Some of the possibilities are c-fold (standard letter), z-fold (accordion fold), double fold, single fold, right-angle fold, and brochure fold.

Such machines can cost as little as a few hundred dollars to thousands of dollars.

Letter-Opening Machines

Letter-opening machines can greatly speed up the opening of mail. Some can process up to 600 envelopes per minute.

What to look for when buying? There are two types of letter openers: chadders and slitters. Chadders open envelopes by cutting one-eighth of an inch from the end. Slitters, while quite a bit more expensive than chadders, cut through the top seam of the envelope and reduce the risk of damaging the contents.

Most models can handle standard #10 envelopes. More expensive models will accommodate different sizes and thicknesses of incoming mail. An automated feeder will send your mail through the machine;

joggers will help settle the contents of the envelope so they don't get cut; counters let you count the number of pieces being processed.

Another feature you may find helpful is an automatic date-and-time stamp to help you keep track of when mail arrives. Because letter openers are usually quite reliable, maintenance contracts are usually not required.

Questions to ask the dealer:

- Does the opener use a chadder or a slitter?
- What sizes of envelopes can the machine handle?
- Does it have an automatic feeder? A jogger? A counter?
- Can incoming mail be time- and date-stamped?

Mail Labelers

Mail labelers quickly affix mailing labels with the use of a hand-held dispenser, desktop model, or heavy-duty floor model, depending on the need for speed and the use of other attachments, such as a tabber, folder, or inserter. They can attach labels to many different types of mail pieces, including postcards, envelopes, catalogs, brochures, sales fliers, and other marketing pieces. Additional features may include the option to use folded label sheets (approximately 30 labels per page) or continuous-feed single label rolls, counters, and different label sizes. If attaching labels using a hand dispenser, the speed will depend on the individual using the device; however, automated labelers can stick on as many as 15,000 labels an hour.

Lease or Buy?

Most of the mailing equipment in this chapter can be rented, leased, or purchased outright. You may prefer to lease to conserve working capital, then upgrade equipment as your business grows. Renting is the easiest method, because if you need to cut costs at any time, you simply hand the equipment back and walk away. If you are leasing, you are obligated to make all the payments specified in the lease. However, leasing offers advantages, including lower rates than renting and the ability to roll the lease over for upgraded equipment.

If a mailing equipment salesperson sells you on leased equipment that ends up being too sophisticated for your needs, some suppliers will purchase the competitor's lease and give you their own equipment. When shopping around for equipment, ask if there are any special promotions available before you sign.

Basic machines lease from about $25 to $45 per month, more sophisticated machines for $60 and up. Anything more expensive than that is usually best suited to large corporations. The average lease is for three to five years and can include maintenance and free postage refills; the average rental agreement is for one year.

Carefully read the contracts you are offered, and, if renting, make sure there is no mention of the word "lease." Also, always ask what options you have if you need to get out of a lease.

e-fyi

Not sure where to start when you need to send a package or overnight letter? iShip.com will provide you with quick and easy shipping solutions without ever picking up the phone. You can compare rates, print labels, order supplies, monitor tracking logs, edit address books, and manage reports conveniently—all from your computer.

Make sure the company is postal-certified with the USPS.

When shopping for mailing equipment, allow the salespeople enough time to make their pitch. The right mailing equipment can save you money, but only if you give the salesperson enough time to analyze your needs.

CHAPTER

21

Charging Ahead

Offering Your Customers Credit

Getting paid for your products or services is what business is all about. These days, there are more options than ever for accepting payment. Whether you are in a B2B or consumer-oriented industry, your choices can include extending credit, taking checks, and accepting credit or debit cards. And there are countless ways to accept payments that don't involve a card—or a cash register. From automatic bank transfers made easy to online services such as PayPal or devices such as Square and other smartphone-based card-payment options, there are many choices.

With so many options, it's easy for a new business owner to get caught up in the excitement of making sales and to forget the necessity of a well-thought-out credit policy. Deciding what forms of payment you will accept, how you will handle them, and what collection methods you'll use to ensure debts are paid is essential to any small business' success.

Establishing a Credit Policy

Credit can make or break a small business. A too-lenient credit policy can set the stage for collection and cash-flow problems later, while a creatively and carefully designed policy can attract customers and boost your business's cash flow.

Many small businesses are reluctant to establish a firm credit policy for fear of losing their customers. What they do not realize is that a consistent credit policy not only strengthens your company, but also creates a more professional image in your customers' eyes.

A well-thought-out credit policy accomplishes four things:

1. Avoids both bad debts and hard feelings
2. Standardizes credit procedures, providing employees with clear and consistent directions
3. Demonstrates to employees and customers that the company is serious about managing credit
4. Helps the business owner define how credit fits into the overall sales and marketing plan

warning

Even the best customers can suddenly become deadbeats. Watch for these warning signs that a customer may be in financial trouble:

- Changes in personnel, especially buyers or management
- Changes in buying patterns, such as purchasing much larger amounts than usual or buying significant amounts off-season
- Failure to return calls with the usual promptness

To establish a smart credit policy, start by investigating the way your competition handles credit. Your goal is to make it easy to buy your products. If your competition offers better terms, they have an advantage. You must meet your competitors' credit terms to attract customers.

At the same time, be cautious not to go too far with your credit policy. Novice entrepreneurs are often tempted to offer lower prices and longer payment terms to take business away from competitors. Credit is a double-edged sword. You want to attract customers with your credit policy, but you do not want to attract customers who are not credit-worthy. Be aware that some troubled companies routinely switch from supplier to supplier whenever they reach their credit limit with one. Others are outright con artists that take advantage of new and naive entrepreneurs.

How to protect yourself? One good way to start is to write a short, simple statement that sums up the intent and spirit of your company's credit policy. For example, a liberal policy might read: "Our credit policy is to make every reasonable effort to extend credit to all customers recommended by sales management, provided a suitable credit basis can be developed."

A conservative policy might say: "Our company has a strict credit policy, and credit lines will be extended only to the most credit-worthy accounts. New customers who fail to meet our credit criteria will need to purchase using cash-on-delivery terms until they establish their ability and willingness to pay on our terms."

Base your policy selection—conservative or liberal—on your industry, the size and experience of your staff, the dollar amount of your transactions, your profit margins, and your tolerance for risk. Also consider the industry to which you're selling. If your customers are in "soft" industries such as construction or computers, for example, you would do well to use a conservative policy.

If you adopt a liberal credit policy for your business, make sure you are prepared to handle the collection calls. Liberal policies will require you to be aggressive when customers do not pay on time.

Give 'Em Credit

The simplest customer credit policy has two basic points: 1) limiting credit risk and 2) diligently investigating each company's credit-worthiness.

No matter how credit-worthy a customer is, never extend credit beyond your profit

tip

When dealing with a new client, it's a good idea to protect yourself by asking for part of your payment upfront. This is an especially good policy if the client is a new or fledgling business.

margin. This policy ensures that if you aren't paid, at least your expenses will be paid. For example, if you mark up your product or service 100 percent, you can then safely risk that amount without jeopardizing your company's cash flow. To gauge a company's credit-worthiness, draft a comprehensive credit application that contains the following:

- Name of business, address, phone, and fax number
- Names, addresses, and Social Security numbers of principals
- Type of business (corporation, partnership, sole proprietorship)
- Industry
- Number of employees
- Bank references
- Trade payment references
- Business/personal bankruptcy history
- Any other names under which the company does business
- A personal guarantee that the business owners promise to pay you if their corporation is unable to

Your credit application should also specify what your credit terms are and the consequences of failing to meet them. Indicate what late fees you'll charge, if any; that the customer is responsible for any attorney's fees or collection costs incurred at any time, either during or prior to a lawsuit; and the venue where such a suit would be filed. Have your credit application form reviewed by an attorney specializing in creditors' rights to make sure it is in line with your state's regulations.

Once a potential customer has completed the application, how do you investigate the information? One way to verify the facts and assess the company's credit history is to call credit-reporting agencies. Some companies' payment histories will also be available through D&B. Because credit agencies' reporting can be

tip

Try this proactive approach to prompt a customer to pay faster: About ten days before payment is due, call to ask if the customer received the bill. Make sure they are satisfied with the product; then politely ask, "Do you anticipate any problems paying your bill on time?"

unreliable, however, it's also a good idea to call others in the industry and try to determine the company's payment record and reputation. Most industries have associations that trade credit information.

Also ask customers how much credit they think they will need. This will help you estimate the volume of credit and the potential risk to your business. Finally, simply use your intuition. If someone doesn't look you straight in the eye, chances are they won't let you see what's in their wallet, either.

Payment Due

Once you've set your credit policy, it's important to stick to it and do your part to ensure prompt payment. The cornerstone of collecting accounts receivable on time is making sure invoices go out promptly and accurately. If you sell a product, get the invoice out to the customer at the same time the shipment goes out. If you're in a service industry, track your billable hours daily or weekly, and bill as often as your contract or agreement with the client permits. The sooner the invoice is in the mail, the sooner you get paid.

To eliminate any possibility of confusion, your invoice should contain several key pieces of information. First, make sure you date it accurately and clearly state when payment is due, as well as any penalties for late payment. Also specify any discounts, such as discounts for payment in 15 days or for payment in cash.

Each invoice should give a clear and accurate description of the goods or services the customer received. Inventory code numbers may make sense to your computer system, but they don't mean much to the customer unless they are accompanied by an item description.

It's also important to use sequentially numbered invoices. This helps make things easier when you need to discuss a particular invoice with a customer and also makes it easier for your employees to keep track of invoices.

> *"The thing women have got to learn is that nobody gives you power. You just take it."*
>
> —Roseanne Barr

>> Collect Call

Having trouble collecting on a bill? Your Better Business Bureau (BBB) may be able to help. Many BBBs now assist with B2B disputes regarding payment as part of their dispute resolution service. BBBs do not operate as collection agencies, and there is no charge beyond standard membership dues.

When the BBB gets involved, there can be three possible outcomes. First, the account may be paid; second, the BBB can serve as a forum for arbitration; third, if the company refuses to pay or arbitrate, the complaint is logged in the BBB's files for three years.

Most businesses find a call from the BBB a powerful motivator to pay up. If the debtor belongs to the BBB and refuses to pay, its membership could be revoked.

To find out if the BBB in your area offers this service, visit bbb.org.

Before sending out an invoice, call the customer to ensure the price is correct, and check to make sure prices on invoices match those on purchase orders and/or contracts.

Know the industry norms when setting your payment schedules. While 30 days is the norm in most industries, in others, 45- or 60-day payment cycles are typical. Learn your customers' payment practices, too. If they pay only once a month, for instance, make sure your invoice gets to them in plenty of time to hit that payment cycle. Also keep on top of industry trends and economic ups and downs that could affect customers' ability to pay.

Promptness is key not only in sending out invoices, but also in following up. If payment is due in 30 days, don't wait until the 60th day to call the customer. By the same token, however, don't be overeager and call on the 31st day. Being too demanding can annoy customers, and this could result in you losing a valuable client. Knowledge of industry norms plus your customers' payment cycles will guide you in striking a middle ground.

Constant communication trains customers to pay bills promptly and leads to an efficient, professional relationship between you and them.

Usually, a polite telephone call to ask about a late payment will get the ball rolling, or at least tell you when you can expect payment. If any problems exist that need to be resolved before payment can be issued, your phone call will let you know what they are so you can start clearing them up. It could be something as simple as a missing packing slip or as major as a damaged shipment.

> **tip** 
> To make sure you get paid for any work performed, it's a perfectly reasonable practice for a business that has out-of-pocket expenses to ask that the client make a deposit at least large enough to cover these expenses.

The first 15 to 20 seconds of the call are crucial. Make sure to project good body language over the phone. Be professional and firm, not wimpy. Use a pleasant voice that conveys authority, and respect the other person's dignity. Remember the old saying "You catch more flies with honey than with vinegar"? It's true.

What if payment still is not made after an initial phone call? Don't let things slide. Statistics show that the longer a debt goes unpaid, the more difficult it will be to collect and the greater chance that it will remain unpaid forever. Most experts recommend making additional phone calls rather than sending a series of past-due notices or collection letters. Letters are easier to ignore, while phone calls tend to get better results.

If several phone calls fail to generate any response, a personal visit may be in order. Try to set up an appointment in advance. If this isn't possible, leave a message stating what date and time you will visit. Make sure to bring all the proper documentation with you so you can prove exactly what is owed. At this point, you are unlikely to get full payment, so see if you can get the customer to commit to a payment plan. Make sure, however, that you put it in writing.

If the customer refuses to meet with you to discuss the issue or won't commit to a payment plan, you may be facing a bad debt situation and need to take further action. There are two options: using the services of an attorney or employing a collection agency. Your lawyer can advise you on what is best to do.

If you decide to go with a collection agency, ask friends or business owners for referrals, or look in the Yellow Pages or online to find collectors who handle your type of claim. To make sure the agencies are reputable, contact the Better Business Bureau or the securities division of your secretary of state's office. Since all collection companies must be bonded with the state, this office should have them on file.

For more information on collection agencies, you can also contact the Association of Credit and Collection Professionals (acainternational.org). Most reputable collection firms are members of this international organization.

e-fyi

For more information on preventing bad checks, visit ckfraud.org. The National Check Fraud Center offers tips for detecting counterfeit checks as well as a rundown of bad check laws for each state.

Many collection agencies take their fee as a cut of the collected money, so there is no upfront cost to you. Shop around to find an agency with a reasonable rate. Also compare the cost of using a collection agency to the cost of using your lawyer. You may be able to recover more of the money using one option or the other, depending on the total amount of the debt and the hourly rate or percentage the lawyer or agency charges.

Accepting Checks

Bounced checks can cut heavily into a small business's profits. Yet a business that doesn't accept personal checks can't expect to stay competitive. How can you keep bad checks out of your cash register? Here are some steps to establishing a check-acceptance policy that works.

- *Start with the basics.* Since laws regarding the information needed to cash checks vary greatly among states (and even within states), begin by contacting your local police department. They can familiarize you with the laws and regulations that govern checks in your state. Some police departments have seminars instructing businesses on how to set up proper check-cashing policies.

  While rules vary among states, there are some good general rules of thumb to follow. When accepting a check, always ask to see the customer's driver's license or similar identification card, preferably one that has a photograph. Check the customer's physical characteristics against his identification. If you have reason to question his identity, ask the customer to write his signature on a separate piece of paper. Many people who pass bad checks have numerous false identifications and may forget which one they are using. Ask for the customer's home and work telephone numbers so you can contact him in case the check bounces. Don't cash payroll checks, checks for more than the amount of purchase, or third-party checks.

- *Be observant.* Desktop-publishing software, laser printers, and scanners have made it easier for people to alter, forge, and duplicate checks. To avoid accepting a forged or counterfeit check, evaluate the document very carefully. Smudge marks on the check could indicate the check was rubbed with moist fingers when it was illegally made. Smooth edges on checks are another sign of a document that may be counterfeit; authentic checks are perforated either on the top or left side of the check. Smudged handwriting or signs that the handwriting has been erased are other warning signs that you might be dealing with an illegal check.
- *Be especially cautious with new checks.* A large majority of bad checks are written on new accounts. Many businesses will not accept checks that don't have a customer's name preprinted on them. If the check is written on a brand-new account (one with a check number, say, below 300), protect yourself by asking to see two forms of ID.
- *Establish a waiting period for refunds.* Merchants can easily be stiffed when a customer makes a purchase by check and returns the merchandise the next day for a cash refund. When the check bounces, the merchant is out the cash paid for the refund. To avoid this scenario, many entrepreneurs require a five-to-seven-business-day grace period to allow checks to clear the bank before cash refunds are paid.
- *Consider getting electronic help.* If you process a large volume of checks, you might benefit from the services of a check-verification company. By paying a monthly fee, which depends on your company's size and volume of checks, you can tap into a company's

database of individuals who write bad, stolen, or forged checks. This is done by passing a customer's check through an electronic "check reader" at your checkout stand. If the check matches a name in the company's database, the check is refused.

> ***"This is the nature of genius, to be able to grasp the knowable even when no one else recognizes that it is present."***
>
> —Deepak Chopra, self-help guru

Using a "check reader" from companies like TeleCheck, a check-verification and check-guarantee company, is quick and efficient. They can approve a check within seconds, which is generally as fast as, or faster than, a merchant getting acceptance for a credit card purchase.

Check-verification companies also offer a check-guarantee service. If a check is approved by a check-verification company and it later turns out to be a bad check, the merchant gets reimbursed for the value of the check. This guarantee service reduces the risk of accepting bad checks. Getting a handle on the bad checks that might pass through your business certainly has its benefits. For small merchants, one bad check can wipe out an entire day's profits.

Another option is an electronic check conversion/acceptance system, which allows merchants to accept checks as easily and safely as credit cards. Here's how it works: When a customer makes a payment with a check, the paper check is run through a check reader, converting it into an electronic item much like the credit card terminal does when swiping a card. Once the transaction is approved, funds are electronically debited from the customer's account and deposited into the merchant's account, usually within 24 to 48 hours. This same technology allows businesses to process checks over the phone or the internet.

Whatever check-acceptance policy you develop, make sure your employees clearly understand the procedure to follow. Also be sure to post your check-acceptance policy prominently where customers can see it. Specify any charges for bounced checks, what forms of ID are required, and what types of checks you will and will not accept. Posting signs helps prevent disgruntlement when customers wait in line, only to find at the register that you can't accept their check.

> **aha!**
> 
> Require employees to sign their initials on checks they accept. No one wants to have their initials on a check that might bounce, so employees will be extra careful about following your check acceptance policy.

What if you do receive a bad check? In most cases, after a check bounces, the bank allows you another attempt to deposit it. After that, the responsibility for collecting the money falls on you.

Contact the customer, either by phone or mail. (Again, consult your local police on the proper procedure; some states require that a registered letter be sent and a specific amount of time elapse before other action can be taken.) Keep your cool; there's nothing gained by being angry or hostile about the situation. Most people bounce checks by accident. Explain the situation, and request immediate payment plus reimbursement for any bank charges you have incurred.

If the person still refuses to pay, or you cannot reach them, you have several options. The first, and probably the easiest, is to hold the check for a short time (up to six months) from the date it was written. Although banks will not allow the check to be deposited a third time, they will cash the check if there are sufficient funds. Call the debtor's bank periodically to see if the funds are there. When they are, cash the check immediately.

Another option is going to the police. Since, through your check-acceptance procedure, you collected all the information needed to prosecute, you should be able to complete the proper paperwork. However, the hassle of hiring a lawyer, identifying suspects, and going to court may be more effort than you want to expend for a $200 check. In that case, your best bet is to use a collection agency. (For more details on this, see the "Payment Due" section starting on page 295).

Accepting Credit Cards

Why should a small-business owner accept credit cards? There are dozens of reasons. First and foremost, research shows that credit cards increase the probability, speed, and size of customer purchases. Many people prefer not to carry cash, especially when traveling. Others prefer to pay with credit cards because they know that it will be easier to return or exchange the merchandise.

Accepting credit cards has several advantages for business owners as well. It gives you the chance to increase sales by enabling customers to make impulse buys even when they do not have enough cash in their wallets or sufficient funds in their checking accounts. Accepting credit cards can improve your cash flow, because in most cases you receive the

>> A Private Affair

MasterCard, Visa, and American Express all have their place. But there's another option you may not have considered: issuing a private-label credit card with your company's name on it.

In addition to all the usual advantages of credit cards, a private-label credit card program allows businesses to focus on who their customers are. For example, your program can gather data about customer purchases, buying patterns, income, and demographics.

Small businesses can save money and eliminate hassles by using an outside administrator that specializes in private-label credit cards. A number of banks have entered this arena; ask your banker if he or she administers such programs. If not, the banker may be able to recommend a private-label credit card administration company.

Administration companies can do everything from setting up the operation to developing specialized marketing programs, designing the credit cards, training employees, and developing lists of potential customers. Fees vary depending on the number of services provided and the size of your customer base.

Before choosing an administration company, talk to other business owners who use private-label credit card programs to see if they're happy with the service and if the administration company does a good job handling customer applications, payments, and the like. Weigh the cost of any program against the benefits you expect to get from it.

money within a few days instead of waiting for a check to clear or an invoice to come due. Finally, credit cards provide a guarantee that you will be paid, without the risks involved in accepting personal checks. And, these days, even though more than 25 million U.S. small businesses don't accept them, credit cards are ubiquitous and you risk losing business if you do not accept them.

Merchant Status

To accept major credit cards from customers, your business must establish merchant status with each of the credit card companies whose cards you want to accept. You'll probably want to start by applying for merchant status with American Express or Discover. For these cards, all you need to do is contact American Express or Discover directly and fill out an application.

However, chances are you'll want to accept Visa and MasterCard, too, since these are used more frequently. You cannot apply directly to Visa or MasterCard; because they are simply bank associations, you have to establish a merchant account through one of several thousand banks that set up such accounts, called "acquiring banks."

The first thing you need to understand about accepting credit cards, explains Debra Rossi of Wells Fargo Bank, is that the bank views this as an extension of credit. "When we give you the ability to accept credit cards, we're giving you the use of the funds before we get them. By the time the money arrives in the cardholder's account, it could be another 30 days," Rossi says. There's also the real concern that if your company goes out of business before merchandise is shipped to customers, the bank will have to absorb losses.

warning

To prevent credit card fraud, follow these steps every time a credit purchase is made:

- Check the signature on the charge slip against the one on the back of the card. This may seem basic, but you'd be surprised at how often it is neglected.
- Verify the card's expiration date.
- Check frequently the credit card companies' updated bulletins listing canceled card numbers. There are automated services for this, too.

While the requirements vary among banks, in general a business does not have to be a minimum size in terms of sales. However, some banks do have minimum requirements for how long you've been in business. This doesn't mean a startup can't get merchant status; it simply means you may have to look a little harder to find a bank that will work with you.

While being considered a "risky business"—typically a startup, mail order, or homebased business—is one reason a bank may deny your merchant status request, the most common reason for denial is simply poor credit. Approaching a bank for a merchant account is like applying for a loan. You must be prepared with a solid presentation that will persuade the bank to open an account for you.

You will need to provide bank and trade references, and estimate what kind of credit card volume you expect to have and what you

>> Skip the Bank and Go Mobile

American consumers conduct 20 billion credit card transactions each year, totaling $1.9 trillion in annual spending, according to Juniper Research—numbers too eye-popping for any merchant to ignore. Yet while shoppers love the convenience of plastic, credit cards are anything but convenient for small businesses. Transaction fees can amount to hundreds or even thousands of dollars each month, dramatically reducing profit margins in the process.

Actually, traditional card processing isn't an ideal option for many types of businesses—food trucks, for example—which translates into any number of missed sales opportunities.

That's why more than 100,000 merchants nationwide sign up with Square each month.

Chances are, you've already encountered mobile payments (and experienced the rush of writing a signature with your finger) in the form of dongle-based technology, recognizable by a card reader that attaches to a mobile device via its audio jack. Such systems are fast becoming a familiar sight, even at some large retailers.

>> Skip the Bank and Go Mobile, continued

The commanding leader in the field is Square, which kicked off the trend in May 2010. Square card readers can be used on smartphones and iPads to swipe credit cards securely, without being given merchant status by a bank. There's a flat 2.75 percent transaction fee for all swiped Square transactions, with a 3.5 percent fee (plus a 15-cent surcharge) when transactions are keyed in manually. There are no additional activation costs, recurring charges, early termination penalties, or hidden fees. That is generally less than bank charges and you can accept any card (no higher fees for, say, accepting American Express).

While Square dominates, there are other card reader device firms, including PayPal and Intuit. Other firms have different pricing—some may charge a monthly fee and slightly lower percentages per charge. As of 2014, there were more than five million devices in use in the U.S. So research all the available services to figure out which is best for your business. For instance, if you do a lot of online and in-person sales, you might prefer PayPal, which will coordinate online payments and credit card swipes with its reader.

think the average transaction size will be. Bring your business plan and financial statements, along with copies of advertisements, marketing pieces, and your catalog, if you have one. If possible, invite your banker to visit your store or operation. Banks will evaluate your product or service to see if there might be potential for a lot of returns or customer disputes. Called "chargebacks," these refunds are very expensive for banks to process. They are more common among mail order companies and are one reason why these businesses typically have a hard time securing merchant status.

In your initial presentation, provide a reasonable estimate of how many chargebacks you will receive, then show your bank why you do not expect them to exceed your estimates. Testimonials from satisfied customers or product samples can help convince the bank your customers will be satisfied with their purchases. Another way to reduce the bank's fear is to demonstrate that your product is priced at a fair market value.

The best place to begin when trying to get merchant status is by approaching the bank that already holds your business accounts. If your bank turns you down, ask around for recommendations from other business owners who accept plastic. You could look in the Yellow Pages for other businesses in the same category as yours (homebased, retail, mail order). Call them to ask where they have their merchant accounts and whether they are satisfied with the way their accounts are handled. When approaching a bank with which you have no relationship, you may be able to sweeten the deal by offering to switch your other accounts to that bank as well.

If banks turn you down for merchant status, another option is to consider independent credit card processing companies, which can be found in the Yellow Pages. While independents often give the best rates because they have lower overhead, their application process tends to be more time-consuming, and startup fees are sometimes higher.

You can also go through an independent sales organization (ISO). These are field representatives from out-of-town banks who, for a commission, help businesses find banks willing to grant them merchant status. Your bank may be able to recommend an ISO, or you can look in the Yellow Pages or online under "Credit Cards." An ISO can match your needs with those of the banks he or she represents without requiring you to go through the application process with all of them.

Money Matters

Enticing your bank with promising sales figures can also boost your case since the bank makes money when you do. Every time you accept a credit card for payment, the bank or card company deducts a percentage of the sale—called a "merchant discount fee"—and then credits your account with the rest of the sale amount.

Here are some other fees you can expect to pay. All of them are negotiable except for the discount fee:

- Equipment costs of $120 to $1,000
- Monthly statement fees of $10 or less
- Transaction fees of 20 to 70 cents per purchase
- The discount rate—the actual percentage you are charged per transaction based on projected card sales volume, the degree of risk,

and a few other factors (the percentage ranges from 2 to 4 percent; rates are usually higher for new, less established businesses)
- Chargeback fees around $25 per return transaction

There may also be some charges from the telephone company to set up a phone line for the authorization and processing equipment. Before you sign on with any bank, consider the costs carefully to make sure the anticipated sales are worth the costs.

Getting Equipped

Once your business has been approved for credit, you will receive a startup kit and personal instruction in how to use the system. You don't need fancy equipment to process credit card sales. You can start with a phone and a simple imprinter that costs under $30. However, you'll get a better discount rate (and get your money credited to your account faster) if you process credit card sales electronically.

Although it's a little more expensive initially, purchasing or leasing a terminal that allows you to swipe the customer's card through for an instant authorization of the sale (and immediate crediting of your merchant account) can save you money in the long run. Cash registers can also be adapted to process credit cards. Also, using your personal computer as opposed to a terminal to get authorization can cut costs per transaction even more.

Once you obtain merchant account status, make the most of it. The credit card and bank industries hold seminars and users' conferences covering innovations in the industry, fraud detection techniques, and other helpful subjects. You can ask a credit card company's representatives for details . . . and keep on top of ways to get more from your customers' credit cards.

aha!

Chargebacks—those sale reversals issued by credit card companies when customers dispute a charge—can really hurt your bottom line. To reduce chargebacks, let your customers know exactly what they will see on their credit card statement, including your company name and sale amount. Also, if you are not sure an order is legitimate, trust your instincts and call the credit card company or issuing bank before finalizing the sale.

Online Payments

Are you selling on the web? If so, you'll need an internet merchant account to accept payments online. An internet merchant account costs more than a regular merchant account because the risk of credit card fraud is greater in an online environment, where no card is physically presented at the point of sale. To cover this risk, your bank or account issuer may charge a higher discount rate (3 to 5 percent per transaction vs. 2 to 4 percent for regular merchant accounts). The service provider may also charge monthly statement and transaction fees on each purchase. When you apply, you'll likely need to estimate the average order size and the average monthly amount you expect to run through the account. You may be asked to keep a percentage of that amount in your account to cover fraud.

Third-party payment processors like PayPal will accept credit card payments on your behalf in return for a percentage of the cost of the transaction. This amount is less than if you have a merchant account—usually under 3 percent plus 30 cents per sale. What's more, you don't have to pay the mandatory monthly fees charged by most merchant account providers. If your business has significant sales volume, it's usually cheaper to process payments through a merchant account.

Accepting Debit Cards

If you foresee a merchant account for accepting credit card payments in your future, then you will be perfectly positioned to accept debit cards, too. The same terminal you will use to process credit card payments can be used for debit card transactions, although you may wish to add a PIN pad terminal to your transaction hardware so customers can type in their PIN. That gives you an extra layer of protection against fraud.

There are a lot of advantages to accepting debit cards. First, because funds are deducted directly from the customer's bank account during a transaction, you will usually get paid faster with debit transactions than you do with credit card payments. Second, rates for PIN-based debit transactions are usually lower than credit card rates because you pay only a flat fee (credit card companies charge a transaction fee and a discount rate of around 2 percent). Finally, merchant account providers may debit the

>> Don't Skimp on Security

Thanks to the internet, small businesses have an unprecedented opportunity to market their products and services to a larger consumer audience than ever before. However, an online presence means little if customers don't feel safe making a transaction on your website. Because identity theft and credit card fraud are running rampant on the internet, many consumers will not buy from a site that doesn't provide secure transactions.

That's where a Secure Sockets Layer (SSL) certificate comes into play. Understanding how SSL affects online security can help unlock your business's ecommerce potential.

SSL technology encrypts your customers' payment information as it travels to you over the internet, protecting credit card data and other sensitive information from hackers during the transaction process. It also verifies to customers that you are who you say you are (a padlock icon is visible, indicating that a secure transaction is underway). This prevents a third party from accepting orders while disguised as your business.

SSL certificates are issued by a Certificate Authority (such as VeriSign, Thawte, GeoTrust, and others). The cost of a standard one-year certificate is $200 to $400.

If you store your customers' data or credit card numbers on your server, a firewall is another vital tool for protecting this information. Many companies expose their customers to hackers by neglecting to implement a proper firewall. If you are uncertain how to install a firewall on your site, consult your web hosting company.

For more information, check out VeriSign's "What Every E-Business Should Know about SSL Security and Consumer Trust." You can request a free copy at verisign.com.

transaction fees at the end of the month rather than with every purchase, as is the case with credit cards. That gives your business extra cash or "float," which is especially helpful for small businesses.

e-fyi

There are many business forms, contracts, and letters available for free or for a nominal fee on the internet. While they can be great resources, caution must be used as to the legality of the business form for your particular situation. If in doubt, it's always best to contact a professional to discuss your situation.

Debit cards are so pervasive these days that pretty much every bank or standalone merchant account supplier offers debit card processing—including online providers—and, in fact, you're likely to be offered the option when you apply for a merchant account. Once your merchant account is approved, all you need to do is buy a PIN pad, which runs as little as $59, connect it to your terminal, and you will be in business. Hypercom and VeriFone are well-known, affordably priced brands.

CHAPTER

22

Cover Your Assets

Getting Business Insurance

One of the most common mistakes startup business owners make is failing to buy adequate insurance for their businesses. It's an easy error to make: Money is tight, and with so many things on your mind, protecting yourself against the possibility of some faraway disaster just doesn't seem that important. "Oh, I will get insurance," you promise yourself, "one of these days." Soon, "one of these days" comes and goes, and you're still uninsured. Only now, your business has gotten much bigger . . . you've put a lot more into it . . . and you have a lot more to lose. Everything, to be exact.

It doesn't take much. A fire, a burglary, the illness of a key employee—any one of these could destroy everything you've worked so hard to build. When you think of all the time, effort, and money you're investing in your business, doesn't it make sense to invest a little extra to protect it?

>> Lost in Cyberspace

Internet businesses have unique needs—and now they have their own unique insurance. Companies like The Hartford or Travelers offer insurance to protect against damage from web-based activities, including viruses and hacking, privacy violations, copyright infringement, and more. Cyber policies are usually added to a business's general liability coverage. Not all businesses qualify for such coverage, though, so talk to your insurance broker.

"The number of (data) breaches in 2013 certainly was the last straw in the camel's back," Robert Parisi, network security and privacy practice leader for insurance broker Marsh USA, a unit of Marsh & McLennan, told CNBC in mid-2014. It was then that well-publicized breaches like the one involving more than 110 million Target customers became big news—and big headaches for businesses.

A 2014 study, "Net Losses: Estimating the Global Cost of Cybercrime," conducted by software security firm McAfee for the Center for Strategic and International Studies, estimated that cybercrime costs the global economy $445 billion a year. The report also forecast the cost will rise as more consumers and businesses connect to the internet. Most states now require companies to notify customers if there is a data breach.

The Ponemon Institute's "2014 Cost of Data Breach Study: United States" found a company with less than 10,000 records is more likely to be hacked than a firm with more than 100,000 records, in part because smaller firms are less likely to have robust defenses against hackers, who Marsh's Parisi said are not discriminating in what they attack.

"Hackers and cybercriminals are very opportunistic," Parisi said. "If they can get 100 records or credit cards from the local dry cleaners they'll do it."

So consider cyber insurance a near-necessity for your business.

Following is a closer look at the types of business insurance available and what most entrepreneurs need, plus tips for keeping costs under control. (Health insurance is covered in Chapter 24.)

Basic Insurance Needs

The basic business insurance package consists of four fundamental coverages—workers' compensation, general liability, auto and property/casualty—plus an added layer of protection over those, often called an umbrella policy. In addition to these basic needs, you should also consider purchasing business interruption coverage and life and disability insurance.

Workers' Compensation

Workers' compensation, which covers medical and rehabilitation costs and lost wages for employees injured on the job, is required by law in all 50 states.

Workers' comp insurance consists of two components, with a third optional element. The first part covers medical bills and lost wages for the injured employee; the second encompasses the employer's liability, which covers the business owner if the spouse or children of a worker who's permanently disabled or killed decides to sue. The third and optional element of workers' compensation insurance is employment practices liability, which insures against lawsuits arising from claims of sexual harassment, discrimination, and the like.

"Employment practices liability protects the unknowing corporation from the acts of the individual," according to a spokesperson at the Independent Insurance Agents of America (IIAA), an industry association. "Whether you need it depends on the size of your business and how much control you have over the daily work of employees." This is something you may need to worry about as your company grows.

According to the IIAA, it is often hard for small companies to get workers' compensation insurance at reasonable rates. Consequently, some states have a risk-sharing pool for firms that can't buy from the private market. Typically state-run and similar to assigned risk pools for car insurance, these pools generally don't provide the types of discounts offered in the voluntary market and thus are an "insurance of last resort."

save

Ask your insurance agent about risk-reduction tactics that you can use to help save money. Altering your business practices—for instance, installing better locks or brighter lights to prevent crime—can cut your premiums (and your risk). You may even want to change your business operations to get rid of a high-risk activity.

Because insurance agents aren't always up-to-date on the latest requirements and laws regarding workers' comp, you should check with your state, as well as your agent, to find out exactly what coverage you need. Start at your state's department of insurance or insurance commissioner's office.

Generally, rates for workers' comp insurance are set by the state, and you purchase insurance from a private insurer. The minimum amount you need is also governed by state law. When you buy workers' comp, be sure to choose a company licensed to write insurance in your state and approved by the insurance department or commissioner.

If you are purchasing insurance for the first time, the rate will be based on your payroll and the average cost of insurance in your industry. You'll pay that rate for a number of years, after which an experience rating will kick in, allowing you to renegotiate premiums.

Depending on the state you are located in, the business owner will be either automatically included or excluded from coverage; if you want something different, you'll need to make special arrangements. While excluding yourself can save you several hundred dollars, this can be penny-wise and pound-foolish. Review your policy before choosing this option, because in most states, if you opt out, no health benefits will be paid for any job-related injury or illness by your health insurance provider.

A better way to reduce premiums is by maintaining a good safety record. This could include following all the Occupational Health and Safety Administration guidelines related to your business, creating an employee safety manual, and instituting a safety training program.

Another way to cut costs is to ensure that all jobs in your company are properly classified. Insurance agencies give jobs different classification ratings depending on the degree of risk of injury.

> *"Be smart, but never show it."*
>
> —Louis Mayer, co-founder of Metro-Goldwyn Mayer

General Liability

Comprehensive general liability coverage insures a business against accidents and injury that might happen on its premises as well as exposures related to its products.

For example, suppose a visiting salesperson slips on a banana peel while taking a tour of your office and breaks her ankle. General liability covers her claim against you. Or let's say your company is a window-sash manufacturer, with hundreds of thousands of its window sashes installed in people's homes and businesses. If something goes wrong with them, general liability covers any claims related to the damage that results.

The catch is that the damage cannot be due to poor workmanship. This points to one difficulty with general liability insurance: It tends to

>> The Name's Bond

Sometimes confused with insurance, bonding is a guarantee of performance required for any business, either by law or by consumer demand. The most common businesses that bond employees are general contractors, temporary personnel agencies, janitorial companies, and companies with government contracts. Bonding helps ensure that the job is performed and that the customer is protected against losses from theft or damage done by your employees.

Although you still have to pay on claims if your employees are bonded, bonding has the side benefit of making your business more desirable to customers. They know that if they suffer a loss as the result of your work, they can recover the damages from the bonding company. The difference between a bond and insurance is that a bonding company ensures your payment by requiring security or collateral in case a claim is made against you.

have a lot of exclusions. Make sure you understand exactly what your policy covers . . . and what it doesn't.

You may want to purchase additional liability policies to cover specific concerns. For example, many consultants purchase "errors and omissions liability," which protects them in case they are sued for damages resulting from a mistake in their work. A computer consultant who accidentally deletes a firm's customer list could be protected by this insurance, for example.

Companies with a board of directors may want to consider "directors' and officers' liability" (D&O), which protects top executives against personal financial responsibility due to actions taken by the company.

How much liability coverage do you need? Experts say $2 million to $3 million of liability insurance should be plenty. The good news is that liability insurance isn't priced on a dollar-for-dollar basis, so twice the coverage won't be twice the price.

The price you'll have to pay for comprehensive general liability insurance depends on the size of your business (measured either by square footage or by payroll) and the specific risks involved.

aha!

Keep detailed records of the value of your office or store's contents off-premises. Include photos of equipment plus copies of sales receipts, operating manuals, and anything else that proves what you purchased and how much was paid. You can even use your smartphone to take a video of the contents—in case you've missed something in a photo. That way, in case of a fire, flood, or other disaster, you can prove what was lost. It's also important to be able to prove your monthly income so you are properly reimbursed if you have to close down temporarily.

Auto Insurance

If your business provides employees with company cars, or if you have a delivery van, you need to think about auto insurance. The good news here is that auto insurance offers more of an opportunity to save money than most other types of business insurance. The primary strategy is to increase your deductible; then your premiums will decrease accordingly. Make sure, however, that you can afford to pay the deductibles should an accident happen. For additional savings, remove the collision and comprehensive coverage from older vehicles in your fleet.

Pay attention to policy limits when purchasing auto coverage. Many states set minimum liability coverages, which may be well below what you need. If you don't have enough coverage, the courts can take everything you have, then attach your future corporate income, thus possibly causing the company severe financial hardship or even bankruptcy. You should carry at least $1 million in liability coverage.

Property/Casualty Coverage

Most property insurance is written on an all-risks basis, as opposed to a named-peril basis. The latter offers coverage for specific perils spelled

>> Package Deal

If figuring out what insurance you need makes your head spin, calm down; chances are, you won't have to consider the whole menu. Most property and casualty companies now offer special small-business insurance policies.

A standard package policy combines liability; fire, wind and vehicle damage; burglary; and other common coverages. That's enough for most small stores and offices, such as an accounting firm or a gift store. Some common requirements for a package policy are that your business occupy less than 15,000 square feet and that the combined value of your office building, operation, and inventory be less than $3 million.

Basic package policies typically cover buildings, machinery, equipment, and furnishings. That should protect computers, phones, desks, inventory, and the like against loss due to robbery and employee theft, in addition to the usual risks such as fire. A good policy pays full replacement cost on lost items.

A package policy also covers business interruption, and some even offer you liability shelter. You may also be covered against personal liability. To find out more about package policies, ask your insurance agent; then shop around and compare.

out in the policy. If your loss comes from a peril not named, then it isn't covered.

Make sure you get all-risks coverage. Then go the extra step and carefully review the policy's exclusions. All policies cover loss by fire, but what about such crises as hailstorms and explosions? Depending on your geographic location and the nature of your business, you may want to buy coverage for all these risks.

Whenever possible, you should buy replacement cost insurance, which will pay you enough to replace your property at today's prices, regardless of the cost when you bought the items. It's protection from inflation. (Be sure your total replacements do not exceed the policy cap.)

For example, if you have a 30,000-square-foot building that costs $50 per square foot to replace, the total tab will be $1.5 million. But if your policy has a maximum replacement of $1 million, you're going to come up short. To protect yourself, experts recommend buying replacement insurance with inflation guard. This adjusts the cap on the policy to allow for inflation. If that's not possible, then be sure to review the limits of your policy from time to time to ensure you're still adequately covered.

Umbrella Coverage

In addition to these four basic "food groups," many insurance agents recommend an additional layer of protection, called an umbrella policy. This protects you for payments in excess of your existing coverage or for liabilities not covered by any of your other insurance policies.

Business Interruption Coverage

When a hurricane or earthquake puts your business out of commission for days—or months—your property insurance has it covered. But while property insurance pays for the cost of repairs or rebuilding, who pays for all the income you're losing while your business is unable to function?

For that, you'll need business interruption coverage. Many entrepreneurs neglect to consider this important type of coverage, which can provide enough to meet your overhead and other expenses during the time your business is out of commission. Premiums for these policies are based on your company's income.

Life Insurance

Many banks require a life insurance policy on the business owner before lending any money. Such policies typically take the form of term life insurance, purchased yearly, which covers the cost of the loan in the event of the borrower's death; the bank is the beneficiary.

Term insurance is less costly than permanent insurance at first, although the payments increase each year. Permanent insurance builds equity and should be considered once the business has more cash to spend. The life insurance policy should provide for the families of the owners and key management. If the owner dies, creditors are likely to take everything, and the owner's family will be left without the income or assets of the business to rely on.

> ***"I never let my mistakes defeat or distract me, but I learn from them and move forward in a positive way."***
>
> —Lillian Vernon, founder of Lillian Vernon Corporation

Another type of life insurance that can be beneficial for a small business is "key person" insurance. If the business is a limited partnership or has a few key stockholders, the buy-sell agreement should specifically authorize this type of insurance to fund a buyback by the surviving leadership. Without a provision for insurance to buy capital, the buy-sell agreement may be rendered meaningless.

The company is the beneficiary of the key person policy. When the key person dies, creating the obligation to pay, say, $100,000 for his or her stock, the cash with which to make that purchase is created at the same time. If you don't have the cash to buy the stock back from the surviving family, you could find yourself with new "business partners" you never bargained for—and wind up losing control of your business.

In addition to the owners or key stockholders, any member of the company who is vital to operations should also be insured.

Disability Insurance

It's every businessperson's worst nightmare—a serious accident or a long-term illness that can lay you up for months, or even longer. Disability insurance, sometimes called "income insurance," can guarantee a fixed amount of income—usually 60 percent of your average earned income—while you're receiving treatment or are recuperating and unable to work. Because you are your business's most vital asset, many experts recommend buying disability insurance for yourself and key employees from day one.

There are two basic types of disability coverage: short term (anywhere from 12 weeks to a year) and long term (more than a year). An important element of disability coverage is the waiting period before benefits are paid. For short-term disability, the waiting period is generally seven to 14 days. For long-term disability, it can be anywhere from 30 days to a year. If being unable to work for a limited period of time would not seriously jeopardize your business, you can decrease your premiums by choosing a longer waiting period.

>> Read All About It

Want to know more about insurance? Check out these publications and websites:

- *Insuring Your Home Business and Insuring Your Business Against a Catastrophe*. Single copies of these brochures are available free from the Insurance Information Institute's website at iii.org.
- *101 Ways to Cut Business Insurance Costs Without Sacrificing Protection*. Written by William Stokes McIntyre, Jack P. Gibson, and Robert A. Bregman, this book is published by the International Risk Management Institute (IRMI) and is available at local and online bookstores or through the IRMI (irmi.com).
- *The Self-Insurance Institute of America Inc.'s blog*. A membership to the group starts at $500 per year. Join at siia.org.
- *WorkersCompensation.com*. This website provides workers' comp information, insurance quotes, and provider names by state, as well as news and information of interest to employers. Go to workerscompensation.com.

Another optional add-on is "business overhead" insurance, which pays for ongoing business expenses, such as office rental, loan payments, and employee salaries, if the business owner is disabled and unable to generate income.

Choosing an Insurance Agent

Given all the factors that go into business insurance, deciding what kind of coverage you need typically requires the assistance of a qualified insurance agent.

Type of Agent

Selecting the right agent is almost as important, and sometimes as difficult, as choosing the types of coverage you need. The most fundamental question regarding agents is whether to select a direct writer—that is, someone who represents just one insurance company—or a broker, who represents many companies.

Some entrepreneurs feel they are more likely to get their money's worth with a broker because he or she shops all kinds of insurance companies for them. Others feel brokers are more efficient because they compare the different policies and give their opinions, instead of the entrepreneur having to talk to several direct writers to evaluate each of their policies. Another drawback to direct writers: If the insurance company drops your coverage, you lose your agent, too, and all his or her accumulated knowledge about your business.

Still, some people prefer direct writers. Why? An agent who writes insurance for just one company has more clout there than an agent who writes for many. So when something goes wrong, an agent who works for the company has a better chance of getting you what you need. Finally, direct writers often specialize in certain kinds of businesses and can bring a lot of industry expertise to the table.

Finding an Agent

To find an insurance agent, begin by asking a few of your peers whom they recommend. If you want more names, a trade association in your state may

> *"Tell the truth, but make it fascinating."*
>
> —David Ogilvy, founder of Ogilvy & Mather

have a list of recommended agencies or offer some forms of group coverage with attractive rates (see the "Cost Containment" section starting on page 364).

Once you have a short list of agencies to consider, start looking for one you can develop a long-term relationship with. As your business grows and becomes more complicated, you'll want to work with someone who understands your problems. You don't want to spend a lot of time teaching the agent the ins and outs of your business or industry.

Find out how long the agency has been in business. An agency with a track record will likely be around to help you in the future. If the agency is new, ask about the principals; have they been in the industry long enough that you feel comfortable with their knowledge and stability?

>> Policy Pointers

Looking for some of the best small-business insurance resources on the web? Check these out:

- *Safeware [safeware.com]*. This company covers computers against damage, theft, power surges, and other high-tech disasters.
- *Insurance Information Institute [iii.org]*. This site puts business insurance news, facts, and figures at your fingertips. Click on "Insurance Topics" for links to a plethora of business insurance information.
- *Cigna [cigna.com]*. Despite its bent toward larger companies, this user-friendly site contains a slew of informative and entertaining insurance-related resources.
- *AllBusiness.com [allbusiness.com]*. This general business site, which is affiliated with D&B, harbors a treasure trove of small-business insurance information. Just search for "Small Business Insurance" or the variation you're interested in to find literally thousands of articles.

One important area to investigate is loss-control service (which includes everything from fire-safety programs to reducing employees' exposures to injuries). The best way to reduce your premiums over the long haul is to minimize claims, and the best way to do that is through loss-control services. Look for a broker who will review and analyze which of the carriers offer the best loss-control services.

Another consideration is the size of the agency. The trend in insurance is consolidation. If you're looking for a long-term relationship, you want to avoid an agency that is going to get bought out. One way to get a handle on whether the agency you are considering is a likely acquiree is by looking at the agency's owner. If he or she is older and is not grooming a successor, there's a chance the agency will get bought out.

Verify the level of claims service each agency provides. When a claim arises, you don't want the agent telling you to call some toll-free number. If that's his or her idea of claims service, keep looking. An agency that gets involved in the claims process and works with the adjuster can have a positive impact on your settlement, while an agency that doesn't get involved tends to minimize your settlement.

tip

The IRS allows self-employed businesspeople to deduct 100 percent of health insurance premium costs. For more information on specific IRS guidelines, request IRS Publication 533, *Self-Employment Tax*, and IRS Publication 502, *Medical and Dental Expenses*, by calling (800) TAX-FORM, or visiting irs.gov, where you can download them instantly.

You want an insurance agency that will stay on top of your coverage and be on the spot to adjust it as your business changes. Of course, it's always difficult to separate promises from what happens after the sale is closed. However, you might ask would-be agents how often they will be in touch. Even for the most basic business situation, the agent should still meet with you at least twice a year. For more complex situations, the agent should call you monthly.

You also want to make sure the company your agent selects or represents is highly rated. While there are numerous rating agencies, the most respected is A.M. Best, which rates the financial strength of insurance companies from A++ to F, according to their ability

>> Staking Your Claim

Though you hope it never happens, you may someday have to file an insurance claim. These tips should make it easier:

- *Report incidents immediately*. Notify your agent and carrier right away when anything happens—such as a fire, an accident, or theft—that could result in a claim.
- *Take steps to protect your property from further damage*. Most policies cover the cost of temporary repairs to protect against further damage, such as fixing a window to prevent looting.
- *If possible, save damaged parts*. A claims adjuster may want to examine them after equipment repairs have been made.
- *Get at least two repair estimates*. Your claims adjuster can tell you what kind of documentation the insurance company wants for bids on repairs.
- *Provide complete documentation*. The insurance company needs proof of loss. Certain claims require additional evidence. For example, a claim for business interruption will need financial data showing income before and after.
- *Communicate with your agent and claims adjustor*. Though your claim is against the insurance company, your agent should be kept informed so he or she can help if needed.

to pay claims and their size. You can find their rating book, Best Rating Guide, at your local library or you can search Best's ratings online at ambest.com. You will have to register with the site for access, but searching is free. Look for a carrier rated no lower than B+.

Also make sure the agent you choose is licensed by the state. The best way to find out is by calling your state insurance department, listed in the telephone book. If you can't find a number there, call the National Insurance Consumer helpline at (800) 942-4242.

Ask for references, and check them. This is the best way to predict how an agent will work with you.

Last but not least, trust your gut. Does the agent listen to you and incorporate your concerns into the insurance plan? Does he or she act as a partner or just a vendor? A vendor simply sells you insurance. Your goal is to find an agent who functions as a partner, helping you analyze risks and decide the best course of action. Of course, partnership is a two-way street. The more information you provide your agent, the more he or she can do for you.

Insurance Costs

As with most other things, when it comes to insurance, you get what you pay for. Don't pay to insure against minor losses, but don't ignore real perils just because coverage carries hefty premiums.

You can lower your premiums with a higher deductible. Many agents recommend higher deductibles on property insurance and putting the money you save toward additional liability coverage.

How much can you afford for a deductible or uninsured risk? Look at your cash flow. If you can pay for a loss out of cash on hand, consider not insuring it.

You can also save money on insurance by obtaining it through a trade group or an association. Many associations offer insurance tailored to your industry needs—everything from disability and health to liability and property coverage. You can also help keep insurance costs down by practicing these good insurance habits:

- Review your needs and coverage once a year. If your circumstances or assets have changed, you may need to adjust your insurance coverage.
- Ask your insurance agent for risk-reduction assistance. He or she should be able to visit your premises and identify improvements that would create a safer facility.
- Check out new insurance products. Ask your agent to keep you up-to-date on new types of coverage you may want.
- Take time to shop for the best, most appropriate coverage. A few hours invested upfront can save thousands of dollars in premiums or claims down the road.

Business Insurance Planning Worksheet

Types of Insurance	Required (Yes/No)	Annual Cost
1. Workers' compensation insurance		
2. General liability insurance		
3. Automotive liability insurance		
4. Property/casualty insurance		
5. Product liability insurance		
6. Errors and omissions liability insurance		
7. Malpractice liability insurance		
8. Web-based business insurance		
9. Fire and theft insurance		
10. Business interruption insurance		
11. Overhead expense insurance		
12. Personal disability		
13. Key person insurance		
14. Shareholders' or partners' insurance		
15. Credit extension insurance		
16. Term life insurance		
17. Health insurance		
18. Directors' and officers' liability insurance		
19. Survivor-income life insurance		
20. Care, custody, and control insurance		
21. Consequential losses insurance		
22. Boiler and machinery insurance		

Figure 22.1. Business Insurance Planning Worksheet

Business Insurance Planning Worksheet

Types of Insurance	Required (Yes/No)	Annual Cost
23. Profit insurance		
24. Money and securities insurance		
25. Glass insurance		
26. Electronic equipment insurance		
27. Power interruption insurance		
28. Rain insurance		
29. Temperature damage insurance		
30. Transportation insurance		
31. Title insurance		
32. Water damage insurance		
Total Annual Insurance Cost		$

Figure 22.1. Business Insurance Planning Worksheet, continued

CHAPTER

23

Staff Smarts

Hiring Employees

To hire or not to hire? That is the question in the mind of the new entrepreneur. You see, hiring even one employee changes everything. Suddenly, you need payroll procedures, rules regarding hours, and a policy for vacation pay. You're hit with a multitude of legal requirements and management duties you'd never have to deal with if you worked solo.

To decide whether you need employees, take a closer look at your ultimate goals. Do you want to create the next Starbucks, or do you simply want to work on your own terms without a boss looking over your shoulder? If your goals are modest, then adding a staff may not be the best solution for you.

If you do need employees, there are plenty of ways to meet your staffing needs—without driving yourself nuts. From temporaries and independent contractors to employee leasing, this chapter takes a closer look at the dos and don'ts of staffing your business. Read it over, and you will have a better idea whether hiring is the right solution for you.

How to Hire

The employees you hire can make or break your business. While you may be tempted to hire the first person who walks in the door "just to get it over with," doing so can be a fatal error. A small company cannot afford to carry dead wood on staff, so start smart by taking time to figure out your staffing needs before you even begin looking for job candidates.

> **e-fyi**
>
> Use the internet to help you find employees:
>
> - CareerBuilder (career builder.com) offers advice, webinars, leadership development, and hiring solutions to employers and job recruiters.
> - Monster.com helps you screen resumes so you can find the right candidate quickly.

Job Analysis

Begin by understanding the requirements of the job being filled. What kind of personality, experience, and education are needed? To determine these attributes, sit down and do a job analysis covering the following areas:

- The physical/mental tasks involved (ranging from judging, planning, and managing to cleaning, lifting, and welding)
- How the job will be done (the methods and equipment used)
- The reason the job exists (including an explanation of job goals and how they relate to other positions in the company)
- The qualifications needed (training, knowledge, skills, and personality traits)

If you are having trouble, one good way to get information for a job analysis is to talk to employees and supervisors at other companies that have similar positions.

Job Description

Use the job analysis to write a job description and a job specification. Drawing from these concepts, you can then create your recruitment materials, such as a classified ad.

Job Analysis

Date: ______________________ Prepared By: ______________________

Title: ______________________ Department: ______________________

Job Title: ______________________

Reporting To: ______________________

Major Responsibilities: ______________________

____

Minor Responsibilities: ______________________

____

Education/Experience Required: ______________________

____

Goals/Objectives of Position: ______________________

____

Knowledge/Skills Required: ______________________

____

Physical Requirements: ______________________

____

Special Problems/Hazards: ______________________

____

Number of People Supervised: ______________________

Reporting To: ______________________

Figure 23.1. Job Analysis

> **tip** 
> It's easy to hire employees who are just like you, but it's often a big mistake. Especially with your first employee, try to find someone who complements your strengths and weaknesses. While personal compatibility is important, hiring a carbon copy of yourself could leave your business ill-prepared for future challenges.

The job description is basically an outline of how the job fits into the company. It should point out in broad terms the job's goals, responsibilities, and duties. First, write down the job title and whom that person will report to. Next, develop a job statement or summary describing the position's major and minor duties. Finally, define how the job relates to other positions in the company. Which are subordinate and which are of equal responsibility and authority?

For a one-person business hiring its first employee, these steps may seem unnecessary, but remember, you are laying the foundation for your personnel policy, which will be essential as your company grows. Keeping detailed records from the time you hire your first employee will make things a lot easier when you hire your 50th.

The job specification describes the personal requirements you expect from the employee. Like the job description, it includes the job title, whom the person reports to, and a summary of the position. However, it also lists any educational requirements, desired experience, and specialized skills or knowledge required. Include salary range and benefits. Finish by listing any physical or other special requirements associated with the job, as well as any occupational hazards.

Writing the job description and job specifications will also help you determine whether you need a part- or full-time employee, whether the person should be permanent or temporary, and whether you could use an independent contractor to fill the position (more on all these options later).

Writing the Ad

Use the job specification and description to write an ad that will attract candidates to your company. The best way to avoid wasting time on interviews with people who do not meet your needs is to write an ad that will lure qualified candidates and discourage others. Consider this example:

> Interior designer seeks inside/outside salesperson. Flooring, drapes (extensive measuring), furniture, etc. In-home consultations. Excellent salary and commission. PREVIOUS EXPERIENCE A NECESSITY. San Francisco Bay Area. Send resume to G. Green at P.O. Box 5409, San Francisco, CA 90842.

This job description is designed to attract a flexible salesperson and eliminate those who lack the confidence to work on commission. The advertiser asks for expertise in "extensive measuring," the skill he has had the most difficulty finding. The job location should be included to weed out applicants who don't live in the area or aren't willing to commute or relocate. Finally, the capitalized "PREVIOUS EXPERIENCE A NECESSITY" underscores that he will hire only candidates with previous experience.

Job Description

Date: ____________________ Prepared By: ____________________

Title: ____________________ Department: ____________________

Job Title: ____________________ Reporting To: ____________________

Job Statement: ____

____

Major Duties

1. ____

2. ____

3. ____

Figure 23.2. Job Description

Job Description

Major Duties

4. ______________________________

5. ______________________________

6. ______________________________

7. ______________________________

Minor Duties

1. ______________________________

2. ______________________________

3. ______________________________

4. ______________________________

5. ______________________________

6. ______________________________

7. ______________________________

Relationships

Number of People Supervised: ______________________________

Person Giving Work Assignments: ______________________________

Figure 23.2. Job Description, continued

To write a similarly targeted ad for your business, look at your job specifications and pull out the top four or five skills that are most essential to the job. Don't, however, list requirements other than educational or experience-related ones in the ad. Nor should you request specific personality traits (such as outgoing, detail-oriented) since people are likely to come in and imitate those characteristics when they don't really possess them. Instead, you should focus on telling the applicants about the excitement and challenge of the job, the salary, what they will get out of it, and what it will be like working for you.

Finally, specify how applicants should contact you.

> ***"My philosophy is, 'When you snooze, you lose.' If you have a great idea, at least take the chance and put your best foot forward."***
>
> —RON POPEIL, FOUNDER OF RONCO INVENTIONS LLC

Recruiting Employees

The obvious first choice for recruiting employees is the classified ad section of your local newspaper, both in the printed and online versions. Place your ad in the Sunday or weekend edition of the largest-circulation local papers.

Beyond this, however, there are plenty of other places to recruit good employees. Here are some ideas:

- *Tap into your personal and professional network.* Tell everyone you know—friends, neighbors, professional associates, customers, vendors, colleagues from associations—that you have a job opening. Someone might know of the perfect candidate.
- *Contact school placement offices.* List your openings with trade and vocational schools, colleges, and universities. Check with your local school board to see if high schools in your area have job training and placement programs.
- *Post notices at senior citizen centers.* Retirees who need extra income or a productive way to fill their time can make excellent employees.
- *Use an employment agency.* Private and government-sponsored agencies can help with locating and screening applicants. Often their fees are more than justified by the amount of time and money you save.
- *List your opening with an appropriate job bank.* Many professional associations have job banks for their members. Contact groups

related to your industry, even if they are outside your local area, and ask them to alert their members to your staffing needs.

- *Use industry publications.* Trade association newsletters and industry publications often have classified ad sections where members can advertise job openings. This is a very effective way to attract skilled people in your industry.
- *Go online.* There are a variety of online job banks and databases that allow employers to list openings. These databases can be searched by potential employees from all over the country. And don't forget LinkedIn, an international professional networking site, where you can post jobs and find candidates through the site's automated talent matching system. Check it out at linkedin.com.

tip

If relevant, ask employees to send samples of their work with their resumes or to bring them to the interview. Another technique: Ask them to complete a project similar to the actual work they'd be doing (and pay them for it). This gives you a strong indication of how they would perform on the job . . . and gives them a clear picture of what you expect from them.

Prescreening Candidates

Two important tools in prescreening job candidates are the resume and the employment application. If you ask applicants to send in a resume, that will be the first tool you use to screen them. You will then have qualified candidates fill out an application when they come in for an interview. If you don't ask for a resume, you will probably want to have prospective employees come in to fill out applications, then review the applications and call qualified candidates to set up an interview.

In either case, it is important to have an application form ready before you begin the interview process. You can buy generic application forms at most office-supply stores, or you can develop your own application form to meet your specific needs. Make sure any application form you use conforms to Equal Employment Opportunity Commission (EEOC) guidelines regarding questions you can and cannot ask (see "Off Limits" on page 339 for more on this).

Your application should ask for specific information such as name, address, and phone number; educational background; work experience, including salary levels; awards or honors; whether the applicant can work full or part time as well as available hours; and any special skills relevant to the job (foreign languages, familiarity with software programs, etc.). Be sure to ask for names and phone numbers of former supervisors to check as references; if the candidate is currently employed, ask whether it is OK to contact his or her current place of employment. You may also want to ask for personal references. Because many employers these days hesitate to give out information about an employee, you may want to have the applicant sign a waiver that states the employee authorizes former and/or current employers to disclose information about him or her.

>> Willing and Able

The Americans with Disabilities Act (ADA) of 1990 makes it illegal for employers with 15 or more employees to refuse to hire qualified people with disabilities if making "reasonable accommodations" would enable the person to carry out the duties of the job. That could mean making physical changes to the workplace or reassigning certain responsibilities.

While the law is unclear on exactly how far an employer must go to accommodate a person with disabilities, what is clear is that it's the applicant's responsibility to tell the employer about the disability. Employers are not allowed to ask whether an applicant has a disability or a history of health problems. However, after the applicant has been given a written or verbal explanation of the job duties, you may then ask whether he or she can adequately perform those duties or would need some type of accommodation.

For further clarification, read the laws, regulations, and enforcement guidance documents available online from the Equal Employment Opportunity Commission at eeoc.gov.

When screening resumes, it helps to have your job description and specifications in front of you so you can keep the qualities and skills you are looking for clearly in mind. Since there is no standard form for resumes, evaluating them can be very subjective. However, there are certain components that you should expect to find in a resume. It should contain the prospect's name, address, and telephone number at the top and a brief summary of employment and educational experience, including dates. Many resumes include a "career objective" that describes what kind of job the prospect is pursuing; other applicants state their objectives in their cover letters. Additional information you may find on a resume or in a cover letter includes references, achievements, and career-related affiliations.

Look for neatness and professionalism in the applicant's resume and cover letter. A resume riddled with typos raises some serious red flags. If a person can't be bothered to put his or her best foot forward during this crucial stage of the game, how can you expect him or her to do a good job if hired?

There are two basic types of resumes: the "chronological" resume and the "functional" resume. The chronological resume, which is what most of us are used to seeing, lists employment history in reverse chronological order, from most recent position to earliest. The functional resume does not list dates of employment; instead, it lists different skills or "functions" that the employee has performed.

Although chronological resumes are the preferred format among HR professionals and hiring managers, functional resumes have increased in popularity in recent years. In some cases, they are used by downsized executives who may be quite well-qualified and are simply trying to downplay long periods of unemployment or make a career change. In other cases, however, they signal that the applicant is a job-hopper or has something to hide.

tip

You should also check a candidate's "online" resume on LinkedIn to see if the paper document and the online presence match up. Note any discrepancies to discuss in an interview. LinkedIn recommendations are also a good place to check to see a candidate's performance—and you can usually contact those recommenders as extra references if needed.

Because it's easy for people to embellish resumes, it's a good idea to have candidates fill out a job application, by mail or in person, and then

>> Off Limits

Equal Employment Opportunity Commission (EEOC) guidelines, as well as federal and state laws, prohibit asking certain questions of a job applicant, either on the application form or during the interview. What questions to sidestep? Basically, you can't ask about anything not directly related to the job, including:

- Age or date of birth (except when necessary to satisfy applicable age laws)
- Sex, race, creed, color, religion, or national origin
- Disabilities of any kind
- Date and type of military discharge
- Marital status
- Maiden name (for female applicants)

Other questions to avoid:

- How many children do you have? How old are they? Who will care for them while you are at work?
- Have you ever been treated by a psychologist or a psychiatrist?
- Have you ever been treated for drug addiction or alcoholism?
- Have you ever been arrested? (You may, however, ask if the person has been convicted if it is accompanied by a statement saying that a conviction will not necessarily disqualify an applicant for employment.)
- How many days were you sick last year?
- Have you ever filed for workers' compensation? Have you ever been injured on the job?

In doubt whether a question (or comment) is offensive or not? Play it safe and zip your lip. In today's lawsuit-happy environment, an offhand remark could cost you plenty.

compare it to the resume. Because the application requires information to be completed in chronological order, it gives you a more accurate picture of an applicant's history.

Beyond functional and chronological resumes, there is another type of resume that's more important to be on the lookout for. That's what one consultant calls an "accomplishment" vs. a "responsibility" resume.

The responsibility resume is just that. It emphasizes the job description, saying things like "Managed three account executives; established budgets; developed departmental contests." An accomplishment resume, on the other hand, emphasizes accomplishments and results, such as "Cut costs by 50 percent" or "Met quota every month." Such a resume tells you that the person is an achiever and has the bottom line firmly in mind.

When reading the resume, try to determine the person's career patterns. Look for steady progress and promotions in past jobs. Also look for stability in terms of length of employment. A person who changes jobs every year is probably not someone you want on your team. Look for people with three- to four-year job stints.

At the same time, be aware of how economic conditions can affect a person's resume. During a climate of frequent corporate downsizing, for example, a series of lateral career moves may signal that a person is a survivor. This also shows that the person is interested in growing and willing to take on new responsibilities, even if there was no corresponding increase in pay or status.

By the same token, just because a resume or a job application has a few gaps in it doesn't mean you should overlook it entirely. You could be making a big mistake. Stay focused on the skills and value the job applicant could bring to your company.

Interviewing Applicants

Once you've narrowed your stack of resumes down to ten or so top candidates, it's time to start setting up interviews. If you dread this portion of the process, you're not alone. Fortunately, there are some ways to put both yourself and the candidates at ease—and make sure you get all the information you need to make a smart decision. Start by preparing a list of basic interview questions in advance. While you won't read off this list like a robot, having it in front of you will ensure you cover all the bases and also make sure you ask all the candidates the same questions.

The initial few moments of an interview are the most crucial. As you meet the candidate and shake his or her hand, you will gain a strong impression of his or her poise, confidence, and enthusiasm (or lack thereof). Qualities to look for include good communication skills, a neat and clean appearance, and a friendly and enthusiastic manner.

Put the interviewee at ease with a bit of small talk on neutral topics. A good way to break the ice is by explaining the job and describing the company—its business, history, and future plans.

aha!

Posting a job on an online job site offers you advantages like 24-hour access to job postings, unlimited text for postings, and quick turnaround. They also allow you to screen candidates, search resume databases, and keep your ad online for a long period of time—30 to 60 days—vs. a newspaper ad, which runs for only one weekend.

Then move on to the heart of the interview. You will want to ask about several general areas, such as related experience, skills, educational training or background, and unrelated jobs. Open each area with a general, open-ended question, such as "Tell me about your last job." Avoid questions that can be answered with a "yes" or "no" or that prompt obvious responses, such as "Are you detail-oriented?" Instead, ask questions that force the candidate to go into detail. The best questions are follow-up questions such as "How did that situation come about?" or "Why did you do that?" These queries force applicants to abandon preplanned responses and dig deeper.

Here are some interview questions to get you started:

- If you could design the perfect job for yourself, what would you do? Why?
- What kind of supervisor gets the best work out of you?
- How would you describe your current supervisor?
- How do you structure your time?
- What are three things you like about your current job?
- What were your three biggest accomplishments in your last job? In your career?

- What can you do for our company that no one else can?
- What are your strengths/weaknesses?
- How far do you think you can go in this company? Why?
- What do you expect to be doing in five years?
- What interests you most about this company? This position?
- Describe three situations where your work was criticized.
- Have you hired people before? If so, what did you look for?

Your candidate's responses will give you a window into his or her knowledge, attitude, and sense of humor. Watch for signs of "sour grapes"

>> Family Affair

Want to get good employees and tax savings, too? Consider putting your family members to work for you.

Hiring family, especially children, enables you to move family income out of a higher tax bracket into a lower one. It also enables you to transfer wealth to your kids without incurring federal gift or estate taxes.

Subject to applicable child labor laws, even preteen children can be put to work stuffing envelopes, filing, or sorting mail. If a child's salary is reasonable, it is considered earned income and not subject to the "kiddie tax" rules that can apply to anyone under the age of 23. And if your business is unincorporated, wages paid to a child under 18 are not subject to Social Security or FICA taxes. That means neither you nor your child has to pay these taxes. Finally, employed youngsters can make tax-deductible contributions to an individual retirement account.

Be sure to document the type of work the family member is doing and pay them a comparable amount to what you'd pay another employee, or the IRS will think you're putting your family on the payroll just for the tax breaks. Keep careful records of time worked, and make sure the work is necessary to the business.

Your accountant can suggest other ways to take advantage of this tax situation without getting in hot water.

about former employers. Also be alert for areas people seem reluctant to talk about. Probe a little deeper without sounding judgmental.

Pay attention to the candidate's nonverbal cues, too. Does she seem alert and interested, or does she slouch and yawn? Are his clothes wrinkled and stained or clean and neat? A person who can't make an effort for the interview certainly won't make one on the job if hired.

Finally, leave time at the end of the interview for the applicant to ask questions—and pay attention to what he or she asks. This is the time when applicants can really show they have done their homework and researched your company . . . or, conversely, that all they care about is what they can get out of the job. Obviously, there is a big difference between the one who says, "I notice that your biggest competitor's sales have doubled since launching their website in January. Do you have any plans to develop a website of your own?" and the person who asks, "How long is the lunch break?" Similarly, candidates who can't come up with even one question may be demonstrating that they can't think on their feet.

End the interview by letting the candidate know what to expect next. How much longer will you be interviewing? When can they expect to hear from you? You are dealing with other people's livelihoods, so the week that you take to finish your interviews can seem like an eternity to them. Show some consideration by keeping them informed.

During the interview, jot down notes (without being obvious about it). After the interview, allow five or ten minutes to write down the applicant's outstanding qualities and evaluate his or her personality and skills against your job description and specifications.

Checking References

After preliminary interviews, you should be able to narrow the field to three or four top candidates. Now's the time to do a little detective work.

It's estimated that up to one-third of job applicants lie about their experience and educational achievements on their resumes or job applications. No matter how sterling the person seems in the interview process, a few phone calls upfront to check out their claims could save you a lot of hassle—and even legal battles—later on. Today, courts are increasingly holding employers liable for crimes employees commit on the job, such as drunk driving, when it is determined that the employer could have been expected to know about prior convictions for similar offenses.

> **aha!**
> Looking to fill an important position, but dreading the hassle of hunting for candidates? Executive recruitment firms, also known as "headhunters" or search firms, can find qualified professional, managerial, or technical candidates for you. Search firms typically charge a percentage of the executive's first-year salary.

Unfortunately, getting that information has become harder and harder to do. Fearful of reprisals from former employees, many firms have adopted policies that forbid releasing detailed information. Generally, the investigating party is referred to a personnel department, which supplies dates of employment, title, and salary—period.

There are ways to dig deeper, however. Try to avoid the human resources department if at all possible. Instead, try calling the person's former supervisor directly. While the supervisor may be required to send you to personnel, sometimes you'll get lucky and get the person on a day he or she feels like talking. You can also contact references and recommenders on a candidate's LinkedIn profile.

Sometimes, too, a supervisor can tip you off without saying anything that will get him or her in trouble. Consider the supervisor who, when contacted by one potential employer, said, "I only give good references." When the employer asked, "What can you tell me about X?" the supervisor repeated, "I only give good references." Without saying anything, he said it all.

Depending on the position, you may also want to do education checks. You can call any college or university's admissions department to verify degrees and dates of attendance. Some universities will require a written request or a signed waiver from the applicant before releasing any kind of information to you.

If the person is going to be driving a company vehicle, you may want to do a motor vehicle check with the department of motor vehicles. In fact, you may want to do this even if he or she will not be driving for you. Vehicle checks can uncover patterns of negligence or drug and alcohol problems that he or she might have.

>> To Test or Not to Test

Personality and skills assessments are increasingly popular as a screen for key employees. This is especially true for sales and customer-facing jobs. According to Psychometrics, a company that leads the pack in offering personality assessments in the workplace, "Personality assessments provide a measure of how individuals work with people, approach their tasks, communicate, approach change, and deal with stress. Differences between people in these various areas can make them more or less effective in different jobs."

There are work personality assessments, skill strength assessments, career value indicators, and more. Psychometrics.com is a good place to start, although other organizations also offer the assessments—and the scoring. A simple questionnaire test might cost as little as $15 to $40 per assessment. More complex assessments can cost $125 or more.

Look for tests that have highly reliable results and those that are most commonly used in your industry. If you can afford the extra cost, personality assessments can be a good extra screen to ensure your new hires have just the right temperament to sell your products, greet your customers, or stay motivated to help you get ahead.

If your company deals with property management, such as maintenance or cleaning, you may want to consider a criminal background check as well. Unfortunately, national criminal records and even state records are not coordinated. The only way to obtain criminal records is to go to individual courthouses in each county, although many now have online records that can be searched if records are publicly available. It's generally sufficient to investigate records in three counties—birthplace, current residence, and residence preceding the current residence.

For certain positions, such as those that will give an employee access to your company's cash (a cashier or an accounting clerk, for instance), a credit check may be a good idea as well. You can find credit reporting bureaus in any Yellow Pages. They will be able to provide you with a

> **save**
> Whenever possible, look for employees you can cross-train for different jobs. A welder with college courses in engineering and a secretary with human resources experience are workers one business owner has successfully cross-trained. Cross-trained employees can fill in when others are absent, helping keep costs down.

limited credit and payment history. While you should not rely on this as the sole reason not to hire someone (credit reports are notorious for containing errors), a credit report can contribute to a total picture of irresponsible behavior. And if the person will have access to large sums of money at your company, hiring someone who is in serious debt is probably not a very good idea.

Be aware, however, that if a credit check plays any role in your decision not to hire someone, you must inform them that they were turned down in part because of their credit report.

If all this background-checking seems too time-consuming to handle yourself, you can contract the job out to a third-party investigator. Look in the Yellow Pages for firms in your area that handle this task, or Google "background checking." A criminal check can cost as little as $20; a full investigation averages $50. There are even better deals online, so be sure to shop around. It's a small price to pay when you consider the damages it might save you.

After the Hire

Congratulations! You have hired your first employee. Now what?

As soon as you hire, call or write the applicants who didn't make the cut and tell them you'll keep their applications on file. That way, if the person you hired isn't the best—or is so good that business doubles—you won't have to start from scratch in hiring your second employee.

For each applicant you interviewed, create a file including your interview notes, the resume, and the employment application. For the person you hire, that file will become the basis for his or her personnel file. Federal law requires that a job application be kept at least three years after a person is hired.

Even if you don't hire the applicant, make sure you keep the file. Under federal law, all recruitment materials, such as applications and resumes, must be kept for at least six months after the employment decision has been made. In today's climate, where applicants sometimes sue an employer who decides not to hire them, it's a good idea to maintain all records related to a hire (or nonhire). Especially for higher-level positions where you narrow the field to two or three candidates, put a brief note or memo in each applicant's file explaining why he or she was or wasn't hired.

> ***"I think people who have a real entrepreneurial spirit, who can face difficulties and overcome them, should absolutely follow their desires. It makes for a much more interesting life."***
>
> —Martha Stewart, founder of Martha Stewart Living Omnimedia

The hiring process doesn't end with making the selection. Your new employee's first day is critical. People are most motivated on their first day. Build on the momentum of that motivation by having a place set up for them to work, making them comfortable and welcome. Don't just dump them in an office and shut your door. Be prepared to spend some time with them, explaining job duties, introducing them to their office mates, getting them started on tasks, or even taking them out to lunch. By doing so, you are building rapport and setting the stage for a long and happy working relationship.

Alternatives to Full-Time Employees

The traditional full-time employee is not your only hiring option. More employers are turning to alternative arrangements, including leased employees, temporary employees, part-timers, and interns. All these strategies can save you money—and headaches, too.

Leased Employees

If payroll paperwork, personnel hassles, and employee manuals sound like too much work to deal with, consider an option that's growing in popularity: employee leasing.

Employee leasing—a means of managing your human resources without all the administrative hassles—first became popular in California in the early '80s, driven by the excessive cost of health-care benefits in the state. By combining the employees of several companies into one larger pool, employee leasing companies (also known as professional employer organizations, or PEOs) could offer business owners better rates on health-care and workers' compensation coverage.

Today, there are more than three million leased employees in the United States, and the employee leasing industry is projected to continue growing at a rate of more than 20 percent each year, according

>> Look Before You Lease

How do you decide if an employee leasing company is for you? The National Association of Professional Employer Organizations (NAPEO) suggests you look for the following:

- Services that fit your human resources needs. Is the company flexible enough to work with you?
- Banking and credit references. Look for evidence that the company's payroll taxes and insurance premiums are up-to-date. Request to see a certificate of insurance.
- Investigate the company's administrative competence. What experience does it have?
- Understand how employees' benefits are funded. Do they fit your workers' needs? Find out who the third-party administrator or carrier is and whether it is licensed if your state requires this.
- Make sure the leasing company is licensed or registered if required by your state.
- Ask for client and professional references, and call them.
- Review the agreement carefully and try to get a provision that permits you to cancel at short notice—say, 30 days.

For a list of NAPEO member organizations in your area, contact the NAPEO at (703) 836-0466 email info@napeo.org, or search their directory online at napeo.org/find/members.cfm.

to the National Association of Professional Employer Organizations (NAPEO).

But today, employee leasing firms do a lot more than just offer better health-care rates. They manage everything from compliance with state and federal regulations to payroll, unemployment insurance, W-2 forms, and claims processing—saving clients time and money. Some firms have even branched out to offer "extras" such as pension and employee assistance programs.

While many business owners confuse employee leasing companies with temporary help businesses, the two organizations are quite different. Generally speaking, temporary help companies recruit employees and assign them to client businesses to help with short-term work overload or special projects on an as-needed basis, according to a spokesperson with the American Staffing Association. With leasing companies, on the other hand, a client business generally turns over all its personnel functions to an outside company, which will administer these operations and lease the employees back to the client.

According to the NAPEO, leasing services are contractual arrangements in which the leasing company is the employer of record for all or part of the client's work force. Employment responsibilities are typically shared between the PEO and the client, allowing the client to retain essential management control over the work performed by the employees.

Meanwhile, the PEO assumes responsibility for a wide range of employer obligations and risks, among them paying and reporting wages and employment taxes out of its own accounts as well as retaining some rights to the direction and control of the leased employees. The client, on the other hand, has one primary responsibility: writing one check to the PEO to cover the payroll, taxes, benefits, and administrative fees. The PEO does the rest.

Who uses PEOs? According to the NAPEO, small businesses make up the primary market for leasing companies since—due to economies of scale—they typically pay higher premiums for employee benefits. If an employee hurts his or her back and files a workers' compensation claim, it could literally threaten the small business's existence. With another entity as the employer of record, however, these claims are no longer the small-

warning 

Be sure you understand the precise legal relationship between your business and a leasing company. Some people consider the leasing company the sole employer, effectively insulating the client from legal responsibility. Others consider the client and the leasing company joint employers, sharing legal responsibility. Have an attorney review your agreement to clarify any risks.

business owner's problem. PEOs have also been known to help business owners avoid wrongful termination suits and negligent acts in the workplace, according to an NAPEO spokesperson.

Having to comply with a multitude of employment-related statutes, which is often beyond the means of smaller businesses, is another reason PEOs are so popular with entrepreneurs. According to the NAPEO, with a leasing company, you basically get the same type of human resources department you would get if you were a Fortune 500 firm.

Before hiring a professional employer organization, be sure to shop around since not all offer the same pricing structures and services. Fees may be based on a modest percentage of payroll (2 to 8 percent) or on a per-employee basis. When comparing fees, consider what you would pay a full-time employee to handle the administrative chores the PEO will take off your hands. (For more information on what to look for, see "Look Before You Lease" on page 348).

Temporary Employees

If your business's staffing needs are seasonal—for example, you need extra workers during the holidays or during busy production periods—then temporary employees could be the answer to your problem. If the thought of a temp brings to mind a secretary, think again. The services and skills temporary help companies offer small businesses have expanded.

Today, some companies specialize in medical services; others find their niche in professional or technical fields, supplying everything from temporary engineers, editors, and accountants to computer programmers, bankers, lab support staff, and even attorneys.

With many temporary help companies now offering specialized employees, many business owners have learned that they don't have to settle for low skill levels or imperfect matches. Because most temporary help companies screen—and often train—their employees, entrepreneurs who choose this option stand a better chance of obtaining the quality employees they need for their business.

In addition to prescreened, pretrained individuals, temporary help companies offer entrepreneurs a slew of other benefits. For one, they help keep your overhead low. For another, they save you time and money on recruiting efforts. You don't have to find, interview, or relocate workers. Also, the cost of health and unemployment benefits, workers' compensation insurance, profit-sharing, vacation time, and other benefits doesn't come out of your budget since many temporary help companies provide these resources to their employees.

How do you find the temporary help company that best suits your needs—from light secretarial to specialized technical support? First, look in the Yellow Pages under "Employment Contractors—Temporary Help." Call a few and ask some questions, including:

- Do you have insurance? Look for adequate liability and workers' compensation coverage to protect your company from a temporary worker's claim.
- Do you check on the progress of your temporaries?
- How do you recruit your temporaries?
- How much training do you give temporaries? (According to the American Staffing Association, nearly 90 percent of the temporary work force receives free skills training of some kind.)
- What benefits do you offer your temporaries?
- Should a temporary fail to work out, does the firm offer any guarantees? Look for a firm that can provide a qualified temp right away.
- How quickly can you provide temporaries? (When you need one, you'll usually need one right away.)

Also ask the company to provide references. Contact references and ask their opinions of the temporary help company's quality level, reliability, reputation, service, and training.

Defining the expected duration of your needs is also very important. While many entrepreneurs bring on a temporary worker for just that—

>> Temporary Treatment

How do you make the most of your temporary workers once they've come on board? For one, don't treat them any differently from your other employees. Introduce them to your full-time workers as people who are there to help you complete a project, to relieve some overtime stress, or to bring in some skills you might not have in-house.

And don't expect temporary workers to be so well-trained that they know how to do all the little (but important) things, such as operating the copier or answering the phone. Spend some time giving them a brief overview of these things, just as you would any new employee.

One strategy for building a better relationship with your temporary workers is to plan ahead as much as possible so you can use the same temporaries for an extended period of time—say, six months. Or try to get the same temporaries back when you need help again. This way, they'll be more productive, and you won't have to spend time retraining them.

temporary work—some may eventually find they would like to hire the worker full time. Be aware that, at this point, some temporary help firms require a negotiated fee for "stealing" the employee away from them. Defining your needs upfront can help you avoid such penalties.

Because a growing number of entrepreneurs purposely use temporary workers part time to get a feel for whether they should hire them full time, many temporary help companies have begun offering an option: temporary-to-full-time programs, which allow the prospective employer and employee to evaluate each other. Temporary-to-full-time programs match a temporary worker who has expressed an interest in full-time work with an employer who has like interests. The client is encouraged to make a

e-fyi

Need to find an employee for your specific industry? Try a trade association's website, many of which have classified sections or job boards. These sites allow you to post job listings at a low cost and receive responses from a very targeted pool of candidates.

job offer to the employee within a predetermined time period, should the match seem like a good one.

Last, but not least, before contracting with a temporary help company, make sure it is a member of a trade association such as the American Staffing Association. This means: 1) the company has agreed to abide by a code of ethics and good practices, 2) it is in the business for the long haul—meaning it has invested in its industry by becoming a member of its

>> The Intern Alternative

Some colleges encourage students to work, for a small stipend or even for free, through internship programs. Student interns trade their time and talents in exchange for learning marketable job skills. Every year, colleges match thousands of students with businesses of all sizes and types. Since they have an eye on future career prospects, the students are usually highly motivated.

Does your tiny one-person office have anything to offer an intern? Actually, small companies offer better learning experiences for interns since they typically involve a greater variety of job tasks and offer a chance to work more closely with senior employees.

Routine secretarial or "gofer" work won't get you an intern in most cases. Colleges expect their interns to learn specialized professional skills. Hold up your end of the bargain by providing meaningful work. Can you delegate a direct-mail campaign? Have an intern help on photo shoots? Ask her to put together a client presentation?

Check with your local college or university to find out about internship programs. Usually, the school will send you an application, asking you to describe the job's responsibilities and your needs in terms of skill level and other qualifications. Then the school will send you resumes of students it thinks could work for you.

The best part of hiring interns? If you're lucky, you'll find a gem who'll stay with your company after the internship is over.

trade association—and 3) it has access to up-to-date information on trends that impact its business.

Part-Time Personnel

Another way to cut overhead and benefits costs while gaining flexibility is by hiring part-time workers. Under current law, you are not required to provide part-timers with medical benefits.

What are the other benefits to you? By using permanent part-timers, you can get more commitment than you'd get from a temp, but more flexibility than you can expect from a nine-to-fiver. In some industries, such as fast food, retail, and other businesses that are open long hours, part-timers are essential to fill the odd hours during which workers are needed.

A traditional source of part-time employees is students. They typically are flexible, willing to work odd hours, and do not require high wages. High school and college kids like employers who let them fit their work schedule to the changing demands of school.

Although students are ideal for many situations, there are potential drawbacks to be aware of. For one thing, a student's academic or social demands may impinge on your scheduling needs. Some students feel that a manicure or a tennis game is reason enough to change their work schedules. You'll need to be firm and set some standards for what is and is not acceptable.

Students are not the only part-timers in town, however. One often-overlooked source of employees is retired people. Often, seniors are looking for a way to earn some extra money or fill their days. Many of these people have years of valuable business experience that could be a boon to your company.

Seniors offer many of the advantages of other part-time employees without the flakiness that sometimes characterizes younger workers. They typically have an excellent work ethic and can add a note of stability to your organization. If a lot of your customers are seniors, they may prefer dealing with employees their own age.

Parents of young children, too, offer a qualified pool of potential part-time workers. Often, these workers are highly skilled and experienced.

>> Contract Only What You Need

The emergence of an entire cadre of people who prefer to work freelance or on contract has opened a big world of project hiring. Websites Odesk.com, Guru.com, and Freelancer.com connect skilled independent workers with businesses who have specific needs. The sites generally allow you to advertise for or search profiles of people for hire, and freelancers can advertise their rates or you can negotiate a rate. These can be a good alternative to temporary workers, or fill in a gap in knowledge that you need—but not full time.

Say you need someone to refine your marketing materials or handle the books for just one product. You might only have ten hours of work per week and you need someone with specific knowledge. These sites connect you with people who specialize in all sorts of work, but want to do it on their own time or prefer to pick and choose projects rather than work for one employer—and you might find a better rate, with fewer employment law worries, than you will at a temporary agency.

Like any hiring, review the potential candidate's work and check references. And remember, if you are paying $10 an hour for a job that should pay $20, you might not get the same quality.

Finally, one employee pool many employers swear by is people with disabilities. Workers from a local shelter or nonprofit organization can excel at assembling products or packaging goods. In most cases, the charity group will work with you to oversee and provide a job coach for the employees. To find disabled workers in your area, contact the local Association of Retarded Citizens office or Easter Seals.

Outsourcing Options

Simply put, this refers to sending certain job functions outside a company instead of handling them in house. For instance, instead of hiring an in-house bookkeeper, you might outsource the job to an independent accountant who comes in once a month or does all the work off-site.

More and more companies large and small are turning to outsourcing as a way to cut payroll and overhead costs. Done right, outsourcing can mean you never need to hire an employee at all!

How to make it work? Make sure the company or individual you use can do the job. That means getting (and checking) references. Ask former or current clients about their satisfaction. Find out what industries and what type of workload the firm or individual is used to handling. Can you expect your deadlines to be met, or will your small business's projects get pushed aside if a bigger client has an emergency?

Make sure you feel comfortable with who will be doing the work and that you can discuss your concerns and needs openly. Ask to see samples of work if appropriate (for example, if you're using a graphic design firm).

If your outsourcing needs are handled by an individual, you're dealing with an independent contractor. The IRS has stringent rules regulating exactly who is and is not considered an independent contractor. The risk: If you consider a person an independent contractor and the IRS later reclassifies him or her as an employee, you could be liable for that person's Social Security taxes and a wide range of other costs and penalties.

For more on independent contractors, see Chapter 41. If you're still in doubt, it always pays to consult your accountant. Making a mistake in this area could cost you big.

CHAPTER

24

Perk Up

Setting Employee Policies and Benefits

Once you have great employees on board, how do you keep them from jumping ship? One way is by offering a good benefits package.

Many small-business owners mistakenly believe they cannot afford to offer benefits. But while going without benefits may boost your bottom line in the short run, that penny-wise philosophy could strangle your business's chance for long-term prosperity. "There are certain benefits good employees feel they must have," says Ray Silverstein, founder of PRO, President's Resource Organization, a nationwide network of peer group forums.

Heading the list of must-have benefits is medical insurance. But many job applicants also demand a retirement plan, disability insurance, and more. Tell these applicants no benefits are offered, and top-flight candidates will often head for the door.

The positive side to this coin: Offer the right benefits, and your business may just jump-start its growth. Give employees the benefits they value, and they'll be more satisfied, miss fewer workdays, be less likely to quit, and have a higher commitment to meeting the company's goals. Research shows that when employees feel their benefits needs are satisfied, they're more productive.

> ***"Take care of your people, and they will take care of your customers."***
>
> —J. Willard Marriott, founder of Marriott International Inc.

Benefit Basics

The law requires employers to provide employees with certain benefits. You must:

- Give employees time off to vote, serve on a jury, and perform military service
- Comply with all workers' compensation requirements (see Chapter 22)
- Withhold FICA taxes from employees' paychecks and pay your own portion of FICA taxes, providing employees with retirement and disability benefits
- Pay state and federal unemployment taxes, thus providing benefits for unemployed workers
- Contribute to state short-term disability programs in states where such programs exist
- Comply with the federal Family and Medical Leave Act (see "Family Matters" on page 360)

You are not required to provide:

- Retirement plans
- Health plans (except in some states)
- Dental or vision plans
- Life insurance plans
- Paid vacations, holidays, or sick leave (except in some localities)

In reality, however, most companies offer some or all of these benefits to stay competitive.

Most employers provide paid holidays for Christmas Day, New Year's Day, Memorial Day, Independence Day, Labor Day, and Thanksgiving Day. Many employers also either allow their employees to take time off without pay or let them use vacation days for religious holidays.

Most full-time employees will expect one to two weeks' paid vacation time per year. In explaining your vacation policy to employees, specify how far in advance requests for vacation time should be made, and whether in writing or verbally.

There are no laws that require employers to provide funeral leave, but most allow two to four days' leave for deaths of close family members. Companies that don't do this generally allow employees to use some other form of paid leave, such as sick days or vacation.

Legally Speaking

Complications quickly arise as soon as a business begins offering benefits, however. That's because key benefits such as health insurance and retirement plans fall under government scrutiny, and it is very easy to make mistakes in setting up a benefits plan.

And don't think nobody will notice. The IRS can discover in an audit that what you are doing does not comply with regulations. So can the U.S. Department of Labor, which has been beefing up its audit activities of late. Either way, a goof can be very expensive. You can lose any tax benefits you have enjoyed, retroactively, and penalties can also be imposed.

The biggest mistake? Leaving employees out of the plan. Examples range from exclusions of part-timers to failing to extend benefits to clerical and custodial staff. A rule of thumb is that if one employee gets a tax-advantaged benefit—meaning one paid for with pretax dollars—the same benefit must be extended to everyone. There are loopholes that may allow you to exclude some workers, but don't even think about trying this without expert advice.

aha!

Want a quick way to save on workers' comp insurance premiums? Some companies offer a 5 percent discount for simply having a written policy prohibiting drugs in the workplace. It's a cheap trick to save big. Ask your workers' comp provider for details.

>> Family Matters

The federal Family and Medical Leave Act (FMLA) requires employers to give workers up to 12 weeks off to attend to the birth or adoption of a baby, or the serious health condition of the employee or an immediate family member.

After 12 weeks of unpaid leave, you must reinstate the employee in the same job or an equivalent one. The 12 weeks of leave does not have to be taken all at once; in some cases, employees can take it a day at a time.

In most states, only employers with 50 or more employees are subject to the Family and Medical Leave Act. However, some states have family leave laws that place family leave requirements on businesses with as few as ten employees, and in the District of Columbia all employees are covered. To find out your state's requirements, visit the Labor Department's website at dol.gov/whd/contacts/state_of.htm.

Such complexities mean it's good advice never to go this route alone. You can cut costs by doing preliminary research yourself, but before setting up any benefits plan, consult a lawyer or a benefits consultant. An upfront investment of perhaps $1,000 could save you far more money down the road by helping you sidestep potholes.

Expensive Errors

Providing benefits that meet employee needs and mesh with all the laws isn't cheap—benefits probably add 30 to 40 percent to base pay for most employees. That makes it crucial to get the most from these dollars. But this is exactly where many small businesses fall short, because often their approach to benefits is riddled with costly errors that can get them in financial trouble with their insurers or even with their own employees. The most common mistakes:

- *Absorbing the entire cost of employee benefits.* Few companies are footing the whole benefits bill these days. The size of employee contributions varies from a few dollars per pay period to several hundred dollars monthly, but one plus of any co-payment plan is that it eliminates employees who don't need coverage. Many employees are covered under other policies—a parent's or spouse's, for instance—and if you offer insurance for free, they'll take it. But even small co-pay requirements will persuade many to skip it, saving you money. These days, many companies charge a much higher rate to cover spouses who could otherwise get coverage from their own employer.

- *Covering nonemployees.* Who would do this? Lots of business owners want to buy group-rate coverage for their relatives or friends. The trouble: If there is a large claim, the insurer may want to investigate. And that investigation could result in disallowance of the claims, even cancellation of the whole policy. Whenever you want to cover somebody who might not qualify for the plan, tell the insurer or your benefits consultant the truth.
- *Sloppy paperwork.* In small businesses, administering benefits is often assigned to an employee who wears 12 other hats. This employee really isn't familiar with the technicalities and misses a lot of important details. A common goof: not enrolling new employees in plans during the open enrollment period. Most plans provide a fixed time period for open enrollment. Bringing an employee in later requires proof of insurability. Expensive litigation is sometimes the result. Make sure the employee overseeing this task stays current with the paperwork and knows that doing so is a top priority.
- *Not telling employees what their benefits cost.* "Most employees don't appreciate their benefits, but that's because nobody ever tells them what the costs are," says PRO's Silverstein. Many experts suggest you annually provide employees with a benefits statement that spells out what they are getting and at what cost. A simple rundown of the employee's individual benefits and what they cost the business is very powerful.
- *Giving unwanted benefits.* A work force composed largely of young, single people doesn't need life insurance. How to know what benefits employees value? You can survey employees and have them rank benefits in terms of desirability. Typically, medical and

financial benefits, such as retirement plans, appeal to the broadest cross-section of workers.

If workers' needs vary widely, consider the increasingly popular "cafeteria plans," which give workers lengthy lists of possible benefits plus a fixed amount to spend.

Health Insurance

Health insurance is one of the most desirable benefits you can offer employees. There are several basic options for setting up a plan:

>> Above and Beyond

What does COBRA mean to you? No, it's not a poisonous snake coming back to bite you in the butt. The Consolidated Omnibus Budget Reconciliation Act (COBRA) extends health insurance coverage to employees and dependents beyond the point at which such coverage traditionally ceases.

COBRA allows a former employee after he or she has quit or been terminated (except for gross misconduct) the right to continued coverage under your group health plan for up to 18 months. Employees' spouses can obtain COBRA coverage for up to 36 months after divorce or the death of the employee, and children can receive up to 36 months of coverage when they reach the age at which they are no longer classified as dependents under the group health plan.

The good news: Giving COBRA benefits shouldn't cost your company a penny. Employers are permitted by law to charge recipients 102 percent of the cost of extending the benefits (the extra 2 percent covers administrative costs).

The federal COBRA plan applies to all companies with more than 20 employees. However, many states have similar laws that pertain to much smaller companies, so even if your company is exempt from federal insurance laws, you may still have to extend benefits under certain circumstances. Contact the U.S. Department of Labor to determine whether your company must offer COBRA or similar benefits, and the rules for doing so.

- *A traditional indemnity plan, or fee for service.* Employees choose their medical care provider; the insurance company either pays the provider directly or reimburses employees for covered amounts.
- *Managed care.* The two most common forms of managed care are the Health Maintenance Organization (HMO) and the Preferred Provider Organization (PPO). An HMO is essentially a prepaid health-care arrangement, where employees must use doctors employed by or under contract to the HMO and hospitals approved by the HMO. Under a PPO, the insurance company negotiates discounts with the physicians and the hospitals. Employees choose doctors from an approved list, then usually pay a set amount per office visit (typically $10 to $35); the insurance company pays the rest.
- *Self-insurance.* When you absorb all or a significant portion of a risk, you are essentially self-insuring. An outside company usually handles the paperwork, you pay the claims, and sometimes employees help pay premiums. The benefits include greater control

>> Health Savings Accounts and Small Business

Employer health-care costs rose an average of 15 percent each year over five years to an average of about $700 per month per employee, according to surveys by The Kaiser Family Institute and The National Association of Health Underwriters. About 45 percent of U.S. small-business owners provide no health-care coverage, in large part because of the cost.

Health Savings Accounts in conjunction with a high-deductible insurance plan can be one way small-business owners can offer health insurance affordably to employees. An HSA allows employees to put money into a savings account (which is invested in funds or interest-bearing accounts) to cover health-care costs. As of 2014, annual out-of-pocket costs could not exceed $6,350 for an individual. Ask your benefits coordinator or get more information by Googling "Health Savings Accounts" or see WageWorks' handy FAQ at www.wageworks.com/employers/benefits/health-savings-account-hsa.aspx.

of the plan design, customized reporting procedures, and cash-flow advantages. The drawback is that you are liable for claims, but you can limit liability with "stop loss" insurance—if a claim exceeds a certain dollar amount, the insurance company pays it.

- *Health savings accounts.* HSAs allow workers with high-deductible health insurance to make pretax contributions to cover health-care costs. A high-deductible plan is one that has at least $1,250 annual deductible for single coverage and $2,500 for family coverage in 2013 and 2014. Furthermore, as of 2014, annual out-of-pocket costs paid under the plan must be limited to $6,350 for individuals and $12,700 for families.

  Employer contributions to HSAs are tax deductible, excludable from gross income, and are not subject to employment taxes. Employees can use these tax-free withdrawals to pay for most medical expenses not covered by the high-deductible plan.

Cost Containment

The rising costs of health insurance have forced some small businesses to cut back on the benefits they offer. Carriers that write policies for small businesses tend to charge very high premiums. Further complicating matters, states are mandating certain health-care benefits so that if an employer offers a plan at all, it has to include certain types of coverage. Mandated benefits increase the cost of basic health coverage from less than 20 percent to more than 50 percent, depending on the state, according to a recent analysis from the Council for Affordable Health Insurance. Employers who can't afford to comply often have to cut insurance altogether.

The good news: Some states have tried to ease the financial burden by passing laws that offer incentives to small-business

e-fyi

Small-business owners can evaluate their options and generate a quote at no charge at BenefitMall.com (benefitmall.com). This site also offers electronic brochures, training videos, and other useful information so you can know what you're looking at when you compare plans for your business.

owners who provide their employees with coverage. There are also ways to cut costs without cutting into your employees' insurance plan. A growing number of small businesses band together with other entrepreneurs to enjoy economies of scale and gain more clout with insurance carriers.

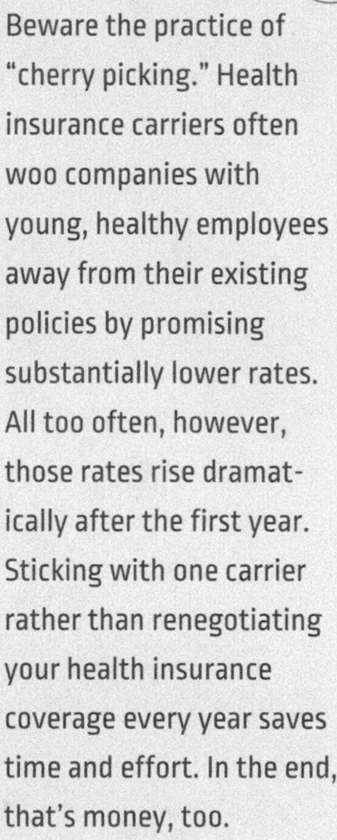

warning

Beware the practice of "cherry picking." Health insurance carriers often woo companies with young, healthy employees away from their existing policies by promising substantially lower rates. All too often, however, those rates rise dramatically after the first year. Sticking with one carrier rather than renegotiating your health insurance coverage every year saves time and effort. In the end, that's money, too.

What's more, the Affordable Care Act has also provided a way, in some states, for employees who aren't offered insurance or who don't like their options, to sign up through health care exchanges administered by the state. The plans are offered at competitive rates and lower-wage earners are offered offsets or stipends. The laws and rules are still changing, so be sure to stay informed.

Many trade associations offer health insurance plans at lower rates for small-business owners and their employees. Your business may have only five employees, but united with the other, say, 9,000 association members and their 65,000 employees, you have substantial clout. The carrier issues a policy to the whole association; your business's coverage cannot be terminated unless the carrier cancels the entire association.

Associations are able to negotiate lower rates and improved coverage because the carrier doesn't want to lose such a big chunk of business. This way, even the smallest one-person company can choose from the same menu of health-care options that big companies enjoy.

Associations aren't the only route to take. In some states, business owners or groups have set up health insurance networks among businesses that have nothing in common but their size and their location. Check with your local chamber of commerce to find out about such programs in your area.

Some people have been ripped off by unscrupulous organizations supposedly peddling "group" insurance plans at prices 20 to 40 percent below the going rate. The problem: These plans don't pay all policyholders' claims because they're not backed by sufficient cash reserves. Such plans often have lofty-sounding names that suggest a larger association of small employers.

How to protect yourself from a scam? Here are some tips:

- *Compare prices.* If it sounds too good to be true, it probably is. Ask for references from other companies that have bought from the plan. How quick was the insurer in paying claims? How long has the reference dealt with the insurer? If it's less than a few months, that's not a good sign.
- *Check the plan's underwriter.* The underwriter is the actual insurer. Many scam plans claim to be administrators for underwriters that really have nothing to do with them. Call the underwriter's headquarters and the insurance department of the state in which it's registered to see if it is really affiliated with the plan. To check the underwriter's integrity, ask your state's insurance department for its "A.M. Best" rating, which grades companies according to their ability to pay claims. Also ask for its "claims-paying ability rating," which is monitored by services like Standard & Poor's. If the company is too new to be rated, be wary.
- *Make sure the company follows state regulations.* Does the company claim it's exempt? Check with your state's insurance department.
- *Ask the agent or administrator to show you what his or her commission, advance, or administrative cost structure is.* Overly generous commissions can be a tip-off; some scam operations pay agents up to 500 percent commission.
- *Get help.* Ask other business owners if they have dealt with the company. Contact the Better Business Bureau to see if there are any outstanding complaints. If you think you're dealing with a questionable company, contact your state insurance department or your nearest Labor Department Office of Investigations.

Retirement Plans

A big mistake some business owners make is thinking they can't fund a retirement plan and put profits back into the business. But fewer than half the employees at small companies participate in retirement plans. And companies that do offer this benefit report increased employee retention and happier, more efficient workers. Also, don't forget about yourself: Many business owners are at risk of having insufficient funds saved for retirement.

To encourage more businesses to launch retirement plans, the Credit for the Small Employer Pension Plan provides a tax credit for costs associated with starting a retirement plan. The tax credit may be claimed for a maximum period of three years. There are four rules you must follow to be eligible for the credit, according to Investopedia.

1. The plan must be a qualified retirement plan, such as pension, profit sharing, stock bonus, or qualified annuity plan; e.g., a 401(k), Simplified Employee Pension (SEP) plan, or SIMPLE.
2. Employers with 100 or fewer employees who received at least $5,000 in compensation for the preceding year are eligible. Part-time employees must be considered part of this group.
3. The plan cannot just be for an owner/employee. It must also cover at least one non-highly compensated employee, who makes $110,000 or less a year and is not an owner of the company.
4. The employer is not allowed to have sponsored a pension plan during the three years preceding the new plan's start date.

The credit is a maximum of $500 in the year the plan starts and $500 in each of the next two years, assuming at least $1,000 of expenses are incurred in both years. Expenses cannot be lumped together.

For more information, see IRS Form 8881, *Credit for Small Employer Pension Plan Start-Up Costs.*

Don't ignore the value of investing early. If, starting at age 35, you invested $3,000 each year with a 14 percent annual return, you would have an annual retirement income of nearly $60,000 at age 65. But $5,000 invested at the same rate of return beginning at age 45 only results in $30,700 in annual retirement income. The benefit of retirement plans is that savings grow tax-free until you withdraw the funds—typically at age 59. If you withdraw funds before that age, the withdrawn amount is fully taxable and also subject to a 10 percent penalty. The value of tax-free investing over time means it's best to start right away, even if you start with small increments.

Besides the long-term benefit of providing for your future, setting up a retirement plan also has an immediate payoff—cutting your taxes.

Here is a closer look at a range of retirement plans for yourself and your employees.

aha!

IRS Publication 560, *Retirement Plans for Small Business*, describes rules for SEP, SIMPLE, and other qualified plans. It's free; visit irs.gov or call (800) TAX-FORM.

Individual Retirement Account (IRA)

An IRA is a tax-qualified retirement savings plan available to anyone who works and/or the person's spouse, whether the individual is an employee or a self-employed person. One of the biggest advantages of these plans is that the earnings on your IRA grow on a tax-deferred basis until you start withdrawing the funds. Whether your contribution to an IRA is deductible will depend on your income level and whether you're covered by another retirement plan at work.

Jeffrey S. Kahn, an employee benefits attorney with Greenberg Traurig in Boca Raton, Florida, says you can't contribute to a traditional IRA after age 70½, and you must begin distributions by April 1 following the year you reach age 70½. There also is a 10 percent penalty for funds withdrawn (with limited exceptions) before age 59.

You also may want to consider a Roth IRA. While contributions are not tax-deductible, withdrawals you make at retirement will not be taxed. The contribution limit in 2014 for both single and joint filers was $5,500 per person or $6,500 for individuals aged 50 and older. After that, contributions are indexed to inflation.

A single person may contribute fully to a Roth IRA with an adjusted gross income (AGI) of under $114,000, with benefits phasing out up to $129,000. For married couples filing jointly, full contributions are possible with an AGI less than $181,000, with benefits being eliminated at $191,000. These limitations are also adjusted periodically.

There's also a retirement savings option known as a Roth 401(k) to consider. It is a 401(k) plan that allows employees to designate all or part of their elective deferrals as qualified Roth 401(k) contributions. Qualified

Roth 401(k) contributions are made on an after-tax basis, just like Roth IRA contributions. Employees' contributions and earnings are free from federal income tax when plan distributions are taken. Regardless of income level, Kahn says you can qualify for a deductible IRA as long as you do not participate in an employer-sponsored retirement plan, such as a 401(k). If you are in an employer plan, you can qualify for a deductible IRA if you meet the income requirements. Keep in mind that it's possible to set up or make annual contributions to an IRA any time you want up to the date your federal income tax return is due for that year, not including extensions. The contribution amounts for deductible IRAs are the same as for Roth IRAs.

e-fyi

Want to know how you're doing on your retirement savings plan? Check out CNN Money's online retirement planning calculators at cgi.money.cnn.com/tools. They provide an easy, accurate way to help you determine how much you'll need and what your chances are of getting there. And if it looks like you'll fall short, suggestions are provided for improving your plan. Best part—it's free!

Savings Incentive Match Plan for Employees (SIMPLE)

SIMPLE plans are one of the most attractive options available for small-business owners. With these plans, you can choose to use a 401(k) or an IRA as your retirement plan.

A SIMPLE plan is just that—simple to administer. This type of retirement plan doesn't come with a lot of paperwork and reporting requirements.

You can set up a SIMPLE IRA only if you have 100 or fewer employees who have received $5,000 or more in compensation from you in the preceding year. Generally, the employer must make contributions to the plan by either matching each participating employee's contribution, dollar for dollar, up to 3 percent of each employee's pay, or by making an across-the-board 2 percent contribution for all employees, even if they don't participate in the plan, which can be expensive.

The maximum amount each employee can contribute to the plan is $12,000 for 2014. After that, the amount will be indexed for inflation.

>> Manual Labor

Sooner or later, every entrepreneur needs to write a manual. Employee policy manuals, procedures manuals, and safety manuals are just a few of the more important ones.

Even if you only have one employee, it's not too soon to start putting policies in writing. Doing so now—before your staff grows—can prevent bickering, confusion, and lawsuits later when Steve finds out you gave Joe five sick days and he only got four.

How to start? As with everything, begin by planning. Write a detailed outline of what you want to include.

As you write, focus on making sure the manual is easy to read and understand. Think of the simplest, shortest way to convey information. Use bullet points and numbered lists, where possible, for easier reading.

A lawyer or a human resources consultant can be invaluable throughout the process. At the very least, you'll want your attorney to review the finished product for loopholes.

Finally, ensure all new employees receive a copy of the manual and read it. Include a page that employees must sign, date, and return to you stating they have read and understood all the information in the manual and agree to abide by your company's policies. Maintain this in their personnel file.

Participants in a SIMPLE IRA who are age 50 or over at the end of the calendar year can also make a catch-up contribution of an additional $2,500 in 2014.

Simplified Employee Pension (SEP) Plan

As its name implies, this is the simplest type of retirement plan available. Essentially, a SEP is a glorified IRA that allows you to contribute a set percentage up to a maximum amount each year. Paperwork is minimal, and you don't have to contribute every year. And regardless of the name, you don't need employees to set one up.

If you do have employees—well, that's the catch. Employees do not make any contributions to SEPs. Employers must pay the full cost of the plan, and whatever percentage you contribute for yourself must be applied to all eligible employees. Generally, the maximum contribution is 25 percent of an employee's annual salary (up to $260,000) or $51,000, whichever is less.

As your company grows, you may want to consider other types of retirement plans, such as Keogh or 401(k) plans.

> ***"When you get into a tight place and everything goes against you, 'til it seems as though you could not hang on a minute longer, never give up then, for that is just the place and time the tide will turn."***
>
> —Harriet Beecher Stowe

Where to Go

With so many choices available, it's a good idea to talk to your accountant about which type of plan is best for you. Once you know what you want, where do you go to set up a retirement plan?

Banks, investment companies, full-service or discount brokers, and independent financial advisors can all help you set up a plan that meets your needs. Many of these institutions also offer self-managed brokerage accounts that let you combine investments in mutual funds, stocks, bonds, and certificates of deposit (CDs).

Low-Cost Benefits

In addition to the standard benefits discussed above, there are plenty of benefits that cost your company little or nothing but reap huge rewards in terms of employee satisfaction and loyalty. Consider these ideas:

- *Negotiate discounts with local merchants for your employees.* Hotels, restaurants, and amusement parks may offer discounts on their various attractions, including lodging and food, through corporate customer programs. Warehouse stores, such as Sam's Club, allow discounted membership to employees of their corporate members. Movie theaters provide reduced-rate tickets for companies' employees. Don't forget to offer employees free or discounted prices on your own company products and services.

- *Ask a local dry cleaner for free pickup and delivery of your employees' clothes.* Or ask a garage for free transportation to and from work for employees having their cars serviced there. Many businesses are willing to provide this service to capture—and keep—new customers.
- *Offer free lunchtime seminars to employees.* Health-care workers, financial planners, safety experts, attorneys, and other professionals will often offer their speaking services at no charge. Education is beneficial for both your employees and your business.
- *Offer supplemental insurance plans that are administered through payroll but are paid for by the employee.* Carriers of health, life, auto, and accident insurance typically offer these plans at a lower rate to employers, so everybody benefits.
- *Offer a prepaid legal services plan administered through payroll but paid for by the employee.* Like insurance, the purpose of the prepaid legal service is to provide protection against the emotional and financial stress of an employee's legal problems. Such services include phone consultations regarding personal or business-related legal matters, contract and document review, preparation of wills, legal representation in cases involving motor vehicle violations, trial defense services, and IRS audit legal services.

  The employer deducts the monthly service fee from the paychecks of those employees who want to take advantage of the service. Typical fees range from $10 to $16 per month per employee and cover most routine and preventive legal services at no additional cost. More extensive legal

tip 

Taking time to thank your employees pays off in performance. Some ways to show appreciation: Send birthday cards to workers' homes. Write congratulatory notes for a job well done. Use food to boost morale—Popsicles on a hot day or hot chocolate in the winter. Small things make a big difference in making employees feel valued.

services are provided at a lower rate when offered in this manner, saving employees money.

- *How about an interest-free computer loan program?* Making it easier for employees to purchase computers for their personal use increases the technical productivity of employees on the job. The employee chooses the computer and peripherals based on the employer's parameters. (For example, the computer must be a Macintosh, and the entire package may not exceed $3,000.) The company purchases the system, allows the employee to take it home, and deducts the payments from his or her paycheck. Although there's some initial capital outlay, it is recouped quickly. Any computer experience an employee can gain at home will most likely enhance his or her proficiency in the workplace.
- *Let employees purchase excess inventory from your business at a significant discount via sample sales or employee auctions.* Arrange these purchases in conjunction with regularly scheduled companywide "yard sales" for employees to buy and sell their personal belongings.

One of the most appreciated but most overlooked benefits is membership in a credit union. There are some 6,000 well-established, state-chartered credit unions throughout the United States and Canada that accept startup businesses as members—at no charge.

The benefits to your employees are threefold: Most likely they'll increase their savings rates (especially if you offer automatic payroll deduction), they'll have access to lower loan rates, and they'll pay lower fees—if any—for services. Services credit unions frequently offer include:

- Automatic payroll deductions
- Individual retirement accounts
- Savings certificates
- Personal and auto loans
- Lines of credit
- Checking accounts
- Christmas club accounts

Only state-chartered credit unions are allowed to add new companies to their membership rosters. To find a credit union that will accept your

>> Perk Up

Consider joining employee discount organizations like WageWorks, NextJump, or Corporate Perks. These companies aggregate discounts and points-based purchasing on everything from local restaurants to theme park tickets to big-box retailers.

NextJump's corporateperks.com program is available to any company with 10 or more employees. According to the company, "Corporate Perks aggregates employees across tens of thousands of corporations to negotiate exclusive offers from top-name merchants, providing a perfect solution for both employees and employers in this economy by stretching the power of employees' paychecks. Active employees save an average of $1,400 a year through the program on items including computers, monthly cell phone bills, pet care, groceries, apparel, home furnishing, and more." Signing up is easy and often costs an employer nothing.

company, call your state's league of credit unions. You can also write to the National Credit Union Administration, 1775 Duke St., Alexandria, VA 22314-3428, or call (703) 518-6300 for more information, or visit their website at ncua.gov for a list of consumer resources.

When comparing credit unions, get references and check them. Find out how communicative and flexible the credit union is. Examine the accessibility. Are there ATMs? Is there a location near your business? Consider the end users—your employees.

Once your company is approved, designate one person to be the primary liaison with the credit union. That person will maintain information about memberships as well as enrollment forms and loan applications. Kick things off by asking a credit union representative to conduct on-site enrollment and perhaps return periodically for follow-up or new sign-ups.

e-fyi

Recruiting firm Robert Half International offers several salary guides that contain data on average starting salaries in accounting, administration, information technology, and legal and creative fields. You can request a complimentary copy at roberthalf.com.

Employee Policies

Now that you have employees, you'll need to set policies on everything from pay rates to safety procedures. Many of these policies are regulated by federal and state laws. Here's what you need to know.

Paying Employees

There are many state and federal laws that regulate the paying of employees, including the calculation of overtime, minimum wage, frequency of payment, and rules for payment upon termination. Because your business may be subject to both state and federal laws (the primary federal law being the Fair Labor Standards Act, or FLSA), which are often quite different and conflicting, you should check with the applicable government agencies, your local chamber of commerce, and appropriate financial and legal experts to determine which laws apply and how to correctly apply them.

Nonexempt and Exempt Employees

Under the FLSA, all employees are classified as either exempt or nonexempt. A nonexempt employee is entitled to a minimum wage and overtime pay as well as other protections set forth in the FLSA.

Exempt employees are not protected under these rules. However, if you wish to classify an employee as exempt, you must pay him or her a salary. Anyone paid on an hourly basis is automatically considered nonexempt; however, there can be nonexempt employees who are paid a salary.

If salary is not the determining factor, what factors determine whether an employee is exempt? Under FLSA and most state laws, an exempt employee is one whose job responsibilities, more than 50 percent of the time, involve the regular exercise of discretionary powers and can be characterized as:

- *Executive*: usually a manager who directs the work of other employees and has the authority to make recommendations affecting the status of those employees (e.g., hiring, firing, promotions, etc.)
- *Administrative*: a person who performs office or nonmanual work under general supervision and which primarily involves special assignments or requires specialized training, experience, or education

- *Professional*: a person who is engaged in a recognized profession such as medicine or law or in a field of learning that is specialized and predominantly intellectual or creative

There are additional exempt categories for more specialized employees, such as professional artist, computer professional, or outside salesperson. In addition, your business may be subject to both federal and often more restrictive state laws governing the exempt status of employees. In those instances, an employee must meet the requirements for exemption under both federal and state law.

aha!

Want to get an idea what others in your industry are paying workers? The Bureau of Labor Statistics offers the National Compensation Survey for most regions of the country. The information is broken down by occupation, industry, and demographics. The bureau also has information about benefits. To access the reports, visit stats.bls.gov/ncs/#tables or call the Bureau of Labor Statistics' regional offices.

Tip Credits

States sometimes set minimum wage laws above or below the federal minimum wage standard. If your business is subject to both state and federal wage laws, you'll have to pay the higher of the two.

Under federal law (the Small Business Job Protection Act of 1996), you may apply tips received by an employee against the employee's minimum hourly wage, provided that: 1) the employee makes at least $30 per month in tips, 2) the employer pays at least 50 percent of the federal minimum wage, 3) the employee has been informed of the applicable law governing minimum wage and tip credits, and 4) the employee retains all the tips received by him or her (unless there's tip pooling with other employees). However, if the hourly wage paid by the employer when added to the tip credit is less than the minimum wage, the employer must make up the difference. In 2014, the maximum tip credit that an employer can currently claim under the FLSA is $5.12 per hour (the minimum wage of $7.25 minus the minimum required cash wage of $2.13), according to the U.S. Department of Labor.

Once again, you will need to make sure there are no contrary state laws governing if and when you can use tip credits to meet your minimum wage obligations. For example, California law requires a higher minimum wage than federal law and thus applies to California employers and employees. Because California law prohibits crediting tips against minimum wage payments, tip credits are unavailable in California. Tip credit is also not allowed in Alaska. For a table of state laws on tip credits, see dol.gov.

Overtime Requirements

Excluding certain industry-specific exceptions, federal and state law requires that nonexempt employees be paid overtime. Under the FLSA, nonexempt employees must be paid one and a half times their normal rate of pay for hours worked in excess of 40 hours during a workweek. A workweek is defined as seven consecutive 24-hour periods. Although a workweek can begin on any day, it must be fixed for that employee and cannot be changed so as to evade applicable overtime laws. Most states also have their own overtime laws, and if they are more favorable to employees, those are the ones you must follow. For example, under California law, employees who work more than eight hours during a single day are entitled to overtime, even if they do not work more than 40 hours during a given workweek (the federal requirement).

Remember, nonexempt employees can be salaried as well as hourly. So don't make the mistake of assuming that just because an employee is salaried, he or she is exempt from overtime.

tip

For a comprehensive look at how to start a successful safety program, read *Workplace Safety: A Guide for Small and Midsized Companies* (Wiley) by Dan Hopwood and Steve Thompson. Besides presenting helpful information about core OSHA regulatory requirements, the book covers workers' comp, disaster and emergency planning, injury investigation and management, best practices, and more.

Workplace Safety

Why worry about safety? Because failing to do so could literally destroy your business. Besides the human loss, workplace accidents cost money and time. You could be liable for substantial penalties that could wipe out your business's cash flow. The Occupational Safety and Health Administration (OSHA) can assess huge fines for willful violations of safety rules, especially when they could result in death or serious physical harm.

OSHA Regulations

All employers, whether they have one employee or 1,000, are subject to federal OSHA requirements. However, in states where a federally certified plan has been adopted, the state plan governs. State standards must be at least as strict as the federal standards.

Businesses that use nonemployee workers, such as independent contractors or volunteers, are not subject to OSHA. Workers are considered employees under OSHA if you:

- Control the actions of the employee
- Have the power to control the employee's actions
- Are able to fire the employee or modify employment conditions

Small employers (with ten or fewer employees) don't have to report injuries and illnesses. However, that doesn't mean they are exempt from OSHA regulations.

Compliance with OSHA

The first step in complying with OSHA is to learn the published safety standards. The standards you must adhere to depend on the industry you're in.

Every business has to comply with general industry standards, which cover things like safety exits, ventilation, hazardous materials, personal protective equipment like goggles and gloves, sanitation, first aid, and fire safety.

Under OSHA, you also have a general duty to maintain a safe workplace, which covers all situations for which there are published standards. In other words, just because you complied with the standards

e-fyi

The Institute for a Drug-Free Workplace is a nonprofit association that provides information, education, and advocacy for companies concerned about controlling illicit drug and alcohol use at work. Learn about drug-testing laws, read model employer guides and more at drugfreeworkplace.org.

that specifically apply to your industry doesn't mean you're off the hook. You also need to keep abreast of possible hazards from new technology or rare situations the government may have thought of and published standards for.

Sound exhausting? Help is available. Start with your insurance carrier. Ask if an insurance company safety specialist can visit your business and make recommendations. Insurers are typically more than happy to do this since the safer your business is, the fewer accident claims you'll file. The government can also help you set up a safety program. Both OSHA and state safety organizations conduct safety consultation programs. Check to see what programs your state safety department offers, too. You'll find local offices of government agencies as well as state organizations listed in the government pages of your phone book, usually under "Labor Department," "Department of Commerce," or a similar name.

Don't forget to tap into the resources of your chamber of commerce, industry trade association, and other business groups. Many offer safety seminars and provide safety training literature free or for a nominal charge. In addition, there are private consultants who can help small businesses set up safety programs that meet OSHA regulatory standards. Your lawyer may be able to recommend a good one in your area.

aha!

Peeved at payroll paperwork? Companies with as few as five employees can benefit from using a payroll service. When comparison shopping, get references, ask about services, and inquire if the payroll service keeps abreast of federal and state payroll regulations. Rates depend on number of employees and frequency of payroll.

Put It in Writing

When you have a safety program in place, put it in writing with a safety manual (see "Manual Labor" on page 370). Your safety manual should explain what to do in the event of a fire, explosion, natural disaster, or any other catastrophe your business may face. Make sure you keep well-stocked fire extinguishers and first-aid kits at convenient locations throughout your building. Also make sure employees know where these are located and how to use them. In addition to emergency procedures, your safety manual should explain proper procedures for performing any routine tasks that could be hazardous. Ask employees for input here; they are closest to the jobs and may know about dangerous situations that aren't obvious to you.

Finally, have an insurance professional, a government representative, and an attorney review the finished manual. You're putting your company's commitment to safety on the line, so make sure you get it right.

Emphasize the importance of safety with meetings, inspections, and incentive programs. These don't have to cost a lot (or anything). Try establishing a "Safe Employee of the Month" award or giving a certificate for a free dinner for winning suggestions on improving safety.

Discriminatory Treatment?

Although sexual harassment is one of the biggest issues facing employers these days, it's not the only type of discrimination you need to be concerned about. Under the Civil Rights Act of 1991, employees who believe they were victims of job discrimination due to race, religion, sex, or disability are entitled to a trial by jury.

While companies with fewer than 15 employees are generally exempt from federal discrimination laws, most states have their own laws prohibiting discrimination, which, in addition to protecting a wider range of categories of employees, include smaller businesses within their scope and procedural and evidentiary standards more favorable to claimants. Apart from the tendency of some juries to award plaintiffs disproportionately high monetary damages, litigation in this area of the law can be extremely costly, even if you prevail. One attorney estimates the average legal fees for defense in a sexual harassment suit, regardless of the verdict, are upwards of $75,000.

warning

Learn to spot some of the signs that sexual harassment may be occurring in your company. Increased absenteeism, drop-offs in productivity, and lackluster performance are all signs that something may be wrong.

Concerns over discrimination are more important than ever in today's increasingly diverse business world. If you run a small business, chances are you will be dealing with employees from many cultures, races, and age groups. How can you keep things running harmoniously and protect your business from legal risk? The best policy is to make sure that everyone in your workplace understands what constitutes harassment and discrimination—and also understands the benefits of a diverse workplace.

Big companies may spend thousands on diversity training, but there are plenty of low-cost options available:

- Learn as much as you can from books on the subject and from exposure to people who are different from you.
- Investigate video series on managing diversity. Many are available for rental or purchase.
- Consider public programs. A growing number of Urban League, chamber of commerce, Small Business Administration, and community college seminars and courses are bringing business owners together to learn about diversity issues.

As the business owner, it's important to set a good example. Some ground rules to help keep you out of trouble:

- Don't touch employees inappropriately.
- Never date someone who works for you.
- Don't demean others or make suggestive comments. Watch your mouth; what seems humorous to some may offend others.
- Be sensitive to diversity of all kinds. Are employees in their 50s making condescending remarks about the "young upstarts" in their 20s? Two white women in their 40s might face a cultural conflict if one is from the Midwest and the other is from the West Coast, or if one has children and the other doesn't.
- If you decorate your office for the holiday season, don't include some religious symbols and leave out others.

> ***"Make the tough decisions and don't look back. As long as you've thought things through and have kept the company's interests at heart, you'll be OK."***
>
> —Katrina Garnett, founder of Crossroads Software Inc.

Many employers use nonreligious décor such as snowflakes and candles.

Put policies regarding discrimination and harassment in writing as part of your employee manual (see "Manual Labor" on page 370). Outline the disciplinary action that will be taken and the process by which employees can make their complaints known.

Hold a brief orientation meeting to introduce employees to your new policy or reacquaint them with the one already in place. Spell out very plainly what is and isn't acceptable. Many employees are especially confused about what constitutes sexual harassment. While you want to follow the law and make a safe environment, you also don't want your staff walking around scared to say hello to one another.

Even if an incident does arise, the good news for business owners is most complaints can be solved at the company level, before the issue comes close to a courtroom. To make this work, however, time is of the essence. Don't put off dealing with complaints, or the victim is likely to stew.

Give both parties a chance to tell their side of the story. Often, the cause is a simple misunderstanding. To cover all your bases, you may want to have a neutral consultant or human resources professional from outside the company investigate the matter.

PART

5

BUY

CHAPTER

25

Buyer's Guide

Business Equipment Basics

When it comes to the day-to-day operation of your business, how you set up your office or workspace is essential. Your goal is to create a work space that's well-lit and will keep you as comfortable as possible, with access to business-related tools and equipment that will allow you to stay organized and productive.

As you'll discover in this chapter, technology plays a tremendous role in creating a well-equipped office on a relatively tight budget. Just a few years ago, for example, if you needed a high-speed laser printer, scanner, copier, and fax machine, these items needed to be purchased separately, at a cost of $400 to $2,000 each. Today, you can walk into any office or electronics superstore and purchase an all-in-one machine for under $300 that's capable of handling all these functions, in addition to the workload of most small or even medium-sized businesses.

What types of equipment do you need? It varies greatly based on the type of business you run as well as your personal work habits. In general, however, there are some basic pieces of equipment most new business owners need (these are discussed in more detail throughout Part 5):

- Computers (desktop, laptop, tablet—and for some people, a sophisticated smartphone)
- Software
- Fax machine
- Laser printer and/or color printer and label printer
- Copier
- Scanner
- Phone
- Voice mail
- Smartphone with wireless ability (such as an Android, BlackBerry, or Apple iPhone)
- Calculator (if the one on your smartphone isn't sophisticated enough)

Look over this list and consider which items you can't live without, which products would be nice to have, and which (if any) you don't need. And note that these days, some of this equipment can be purchased all in one (printer, fax, scanner, copier, for example). When equipping a startup business, you must tread a fine line. Most people race out and purchase the best office equipment possible and often feel the compulsion to buy the latest tools simply because they're cutting-edge. These entrepreneurs often end up spending way beyond their budgets, only to find that the items they bought aren't necessary, don't make them more productive, aren't compatible with their existing equipment, or contain so many bells and whistles that the equipment is too confusing and time consuming to fully use.

At the other end of the spectrum are those entrepreneurs who try to make do with the bare bones. In an effort to save a few dollars, these business owners sacrifice efficiency and productivity, chugging along with a prehistoric computer, a one-line phone, or an internet connection that moves at a snail's pace. In short, they're penny-wise and pound-foolish.

Today's business climate is so fast-paced, clients won't do business with you if you can't keep up. Assess each item, and determine how it could benefit your business. Would you use a color laser copier often enough to make it worth the cost? Or for that occasional color copy, can you head over to Staples or a FedEx Kinko's? Do you really need the cutting-edge $2,000 laptop from Apple, or would you be just as productive using a $400 iPad when you're on the go?

e-fyi

Save time and money with virtual fax machines. Rather than purchasing a standalone fax machine, online services, such as eFax.com, will forward faxes to your email account and allow you to send faxes directly from your word processor or web browser.

Choose what technology and office equipment you absolutely need, then purchase the best quality equipment you can afford. When it comes to purchasing technology, you may be better off spending a bit extra now to ensure the item will last two to three years rather than purchasing something that will quickly become outdated or need to be replaced in just 12 to 18 months.

Cost Cutters

Technology is far less expensive than it was just three to five years ago. For example, you can purchase a powerful, PC-based desktop computer for under $1,000. Even five or six years ago, a similar machine might have cost $3,000 or more. That being said, equipping your business can still be a costly proposition. Fortunately, there are several different avenues you can take to keep the expenses to a minimum.

Financing Plan

If you're buying expensive equipment, consider having the manufacturers "lend" you money by selling the equipment to you over a period of time.

save

How can you keep equipment costs way down? Consider launching from a business incubator, where services, facilities, and equipment are shared among several businesses. Often the incubator provider—a university or a startup or research group—provides most of the equipment for free. (For more on incubators, see Chapter 17.)

There are two types of credit contracts commonly used to finance equipment purchases: the conditional sales contract, in which the purchaser does not receive title to the equipment until it is paid for; and the chattel-mortgage contract, in which the equipment becomes the property of the purchaser on delivery, but the seller holds a mortgage claim against it until the contract amount is fully paid.

There are also lenders who will finance 60 to 80 percent of a new equipment purchase, while you pay down the balance as a down payment. The loan is repaid in monthly installments, usually over one to five years, or the usable life of the equipment. (Make sure the financing period doesn't extend past the usable life of the equipment; you don't want to be paying for something you can no longer use.)

By using your equipment suppliers to finance the purchase, you reduce the amount of money you need upfront.

When Lease Is More

Another way to keep equipment costs down is to lease instead of buy. These days, just about anything can be leased—from computers and heavy machinery to complete offices. The kind of business you're in and the type of equipment you're considering are major factors in determining whether to lease or buy.

If you're starting a one-person business and need just one computer, for instance, it probably makes more sense to buy. On the other hand, if you're opening an office that will have several employees, and you require a dozen computers, you may want to look into leasing.

According to the Equipment Leasing Association of America (ELA), approximately 80 percent of U.S. companies lease some or all of their equipment, and there are thousands of equipment-leasing firms nationwide catering to that demand. "[Leasing is] an excellent hedge against obsolescence," explains a spokesperson at the ELA, "especially if you're leasing something like computer equipment and want to update it constantly."

Other leasing advantages include: making lower monthly payments than you would have with a loan, getting a fixed financing rate instead of a floating one, benefiting from tax advantages, conserving working capital

>> Package Deal

As you put together an equipment leasing package, consider these issues:

- > What equipment do you need and for how long?
- > Do you want to bundle service, supplies, training, and the equipment lease itself into one contract?
- > Have you anticipated your company's future needs so you can acquire adequate equipment?
- > What is the total payment cost?

Also ask the following questions about each leasing source you investigate:

- > Who will you be dealing with? Is there a separate company financing the lease? (This may not be desirable.)
- > How long has the company been in business? As a general rule, deal only with financing sources that have been operating at least as many years as the term of your proposed lease.
- > Do you understand the terms and conditions during and at the end of the lease?
- > Is casualty insurance (required to cover damage to the equipment) included?
- > Who pays the personal property tax?
- > What are the options regarding upgrading and trading in equipment before the lease period expired?
- > Who is responsible for repairs?

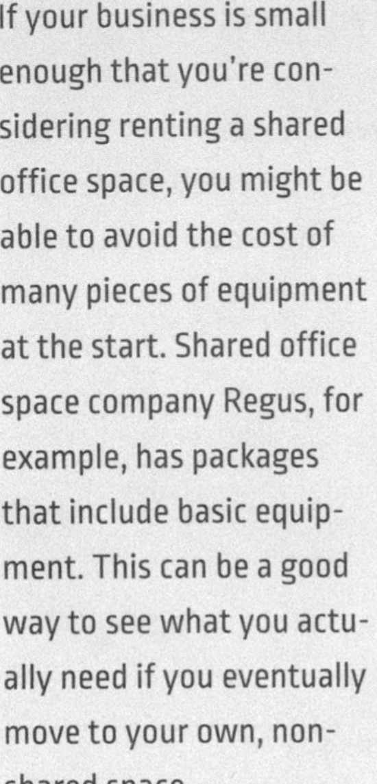

save

If your business is small enough that you're considering renting a shared office space, you might be able to avoid the cost of many pieces of equipment at the start. Shared office space company Regus, for example, has packages that include basic equipment. This can be a good way to see what you actually need if you eventually move to your own, non-shared space.

and avoiding cash-devouring down payments, and gaining immediate access to the most up-to-date business tools. The equipment also shows up on your income statement as a lease expense rather than a purchase. If you purchase it, your balance sheet becomes less liquid.

Leasing also has its downside, however: You'll pay a higher price over the long term. Another drawback is that leasing commits you to retaining a piece of equipment for a certain time period, which can be problematic if your business is in flux (although some leases do allow for upgrades or pre-lease termination, with a fee).

Every lease decision is unique, so it's important to study the lease agreement carefully. Compare the costs of leasing to the current interest rate, examining the terms to see if they're favorable. What's the lease costing you? What are your immediate and long-term savings? Compare those numbers to the cost of purchasing the same piece of equipment, and you'll quickly see which is the more profitable route.

Because startups tend to have little or no credit history, leasing equipment is often difficult or even impossible. However, some companies will consider your personal, rather than business, credit history during the approval process.

If you decide to lease, make sure you get a closed-end lease, without a balloon payment at the end. With a closed-end lease, nothing is owed when the lease period ends. When the lease period terminates, you just turn the equipment in and walk away. With an open-end lease, it's not that simple. If you turn in the equipment at the end of the lease, but it's worth less than the value established in the contract, then you're responsible for paying the difference. If you do consider an open-end lease, make sure you're not open to additional charges, such as wear and tear.

Finally, balloon payments require you to make small monthly payments with a large payment (the balloon) at the end. While this allows you to conserve your cash flow as you're making those monthly payments, the bad news is, the final balloon payment may be more than the equipment is worth.

There are many different avenues through which you can secure an equipment lease, including:

- Banks and bank-affiliated firms that will finance an equipment lease may be difficult to locate, but once found, banks may offer some distinct advantages, including lower costs and better customer service. Find out, however, whether the bank will keep and service the lease transaction after it's set up.
- Equipment dealers and distributors can help you arrange financing using an independent leasing company.
- Independent leasing companies can vary in size and scope, offering many financing options.
- Captive leasing companies are subsidiaries of equipment manufacturers or other firms.
- Broker/packagers represent a small percentage of the leasing market. Much like mortgage or real estate brokers, these companies charge a fee to act as an intermediary between lessors and lessees.

For more information on leasing, the ELFA in Arlington, Virginia (elfaonline.org), and the Business Technology Association (BTA) in Kansas City, Missouri (bta.org), offer member directories. The ELFA allows you to personalize your directory and pay for only the information you need, which could result in paying well under $100 or well over. The BTA offers informative resources and

save

Turning off your computer at night, on average, can save you more than $100 a year, and using more energy-efficient lights can reduce your lighting costs by two-thirds. However, certain types of fluorescent lights cause added eye strain, so if you'll be spending 8 to 12 hours per day in a work space with minimal natural light, you might want to splurge on lighting that won't give you a headache or cause added eye stress over time.

publications to the public for free; however, only subscribing members have access to its membership database.

Wise Buys

If your calculations show that buying makes more sense for you, you've still got some decisions to make. First and foremost, where to buy?

Buying New Equipment

The same piece of new equipment that costs $400 at one store can cost $1,000 at another. It all depends on where you go. Here are some of the most common sources for new equipment, with a look at the pros and cons of each.

- *Superstores.* Office or electronics superstores usually offer competitive retail prices because they buy from manufacturers in volume. Most superstores offer delivery, installation, and ongoing service contracts for the equipment they sell. However, you're unlikely to find knowledgeable salespeople at superstores, and the prices will almost always be higher than shopping online. It is convenient, however, to walk into a store and walk out with your purchase a few minutes later. You can see and touch the products before buying—and if you decide to wait and buy online, you'll know what you are getting.
- *Specialty stores.* Small electronics stores and office equipment retailers are likely to offer more assistance in putting together a package of products. Salespeople will typically be more knowledgeable than at superstores, and service will be more personal. Some even offer service plans. On the downside, prices go up accordingly. Unfortunately, many of these smaller, independently owned and operated specialty stores are going out of business because they can't compete with online vendors or the superstores.
- *Dealer direct sales.* Many manufacturers choose this option as a way of maintaining their service-oriented reputation. On the plus side, you'll get assistance from highly knowledgeable salespeople

who can help you put together the right system of products. You may also get delivery, installation, and training at no extra cost. Many entrepreneurs swear by this method of buying. The downside: Since you're dealing with one manufacturer, you won't get to compare brands. Apple is the perfect example of a major computer company that has its own chain of retail stores, plus sells directly to consumers online. If you go this route, make sure you've thoroughly researched all the competitor manufacturers so you've come to a solid decision about which to go with.

- *E-tailers.* Without incurring the overhead of a brick-and-mortar store, online equipment sellers are able to offer brand names at much lower prices than retail stores. To shop efficiently online, you must know exactly what you want to purchase (make and model numbers, for example), then shop around for the best prices and the most reputable online dealers. Use price-comparison websites, such as Nextag (nextag.com), to compare multiple vendors and their prices, and you could wind up saving 20 to 60 percent off your purchase. Shopping online also works for office supplies, such as toner or ink cartridges. A toner cartridge for a brand-name laser printer might sell at Staples or Office Max for $89 but be available online for $29 (or less).

save

If you purchase all your equipment from a single supplier, you may be able to negotiate volume discounts, free shipping, and other extras. Be aware, though, that purchasing from a single vendor also limits your options. For example, the merchant you choose for your computer system may not offer the brand of printer you want, or you could run into a problem if your sole vendor winds up going out of business.

No matter what source you buy your equipment from, be sure to investigate the type of service and support you'll get before you whip out your wallet. A tempting price may seem like a compelling reason to forgo solid service when you buy, but it won't seem like such a good deal when the equipment grinds to a halt in the middle of an urgent project. . . and the vendor is nowhere to be found.

In terms of computers, many businesses are considering Apple as a good alternative to traditional PC-based systems. With the AppleCare program, at any time, you can visit an Apple Store or call Apple's toll-free number and quickly receive technical support by a knowledgeable expert. In addition, most repairs and replacement equipment are covered for three years. This is something Dell, Acer, HP, Lenovo, and other PC-based computer manufacturers have begun to offer mostly as an add-on services (for an annual or monthly fee).

To get the most from your equipment vendors, it's important to lay the proper groundwork and let them know you're a valuable customer. One way to do this is to make sure you send in the service registration card that comes with the product. Contact the vendor before problems arise to ask for all the relevant telephone and tech support websites, so you know what to do if disaster strikes. Maintain contact with the vendor by asking questions as they come up and giving the vendor any comments or ideas that might improve the product. This identifies you as an active user and builds your relationship with the vendor.

Before you buy, prioritize what's important to your company; then get the answers to these questions:

- How long does the warranty last?
- Does the vendor offer a money-back guarantee? Many computer peripherals, for instance, come with 30-day money-back guarantees. Use this time to make sure the item works with the rest of your system.
- Does the vendor charge a restocking fee? Even when a company offers a money-back guarantee, the company may charge a restocking fee of up to 20 percent of the product's cost on returns. Some states prohibit such charges if merchandise is defective.
- What fees, if any, does the vendor charge for technical support?
- How easy is it to reach technical support? Try calling before you buy the product to see how long you're put on hold and whether the company returns calls. Many companies outsource their technical support overseas, so you should also make sure you can understand the support personnel.
- What hours is technical support available? Be aware of time zones.

If you're in California and your East Coast vendor shuts down at 5 P.M., you could be out an afternoon's work if your computer breaks down after 2 P.M. California time.

- How quickly can the vendor fix problems? What are the repair costs and time frames (on-site repair, 24-hour turnaround, etc.)? Who pays shipping costs if items need to be returned to the manufacturer for repair during the warranty period?
- Does the vendor offer any value-added services?

Buying Used Equipment

If new equipment is out of your price range, buying used equipment can be an excellent cost-cutter. But with technology changing so rapidly, you'll want to make sure you're buying used equipment that will meet your needs now and in the future. Some older computers, for example, won't run the current Windows or Mac operating system, or the current versions of software you may absolutely need.

There are several sources for buying used. Asset remarketers, for example, work with equipment leasing companies to resell repossessed office equipment through a network of dealers and wholesalers—and sometimes directly to business owners. The prices are a fraction of the cost of buying or leasing brand-new equipment.

It is also simpler buying repossessed equipment through an asset remarketer than going to a bankruptcy auction. As in most auctions, the asset remarketing company accepts bids—but that is where the similarities end. Asset remarketers keep equipment in warehouses, which buyers visit at their convenience as they would a discount office equipment retailer. Often, the remarketer has a price sheet showing the equipment's original price and its approximate resale value. Use this price sheet as a guideline in making your offer.

e-fyi

InterSchola (interschola.com) sells used equipment from an unlikely source: school districts. The company works with public and private school systems to help them sell their surplus equipment using an online auction sales model. You can often find amazing deals on used computers and office equipment. And, the group also has eBay sellers.

>> Lemon Alert

Whether you're buying used equipment from an individual or a business, take these steps to make sure you don't get stuck with a lemon.

- *Know the market*. Do some research before you make an offer. Read the classifieds to learn the going rates for the item(s) you want. Notice how quickly items move. Is it a seller's market, or do you see the same ads run again and again?
- *Try before you buy*. Just as you would with new equipment, it's essential to "test drive" used equipment. Run diagnostic tests; make sure all the parts are working; ask about any problems. (Sometimes, an item may still be still worth buying, even with the cost of repairs.)
- *Bring a buddy*. If you're a novice, it helps to take a more experienced friend or colleague with you when you test the equipment. He or she can ask questions you may not think of and pinpoint problems you might miss.
- *Don't buy if you don't feel comfortable*. Never let anyone talk you into a purchase or make you feel guilty. If you don't feel good about it, walk away.

Leasing companies and asset remarketers must resell equipment at a fair market price, so three bids are usually required. But you'll want to move quickly to "win" the bid.

If you want to buy, make an offer to the asset remarketing firm, which then sends it to the leasing company's asset recovery manager. Some asset remarketers may require a $100 deposit when the leasing company accepts the bid; you'll then need to pay with cash, certified funds, or cashier's check within a few days.

While finding asset remarketing companies is as easy as calling a local repossession company, be careful to find a reputable company. While some states regulate asset remarketing or repossession firms, there are unscrupulous remarketers in many states who hang out their shingle, pocket consumers' deposits, and then disappear. The safest way to find an honest asset remarketer is to call a leasing company's asset recovery manager and ask for the name of a local firm. Some leasing companies prefer to sell to end users directly, and they may ask for a description of the equipment you want to purchase.

In addition to asset remarketers and leasing companies, you can also buy used equipment from individuals (look in the local classifieds) or check online for used equipment retailers in your area. Also, be sure to check popular used equipment websites like Craigslist.org or Freecycle.com. Another great resource for finding affordable equipment are auction sites, such as eBay (ebay.com), Bid4Assets (bid4assets.com), Liquidation.com, and DellAuction.com, which allows you to buy used and refurbished computers, peripherals, and software of any brand. The resale of used equipment is becoming more common, so in most cities, you'll have several sources to choose from.

CHAPTER

26

Business 24/7

Using Technology to Boost Your Productivity

If you're like most businesspeople, you probably have a main base of operations you call your "office." It may not be an office per se; it could be a retail store, a factory floor, or a trailer on a construction site. It could also be a room in your home or a cubicle within a larger office complex. But it's where you can usually be found from 9 to 5, or whatever your typical office hours might be.

Correction: It used to be where you were usually found. These days, your exact location could vary widely. Nowadays, entrepreneurs and employees alike are just as likely to be found working from home, at a client's office, from a hotel room, or while on board an airplane or train. In fact, according to wide-ranging studies by The Dieringer Research Group, more than 21 million of us frequently work from our cars. And some 15 million of us

> **save**
> 
> Don't need new? The best place to find used equipment is eBay. There are other auction sites, but eBay's advantage is the sheer size of its worldwide community. Amazon.com also has a growing community of resellers.

often work from parks and other recreational sites, according to Industrial and Technology Assistance Corporation (ITAC).

Widespread use of devices such as smartphones, tablets, and laptops means your office can be virtually anywhere, and you can stay connected to your co-workers, clients, and customers anywhere, anytime. Cloud computing has also allowed data to be stored remotely, in the cloud, and be accessed from any of your devices, from anywhere at any time.

Business that's conducted away from the traditional office goes by a lot of names, such as mobile working or telecommuting—the latter term underlining the importance of telecommunications in enabling this activity (see Chapter 28). Another way to think about it is that, in reality, the office is you—or, at the very least, it becomes whatever workspace you happen to be occupying at the moment. Work is now something you do, rather than a place you go to.

In today's business world, you're no longer chained to a desk by a fixed phone number (that only rings at your office), and you're not required

>> Virtually on the Road

Thanks to the latest technology, there's a wide range of products and online services to help you become more productive. The Apple iPhone and iPad, for example, offer thousands of business-oriented applications that allow users to truly customize their phones and transform them into the ultimate time management, contact management, and personal productivity tools.

For the on-the-go entrepreneur, the trick is to choose technology-based tools, whether it's an iPhone, iPad, Samsung Galaxy, BlackBerry, netbook or laptop, that best fits your work habits and style, and that you're most comfortable using. After all, you want to boost your productivity, not drown yourself in technology that's not appropriate or overly complicated for what you need it to do.

to use an oversized desktop computer that contains all your important data. Internet connectivity, powerful mobile versions of office tools, and new phone services (not to mention the latest smartphones and wireless tablets) are loosening the ties that bind and making physical location more about convenience than necessity.

> **tip** 
>
> While computers and mobile devices run using a wide range of different operating systems, most are designed to operate seamlessly in a work environment. So if you're using an Apple MacBook Pro laptop, for example, you'll have no trouble transferring data and files with co-workers or clients using Windows-based computers. In fact, you can even run Windows-based software on the latest Macs, and Microsoft Word for iPad has gone a long way to making the iPad a virtual office, too.

Many entrepreneurs have the equivalent of fully equipped virtual offices in the laptops, smartphones, tablets, and other devices they carry around. Some enterprises have even become virtual companies with workmates spending most of their time in separate locations and meeting only occasionally. Basically, you're "in the office" whenever you're telecommuting.

The goal isn't always to do away with the traditional "office," it's to use networking and communications technologies to turn it into your "extended office." Your extended office isn't a real, physical location; it's virtual, just like the internet is virtual.

People have been teleworking for decades, but our current degree of mobility is a direct outgrowth of the internet and the mobile devices that allow us to easily connect to the internet from anywhere.

Equipping Your Virtual Office

Even though you may be starting your first business, you're probably fairly experienced with desktop and laptop computers, tablets, wireless PDAs, and smartphones, as well as other productivity equipment needed to get your enterprise off the ground.

One unfailing characteristic of consumer and small-business technologies is that each new iteration delivers more for less. Depending on how much mobility you need, you may find yourself buying more individual pieces of equipment than in years past, but the price tag on each one is guaranteed to be lower than last year and the year before that. In fact, prices fall so rapidly that office technologies depreciate at an unusually high rate. It's not that they're shoddy—quite the contrary. But their resale values are continuously being undercut by cheaper and more powerful successors.

save

Depending on your needs, you might not need to invest $1,500 to $2,500 for a state-of-the-art laptop. If your main tasks when traveling include surfing the web, word processing and spreadsheet management, for example, a less cumbersome, smaller, and lightweight netbook may work for you just fine. The latest netbooks cost only around $300. Or, you might find a tablet, like an iPad or Samsung Galaxy, is all you need for the office. Those can cost between $400 and $900.

Therefore, you should think about office tools and technology slightly differently than you do other durables. Here are a few truisms that need to be taken into account when buying hardware (although they don't necessarily apply to software):

- Even the most expensive office item, the desktop or laptop computer, is dirt cheap by historical measures.
- Whatever you buy and whenever you buy it, it will appear expensive and underpowered compared to succeeding versions. New computer technology is available every three to six months. The computer you purchase brand-new today will be outdated by more powerful equipment within months and will probably need to be replaced altogether within two to three years if you want to stay current.
- Theoretically, office equipment pays for itself in a very short time by enhancing your productivity; it then helps you make money by letting you do whatever you do faster and better.

Treat your current technology-related purchases as a simple business expense rather than the investment in capital equipment it actually is. Irrespective of how you treat these items on your tax return, don't try to extract the value of this equipment over years. Yes, the products will work just fine and continue to deliver productivity for years. But their costs are likely recovered within weeks or months—no depreciation calculations required (see "It's Now or Never" on page 407).

That's not to say you shouldn't get the best buy you can. Cash is always precious. But so is your time, and price tags are usually overshadowed by the return on investment from most office products. The real issue when shopping for office equipment is whether the new machine will deliver a higher rate of productivity than the old. It's a mistake to try to squeeze the last bit of usefulness out of older equipment when a change could result in higher levels of moneymaking. Keep it only until something comes along that will deliver still higher productivity.

Being Well-Connected

The first concern in equipping yourself and your office (virtual or otherwise) is connectivity. You have an expanding constellation of stuff, and it's more important than ever that it all work together for maximum effect. Efficiency today means being well-connected—both inside and outside the walls of your company.

Even if you start off as a solo operator working from a home office, you'll want to connect electronically to clients and suppliers and possibly share proposals, spreadsheets, and other data files. This not only requires phone, fax, and instant messaging (IM) connections but usually some level of compatibility among productivity software, IM services, and handheld wireless devices. That used to mean sticking with only the most popular operating systems and applications for seamless data transfer among employees and business partners.

Today, however, PCs can communicate easily with Macs and BlackBerrys and with iPhones; any peripheral that connects to a computer via a USB connection will most likely work with all computers on a network. Sure, you may still encounter minor compatibility issues, but for the most part, exchanging data and files is easier than ever, regardless of what type(s) of computer equipment is being used.

What's more, Google's rise in the shared document space has been tremendous. It's easy to selectively share—and set parameters around

>> The Cloud and You

Simply put, the cloud means applications and services that people access via the internet instead of installing software on their computers. If you're online, you're somewhere in the cloud. If you use Facebook or Gmail or Twitter, you're using the cloud. Many valuable services that once required installing applications have become available as cloud services, explains Mikal Belicove, a market positioning, social media, and management consultant specializing in website usability and business blogging. Often, businesses can use free versions of these applications in the cloud, while full-featured versions are available at low subscription rates, he says.

"The cloud is more heavy-duty and provides more utility than initially perceived," Belicove says. You can access customer relationship management tools like those offered by Salesforce.com and SugarCRM.com, but also project management applications and many other types of helpful programs and utilities, he says.

who can edit and who can simply view—spreadsheets, Word documents, PowerPoint presentations, and many other kinds of documents through Google Docs and Google Drive. Free or low-cost services like DropBox, weTransfer, and Box have also made it possible to skip the USB and thumb drives altogether by acting as a transfer service.

At your office, the network is the thing that helps you coordinate your tools—both those inside the office and out—and share them and the data on them among co-workers and partners. Networks include your local area network, Bluetooth connections between devices, cellular connections over a wide area, and, of course, the ultimate backbone, the internet. Increasingly, these things are all backed up by "the cloud."

It's not really our portable devices—laptop computers, smartphones, wireless PDAs, netbooks, and tablets—that extend our office. It's this infrastructure that networks all our devices together and provides quick and easy access to shared information, both in-house and outside, via global network providers.

It Takes Two

Even if you're starting as a sole proprietor, you really should have at least two connected computers. It doesn't have to be two desktop computers. If you travel a lot, one could be a laptop computer or netbook.

It's only a matter of time before your hard drive crashes, you get a virus, or there's some inscrutable problem with the first PC's on/off button—whatever. Computers are very durable, but all equipment can fail.

What will you do if the machine holding your critical business information happens to be among the 100,000 computers lightning strikes every year? Even if you're among that fraction of users who have their data backed up somewhere, how long will it take you to run out and buy a new computer, and add all your usual software configured the way you like it so that data can be read? How many hours or days can your business be offline from customers and business partners?

Realistically, you need at least one duplicate of your main computer that you can immediately turn to without losing a step. Ideally, there will be a third, and more portable option—a hard drive or an automatic cloud backup storage option (you'll pay an annual fee of between $40 and $150, depending on what it is you need to back up and how much data you'll need to store). For some businesses, cloud backup is enough to make a second backup computer unnecessary. But, be aware: The cloud isn't infallible. Some services have experienced outages that can last an hour or two—or up to 12 hours.

> **tip**
>
> 
>
> Remote backup services, such as Carbonite.com, and the extremely low cost of high-capacity external hard drives make it easy and inexpensive to automatically and continuously back up your data. Now you have no excuse for not properly backing up your data so if something happens to your primary computer, you can be back up and running, without losing any data, within minutes or hours—not days or weeks.

Serving It Up

Ultimately, you want to build a virtual network that ties your office and its equipment to all those other places and devices you use for work. Thanks to wireless networking, your home, back deck, a local coffee shop, park, and automobile can be part of your extended office.

But the most logical place to start is by connecting your main computer and its backup. Your primary workstation will likely become the heart of your operation, where you generate spreadsheets, keep your books, create sales presentations, surf the net, and do your word processing. If yours is a one-person operation, that's usually where the master copy of everything is kept—and, if you have help, no one but you should have full access to its data.

Again, even if you're a one-person operation, you need another computer mirroring that system (or a very reliable data backup solution). As your company grows, you might find it cheaper and more convenient to keep master copies of software and even data on a central computer, and give different workstations access to more or less of it, depending on the needs of individual employees.

Any computer that serves up data and other services to other devices is referred to as a server, and the computers that get information from it are the clients, arranged in a client/server architecture. As networks and the demands on them grow, computers with specialized characteristics are chosen for servers. But you don't need to worry about shopping for server hardware at this stage.

By the way, the word *server* also is used to refer to the operating system that makes connections possible—software like Windows, Mac OS, or Linux. These operating systems include all the special software features to connect your computers in a network.

save

If you're looking to create a network and link multiple computers and peripherals within your home office, many computer retailers will help you set this up for free (or for a small fee) when you purchase equipment from them. When shopping for computer equipment, ask what support services are available directly from the retailer. For example, Best Buy (bestbuy.com) offers its Geek Squad Computer Set-Up and Support services, starting at a flat fee of $99.

Networking

The traditional way to create your LAN (Local Area Network) is to string very inexpensive Category 5 cable between the Ethernet adapters of two or more computers. You may need to buy a small and inexpensive Ethernet card to plug into one or more of your computers, if any of them is old. Most computers today come with built-in Ethernet adapters.

Easier still is to network your computers wirelessly using wifi network adapters. These come in a variety of network speeds and adapter styles—Ethernet or USB ports, or as an add-in card—for connecting computers. These wifi transceivers have become hugely popular, a standard feature of laptops and available in all smartphones and wireless PDAs. More U.S. households now use wifi wireless technology for home networking than cabled Ethernet, according to a study by Parks Associates. Wifi hot spots in airports, hotels, coffee shops, and other public places deliver this connectivity on the road. And most smartphones have wifi hot spot capabilities for a small, additional, monthly fee on your wireless plan.

Broadband data channels on cellular networks are providing much wider connectivity. Formerly limited to carrying voice, cell phone networks are

>> It's Now or Never

In most cases, you'll probably find it more advantageous—and certainly more convenient—to expense, rather than depreciate, computer and telecommunications equipment on your tax returns. That way, there's less paperwork and no mind-bending depreciation calculations that change every year. Also, the time value of money tells us that a lump-sum refund to you today is always worth more than pro rata shares over the next three to five years.

Uncle Sam has been cooperating in recent years by raising the amount of business equipment you can expense rather than depreciate. No, he isn't getting soft and generous. Why then? Adam Smith, the father of modern economics, said it first: New equipment generates new [higher] levels of productivity, which generates increased profits, which generates increased taxes. Speak with your accountant about the latest tax deductions and allowances available.

increasingly able to transfer data at lightning-fast speeds. This technology works with cell phones, wireless PDAs, netbooks, and laptops—making the net available anywhere, regardless of whether there's a nearby electrical outlet or wifi hotspot.

Choosing Partners

There are two things on which you can rely these days when buying just about any individual piece of office equipment:

1. The minimum configuration is going to support 95 percent (or more) of what you want to do.
2. Prices will be so low as to eliminate just about all chance of buyer's remorse.

Add to that the ease with which internet shopping sites let you comparison shop, and you have a confluence of factors that make it pretty hard to go wrong when buying office equipment. Computers and peripherals are constantly evolving, but the choice of models and features are broad and deep.

When it comes to PCs, you can choose from dozens of well-known manufacturers, such as Dell, HP, or Lenovo, all of which run the Windows operating system.

Apple offers greater ease of use, superior technical support, the availability of Apple retail stores nationwide, and a sleeker design than most PCs, but they're also typically a bit more expensive. On that note, there is no one "right" computer brand, printer type, phone system, or fax solution for everyone, any more than everyone needs the same model Chevy or Ford. You're unique, and your business idea probably is, too. Your enterprise will have its own unique set of equipment needs that probably differ from those of the business next

e-fyi

Looking to purchase used equipment or other items? For some large items that cost a lot to ship, or when you're looking for something unusual in your own town, it's hard to beat Craigslist (craigslist.org). Instead of just one website and worldwide marketplace, Craigslist is a collection of cyber marketplaces arranged by city, where anyone can post just about anything for free. It's not yet in every city, but where it is, craigslist is a virtual version of the local paper's classified ads.

door. Not a problem. Web shopping sites let you quickly find just what you need.

Flying Business Class

Personal computers, whether PCs or Macs, are less expensive than ever. For about $1,500 (usually much less), you can buy a powerful, nicely equipped, state-of-the-art PC. For less than $2,500, you can purchase an extremely powerful Mac-based desktop (an iMac) that will meet all your business-related needs.

Your goal when purchasing computer equipment should be to select items that not only meet all your computing needs today but will also grow with you over the next two to three years until your next upgrade. Buy more than you need now so you'll be able to continue to run the latest versions of the software and applications you need to properly manage your business.

You'll want a business-class, rather than a first-class, computer. That means instead of going for the cutting-edge graphics and processor speeds preferred by enthusiasts of multimedia entertainment, gaming, and other photographic activities, a business user's money is better spent getting just a little more of all the standard stuff—memory, storage, a higher resolution or larger display, those things that not only make computing more pleasing but also enhance your productivity.

They can help you do more in less time, and, if you're in business, time is money. Things like waiting for databases to update, web pages to download, and insufficient memory errors waste your time and can interfere to different degrees with your efficiency. You want to have the best business productivity enhancer you can afford.

save

How long will a computer last? To maximize your return on investment, replace it every three years, advises the Information Technology Solution Providers Alliance. Older computers negatively impact security and productivity and cost considerably more per year to support and maintain—often twice the cost of newer technology.

Take Note

As mentioned, if you travel or work from home and the office, or different spots around your home, you may prefer that your second computer be a laptop or netbook. Portables come in all shapes and sizes today, and you can easily find one powerful enough to perform any or all the desktop duties described earlier.

When it comes to laptops, focus on their computing power (processor speed, memory, hard-drive capacity, available ports, DVD/CD drive, etc.) and battery life as well as the overall size and weight of the unit. A laptop that weighs five pounds or less is a lot easier to lug around when you're traveling than a larger laptop that weighs six to eight pounds.

However, if your laptop computer will be your primary backup computer, and you'll need serious computing power while on the go, you may want to spend more (up to $2,500) for a unit with a larger display and extra computing muscle. On the flip side, if you'll want a small, lightweight computer, a netbook (priced under $300) might be the perfect solution.

A typical laptop will generally run a few hundred dollars more than an equivalent desktop model, but name-brand laptops can easily be found for as little as $500. Laptops suitable for serious business users typically range between $1,000 and $2,500.

The Well-Dressed Computer

The minimum you should look for in terms of technical specifications for a desktop or laptop changes constantly. As a general rule, look for a computer with a fast processing speed, graphics card, and DVD/CD drive; sizeable amount of memory; large-capacity hard drive; powerful sound card; and plenty of ports.

Every six to 12 months, Apple overhauls its lineup of iMac and MacBook computers with improved specifications. For descriptions of the latest desktops and laptops available, visit any Apple store or apple.com. Plan on spending between $999 and $2,500 for a MacBook or MacBook Pro

tip

Need it fixed? Most computer retail stores have on-site repair departments to fix or install new hardware, even if you purchased the original computer elsewhere. The price to have a professional debug your PC or install an upgrade is $50 to $150 per hour. Add-on services and repairs for Macs cost about the same, but are typically billed by service, not hourly.

laptop and between $1,100 and $2,500 for an iMac or Mac Pro desktop that runs both Windows and Mac-based software applications.

Office Productivity Software

A computer is useless without the right software to support your business activities. The most popular suite of business-related applications is, without a doubt, Microsoft Office. It's available for both PCs and Macs. There are, however, other business application suites that also offer word processing, spreadsheet, database management, scheduling, contact management, and presentation tools.

One of these software suites alone could cost $150 to $400 or more, depending on the components included. Computers are so cheap that not many computer manufacturers include an office suite on a standard hard drive, but most will offer Microsoft Office preinstalled as an upgrade.

After that, two other kinds of software you can't live without are a security suite and accounting program. You'll want an all-encompassing security suite, such as those offered by companies like Symantec (symantec.com), McAfee (mcafee.com), Zone Labs (www.zonealarm.com/security/en-us/home.htm), Trend Micro (trendmicro.com), and Panda Labs (www.pandasecurity.com/usa/) that include a firewall, regularly updated anti-virus and anti-spyware definitions, email scanning and other protections for $50 to $90. If you're running Mac-based computers, different types of security software may be needed, depending on how you'll be using the computer.

Whether or not you use an accounting professional, you also need a good basic

warning

Got a cash-flow problem? Who doesn't? Don't solve it by succumbing to the gazillion counterfeit software offers filling your email inbox. If you get caught purchasing these low-cost knock-offs, you'll be fined heavily and could face criminal charges. Instead, look into using open source software, which is just as powerful as the higher priced commercial software you pay for, only it's 100 percent free, with no strings attached. SourceForge (sourceforge.net) is an excellent resource for finding and downloading a wide range of open source software for any operating system.

accounting program, from a company like Intuit (intuit.com), Sage 50 Accounting (http://na.sage.com/us/sage-50-accounting), or Microsoft (microsoft.com), to keep up with your checkbooks, bank accounts, invoices, bills, taxes, and inventory. Most of these programs let you pay bills and download bank account information electronically, use your printer to create checks, and link to tax preparation software so you can minimize your tax liability. Some popular programs are: Intuit's QuickBooks Pro, Bookkeeper, and Sage 50 Complete Accounting.

Peripherals

There are any number of things you can hang off a computer these days—or, more likely, wirelessly connect to your office network. The basics include printers, scanners, copiers, webcams, external hard drives, thumb drives, digital cameras, speakers, and fax machines. If you have an iPhone, Android, or BlackBerry, you can also connect these devices to your computer to sync data.

Most businesses need at least one good-quality laser printer; however, if your printing needs involve color or photo-quality output, an inkjet or high-end photo printer will also be useful. When choosing printers, look at the unit's resolution, print speed, and paper-tray size.

For most small businesses, an all-in-one device (sometimes referred to as a multifunction device, or MFD) that includes a printer, scanner, fax machine, and copier is ideal. Plus, you'll definitely want to invest in an external hard drive to back up important data.

tip

To buy online or not to buy online, that's the question. If you're not techno-savvy and need after-sales support, the superstores are a good option for purchasing equipment. If you're looking to save money and don't need support, buying online is the way to go.

Most peripherals these days connect to a computer via FireWire, or a USB or Bluetooth wireless connection. It's common for a desktop computer to have up to ten or more devices and peripherals connected to it, all of which work seamlessly with your software.

As a general rule, focus first on your needs, and then shop around for the most advanced technology you can afford. If you don't need a color laser printer, for example, opt for a less expensive black-and-white laser printer with a faster print speed and larger paper tray. Or if you're choosing between laser printers and inkjet printers, consider not only the cost of the hardware (the printer itself) but also the ongoing cost of toner or ink cartridges, as well as the printer's speed. If you'll frequently be producing 100-page reports, a printer that churns out 15 to 30 pages per minute is much more useful than one that prints just 8 pages per minute with a feeder that holds just 25 sheets.

Once you determine your needs, shopping for computer peripherals online will always save you a fortune. Reserve a visit to the local consumer electronics or office supply superstore to see and touch the latest technology firsthand before making your purchases.

In the past, any one of these peripherals could have been priced in the thousands, and, of course, you can still pay as much as you want to get all the buzzers and bells. But a personal laser printer will only set you back around $100—ditto for a scanner and a fax. And while a copier appointed for business can run into the thousands, you can find very capable ones for $200.

MFDs didn't used to be the best alternative for growing businesses when prices were high and the technologies of these devices were evolving at different rates. You could find yourself locked behind the curve on one or more, and, since MFDs cost in the thousands, their purchase became a complex decision.

Not so anymore. There are any number of MFDs priced between $100 and $300—from companies such as HP, Canon, Brother, Epson, and Kyocera—that pack an incredible amount of functionality. For example, HP—the longtime quality leader and high-priced spread in printing peripherals—has

save

Printers are relatively cheap. What's expensive is the toner or ink cartridges you must use with the printer. You can shop for name-brand cartridges at retail stores and pay a fortune, or you can shop online for compatible, no-name cartridges—that cost up to 80 percent less. Just go to a price comparison website, such as Nextag.com, and enter the make and model of your printer. Also check out eBay. In most cases, the cartridges are the same or better quality than their name-brand counterparts.

Office Equipment Budget

The following are rough estimates for what it will take to outfit a single entrepreneur with basic computer and telecommunications equipment, along with related services for the first year. More expensive options are always available, and you may not need every item on this list. Plus, some items can serve more than one individual without additional cost.

Basic Office Equipment	First-Year Low Cost	First-Year High Cost
Basic office furniture and accessories	$1,000	$2,000
1 Desktop computer	1,000	3,000
1 Laptop computer	1,100	2,000
Printer, scanner, copier, fax combo	100	500
Label printer	100	300
Software (office suite, security, accounting)	Free	2,500
Remote data backup service	100	500
Uninterruptible power supply	150	500
Miscellaneous supplies	500	1,000
Three-node wifi wireless LAN	50	250
High-speed internet access	500	1,000
2 Telephone lines	200	1,200
1 Smartphone with data access	800	1,200
Website domain hosting	60	300
Website design (simple site)	500	1,500
Total Startup Expenses	**$6,160**	**$17,750**

Figure 26.1. Office Equipment Budget

Office Shopping List

Use this shopping list to help price and compare your office equipment and service alternatives.

Expense	Price 1	Price 2
Desk, chair, filing cabinet		
Desktop computer		
Laptop/Netbook/Tablet		
Smartphone		
Laser printer		
Scanner		
Copier		
Fax machine		
Multifunction printer/scanner/copier		
Uninterruptible power supply		
Office productivity suite (software)		
Security software		
Accounting software		
Desktop or web publishing software		
Multiline telephone, plus two landlines		
Answering service		
Cell phone service		
High-speed internet access		
Website hosting		
Paper, cables, miscellaneous supplies		
Total Startup Expenses	$	$

Figure 26.2. Office Shopping List

an absolutely amazing MFD line with several models designed for entrepreneurs that print, scan, and copy for less than $200.

In some cases, it might be useful to think of these categories of peripherals as supplies, rather than equipment, because, in fact, the replacement toner cartridges for MFDs and individual copiers and printers can cost as much as the hardware itself. Today, an MFD is almost an impulse buy.

Suffice to say, entrepreneurship is no longer a stationary activity. Entrepreneurs go where the action is, stay productive en route, and use technology to adapt to changing market conditions and ad hoc business needs. Now you can make the most of what is available wherever you are.

CHAPTER

27

Net Works

Building Your Company Website

Why put your business online? The answer is simple. Because in today's business world, it's essential that your business have an online presence if you want to stay competitive. Your prospective and existing customers use the internet for a wide range of purposes, such as researching products they need, then purchasing those items from the comfort of their homes or offices, or anywhere else they may be. Chances are, your competition is already online and is using their internet presence as an extremely powerful sales, marketing, and promotional tool. Not being online puts your business at a serious disadvantage.

A web presence allows you to communicate with anyone, anywhere (or thousands of people at once) with email, a blog, an electronic newsletter, or directly through your website. Your website can also be an electronic brochure (that's available

24/7) to show and promote your wares to prospective customers, offer interactive customer service, allow them to make immediate purchases, then back up those sales with technical support.

Sounds Like a Plan

If you plan to sell anything online, having an ecommerce plan is as important as your original business plan. Because you're exploring new territory, making decisions about technology and marketing, and establishing a new set of vendor relationships, a well-thought-out plan will serve you well.

The first step in writing an ebusiness plan is to decide what kind of experience you want your online customers to have. Think not only about today but also two and five years down the road.

Your ecommerce plan starts with website goals. Who are your target customers? What do they need? Are they getting information only, or can they buy products at your site? These key questions, asked and answered early, will determine how much time and money you'll need to develop and maintain an online presence.

Second, decide what products or services you will offer. How will you position and display them? Will you offer both online and offline purchasing? How will you handle shipping and returns? Additionally, don't overlook the customer's need to reach a live person. A toll-free phone number should be prominently displayed that customers can call anytime to get their questions answered by a live person.

As you explore the web for vendors to support your e-business, have a clear idea of how you want to handle the "back end" of the business. If you decide to sell online, you'll need a shopping cart component,

tip

Building and maintaining a well-designed online presence, particularly a website with an ecommerce component, requires a significant time and financial commitment. For more details on how to accomplish this successfully and professionally without spending a fortune, pick up a copy of *Start Your Own eBusiness, Third Edition* (Entrepreneur Press) by Entrepreneur Press and Rich Mintzer.

which is a means of handling credit card processing, and an organized order fulfillment process. However, you may decide that your site is informational only, and that you will continue to process transactions offline.

Finally, even if you build an amazing website, don't assume people will find you on their own. If you simply build it, they will not come. If you want to develop a consistent flow of traffic to your site, it's essential that you plan, execute, and maintain an ongoing and multifaceted promotional strategy that's carefully targeted to your audience. This is in addition to the promotions, advertising, and marketing you already do for your brick-and-mortar business.

"The website should be viewed as an integral part of the marketing effort—as another 'front door,' if you will, into the business," says Frank Catalano, an Auburn, Washington, marketing strategy consultant and co-author of *Internet Marketing for Dummies*. "After all, the site is a way to distribute information, gather customer feedback, and even sell a product or service. Just promoting a website without regard to overall business goals and other marketing efforts is pointless."

save

Many domain registration services offer additional free or low-cost options. Domain parking, which holds your registered domain name at no charge until you're ready to launch, is one feature.

Email forwarding allows you to use your new domain name to receive email, while domain forwarding directs traffic to an existing site or web page. You can also save money if you pre-register your domain name for multiple years.

The Name Game

Once you've decided to have a website, one of your first "to-do" items is to make a list of possible website names or URLs. Then run, don't walk, to the nearest computer, log on to the internet, go to your favorite search engine, and type in "domain registration." You will find a list of companies, such as NetworkSolutions.com, GoDaddy.com, and Register.com, that will guide you through the simple domain registration process. For a modest fee ($8 to $75), you can register a domain name for one or more years. You'll probably discover that GoDaddy.com offers the most competitive rates for domain name registration, plus the widest range of online tools and services that will help you plan, design, publish, manage, and promote your online presence.

If the name you decide on is taken, you'll want to have at least two or three backup options. Let's say that you sell flowers, and you would like to register your online name as flowers.com. A search shows that flowers.com is taken. Your second choice is buyflowers.com, but that's already spoken for as well. Many of the domain name registrars, like GoDaddy.com or Register.com, offer several alternatives that are still available.

From the available names, choose one that's easy to spell and remember, and describes what your company does. Make sure, however, you're not imposing on someone else's trademark or copyrighted name. In many cases, the name of your company, with the addition of dot-com (www.[YourCompanyName].com) is a suitable domain name that you should definitely register.

If you choose a domain name that's difficult to spell or that might easily be confused with something else, also register the most common misspellings, or what you think people might accidentally type into their browser to find your website. If you don't do this, your competition might, and they could wind up stealing some of your website traffic.

Once you've chosen a name, prompts on the domain registration site will guide you through a simple registration procedure. You'll generally be offered one-, two-, or three-year registration packages. Once you pick a domain name and start promoting it, you'll want to stick with it. Otherwise, you'll confuse your customers and could lose web traffic. However, it is appropriate to have several domain names linking to the same website. These different domain names can be used as part of separate marketing and promotional plans that target an audience.

Why is domain name registration imperative? Everyone wants a catchy name, so registering yours ensures that no one else can use it as long as you maintain your registration. For a small investment, you can hold your place on the internet until you're ready to launch.

With your ecommerce name established, start telling people your domain name and promoting it heavily. Make sure you've done everything you can do offline to tell people about your site at the same time you actually go online. Print your web address on your business cards, brochures, letterhead, invoices, and press releases as well as on your product packaging and within product user manuals and advertisements. Stick it on other items, too, such as mouse pads, T-shirts, promotional key chains, and even your company's van.

Website Basics

Once you've registered your domain name and have a plan in place for what you want to offer prospective and existing customers online, the next major challenge is designing and building your actual website or online presence.

What makes a good website? Before getting enmeshed in design details, get the big picture by writing a site outline. In addition to basic text, your website can incorporate photos, illustrations, animation, videos, audio clips, music, and a plethora of other multimedia elements or content that will convey your information to your target audience in an easy-to-understand, visually appealing and appropriate manner. The content you develop and publish should directly relate to and help you achieve the goals and objectives you've set for your website.

A well-thought-out site outline includes:

- *Content.* The key to a successful site is content. Give site visitors lots of interesting information, incentives to visit and buy, and ways to contact you. Once your site is up and running, continually update and add fresh content to keep people coming back.
- *Structure.* Decide how many pages to have and how they'll be linked to each other. Choose graphics and icons that enhance the content.

tip

Even if you work from home or have a day job and are starting an e-business on a shoestring, customers need to be able to reach you. An answering machine or a voice-mail box that says "We are not in the office at this time. Our business hours are from blank to blank. Please leave your name and number and a brief message, and we'll get back to you" is a simple solution. You should also set up an email auto-responder that will guarantee customers that they'll hear back from you on the next business day.

- *Design.* With the content and structure in place, site design comes next. Whether you're using an outside designer or doing it yourself, concentrate on simplicity, readability, and consistency. Remember to focus on what you want to accomplish.
- *Navigation.* Make it easy and enjoyable for visitors to browse the site. For example, use no more than two or three links to major areas and never leave visitors at a dead end.
- *Credibility.* This is an issue that shouldn't be lost in the bells and whistles of establishing a website. Your site should reach out to every visitor, telling that person why he/she should buy your product or your service. It should look very professional, and give potential customers the same feeling of confidence they would get with a phone call or face-to-face visit with you. Remind visitors that you don't exist only in cyberspace. Your company's full contact information—company name, complete address, telephone, fax, and email—should appear on all or most of your individual web pages and be displayed prominently on your site's homepage.

An outline helps you get the most out of your website design/ecommerce budget. It will also help you determine whether you, or someone in your company, can design portions of the website, or if you need to solicit outside help. That way, when you hire someone, it will be for only the parts of the job that you'll need to have outsourced.

At this point, you have two options: You can bring your detailed outline to a prospective web designer, or you could go the do-it-yourself route. Once a designer has your outline, the process will be more efficient, but creating a website from scratch can still be costly and time-consuming. Consider researching one of the many website or ecommerce turnkey solution services, which allow you to design, publish, and manage a website or ecommerce site by customizing website templates using online design and management tools. These services are inexpensive, powerful, and allow you to create highly professional websites with no programming skills.

There are only a few possible reasons why you'd want to hire a website designer and/or programmer to have your site created from scratch vs. using a turnkey solution. One reason would be if you absolutely require

> *"A dream is just a dream. A goal is a dream with a plan and a deadline."*
>
> —Harvey MacKay, founder of MacKay Envelope Co.

specialized functionality (either on the front or back end of the site) that isn't offered by the turnkey solutions. Many startups initially spend too much on a custom-designed site that wasn't really required, and, ultimately, regret the decision since their financial resources could have been put to better use elsewhere. Instead, it's best to rely on an inexpensive turnkey solution for creating, publishing, and managing your website. As your company grows and becomes successful, it's then possible to transition to a custom-designed site, if the need arises.

Once you know what tools and resources you'll use to create and manage the site, the next step is to organize your site's potential content into a script. Your script is the numbered pages that outline the site's content and how web pages will flow from one to the next. Page one is your homepage, the very first page that site visitors see when they type in your URL. Arrange all the icons depicting major content areas in the order you want them. Pages two through whatever correspond to each icon on your homepage.

Writing a script also ensures your website is chock-full of appropriate content that's well-organized. Offer your visitors content that's valuable, informative, and engaging—make it worth their while to spend time on your site. Provide regular opportunities for visitors to get more content.

>> Research Made Perfect

Research is what makes an effective website. Some good resources are:

- *Entrepreneur.com's Online Business How-To Guides* (www.entrepreneur.com/ebusiness/howtoguides/). This series of articles offers everything you need to know about starting, running, and growing your online business.
- *E-Commerce Guide's Starting an Online Store: The Essential Checklist* (ecommerce-guide.com). These articles list everything you'll need to get your online store off the ground.

> **tip**
>
> When creating and designing your web content, you won't go wrong if you follow three basic design rules:
>
> 1. Put the most important pages near the top.
> 2. Eliminate extraneous words and visual clutter from the content.
> 3. Use headlines, icons, bullets, boldface words, and color only to draw attention to important content, not to distract or confuse the web surfer.

Whether you offer a blog, free electronic newsletter, a calendar of events, columns from experts, or book reviews, your content and the site's structure become the backbone of your website.

As part of your website design, use graphics, colors, and fonts that make sense (not just to you but to your target audience as well). Subtle visual cues make all the difference in how visitors respond to your website. Surf the net to research what combinations of fonts, colors, and graphics appeal to your audience, and incorporate pleasant and effective design elements into your site.

If your target audience is comprised of tween or teenage girls, using a color combination of pinks, reds, and other feminine or pastel colors, along with more decorative (yet easy-to-read font) makes sense. However, if you're targeting middle-age businessmen, a more masculine color scheme, combined with traditional fonts, should be used.

To create a successful website, all the elements must work seamlessly. Sure, having top-notch content is essential, but it must be displayed in a manner that's easy to understand, visually appealing, simple to navigate, and of interest to your target audience. How you present your information is important. It's not just about what you have to say, but it's also the manner in which you present that content that will either attract or repel your audience.

Handy Tools

Your website is your online presence and your connection to the world, so give it your very best shot, making sure it conveys the image and message you want and need your customers to see. Fortunately, there are loads of tools to help you improve your website's appearance.

>> Success by Design

For a successful website, follow these general dos and don'ts of site design.

Do:

- Make your site easy to navigate.
- Use a consistent look, layout, design, and feel throughout your site.
- Make sure your website works with all the popular web browsers (Explorer, Safari, Foxfire, Chrome, etc.).

Don't:

- Use text and color combinations that are too busy or distracting. Anything that makes your site confusing or hard to read should be eliminated immediately.
- Allow the content or links on your website to become outdated; update, fine-tune and proofread regularly.

For those of you who love the feel of a book, two good ones about building websites are *The Unofficial Guide to Starting a Business Online* (Wiley) by Jason R. Rich and Entrepreneur's startup guide *e-Business: Step-By-Step Startup Guide, 3rd Edition* (available at bookstore.entrepreneur.com). They both give detailed, hands-on advice about website design, as well as plenty of helpful dos and don'ts.

Finding the Host with the Most

Now that you have your site's design and content creation well underway, the next step is publishing your site on the net. For this, you have three basic options. The first is to host it yourself on a computer that can be dedicated as a web server (or a computer that's permanently connected to the internet) and has a broadband internet connection. This will prove costly to set up and maintain. For most online businesses, this isn't the best option, at least in the beginning.

The second option is to use an established and reputable web hosting company, which stores and manages websites for businesses, among other

aha! 

If you know what you want to say but are not sure how to best say it, one option is to hire a copywriter to transform your idea into compelling text. If, however, you opt to do the writing yourself, the book *Letting Go of the Words: Writing Web Content That Works* (Morgan Kaufmann) by Janice Redish is an excellent resource, as is *Killer Web Content* (A&C Black) by Gerry McGovern.

services. There are several large and well-established web hosting companies that cater to a worldwide audience, including Yahoo!, Google, and GoDaddy.com.

Some companies, however, prefer local, small-hosting providers, since they offer a direct contact—especially important if your site goes down. Most of these companies also offer domain name services, which we mentioned above, so you can sign up when you choose your name.

A third option—and the most popular (as well as least expensive)—is to use a website turnkey solution. As we mentioned above, this is a company that provides all the site development tools and hosting services in one easy-to-use, low-cost, bundled service, which is entirely online-based. In other words, to create, publish, and manage your website, you don't need to install any specialized software, and no programming is required. Using an internet search engine, enter the phrase "website turnkey solution" or "ecommerce turnkey solution." Also, check out what's offered by Yahoo!, Google, GoDaddy.com, and eBay.com.

Whether buying from a large or small provider, basic hosting service—along with standards like domain name registration and email accounts—starts at about $10 per month but can go up considerably, depending on your needs.

Still not sure which host to choose? Log on to Compare Web Hosts (comparewebhosts.com), where you can compare hosts based on price. Other variables include amount of disk space allocated to you, available bandwidth, number of email services offered, customer service support availability, database support, and setup fees. For even more information, check out CNET Editors' web hosting guide, with discount codes for some, at cnet.com/web-hosting.

How much disk space do you need to store your website? Generally, 1MB can hold several hundred text pages, fewer pages when images and multimedia content are included. Web hosts typically offer between 10MB and 50MB of free storage. The better web host contracts offer more than 100MB of disk space, which should be adequate for most situations. If you're unsure how much disk space or bandwidth you need, check with your website designer or computer consultant before you sign on a web server's dotted line.

aha!

Although people have gotten increasingly comfortable with the internet as a secure place for credit card transactions, a little reassurance doesn't hurt. Have whomever sets up your shopping cart component provide a message to customers that details your company's policy for protecting credit card information and customer/client privacy.

Ka-ching

The best part of ecommerce is that customers do the work while you make the sales. You've probably noticed that companies of all sizes, from SOHOs to the Fortune 500, use sticks and carrots to encourage web

>> Keeping Up Appearances

Unless you're careful when designing and programming your website, it might behave differently to different people. This is because web browsers (the software that enables net users to navigate the web) differ somewhat in how the websites they access perform. Make sure your website is fully compatible with Explorer, Safari, Firefox, and Chrome, which are the most popular web browsers. Also make sure the content works well and looks good on the screen of a smartphone (Android and iPhone), tablet, and desktop computer.

So how do you know how your site is behaving? Whenever you have the chance to use computers with different browsers, check your site. Note differences in appearance, ease of navigation, and speed. Be sure to check compatibility issues with all browsers (and all versions of each browser) before launching your site. Nothing destroys your credibility like computer mishaps.

usage vs. telephone support for all sorts of transactions. Every time you serve yourself on the internet, whether it's to purchase an airline ticket, a can of cat food, or 100 shares of stock, you've saved the seller money on salaries and, ultimately, office space and phone charges. Nevertheless, business owners should consider carefully how many sales support services they want to handle themselves.

> **warning**
>
> 
>
> You can create the most incredible website in the history of the internet and then incorporate cutting-edge content, but if your text is filled with grammatical errors, misspelled words, inappropriate language, or misused words, it will immediately destroy your reputation and credibility. Make sure you have your site edited and proofread before you launch it.

In fact, many ecommerce entrepreneurs turn to the web hosting companies we mentioned above to solve all their ecommerce needs, such as handling credit card transactions, sending automatic email messages to customers thanking them for their orders, and forwarding the order to them for shipping and handling—and of course, domain registration and hosting.

Another option is to incorporate an electronic shopping cart module, which allows people to place their orders online and process their credit card payment transactions. A site using a shopping cart module should have these four components:

1. *Catalog*. Customers can view products, get information, and compare prices.
2. *Shopping cart*. The icon works like the real thing. It tracks all the items in the basket and can add or delete items as the customer goes along. It's like an online order form.
3. *Checkout counter*. The shopper reviews the items in her cart, makes changes, and decides on shipping preferences, gift-wrapping, and the like.
4. *Order processing*. The program processes the credit card (or payment option), verifies all information, and sends everything to the database.

Final Check

You're now just about ready to launch your online business (or the online component to your traditional business). Here's a checklist to keep you on track:

- Keep your online and ecommerce strategy in focus.
- Put full contact information on your homepage.
- Make sure your online message is clear.
- Keep graphics clean and eye-catching.
- Make sure your website is free of glitches, typos, and dead ends that frustrate visitors.
- Ensure your site meets its objectives.
- Enable visitors to get information quickly and easily.

Make sure your website meshes with the rest of your business.

Once your website is up and running, it's time to get to the really important jobs. The first is getting visitors to your site (generating traffic), followed by encouraging them to become paying customers. Promoting and advertising your site properly, and on an ongoing basis, will be essential for its success. To learn how to do all this and more, turn to Chapter 34.

aha!

Here's another idea to give your customers peace of mind: Look into third-party certification seal programs that let you post a symbol to signify that your website is using effective privacy practices. Leading firms offering these programs are the Better Business Bureau Online (bbb.org) and TRUSTe (truste.org). Or you could display the VeriSign seal, which verifies that your business has been approved to protect confidential information with industry-leading SSL encryption.

CHAPTER

28

Keep in Touch

Using Technology to Stay Connected

These are exciting times for mobile entrepreneurs. Laptop computers have become smaller and far more powerful, and clunky cell phones have transformed from being devices simply for talking into sleek smartphones capable of a wide range of wireless interactivity. In addition, the cost of traditional long-distance phone service has plummeted, and the option to use the internet as a phone (using voice over internet protocol, or VoIP) has become extremely viable for saving a fortune on calls (as well as making video conferencing an affordable option for everyone).

Thanks to the wireless web, we can connect to the internet anywhere and anytime and have a high-speed connection from a laptop computer, netbook, smartphone, or wireless PDA or tablet.

While the technology that allows us to communicate more effectively is becoming increasingly powerful, the price for all this power is decreasing. Today, just about any startup entrepreneur can afford the latest Android or iPhone, netbook or laptop with wireless connectivity, or a new iPad or Samsung tablet. These technologies allow us to talk, video conference, email, IM, or communicate in ways never before possible—from anywhere we happen to be. We're no longer held down by cables or phone lines or the need to find wifi hotspots or electrical outlets. We can conduct business as efficiently as if we were sitting at our office desk.

tip 

When selecting a cell phone, smartphone, or wireless PDA, don't just look at the equipment in terms of its features and functionality. Determine what types of service plans are available, what fees are associated with those plans, and what downloadable apps you might want to use.

Do Your Homework

Yes, the technology to do these incredible things exists, but it's your responsibility to discover what's out there, then determine the best ways to use it to make you more productive—and competitive. Everyone's needs are different. While a netbook might be the ultimate solution for one person, a full-powered laptop computer or the latest Apple iPad might be a more useful tool for someone else.

Once you pinpoint which technology is best for you, it's up to you to become proficient using that equipment. For some, overcoming the learning curve associated with the latest technologies, as well as an inherent fear of them, is a debilitating hindrance. In order to ensure your success in today's business world, you must possess the knowledge, skills, and experience to fully use the latest emerging technologies and the well-established ones.

The best way to acquire this knowledge and proficiency is to read the equipment manuals, visit related websites that offer interactive tutorials, and then invest some time in using your new equipment. For example, before loading your phone with crucial work-related data, spend a few days actually using all its features without the fear of corrupting or losing important information.

As you invest the time and energy to learn about the latest tools, don't just buy the hottest gadget so your colleagues, clients, and customers will be impressed. Focus on which of these technologies will make you more organized, efficient, productive, and available to current and prospective customers. Determine which mobile technology will be the biggest time and money saver. To accomplish this goal, you'll need to study your current work habits and how you spend your time, then choose appropriate technologies so you can stay compatible and competitive in today's fast-paced work environment.

tip

If you want to become proficient using an Apple iPhone or iPad quickly, visit the Apple.com website and watch the video tutorials that explain how to use the phone's most popular features. Samsung tablet users should check out androidforums.com for tutorials and easy-to-understand "how-to" and "getting started" information.

Just the Beginning

There are so many different technologies out there that can be used for communicating and staying connected, it's impossible to write about all of them or to focus on all the different ways they can be used in conjunction to make you better and more efficient.

For example, if you travel a lot for your business, you can have one single phone number that follows you anywhere in the world, or that rings in certain places at certain times of the day or night. If you're not available to answer the phone, the caller can automatically be sent to voice mail, and that message can be listened to at your convenience or automatically translated into an email message and sent to your smartphone, laptop, computer, or iPad. Many phone service companies offer "Follow Me" functionality, including Google Voice (google.com/voice) and Vonage (vonage.com). Even many cable providers now offer this.

tip

If you're using the latest technologies to be more productive while driving, be smart about it by taking advantage of a high-quality Bluetooth headset or hands-free device. The cost of a high-end Bluetooth headset with the latest noise-cancelling technologies will be $80 to $230.

Likewise, if someone needs to send you a fax, you no longer have to sit at your office next to the fax machine waiting for it to ring. With a virtual fax machine (like eFax.com), you can receive faxes as email messages (in PDF format, for example), and access those incoming faxes from anywhere, plus print them from your computer. You can also send a fax to any traditional fax machine directly from your word processor or web browser. That is, if an email message or IM won't suffice.

Your cell phone, smartphone, notebook computer, netbook, or iPad can handle many tasks: It can be used as a plain old telephone or as a full-featured voice-mail system that also sends/receives emails, faxes, and instant messages, or in some cases, allows for real-time video conferencing . . . and that's just the beginning.

tip

Never send or read text messages, IMs, emails, or surf the web while driving—no matter how appealing the concept of multitasking in this situation might be. If you're distracted, even for a second, the consequences can turn deadly.

Talk Is Cheap

The kind of productivity boom that personal computers and other office machines brought to business in the 1980s and '90s are antiquated. Technological advancements in the 21st century offers us cheap home and office phone systems, powerful mobile smartphones, mobile broadband (for high-speed internet access from virtually anywhere), plus various kinds of text messaging and video communications. In fact, research shows that more and more people are giving up their traditional landlines altogether in favor of using wireless cell phone technology as their primary home or office phone line(s).

Whether you use a landline or cell phone, most service plans these days offer unlimited local and long-distance calling for a flat rate (typically between $30 and $100 per month). Thus, from a business perspective, your telecom budget line item went from a variable to a fixed expense. Add in plummeting telecom costs, and you have what amounts to cold, hard cash in your pocket, plus much greater communications tools at your disposal.

Even the cost of internet access has dropped significantly in recent years, thanks to DSL, broadband, FIOS, and wireless 3G and 4G technologies. For a flat monthly fee, anyone can have unlimited internet access from their home, office, or mobile device, usually for well under $50 per month.

Which Smartphone Is the Smartest?

Just about all cell phones have the ability to send and receive text messages and surf the web. However, it's the true smartphones and wireless smartphones, such as Apple iPhones, Android, and Google phones, that offer truly powerful and seamless voice and data communications capabilities—all from a single handheld device.

You can use a smartphone for a wide range of tasks, including sending/receiving calls, voice mails, emails, text, and instant messaging. You can also surf the web, and use it as a powerful GPS navigational system as well as a personal productivity tool for managing your contacts, schedule, expenses, and other data.

Choosing which smartphone is right for you is a matter of personal preference, based on your unique work habits, communication and connectivity needs, and budget. Once you know how you'll be using your smartphone, consider what features and functionality you want and need, then take a look at the various iPhone, Android, BlackBerry, Google, and other smartphone models available. (If you're going to have employees, consider compatibility issues as well to ensure data from your smartphone will be transferable to your staff and vice versa.)

Also, consider the phone's design, battery life, screen readability, keyboard size (or virtual keyboard), overall size and weight, and price. Also, ask about repair/replacement service plans, insurance options, and the warranty.

While you should certainly consider the cost of the device when shopping for a smartphone, you'll also want to look at:

e-fyi

Don't have a cellular wireless card for your laptop computer yet, and need wifi web access while on the go? Most hotels, airports, coffee shops, and bookstores offer free or fee-based wifi. You can quickly find local wifi hotspots throughout the United States or abroad on wififreespot.com, ipass.com/find-mobile-hotspot/, openwifispots.com, and youcanworkfromanywhere.com/wi-fi/.

- What the various cell phone carriers (AT&T, Sprint, Verizon, T-Mobile, etc.) offer in terms of monthly service plans
- The cost of the monthly service plan (with all of the extras you'll want and need, such as unlimited talk minutes, data usage, and text messaging)
- The length of the service contract you'll need to commit to (usually one or two years); if you cancel prematurely, you'll be charged an early termination fee between $150 and $300, depending on the carrier
- The level of national and international roaming service offered, based on the areas where you'll use your smartphone the most. For example, even the most advanced wireless carriers don't yet offer true high-speed wireless internet coast to coast. Depending on the carrier, the latest 3G or 4G service may only be available in or near major cities. Be sure to study the carrier's most current service coverage map.

save

To save money on cell phone usage and international roaming fees when traveling overseas, consider purchasing an inexpensive, prepaid cell phone in the country you're visiting. This means you pay for the phone and a predetermined number of talk minutes or data usage, then you can pay as you go for service and can cancel it at any time.

At Your Service

When choosing a service plan for your smartphone, shop around for the best deals based on the functionality you actually want and need. If, for example, you need a lot of talk time but don't plan to send/receive text messages or surf the web too much, the service plans you should look at will be very different from someone who relies on their phone to surf the web and check email while on the go.

Your comparison shopping should focus on three components—voice, data, and text messaging. For a voice plan, things to consider include how many minutes per month of talking (sending or receiving voice calls) a plan includes and whether or not the plan differentiates between peak and off-peak minutes (based on the time of day or day of the week calls are sent/received). You'll want to look for a voice plan that includes unlimited local and long-distance (domestic) calls 24/7.

As for the data component, carriers charge based on the amount of data sent/received. This is the least desirable option. Instead, either choose a data plan that includes a predetermined amount you can send/receive per month, such as 25MB, or choose an unlimited plan for a flat fee, which is usually the best deal for business users.

Finally, most carriers will either charge you per text message sent/received or offer a plan that allows for a predetermined number of text messages to be sent/received. The best option is a plan that offers unlimited texting each month.

To stay competitive, many carriers now offer unlimited voice, high-MB data, and unlimited text plans for a monthly fee of $69 to $130 per month. You can often share lines—that is, add another mobile phone or device—for as little as $20 more per smartphone. This could be a great option for multiple employees in an office where you're most often out and about, rather than at a desk. However, keep in mind that there are also additional charges you may incur for various extras, such as the ability to turn your phone into a mobile wifi hotspot so that you can connect your laptop or other devices to the internet.

And keep in mind that most U.S.-based cell phones and smartphones will automatically work when you travel overseas, thanks to international roaming. However, unless you have an international roaming plan, you'll be charged $2 to $5 (or more) per minute to make or receive calls while overseas, plus you'll be charged up to $1 for each text message sent/received, and up to $20 (or more) per megabyte of data sent/received. If you plan to travel overseas and use your cell phone or smartphone, inquire about

save

Another option for international calling is to forgo a cell phone altogether and rely on a VoIP service, such as Skype, to make free (or really cheap) calls from your laptop computer or iPad, which is connected to a high-speed wifi internet connection in your hotel, for example. If you own an iPad or iPhone, you can also use wireless connections to Skype or video chat via programs like FaceTime, without incurring extra charges.

international roaming packages, which can save you a bundle if activated before you leave the country.

Wireless Wonders

All laptop computers and smaller netbooks allow users to connect to the web via wifi (assuming a wifi hotspot is available) by connecting an

>> The iPad

The Apple iPad was released in 2010. It allows for wireless web surfing and the use of a wide range of other internet-related applications. Plus it runs all third-party Apple iPhone apps and iPad-specific apps from third-party developers—all from a device that's larger than a smartphone but smaller than a netbook or laptop.

The iPad, which starts at $499, connects to the web via any wifi hotspot. However, for a bit more money, you can purchase an iPad that also offers web connectivity, meaning you can access the internet using a wireless internet connection offered by a major carrier, such as AT&T, for a monthly fee of less than $30. (Best part: Long-term service contracts aren't usually required.) Its competitors include Samsung, Microsoft, and Google, all of which have tablets as an offering. Even so, the iPad is the most ubiquitous of the tablet computers.

While these tablet offerings aren't phones, they offer the ability to surf the web with a large screen from almost anywhere. The tablet is incredibly lightweight and portable. There's also a virtual keyboard, so you don't need a separate keyboard or mouse to use the unit, although you can buy a small external keyboard for about $100. Apps available for the iPad are office-friendly and becoming more so every day. Other manufacturers also offer apps for Windows, too.

Like a netbook or smartphone, a tablet won't meet everyone's needs; however, it can be a powerful business tool that will help many people become more productive, accessible, organized, and competitive in today's business world.

Wireless Protocols

When it comes to communicating wirelessly, you'll hear a lot of buzzwords as technology evolves and changes. Here are some of the current and popular wireless protocols used in business today.

Protocol	Range	Bandwidth	Common Uses
3G Cellular	>30 miles	Up to 2.4Mbps	High-speed voice and data transmission via cell phones, smartphones, wireless PDAs and wireless modems (used with laptop computers); replaced slower 2G technology, which is pretty much outdated at this point
4G Cellular	>30 miles	Up to 100Mbps	Even higher speed voice and data transmission via cell phones, smartphones, wireless PDAs, and wireless modems (used with laptop computers)
802.11g	300 feet	Up to 54Mbps	Wireless LANs (including wifi hotspots and home wireless networks)
202.11n	300 feet	Up to 300Mbps	Wireless LANs (including wifi hotspots and home wireless networks)
Bluetooth	300 feet	700Kbps	Short-range audio and data transmission for cell phones, computers, digital cameras, etc.; used for connecting a cell phone to a wireless headset, or a computer to a printer without cables
Ultra Wideband	30 feet	480Mbps	Replaces the need for cables when connecting computers to equipment, such as printers, speakers, and other devices

Figure 28.1. Wireless Protocols

internet cable to the computer directly or via an optional wireless internet card.

A wireless internet card is a cell phone modem for your computer. It allows the computer to connect to the internet via a cell phone connection, so no wifi hotspot is required. You just need to be within the service area of a wireless data provider with whom you have a data plan.

All the wireless service providers—AT&T, Sprint, Verizon, T-Mobile, etc.—offer wireless modem cards for laptop and netbook computers (if the computer doesn't have the technology built in). These modems connect to the computer, usually via a USB connection. To gain wireless access to the web, you'll need to sign up for a provider's data-only service plan. This can cost $40 to $60 per month—less if you've got a wireless contract for your smartphone with the provider already—depending on the data amount you need.

You might be better off activating mobile wifi hotspot capabilities for your smartphone, which can cost as little as $20. But, with some carriers, when other devices are connected to your phone, you won't be able to make calls. Be sure to ask for details.

Adding a wireless modem and service plan to your laptop allows you to surf the web (via a high-speed 3G or 4G wireless connection) from anywhere there's wireless data service from your provider. You don't need to hunt down a wifi hotspot or connect your computer to a modem. This gives you tremendous freedom to access the web anywhere, any time.

I'm IMing

Instant messages (also referred to as *IMing*) allow people to communicate in real time without speaking. While cell phones allow us to roam freely and wirelessly, they're still used primarily for real-time conversations. Other internet-based communications methods let the two halves of the conversation proceed at the pace preferred by each participant. Welcome to the world of instant messages (IMs) and text messages. These are two different technologies that have similar uses.

IMing is used while you're online and surfing the web to instantly send text-based messages (and potentially attached files or links) to a recipient, who receives your IM instantly on his/her desktop computer, laptop, netbook, iPad, or smartphone (assuming it's connected to the web). To use IMs, both the sender and the receiver must participate in the same (or on a compatible) IM service, such as G-Chat from Google, Yahoo Messenger, or MSN (Microsoft) Messenger. A real-time, text-based conversation can be held between two or more people.

The benefit to IMing is that you can participate in an unlimited number of conversations simultaneously, plus it's quicker than picking up the phone or sending a full-length email. Text messaging works in much the same way as IMing; however, to send and receive a text message, you use a cell phone or smartphone. You can send a text message to anyone with a cell phone, as long as you know their phone number, regardless of what carrier they use, and assuming you both have a text messaging plan as part of your cell phone service.

e-fyi

While IMing is one method to have quick nonverbal communication, many people today are hooked on Twitter (twitter.com). Twitter allows people to post short messages—140 characters in length, plus a website link or photo—which their "followers" can read in real-time, or at their convenience. (See Chapters 35 and 36 for more details.)

Web Calling

Instead of using traditional phone lines to make and receive calls, anyone with any type of high-speed internet connection can take advantage of VoIP technology to make and receive calls from the web. Calls originating from the web can be placed to traditional phone lines, often at a fraction of the cost of making a traditional long-distance call (and sometimes free of charge, depending on the service you use).

Using a VoIP service gives you access to a wide range of calling services and features, from caller ID and voice mail to call forwarding and conference calling. As long as you have a stable, high-speed internet connection, the calls will be clear.

There are many VoIP services that offer different types of features of interest to entrepreneurs. For example, there's Skype (skype.com), MagicJack (magicjack.com), and Vonage (vonage.com). You can find a worldwide list of VoIP services by visiting voipproviderslist.com.

For people who need to make international calls, either from the United States to an overseas country or who travel overseas and need to call home to the United States, VoIP offers a tremendous savings over traditional phone or cellular phone services. In fact, using VoIP, you can typically call anywhere in the world, any time, for less than a few cents per minute (and sometimes for free).

With VoIP, you're assigned your own phone number, plus you can receive calls at that number any time you're connected to the internet—from anywhere—or have calls forwarded to your cell phone or a landline. Most VoIP services charge a flat monthly fee up to $30 for unlimited service, or waive the monthly fee but charge a low, per-minute fee per call.

It's Your Turn

Technology is changing rapidly and almost daily. New devices and tools are constantly being introduced. New software upgrades to existing devices, such as the iPhone or Android, are allowing for greater functionality. Plus, prices are dropping fast!

If you want to be competitive in today's business world, it's no longer a matter of whether you need a smartphone and/or a netbook, laptop (with wireless capabilities), or an iPad—it's a matter of which model you need right now and how you'll be able to get the most use out of each technology or device as you juggle your daily work and personal responsibilities, plus deal with the growing need to be accessible virtually 24/7.

This chapter offered just a short introduction to the communications and connectivity technology that's available. How you use this technology is up to you! So put on your thinking cap, be creative,

tip

Having a handheld device can keep you connected 24/7, and in the spirit of increased productivity, it's easy to get into the habit of constantly checking your emails and voice mails, making it difficult to disconnect from your work-related responsibilities at the end of the day. As you incorporate these new technologies into your life, also develop the discipline to use them in moderation.

and discover ways you can use it to become more productive, accessible, and competitive in today's business world.

New technologies and phone models are introduced almost every month. One of the best ways to learn about the latest gadgets, gizmos, and technologies businesspeople use to communicate is to visit a consumer electronics superstore, such as Best Buy, or at least two different cell phone stores (representing different service providers, like AT&T Wireless, Verizon, Sprint, and/or T-Mobile). If you're interested in Apple products (e.g., the iPhone or iPad), visit an Apple store. By visiting a retail store that showcases the latest products, you can try them out firsthand, learn about their features, and more easily compare pricing.

GO!

All systems are go. You're ready to launch your new business. To make sure the launch is successful, Part 6, "Market," shows you how to spread the word about your company. First, you'll learn how to create a brand identity that will get your new business noticed. Then, you'll find out how to create a marketing and advertising campaign that works . . . without spending a fortune. From print ads and direct mail to TV, radio, and social media websites like Facebook, we share smart strategies to build buzz about your business. You'll also learn about the single best way to promote your business: public relations. From special events and community projects to media coverage, we show you dozens of ways to get your business noticed—many of them virtually free!

If the idea of selling scares you, you're not alone. That's why we provide everything you need to know to sell like a pro. Learn how to get over your fear of cold calls, techniques for overcoming objections, how to spot hot prospects, and how to close the sale. Once you've made the sale, the game isn't over: You've got to keep the customer coming back. Our secrets to great customer service will give you the edge you need to win repeat business . . . over and over again.

No marketing and advertising plan is complete today without including the internet. In Part 7, "Engage," we introduce you to the brave new world of social media and online advertising and marketing. We start by showing you how to get visitors to your website, keep them there, and, when they leave, make sure they return for more. From search engine marketing and paid search services to email marketing and affiliate promotions, you'll learn valuable tips and techniques to make your website a roaring success.

What's all the buzz about social media and why should you be listening? Social media has changed the conversation between businesses and customers. It's also changing the way brands are marketed and the way customers engage with your company. We show you how to use social tools to network with potential customers and connect and engage with your audience—because in today's marketing landscape, that's how brands are built. We cover all the social sites you've probably heard of, such as Twitter, LinkedIn, Facebook, and Pinterest, plus numerous other tools to help you reach out and connect with your target audience.

If you're doing everything right, you'll be dealing with a bundle of money. In Part 8, "Profit," we show you the strategies to make the most of your money. Whether or not you're a math whiz, you'll want to read our bookkeeping basics, which contain everything you need to know to keep track of your finances. You'll learn the accounting methods that can make a difference come tax time, what records to keep and why, and whether to computerize or do it by hand. Check out our step-by-step look at creating financial statements, income statements, cash-flow statements, and other important indicators that help you measure your money. Then learn ways to manage your finances, including secrets to pricing your product or service; how to get short-term capital infusions when you're low on cash; and how to determine your overhead, profit margin, and more. We'll answer your most burning question—how much (and how) to pay yourself. We also show you how to stay out of trouble when the tax man comes calling. Get the inside scoop on payroll taxes, personal vs. corporate tax returns, and what to file when. We'll also cover what you can deduct . . . and what you can't.

Finally, at the end of the book, you'll find a handy glossary of terms in case you need a refresher on any of the concepts we've covered in the book, as well as an appendix chock full of helpful business resources.

PART

6

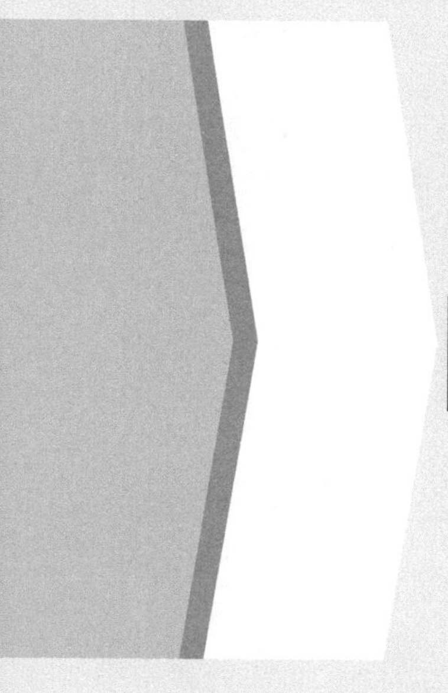

MARKET

CHAPTER

29

Brand Aid

Building a Brand

You're really excited about your concept for a new product or service. But do you have a potential brand in the making?

Unfortunately, it's a question too many small-business owners ask far too late, or never ask at all—not a good idea in a world full of savvy consumers and big companies that have mastered the branding game. Great brands are all around us, and it's no accident they make us think of certain things. Think FedEx, and think overnight delivery. Apple Computer brings to mind cutting-edge products and now, music and must-have phones and devices.

Even celebrities are brands. Would you describe Bradley Cooper the same way you would Jack Nicholson? Their differences—charming vs. gruff, refined vs. rough and rugged—helped to define their particular acting "brands" and let the public get a grasp on their personas. Corporate brands are no different. They have their own "personalities."

We like to categorize everything, whether we're talking about people, printers, or pizza places. Test this theory yourself. What draws you to one local business instead of another selling a similar product? One local restaurant might strike you as cute and inviting; another might make you lose your appetite without setting a foot inside—even though both restaurants serve the same type of food. You're not alone if you find yourself categorizing each business you pass.

As a startup entrepreneur, you'll be branding whether you're even trying. If you don't have a clear idea of what your new company is about, your potential customers will decide on their own—a risky move for a new company without many, or any, customers. You'll need to have a branding strategy in place before you hang up your shingle. However, before we start strategizing, let's answer the most basic question of all.

tip

Make your company's website more than just a boring online brochure by adding an e-newsletter, message board, a monthly podcast from the founder—anything that conveys your brand's personality and humanizes your company in the eyes of potential customers. People want to know who they're buying from, especially if it's a new company.

What Is Branding, Exactly?

Branding is a very misunderstood term. Many people think of branding as just advertising or a really cool-looking logo, but it's much more complex—and much more exciting, too.

- *Branding is your company's foundation.* Branding is more than an element of marketing, and it's not just about awareness, a trademark, or a logo. Branding is your company's reason for being, the synchronization of everything about your company that leads to consistency for you as the owner, your employees, and your potential customers. Branding meshes your marketing, public relations, business plan, packaging, pricing, customers, and employees (the last element is often the most overlooked; read "In the Loop" on page 452 for more on this).

> ***"Success is often achieved by those who don't know that failure is inevitable."***
>
> —GABRIELLE "COCO" CHANEL, FOUNDER OF CHANEL INC.

- *Branding creates value.* If done right, branding makes the buyer trust and believe your product is somehow better than those of your competitors. Generally, the more distinctive you can make your brand, the less likely the customer will be willing to use another company's product or service, even if yours is slightly more expensive. "Branding is the reason why people perceive you as the only solution to their problem," says Rob Frankel, a branding expert and author of *The Revenge of Brand X: How to Build a Big Time Brand on the Web or Anywhere Else*. "Once you clearly can articulate your brand, people have a way of evangelizing your brand."
- *Branding clarifies your message.* You have less money to spend on advertising and marketing as a startup entrepreneur, and good branding can help you direct your money more effectively. "The more distinct and clear your brand, the harder your advertising works," Frankel says. "Instead of having to run your ads eight or nine times, you only have to run them three times."
- *Branding is a promise.* At the end of the day, branding is the simple, steady promise you make to every customer who walks through your door—today, tomorrow, and ten years from now. Your company's ads and brochures might say you offer speedy, friendly service, but if customers find your service slow and surly, they'll walk out the door feeling betrayed. In their eyes, you promised something that you didn't deliver, and no amount of advertising will ever make up for the gap between what your company says and what it does. Branding creates the consistency that allows you to deliver on your promise over and over again.

Building a Branding Strategy

Your business plan should include a branding strategy. This is your written plan for how you'll apply your brand strategically throughout the company over time.

At its core, a good branding strategy lists the one or two most important elements of your product or service, describes your company's ultimate purpose in the world, and defines your target customer. The result is a blueprint for what's most important to your company and to your customer.

Don't worry; creating a branding strategy isn't nearly as scary or as complicated as it sounds. Here's how:

- *Step one.* Set yourself apart. Why should people buy from you instead of the same kind of business across town? Think about the intangible qualities of your product or service, using adjectives from "friendly" to "fast" and every word in between. Your goal is to own a position in the customer's mind so they think of you differently than the competition. "Powerful brands will own a word—like Volvo [owns] safety," says Laura Ries, an Atlanta marketing consultant and co-author of *The 22 Immutable Laws of Branding: How to Build a Product or*

>> In the Loop

Many companies large and small stumble when it comes to incorporating employees into their branding strategies. But to the customer making a purchase, your employee is the company. Your employees can make or break your entire brand, so don't ever forget them. Here are a few tips:

> *Hire based on brand strategy.* Communicating your brand through your employees starts with making the right hires. Look to your brand strategy for help. If your focus is on customer service, employees should be friendly, unflappable, and motivated, right? Give new hires a copy of your brand strategy, and talk about it.

> *Set expectations.* How do you expect employees to treat customers? Make sure they understand what's required. Reward employees who do an exceptional job or go above and beyond the call of duty.

> *Communicate, then communicate some more.* Keeping employees clued in requires ongoing communication about the company's branding efforts through meetings, posters, training, etc. Never, ever assume employees can read your mind.

Service into a World-Class Brand. Which word will your company own? A new hair salon might focus on the adjective "convenient" and stay open a few hours later in the evening for customers who work late—something no other local salon might do. How will you be different from the competition? The answers are valuable assets that constitute the basis of your brand.

- *Step two.* Know your target customer. Once you've defined your product or service, think about your target customer. You've probably already gathered demographic information about the market you're entering, but think about the actual customers who will walk through your door. Who is this person, and what is the one thing he or she ultimately wants from your product or service? After all, the customer is buying it for a reason. What will your customer demand from you?
- *Step three.* Develop a personality. How will you show customers every day what you're all about? A lot of small companies write mission statements that say the company will "value" customers and strive for "excellent customer service." Unfortunately, these words are all talk, and no action. Dig deeper and think about how you'll fulfill your brand's promise and provide value and service to the people you serve. If you promise quick service, for example, what will "quick" mean inside your company? And how will you make sure service stays speedy? Along the way, you're laying the foundation of your hiring strategy and how future employees will be expected to interact with customers. You're also creating the template for your advertising and marketing strategy.

Your branding strategy doesn't need to be more than one page long at most. It can even be as short as one paragraph. It all depends on your product or service and your industry. The important thing is that you answer these questions before you open your doors.

warning

A lot of new companies try to be everything to everyone, but this strategy will make it impossible to communicate your brand. Instead, identify your most likely customer and build your brand on what this person wants.

Bringing It All Together

Congratulations—you've written your branding strategy. Now you'll have to manage your fledgling brand. This is when the fun really begins. Remember, FedEx was once a startup with an idea it had to get off the ground, too. Here are some tips:

- *Keep ads brand-focused.* Keep your promotional blitzes narrowly focused on your chief promise to potential customers. For example, a new bakery might see the warmth of its fresh bread as its greatest brand-building asset. Keep your message simple and consistent so people get the same message every time they see your name and logo.

>> Many Happy Returns?

It can be hard to put a dollar figure on what you're getting in return for your investment in branding. Branders talk about this dilemma in terms of "brand equity": The dollar value your brand generates over decades in terms of the demand it drives and the customer loyalty it creates. Coca-Cola's brand equity, for example, is estimated in the billions of dollars.

Think about conducting a simple "brand audit" at least once a year. This means looking at how your product or service is marketed and branded (your marketing messages, etc.), analyzing your brand positioning (i.e., asking customers what they think of your brand), and then comparing the two (your branding efforts vs. customer perceptions) to see how well the two connect.

A simple customer survey with questions like "When you think about our company and our product, what words come to mind?" can tell you volumes about the strengths and weaknesses of your branding. A new coffee shop owner, for example, might think she serves the best coffee in town, while convenience or ambience—say, the type of music played over the sound system—turns out to be as much, or more, of a selling point from the customer's perspective. A brand audit will help keep you on track and help you build on what you already do well.

- *Be consistent.* Filter every business proposition through a branding filter. How does this opportunity help build the company's brand? How does this opportunity fit our branding strategy? These questions will keep you focused and put you in front of people who fit your product or service.
- *Shed the deadweight.* Good businesses are willing to change their brands but are careful not to lose sight of their original customer base and branding message. Consider Starbucks, which changed the way it made lattes to speed up the process. "You have to give up something to build a brand," Ries says. "Good brands constantly get rid of things that don't work."

Read All About It

Luckily, there are tons of books on the topic of branding. Here are just a few of them, along with a major trade magazine:

- *The Business of Brands.* Written by Jon Miller and David Muir and published by John Wiley & Sons, this book discusses creating value around a brand as well as brand strategy.
- *Brandweek.* This trade magazine is a good source of news and information about branding trends. Visit brandweek.com to subscribe.
- *Designing Brand Identity: A Complete Guide to Creating, Building, and Maintaining Strong Brands.* This John Wiley & Sons book by Alina Wheeler discusses branding fundamentals and also provides a number of case studies.
- *Emotional Branding: The New Paradigm for Connecting Brands to People.* Written by Marc Gobé, this book delves into creating a strong brand personality, among other things.
- *The 22 Immutable Laws of Branding: How to Build a Product or Service into a World-Class Brand.* This Harper Business book by Al Ries and Laura Ries includes tips for branding as well as numerous examples of how successful companies have built their brands.

There's a lot of work that goes into launching and building a world-class brand, but it pays off. Nike once ran its business out of the back of

Branding Checklist

Test your branding savvy by answering "yes" or "no" to these statements. Hint: The more you answer "no," the more you'll need to bone up on your knowledge of branding.

Yes	No	
❑	❑	I know what branding means, exactly.
❑	❑	I've added a simple branding strategy to my business plan.
❑	❑	I understand the one thing the customer ultimately wants from my product or service.
❑	❑	I know what our straightforward and consistent message will be to the customer, today and 20 years from now.
❑	❑	I've thought about how my company will ultimately provide value and service to the customer.
❑	❑	I'll rely on the company's brand strategy when hiring future employees.
❑	❑	The company's brandmark (logo), packaging, stationery, slogan, and approach to customer service all reflect our company's main promise to the customer.
❑	❑	I plan to measure the effectiveness of our branding strategy through an annual brand audit.

Figure 29.1. Branding Checklist

a car, but now it's a global brand worth billions of dollars. Think of your fledgling brand as a baby you have to nurture, guide, and shape every day so it grows up to be dependable, hardworking, and respectable in your customers' eyes. One day your company's brand will make you proud. But you'll have to invest the time, energy, and thought it takes to make that happen.

CHAPTER

30

Marketing Genius

Advertising and Marketing Your Business

You may know how to build the perfect product or provide excellent service, but do you know how to market your business? If not, all your expertise won't help keep your business afloat. Without marketing, no one will know your business exists—and if customers don't know you're there, you won't make any sales.

Advertising doesn't have to mean multimillion-dollar TV commercials. There are plenty of ways to market your business that are affordable or even free. All it takes is a little marketing savvy and the dedication to stick with a year-round program that includes a solid mix of proven tactics.

> *"If you can dream it, you can do it."*
>
> —Walter Elias Disney, founder of Walt Disney Co.

Creating a Marketing Plan

Everyone knows you need a business plan, yet many entrepreneurs don't realize a marketing plan is just as vital.

Unlike a business plan, a marketing plan focuses on winning and keeping customers. A marketing plan is strategic and includes numbers, facts, and objectives. Marketing supports sales, and a good marketing plan spells out all the tools and tactics you'll use to achieve your sales goals. It's your plan of action—what you'll sell, who will want to buy it, and the tactics you'll use to generate leads that result in sales. And unless you're using your marketing plan to help you gain funding, it doesn't have to be lengthy or beautifully written. Use bulleted sections, and get right to the point.

Here's a closer look at creating a marketing plan that works.

Step One: Begin with a Snapshot of Your Company's Current Situation, Called a "Situation Analysis"

This first section of the marketing plan defines your company and its products or services, then shows how the benefits you provide set you apart from your competition.

>> Position Power

The right image packs a powerful marketing punch. To make it work for you, follow these steps:

- *Create a positioning statement for your company*. In one or two sentences, describe what distinguishes you from your competition.
- *Test your positioning statement*. Does it appeal to your target audience? Refine it until it speaks directly to their wants and needs.
- *Use the positioning statement* in every written communication to customers.
- *Integrate your company's positioning message* into all your marketing campaigns and materials.
- *Include your team in the positioning effort*. Help employees understand how to communicate your positioning to customers.

Target audiences have become extremely specialized and segmented. For example, there are hundreds of special-interest magazines—each targeted to a specific market segment. No matter your industry, from restaurants to professional services to retail clothing stores, positioning your product or service competitively requires an understanding of your niche market. Not only do you need to be able to describe what you market, but you must also have a clear understanding of what your competitors are offering and be able to show how your product or service provides a better value.

tip

Your business plan and your marketing plan have a lot in common, but make sure to keep them separate. Your business plan should show how you're going to support your marketing efforts. At the same time, your marketing plan should be a concrete working-out of the ideas in your business plan.

Make your Situation Analysis a succinct overview of your company's strengths, weaknesses, opportunities, and threats. Strengths and weaknesses refer to characteristics that exist within your business, while opportunities and threats refer to outside factors. To determine your company's strengths, consider the ways that its products are superior to others, or if your service is more comprehensive, for example. What do you offer that gives your business a competitive advantage? Weaknesses, on the other hand, can be anything from operating in a highly saturated market to lack of experienced staff members.

Next, describe any external opportunities you can capitalize on, such as an expanding market for your product. Don't forget to include any external threats to your company's ability to gain market share so that succeeding sections of your plan can detail the ways you'll overcome those threats.

Positioning your product involves two steps. First, you need to analyze your product's features and decide how they distinguish your product from its competitors. Second, decide what type of buyer is most likely to purchase your product. What are you selling—convenience? Quality? Discount pricing? You can't offer it all. Knowing what your customers want helps you decide what to offer, and that brings us to the next section of your plan.

Step Two: Describe Your Target Audience

Developing a simple, one-paragraph profile of your prospective customer is the second step in an effective marketing plan. You can describe prospects in terms of demographics—age, sex, family composition, earnings, and geographic location—as well as lifestyle. Ask yourself the following: Are my customers conservative or innovative? Leaders or followers? Timid or aggressive? Traditional or modern? Introverted or extroverted? How often do they purchase what I offer? In what quantity?

If you're a business-to-business marketer, you may define your target audience based on their type of business, job title, size of business, geographic location, or any other characteristics that make them possible prospects. Are you targeting the owners of businesses with 25 or fewer employees or mid-level managers in Fortune 100 companies? No matter who your target audience is, be sure to narrowly define them in this section, because it will be your guide as you plan your media and public relations campaigns. The more narrowly you define your target audience, the less money you'll waste on ads and PR in poorly targeted media and the unqualified leads they would generate. (Chapters 6 and 7 explain in detail how to define your target customer.)

Step Three: List Your Marketing Goals

What do you want your marketing plan to achieve? For example, are you hoping for a 20 percent increase in sales of your product per quarter? Write down a short list of goals—and make them measurable so that you'll know when you've achieved them.

Step Four: Develop the Marketing Communications Strategies and the Tactics You'll Use

This section is the heart and soul of your marketing plan. In the previous sections, you outlined what your marketing must accomplish and identified your best prospects; now it's time to detail the tactics you'll use to reach these prospects and accomplish your goals.

A good marketing program targets prospects at all stages of your sales cycle. Some marketing tactics, such as many forms of advertising, public relations, and direct marketing, are great for reaching cold prospects.

Warm prospects—those who have previously been exposed to your marketing message and perhaps even met you personally—will respond best to permission-based email, loyalty programs, and customer appreciation events, among others. Your hottest prospects are individuals who've been exposed to your sales and marketing messages and are ready to close a sale. Generally, interpersonal sales contact (whether in person, by phone, or email) combined with marketing adds the final heat necessary to close sales.

warning

Don't mess with success. Once you find an advertising idea that works for you, stick with it. Repetition is the key to getting your message across.

To complete your tactics section, outline your primary marketing strategies, then include a variety of tactics you'll use to reach prospects at any point in your sales cycle. For example, you might combine outdoor billboards, print advertising, and online local searches to reach cold prospects but use email to contact your warm prospects. Finally, you can use one-on-one meetings to close the sale. Don't overlook complementary materials that support sales: For instance, if you plan to meet with prospects to follow up on leads you've generated, you'll need brochures and presentation materials.

To identify your ideal marketing mix, find out which media your target audience turns to for information on the type of product or service you sell. Avoid broad-based media—even if it attracts your target audience—if the content is not relevant. The marketing tactics you choose must reach your prospects when they'll be most receptive to your message.

Step Five: Set Your Marketing Budget

You'll need to devote a percentage of projected gross sales to your annual marketing budget. Of course, when starting a business this may mean using newly acquired funding, borrowing, or self-financing. Just bear this in mind—marketing is absolutely essential to the success of your business. And with so many different kinds of tactics available for reaching out to every conceivable audience niche, there's a mix to fit even the tightest budget.

Market Planning Checklist

Before you launch a marketing campaign, answer the following questions about your business and your product or service:

- ❑ Have you analyzed the total market for your product or service? Do you know which features of your product or service will appeal to different market segments?
- ❑ In forming your marketing message, have you described how your product or service will benefit your clients?
- ❑ Have you prepared a pricing schedule? What kinds of discounts do you offer, and to whom do you offer them?
- ❑ Have you prepared a sales forecast?
- ❑ Which media will you use in your marketing campaign?
- ❑ Do your marketing materials mention any optional accessories or added services that consumers might want to purchase?
- ❑ If you offer a product, have you prepared clear operating and assembly instructions if required? What kind of warranty do you provide? What type of customer service or support do you offer after the sale?
- ❑ Do you have product liability insurance?
- ❑ Is your packaging likely to appeal to your target market?
- ❑ If your product is one you can patent, have you done so?
- ❑ How will you distribute your product?

Figure 30.1. Market Planning Checklist

As you begin to gather costs for the marketing tactics you outlined in the previous section, you may find that you've exceeded your budget. Not to worry. Simply go back and adjust your tactics until you have a mix that's affordable. The key is to never stop marketing—don't concern yourself with the more costly tactics until you can afford them.

So what should you spend on marketing? There's no hard-and-fast guideline. In fact, the amount varies based on your industry, the amount of competition you must overcome, and the type of media you have to use to reach your audience. A particularly complex message will also require a bigger marketing budget because prospects will need to be guided through the education phase, which involves more advertising and an increase in the repetition of your message. One study showed that major advertisers with well-established brand names, including General Mills, Kodak, Dunkin' Donuts, and Kraft Foods, spend an average of 11.6 to 12.4 percent of sales on marketing. On the other hand, many successful small businesses that are competing for brand recognition and market share budget approximately 15 to 19 percent of sales. The rule of thumb, according to most studies, is between 6 and 12 percent.

tip

Dream the dream. Your marketing plan should include a "blue sky" section in which you put your feet back and look at where you think you'll be in a couple of years. Especially in small businesses, it's a waste of time to formulate marketing thoughts that go out more than two or three years. But dreams are important—and they can be fun, too.

Where to Advertise

Once you know your target audience, it'll be easier to determine which media will work well for you. Much of this is just common sense, based on your product or service, method of sales, and audience.

Sure, it would be great if you could afford to buy a full-page color ad in *Time* magazine or a 60-second commercial during the Super Bowl. But in addition to being beyond your budget, such ads aren't even the most effective way to go for a small company.

Small companies succeed by finding a niche, not by targeting every Tom, Dick, and Harry. (Remember the "Choose Your Target" chapter in Part 2?) Similarly, you need to focus your advertising as narrowly as possible on the media that will reach your customers. Your customers' location, age, income, interests, and other information will guide you to the right media.

> *"All you need in this life are ignorance and confidence, and then success is sure."*
>
> —Mark Twain

Suppose you ran a business selling model train supplies nationwide online and by mail order. It would make sense to advertise in a mix of national specialty magazines, on websites targeting aficionados, and in specialty e-newsletters catering to the hobby rather than advertising in, say, *The New York Times*. On the other hand, if you sold model trains from a hobby shop rather than online or via mail order, the vast majority of your customers would be drawn from your local area. Therefore, advertising in national hobbyist magazines would net you only a few customers. In this case, it would make more sense to advertise in local phone directories (both online and offline), area newspapers, or magazines that carry related editorial sections online and in print, or by commercials on carefully selected cable TV programming targeting the local area.

Like any aspect of running a business, marketing involves a measure of trial and error. As your business grows, however, you'll quickly learn which advertising media are most cost-effective and draw the most customers to your company. Here's a closer look at the different types of advertising methods and tips for succeeding with each.

Print Advertising

The print ad is the basic unit of advertising, the fountainhead from which all other forms of advertising spring. Knowing the principles of creating print ads will help you get results in any other advertising media you use. Print ads have helped launch some of the most successful products and services we know. And there's no reason they can't work for you, too—if you observe a few hard-and-fast rules.

> **tip** 
>
> Make sure all your ads answer every customer's number-one question: "What's in it for me?"

Most print ads out there are poorly conceived and, as a result, perform badly. If an ad lacks a strong motivating message, especially in the crowded marketplace of a newspaper or magazine, it becomes a costly lesson—one your business will be lucky to survive. The good news? With so many bad ads out there, if you can put together a good one, you're way ahead of the game.

Whether you are developing an ad yourself or having someone else craft it for you, make sure it follows the five fundamentals of successful ads.

1. *It should attract attention.* That sounds obvious, but nothing else matters unless you can do this. And that means having a truly arresting headline and visual element.
2. *It should appeal to the reader's self-interest or announce news.* An ad that takes the "you" point of view and tells readers how they'll benefit from your product or service piques and keeps their interest.

>> Go for the Pros

Can you create your own advertising copywriting and design? If you have a background in marketing and advertising, the answer may be yes. If not, however, you're better off hiring professionals. No matter how creative you are, a commercial artist or a graphic designer can vastly improve almost any ad created by an entrepreneur.

However, since no one knows your business better than you, it's a good idea to develop your own rough draft first. Think about the key benefits you want to get across, what makes your company different from and better than the rest, and the major advantages of doing business with you.

If you're reluctant to spend the money on a copywriter and a graphic designer, don't be. Printing, distributing, and placing your advertising and marketing materials are going to be costly. If the materials you're paying to have printed aren't well-written, eye-catching, and effective, you're wasting your money.

Graphic design and copywriting are two areas where it's possible to get good work at substantial savings. Plenty of freelance, one-person graphic design and copywriting businesses exist, many of them quite reasonably priced. Ask friends, other business owners, or your chamber of commerce for referrals. Many copywriters and designers will cut you a price break on the first project in hopes of winning your business in the future.

And if, in addition, it has news value ("Announcing a bold new breakthrough in moisturizers that can make your skin look years younger"), your ad has a better than fighting chance.

3. *It should communicate your company's unique advantage.* In other words, why should the prospect pick your firm over a competitor's?
4. *It should prove your advantage.* One convincing way to do that is through testimonials and statistics.
5. *It should motivate readers to take action.* This is usually accomplished by making a special offer that "piggybacks" your main sales thrust. Such offers include a free trial, a discount, or a bonus.

An ad doesn't have to do a "hard sell" as long as it is an all-out attempt to attract, communicate with, and motivate the reader. That process starts with the single most important element of any ad: the headline.

Headlines That Work

Some of the biggest flops in advertising contained convincing copy that never got read because the ads lacked a great headline or visual element to hook the passing reader.

David Ogilvy, founding partner of legendary ad agency Ogilvy & Mather, said that on the average, five times as many people read the headlines of ads as read the body copy. Headlines that work best, according to Ogilvy, are those that promise the reader a benefit—more miles per gallon, freedom from pimples, or fewer cavities.

Flip through a magazine or a newspaper and see what you notice about the ads. Typically, it is the headlines that your eyes go to first. Then notice how many of those headlines promise a benefit of some kind.

However, expressing a benefit is not enough if the way you communicate it is dull and hackneyed. Your headline should be unusual or arresting enough to get interest. Here are some examples of headlines that got noticed:

- "When doctors feel rotten, this is what they do."
- "Why some foods explode in your stomach."
- "How a fool stunt made me a star salesman."

John Caples, co-author of the classic guide *Tested Advertising Methods*, recommends beginning headlines with such words or phrases as "New,"

"Now," "At last," "Warning" or "Advice" to pique interest. He also suggests using one- or two-word headlines and giving readers a test in the headline to get them involved (such as "Do you have an iron deficiency? Take this simple test to find out").

Whatever you do, don't use your company name as the headline for your ad. This is one of the most common mistakes small companies make. Would you read an ad whose most eye-catching element was "Brockman Financial Services"? Probably not.

tip

Can't come up with ideas for your ad? Try a brainstorming session. Jot down words or phrases related to your product or service and its benefits. Then see what associations they trigger. Write down all the ideas you can think of without censoring anything. From those associations—whether words, phrases, or visual images—come ideas that make good ads.

Ads That Stand Out

Imagine scanning a convention half full of people dressed in formal attire and suddenly noticing that one brazen attendee is wearing overalls and a red flannel shirt. Is it safe to say your eyes would be riveted to that individual? Your first reaction might be "How dare he?" but you'd also probably be curious enough to walk over and find out what this audacious character was all about.

Such nonconformity can have the same riveting effect in advertising. Imagine scanning a newspaper page full of ho-hum little ads and then noticing that one of them stands out from the crowd. All of a sudden, the other little ads become invisible, and the unique one grabs all the attention. That ad has accomplished the single most difficult task small-business advertising faces—simply getting noticed.

Ideally, your advertising should reflect your company in both look and message. An ad represents you and what you have to offer. If it's generic, it won't have the power to grab attention or persuade prospects to take action.

Even a small ad, if it exhibits something a little unexpected, can steal the thunder of larger, more traditional ads that surround it. But what can you say in a small space that gets noticed and makes an impression? Here are a few ideas that could work with a variety of products or services.

- *For a restaurant.* Use a large but short headline that can't help but arouse curiosity, such as "Now, that's enormous!" This would then be followed by an explanation that this is usually the reaction when one of Francisco's Super-Subs (or whatever large-serving entrée) is placed in front of a customer.
- *For a beauty salon.* Use a small ad with the headline "Can we have your autograph?" in quotes. Follow with copy that reads: "Be ready to draw the attention of admirers when you leave Noreen's Cut 'n' Curl—for people are sure to recognize you as the star you are."
- *For a carpet cleaner.* Try a small ad that shows a blowup of a dust mite with the headline "They're hiding in your carpet." The body copy then explains that these bugs are invisible to the naked eye but are accumulating by the thousands in your uncleansed carpet.

tip

Sometimes the story of your business can make an interesting "hook" for a print ad or a brochure. The social worker who started a maid service could use a headline like "Why I gave up social work to rid the world of dust balls." If your story's intriguing enough, it could get readers hooked.

Ad Placement

There are two principal publication categories to consider for print advertising. The first, the newspaper category, has a positive and a negative side. On the plus side, you can get your ad in very quickly. That enables you to run an ad, for example, that capitalizes on some market turn of events that saves your prospects money if they act fast and buy from you. This could be very exciting news for them, and that's perfect because they are in a "newsy" frame of mind when they read the newspaper.

On the downside, newspapers usually have a shelf life of just 24 hours. Therefore, if you run your ad on Monday, you can't count on anyone discovering that ad on Tuesday. As the saying goes, "Nobody wants to read yesterday's news." (Of course, if your ad runs online at the paper's website, too, you'll likely get a multiple-day run and more bang for your buck.)

Just as with most media, your budget must allow for multiple insertions—it's essential to run your ad with enough frequency for its message to penetrate. Regular exposure of the ad builds recognition and credibility. If some of your prospects see your ad but don't respond to

>> The Good Word

Third-party praise—whether from a customer, an industry organization or a publication—is one of the most effective tools you can use to give your ad, commercial, or direct-mail package added credibility. This can take a variety of forms:

> If your business has received some kind of prize, mention in the press, or other honor, don't hesitate to put it in your advertising. "Rated #1 By Dog Groomers Monthly" or "Voted 'Best Value' by The Chagrin Falls Gazette" are good ways to establish your product or service's benefit in customers' eyes.

> Testimonials from individual customers carry weight, too. "Wanda's Party Planners Gave My Son the Best Birthday Ever!—Jane Smith, Wichita, Kansas," attracts customers' attention. How to get testimonials? If a customer says something nice about your business, don't let the compliment slide—ask, then and there, if you can use the testimonial in your sales materials. (You may want to get this in writing, just to be on the safe side.) Most customers will be happy to comply.

> Even if your company hasn't gotten recognition, perhaps you can use a part, a process, or an ingredient from one of your suppliers that has received praise. For example, you could say "Made with the Flame Retardant Rated #1 by the American Fire Safety Council." This tells your customers you think highly enough of them to provide them with such a great product or ingredient.

> If you're a member of the Better Business Bureau, that's an implied endorsement, too. Be sure to post your BBB plaque prominently on your store or office wall, or use the logo on your letterhead.

your first insertion, they may well respond to your second or third. If you have confidence in your ad's message, don't panic if the initial response is less than what you wanted. More insertions should bring an improved response.

The second type of publication is magazines, for which there are specialty categories of every kind. This allows you to target any of hundreds of special-interest groups. Another advantage of magazines, especially monthlies, is that they have a longer shelf life; they're often browsed through for months after publication and also often have pass-along readership. So your ad might have an audience for up to six months after its initial insertion. Of course, an effective campaign requires multiple insertions. After all, readers can't be expected to see and recall every ad in each issue, and smaller space ads may require even higher frequency than larger ads to get noticed over time.

Researchers have found the following about magazine ads:

- Full-page ads may attract about 70 percent more readers than fractional-page ads.
- Adding a photograph or illustration dramatically increases an ad's power to draw readers.
- Many successful ads use photographs unrelated to the subject matter.
- It's crucial to maintain a balance between the space devoted to photos or illustrations and copy.
- There must be sufficient text to draw readers' attention, which is crucial to advertising success.

aha!

The most persuasive words in advertising: "free," "you," "now," "new," "win," "easy," "introducing," "save," "money," "today," "guarantee," "health," "safety," and "discovery."

When planning advertising in any print medium, contact the publication first and ask for a media kit. This contains rate information for various sizes of ads as well as demographic information about the publication's readership—age, income, and other details—to help you decide if this is where your buyers are. The media kit also indicates specifications for the format in which you'll have to deliver your ad to the publication.

Radio and TV Advertising

Many entrepreneurs believe that TV and radio advertising are beyond their means. But while advertising nationally on commercial network TV may be too costly for many entrepreneurs, advertising on local stations and especially on cable TV can be surprisingly affordable. Armed with the right information, you may find that TV and radio advertising deliver more customers than any other type of ad campaign. The key is to have a clear understanding of your target audience and what they want or listen to so the money spent on broadcast advertising is invested in programming that reaches them in the right way and in the right context.

"A lot of advertising decisions are made more from the heart than from the head," says William K. Witcher, author of *You Can Spend Less and Sell More*, the classic guide to low-cost advertising. Witcher warns entrepreneurs not to get so swept up in the idea of advertising on TV or radio that they neglect to do the necessary research.

save

Considering advertising on cable? Look into a "cable co-op," where several companies collaborate on an ad package that promotes all their services or products.

Sitting down and coming up with a well-thought-out advertising plan is crucial, Witcher says. "Don't feel that you can simply throw a bunch of dollars into the advertising mill and create miracles."

Planning is essential if you're approaching broadcast advertising for the first time. Experts suggest entrepreneurs take the following steps before diving in:

- *Use the target audience description from your marketing plan as the basis for your broadcast buy.* Steer clear of any media or programming that doesn't help you reach your audience with as little waste as possible.
- *Set a rough budget for broadcast advertising.* Come up with an amount that won't strain your business but will allow you to give

broadcast advertising a good try. Many stations suggest running ads for at least three months. A good rule of thumb for a cable TV buy is to budget a minimum of $1,500 per month, plus production. The rates for radio time will vary depending on the size of the market, the station's penetration, and the audience of the shows on which you want to advertise.

- *Contact sales managers at TV and radio stations in your area and arrange to have a salesperson visit you.* Ask salespeople for a list of available spots that air during hours that reach your target audience.
- *Talk to other businesspeople in your area about their experiences with broadcast advertising.* While salespeople from TV and radio stations can be helpful, they are, after all, trying to sell you something. It is your responsibility to be a smart consumer.
- *Ask about the "audience delivery" of the available spots.* Using published guides (Arbitron or Nielsen), ask the salesperson to help you calculate the CPM (cost per thousand) of reaching your target audience. Remember, you are buying an audience, not just time on a show, and you can calculate pretty exactly how much it's going to cost you to reach every single member of that audience.

>> The Small Stuff

Should you use your limited advertising budget to create larger, more visible ads that restrict you to advertising less frequently, or smaller, less visible ads that you can afford to run more frequently?

The answer: smaller ads more frequently. The reason is that most people—even those who are likely candidates for your product—typically don't respond to ads the first time they see them. Prospects may have to notice an ad a number of times and develop a level of comfort with it (especially if the product or service is new to them) before they take action. The more often prospects see your ad, the more comfortable they'll become and the better the chance they'll respond to it. Of course, if your ad is too small, it may not be seen at all, so be sure to pick an ad size that allows you to shine and still maintain a frequency you can afford.

- *Inquire about the production of your commercial.* Fortunately, major cable companies are now offering production assistance to small-business owners with rates that can be as little as $600 to $1,500 per spot. And some independent TV stations will offer low-cost or free production if you enter into an agreement to advertise for at least three months. With a similar contract, some radio stations will provide a well-known personality to be the "voice" of your business at no extra cost. However, for multivoice, high production value spots, you'll want to enlist an outside production company. That could cost you between $4,000 and $15,000, depending on how complex your spot is.

save

Get your ad on the radio—for free—by bartering your products or services for air time. Called "trade-out," this practice is common. Radio stations need everything from janitorial services and graphic designers to products they can give away as on-air prizes, so whatever you sell, you're likely to find a ready market.

- *Compare the various proposals.* Look at the CPMs, and negotiate the most attractive deal based on which outlet offers the most cost-effective way of reaching your audience. Buying time well in advance can help lower the cost. For TV ads, stick with 30-second spots, which are standard in the industry. And keep in mind that the published rates offered by TV and radio stations are often negotiable. Generally, rates vary widely during the first quarter of the year, and sometimes during the third quarter or late in the fourth quarter, traditionally slow seasons for many businesses. But expect to pay full rates during the rest of the year or during popular shows or prime time.

Getting Help

Once you've gone through all these steps, you should have a good idea what is involved in broadcast advertising. But learning to be a smart consumer in the TV and radio market isn't always easy. If you're worried about making the right choice on your own, consider hiring a consultant or an advertising agency to guide you.

>> Right Place, Right Time

Today, marketing messages can go anywhere and everywhere people do, thanks to "out-of-home" advertising. You can reach boaters with advertising at marinas, golfers out on the links with signage on hospitality carts, or health-conscious consumers while they exercise at their local gyms.

Traditional out-of-home advertising encompasses billboards—including the now more ubiquitous LED boards on which messages can be changed frequently, even based on the time of day—and transit advertising, from bus-backs to subway posters and taxi-top ads.

Then there's alternative out-of-home, generally called "place-based advertising." This is where things really get interesting. The "street furniture" category includes bicycle-rack displays and posters on bus shelters and trash receptacles. Other place-based media include newsstand, convenience store, and shopping mall displays. You can even try placing posters above diaper changing stations or in college campus laundry rooms. Your choices and locations are virtually endless.

Follow these three rules for picking the right out-of-home advertising opportunity for your business:

> *Rule one.* The advertising must reach a high percentage of your best prospects. For example, a poster on a bus shelter at a busy intersection can boost sales for a nearby retailer if it is seen often enough by a majority of the store's customers and prospects.

> *Rule two.* The place-based ad must be in an appropriate venue. The posters you find in the restrooms of popular bars and restaurants typically carry ads for other entertainment-oriented businesses because their messages are compatible with the venue.

> *Rule three.* Your ad must reach prospects at the right time. From billboards promoting business services directed at commuters on their way to work to posters for beauty products in neighborhood hair salons, out-of-home advertising should target your prospects at the time when they'll be most receptive to your message.

When approaching radio stations, it's important to learn their demographics, and look at how closely they match your target market. Sorting out demographics is one area where hiring an ad agency or consultant can really help. Every radio station in the country says they are number one in a certain time spot or with a certain audience, so it helps to have an insider on your team.

Microtargeting

Radio can be a good option if you only need to reach a small geographic area, such as a single city or town. Another option that can help an advertiser pinpoint a small geographic area is cable TV. With networks featuring all-news, sports, music, weather, and other specialized topics, cable lets you microtarget the groups that fit your customer profile. Plus, cable TV allows you to reach your target audience in specific towns, without wasting money covering viewers who are too far away to use your products or services. Major cable system providers, such as Comcast, Cablevision, Verizon FiOS, and Time Warner, allow you to buy advertising on cable programming within geographic zones that can be as small as five miles or in multiple zones to reach an entire major metropolitan area. So it's easy to target both geographically and based on the special viewing interests of your audience.

For example, a business owner looking to reach upscale members of the community might try advertising on CNN. A sporting goods store might make a big splash by advertising locally during the national broadcast of "Monday Night Football," carried by ESPN.

But what if you want to target prospects beyond your local broadcast area? You can still use cable TV and radio to achieve your goals. Rather than advertise on your local cable TV provider, for example, you could go directly to national cable networks—from HGTV to ESPN 2—and negotiate for a spot schedule on programs that are targeted to your audience.

warning

Don't wait to market. Fight the tendency to pay too little attention to your customers and to resist marketing until you're in trouble. Market when times are good, and you're more likely to keep the good times rolling.

Today, there are more options than ever to reach national audiences using radio advertising. Thousands of radio stations now simulcast on the internet, and there are networks of internet-only radio stations to suit every breed of listener. If your startup is well-capitalized and you can budget at least $2,000 for a national radio campaign as part of your media mix, you can reach an affluent audience online.

The monthly audience for internet radio tops an estimated 159 million, and a study from Arbitron and Edison Media Research showed online radio listeners are twice as likely to live in households with annual household incomes of more than $100,000. There are other advantages as well: Nearly 80 percent of internet radio listeners tune in while they're at work. So when your spot plays, your prospects are just one click away from your website. In addition to running audio advertising, it's often possible to place online ads your prospects will see while listening.

The challenge is to book the best stations that can reach your audience in sufficient numbers to produce results.

Direct Mail

Direct mail encompasses a wide variety of marketing materials, including brochures, catalogs, postcards, newsletters, and sales letters. Major corporations know that direct-mail advertising is one of the most effective and profitable ways to reach out to new and existing clients.

What's the advantage? Unlike other forms of advertising, in which you're never sure just who is getting your message, direct mail lets you communicate one-on-one with your target audience. That allows you to control who receives your message, when it is delivered, what is in the envelope, and how many people you reach.

To create an effective direct-mail campaign, start by getting your name on

e-fyi

Get your business on target with these two direct-mail websites:

1. *Chief Marketer*, at www.chiefmarketer.com/direct-marketing, offers case histories, mailing list resources, and e-newsletters, including Chief Marketer Listline for direct marketers.
2. *Dmnews* (dmNews.com) offers business updates, a blog, white papers, and email newsletters.

as many mailing lists as possible. Junk mail isn't junk when you're trying to learn about direct mail. Obtain free information every chance you get, especially from companies that offer products or services similar to yours. Take note of your reaction to each piece of mail, and save the ones that communicate most effectively, whether they come from large or small companies.

The most effective direct-mail inserts often use key words and colors. Make sure the colors you use promote the appropriate image. Neon colors, for example, can attract attention for party-planner or gift basket businesses. On the other hand, ivory and gray are usually the colors of choice for lawyers, financial planners, and other business services.

To involve the reader in the ordering process, many mailers enclose "yes" or "no" stickers that are to be stuck onto the order form. Companies such as Publisher's Clearing House take this technique further by asking recipients to find hidden stickers throughout the mailing and stick them on the sweepstakes entry. It also asks customers to choose their prizes, which gets them even more involved.

Next, read up on the subject. A wealth of printed information is available to help educate you about direct mail. Two of the better-known publications are *DM News*, a bimonthly trade paper, and *Direct Magazine*, a monthly.

The Direct Marketing Association (DMA) in New York City is a national trade organization for direct marketers. For a catalog that highlights many of the direct marketing industry's books, a free brochure that lists a variety of direct marketing institutes and seminars across the country, or more information about joining, call the DMA at (212) 768-7277 or email info@the-dma.org. You can also visit the group's website at the-dma.org.

Mailing Lists

No matter what type of direct mail you send out, you'll need a mailing list. The basic way to build a mailing list is by capturing name and address information for everyone who buys or shows interest in your product. If you sell by mail, you'll already have this information. If not, you can get it off customers' checks. Hold a drawing and ask customers to fill out an entry card or drop their business cards in a bowl. Or, if you're a retailer, simply put a mailing list book next to your cash registers where customers can sign up to receive mailers and advance notices of sales. One of the best ways to build a mailing list is to compile a database using the leads generated by your other forms of advertising.

aha!

A growing number of list publishers sell lists on CD. Since these lists may not be updated as regularly as other list sources, be sure to ask how current the list is before you buy.

The list you develop using your own customers' names is called your "house list." Of course, when you're starting out, your house list is likely to be skimpy. To augment it, one way to go is to rent a mailing list. There are two ways to rent a mailing list: approaching the company you want to rent from directly or using a list broker.

Any company that mails merchandise or information to its customers—catalog companies, magazine publishers, manufacturers, etc.—usually has a list manager who handles inquiries and orders for the mailing list. If, for example, you know that subscribers to *Modern Photography* magazine are likely to be good prospects for your product, then you can rent the subscriber list directly. Another good source is local newsletters or group membership lists. Many organizations will let you use their member lists; these can be very cost-effective.

If you aren't sure whose list you want, then call a mailing list broker. List brokers know all the lists available and can advise you on what type of list would work best for your business. Many can also custom-create lists based on your requirements. You can find brokers in the Yellow Pages under "Mailing Lists" and "Mailing Services," and in the classified sections of mail order trade magazines. The DMA can also refer you to brokers. Another source is the monthly directory Standard Rate and Data Service Direct Marketing List Source, available in major reference libraries.

Some list companies let you sample a list before making a purchase. Rental costs typically range from a low of $50 per thousand (CPM) for the most basic compiled lists to $250 CPM for names with multiple selections, such as recipient's name, job title, type of business, or number of children, for example. This is for a one-time use only. (List owners typically "seed" their lists with their own names and addresses so they can tell if you use the list more than once.)

> **save**
>
> 
>
> Keep your house mailing list up-to-date by cleaning it regularly. To do this, send out mailers with the notation "Address Correction Requested." The post office won't charge you for sending you the new addresses of your customers when the cards are returned.

A list will typically be provided in an electronic format or on pre-printed mailing labels and sent directly to the vendor you want to do the final mailing. Consider using a mailing house. Mailing houses have the equipment to professionally cut and apply preprinted labels or to download electronic files and rapidly create and affix labels by the thousands to your envelopes. A large mailing house can also personalize and print your letter and envelope, handle the folding and insertion, and do everything else associated with assembling your direct-mail package. Depending on the level of service you need, rates may range from a few hundred to several thousand dollars for a 5,000-piece mailing.

Most experts agree renting fewer than 5,000 names isn't worthwhile, primarily because a large mailing doesn't cost much more per piece than a small mailing, and the returns are higher. Start with about 5,000 names for your first mailing, and consider it a test.

Entrepreneurs inexperienced with direct mail are often surprised to learn that the average positive response rate is between 2 and 3 percent. In some industries or with some types of products and services, a 1-percent response rate may be considered positive. If you believe your responses are less than stellar, it may be that the market isn't right for your product, your mailer isn't attention-grabbing enough, or your prices are too high. If you get a response of 2 percent or higher, then you're on the right track.

Once you develop a complete mailer, continue to test your enclosures by adding or eliminating one important element at a time and keeping track of any upward or downward changes in response.

Brochures

For many businesses, especially service companies, a brochure is the building block of all marketing materials. A brochure is an information piece that doubles as an image maker. The look and feel of the brochure don't only describe the benefits of your product or service, but also convey your legitimacy and professionalism. A brochure can make your small company look just as substantial as a more established rival, making it a great equalizer.

The good news is that a brochure doesn't have to be expensive. It can be almost as cheap to produce as a flier. A brochure can be as uncomplicated as a piece of folded paper—the same piece of letter-sized paper that would otherwise be a flier. By folding it twice, as you would a letter, then turning it upright so it opens like a book, you have the basis for a brochure.

The magic of the brochure format is that it allows for a more dramatic presentation of the material than does a flier. Think of your brochure cover as the stage curtain, creating anticipation of the excitement that lies inside. An eye-catching headline on the cover is like the master of ceremonies, piquing the prospect's interest about what's behind the "curtain." Inside, you first need to pay off the promise, or claim, in the cover headline with another headline, then use the remaining space for elaboration.

The principles of writing successful brochures are basically the same as those for writing print ads (see the "Print Advertising" section starting on page 464). However, brochures offer more room than ads, so there is a tendency to get long-winded and wordy. Keep your brochure brief, with enough information to interest readers but not so much repetition that they get bored. Use benefit-laden headlines and subheads, and "explain" your benefits by detailing all your features in the body copy.

The sample on pages 482 and 483 shows a "before and after" makeover of a brochure for a company called My Right Hand that provides business support services. The first step in boosting this brochure's appeal was

save

Go to direct-mail school in your mailbox. Each day your mail brings a handful of direct-mail solicitations you can use for hands-on education. Study the letters, use design ideas from the fliers, and keep copies of different types of reply cards. Big-time direct-mail companies spend millions refining their mailing techniques. You can use that information just for the price of tearing open the envelope.

coming up with a tempting headline for the cover. The goal is to arouse the interest of potential clients—the harried sole proprietor who needs help with the detailed paperwork involved in running a business alone. The revised headline "How to Free Your Business from Paperwork Purgatory" accomplishes that goal.

In this or any other headline, it's important to go beyond the ordinary. Give your headline an unexpected word or phrase that expresses the idea in a memorable fashion. Adding the word "purgatory" gives this headline extra drama and emotion and puts the worst face on paperwork.

When the prospect flips the page, he or she finds a short-story-length headline that builds on the cover: "PAPERWORK. It ties you up. It slows you down. It ticks you off. All good reasons to delegate it to us . . . a service you'll feel confident calling MY RIGHT HAND."

This headline pushes the prospect's buttons (i.e., sensitivities) by emphasizing that paperwork is a grind, a bore, and a frustration. The buzzword "delegate" is used because delegation is recognized as essential to entrepreneurial success when a business has grown too big for one person to handle. And since confidence and trust are essential when giving your business papers to an unknown company, the headline also emphasizes the company's trustworthiness by using the word "confident."

The overall look of a brochure is the key to making a good impression on prospective customers. Here are some tips to make sure yours is inviting to the eye:

- *Use a fairly large size type for the descriptive copy.* There's no bigger turnoff for a prospect than squinting at tiny printing.
- *Use light-colored paper.* This, too, makes the brochure easier to read.
- *Break up the copy with subheads.* This makes the overall brochure less intimidating to read.
- *Add something visually unexpected.* One idea is to use a striking photo or graphic on the cover.

tip

Even if you do most of your business by mail or over the phone, customers like to see who they're doing business with. Put your photo on your brochures or mailings. It conveys friendliness and builds confidence in your company.

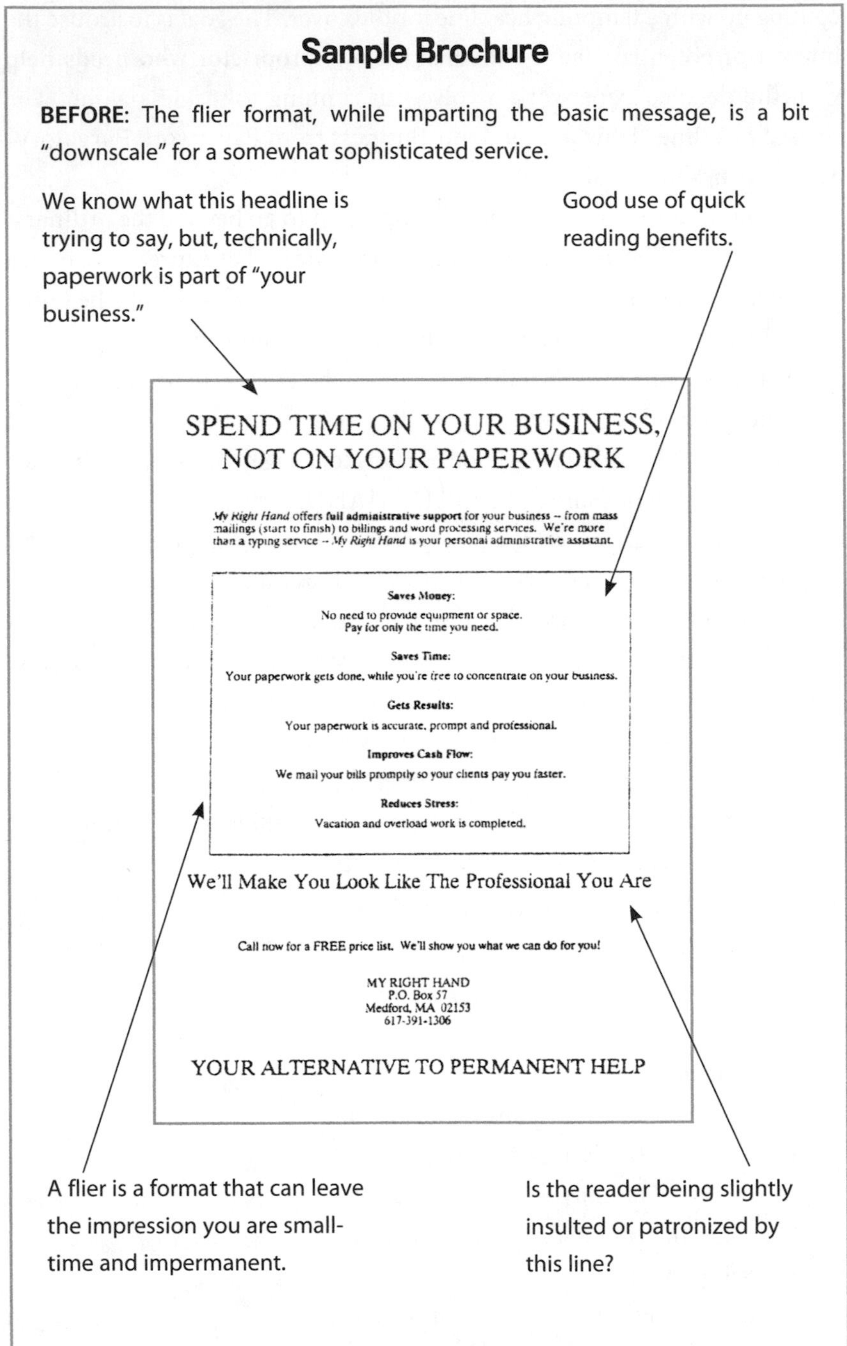

Sample Brochure

BEFORE: The flier format, while imparting the basic message, is a bit "downscale" for a somewhat sophisticated service.

SPEND TIME ON YOUR BUSINESS, NOT ON YOUR PAPERWORK

My Right Hand offers **full administrative support** for your business -- from mass mailings (start to finish) to billings and word processing services. We're more than a typing service -- *My Right Hand* is your personal administrative assistant.

Saves Money:

No need to provide equipment or space.
Pay for only the time you need.

Saves Time:

Your paperwork gets done, while you're free to concentrate on your business.

Gets Results:

Your paperwork is accurate, prompt and professional.

Improves Cash Flow:

We mail your bills promptly so your clients pay you faster.

Reduces Stress:

Vacation and overload work is completed.

We'll Make You Look Like The Professional You Are

Call now for a FREE price list. We'll show you what we can do for you!

MY RIGHT HAND
P.O. Box 57
Medford, MA 02153
617-391-1306

YOUR ALTERNATIVE TO PERMANENT HELP

Figure 30.2. Sample Brochure

Sample Brochure

AFTER: A brochure gives you a more polished image. It says you are seasoned, sophisticated, and professional.

A brochure allows you to manage the information in a way that gives each element special importance.

A brochure adds a lot to your image, without costing much more than a flier.

Figure 30.2. Sample Brochure, continued

- *Use the back of your brochure for a "business biography."* This is a good place to talk about how your company got started, how it has succeeded and where it is today.
- *Always use endorsements*, testimonials, industry affiliations or other credibility-raising elements.
- *Spend a little extra money*. It's worth it to have your brochure printed on cover stock or quality heavyweight paper because it makes a better impression in a customer's hand.

Sales Letters

Whether you send it out solo or as part of a direct-mail package (see "Package Deal" on page 498), a sales letter can be one of your most effective marketing tools, allowing you to speak one-on-one to prospects and customers. What makes a good sales letter? There are three key rules:

1. *Start with a hook.* Begin your letter with a provocative thought or idea that hooks readers and makes them want to keep reading.
2. *Give them the facts fast.* Quickly list the top two or three benefits of doing business with your company.
3. *End persuasively.* Close the letter with a strong argument that compels readers to respond.

How long should a sales letter be? The standard answer is "long enough to do the job." And yes, it takes longer to persuade a prospective customer to buy than to merely get him to inquire further. But in today's high-tech age, people become impatient with anything that takes much longer than an eye blink to read.

Does this mean the sales letter is dying out? No; people will still read sales letters. However, they don't like it when you make them work at it—so keep it lean and mean.

Equal in importance to your message (some would say more important) is the

tip

Trial sizes and sampling work. Have employees pass out product samples in front of your store; if you provide a service, offer a free trial period or consultation.

>> Added Dimension

Add dimension to your sales letters—literally—by attaching some type of small item to the letter. Make it something that ties in to the letter's headline or subject. For example:

- A plumber could stick a minipacket of aspirin to a letter with a headline reading "Pipes giving you a headache? Take two of these, and call us in the morning."
- Child's plastic play scissors attached to the letter could be combined with a "Cut your costs . . ." message.
- Or try a packet of coffee with a headline like "Sit down, have a cup of coffee on us, and learn how you can profit from stocking Steve's Safety Bolts."

A 3-D item inside gives your direct-mail package bulk. Recipients are curious and more likely to open the letter. Once they see what's inside, they'll read on to find out the connection between the item and the words.

look of your letter. It should be visually inviting. If it's crammed with words, readers will get a negative impression right away.

To have the best chance of being read, your letter should be open and airy-looking with short paragraphs—including some that are one sentence or even one word long. (A one-word paragraph? Here's how: Write something like "I have one word for suppliers who say they can't offer you a one-year guarantee." Follow that with a one-word paragraph such as "Baloney!" or any similar word you want to use. It is a real attention-getter.)

Strip your sales message down to the essentials so readers can breeze through it. This may mean hacking out words and phrases you have slaved over. But each extra bit you take out increases your chances of actually getting a response.

Last but not least, be sure to use "you." This is a good rule of thumb in any form of advertising, but especially in a sales letter, where you are, in a sense, talking to the prospect face-to-face. Always talk about your

A Little Surgery Can . . .

This company's old letter is a good first start. It's persuasive and has immediacy. All it needs is some additional structure and a little nipping and tucking to make it work even harder.

BEFORE

It's not too late to lower your property tax.

1) Dec. 26 deadline: The town of Plainville just mailed the Fiscal Year 2001 Real Estate Tax Bills. You have until December 26 to contest your assessed valuation and get an abatement that would lower your taxes.

2) Get an expert: Property owners can obtain abatements on their own; however, the adjustment is usually nominal. For substantial reduction of property taxes, the services of a professional CPA and real estate tax expert is advised to substantiate your case.

3) No-risk contingency fee: My firm, Property Tax Associates, only gets paid if I successfully reduce your property tax. I know what method is currently being used in Plainville to assess your property. I know how similar properties are assessed. And I can evaluate whether your assessment is taking advantage of the full depreciation deductions to which you are entitled and apply declining value multipliers. In a word, I am a property tax abatement expert and have successfully lowered the property taxes of my clients by thousands of dollars.

4) Free evaluation: I know the Plainville real estate market and can quickly evaluate your current assessment and tax situation, at no obligation to you. I will not take your case if I do not believe I can substantially reduce your real estate taxes. My fee is based on a percentage of your actual tax reduction. So it is in my interest as well to make sure your taxes are lowered to the full limit of the law.

5) You must act quickly: State law limits the number of days during which an abatement application can be filed. Call me at (508) 429-2527 for an appointment now so there will be enough time to properly and legally substantiate your tax reduction request.

Property Tax Associates
Rocco Beatrice, CPA, MST, MBA
156 Mitchell Road
Holliston, MA 01746
(508) 429-2527

RECOMMENDATIONS

A. Headline transplant:
The old headline telegraphs a strong benefit—but may work better as a subhead, beneath the new headline.

B. Personalization implant:
Who are you talking to? With no salutation, this letter doesn't draw readers in.

C. Pace lift:
The old letter opens a little slowly and dully. That can be a turnoff to the impatient, indifferent reader.

D. Paragraph liposuction:
The old letter has a few oversized paragraphs that look formidable to read. That immediately disinvites the reader.

A letter with potential . . .

Figure 30.3. Sample Sales Letter

. . . Make a Letter Better

AFTER

Property Tax Associates
Rocco Beatrice, CPA, MST, MBA
156 Mitchell Road, Holliston, MA 01746 · (508) 429-2527

Will you OVERPAY Your Property Tax Again This Year?

It's not too late to lower it if you act by the December 26th deadline.

Mr. George Wagner
R-B Electronics
1313 Azure Blvd.
Plainview, MA 01746

Dear Mr. Wagner,

Will you be "nailed" again this year?

Amazingly, six out of every 10 property owners overpay on their property taxes . . . and you could be one of them.

If you act by December 26th—the deadline for contesting your assessed valuation—you can get an abatement that will lower your taxes.

Why you should call Property Tax Associates:

1) get a larger abatement.You can expect a much larger cut than you could obtain on your own because of our special understanding and knowledge of the abatement process.

2) pay only if you get a reduction. You don't pay us unless we successfully reduce your tax. And our fee is based on a percentage, so it is in our interest to get your taxes reduced as low as possible.

3) get a free evaluation. It costs you nothing to learn if you have a chance for an
abatement. We know the Plainview real estate market and can quickly evaluate your assessment and tax situation, without obligation.

We've helped many owners like you save thousands on their property taxes. And we can do the same for you.

MAKE NO MISTAKE: The city will not reduce your tax automatically. You must apply by December 26th for a reduction—or overpay again. Call me at (508) 429-2527 today so there is enough time to evaluate and prepare your request.

Sincerely,

Rocco Beatrice

Rocco Beatrice
Certified Public Accountant

RECOMMENDATIONS

A. Headline transplant: The new headline pushes an emotional "hot button" that gets prospects riled up—and ready to act.

B. Personalization implant: A letter with opening personalization enables you to bond one-to-one with the reader. That connection is the same that a sales rep hopes to achieve. And a letter is a sales rep.

C. Pace lift: The new letter opens with a provocative, one-sentence "hook," then quickly hops from point to point.

D. Paragraph liposuction: The new letter keeps paragraphs lean, mean, and easy to read.

. . . Potential released!

Figure 30.3. Sample Sales Letter, continued

product or service in terms of its benefit to the reader, such as "You'll save more than 50 percent." Sounds obvious, but it's easy to lapse into the impersonal "we" mode, as in "We offer our customers discounts of more than 50 percent."

> **tip** 
>
> It's easy to get caught up in marketing campaigns that bring sales from new customers yet overlook the importance of retaining existing customers. It's less expensive to upsell an old customer than to win a new one, so you need to strike a balance between acquisition and retention tactics, such as loyalty programs.

Postcards

The humble postcard has the power to beat all other direct-marketing formats when it comes to generating sales leads. Why is the postcard so effective? It's much less costly to prepare and mail than other direct-mail efforts, but that's not its greatest strength. It can be mailed out practically overnight, but that's not its greatest strength, either.

The real power of a postcard is that it takes only a flip of the wrist for recipients to get your message. They read their name on it, then flip it over to see what's on the other side. Simple, but incredibly powerful. Why? Because a huge percentage of direct mail never even gets opened. That's the key word—"opened." A postcard never has to overcome that obstacle. Even a folded flier has to be unfolded, while all a postcard requires is a flip of the wrist.

More than letters, postcards convey a sense of urgency, making them an ideal way to notify customers of a limited-time offer or special sale. Don't restrict yourself to the standard 4-by-6-inch postcard format, either. Postcards can be as big as a letter-sized piece of paper, and many really benefit from that extra size. This costs more (although still not as much as a full direct-mail package), but it gives you more room to dramatize your offer. If you do use a larger size, you can make it a picture postcard, with just a large visual on the front and words on the back next to the recipient's name and address.

Consider the "before and after" makeover (starting on page 490) on a postcard for SWD Truck Repair. Like many service businesses, SWD's services aren't an impulse purchase—meaning buyers usually don't leap for the phone right after getting the promotional mailer.

> *"A life spent making mistakes is not only more honorable but more useful than a life spent doing nothing."*
>
> —George Bernard Shaw

What's a great way to get more attention in the nanosecond of time it takes the recipient to turn the postcard over? First, the company needs a catchier nickname to use for the purposes of advertising. In this case, "The Truck Doctor" fits the bill perfectly. Nicknames can work for many types of service businesses. Some examples:

- For a wedding planner: The Marriage Maestro
- For an auto mechanic: The Car Medic
- For a party planning service: The Party Smarty
- For a carpenter: The Wood Wizard

You get the idea. Next, add an eye-catching graphic on the front of the postcard, along with a provocative headline or teaser that conveys the company's benefit. In this example, the illustration shows a struggling truck, and the headline urges "Call For A Free Checkup At The Truck Doctor." It's a nice play on words that offers a benefit few can resist—a free service. Cartoons with copy balloons, as shown in the makeover, are an excellent way to cut through the advertising clutter and grab the reader's attention.

Fliers

A hybrid of the postcard and brochure, fliers give you more room to get your message across than a postcard but are cheaper (and easier to design) than a brochure.

Fliers are ideal for certain situations, such as for posting on a bulletin board or handing out at an event. They are also a good tool to enclose with a sales letter if, for example, you want to notify recipients about a short-term sale or upcoming special event.

Because fliers' primary benefit is that they convey information quickly, make sure yours is easy to read and stands out (see the sample on page 491). Try bright colors to grab the viewer's eye, and use large type so

Sample Postcard

BEFORE: This postcard has the basics—for a business card. But it's supposed to grab attention as an advertisement, and it doesn't.

What makes this company special? What makes it worth remembering? There's no telling from this card.

AFTER: This approach catches your eye with the cartoon, the contrasting panels, and the proposition.

This headline makes an attractive offer from a memorably named mechanic.

The relevant cartoon makes your message interesting and more palatable.

Figure 30.4. Sample Postcard

Sample Flier

WHY STAND IN LINE AT THE POST OFFICE?

When we can box and ship anything, anywhere, and we won't make you wait.

Pacific Packaging & Shipping

555 Piedmont Dr., Bakersfield, CA 91054, (805) 555-1215

Figure 30.5. Sample Flier

information can be seen from a distance. Keep type brief and to the point. A crowded flier won't get anyone's attention.

Don't use fliers as your only direct-mail tool, or you could come off looking amateurish.

Catalogs

For mail-order entrepreneurs, a catalog is the backbone of their businesses. But even if selling by mail is only a small part of your business, you'll be surprised to find out how much you can benefit from a catalog.

If you're picturing the hefty Spiegel catalog or a glossy magazine like those sent by Pottery Barn, don't despair. A catalog can be significantly briefer and still be successful. Here are five tips to ensure yours is, too:

1. *Keep it simple.* Don't try to reinvent the wheel. Catalogs look the way they do for a reason. Almost every format you can imagine has been tested numerous times, and those you see most often are the most effective. Choose one of the most common sizes.
2. *Borrow from the best.* The surest way to plot your catalog layout is to study other catalogs—at least 20 or 30. You'll then have a collection of the best ideas from the best designers and copywriters money can buy. Study the catalogs, and note any useful ideas.
3. *Choose a production route.* With the abundance of high-quality desktop publishing programs, chances are you can easily create your own camera-ready catalog design. Microsoft Publisher, for example, includes a design "wizard" that shows you how to easily lay out your catalog pages. The real challenge is to create hard-working copy that's professional, clean, and motivates customers to purchase the featured products. If you're up to the task, you can save considerable production costs by completing this step on your own. If not, you should look for a professional design team

warning

Don't launch a direct-mail campaign (especially a catalog) until you're sure you can handle the orders you might receive. If fulfillment systems aren't in place and orders don't get sent out, you'll lose credibility—and future business.

that's experienced in catalog production. Or, you may want to hire a copywriter to review your initial efforts and improve them before having a catalog printed. After all, with the cost of printing, postage, and rental lists, sending a poorly produced piece is a costly mistake.

4. *Find the perfect printer.* Shop around—you'll be amazed at the range of prices printers will quote you for the same job. If you live in a small town, call large printers in nearby metropolitan areas since they often offer substantial savings and give quotes over the phone. And don't overlook the internet when it comes to shopping for the best printer. Some of the country's largest printers have made it easy to order online, and this is where you may find the most attractive pricing. You can email them your artwork and often receive a free or very low-cost sample before you commit to buy in bulk. It's a good idea to get at least three bids on any print job you plan to run, and get six or more on a big one, typically over 1,000 items.

>> Gifts That Keep on Giving

Do you offer customers gift certificates or gift cards? Many entrepreneurs don't, not realizing how this can boost sales. Here are some suggestions to make the most of this sales tool and also prevent fraud:

- *Don't buy generic gift certificates from stationery or office supply stores.* These can easily be duplicated. Invest in custom-designed certificates.
- *Avoid cash refunds.* State on the certificate that if more than $5 in change is due, it will be issued in the form of another gift certificate.
- *Keep a log.* Record the number, date of sale, and dollar amount of each gift certificate sold. Be sure to note when the certificate is redeemed.
- *Use security features* like an embossed logo or watermark to prevent photocopying.

Properly used, certificates are like money in the bank for your business since customers often don't redeem them until months after they're purchased.

The printers will want to know the physical dimensions of your catalog, whether it will be in four-color, the number of pages to be printed, the kind of paper you want, and the number of catalogs you plan to order. The more catalogs you print, the cheaper your cost per unit. In addition to the catalogs you mail out, you need to include a fresh catalog with each order shipped, give away catalogs to customers or at events, and have extras to send when someone expresses interest—so print a generous quantity.

5. *Put it all together.* You can spend tens of thousands of dollars on a mail order catalog—but if you do as much as you can yourself, you won't have to. Today's technology—from digital cameras to simple desktop publishing programs—makes catalog production and layout simpler than ever.

   Of course, the real key to catalog success doesn't lie exclusively in technology—it's understanding your customers. Show them why they should buy from you and no one else. Target them with the right mailing lists. And remember, the more you do yourself, the more you save.

Need more help? The Direct Marketing Association can refer you to catalog consultants in your area.

>> Direct Hits

Try these attention-getting direct-mail ideas to power up your business:

> *Reactivation voucher.* Mail a $20 no-strings-attached voucher to any customer you haven't seen in six months or longer. Few can turn it down . . . and even fewer will spend only $20.

> *Magalog.* If you have a catalog, give it more value by enhancing it with problem-solving editorial content. This creates a combination magazine and catalog.

> *We've missed you.* Send a card to clients you haven't seen in a year telling them they're missed. Include a discount coupon.

> *Birthday call.* Record all customers' birth dates, and make sure that they get a special call or card from you.

Newsletters

Publishing a company newsletter is a great way to get the word out about your business, and keep past customers coming back. While many small-business owners have changed from printed newsletters to e-newsletters, which are sent via email, there are still some target audiences, such as seniors, that respond best to old-fashioned snail mail. If your newsletter becomes well-known for valuable content, your readers will spend time with it rather than pitch it into the trash as junk mail.

"The primary benefit of a customer newsletter is keeping your existing customers informed about what you're doing," says Elaine Floyd, author of *Marketing with Newsletters.* Newsletters are also a good way to reach new customers because, if done correctly, they come off as more informative and with less sales hype than most items consumers receive in the mail. In addition to telling readers about your product or service, newsletters inform them about developments in your industry or theirs and share information that affects them. "People might not think they need your product or service," says Floyd. "Reading an informative newsletter helps convince them they do."

tip 

Consider a loyalty program for customers. It could be in the form of a punch card—buy a certain number of items of products and receive a discount or free item. It's a popular scheme with ice cream and coffee shops, where customers make a purchase 10 or 12 times and then receive a free ice cream or coffee by turning in the card. Just be sure to put a price limit on the freebie, or be willing to watch some customers pile their ice cream sky-high with toppings. You can also offer a loyalty card, similar to those found at local grocery stores. These customers could get discounts or accumulate points for a discount or free item.

The businesses that benefit most from newsletters are those that have to educate customers about the advantages of using their product or service. If you own a candy shop, for example, you might not have enough pertinent information for customers to justify a newsletter. On the other hand, a computer consultant could do a real service by publishing a newsletter about the latest software and hardware.

Your newsletter doesn't have to be all information. Including a coupon, a special offer, or other call to action helps get people to buy. Also, always give upcoming sales or promotions a prominent place in your newsletter. "The promotional aspects of your newsletter should be woven in with the informational," advises Floyd. If you're reporting on your industry, talk about your company's place within the industry. If you're talking about a trend in the economy—the rising gas prices, let's say—then tie in the fact that using your company's service helps customers save money.

tip 

Although newsletters give you room for lengthier articles, keep the bulk of your newsletter limited to short pieces, so they are very scannable. You want lots of different items in the hope of providing something interesting to every reader.

Floyd recommends using the following formula, which she calls RISE, to be sure your newsletter covers all the bases:

- *Recognition*. Your newsletter should tell people who you are, what you do, and where they can find you. If consumers have to read through two pages of text to find the name of your company, you're not increasing your name recognition. Use your company logo on the newsletter.
- *Image*. Your newsletter is an important branding tool that can enhance your company's image. If it's interesting and professional-looking, customers will think well of your business. If it's not, they may doubt your credibility. Floyd says most people can create their own professional-looking newsletter with desktop publishing programs or have it done affordably by a freelancer.
- *Specifics*. Give your readers specific reasons why they should choose your product or service. Vague assertions like "We're the best" don't work nearly as well as matter-of-fact details about exactly what you can do for them.
- *Enactment*. Make the reader take action—whether by picking up the phone, mailing in a reply card, or coming down to your store.

Strapped for things to write about—or don't have time to write it yourself? Try asking your industry trade association for news services that provide copy in return for a monthly subscription fee. This also ensures the articles are professionally written.

>> Premium Prospects

Whether you call them premiums or advertising specialties, gifts are a marketing tool that works with all demographic groups. Studies show that 40 percent of people remember an advertiser's name up to six months after receiving a promotional product as a gift.

Premiums carrying your company name, logo, or message can be used to generate leads, build name awareness, thank customers, increase store traffic, introduce new products, motivate customers, and create an unconscious obligation to buy. Premiums can be used at trade shows, open houses, special events and grand openings, and in direct mail.

Classic premiums include T-shirts, baseball caps, jackets, headbands, writing instruments, desk and office accessories, scratch pads, and mugs. Mouse pads and high-tech devices, such as USB memory drives, are some of the more recent premiums gaining popularity.

How to make a premium work for you? Research it first. Make sure the item is matched with your target audience. Also make sure the item is good quality. A cheap premium that breaks or doesn't work in the first place makes a negative impression—just the opposite of what you want.

When choosing a premium, ask five questions:

1. How many people do I want to reach?
2. How much money do I have to spend?
3. What message do I want to print?
4. What gift will be most useful to my prospects?
5. Is this gift unique and desirable? Would I want it?

You can find specialty advertising firms listed in the Yellow Pages. Ask to see their catalogs; compare sample quality and prices.

While the gift is being offered, focus your marketing and advertising efforts on it. There's no more powerful word in advertising than "free," so put the power of freebies to work for you.

If you can't find a news service, use a clippings service to get story ideas. Though clippings from other publications can't be reprinted without the writer's permission, they can give you ideas for articles of your own and keep you updated on hot industry topics.

Tap clients for copy by featuring a "Client of the Month," showing how your product or service solved a problem they were facing. Or you can team up with related businesses; for example, an interior designer could have guest columns written by florists or furniture store owners.

Easy ways to get clients to contribute? Conduct a survey—and print the results. Start a "Letters to the Editor" column. Add a "Q&A" column, where customers can pose their problems and other customers can write in with solutions.

>> Package Deal

While direct mail can mean everything from a postcard to a catalog, many business owners get the best response from sending out a direct-mail "package." In addition to the sales letter and brochure (see the "Sales Letters" and "Brochures" sections earlier in this chapter), this typically includes three other elements:

1. *The outside envelope.* There are two schools of thought on this. One school swears that "teaser" copy on the envelope can get recipients to open it. On the other hand, some people throw away anything that looks like junk mail. The opposite strategy is to trick readers into opening your mail by sending direct mail that looks like personal letters. Software programs can print addresses so they look like handwriting.
2. *A response form.* The form should be easy to fill out. Be sure to include your phone number in case the prospect wants to ask a question or order by phone.
3. *A reply envelope.* Enclosing postage-paid reply envelopes helps get orders. Even if you can't afford postage-paid envelopes, include a pre-addressed reply envelope.

Keep your writing style simple, and make sure you get help proofreading if your skills aren't up to snuff. A newsletter full of typos or grammatical errors shows clients you're a careless amateur.

Newsletters can be monthly, semimonthly, or quarterly, depending on what your budget is, how much time you have, and how fast-paced your industry is. Quarterly publications are generally sufficient to get your name in front of customers; then increase frequency if needed. The key is to be consistent, so don't take on more than you can handle.

Renting a mailing list isn't generally a good idea for newsletters, says Floyd. "Your newsletter will be better received if the reader knows about you or needs your product," she says. Floyd recommends sending newsletters only to current customers, qualified leads, and referrals. When someone gives you a business card, send him or her a newsletter. Then you or a salesperson can call the person later, using the newsletter as a starting point to ask about products or services they might need.

e-fyi

Consider adding a connected element to your mailings and promotions by encouraging recipients to "check-in" on Foursquare or other location-based services on their smartphones. You could offer a discount, a prize for becoming "mayor" of a location the customer checks in at often, or the like. Many smartphone users habitually enter their location on such services, as well as Facebook and other social media.

Classified Ads

Classified ads are a smart way to reach prospects who are looking for—and are prepared to buy—what you sell. And since they demand neither the eye-catching design of a display ad nor the clever wording of a direct-mail campaign, almost anyone can write them.

What should your ad say? The Newspaper Association of America (NAA) recommends listing your product or service's main benefit. Does it make people money? Improve their self-image? Use a catchy statement, such as "Feel Good Now!" to create an impact. Not every reader is looking for the same benefit, so list as many as you can afford. The more readers know about your business, the more they'll trust you.

> *"The workplace should primarily be an incubator for the human spirit."*
>
> —Anita Roddick, founder of The Body Shop

Experts also recommend using white space to make your classified ad stand out from the competition. White space works especially well in newspapers, which sell ads for pennies a word or by the line. If you place just a few words in each line—the first line listing a benefit, the second the name of your company, the third your address, for example—you have a striking, centered ad surrounded by white space.

These brief ads work best when they offer a commonly sold product or service such as tax preparation or catering. Listing the benefits of each isn't essential because the public knows what to expect. White space in classifieds is also effective when you offer a catalog or another form of literature describing your product. In this case, you might place the main benefit in an opening line that's designed to grab the reader's attention, and below the benefit list how to send for the information, noting its price, if any. For example, "Play Backgammon Like a Pro" would be a good benefit line in an ad offering free information about a booklet that shows backgammon players how to improve their game.

Ads that use white space are less common in magazines since these ads are often twice as costly as a typical newspaper classified. However, they are often more effective as well—even more so than in a newspaper because few other white space ads will be competing for readers' attention.

Before placing your classified ad, contact the publication and ask for a media kit. They should include guidelines that will help you construct your ad and give you tips on choosing the main benefit, consolidating words, or determining whether the tone should be boldly stated or instead employ a conservative description and a list of benefits. Most media kits also list demographic information about the readers—essential information to determining if the publication is right for you.

Finally, repeat your ad as often as possible, so long as it brings in enough money to justify its expense. Repeating ads helps customers gain familiarity with your product or service and helps break down sales resistance. Once the ad stops pulling in new accounts, it's time to develop a new ad. A classified that uses fewer words will cost less to run, so it doesn't have to pull as well to justify itself. But sometimes adding more words can help your sales, too. It doesn't hurt to experiment.

How much profit do you need to make on classifieds? Unless you're running a one-product, one-sale business, you can build a profitable operation through classifieds just by breaking even, or even by coming in a little under the money since many of those buyers will become your repeat customers.

Co-Op Advertising

How can small retailers or distributors maintain a high profile without spending lots of money? One answer is co-op advertising.

Co-op advertising is a cooperative advertising effort between suppliers and retailers—such as between a soda company and a convenience store that advertises the company's products.

Both retailers and suppliers benefit: retailers because co-op advertising increases the amount of money they can spend on ads, and suppliers through increased local exposure and better sales.

Although each manufacturer or supplier that uses co-op advertising sets up its own individual program, all co-op programs run on the same basic premise. The retailer or distributor builds a fund (called accrual) based on the amount of purchases made by the supplier. Then, when the retailer or distributor places ads featuring that supplier's products, the supplier reimburses all or part of the cost of the ad, up to the amount accrued.

To start using co-op advertising, begin by asking your suppliers what co-op programs they offer. Follow their rules to be sure you get reimbursed. Some suppliers require that ads feature only their products, not any other supplier's. Others ask that no competing products be included.

Though procedures may vary, there are three basic steps to filing a claim for reimbursement. First, show "proof of performance." For print ads, this is just a copy of the ad exactly as it was printed. If you buy TV or radio ads, you'll need a copy of the script with station affidavits of the dates and times aired.

Next, document the cost of the advertising—usually with copies of applicable invoices from the publication or station where you ran the ad.

>> Coupon Cutters

If you want to attract and keep customers, you need to offer an incentive. A coupon for a free sample or service, or a discount on your normal prices, can be just the nudge a customer needs to try your new business. Coupons help you achieve many goals: introducing a new product or service, increasing repeat business, beating the competition, and more.

One of the most powerful ways to use coupons is through direct mail. This method is especially good for occasions such as grand openings or new product/service introductions. How to make the most of your direct-mail coupon campaign? Keep these tips in mind:

- Coupons can be offered as a "Thank you for buying from us" or a "Stop by and try us" message.
- A coupon can be a single item for a one-shot promotion or used in combination with other offers.
- The value must be substantial enough to make it worthwhile. Better to err on the side of giving too big a discount than to seem cheap.
- Use coupon promotions sparingly. They wear themselves out if overused. And customers begin to expect a coupon and might delay purchases until they get one.
- Be clear. State exactly what the offer is, how long it lasts, and the terms of redemption.
- Color-code your coupons if a variety of groups will receive them. For example, if you're mailing to six ZIP codes, color-code them differently so you know how many were redeemed from each area.

You can also distribute coupons on the internet. Add a registration box to the main page of your website so people can sign up to receive coupons. This way, you can build a permission-based email list of people who want to receive ongoing offers and rewards. Or consider using a web coupon service, which offers coupons in booklets by mail or online for consumers to download and print out themselves.

Third, fill out and submit a claim form, which you can get from the supplier.

Other steps to make the most of co-op advertising:

- Keep careful records of how much you have purchased from each supplier.
- If you try something unusual, such as a sales video or a catalog, get prior approval from each vendor before proceeding.
- If you're preparing your own ads, work with an advertising professional to prepare an ad you think will appeal to the manufacturer. Keep in mind the image the manufacturer presents in its own ads.
- Make sure your company's name stands out in the ad. Your goal is not so much to sell the supplier's product but to get customers into your store.
- If there's no established co-op program, pitch your ad campaign to the vendor anyway.
- Expect vendors to help out; after all, you're bringing them business. If your vendor doesn't offer advertising co-op money, you should look for another vendor that does.
- Be sure to follow up. Money goes only to those who submit claims.

tip 

Your marketing plan is an ongoing process. Market conditions change. Some of tomorrow's challenges you can predict today, while others you can never anticipate. You should take a look at your plan at least every three months and on a formal basis every six months. If you aren't on track, why not? Has your thinking changed or has the market thrown you a curve?

Measuring Advertising Effectiveness

Just as important as creating a strong marketing plan is following through on the results. How will you know which ads are working if you don't analyze the results? Check the effectiveness of your advertising programs regularly by conducting one or more of the following tests:

- *Run the same ad in two different publications with a different identifying mark on each one.* Ask customers to clip the ad and bring it in for a discount or a free sample. Or, if you are running an ad that asks customers to order by mail, put a code in your company address such as "Dept. SI." By looking at the marks on the clipped ads or the addresses on the mail-in orders, you'll be able to tell which ad pulled better.

- *Train everyone in your company who answers the phone to ask customers where they heard about you.* Create a one-page form with checkboxes so this process is simple to follow and the results are easy to evaluate. Just bear in mind that customers will sometimes get it wrong—they may say they saw you on TV when you don't run a TV campaign. But overall, asking for this information will be valuable.
- *Offer a product at different prices in different magazines.* This has the added benefit of showing whether consumers will buy your product at a higher price.
- *Advertise an item in one ad only.* Don't have any signs or otherwise promote the item in your store or business. Then count the calls, sales, or special requests for that item. If you get calls, you'll know the ad is working.
- *Stop running an ad that you regularly run.* See if dropping the ad affects sales.
- *Always check sales results.* This is especially important when you place an ad for the first time.

Checks like these will give you some idea of how your advertising and marketing program is working. Be aware, however, that you can't expect immediate results from an ad. Advertising consistently is important, especially if you run small-space ads, which are less likely to be seen and remembered than larger ads.

One study showed that attention to an ad is significantly impacted by its size—in fact, a one-percent increase in ad size leads to the same percentage increase in attention. You must also run your ad in multiple issues (at least three) before readers will notice your ad and buy what you're selling.

> ***"No person can get very far in life working 40 hours a week."***
>
> —J. WILLARD MARRIOTT, FOUNDER OF MARRIOTT INTERNATIONAL INC.

Advertising Checklist

Overview

- ❑ Have you defined your advertising objectives and written them down?
- ❑ Have you developed an advertising strategy?
- ❑ What exactly do you want to communicate to your potential customers?
- ❑ Are you communicating buyer benefits?
- ❑ Is the timing right?
- ❑ Do you have a planned advertising budget?
- ❑ Are you prepared for a successful response?
- ❑ Have you asked suppliers about cooperative programs?
- ❑ Have you made sure that employees (if any) are informed of your goals?
- ❑ Have all appropriate employees been familiarized with your advertising and trained how to respond to customers?
- ❑ What is your lead time for ad placement? Some newspapers require only a few days; some magazines require two months or longer.
- ❑ How will you measure the effectiveness of your ad?

Specifics

- ❑ Does your ad present a central idea or theme?
- ❑ Does your message require a response?
- ❑ Have you told customers where and how to reach you?
- ❑ Is your ad clear and concise?
- ❑ Is your ad consistent with your desired business image?

Figure 30.6. Advertising Checklist

Advertising Checklist

Files

- ❑ Are you keeping files on all aspects of each ad?
- ❑ Where did the ad run? What were the results? (Number of sales? Sales increases?)
- ❑ Have you reflected/brainstormed/evaluated?
- ❑ What variables (the economy, competition, etc.) have you targeted for further study?

Competitors and Customers

- ❑ Are you watching competitors? (If advertisers repeat ads, try to determine why.)
- ❑ Are you listening to your customers? What do they want? What's important to them?
- ❑ Which media are most cost-effective for reaching your customers?

Figure 30.6. Advertising Checklist, continued

Evaluate an ad's cost-effectiveness, too. Consider the CPM. A cheaper ad is no bargain if it doesn't reach many of your prospects.

CHAPTER

31

Talking Points

How to Promote Your Business

Paid advertising isn't the only way to spread the word about your business. In fact, one of the best ways to get your business noticed does not have to cost you a dime. We are talking about public relations.

Public relations is a broad category, spanning everything from press releases and networking at chamber of commerce meetings to sponsoring contests or holding gala special events. This chapter will show you the basics of public relations and give you plenty of ideas to get started. And ideas are what it's all about, because when it comes to public relations, you are limited only by your own imagination.

Getting Publicity

Just what is public relations? And how does it differ from advertising? Public relations is the opposite of advertising. In advertising, you pay to have your message placed in a newspaper, TV, or radio spot. In public relations, the article that features your company is not paid for. The reporter, whether broadcast or print, writes about or films your company as a result of information he or she received and researched.

tip 

Find out the lead times for the media in which you want to run your promotional piece. Magazines, for instance, typically work several months in advance, so if you want to get a story about your business in the December issue, you may need to send your idea in June.

Publicity is more effective than advertising, for several reasons. First, publicity is far more cost-effective than advertising. Even if it is not free, your only expenses are generally phone calls and mailings to the media.

Second, publicity has greater longevity than advertising. An article about your business will be remembered far longer than an ad.

Publicity also reaches a far wider audience than advertising generally does. Sometimes, your story might even be picked up by the national media, spreading the word about your business all over the country.

Finally, and most important, publicity has greater credibility with the public than does advertising. Readers feel that if an objective third party—a magazine, newspaper, or radio reporter—is featuring your company, you must be doing something worthwhile.

Why do some companies succeed in generating publicity while others don't? It's been proved time and time again that no matter how large or small your business is, the key to securing publicity is identifying your target market and developing a well-thought-out public relations campaign. To get your company noticed, follow these seven steps. You'll notice that many are similar or identical to steps you went through when developing your marketing plan.

1. *Write your positioning statement.* This sums up in a few sentences what makes your business different from the competition.

2. *List your objectives.* What do you hope to achieve for your company through the publicity plan you put into action? List your top five goals in order of priority. Be specific, and always set deadlines. Using a clothing boutique as an example, some goals may be to:
   - Increase your store traffic, which will translate into increased sales
   - Create a high profile for your store within the community
3. *Identify your target customers.* Are they male or female? What age range? What are their lifestyles, incomes, and buying habits? Where do they live?

aha!

When considering media that can publicize your business, don't forget the "hidden" media in your community. These can include free publications for singles and seniors, for tourists, for local companies' employees, and for social or charitable organizations like the Junior League.

4. *Identify your target media.* List the newspapers and TV and radio programs in your area that would be appropriate outlets. Make a complete list of the media you want to target, then call them and ask whom you should contact regarding your area of business. Identify the specific reporter or producer who covers your area so you can contact them directly. Your local library will have media reference books that list contact names and numbers. Make your own media directory, listing names, addresses, and telephone and fax numbers. Separate TV, radio, and print sources. Know the "beats" covered by different reporters so you can be sure you are pitching your ideas to the appropriate person.
5. *Develop story angles.* Keeping in mind the media you're approaching, make a list of story ideas you can pitch to them. Develop story angles you would want to read about or see on TV. Think back to the last story about a company that kept your attention. What angle and interest was in that story and others that caught your eye? Plan a 45-minute brainstorming session with your spouse, a business associate, or your employees to come up with fresh ideas.

   If you own a toy store, for example, one angle could be to donate toys to the local hospital's pediatric wing. If you own a clothing store, you could alert the local media to a fashion trend in your area. What's flying out of your store so fast you can't keep it in stock? If it's shirts featuring the American flag, you could talk to the media about the return of patriotism. Then arrange for a reporter to speak with some of your customers about why they purchased that particular shirt. Suggest the newspaper send a photographer to take pictures of your customers wearing the shirts.

aha!

Sending out publicity photos with your press release or kit? Make them fun, different, and exciting. Editors and reporters see thousands of dull, sitting-at-the-desk photos every year. Come up with a creative way to showcase something photogenic about your business . . . and make it stand out from the pack.

6. *Make the pitch.* Put your thoughts on paper, and send them to the reporter in a "pitch letter." Start with a question or an interesting fact that relates your business to the target medium's audience. For instance, if you were writing for a magazine aimed at older people, you could start off "Did you know that more than half of all women over 50 have not begun saving for retirement?" Then lead into your pitch: "As a Certified Financial Planner, I can offer your readers ten tips to start them on the road to a financially comfortable retirement . . ." Make your letter no longer than one page; include your telephone number and email address so the reporter can contact you.

   If appropriate, include a press release with your letter (see "Meet the Press" on page 511). Be sure to include your positioning statement at the end of any correspondence or press releases you send.
7. *Follow up.* Following up is the key to securing coverage. Wait four to six days after you've sent the information, then follow up your pitch letter with a telephone call. If you leave a message on voice mail and the reporter does not call you back, call again until you get him or her on the phone. Do not leave a second message within five days of the first. If the reporter requests additional information, send it immediately and follow up to confirm receipt.

>> Meet the Press

Think of a press release as your ticket to publicity—one that can get your company coverage in all kinds of publications or on TV and radio stations. Editors and reporters get hundreds of press releases a day. How to make yours stand out?

First, be sure you have a good reason for sending a press release. A grand opening, a new product, a record-setting sales year, a new location or a special event are all good reasons.

Second, make sure your press release is appropriately targeted for the publication or broadcast you're sending it to. The editor of *Road & Track* is not going to be interested in the new baby pacifier you've invented. It sounds obvious, but many entrepreneurs make the mistake of sending press releases at random without considering a publication's audience.

To ensure readability, your press release should follow the standard format: typed, double-spaced, on white letterhead with a contact person's name, title, company, address and phone number in the upper right-hand corner. Below this information, put a brief, eye-catching headline in bold type. A dateline—for example, "Los Angeles, California, April 10, 2014—" follows, leading into the first sentence of the release.

Limit your press release to one or two pages at most. It should be just long enough to cover the six basic elements: who, what, when, where, why, and how. The answers to these six questions should be mentioned in order of their importance to the story to save the editor time and space.

Don't embellish or hype the information. Remember, you are not writing the article; you are merely presenting the information and showing why it is relevant to that publication in hopes that they will write about it. Pay close attention to grammar and spelling. Competition for publicity is intense, and a press release full of typos or errors is more likely to get tossed aside.

Some business owners use attention-getting gimmicks to get their press releases noticed. In most cases, this is a waste of money. If your release is

>> Meet the Press, continued

well-written and relevant, you don't need singing telegrams or a bouquet of flowers to get your message across (and most reporters won't take such shenanigans seriously).

If you have the money to invest, you may want to try sending out a press kit. This consists of a folder containing a cover letter, a press release, your business card, and photos of your product or location. You can also include any other information that will convince reporters your business is newsworthy: reprints of articles other publications have written about your business, product reviews, or background information on the company and its principals. If you do send out a press kit, make sure it is sharp and professional-looking and that all graphic elements tie in with your company's logo and image.

Talking to the Media

Once you reach the reporter on the telephone, remember that he or she is extremely busy and probably on deadline. Be courteous, and ask if he or she has time to talk. If not, offer to call back at a more convenient time. If the reporter can talk to you, keep your initial pitch to 20 seconds; afterward, offer to send written information to support your story ideas.

The following tips will boost your chances of success:

- If a reporter rejects your idea, ask if he or she can recommend someone else who might be interested.
- Know exactly what you're going to say before you telephone the reporter. Have it written down in front of you—it's easier, and you'll feel more confident.
- Everyone likes a compliment. If you've read a story you particularly enjoyed by the reporter you're contacting, let him or her know. This will also show that you're familiar with the reporter's work.
- Be persistent. Remember, not everyone will be interested. If your story idea is turned down, try to find out why and use that information to improve your next pitch. Just keep going, and don't give up. You will succeed eventually.

- Don't be a pest. You can easily be persistent without being annoying. Use your instincts; if the reporter sounds rushed, offer to call back. Daily newspaper reporters face deadlines in the early afternoon. It's best to call between about 2:30 P.M. and 5:30 P.M.
- Be helpful and become a resource by providing reporters with information. Remember, they need your story ideas. There are only so many they can come up with on their own.
- Always remember that assistants get promoted. Be nice to everyone you speak with, no matter how low they are on the totem pole. After you establish a connection, keep in touch; you never know where people will end up.
- Say thank you. When you succeed in getting publicity for your business, always write a thank-you note to the reporter who worked on it with you. You'd be surprised how much a note means (and how few of these reporters receive).

aha!

Capitalize on old-fashioned publicity stunts. No, you don't have to swallow goldfish or sit atop a telephone pole, but consider the landscaping company whose precision lawn-mowing team shows off its fancy footwork while marching in local parades.

Plan your publicity efforts just as carefully as you plan the rest of your business. You'll be glad you made the effort when you see your company featured in the news—and when you see the results in your bottom line.

Special Events

Ever since the first Wild West Show was staged to sell "Doctor Winthrop's Miracle Elixir," businesspeople have understood the value of promotional events. Even the most obscure product or service takes on new cachet when accompanied by a dash of showmanship. From "fun runs" to fashion shows, contests to concerts, businesses have learned it pays to be associated with special events.

In fact, special events are one of the fastest-growing areas of marketing today. And while large corporations shell out billions each year to host events, small companies, too, can use promotions to reach their market in a way no conventional method could.

No matter how spectacular an event is, however, it can't stand alone. You can use advertising or public relations without doing a special event, but you need both advertising and public relations to make your event work. How do you put together the right mix to make your event successful?

First, you must know what you want to accomplish. The desired outcome of event marketing is no different from that of any other marketing effort: You want to draw attention to your product or service, create greater awareness of it, and increase sales.

While the number of special event ideas is infinite, some general categories exist. Following are some of the most popular.

Grand Openings

You're excited about opening your new business. Everyone else will be, too . . . right? Wrong. You have to create the excitement, and a knockout grand opening celebration is the way to do it. From start to finish, your event has to scream "We're here. We're open. We're ready to go. We're better than, different from, and more eager to serve you than our competitors. We want to get to know you and have you do business with us."

A grand opening is one of the best reasons to stage a special event. No one thinks twice about why you're blowing your own horn. What you want people to think about is what a great time they had at your event.

That means no run-of-the-mill, garden-variety ribbon-cutting. Be original. If you own an electronics store, open your doors via remote control. If you are opening a yarn store, unravel a huge knitted ribbon. If you sell sporting goods, reel in both ends of an enormous bow until the ribbon is untied. Whatever your specialty, do something unusual, entertaining, and memorable.

Design a terrific invitation, do plenty of publicizing, provide quality refreshments and entertainment, select a giveaway that promotes your business (and draws people into the store to get it), and incorporate some way of tracking who attended your event (contest entry forms, coupons, free newsletter subscriptions, birthday club sign-ups, and so on).

>> Social Graces

Does your business use recycled paper products or donate to a homeless shelter? Today, many consumers consider such factors when deciding whether to patronize your business. A business's "social responsibility" quotient can make a difference in its bottom line.

If you think getting involved in social causes would work for your business, here are some things to consider. First and foremost, customers can smell "phony" social responsibility a mile away, so unless you're really committed to a cause, don't try to exploit customers' concerns to make a profit.

Consider these steps for making social responsibility work for you—and your community:

> *Set goals*. What do you want to achieve? What do you want your company to achieve? Do you want to enter a new market? Introduce a new product? Enhance your business's image?

> *Decide what cause you want to align yourself with*. This may be your toughest decision, considering all the options out there: children, the environment, senior citizens, homeless people, people with disabilities—the list goes on. Consider a cause that fits in with your products or services; for example, a manufacturer of women's clothing could get involved in funding breast cancer research. Another way to narrow the field is by considering not only causes you feel strongly about, but also those that your customers consider significant.

> *Choose a nonprofit or other organization to partner with*. Get to know the group, and make sure it's sound, upstanding, geographically convenient, and willing to cooperate with you in developing a partnership.

> *Design a program, and propose it to the nonprofit group*. Besides laying out what you plan to accomplish, also include indicators that will measure the program's success in tangible terms.

> *Negotiate an agreement with the organization*. Know what they want before you sit down, and try to address their concerns upfront.

>> **Social Graces, continued**

> *Involve employees*. Unless you get employees involved from the beginning, they won't be able to communicate the real caring involved in the campaign to customers.

> *Involve customers*. Don't just do something good and tell your customers about it later. Get customers involved, too. A sporting goods store could have customers bring in used equipment for a children's shelter, then give them a 15 percent discount on new purchases. Make it easy for customers to do good; then reward them for doing it.

Entertainment and Novelty Attractions

Time, space, and popular appeal are three things to consider if and when you host or sponsor a one-time special attraction. If space permits and a beach motif fits your business, having a huge sand castle built in your parking lot might draw attention and business for the entire time it takes to construct it.

Just keep in mind that the novelties and entertainment shouldn't last so long or be so distracting that no one finds the time or inclination to do business with you. Think of these events as the appetizer, with your product or service as the main course.

aha!

Whenever possible, tie your business to a current event or trend. Does your product or service somehow relate to the Olympics, the presidential election, the environment, or the hot movie of the moment? Whether you're planning a special event or just sending out a press release, you can gain publicity by association.

Holidays and Seasons

Some of the most common and easily developed special events are based on holidays or times of year.

Again, when planning an event tied to a holiday or season, make originality your motto. If the average December temperature in your city is a balmy 76 degrees, then don't dredge up icicles and fake snow for the store. Take a cue from your locale: Put antlers on pink flamingos and dress Santa in shorts and sunglasses.

Celebrity Appearances

Working with celebrities is like buying a volatile stock—high risk but high return. If you are willing to go out on a limb, you may harvest the sweetest fruit. Many celebrities are affable, cooperative, and generous if they are treated professionally and supplied with all the necessary details in advance.

The key to using a celebrity to promote your business is knowing what kind of "personality" is appropriate for your company and marketing goals. Think about whom you want to attract, what kind of media coverage you want to generate, and what kind of impression you want to create.

Whether you are seeking soap stars, sports stars, or movie stars, it's usually best to contact their agents first. If you don't know who a star's agent is, contact a talent agency or the organization the celebrity works for.

Unless you know celebrities personally, you must consider the arrangement a commercial venture for them. There are literally hundreds of details to work out and opportunities at every turn for something to go wrong unless you are experienced in dealing with celebrities or you have contacted a reputable talent or public relations agency to help you.

Celebrities don't have to be nationally known names, either. Think about local celebrities in your community who might be willing to be part of your special event. A politician, well-known businessperson, or community leader can be an excellent addition to your big day.

Co-Sponsoring

You can partner with complementary businesses to host an event, or you can take part as a sponsor of an established charity or public cause. Sporting events, fairs, and festivals have proved to be popular choices with good track records for achieving marketing goals. Keep in mind, not every event is right for every business. As with any marketing strategy, your event must be suited to your customers' needs.

>> You're the Expert

As an entrepreneur, it's your responsibility to get your business noticed—which means you've got to toot your own horn. You need to do whatever it takes to let others know you exist and that you are an expert source of information or advice about your industry.

Being regarded as an industry expert can do wonders for your business. How can you get your expertise known?

- Start by making sure you know everything you can about your business, product, and industry.
- Contact experts in the field and ask them how they became experts.
- Talk to as many groups as possible. (If public speaking strikes fear in your heart, you'd better get over it. This is one skill you're going to need as an entrepreneur. Try a Toastmasters group or practice among friends to boost your confidence and skills.) Volunteer to talk to key organizations, service clubs, business groups . . . whoever might be interested in what you have to say. Do it free of charge, of course, and keep it fun, interesting, and timely.
- Contact industry trade publications and volunteer to write articles, opinion pieces, or columns. (If you can't do that, write a letter to the editor.)
- Offer seminars or demonstrations related to your business (a caterer could explain how to cook Thai food, for instance).
- Host (or guest on) a local radio or TV talk show.

Do all this, and by the time you contact media people and present yourself as an expert, you'll have plenty of credentials.

Think about how your company can benefit any event. If you are a florist, for instance, you could provide flowers for a wide range of charity luncheons or galas. A health-food retailer could provide free energy bars to participants in a local 10K race. Whatever you do, be sure to promote it with press releases, a sign in your window, or a mention in the event's program.

Anniversary Celebrations

This is one special event most people can relate to. Staying in business for a number of years is something to be proud of, so why not share the achievement with others? Throw a party and invite current, past, and prospective customers to enjoy your anniversary, too.

Games and Contests

From naming a mascot to guessing the number of jelly beans in a jar, contests are a proven means of attracting attention. But they pay off big only when they're properly promoted and ethically managed. Be sure your prizes are first-rate and that you get the word out in a timely and professional manner. Let people know how and when they can participate. Think through all the ramifications of judging and selecting and awarding a prize. Check out the need for special permits or licenses well before staging any contest (it never hurts to get a legal opinion just to be on the safe side). Above all, deliver on your promises.

warning

Before sponsoring a contest or giving away a prize, make sure you contact the FTC, a lawyer specializing in games and promotions, or your secretary of state's office to check out the FTC guidelines governing different types of promotions.

Networking

The ability to network is one of the most crucial skills any startup entrepreneur can have. How else will you meet the clients and contacts necessary to grow your business?

But many people are put off by the idea of networking, thinking it requires a phony, glad-handing personality that oozes insincerity. Nothing could be further from the truth.

Think a moment. What does a good networker do? How does he or she act? What is his or her basic attitude? You'll probably be surprised at how much you instinctively know about the subject.

You may decide, for example, that a good networker should be outgoing, sincere, friendly, supportive, a good listener, or someone who follows up and stays in touch. To determine other skills an effective networker needs, simply ask yourself "How do I like to be treated? What kinds of people do I trust and consider good friends?"

Now that you have an idea of what attributes a good networker must have, take an objective look at your own interactive abilities. Do you consider yourself shy and regard networking groups as threatening? Do you tend to do all the talking in a conversation? Do you give other people referrals and ideas without a thought to your own personal gain? Can people count on your word?

tip 

After you finish talking to someone at a networking event, take a few seconds to jot down pertinent information on the back of their business card. This can be anything from their business's biggest problem to the college their daughter attends—whatever will give you a "hook" to follow up on when you call them later.

Many people go to networking events, but very few know how to network effectively. Networking is more than just getting out and meeting people. Networking is a structured plan to get to know people who will do business with you or introduce you to those who will.

The best way to succeed at networking is to make a plan, commit to it, learn networking skills and execute your plan. To make the best plan, ask yourself: What do I want to achieve? How many leads (prospects) do I want per month? Where do my customers and prospects go to network? What business organizations would benefit my business? How can I build my image and my business's image? What would I like to volunteer to do in the community?

Make a five-year networking plan listing your five best customers, five targeted prime prospects, and five targeted organizations. Next, set goals for involvement in each organization, determine how much time you will need to commit to each organization and prospect, and decide what kinds of results you expect.

Now that you have a plan, get committed. Tell yourself that you will devote enough time and effort to make it work. Half the battle of networking is getting out there and in the swim.

The other half of the battle is learning to network effectively. Typically, ineffective networkers attend several networking groups but visit with the same friends each time. Or they get involved and expect only to receive invitations and information, rather than participate and bring something to the table, too. Obviously, this behavior defeats the entire purpose of networking. If you stick with familiar faces, you never meet anyone new. And since most people stay within their circle of friends, newcomers view the organization as a group of cliques. This is one reason people fear going to new organizations by themselves—they're afraid no one will notice them.

aha!

Always be alert to networking opportunities. Don't rule out traffic school, Little League games, aerobics class, and other nonbusiness events as chances to share your story. Leisure activities provide a natural setting for networking and encourage relationship-building.

The trick with networking is to become proactive. This means taking control of the situation instead of just reacting to it. Networking requires going beyond your comfort zone and challenging yourself. Try these tips:

- *Set a goal to meet five or more new people at each event.* Whenever you attend a group, whether a party, a mixer, or an industry luncheon, make a point of heading straight for people you don't know. Greet the newcomers (they will love you for it!). If you don't make this goal a habit, you'll naturally gravitate toward the same old acquaintances.
- *Try one or two new groups per month.* You can attend almost any organization's meetings a few times before you must join. This is another way to stretch yourself and make a new set of contacts. Determine what business organizations and activities you would best fit into. It may be the chamber of commerce, the arts council, a museum society, a civic organization, a baseball league, a computer club, or the PTA. Attend every function you can that synergizes your goals and customer/prospect interaction.
- *Carry your business cards with you everywhere.* After all, you never know when you might meet a key contact, and if you don't have your cards with you, you lose out. Take your cards to church, the gym, parties, the grocery store—even on walks with the dog.

>> Image Power

Throughout this book, we've touched on various aspects of developing a corporate image. Your business cards, logo, signage, and letterhead all tie into that image. So do your marketing materials and ads. It's equally important to keep your image in mind when planning a publicity campaign.

Any events or causes you participate in should be in keeping with your business image. If your company is in a fun, creative industry, like the toy business, you can get zany and silly with special events like a balloon-popping race or pot-bellied pig races. On the other hand, if you're in a serious industry like medical transcription or accounting, it makes more sense to take part in more serious events like a 10K walk or a blood drive.

The publications and broadcast stations you target with your publicity must fit your image, too. A company that makes clothes targeted at teenage skateboarders would prefer publicity in a cutting-edge lifestyle magazine rather than in a mainstream publication aimed at middle-aged moms. Think about how the publication or broadcast will affect your image, and make sure the results will be positive.

Don't forget the most important parts of your public image: yourself and your employees. Your marketing materials and corporate sponsorships can tout your socially responsible, kind-hearted company . . . but if your employees are rude and uncaring toward customers, all your efforts to promote that image will be in vain.

Make sure your employees understand the image you are trying to convey to customers and how they contribute to creating that image. Show them by example how you want them to behave whenever they're in the public eye.

- *Don't make a beeline for your seat.* Frequently, you'll see people at networking groups sitting at the dinner table staring into space—half an hour before the meal is due to start. Why are they sitting alone? Take full advantage of the valuable networking time before you have to sit down. Once the meeting starts, you won't be able to mingle.

- *Don't sit by people you know.* Mealtime is a prime time for meeting new people. You may be in that seat for several hours, so don't limit your opportunities by sitting with your friends. This is a wonderful chance to get to know new people on either side of you. Remember, you are spending precious time and money to attend this event. Get your money's worth; you can talk to your friends some other time.

>> The Meet Market

To make the most of any networking situation, make sure to heed the following dos and don'ts:

> *Don't spend too much time with one person, or you defeat the purpose of networking.* Your objective is to take advantage of the entire room. If you spend three minutes with a prospect, that gives you a possibility of 20 contacts per hour. Spending five minutes with each person reduces that to 12 contacts and so on.

> *Do give others the chance to sell, too.* At a networking event, everyone wants to sell. You may have to play buyer to get a chance to be a seller. You must be able to wear both hats.

> *Do know the kinds of problems you can solve rather than a bunch of boring facts about your product or service.* Talk in terms of how you benefit customers rather than the product or service you offer.

> *Don't be negative.* Never complain about or bad-mouth a person or business. You never know whether the prospect you're talking to has some connection, interest, or affiliation with the people, company, or product you're slamming.

> *Don't forget your manners.* "Please" and "thank you" go a long way toward creating a good impression.

> *Do be prepared.* When people ask you what you do, be ready to describe your business in one short, interesting sentence that intrigues and enlightens.

- *Get active.* People remember and do business with leaders. Don't just warm a chair—get involved and join a committee or become a board member. If you don't have time, volunteer to help with hospitality at the door or checking people in. This gives you a reason to talk to others, gets you involved in the inner workings of the group, and provides more visibility.
- *Be friendly and approachable.* Pretend you are hosting the event. Make people feel welcome. Find out what brought them there, and see if there's any way you can help them. Introduce them to others, make business suggestions, or give them a referral. Not only will you probably make a friend, but putting others at ease eliminates self-consciousness. A side benefit: If you make the effort to help others, you'll soon find people helping you.
- *Set a goal for what you expect from each meeting.* Your goals can vary from meeting to meeting. Some examples might be: learning from the speaker's topic, discovering industry trends, looking for new prospects, or connecting with peers. If you work out of your home, you may find your purpose is simply to get out and talk to people face to face. Focusing your mind on your goal before you even walk into the event keeps you on target.
- *Be willing to give to receive.* Networking is a two-way street. Don't expect new contacts to shower you with referrals and business unless you are equally generous. Follow up on your contacts; keep in touch; always share information or leads that might benefit them. You'll be paid back tenfold for your thoughtfulness.

Now that you know how to network in person, learn the fine art of social media networking in Part 7, Chapter 36.

CHAPTER

32

Sell It!

Effective Selling Techniques

No matter what business you're in, if you're an entrepreneur, you're in sales. "But I hate to sell," you groan. You're not alone. Many people are intimidated by selling—either because they're not sure how to proceed or they think they don't have the "right" personality to sell.

Well, guess what? Anyone can sell—anyone, that is, who can learn to connect with the customer, listen to his or her needs, and offer the right solutions. In fact, as your business's founder, you're better positioned than anyone else to sell your products and services. Even if you have a team of crack salespeople, there's no one else who has the same passion for, understanding of, and enthusiasm about your product as you do. And once you finish reading this chapter, you'll have plenty of sales skills as well.

Understanding Your Unique Selling Proposition

Before you can begin to sell your product or service to anyone else, you have to sell yourself on it. This is especially important when your product or service is similar to those around you. Very few businesses are one of a kind. Just look around you: How many clothing retailers, hardware stores, air conditioning installers, and electricians are truly unique?

The key to effective selling in this situation is what advertising and marketing professionals call a "unique selling proposition" (USP). Unless you can pinpoint what makes your business unique in a world of homogeneous competitors, you cannot target your sales efforts successfully.

Pinpointing your USP requires some hard soul-searching and creativity. One way to start is to analyze how other companies use their USPs to their advantage. This requires careful analysis of other companies' ads and marketing messages. If you analyze what they say they sell, not just their product or service characteristics, you can learn a great deal about how companies distinguish themselves from competitors.

For example, Charles Revson, founder of Revlon, always used to say he sold hope, not makeup. Some airlines sell friendly service, while others sell on-time service. Neiman Marcus sells luxury, while Walmart sells bargains.

aha!

Want to boost sales? Offer a 100 percent guarantee. This minimizes customer objections and shows you believe in your product or service. Product guarantees should be unconditional, with no hidden clauses like "guaranteed for 30 days." Use guarantees for services, too: "Satisfaction guaranteed. You'll be thrilled with our service, or we'll redo it at our expense."

Each of these is an example of a company that has found a USP "peg" on which to hang its marketing strategy. A business can peg its USP on product characteristics, price structure, placement strategy (location and distribution), or promotional strategy. These are what marketers call the "four P's" of marketing. They are manipulated to give a business a market position that sets it apart from the competition.

Sometimes a company focuses on one particular "peg," which also drives the strategy in other areas. A classic example is Hanes

>> Star Power

You can find salespeople of all ranges, temperaments, and styles of selling. Some are more aggressive than others. Some are more consultative. Some are highly educated, some not so. But they're all champs because they're the ones who consistently build the business, keep the territory, and retain their customers. And they share these three traits:

1. *Attitude*. Attitude makes all the difference. Sales champs set priorities and keep things moving forward, ending each day with a sense of accomplishment. Sales champs don't let losing a deal get them down. If they can't change a situation, they change their attitude about it. In sales, you've got to make things happen for your business—and the best salespeople can't wait to get started every day.
2. *Tenacity*. When sales champs know they have something of value for a prospect or client, they don't give up. They learn more about the situation, the potential customer, and the customer's company. They study what went wrong and improve their approach for the next time so they can come back with new ideas. They are not easily defeated. However, sales champs understand when they're wasting time and when it's best to move on to the next tactic or even the next sale. If you get smarter each time you come back, you will succeed. When prospects see how much you believe in your vision and in their goals they, too, will be enthusiastic about what you have to offer.
3. *Follow-through*. A broken promise makes it extremely difficult to regain a customer's trust. Sales champs don't make promises they can't keep. They don't try to be everything to everybody. But once they give their word, they stick to it.

A sales champ doesn't exhibit all these traits all the time. But they know that in the end, the harder they work at sharpening these traits, the better these traits will work for them.

L'Eggs hosiery. Back in an era when hosiery was sold primarily in department stores, Hanes opened a new distribution channel for hosiery sales. The idea: Since hosiery was a consumer staple, why not sell it where other staples were sold—in grocery stores?

That placement strategy then drove the company's selection of product packaging (a plastic egg) so the pantyhose did not seem incongruent in the supermarket. And because the product did not have to be pressed and wrapped in tissue and boxes, it could be priced lower than other brands.

Here's how to uncover your USP and use it to power up your sales:

- *Put yourself in your customer's shoes.* Too often, entrepreneurs fall in love with their product or service and forget that it is the customer's needs, not their own, that they must satisfy. Step back from your daily operations and carefully scrutinize what your customers really want. Suppose you own a pizza parlor. Sure, customers come into your pizza place for food. But is food all they want? What could make them come back again and again and ignore your competition? The answer might be quality, convenience, reliability, friendliness, cleanliness, courtesy, or customer service.

  Remember, price is never the only reason people buy. If your competition is beating you on pricing because they are larger, you have to find another sales feature that addresses the customer's needs and then build your sales and promotional efforts around that feature.
- *Know what motivates your customers' behavior and buying decisions.* Effective marketing requires you to be an amateur psychologist. You need to know what drives and motivates customers. Go beyond the traditional customer demographics, such as age, gender, race, income, and geographic location, that most businesses collect to analyze their sales trends. For our pizza shop

warning

Want to know the best way to talk yourself out of a sale? Overselling—pushing your features and benefits too hard—is a common problem for salespeople. The problem is that you aren't hearing the customer's needs. Shut up and listen. Then start asking questions. Keep asking questions until you can explain how your product or service meets the customer's needs.

example, it is not enough to know that 75 percent of your customers are in the 18-to-25 age range. You need to look at their motives for buying pizza—taste, peer pressure, convenience, and so on.

- *Cosmetics and liquor companies are great examples of industries that know the value of psychologically oriented promotion.* People buy these products based on their desires (for a prettier face, luxury, glamour, and so on), not on their needs.
- *Uncover the real reasons customers buy your product instead of a competitor's.* As your business grows, you'll be able to ask your best source of information: your customers. For example, the pizza entrepreneur could ask them why they like his pizza over others, plus ask them to rate the importance of the features he offers, such as taste, size, ingredients, atmosphere, and service. You will be surprised how honest people are when you ask how you can improve your service.
- *Since your business is just starting out, you won't have a lot of customers to ask yet, so "shop" your competition instead.* Many retailers routinely drop into their competitors' stores to see what and how they are selling. If you are really brave, try asking a few of the customers after they leave the premises what they like and dislike about the competitors' products and services.

Once you have gone through this three-step market intelligence process, you need to take the next—and hardest—step: clearing your mind of any preconceived ideas about your product or service and being brutally honest. What features of your business jump out at you as something that sets you apart? What can you promote that will make customers want to patronize your business? How can you position your business to highlight your USP?

Do not get discouraged. Successful business ownership is not about having a

tip 

Tips for better cold-calls: Stand up when you talk on the phone. It puts power and confidence in your voice. Smile when you say hello. It makes you sound relaxed and confident. Prospects can't see these telephone tricks, but they'll hear and feel the difference in your tone—and in your persuasive powers.

unique product or service; it's about making your product stand out—even in a market filled with similar items.

Cold-Calling

The aspect of selling that strikes the greatest fear in people's hearts is usually cold calls. A good way to make cold calls more appealing is to stop thinking of them as "cold" calls. Try thinking of them as "introductory" calls instead. All you are trying to do is introduce yourself and your business to the prospect.

It's important to understand the purpose of introductory calls so you have a realistic attitude about this type of business development activity. Phone prospecting takes longer to pay off than other types of marketing efforts, so go into it knowing you're exploring a new frontier, and it's going to take some time to get results.

Just as with any marketing method, you should never make introductory calls without a plan. First, always use a targeted list of prospects when making your calls. If your product is household cleaning services, why call a random neighborhood if you have no knowledge of income levels, number of household wage earners, or number of children? If you sell nutritional products to hospitals, why call nurses or doctors if a third-party pharmacy makes all the buying decisions? Get the right list of prospects.

You can obtain information about prospects from the list broker who provides you with the list; if you are working from your house list, you should already have the information. If for some reason you don't, try an introductory call like the following: "We provide mobile pet grooming for dogs and cats. Would that be a service your customers would want to know about, Dr. Veterinarian?"

Next, determine the best time frames for calling. If you are selling financial services to upper-income CEOs or entrepreneurs, wouldn't it be nice to know when their corporate fiscal years end? Perhaps most of their investment purchases are made two to four weeks prior to that year-end close-out. That's when they know how much extra income needs to be sheltered in a pension plan.

Sometimes timing is your ace in the hole. Granted, follow-up calls throughout the year may make that one important sale possible, but knowing when to instigate the first call is a priceless piece of information.

Third, plan by preparing a "sales script" ahead of time. Write down what you are going to say, what responses the prospect is likely to have, and how you will reply to them. No, you're not going to follow this word for word, but if you're nervous about making calls, it helps to have something in front of you. Chances are, after you get beyond the opening sentences, you'll be able to "wing it" just fine.

If preparation for cold-calling is easy but actually making calls is painful for you, here are seven easy steps to get you on the phone fast.

1. *Personalize each call by preparing mentally.* Your mind-set needs to be aligned with your language, or the conversation will not ring true. You need to work on developing a warm but not sugarcoated telephone voice that has that "Don't I know you?" ring to it.
2. *Perfect your phone style alone before making any calls.* If you are self-conscious about calling, you need to feel safe to act uninhibited. Try this: Gather a voice recorder, a mirror, a sales journal of incoming and outgoing phone scripts, a pen, and a legal-sized pad. Either write or select a favorite phone dialogue; then talk to yourself in the mirror. Do you look relaxed, or are your facial expressions rigid? Our exteriors reflect our inner selves. If you look like you're in knots, your voice will sound strained as well.

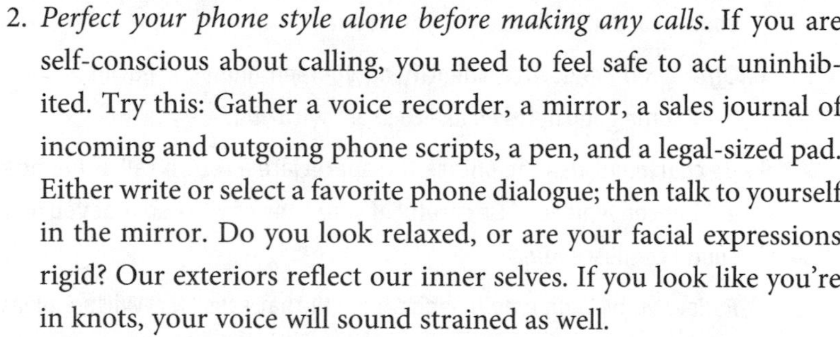

   Press the "record" button on your recorder, and pretend you're talking to a new prospect. Play back the recording, and listen to your conversation. Ask yourself how you could improve your delivery. If your voice seems unnatural and the dialogue contrived, do not despair. As you practice and participate in real phone experiences, you will improve. Mastering the art of cold-calling is no different than improving your golf swing or skiing technique.

aha! 

Got cold-call phobia? Psych yourself up with a numbers game: If every sale brings you $200 profit and it takes an average of 10 calls to make one sale, then each "no" is worth $20. Or try the "immersion" technique: Make 100 cold calls without worrying about the results. When it's over, you'll have learned a great deal about selling . . . and your fear of cold calls will be history.

3. *Create familiarity all around you.* Use family photos, framed testimonial letters, motivational quotes, or whatever gets you in a positive, enthusiastic mood. If you like, play some music that inspires you.
4. *Use your imagination.* Pretend you are a prospective customer calling a bookstore to see if they have a book in stock. If it helps, record how you sound to get the feel of your inquiring phone voice. It's always easier to imagine you're a customer in need of information than a salesperson trying to force your way into the customer's

>> Voice-Mail Victories

When making cold calls, always leave voice-mail messages if possible instead of leaving messages with an assistant. No one can transmit your enthusiasm for your products or services the way you can. Here are some tips to make the most of voice mail.

> *State your business.* Clearly tell prospects who you are and why they should be interested in talking to you. "Hello, my name is Jane Smith, and I'm with the Smith Co. We're the people who conduct one-day Sales Power seminars all over the country. Our seminar is coming to your area, and I'd like to tell you about it."

> *Offer good news.* After identifying yourself and your business, say "I have some good news I'd like to share with you."

> *Be courteous.* Use the phrase "I'd appreciate a return call at (number) at your convenience." Be careful of your tone of voice so that you don't sound condescending.

> *Follow up with an email.* Send an email that says "Mr. Wilson, please check your voice mail for an important message." Or leave a voice-mail message saying "I'm emailing you the information; if it is of interest to you, please give me a call."

> *Always leave your phone number—twice.* Repeat your number near the end of the message. Practice writing it down as you talk so you don't go too quickly.

time. The inquiry call is good practice because the tone of the conversation is "Can you help me?" or "I need some information." Try to convey that same attitude when you use the phone to contact future customers.

5. *Watch your tone of voice.* You do not want to sound sheepish and embarrassed, nor do you want to be arrogant. The ideal tone is warm, businesslike, curious, and straight to the point. A good option is a question or a cut-to-the-chase statement such as: "I've got a question. We are offering a two-for-one special during the next 30 days on all our coffee drinks, just to get people into the store. I need to know if you have ever stopped in while shopping at the mall, and, if not, why not? We have got the greatest ice-blended mochas in town."
6. *Make your goal a fast "50 in 150"—that is, 50 calls in 150 minutes.* Three minutes per call is all you need. With so many voice-mail systems intercepting calls today, this should be easy. Never give people the impression you have time to chat. Chatting is not prospecting. You're on a mission. Get to the point, then move to the next prospect.
7. *Take five after 15.* After 15 calls, take a five-minute break—stretch, eat, sip a soda, turn on some tunes, and pat yourself on the back because you're making it happen. Then grab the phone for 15 more calls.

Following Up

Your initial cold call typically will not result in a sale, or even in an appointment to make a sales presentation. One study shows it takes an average of seven contacts, impressions, or follow-ups to make a sale. (That's only one more time than the number of times experts say a child must be introduced to a new food before they try it—so don't be daunted.)

Think of each follow-up contact as a chance to get closer to the prospect and change his or her mind about meeting with you. Plan your follow-up contacts carefully, and be flexible and creative.

How do you start the follow-up call? Here are some lead-in lines:

- "I thought of a few things that might help you decide . . ."

>> Team Work

The right sales team—whether they are in-house employees or outside sales representatives—makes a big difference in how quickly your company grows. How to make sure you're hiring the right people? Try these tips:

> *Don't rely solely on resumes*. Good salespeople sell themselves so well, they might not even need resumes.

> *Try placing a classified ad that says "send resume to [address] or call [number]."* Don't even look at the resumes; just interview the people who call. These are the people who won't be afraid to pick up the phone and make cold calls for your company.

> *In the first phone contact, if the applicant doesn't ask for an appointment, stop right there*. If the person doesn't ask for an interview now, he or she won't ask for orders later.

> *Does the person sound like someone you want to spend time with?* If you don't want to, neither will your customers.

> *When they first call, tell them you're busy and will call them back.* Then don't. If they don't call back, they lack the persistence you need in a salesperson.

> *Does the applicant listen?* If they're too busy talking, they'll be too busy to listen to your customers.

> *At the end of the call, say you plan to talk to several candidates and will get back to them*. Wait until one says "You don't need to talk to more people. I'm the one you want." That's the kind of person you need.

- "Something recently happened that I thought you might want to know about . . ."
- "There has been a change in the status of . . ."
- "I just was thinking about you recently and I wanted to tell you about . . ."

Here are other sales tools you can use in follow-up situations:

- *A personal note.* A handwritten note on your company note cards is far more effective than a typed business letter.
- *An endorsement from a mutual friend.* A friend or mutual business acquaintance is far more influential than you are.
- *An article about your company.* Something in print can work wonders. You can even send articles about the prospect's company or, better yet, about a personal interest of the prospect. "Thought you might be interested in . . ."
- *An invitation to visit your facility.* Bring the prospect to your home turf.
- *A meal.* Meetings in a nonbusiness environment are powerful and help you build personal relationships that lead to sales.

tip 

Sell to the people most likely to buy. Your best prospects have a keen interest in your product or service and the money to purchase it. If you're selling office espresso machines, don't try to sell to people who have never bought one. Sell to those who already have one or those you know are interested in buying one. Show them how yours is superior.

Making Sales Presentations

Your cold calls and follow-up efforts have paid off, and you have made an appointment to visit a prospect in person and make a sales presentation. How can you make sure it's a success? Four elements determine whether a sale will be made or not:

1. *Rapport*: putting yourself on the same side of the fence as the prospect
2. *Need*: determining what factors will motivate the prospect to listen with the intent to purchase
3. *Importance*: the weight the prospect assigns to a product, feature, benefit, price, or time frame
4. *Confidence*: your ability to project credibility, to remove doubt, and to gain the prospect's belief that the risk of purchase will be less than the reward of ownership

Here is a closer look at the steps you can take to make your sales presentation a success.

Before the Presentation

1. *Know your customer's business.* Potential clients expect you to know their business, customers, and competition as well as you know your own product or service. Study your customer's industry. Know its problems and trends. Find out who the company's biggest competitors are. Some research tools include the company's annual report, brochures, catalogs, and newsletters; trade publications; chamber of commerce directories; and the internet.
2. *Write out your sales presentation.* Making a sales presentation isn't something you do on the fly. Always use a written presentation. The basic structure of any sales presentation includes five key points: Build rapport with your prospect, introduce the business topic, ask questions to better understand your prospect's needs, summarize your key selling points, and close the sale. Think about the three major selling points of your product or service. Develop leading questions to probe your customer's reactions and needs.
3. *Make sure you are talking to the right person.* This seems elementary, but many salespeople neglect to do it. Then, at the last minute, the buyer wriggles off the hook by saying he or she needs a boss's, spouse's, or partner's approval. When you are setting the appointment, always ask "Are you the one I should be talking to, or are there others who will be making the buying decision?"

> **aha!**
>
> Condition prospects to say yes by asking questions they will agree with. "It's a great day, isn't it?" or "You got an early start today, didn't you?" Little questions like these help start customers on a momentum that builds trust. Subconsciously, because they are agreeing with you, they begin to trust you.

In the Customer's Office

- *Build rapport.* Before you start discussing business, build rapport with your prospect. To accomplish this, do some homework. Find out if you have a colleague in common. Has the prospect's company been in the news lately? Is he or she interested in sports? Get a little insight into the company and the individual so you can make the rapport genuine.

>> Presentation Perfect

Want to improve your sales presentation skills? Use these strategies to hone your speaking abilities:

> *Tag-team-sell for evaluation purposes*. Have a colleague go on sales calls with you once a week to listen to your presentation. Create a review form for them to fill out immediately after your performance. (Include your strengths as well as your weaknesses.) Read it right away, and talk about what you can do to improve.

> *Record your telephone sales conversations*. Use them as a self-monitor of your ability to present a clear and confident message. Play them back. If you can't stand your voice, change your pitch. Or, ask a trusted friend or mentor to listen to your tone and give feedback—sometimes we are really our own worst critics and many people cringe at the sound of their own voice for no real reason.

> *Read a chapter from a sales book aloud, and make an audio recording of it*. Play it in your car. You'll learn about sales and about how you present your pitch. Would you buy from yourself? If not, record another version with style and emotion.

> *Videotape the first five minutes of your sales presentation*. Ask a friend or colleague to be the prospect. Watch the video together, and rate your performance. Repeat the process once a week for two months. Work to eliminate your two worst habits; at the same time, work to enhance your two best strengths.

> *Above all, be yourself*. Don't put on an act. Your personality will shine if you believe in what you are saying. Being genuine will win the prospect's confidence . . . and the sale.

- *Ask questions.* Don't jump into a canned sales spiel. The most effective way to sell is to ask the prospect questions and see where he or she leads you. (Of course, your questions are carefully structured to elicit the prospect's needs—ones that your product just happens to be able to fill.)

  Ask questions that require more than a yes or no response, and that deal with more than just costs, price, procedures, and the technical aspects of the prospect's business. Most important, ask questions that will reveal the prospect's motivation to purchase, his or her problems and needs, and the prospect's decision-making processes. Don't be afraid to ask a client why he or she feels a certain way. That's how you'll get to understand your customers.
- *Take notes.* Don't rely on your memory to remind you of what's important to your prospect. Ask upfront if it's all right for you to take notes during your sales presentation. Write down key points you can refer to later during your presentation.
- *Be sure to write down objections.* This shows your prospect you are truly listening. In this way, you can specifically answer objections by showing how the customer will benefit from your product or service. It could be, for instance, by saving money, raising productivity, increasing employee motivation, or increasing his or her company's name recognition.
- *Learn to listen.* Salespeople who do all the talking during a presentation not only bore the prospect, but also generally lose the sale. A good rule of thumb is to listen 70 percent of the time and talk 30 percent of the time. Don't interrupt. It's tempting to step in and tell the prospect something you think is vitally important. Before you speak, ask yourself if what you're about to say is really necessary.

  When you do speak, focus on asking questions. Pretend you are Barbara Walters interviewing a movie star: Ask questions; then shut up. You can improve your listening skills by taking notes and observing your prospect's body language, not jumping to conclusions.
- *Answer objections with "feel," "felt," and "found."* Don't argue when a prospect says "I'm not interested," "I just bought one," or "I don't

have time right now." Simply say "I understand how you feel. A lot of my present customers felt the same way. But when they found out how much time they saved by using our product, they were amazed." Then ask for an appointment. Prospects like to hear about other people who have been in a similar situation.

- *Probe deeper.* If a prospect tells you "We're looking for cost savings and efficiency," will you immediately tell him how your product meets his need for cost savings and efficiency? A really smart salesperson won't—he or she will ask more questions and probe deeper: "I understand why that is important. Can you give me a specific example?" Asking for more information—and listening to the answers—enables you to better position your product and show you understand the client's needs.
- *Find the "hot button."* A customer may have a long list of needs, but there is usually one "hot button" that will get the person to buy. The key to the hot button is that it is an emotional, not practical, need—a need for recognition, love, or reinforcement. Suppose you are selling health club memberships. For a prospect who is planning a trip to Hawaii in two months, the hot button is likely to be losing a few pounds and looking good in a bikini. For a prospect who just found out he has high blood pressure, the hot button could be the health benefits of exercise. For a busy young mother, the hot button may be the chance to get away from the kids for a few hours a week and reduce stress.
- *Eliminate objections.* When a prospect raises an objection, don't immediately jump in with a response. Instead, show empathy by saying "Let's explore your concerns." Ask for more details about the objection. You need to isolate the true objection so you can handle it.

aha!

Offer a first-time incentive to help clinch the sale. If prospects like your product or service, they'll be inclined to make a decision now rather than wait a few days or put off the decision indefinitely. First-time incentives might include "10 percent off with your purchase today" or "With today's purchase, you'll receive one free hour of consultation."

Here are some ways to do that:

1. *Offer a choice.* "Is it the delivery time or the financing you are concerned about?"
2. *Get to the heart of the matter.* "When you say you want to think about it, what specifically did you want to think about?"
3. *Work toward a solution.* Every sale should be a win-win deal, so you may need to compromise to close the deal: "I'll waive the delivery charge if you agree to the purchase."

tip 

Trying to scare up business? If your product isn't very appealing or exciting, one way to motivate customers is by describing the consequences of not using your product. For products that increase security or safety or improve health, fear can be an effective business-boosting tool.

As you get more experience making sales calls, you'll become familiar with different objections. Maintain a list of common objections and ways you have successfully dealt with them.

- *Close the sale.* There is no magic to closing the sale. If you have followed all the previous steps, all you should have to do is ask for the customer's order. However, some salespeople make the mistake of simply not asking for the final decision. It's as if they forget what their goal is!

  For some, "closing" sounds too negative. If you're one of them, try changing your thinking to something more positive, such as "deciding." As you talk with the customer, build in the close by having fun with it. Say something like "So how many do you want? We have it in a rainbow of colors; do you want them all?" Make sure to ask them several times in a fun, nonthreatening way; you're leading them to make the decision.

After the Sale

- *Follow up.* What you do after the sale is as crucial as what you do to get it. "Nearly 85 percent of all sales are produced by word-of-mouth referrals," says sales guru Brian Tracy. "In other words, they're the result of someone telling a friend or associate to buy a product or service because the customer was satisfied." Concentrate on developing future and referral business with each satisfied customer. Write thank-you notes, call the customer after the sale to make sure he or she is satisfied, and maintain a schedule of future communications. Be in front of that client, and always show attention and responsiveness. (For more on retaining customers, see Chapter 33.)

tip 

What's the best way to reach a prospect? Send a letter and follow it up with a phone call. Next best is a referral. Then comes a cold call, then a personal visit. Least effective is a direct-mail piece.

>> The Price Isn't Right

How do you overcome that most common objection, "Your price is too high"? Lawrence L. Steinmetz, author of *How to Sell at Prices Higher Than Your Competitors*, says you need to learn how to acknowledge that your price is higher than competitors' and use that as a selling tool.

Showing that customers get more services, better warranties, or higher-quality products for the extra cost makes the higher price seem less imposing. Telling them why the competition's services or products don't measure up differentiates you from the competition and convinces customers you're worth the extra money.

Whatever you do, don't be too willing to negotiate or slash prices. "When you ask a customer 'Is that too much?' you are encouraging him or her to beat you up," says Steinmetz.

With the right ammunition, you can turn price problems into selling points.

For instance, customers often say that Verizon's wireless contracts are more expensive than its competitors. But, many also stick with the pricier contract or sign up for the first time because the company is known to have the largest coverage area in the country.

- *Ask for feedback.* Ask customers what you need to do to maintain and increase their business. Many customers have minor complaints but will never say anything. They just won't buy from you again. If you ask their opinions, on the other hand, they'll be glad to tell you—and, in most cases, will give you a chance to solve the problem.

Speaking Effectively

The difference between good and great salespeople is the way they deliver their messages. You can have the greatest sales pitch in the world, but if you deliver it with no enthusiasm, sincerity, or belief, you will lose the sale.

Here are some suggestions to improve your speaking skills and power up your presentations:

- *Speak clearly.* If the prospect doesn't understand you, you won't get the sale.
- *Lean forward.* Leaning into the presentation gives the prospect a sense of urgency.
- *Don't fidget.* Knuckle-cracking, hair-twirling, and similar nervous habits detract from your presentation.
- *Don't "um," "ah," or "er."* These vocal tics are so irritating, they make the prospect focus on the flaws rather than the message. Best cure? Practice, practice, practice.
- *Be animated.* Act as if the best thing in the world just happened to you.
- *Vary your voice.* Don't drone on in a monotone. Punch the critical words. Go from high to low tones. Whisper some of the key information as if it's a secret. Get the prospect to lean

tip

Sell benefits, not features. The biggest mistake entrepreneurs make is focusing on what their product or service is (its features). Rather, it's what it does (its benefits) that's important. A health-food product contains nutrients that are good for the body. That's what it is. What the product does is make the customer thinner, more energetic, and able to do more with less sleep.

>> Pass It On

Referrals are among a salesperson's best weapons. Yet many salespeople fail to take advantage of this powerful marketing tool. Here are secrets to getting and making the most of referrals:

> *Ask for specific referrals*. Many salespeople ask for referrals by saying "Do you know anyone else who might be interested in my product?" The prospect replies "Not off the top of my head, but I'll let you know if I think of anyone." And that's where it ends. More effective is to ask for a specific referral that deals with a need your business addresses. For instance, ask "Steve, at your last Rotary Club meeting, did you talk to anyone who was thinking about moving or selling a home?"

> *Gather as much information about the referral as possible*. Use this to prepare for the cold call.

> *Ask your customer for permission to use his or her name when contacting the referral.*

> *Ask your customer to help you get an appointment with the referral.*

> *Contact the referral as soon as possible.*

> *Inform your customer about the outcome of the referral*. People like to know when they have been of help.

> *Prospect for referrals just as you would for sales leads.*

into your words. Make him or her feel fortunate to be receiving this message.

- *Look prospects in the eye.* Eye contact signals credibility and trustworthiness.
- *Follow the prospect's lead.* Keep your tone similar to his or her tone. If the prospect is stuffy and conservative, do not get too wild.
- *Relax.* High anxiety makes prospects nervous. Why do salespeople get nervous? Either they are unprepared or they need the money from the sale. Calm down. Never let them see you sweat.

CHAPTER

33

Now Serving

Offering Superior Customer Service

To the ordinary entrepreneur, closing and finalizing the sale is the completion of serving the customer's needs. But for the pro, this is only the beginning. Closing the sale sets the stage for a relationship that, if properly managed by you, the entrepreneur, can be mutually profitable for years to come.

aha!

To ensure you don't drop the ball on follow-up, check out one of the many contact management or sales software programs on the market. These little wonders can remind you of everything from a big client's birthday to an important sales call.

Remember the "80-20 rule" discussed in an earlier chapter? The rule states that 80 percent of your business comes from 20 percent of your customers.

Repeat customers are the backbone of every successful business. So now that you know how to land customers, it is time to learn how to keep them.

Building Customer Relationships

It's tempting to concentrate on making new sales or pursuing bigger accounts. But attention to your existing customers, no matter how small they are, is essential to keeping your business thriving. The secret to repeat business is following up in a way that has a positive effect on the customer.

Effective follow-up begins immediately after the sale, when you call the customer to say "thank you" and find out if he or she is pleased with your product or service. Beyond this, there are several effective ways to follow up that ensure your business is always in the customer's mind.

- *Let customers know what you are doing for them.* This can be in the form of a newsletter mailed to existing customers (see Chapter 30), or it can be more informal, such as a phone call. Whichever method you use, the key is to dramatically point out to customers what excellent service you are giving them. If you never mention all the things you're doing for them, customers may not notice. You are not being cocky when you talk to customers about the work you have done to please them. Just let them know they don't have to worry because you handled the paperwork, called the attorney, or double-checked on the shipment—one less thing they have to do.
- *Write old customers personal, handwritten notes frequently.* "I was just sitting at my desk, and your name popped into my head. Are you still having a great time flying all over the country? Let me know if you need another set of luggage. I can stop by with our latest models anytime." Or, if you run into an old customer at an event, follow up with a note: "It was great seeing you at the CDC Christmas party. I will call you early in the new year to schedule a lunch."
- *Keep it personal.* Voice mail and email make it easy to communicate, but the personal touch is lost. Don't count these as a legitimate follow-up. If you're having trouble getting through, leave a voice-

mail message that you want to talk to the person directly or will stop by his or her office at a designated time.

- *Remember special occasions.* Send regular customers birthday cards, anniversary cards, holiday cards . . . you name it. Gifts are excellent follow-up tools, too. You don't have to spend a fortune; use your creativity to come up with interesting gift ideas that tie into your business, the customer's business, or his or her recent purchase.
- *Pass on information.* If you read an article, see a new book, or hear about an organization that a customer might be interested in, drop a note or make a quick call to let them know.
- *Consider follow-up calls business development calls.* When you talk to or visit old clients or customers, you'll often find they have referrals to give you, which can lead to new business.

e-fyi

Feeling alone? Wish you had someplace to advise you on better customer service? Try the International Customer Service Association's website (icsatoday.org). You're required to join the organization to reap the benefits, but there are plenty of them—from networking opportunities to customer service training programs.

With all that your existing customers can do for you, there's simply no reason not to stay in regular contact with them. Use your imagination, and you'll think of plenty of other ideas that can help you develop a lasting relationship.

Customer Service

There are plenty of things you, the entrepreneur, can do to ensure good customer service. And when you're a one-person business, it's easy to stay on top of what your customers want. But as you add employees, whether it's one person or 100, you are adding more links to the customer service chain—and creating more potential for poor service along the way.

That's why creating a customer service policy and adhering to it is so important. Here are some steps you can take to ensure that your clients receive excellent service every step of the way.

- *Put your customer service policy in writing.* These principles should come from you, but every employee should know what the rules are and be ready to live up to them.
- *Establish support systems that give the employees clear instructions for gaining and maintaining service superiority.* These systems will help you outservice any competitor by giving more to customers and anticipating problems before they arise.
- *Develop a measurement of superb customer service.* Then reward employees who practice it consistently.

>> Go to the Source

Excellent customer service is more than what you say or do for the customer; it also means giving customers a chance to make their feelings known. Here are some suggestions for finding out what your customers want, need, and care about:

> *Attend trade shows and industry events that are important to your customers.* You'll find out what the competition is doing and what kinds of products and services customers are looking for.

> *Nurture a human bond, as well as a business one, with customers and prospects.* Take them out to lunch, dinner, the ballgame, or the opera. In the relaxed atmosphere of socializing, you'll learn the secrets that will allow you to go above and beyond your competition.

> *Keep alert for trends; then respond to them.* Read industry trade publications; be active in trade organizations; pay attention to what your customers are doing.

> *Ask for feedback.* Survey your customers regularly to find out how you're doing. Send postage-paid questionnaire cards or letters; call them by phone; set up focus groups. Ask for suggestions; then fix the trouble areas revealed.

Whatever you do, don't rest on your laurels. Regularly evaluate your product or service to be sure it is still priced, packaged, and delivered right.

- *Be certain that your passion for customer service runs throughout your company.* Your employees should see how good service relates to your profits and to their future with the company.
- *Be genuinely committed to providing more customer service excellence than anyone else in your industry.* This commitment must be so powerful that every one of your customers can sense it.
- *Share information with people on the front lines.* Meet regularly to talk about improving service. Solicit ideas from employees—they deal with the customers most often.
- *Act on the knowledge that customers value attention, competence, promptness, and dependability.* They love being treated as individuals and being referred to by name. (Don't you?)

Interacting with Customers

Principles of customer service are nice, but you need to put those principles into action with everything you do and say. There are certain "magic words" that customers want to hear from you and your staff. Make sure all your employees understand the importance of these key words:

- *"How can I help?"* Customers want the opportunity to explain in detail what they want and need. Too often, business owners feel the desire or the obligation to guess what customers need rather than carefully listening first. By asking how you can help, you begin the dialogue on a positive note. And by using an open-ended question, you invite discussion.
- *"I can solve that problem."* Most customers, especially B2B customers, are looking to buy solutions. They appreciate direct answers in a language they can understand.
- *"I don't know, but I'll find out."* When confronted with a truly difficult question that requires research on your part, admit it. Few things ruin your credibility faster than trying to answer a question when you are unsure of all the facts. An honest reply enhances your integrity.

aha!

Make it easy for customers to contact you—by phone, fax, or email—to share ideas, frustrations, and suggestions.

>> Complaint Department

Studies show that the vast majority of dissatisfied customers will never tell you they're dissatisfied. They simply leave quietly, then tell everyone they know not to do business with you. So when a customer does complain, don't think of it as a nuisance—think of it as a golden opportunity to change that customer's mind and retain his or her business.

Even the best product or service meets with complaints or problems now and then. Here's how to handle them for positive results:

> Let customers vent their feelings. Encourage them to get their frustrations out in the open.

> Never argue with a customer.

> Never tell a customer "You do not have a problem." Those are fighting words.

> Share your point of view as politely as you can.

> Take responsibility for the problem. Don't make excuses. If an employee was sick or a third-party supplier let you down, that's not the customer's concern.

> Immediately take action to remedy the situation. Promising a solution then delaying it only makes matters worse.

> Empower your front-line employees to be flexible in resolving complaints. Give employees some leeway in deciding when to bend the rules. If you don't feel comfortable doing this, make sure they have you or another manager handle the situation.

> Imagine you're the one with the complaint. How would you want the situation to be handled?

- *"I will take responsibility."* Tell your customer you realize it's your responsibility to ensure a satisfactory outcome to the transaction. Assure the customer you know what she expects and will deliver the product or service at the agreed-upon price. There will be no unexpected expenses or changes required to solve the problem.

- *"I will keep you updated."* Even if your business is a cash-and-carry operation, it probably requires coordinating and scheduling numerous events. Assure your customers they will be advised of the status of these events. The longer your lead time, the more important this is. The vendors that customers trust the most are those that keep them apprised of the situation, whether the news is good or bad. And make sure you follow up with updates.
- *"I will deliver on time."* A due date that has been agreed upon is a promise that must be kept. "Close" does not count.
- *"Monday means Monday."* The first week in July means the first week in July, even though it contains a national holiday. Your clients are waiting to hear you say "I deliver on time." The supplier who consistently does so is a rarity and well-remembered.
- *"It will be just what you ordered."* It will not be "similar to," and it will not be "better than" what was ordered. It will be exactly what was ordered. Even if you believe a substitute would be in the client's best interests, that's a topic for discussion, not something you decide on your own.
- *"The job will be complete."* Assure the customer there will be no waiting for a final piece or a last document. Never say you will be finished "except for . . ."
- *"I appreciate your business."* This means more than a simple "Thanks for the order." Genuine appreciation involves follow-up calls, offering to answer questions, making sure everything is performing satisfactorily, and ascertaining that the original problem has been solved.

Neglecting any of these steps conveys the impression that you were interested in the person only until the sale was made. This leaves the buyer feeling deceived and used, and creates ill will and negative advertising for

tip 

When customers are happy with your service, ask them for a testimonial letter. Get permission to use quotes from the letters in your print ads and brochures. Also ask if you can give past customers' phone numbers to certain qualified prospects so they can get a solid recommendation about your business firsthand.

your company. Sincerely proving you care about your customers leads to recommendations . . . and repeat sales.

Going Above and Beyond

These days, simply providing adequate customer service is not enough. You need to go above and beyond the call of duty to provide customer service that truly stands out. How to do this?

Begin by thinking about your own experiences as a customer—what you have liked and disliked in certain situations. Recall the times you were delighted by extra efforts taken to accommodate your needs or outraged by rudeness or negligence. This will give you greater insight into what makes for extraordinary customer service.

To put yourself in the customer's shoes, try visiting a wide range of businesses your customers are likely to frequent. This could include your direct competitors, as well as companies that sell related products and services. Observe how customers are treated in addition to the kinds of services that seem to be important to them. Then adapt your business accordingly.

Going above and beyond is especially important when a customer has complained or if there is a problem with a purchase. Suppose an order is delayed. What can you do?

- Call the customer personally with updates on the status of the order and expected arrival time.
- Hand-deliver the merchandise when it arrives.
- Take 20 or 30 percent off the cost.
- Send a note apologizing for the delay . . . tucked inside a gift basket full of goodies.

aha!

Create external incentives to keep customers coming back. Offer customers free merchandise or services after they buy a certain amount. This gets them in the habit of buying again and again.

Going above and beyond doesn't always mean offering deep discounts or giving away products. With a little ingenuity and effort, you can show customers they are important at any time. Suppose you've just received the newest samples and colors for your home furnishings line. Why not invite your best customers to a private showing, complete with music, appetizers, and a coupon good for one free hour of consultation?

Emergency orders and last-minute changes should be accommodated when possible, especially for important occasions such as a wedding or a big trade show. Customers remember these events . . . and they will remember your flexibility and prompt response to their needs, too.

Being accessible also wins loyalty. One entrepreneur who runs a computer chip company has installed a customer service line on every employee's telephone, from the mail room clerk on up. This means every caller gets through to a real person who can help him or her, instead of getting lost in a voice-mail maze.

Customer loyalty is hard to win and easy to lose. But by going above and beyond with your customer service, you'll soon see your sales going above and beyond those of your competitors.

PART

7

ENGAGE

CHAPTER

34

Net Sales

Online Advertising and Marketing

Your website is up and you have promoted it on everything from business cards to T-shirts. Your shopping cart program is primed for action. There's only one problem—nobody shows up.

The net is littered with tens of thousands of dead sites, abandoned because no one visited. You can always tell a dead site—it was last updated on its launch date. So how can you make yours successful?

Throw some money at it—judiciously. "It's a good idea to stick with low-cost, grass-roots techniques," says Jim Daniels, president of JDD Publishing in Smithfield, Rhode Island. Daniels has written several books about internet marketing and publishes the Bizweb eGazette newsletter, which has more than 110,000 subscribers worldwide and is accessible at bizweb2000.com.

Also, if you can afford one, hire a PR firm. In general, raising your firm's visibility through media exposure lets you talk about your website to a broad range of potential customers.

A Marketing Tool

Think of your website as a marketing tool like the others you use to promote your business. Because its return is hard to gauge, your job is to learn how to get the most from the web. "Why would someone want to visit my site?" That's your key question. If your site talks only about your company and how great you are, chances are, no one will come back. Attracting visitors requires magnets: things that excite people and make them return for more.

Savvy marketers master permission marketing, which provides incentives for customers to learn more about your product or service. Let's say you run the Clicks and Bricks Bed and Breakfast in Vermont. Spring and fall are your off seasons. You'd like to reach out to former visitors and those who have sent emails inquiring about the Clicks and Bricks B&B.

Using the principles of permission marketing, you can:

- Use your database of customer and prospect emails to build an audience for a promotional campaign.
- Recognize that those consumers have indicated a willingness to talk to you. So find something to say to them. You could offer them a "three nights for the price of two" promotion or run a contest for a free two-night midweek stay. It's offers like these that keep customers and prospects engaged.

tip

Before you publicize your site, make sure you have an opt-in box on the homepage and throughout your site by using email capture software, also called an autoresponder system. This is a great way to develop customers and build your email list so you can send them valuable offers, tips, and resources. For more details on setting up email captures, visit AWeber at aweber.com and check out the opt-in tutorial. Click on "Support," then "Videos."

- Encourage a learning relationship with your customers. Send emails or print brochures about upcoming local events such as the annual Fuzzy Worm Festival, or offer two-for-one coupons for an upcoming art show. Remind them of Vermont's allure in the spring and fall.
- Deepen your communication as site visitors become customers and first-timers become return visitors. Send birthday or anniversary cards. Reward them with a glossy national B&B directory. Show them that you value their patronage.

Attracting Visitors to Your Site

The number of websites is well over the million mark with the potential of crossing into the billions. According to the *2014 Domain Name Industry Brief*, published by VeriSign, the internet boasted more than 271 million domain names, more than 35 billion pages, and well over 183 million websites. With millions of websites out there, getting visitors to your individual site is often the biggest challenge. Your strategies for doing so may include search engines, paid search services, and affiliates. Let's consider them one at a time.

tip

Using search engines is a matter of personal preference. Try some engines listed in this chapter to discover which return the most "hits," or matches, with your keywords.

Search Engines

Search engines have become a ubiquitous part of American culture. Every day millions of Americans go online to search the internet or "Google" something or someone. According to a 2014 report from the Pew Internet & American Life project—which produces reports that explore the impact of the internet—87 percent of American adults use the internet, and 84 percent look online for information about a service or product they're thinking of buying.

Perhaps the most important—and inexpensive—strategy in getting people to your website is to rank high for your preferred keywords on the main search engines in "organic" or "natural" searches (as opposed to paid ads, also known as "sponsored links," which are often found on the right side of search pages or clearly marked as a "sponsored link"). In general, achieving a high rank is based on three criteria: competition, relevancy, and content.

> **tip** 
>
> Adding widgets to your website and staying active on social sites, such as Facebook, LinkedIn, and Twitter, helps increase organic SEO rankings. What's a widget? It's a live stream of updates from your social sites that feed directly into your website. For more information on embedding widgets, type in "widgets" in the search box on each social site.

Think of "competition" like popularity. The more popular (talked about, linked to, and clicked on) your offer or website is, the more competitive you are. "Relevancy" is based on how well your offer or site matches the keywords. Your site should include the keyword, or be as close as possible to the keyword that's being searched. Finally, your "content" should address the question being asked. Your goal is to answer the query as directly as possible. You want the end user to say "Yes, this is the answer I'm looking for." The sooner you master these three criteria, the higher rank you'll be able to achieve in search results. Mastering the art of search is not impossible; it just takes practice and time. Take the time to think about what your potential customers are really asking and how your offer or website answers their questions. Be persistent and consistent, work through the learning curve, and you'll find yourself with a high rank in the search engines.

Search engine marketing (SEM) is also a rapidly growing and profitable segment of the internet. According to a study from Search Engine Marketing Professionals Organization, conducted in partnership with Radar Research, SEM expenditures reached $26 billion in 2013, which is close to 10 percent of total U.S. advertising spending for 2013. Increasingly, ad budgets are being shifted away from offline marketing, such as print, direct-mail, and TV advertising, and directed toward online marketing.

There are many search engines out there, and they all differ in structure, search strategy, and efficiency. According to a recent report from online internet research firm Hitwise, most searches take place on the following sites:

- Google-owned sites, such as Google.com or Google Image Search
- Yahoo!'s Yahoo.com
- MSN-operated sites, such as Bing.com, which is Bing and Yahoo!'s merged search engine
- IAC-owned sites, such as Ask.com

For the best exposure, be sure your website is listed on most of these sites. To use search engines effectively to draw visitors to your site, the keywords you choose in your domain name, title tag, and the text of your main page can spell the difference in your search engine rankings. Keyword-rich domain names, title tags, and main pages boost traffic. And when using keywords, remember it's important to have them appear naturally. You can check Google AdWords and Google Insights to get a good idea of what sort of words and phrases people search for in your category. You might even consider looking on Twitter at its trending topics for the prior few months for hints as to what people are talking about around the products or services you offer.

The easiest way to get ranked on search engines is to submit your domain name to various search engines. Maximizing the number of times your URL comes up in a search result is an ongoing process. It takes patience to monitor the search engines by visiting them frequently and studying your log files to see which search engines send you the most traffic. If you need to make changes in your website, particularly your opening page, to move up in the search engine rankings, do so. Spend your time submitting to the most-popular and frequented search engines.

Also check out SelfPromotion.com, a free resource for do-it-yourself web promotion. Here you can find information and tips about search engine submission, along with automatic submission tools that help you submit your URL to all the major search engines. Once listed, you can use free online tools, including:

tip

Think of all the keywords and phrases for your product or service, and put them in your URL. For example, try discountchairstore, discount-sofas-and-chairs, or buydiscountfurniture. The search engines are likely to pick up multiple keywords, thereby boosting your rankings.

- *SiteRankChecker.com*: gives you an overview of where you rank on top search engines (and don't be alarmed by the code that appears at the top of the page—your results are underneath)
- *SiteReportCard.com*: compares your site with your competition in SEO-friendliness
- *LinkPopularity.com*: lists all sites that have linked back to your domain name

If you get good results with Yahoo! Search using one set of keywords and do well with Google using another set of keywords, that's fine. But keep in mind that Google's share of search is well over 60 percent, so it's important to spend time refining your keywords for Google success—that's the engine where you get the most bang for your buck if you succeed in search.

Also keep in mind that the narrower the category, the better your chance of scoring unique visitors; for example, "percussion instruments" and "ice skating dresses" are more specific than "drums" and "sports attire" and have a better chance of scoring clicks.

Paid Search Services

Many companies are also using paid search services as a supplement to SEM. These services basically allow you to pay to have your website be part of the results of a user's query on a search engine site. There are three types of paid search services: paid submission, pay-for-inclusion, and pay-for-placement.

In paid submission, you can submit your website for review by a search service for a preset fee with the expectation that the site will be accepted and included in that company's search engine—provided it meets the stated guidelines for submission. Yahoo! is the major search engine that accepts this type of submission. While paid submissions guarantee a timely review of the submitted site and notice of acceptance or rejection, you're not guaranteed inclusion or a particular placement order in the listings. Yahoo! charges $299 annually (non-refundable) for this service, which it calls Yahoo! Directory Submit.

Paid inclusion programs allow you to submit your website for guaranteed inclusion in a search engine's database of listings for a

> *"Many a small thing has been made large by the right kind of advertising."*
>
> —Mark Twain

set period of time. While paid inclusion guarantees indexing of submitted pages or sites in a search database, you're not guaranteed that the pages will rank well for particular queries.

In pay-for-placement, you can guarantee a ranking in a search listing for the terms of your choice. Also known as paid placement, paid listings, or sponsored listings, this program guarantees placement in search results. The leaders in pay-for-placement are Google, Yahoo!, and Bing. These programs allow you to bid on the terms you wish to appear for; you then agree to pay a certain amount each time someone clicks on your listing. Costs for pay-for-placement start at around a nickel a click and go up considerably based on how high you want your site to appear—and competition for keywords has the biggest bearing on that. For example, a bid on "web hosting" will result in payment of a few bucks a click if you want to get on the first page of results. But if you're promoting, say, lighthouse tours, you may be able to get on top paying just a dime a click.

In the Google AdWords program, Google sells paid listings that appear above and to the side of its regular results, as well as on its partner sites. Since it may take time for a new site to appear within Google, these advertising opportunities offer a fast way to get listed with the service.

In the Google AdWords program, the cost of your campaigns really depends on how much you're willing to pay and how well you know your audience. It all boils down to knowing your own goals and letting Google know what they are. Google will grant the highest position to the advertiser with the highest bid for keywords and the highest clickthrough rate. Minimum costs per click start at just a penny.

> **tip**
>
> 
>
> What's the best day to send email marketing messages? According to Infusionsoft, a leading email marketing provider, in general the prime days are Tuesdays and Thursdays between 10 A.M. and 2 P.M.

The Bing Search, known as Bing Ads, doesn't charge you to create an account; you only pay when someone clicks on your ad. The highest position is given to the advertiser with the highest bid for keywords and the highest clickthrough rate.

Yahoo! allows you to bid on the keywords for which you wish to appear and then pay a certain amount each time someone clicks on your listings. For example, if you wanted to appear in the top listings for "clocks," you might agree to pay a maximum of 25 cents per click. If no one agrees to pay more than this, then you would be in the No. 1 spot. If someone later decides to pay 26 cents, then you fall into the No. 2 position. You could then bid 27 cents and move back on top if you wanted to. In other words, the highest bid gets the highest position on Yahoo!'s results.

Yahoo! displays its listings on its own search results, in addition to other partner sites.

Yahoo!'s minimum bid requirement is 10 cents. By carefully selecting targeted terms, you can stretch that money for one or two months and get quality traffic.

Another paid search program to check out is from Miva Merchant Inc. (mivamerchant.com), which is a major search player and also offers software and other solutions for small businesses just getting started on the web.

tip

If you're willing to experiment with mobile advertising, you can use either paid search engines or display mobile advertising companies, such as AdMob, Smaato, Ad Infuse, InMobi, or Mojiva. Google AdWords has allowed marketers to select "mobile" as one of its ad distribution channels for some time. If you're not sure if your mobile setting is on or off, log into your AdWords account and check your campaign settings.

Local Search

Want local customers to find you? Then try local search engine advertising, which lets you target ads to a specific state, city, or even neighborhood. A growing number of small businesses are using local search. Yelp found in 2012 that 85 percent of consumers use search engines first to find information online. Ipsos MediaCT and Google released a study which stated 88 percent of smartphone users and 84 percent of tablet owners turn to the web to search for local businesses, and another study showed such searchers are willing to drive up to 17 miles to get to a business they found in their search.

Like other search engine advertising, the local variety lets you track your account closely to find out which keywords are most successful at drawing customers and how much you're spending each day.

As you can imagine, the major search engine companies offer local search options, too. You'll find them offered on the main search marketing pages for each site.

Affiliates

Firms that sell products and services on their websites for commissions offer another way to draw site visitors. The web is democratic; a SOHO (small office home office) can be an affiliate of a Fortune 500 firm, as can other corporate giants, midsized businesses, and even charities.

Affiliates place merchant promotions on their websites to sell goods or services. They control the type of promotion, location on the site, and the length of time it runs. In return, the affiliate earns commission on clickthroughs, leads, or purchases made through the site. For example, your town's Big Bank is the affiliate looking for local merchants to advertise on its site. It has a restaurant, an office supply store, a realtor, a law firm, and an accounting firm with ads or promotions on its site. Depending on what they negotiated with Big Bank, they'll receive commissions on sales that initiated from their website. For every clickthrough that results in a sale, you'll earn a commission, anywhere from 1 to 10 percent for multichannel retailers, or 30 to 50 percent in the software sector.

tip

Want to know more about search engines? Searchenginewatch.com can answer your questions. It compares the major search engines and tells you how to get listed. It also provides tips for searchers so you can learn to think like your customers and make it easier for them to find you. Plus, you can get a free newsletter.

You may want to consider joining an affiliate program network, which provides all the tools and services affiliates and merchants need to create, manage, and optimize successful affiliate marketing programs. Sites that offer quality programs include Rakuten Affiliate

Network (marketing.rakuten.com)—which offers deals with Best Buy, 1-800-Flowers.com Inc., Lego, and Foot Locker, among others—and CJ Affiliate by Conversant (cj.com). Another route is using your favorite search engines to find companies that have potential as affiliates. For example, if you own a gym and sell workout products, you might want to affiliate partner with nutritionists, personal trainers, sports drinks, and vitamin and health-food partners. If you decide to run your own affiliate programs, Infusionsoft (infusionsoft.com) offers a complete email marketing system and everything you'll need to run a successful affiliate program.

>> Reach Out and Email Someone

The Direct Marketing Association offers some practical advice on how to be more successful at reaching current and potential customers through email:

- Encourage customers and prospects to add your email address to their personal "approved list/address book." Being an "approved" sender yields higher response rates and generates fewer complaints and blocking issues.
- Carefully consider the content and presentation of your marketing messages because recipients are increasingly labeling any email communication that's not relevant or looks suspicious as spam.
- Click the "spam check" button in your email program to see if your email is at risk for being marked as spam. A growing number of ISPs use spam-filtering software. This technology uses algorithms to determine whether incoming messages qualify as junk email and filters them out before they get to a client's inbox. In addition, you should register for all mailbox provider feedback loops. In general, aim to keep complaint rates (total complaints divided by total delivered email) below 0.1 percent to avoid temporary or long-term blocks.
- Adopt good list-hygiene and list-monitoring practices that help facilitate message delivery. Monitoring campaign delivery and open and clickthrough rates is essential because low open rates or high bounce-back rates may indicate a delivery problem.

Keeping Visitors at Your Site

A good website design and strategy for attracting visitors takes you three-quarters of the way to success. The final step is getting people to try your offerings and to come back for more. The best way to do that is to treat each customer as unique. Fortunately, the web lends itself to the kind of personalization that's relatively easy and inexpensive for even the smallest business.

With a little effort, you can address each site visitor's needs effectively. Combined with offline strategic work—such as hitting customers every other week with a free newsletter or offering them a two-for-one special if they haven't visited your site in two months, readily available ecommerce tools enable you to personalize as nothing else can.

The basis for customization is the cookie—a morsel of information that lets sites know where customers go. A cookie is a piece of data that's sent to the browser along with an HTML page when someone visits a site. The browser saves the cookie to the visitor's hard drive. When that customer revisits the site, the cookie goes back to the web server along with his new request, enabling your site to recognize the return visitor.

Here are some ideas for marketing programs you can create from an analysis of stored cookies and email:

- Send a postcard to customers who haven't bought anything online in three months, offering a $10 or $20 reward for shopping online.
- Send an email with a new promotion a few weeks or months after a customer makes a purchase.
- Offer a chance to win something and make it easy for visitors who drop in at least once a week to enter the contest.

save

Jim Daniels of JDD Publishing advises teaming up with other sites in your niche by forming joint ventures. Search for sites that serve a similar customer base, and get their mailing addresses. Then mail them a letter offering to send them your best product or service at no charge so they can try it out. If they like it, you'll pay them a commission if they'll recommend it to their site visitors and newsletter subscribers. If you found them easily on the web, chances are, they have lots of website traffic.

If personalization seems too complicated, you can still design your website to speak to different groups of people. Let's say you're a realtor wanting your site to meet several needs. Create a screen with button bars like these:

- If you're a buyer, click here.
- If you're thinking of listing your house for sale, click here.
- If you're a Realtor from outside the area, click here.
- If you want to join our team, click here.

This form of customization addresses the needs of different groups. You have made an effort to provide information tailored to each market segment. It doesn't cost a million dollars, yet increases your credibility and efficiency.

Getting visitors to stick around long enough to explore your site is just as important as tempting them to visit in the first place. Here are some tips on capturing your visitors' attention.

- *Make connections.* Hyperlink your email address; this means most visitors can simply click to open a blank message and send you a note.
- *Have fun.* People who surf the internet are looking for fun. You don't have to be wild and wacky (unless you want to). Just make sure you offer original content presented in an entertaining way.
- *Add value.* Offering something useful that customers can do adds tremendous value to your site. For example, customers can track their own packages at the FedEx site or concoct a recipe for a new drink at the Stolichnaya vodka site. While it doesn't have to be quite so elaborate, offering users the ability to download forms, play games, or create something useful or fun will keep them coming back.
- *Keep it simple.* Don't build a site that's more than three or four levels deep. Internet users love to surf, but they get bored when they have to sift through loads of information to find what they're looking for.
- *Provide a map.* Use icons and button bars to create clear navigational paths. A well-designed site should have a button at the

bottom of each subpage that transports the visitor back to the site's homepage.

- *Stage a contest.* Nothing is more compelling than giving something away. Have the contestants fill out a registration form so you can find out who's coming to your site.
- *Make payment a snap.* If you're setting up an online storefront, give customers an easy way to pay you. Consider including an online order form, toll-free ordering number, or fax line.

tip

If you want to get noticed online, offer to provide content to others. Electronic newsletters and magazines always need new information. One of the best ways to create an online presence is to email sites and volunteer content on a regular basis.

The Ad-Free Zone

When you design your website's marketing plan, remember that the internet is a community with its own set of rules that you as an entrepreneur must understand to be successful. The primary rule is: Don't send spam.

Not only is it annoying to recipients, it is also illegal. In 2004, Controlling the Assault of Non-Solicited Pornography and Marketing Act (or Can-Spam Act of 2003) was signed into law. The law requires commercial email messages to be labeled and to include opt-out instructions as well as the sender's physical address. It also prohibits the use of deceptive subject lines and false headers. A good way to get folks to opt in to your email list—which of course they'll have the option of opting out of—is to offer a free monthly email newsletter.

Content is wide open, but effective newsletters usually mix news about trends in your field with tips and updates on sales or special pricing. Whatever you do, keep it short. Six hundred words is probably the maximum length. Another key: Include hyperlinks so that interested readers can, with a single mouse click, go directly to your site and find out more about a topic of interest.

Another tip to keep in mind: Don't post commercial messages to newsgroups that have rules against these types of messages. For example, on the social networking site LinkedIn, don't post massive messages that sound like sales pitches to any of the groups. However, if you're offering valuable content and resources or if you're looking to start a discussion on a topic, then by all means post away.

CHAPTER

35

Social Studies

Social Media Marketing

Social media has become a necessary tool to connect and engage with your audience—and in today's marketing landscape, that's how brands are built.

Social media marketing is simply using social sites, such as Facebook, LinkedIn, Pinterest, Instagram, Twitter, and YouTube, to market your business—and, when possible, to create a community of people excited about your brand. This new marketing medium is more demanding on businesses because to promote and build a brand, you must engage in conversations with your target market.

The *2014 Social Media Marketing Industry Report*, by social media researcher Michael Stelzner at socialmediaexaminer.com, confirms that 92 percent of businesses using social media marketing indicated that their efforts have generated significant exposure for their brand. Improving traffic and growing lists was the second major benefit listed—with 80 percent having success, followed by developing loyal fans, at 72 percent.

The number-one benefit of social media marketing was gaining those all-important eyeballs and an increase in sales (reported by more than 60 percent of respondents); an unexpected benefit was a rise in search engine rankings reported by more than half the participants in the study.

aha! 

Google Alerts are a great way to keep track of buzz and conversations happening about you and your company. Go to google.com/alerts and enter your company name and any keywords that might come up in a conversation about your brand. Whenever something is posted on the internet with those keywords, Google will send you an email with the link. You can set this up to keep an eye on your competitors, too.

Engaging Online Tools

There are hundreds of engagement tools on the internet that can help you not only start and conduct conversations with your brand's audience but also monitor and deepen them. One of the most powerful is blogging. Blogging is derived from the word "web log," and it's a type of website that's usually maintained by an individual who regularly enters commentary, descriptions of events, or other material, such as graphics or video.

Websites can become static and dated, in addition to not being interactive, which means you're not engaging or talking with your customers or clients. Putting a blog on your website allows you to engage in a two-way conversation with your market. To start the conversation, you can post valuable tips, content, discussions, resources, thoughts, and reviews on your blog.

Blogging, which dates to the early '90s, gained popularity in the beginning of 2000 and today is one of the most powerful interactive tools on the net. Whether you already have a blog or you need to set one up, there's one thing you need to do . . . become active on it. Some 69 percent of respondents in the Social Media Marketing Industry report who blogged for at least one year cited a loyal fan base as the biggest benefit to doing so. The key to building readers and followers for your blog is to be active and post valuable and compelling information on a regular basis. Serious bloggers post and market their blogs on social sites daily. Although this is a powerful and effective way to build readers and followers, daily posting isn't necessary to grow your blog. All you need to do is allocate posting time that fits within your marketing schedule—and stick to it. Consistency is key when you launch and operate a blog. Your readers will begin to expect and look forward to your posts. Be sure to optimize your blog for mobile, as more and more people view the internet from smartphones and tablets.

The first thing you need to do is find a blog platform. A blog platform is a site that allows you to set up, design, and even host your blog. Most are free, although some offer upgrade capabilities and options.

A few top blog platforms include:

- *WordPress*: wordpress.com
- *Tumblr*: tumblr.com
- *Blogger*: blogger.com/start, a Google platform
- *TypePad*: typepad.com

Video Marketing

Just as marketing has evolved, so has the internet. What started as static, text-heavy sites are now evolving into interactive and informative video pages. "Videos are by far the best lead-generation tool on the net," according to founder and CEO Mike Koenigs of TrafficGeyser.com, a website traffic generator. "Videos are often misunderstood: Most people think that they need to invest in a big production of storyboards and high-end video equipment to make quality viral videos; however, the opposite is true. The more fun, humorous, and engaging they are, the more likely they will become viral."

Some 86 percent of internet traffic is

e-fyi

More than half the respondents in the Social Media Marketing Industry report said Facebook (54 percent) was their most important platform, followed by LinkedIn, at 17 percent, and Twitter, at 12 percent. And those who spend six hours a week or more concentrating on their social media efforts cited the biggest return for their investment in terms of sales and exposure.

> **e-fyi**
> Check out TubeMogul.com. You can use this company to upload and post videos to the top 30 to 40 video sites, depending on what the content of your video is.

expected to be video by 2016, according to Cisco's Visual Networking Index, and according to YouTube, the average video viewed on the site was 4 minutes and 20 seconds in 2014, but typically ranges between 3 minutes and 50 seconds and 5 minutes, which is surprising when the general marketing rule has been no more than two-minute clips, or you'll lose them. Furthermore, YouTube reports that more than six billion hours of videos are watched in the United States every month. Some 40 percent of that traffic comes from mobile device users. Another reason why videos are so powerful in marketing is the fact that they connect with the consumer's three vital learning gateways—the auditory, visual, and kinesthetic.

One of the quickest, most affordable ways to create a video is to use a Flipcam and record short videos for your target market. They don't have to be fancy; they just have to be fun and informative. A quick and easy way to launch a video campaign and make it viral is to do short video clips two to three minutes in length that are frequently asked and answered questions from your customers. The complete video marketing formula can be found on TrafficGeyser's blog at trafficgeyser.com/blog.

Overview of Social Bookmarking Sites

Traffic from social bookmarking sites can give your site a huge boost in traffic, delivering thousands of visitors in just a few hours. While the initial effects can be temporary, if you give people a reason to come back to your website, you'll certainly notice a positive cumulative effect. We'll cover how to do this in the "Content Marketing Online" section starting on page 575.

What is social bookmarking, how does it work, how can you get people to bookmark you, and what can you expect? A social bookmarking service is a website that allows members to add page links as bookmarks, categorize those links, and provide added commentary. These bookmarks are then made available to the other community members, who are also generally allowed to make their own comments on the bookmarked page.

The service that kicked off the social bookmarking craze in 2003 was Del.icio.us. Since that time, hundreds of other social bookmarking services have been launched, with the most popular being Digg, Reddit, and StumbleUpon. All these services have the ability to deliver hundreds or thousands of targeted visitors to your site within a very short time; sometimes within hours of your page having been bookmarked if the wider community finds the entry of interest.

e-fyi

Check out services like onlywire.com or socialmaximizer.com for automated (or manually curated) social bookmarking options.

Make it easy for site visitors to bookmark you by using a service called AddThis, which offers a free one-step click-and-add button for bookmarking sites. Site visitors simply click on the "Bookmark" icon on your site, and choose which of their social networks to post your content to, from Twitter and Facebook to LinkedIn and StumbleUpon.

AddThis keeps the list of bookmarking options current; plus, the service provides you with stats, such as tracking how your users are sharing your content. When you install AddThis, you'll begin to receive analytics once your visitors start sharing your content. After you begin to receive analytics information, you can use filters to refine your data by domain, time period, and other options. AddThis offers several different analytics reports to help you understand how visitors are sharing your content. These reports include information about popular content, services usage (such as Facebook, Twitter, etc.), and geographic summaries. Your analytics data can even be integrated into your Google Analytics reports.

Another must-have on your site is ShareThis, a little green button found at ShareThis.com. This is another icon that makes it easy to share ideas, articles, and content online. It's a great tool to increase traffic and engagement, and with one click of this green button, visitors can share your content with all their online networks.

Content Marketing Online

Article marketing is a type of content marketing in which businesses write short articles related to their respective industries. These articles are made available for distribution and publication in the marketplace. Each article contains a bio box and byline that includes references and contact information for the author's business. Well-written content articles released for free distribution have the potential of increasing the business's credibility within its market as well as attracting new clients.

If writing is not your forte and you're worried about creating powerful articles or content, there are hundreds of sites that offer writing services, such as WritersForHire.com, Guru.com, or ODesk.com, where you can set a budget for a project and post the job for hire. Another great resource for writers is right in your hometown at the local university or college. Interns are starving for more experience and would jump at the opportunity to write articles for credit. You can post writing jobs in the college career center, or call on the intern division in the marketing department.

Before you submit your articles online, make sure you read submission guidelines to ensure timely approval and posting. There are hundreds of article marketing sites on the net. Here are a few top sites:

- *Businessknowhow.com.* If your content can help businesses grow, then this is a great site to submit articles and tips to. Business Know-How is known for providing practical information, tools, and resources for starting, growing, and managing small and homebased businesses. The Business Know-How website reaches about three million individuals each year.
- *Ezinearticles.com.* This is a matching service that brings real-world experts and ezine publishers together. Experts, authors, and writers are able to post their articles on this member site. The site's searchable database of hundreds of thousands of quality original articles allows email newsletter publishers that need fresh content to find articles that they can use

tip

Post articles to chosen sites and link back to your blog, client, or marketing campaign site. Make sure to include tags and keywords relevant to your content topic when posting. Develop a list of relevant industry blogs, e-newsletters, and Twitter feeds and send your link to those, too.

>> Words Heard Round the World

Here are a few quick tips on how to take an article and make it viral on the net:

> *Post on discussion boards and forums*. Post snippets of your article or the article title in forums and on discussion boards that are related to your target market or topic focus. Don't forget to include your full name and website or blog URL where the article is located.

> *Tweet it—and include influential Twitter handles in your posts*. Make a 100-character, pithy summary and use the @ handles of people with many followers (that could be a few thousand in a smaller industry or tens of thousands in a big one) in your industry or reviewers in your product or service space.

> *Compile articles into an ebook*. Compile the articles into an ebook. For example, if you own a gym and want to get more people in to work out, offer an ebook on the top ten ways to motivate yourself to get to the gym. Take these ebooks and distribute them either through your website, to your email list, or via safelists. Give your readers the right to distribute them as well. This is viral marketing at work. If your ebook is for sale, offer to share revenue if readers distribute it to their list and sell it. This is called an affiliate marketing program.

> *Write a variety of articles*. The trick to reaching a massive amount of people is to create a variety of articles. For example, if you want to promote your public relations service, you could post content on how to write an article, how to come up with attractive article titles, what's the right format and ideal word count, how and where to distribute the articles, how to submit to hundreds of article directories within the shortest time, etc.

> *Add a disclosure in each article at the end or bottom of the article*. Your disclosure statement should say something like this: "This article may be freely reprinted or distributed in its entirety in any ezine, newsletter, blog, or website. The author's name, bio, and website links must remain intact and be included with every reproduction."

for inclusion in their next newsletter or blog post.

- *Goarticles.com.* With a membership exceeding 135,000 authors, this article search engine and directory boasts more than 1.5 million indexed articles. Their goal is to provide authors, publishers, and visitors with the best and largest free content article database on the web.
- *Articlealley.com.* This free article directory was started to help authors promote and syndicate their content. This site allows authors and promoters to get their articles out with the potential of being read by millions. They now have a loyal author base of more than 500,000 active authors and more than half a million pages of content.

Once you've posted your content on the article publishing sites, you'll want to track their success. If you posted your content on EzineArticles.com, you can get a fairly good idea how many people are republishing your articles in newsletters or other nonwebsite sources. On each article, there's a quick-publish button that spits out an HTML-formatted version of the article, allowing publishers to copy and paste the content into a website or email. Authors are provided with statistics on how many times the button is clicked as well as how many times the article has been viewed, forwarded by email, and a few other neat statistics. Total views (page views) are also included in the statistic. Top authors report figures in the hundreds of thousands; however, they're publishing more than 100 articles per month. You get back multiples of what you put in, and depending on keywords, titles, and subject matter, you can expect varying results.

Another great analytics tool you can use to track where visitors are coming from, what article pages they visit on your site, and how long they stay is Google Analytics. It's a free service and fairly simple to set up. Go to google.com/analytics to set up an account. The analytics site offers a complete tutorial; however, if you're still unsure how to use it, you can ask a web programmer to set it up for you in a matter of minutes.

Social Marketing Automation

With all the social site tools available, often the best way to be effective with your social marketing is to automate the process. First, you need to decide whether automation is right for you and, if so, which automation you should set up. Automation can be key in turning your contacts into profits because you can post less, but at the same time, you get more exposure. Social automation, however, can be considered spamming, so be careful with how you set it up.

How does social network automation work? There are tools like Hootsuite (hootsuite.com) and SocialFlow (socialflow.com) where you can automate your social networking sites or TubeMogul.com to automate your video posting. These sites can submit a link or post to not just one or two sites but, in some cases, up to 60. Sometimes, though, the link posted isn't relevant for the site it goes out to. In other words, the links aren't even relevant for the members of the network, and sometimes they're not properly tagged or categorized. This eventually leads to negative votes on the article or post submitted, so make sure you set up your automation properly.

There are many automation capabilities and options available. Here are some automation suggestions to get you started:

- *Twitter to Facebook.* Every time you post on Twitter, it will automatically post to your personal Facebook newsfeed. While some media professionals have gotten away from this since the @ Twitter handles are "dead links" when they move to Facebook, it can still be a fast and efficient way to automate. However, if Facebook is your primary source of engagement, consider the other way around for automation (see next bullet).
- *Facebook Fan Page to Twitter.* Every time you post to your Facebook fan page, it can post to Twitter, which will, in turn, post to your personal Facebook newsfeed.
- *Link your blog to Facebook.* Click on the NetworkedBlogs application in Facebook (facebook.com/games/blognetworks), and add your blog information as prompted. There's a verification process that Facebook will walk you through to make sure you're the author of the blog.
- *Link your blog to LinkedIn.* Go to Applications and click on WordPress if you have a WordPress blog, or go to Applications then Blog Link if you have a TypePad blog. LinkedIn will walk you through the process step by step.
- *Link your blog to Twitter.* Twitterfeed (twitterfeed.com) is a handy,

free website and application that will "feed your blog to Twitter." Go to Twitterfeed, sign up for an account, verify and log in, then click "Create New Feed" button, and add your blog. It might take a couple of hours to start working. Once going, it's fairly reliable unless Twitter goes down or has API issues. Check the stream once a week.

- *Use a service like Hootsuite, where you can schedule posts months in advance.* You can also use the service to link to all of your social media accounts, from Twitter to Facebook, to LinkedIn, Google+, and even Pinterest. Your most popular articles or blog posts can be "socialed" months into the future to give them new life. Just be sure to make clear that they're older posts (add the phrase "In case you missed it," or ICYMI in Twitterspeak, or are evergreen).

Another way to automate your blog so it posts to the social sites you're active on is to set up widgets and add plugins. You can do this for sites like Twitter, Facebook, LinkedIn, YouTube, Squidoo, Delicious, Digg, and many more. The way a widget works is every time you post on one social site it will go out to your blog as an update. First, you need to make sure your blog allows widgets. Some blogs won't allow widgets unless you host the blog on your own site. Once you determine whether you can add these widgets, log in to each of the sites you want to add a widget to and go to the search box, type in widget, and that will take you to the most current directions on how to upload or generate the HTML code needed to post widgets to your blog.

Plugins are applications that can enhance the capabilities of your blog, such as the All in One SEO plugins available on WordPress, which helps you optimize your blog for search engines, or the WPtouch iPhone Theme on WordPress that transforms your WordPress blog into an iPhone application-style theme. There are thousands of plugins available, and they're usually found on your blog platform under "plugin."

CHAPTER

36

Can You Relate?

Social Media Networking

The days of in-person networking are quickly being overpowered by connecting on the internet. In the past five years, connecting on social networking sites has rocketed from a niche activity into a phenomenon that engages tens of millions of internet users.

According to Nielsen Online, a global research company, "member communities" are now visited by nearly three-quarters of the global online population, which includes both social networks and blogs. It has become the third most popular online category—ahead of email—and it's growing twice as fast as any of the other four largest sectors (search, portals, PC software, and email).

Throughout this social movement, this new approach to networking has continued to be overlooked as a marketing vehicle for business owners. Now, instead of connecting at an in-person event, you can reach hundreds, even thousands, of potential customers online. Social networking can help you reach new markets and enhance your customer service.

High-Level Networking

In today's networking space, you need to be efficient with your time and even more effective in regard to whom you choose to connect with. It's important to know how to choose whom to connect with online. There are two different types of networkers online—the posters and the seekers. Your business is a poster, which means you actively post valuable information, resources, tips, and offers. The seekers are your customers—they're actively seeking your products and or services. You'll find seekers in discussion areas, forums, groups, and engaging on fan pages.

When searching for quality contacts to network with online, start with connection sites, such as LinkedIn or Xing, and look for high-level networkers (HLN). You'll know an HLN when you see one; they're active online, have at least 500 connections, and have powerful profiles, which means that their profiles are set up completely. Make sure these contacts have at least one of the three criteria before you connect with them online. Some examples of HLNs would be decision makers, executives, the media, and the movers and shakers in your industry. Don't let the fact that you don't yet know the person hold you back from sending an invite to connect. Simply be transparent, and let them know why you'd like to connect with them online. Whether you're offering your help, sending them a resource, or introducing them to one of your connections, make sure that you make it about how you can help them and not how they can help you.

e-fyi

Check out Meetup.com, an online networking site that facilitates offline networking. Members can create and join groups of people with similar interests who live in their area, and they can easily organize real-life meetings. It's a great way to meet potential business partners and clients. It's usually free to participate in monthly meetup events, although some events come with a nominal organization fee or participation cost.

Target Market Connections

Target market connections (TMC) are a group of consumers at which your company aims its products and services. They're found by using keywords in the search section on social sites as well as in groups and discussion areas in your area of interest or focus. TMCs are mostly seekers that chat and seek out information by posting questions online. In the most basic terms, they're seeking you. The key is to join in the groups and discussions where your target market is talking and engage with them. You can also send them an invite to connect and let them know that you sent them the invite because you have similar interests and you're looking to expand your professional network. You can also find these groups in sites like LinkedIn. Search for groups that match what you have to contribute and then check to see which have not just the largest member numbers, but also the most active discussions.

Another way to find your target market online is to investigate competitors' marketing methods. See where another business that offers the same or similar products and services advertises their links and posts on social sites. Be sure each location makes sense and has a large contingent of people in your targeted market. Searching in your field will often turn up places where your audience goes when they're looking for something in your industry.

The top three social sites to get started with or choose from are LinkedIn, Facebook, and Twitter. These sites are massive online communities filled with potential high-level networkers and target market connections. To get started, set up your profile and navigate to get familiar with the sites' offerings. To stay informed on any social site changes or updates, be sure to bookmark Mashable (mashable.com), the leading source for all social networking news and updates.

e-fyi

If someone is looking for house cleaning services in Orlando, Florida, you should know what he or she is likely to type into the search engine. You can find out this information by researching how people search. Good Keywords (goodkeywords.com) offers some great keyword-related software for brainstorming, researching, analyzing, and managing keywords. Free trials are available.

Groups and Discussions

Even the most unsociable entrepreneur can interact on message boards and blogs. Groups and discussion areas on social sites are all over the internet from LinkedIn and Xing to Twitter and Facebook. Most social networking sites have community areas for people who have similar interests to gather and connect (even Twitter has groups, or you can join people in discussions around # hasthtags on a topic—or create your own). It's important to find a dozen or so of these groups and discussion areas and not only join and monitor them but engage in the conversations as well.

Blogs are another type of discussion forum on the internet. A blog isn't just a type of website; it's quickly becoming a place to interact with your target market. Technorati (technorati.com), a site focused on helping people find great blogs and content specific to their industry or topic, was recently ranked as the fifth largest social media site by comScore, an internet market research company. Technorati manages a list of the top 100 blogs, which is a great place to find the world's most popular blogs on subjects you're interested in. Not only can you find connections and blogs on this site, but you can also list your own blog so that people can search and find you.

Blogs are a great way to find HLNs to connect with online as well as partner with. For example, if you're a restaurant, you could connect with

>> Keep It Separated

It's critically important, in most instances, to keep your personal social media accounts separate from your business accounts. Many people do blur the line between professional and personal, but when you own a business, it's more important to be concerned about offending a professional contact with your personal photos or posts. It's best to keep separate Facebook and Twitter accounts, in particular. And if you are a heavy YouTube user, keep your accounts separate there, too. LinkedIn, which is professional in nature to begin with, can be the exception, if you keep your posts related to your industry or work.

food and review writers, vendors that are blogging, or food enthusiasts, and share their posts and content on your site or blog. This not only builds relationships but can expose you to their markets, followers and fans.

tip 

When looking for groups to join, search for groups that have at least 500 members, unless they're industry-specific. Most groups that are under 500 might not be as active or updated and visited frequently enough for it to be worth your posting time. If you find a group with fewer members, be sure to keep an eye on how active its members are before you spend much time on involvement.

Fan Pages

With any social media platform, you need to be creative and find ways to provide value and engage your target market. One of the best ways to accomplish this and position yourself as an industry leader is to build and launch a Facebook fan page. If you're an entrepreneur, you can't afford to ignore this powerful tool. Fans are enthusiastic, and if they like what they see and read, they'll connect with you, become loyal supporters, and tell their friends. This is how word-of-mouth will grow. The Social Media Industry Marketing report showed that 54 percent of respondents find Facebook their most valuable social networking platform in 2014. That was up dramatically from just two years earlier, when only 40 percent said the same.

It's very simple to set up a fan page on Facebook—just a few clicks and you're ready to go. You can either create a fan page from your homepage on the Facebook site or there are tutorials available in the help section on the site. Once you get your fan page up and running, pay attention to your analytics, or what Facebook calls "Insights." You can view specific demographic information, such as where your fans are from, their gender, and their age. Monitor who's becoming your fan, how they're interacting, and how often they're posting. This will help you figure out who and where else you should be targeting online.

To enhance the look and brand image of your fan page, use a horizontal image that covers the top of the page invitingly. You should use a smaller logo or image for the inset image that will show up as your page profile photo in fan newsfeeds. You can also set your fan page to have a vanity

warning 

Be aware of "trolling" (aka trolls) on the net: A troll is someone who posts inflammatory or off-topic messages in an online community, such as a discussion forum, group, or blog, with the primary intent of provoking other users into an emotional response or of otherwise disrupting normal on-topic discussion.

URL, which is a personalized web name. This will take your fan page URL from facebook.com/#/pages/brandnamehere/180746308742 to facebook.com/brandnamehere.

One of the main differences between a Facebook profile and a fan page is you can send bulk messages to all your fans. You can also "Suggest to Friends" that they join you on your fan page. Obviously, this is a feature you need to use wisely, and be careful not to annoy your audience. But it's a great way to connect with your target market, especially since these are connections that have opted-in to become a part of your community. They want to hear from you and talk with you.

After you have your fan page published live, you can use the little ads you see in the margins on your profile page to increase your fan base, mostly to kick it off at the beginning. Facebook advertising is very affordable; you can set up campaigns of any size and on any budget, and they're highly targeted. People usually assume that advertising is expensive, but don't let that scare you. Give it a try.

You can boost a few posts and promote your page—and gain hundreds and even thousands of fans, not to mention expose your brand—for a few hundred dollars, sometimes even less. Facebook keeps track of the success of your campaign and you set targets for viewers and interactions. So you can quickly see the ROI of any post you've boosted or the value of the page promotion parameters you choose. Because ads and post-boosting are able to be finely targeted, you can also be sure your target audience (all the way down to location and age range) sees your page and posts.

> ***"A terrible thing happens without publicity . . . nothing!"***
>
> —P.T. Barnum

Media Connections on Social Sites

The media is an effective conduit for delivering your messages and story to the

>> Fan Page Workout

Social media news site Mashable suggests the following tips to enhance and build out your fan page:

- *Twitter integration*. Link your fan page to Twitter so every time you post, it will automatically be posted to your Twitter account as well. (For more on automating your content, see Chapter 35.) One caveat: If you find your Twitter audience has different interests than your Facebook fans, you might want to consider turning the auto-feed to Twitter off, so as to not alienate those followers.
- *Fan page blog widget*. Add a fan page widget to your blog to help drive blog traffic and connections to your fan page. Facebook provides you with the necessary code. (For more details on widgets, see Chapter 35.)
- *Blog promotion*. Take your blog to the next level, and add your blog to your fan page. Blogging networks, such as NetworkedBlogs (networkedblogs.com) or Blogged (blogged.com), allow you to integrate a feed and give your fans a little taste of your blog. At the same time, your blog is now part of a network and that can translate into some additional traffic and followers.
- *Facebook apps*. There are many great applications that you can integrate into your page to help promote audience interaction. Some of them, like the video app, are already a default on your page. Be sure to browse through them, and you'll most likely find something great for your industry or business. Don't be afraid to test different ones; you can always remove them. Consider polls and questions as a good addition—Facebook users like to interact and you can use the polls to gauge interest in everything from products and services to events.

people you want to reach and can be vital to gaining word-of-mouth online and off. A majority of journalists have switched to social sites because they don't have the time to read lengthy email pitches and press releases. With the help of social networking sites, you can search for media contacts on sites such as LinkedIn and reach out to them directly. You can also pitch journalists on blogs and Twitter, and get up-to-date information

> **tip** 
>
> The number of PR and marketing people on Twitter is astounding. Use their collective wisdom and networks to create buzz and support for you and/or an event.

about a media outlet and what it's looking for. Look for trending topics in your area or industry and use the prevailing hashtags to get your expertise or product in the conversation when it comes up.

Start by identifying the media outlets you want to target, and visit the website for each one to research it thoroughly. Keep your list brief so follow-up is manageable. Once you've built your list, search for key contacts at those outlets on LinkedIn. LinkedIn is a great resource for finding professional journalists and segment producers. With LinkedIn's new search features, you can dive deeper into user data to find contacts that fit your criteria. For example, you can create a search to find contacts with "reporter" as their professional title within a 50-mile radius of your ZIP code. You can easily

>> Media Matters

To find media outlets in your industry or topic area, check out the following sites:

- *ipl2 (ipl.org/div/news/) is a merger of the Internet Public Library and the Librarians' Internet Index*. It includes a list of popular magazines and newspapers organized by their respective subject area or geographic focus. Each listing includes a brief description of the outlet's coverage area, along with a link to the website.
- *Yahoo! News and Media Directory (dir.yahoo.com/News_and_Media)*. You can search news and media by format (newspaper, magazine, blog, etc.) or by subject. This site also lists how many outlets are available under each category.
- *HARO (Help a Reporter Out) at helpareporter.com* is a free service that connects journalists with expert sources. Each email (there are three a day) includes reporter queries you can respond to (provided you have a relevant pitch or expert to offer).

narrow each search by limiting other fields or adding a keyword, such as "business" or "features." LinkedIn also lets you save a certain amount of searches so you can be alerted to new contacts that join LinkedIn matching your criteria.

Key media contact titles include:

- Editor
- Segment producer
- Journalist
- Reporter
- Assignment desk editor

Center of Influence List

One of the fastest ways to build referrals and relationships online through social networking is by reconnecting with past friends and family members or simply by reaching out to the top people in your center of influence that respect and admire you. This could be friends from grammar or high school, college, past co-workers, family members, bestselling authors, media contacts, etc.

eMarketer.com, a digital marketing and media researcher, reports that more than half (53 percent) of internet users have visited websites referred by friends or family members in the previous 30 days. People trust people that they already know, and your friends and family will most likely recommend you if the situation is right. Referrals have always been an extremely powerful way of gaining customers. With the web, trust levels can be very low for new visitors. In this environment, a referral from a trusted source can make all the difference in converting a contact into a customer.

tip

Twitter is a great site to meet media contacts from around the world. Once you build a following, try to attend a local tweetup. A tweetup is an event where people who use Twitter come together to meet in person; they're great for walking away with a lot of contacts and leads. At a tweetup, you meet the people you might only otherwise know virtually, plus the media often attends.

>> Forget Me Not

It is vital that you create a powerful "stay connected" plan to keep your brand at top of mind with your contacts. Set aside half a day to reach out to your connections at least once every three months by using one of the following approaches:

- Send them an email once a month to announce something new in your business and simply to touch base.
- Phone (or Skype) them to say hello. Ask them how they are first, and keep notes so you have a point of contact for the next call. You can close with an event or big announcement about your company, product, or service.
- A personal note works very well for developing this type of relationship. Notes take time, which shows that you value this relationship. SendOutCards.com is a great site that can help you automate card sending—and we're talking real printed cards, not e-cards.
- Don't tell them, show them how important they are. If this relationship doesn't include reciprocity, it will degenerate into a "what's in it for me" situation that won't stand the test of time. Send them thank-you gifts or online gift cards (a small amount will do just fine) to let them know you're grateful for them and any referrals that they've sent your way.

Develop that trusting relationship with people who are well positioned to help you. You must earn their referrals. When you do, your marketing will become supercharged with what's clearly the best form of advertising—positive word-of-mouth.

Facebook is one of the best sites to connect with friends and family as well as past co-workers and your online center of influence. Once you've determined who these contacts are and connect with them online, you need to not only reach out to them but keep in touch with them. Have you ever had someone you know buy what you sell from a competitor because they just didn't know you sold it? That means that you're not at the top of their mind.

PART

8

PROFIT

CHAPTER

37

Keeping Score

The Basics of Bookkeeping

By J. Tol Broome Jr., Freelance Business Writer and Banker with 33 Years of Experience in Commercial Lending

So you say you would rather wrestle an alligator with one hand tied behind your back than get bogged down in numbers? Well, you aren't alone. Many small-business owners would rather focus on making and selling their products than on keeping their books and records in order. However, bookkeeping is just as important as production and marketing. Many a great business idea has failed due to a poor bookkeeping system.

Simply put, a business's bookkeeping system tracks the money coming in vs. the money going out. And, ultimately, you won't be able to keep your doors open if you have more dollars going out than coming in.

Aside from every business owner's inherent desire to stay in business, there are two other key reasons to set up a good bookkeeping system:

1. It is legally required.
2. Bookkeeping records are an excellent business management tool.

Of course, staying out of jail is a good thing. And a good basic accounting system will provide useful financial information that will enable you to run your business proactively rather than reactively when it comes to important financial decisions.

tip 

"The check is in the mail." Or so they say—but is it really? If you switch to electronic billing and payment, you'll always know for sure. Another advantage is a reduction in errors. If you want to start e-billing, you'll need software and some training. Or you can find a service provider for a one-time setup fee and per-transaction charges.

The Bookkeeping Advantage

As a new business owner, you are in an enviable position in setting up a bookkeeping system for your venture. You are not bound to the "we've always done it that way" mentality that bogs down many businesses. For your new endeavor, you have the advantage of being able to develop the bookkeeping system that is most compatible with your business type as well as your financial management skills.

Few new businesses—and even most older ones—still operate using a manual (checkbook and receipts) bookkeeping system, and it is not a good idea for a new business to use this type of system. It is far more efficient to go with an automated system, and there are now many bookkeeping software packages on the market that won't break your wallet.

For a financially complex business such as a manufacturing concern, you can buy industry-specific software, but there also are generic programs available that would suffice for most new businesses (see "It All Adds Up" on page 608).

A good accounting system meets three criteria. First, it is accurate; the numbers must be right. Automation will help ensure accuracy, but it won't guarantee it. Bookkeeping numbers should be checked and rechecked to maintain accuracy.

Second, a good accounting system is relevant. The system provides information that is required and needed. The law requires that certain pieces of financial information be tracked for tax-reporting purposes. Obviously, these items (which compose a basic income statement and balance sheet) must be measured and tracked. However, it's equally important to include information that you'll need to run your business successfully.

> **e-fyi**
>
> 
>
> The website of the American Institute of Certified Public Accountants (aicpa.org) provides links to news updates, legislative activities, state CPA societies, and a "financial literacy" tutorial.

Third, a good accounting system is user-friendly. It should not require a CPA to operate and interpret. Most of the Windows-based bookkeeping software packages are pretty user-friendly. They include tutorials and help screens that walk you through the programs. Find one with which you are comfortable, even if it doesn't have some of the bells and whistles of more complicated programs.

Basic Accounting Principles

Most businesses typically use one of two basic accounting methods in their bookkeeping systems: cash basis or accrual basis. While most businesses use the accrual basis, the most appropriate method for your company depends on your sales volume, whether or not you sell on credit, and your business structure.

The cash method is the most simple in that the books are kept based on the actual flow of cash in and out of the business. Income is recorded when it is received, and expenses are reported when they are actually paid. The cash method is used by many sole proprietors and businesses with no inventory. From a tax standpoint, it is sometimes advantageous for a new business to use the cash method of accounting. That way, recording income can be put off until the next tax year, while expenses are counted right away.

With the accrual method, income and expenses are recorded as they occur, regardless of whether or not cash has actually changed hands. An excellent example is a sale on credit. The sale is entered into the books when the invoice is generated rather than when the cash is collected. Likewise, an

>> Make No Mistake

When setting up your bookkeeping system, keep the following four points in mind:

1. *Competency*. To run a small business effectively, you must become familiar with your bookkeeping system as well as the financial reports it will generate. Even if you hire an internal bookkeeper on Day One, it is critical that you understand the numbers. Don't make the mistake of focusing all your efforts on marketing and production/operations while leaving the financial job in someone else's hands. Successful entrepreneurs are proficient in all aspects of their ventures, including the numbers. Most community colleges offer basic accounting and finance courses. If numbers aren't your thing, sign up for a class. It will be well worth the time investment.
2. *Computerization*. Don't let your lack of computer skills keep you from automating your bookkeeping system. If you aren't computer-literate, community colleges also offer a host of classes that provide training both in general computer use as well as specific software programs (such as Microsoft Office or Lotus).

   You have to think long term here. Just because a manual system might suffice in the early stages of your operation doesn't mean that you should ignore automation. Think about what will be needed three to five years down the road. Converting from a manual to an automated system is no fun—you can avoid this costly time drain by going automated upfront.
3. *Consistency*. When deciding on a computer software package for your bookkeeping system, don't just consider the price. The important issues to consider when buying bookkeeping software are: a) the track record of the software manufacturer, b) the track record of the software system itself (even Microsoft releases flops every now and then), and c) the amount of technical assistance provided by the manufacturer.

>> **Make No Mistake,** continued

4. *Compatibility.* Before you make a final bookkeeping software decision, check to see if the system is compatible with the other software you plan to use in your venture. Imagine the frustration you would experience if the spreadsheets you create in Microsoft Excel, say, for payroll tracking couldn't be exported into your bookkeeping system.

expense occurs when materials are ordered or when a workday has been logged in by an employee, not when the check is actually written. The downside of this method is that you pay income taxes on revenue before you've actually received it.

Should you use the cash or accrual method in your business? The accrual method is required if your business's annual sales exceed $5 million and your venture is structured as a C corporation. In addition, businesses with inventory must also use the accrual method. It also is highly recommended for any business that sells on credit, as it more accurately matches income and expenses during a given time period.

The cash method may be appropriate for a small, cash-based business or a small service company. You should consult your accountant when deciding on an accounting method.

Accounting System Components

Every accounting system has key components. Even if you decide to farm out all your bookkeeping work, you should still understand the basic elements of an accounting system. While some may vary depending on the type of business, these components typically consist of the chart of accounts, general ledger, accounts receivable, inventory, fixed assets, accounts payable, and payroll.

Chart of Accounts

The first step in setting up an accounting system for your new business is deciding what you want to track. A chart of accounts is kept by every business to record and follow specific entries. With a software program, you can customize the chart of accounts to your business. Account numbers are used as an easy account identification system. For most businesses, a three-number system will suffice; however, a four-number system is sometimes used for more complex ventures.

The chart of accounts is the fuel for your accounting system. After the chart of accounts, you establish a general ledger system, which is the engine that actually runs your business's accounting system on a daily basis.

tip

The chart of accounts is the foundation on which you will build your accounting system. Take care to set up your chart of accounts right the first time. Keep your account descriptions as concise as possible. And leave room in your numbering system to add accounts in the future.

General Ledger

Every account that is on your chart of accounts will be included in your general ledger, which should be set up in the same order as the chart of accounts. While the general ledger does not include every single accounting entry in a given period, it does reflect a summary of all transactions made.

If your new business will be a small, cash-based business, you can set up much of your general ledger out of your checkbook. The checkbook includes several pieces of information vital to the general ledger—cumulative cash balance, date of the entry, amount of the entry, and purpose of the entry. However, if you plan to sell and buy on account, as most businesses do, a checkbook alone will not suffice as a log for general ledger transactions. And even for a cash-based business, a checkbook cannot be your sole source for establishing a balance sheet.

An important component of any general ledger is source documents. Two examples of source documents are copies of invoices to customers and invoices from suppliers. Source documents are critical in that they provide an audit trail in case you or someone else has to go back and study financial transactions made in your business.

For instance, a customer might claim that he never received an invoice from you. Your source document will prove otherwise. And your source documents are a required component for your accountant at tax time. Other examples of source documents include canceled checks, utility bills, payroll tax records, and loan statements.

All general ledger entries are double entries. And that makes sense. For every financial transaction in your business, the money (or commitment to pay) goes from one place to another. For instance, when you write your payroll checks, the money flows out of your payroll account (cash) into the hands of your employees (an expense). When you sell goods on account, you record a sale (income) but must have a journal entry to make sure you collect that account later (an account receivable). The system used in recording entries on a general ledger is called a system of debits and credits. In fact, if you can gain even a basic understanding of debits and credits, you will be well on your way to understanding your entire accounting system.

As outlined above, for every debit, there should be an equal and offsetting credit. It is when the debits and credits are not equal or do not offset each other that your books don't balance. A key advantage of any automated bookkeeping system is that it will police your debit and credit entries as they are made, making it far more difficult not to balance. It won't take many 3 A.M. error-finding sessions in a manual system to persuade you to automate your bookkeeping system!

All debits and credits either increase or decrease an account balance. These basic relationships are summarized in the chart below:

Account Type	Debit	Credit
Asset	Increases	Decreases
Liability	Decreases	Increases
Stockholder's Equity	Decreases	Increases
Income	Decreases	Increases
Expense	Increases	Decreases

In a general ledger, debits always go on the left and credits always go on the right. (For examples of general ledger debit-and-credit entries, see the chart on page 600).

While many double entries are made directly to the general ledger, you'll find it's necessary to maintain subledgers for a number of accounts

>> General Ledger Entries

While the bookkeeping process for your business can be rather intricate, single debit and credit entries are really quite basic. Remember that for every entry, there is an equal and offsetting co-entry. Also keep in mind that the different types of accounts have both debits and credits depending on whether the account is increased or decreased (see the chart on page 599). Here are five examples of equal and offsetting general ledger entries for a sock manufacturing business:

1. Purchasing a delivery truck	**Debit**	**Credit**
Cash (Asset)	$20,000	
Fixed Asset (Asset)		$20,000
2. Purchasing yarn on account to make the socks		
Accounts Payable (Liability)	$25,000	
Inventory (Asset)		$25,000
3. Selling a sock order to a customer on account		
Accounts Receivable (Asset)	$10,000	
Sales (Income)		$10,000
4. Collecting the account receivable from the same customer		
Accounts Receivable (Asset)		$10,000
Cash (Asset)	$10,000	
5. Funding payroll at the end of the month		
Payroll Expense (Expense)	$20,000	
Cash (Asset)		$20,000

in which there is regular activity. The information is then taken in a summary format from the subledgers and transferred to the general ledger. Subledgers showing cash receipts and cash disbursements are pretty easy to follow. However, some subledgers, such as accounts receivable, inventory, fixed assets, accounts payable, and payroll can prove to be a challenge in their daily maintenance.

Accounts Receivable

If you plan to sell goods or services on account in your business, you will need a method of tracking who owes you how much and when it is due. This is where the accounts receivable subledger comes in. If you will be selling to a number of different customers, then an automated system is a must.

A good bookkeeping software system will allow you to set up subledgers for each customer. So when a sale is made on account, you can track it specifically to the customer. This is essential to ensure that billing and collection are done in a timely manner.

aha!

If you'll be selling on credit, your accounts receivable system will be vital. Here are five key components of a good accounts receivable system:

1. Verify accounts receivable balances. Use source documents such as invoices to keep balances accurate.
2. Send accurate and timely invoices.
3. Generate accounts receivable reports. Determine which customers are past due and track credit limits.
4. Post paid invoices to track who pays you when.
5. Match up your customer records totals, your general ledger, and subledgers.

Inventory

Unless you are starting a service business, a good inventory-control feature will be an essential part of your bookkeeping system. If you are going to be manufacturing products, you will have to track raw materials, work-in-progress, and finished goods, and separate subledgers should be established for each of these inventory categories. Even if you are a wholesaler or a retailer, you will be selling many types of inventory and will need an effective system to track each item offered for sale.

Another key reason to track inventory very closely is the direct relationship to cost of goods sold. Since nearly all businesses that stock inventory are required to use the accrual method for accounting, good inventory records are a must for accurately tracking the material cost associated with each item sold.

>> Stocking Up

If your business will produce or sell inventory, your inventory management system will be crucial to your business' success. Keeping too much inventory on hand will cost you cash flow and will increase the risk of obsolescence. Conversely, a low inventory level can cost you sales.

Here are some suggestions to help you better manage your inventory:

- *Pay attention to seasonality*. Depending on the type of business you are starting, you may have certain inventory items that sell only during certain times of the year. Order early in anticipation of the peak season. Then make sure you sell the stock so that you don't get stuck holding on to it for a year.
- *Rely on suppliers*. If you can find suppliers that are well-stocked and can ship quickly, you can essentially let them stock your inventory for you. "Just in time" inventory management can save valuable working capital that could be invested in other areas of your business.
- *Stock what sells*. This may seem obvious, but too many business owners try to be all things to all people when it comes to inventory management. When you see what sells, focus your purchasing efforts on those items.
- *Mark down stale items*. Once you're up and running, you will find that certain items sell better than others. Mark down the items that don't sell, and then don't replace them.
- *Watch waste*. Keep a close eye on waste. If production mistakes aren't caught early, you can ruin a whole batch of inventory, which can be extremely costly.

From a management standpoint, tracking inventory is also important. An effective and up-to-date inventory-control system will provide you with the following critical information:

- Which items sell well and which items are slow-moving
- When to order more raw materials or other items
- Where the inventory is stored when it comes time to ship
- Number of days in the production process for each item
- The typical order of key customers
- Minimum inventory level needed to meet daily orders

(For more information on inventory-control systems, see Chapter 19.)

Fixed Assets

Fixed assets are items that are for long-term use, generally five years or more. They're not bought and sold in the normal course of business operation. Fixed assets include vehicles, land, buildings, leasehold improvements, machinery, and equipment.

In an accrual system of accounting, fixed assets aren't fully expensed when they are purchased but rather they are expensed over a period of time that coincides with the useful life (the amount of time the asset is expected to last) of the item. This process is known as depreciation. Most businesses that own fixed assets keep subledgers for each asset category as well as for each depreciation schedule.

In most cases, depreciation is easy to compute. The cost of the asset is divided by its useful life. For instance, a $60,000 piece of equipment with a five-year useful life would be depreciated at a rate of $12,000 per year. This is known as straight-line depreciation.

There are other more complicated methods of fixed-asset depreciation that allow for accelerated depreciation on the front end, which is advantageous from a tax standpoint. You should seek the advice

save

For more information on setting up your bookkeeping system, you can download *Starting a Business and Keeping Records* (Publication 583) for free from the IRS website at irs.gov.

of your CPA before setting up depreciation schedules for fixed-asset purchases.

Accounts Payable

The accounts payable subledger is similar to that used to track accounts receivable. The difference is, accounts payable occur when you purchase inventory or other assets on credit from a supplier rather than tracking a specific sale to a customer.

It is important to track accounts payable in a timely manner to ensure that you know how much you owe each supplier and when payment is due. Many a good supplier relationship has been damaged due to a sloppy accounts payable system. Also, if your suppliers offer discounts for payment within ten days of invoice, a good automated accounts payable system will alert you when to pay to maximize the discounts earned.

Payroll

Payroll accounting can be quite a challenge for the new business owner. There are many federal and state laws regulating what you have to track related to payroll (see Chapter 41). Failure to do so could result in heavy fines—or worse.

Many business owners use outside payroll services. These companies guarantee compliance with all the applicable laws. This keeps the business owner out of trouble with the law and saves time that can be devoted to something else in the business. If you choose to do your own payroll, it's recommended that you purchase an automated payroll system. Even if the rest of your books are done manually, an automated payroll system will save you time and help considerably with compliance.

warning

All businesses are subject to laws governing the payment of federal and state withholding taxes. Here are three rules that must never be violated in your business:

1. Make sure you have current withholding tax tables.
2. Always make your payroll deposits on time.
3. Stay up-to-date and accurate with payroll record-keeping reporting requirements.

There's not a lot of margin for error when you're dealing with the federal government!

Cost Accounting

Cost accounting is the process of allocating all costs associated with generating a sale, both direct and indirect. Direct costs include materials, direct labor (the total wages paid to the workers who made the product), foreman/plant manager salaries, and freight. Indirect costs include all other costs associated with keeping your doors open.

As profit margins have shrunk in many businesses, particularly manufacturing ventures, cost accounting has become an increasingly valuable tool. By knowing the total costs associated with the production of a product, you can determine which inventory items are the most profitable to make. This will enable you to focus your sales efforts on those inventory items rather than on products that offer little or no bottom-line enhancement.

To set up an effective cost accounting system, you should seek input from your CPA. Cost accounting can get fairly complicated, and the money you might spend for a CPA will be more than made up for in the expertise he or she will provide in customizing a cost accounting system for your business.

Under Control

Do you know any business owners who have suffered significant losses due to employee theft or embezzlement? They probably did not have an effective internal-control system in place. Many successful ventures have been set back or even put out of business by an unscrupulous employee or financial service provider. And it is often someone whom the business owner least suspected of wrongdoing.

When setting up a bookkeeping system, you need to focus a good deal of effort on instituting a sound system of policies and procedures governing internal control. Here are ten areas where you need internal control:

1. *You need a written policy that clearly spells out your internal control system.* Make sure all employees read this policy. Having a policy

not only spells out the procedures to be followed, but it also lets your employees know you are serious about internal controls.

2. *On a regular basis, review the internal control policy to ensure it is up-to-date.* When changes are made, hold meetings with employees to discuss the changes and to maintain a focus on this vital area.
3. *Make sure all employees take at least one week of vacation each year.* This is often the time during which embezzlement is discovered.
4. *Cross-train others in the company to handle bookkeeping.* If the person who is stealing from you is sick or on vacation, you'll have a hard time catching him if you let the work go unprocessed until his or her return.
5. *Perform background checks before hiring new employees.* This may sound obvious, but dishonest employees often are hired by unsuspecting employers who failed to check references before making the offer.
6. *Use dual control.* You're asking for trouble if you have the same person running the accounts payable system, making journal entries, printing and signing checks, and reconciling the checkbook.
7. *Have your CPA or outside bookkeeper perform unannounced spot audits.* You may be uncomfortable performing these audits yourself, but if your policy calls for periodic audits, the CPA looks like the bad guy.
8. *Be careful who you hire as an outside financial services provider.* There are countless stories of entrepreneurs being ripped off by

warning

Here are seven signs that you might be experiencing embezzlement or employee theft:

1. Employees who don't want a vacation.
2. Employees who refuse to delegate certain tasks.
3. Ledgers and subledgers that don't balance.
4. Financial statements that don't balance.
5. Lack of audit trails.
6. Regular customer complaints that inventory shipments aren't complete.
7. Bookkeeper or accountant who won't share information.

supposedly trusted professional service providers such as accountants and attorneys. Don't relinquish total control of your cash to an outside bookkeeper. And if he or she seems reluctant to share information with you when you ask for it, this could be a sign of deceptive financial advisory practices.

9. *Back up your computer information regularly*. This is an important function for all aspects of your business. If you begin to suspect an employee of stealing, the ability to study past transactions will be vital in finding out if your suspicions are justified.
10. *In the early stages of your business, you may be able to monitor much of the cash-control procedures yourself.* However, as your business grows, you will be forced to delegate certain internal control functions. When you do, make sure you choose qualified, well-trained employees who have proved to be trustworthy. And make sure your policy clearly stipulates the person who is authorized to perform internal-control tasks such as processing invoices and signing checks.

save

Following are three tips for your accounts payable system that will improve your business's cash flow:

1. Take discounts whenever feasible. Saving 1 or 2 percent on an order can be significant.
2. If discounts aren't offered, don't pay early. There's no need to drain your cash flow unnecessarily.
3. Keep your suppliers informed. If you do fall behind, keep the lines of communication open with your suppliers. You can ill afford to get put on c.o.d.

Financial Statements

One of the primary benefits of a good bookkeeping system is the generation of timely and useful financial statements. Most automated software packages offer the capability of producing monthly financial statements. This information includes a balance sheet, an income statement, and a cash-flow statement. These monthly reports provide invaluable information on

>> It All Adds Up

In the not-too-distant past, to set up an automated bookkeeping system you had to spend countless hours yourself or hire a programmer to customize an accounting system for your business. And since most new business owners did not have the time to do it themselves or the financial resources to hire a programmer, cumbersome manual systems were used, or the bookkeeping function was completely outsourced to an accountant or bookkeeping service.

Fortunately, those days are over. In today's market, new business owners will find a number of very affordable and full-featured accounting software packages from which to choose. These popular accounting packages not only allow business owners to track and manage every aspect of their companies' finances, but they also reduce accounting expenses by saving accounting firms time and effort in producing companies' year-end tax returns and/or financial statements.

Here are some of the most popular "canned" accounting software packages: Intuit's QuickBooks Pro, Bookkeeper, and Sage 50 Complete Accounting. They range in price from $200 to $450. Regardless of which package you buy, it will be one of the most beneficial purchases you make in starting your small business.

the historical measures you need to make the financial decisions that will positively impact your business tomorrow.

Refer to the next chapter for a look at these financial statements in detail and how you can use them for effective short- and long-term financial planning.

To be an effective and proactive business owner, you will need to learn to generate and understand the financial management tools discussed in this chapter. Even if you don't consider yourself a "numbers person," you will find that regular analysis of your financial data will be vital as you start and grow your business.

For the Record

As you set up your bookkeeping system, you will need to establish procedures for keeping financial records. The IRS requires that you keep records on hand for certain specified periods of time. And with some financial records, it just makes good business sense to keep them so you can access them at a later date.

One key point here is to make sure these records are kept in a safe place. Whether you store them on-site or at a remote location (some business owners use self-storage units), make sure you use a fireproof cabinet or safe.

Another recommendation is to minimize paper buildup by storing as much as possible on CDs, microfilm, or DVDs. Here is a list of what you need to save and for how long, as recommended by accounting firm PricewaterhouseCoopers:

Record Type	How Long?
Income tax reports, protests, court briefs, appeals	Indefinitely
Annual financial statements	Indefinitely
Monthly financial statements	3 years
Books of account, such as the general ledger	Indefinitely
Subledgers	3 years
Canceled payroll and dividend checks	6 years
Income tax payment checks	Indefinitely
Bank reconciliations, voided checks, check stubs, and register tapes	6 years
Sales records such as invoices, monthly statements, remittance advisories, shipping papers, bills of lading, and customers' purchase orders	6 years
Purchase records, including purchase orders and payment vouchers	6 years

Figure 37.1. For the Record

For the Record

Record Type	How Long?
Travel and entertainment records, including account books, diaries, and expense statements and receipts	6 years
Documents substantiating fixed-asset additions, depreciation policies, and salvage values assigned to assets	Indefinitely
Personnel and payroll records, such as payments and reports to taxing authorities, including federal income tax withholding, FICA contributions, unemployment taxes, and workers' compensation insurance	6 years
Corporate documents, including certificates of incorporation, corporate charter, constitution and bylaws, deeds and easements, stock, stock transfer records, minutes of board of directors meetings, retirement and pension records, labor contracts, and license, patent, trademark, and registration applications	Indefinitely

Figure 37.1. For the Record, continued

CHAPTER 38

Making a Statement

How to Create Financial Statements

By J. Tol Broome Jr., Freelance Business Writer and Banker with 33 Years of Experience in Commercial Lending

In the last chapter, we explored establishing a good bookkeeping system for your new business. And while a well-organized bookkeeping system is vital, even more critical is what you do with it to establish your methods for financial management and control.

Think of your new bookkeeping system as the body of a car. A car body can be engineered, painted, and finished to look sleek and powerful. However, the car body won't get anywhere without an engine. Your financial management system is the engine that will make your car achieve peak performance.

You may be wondering what exactly is meant by the term "financial management." It is the process you use to put your numbers to work to make your business more successful. With a good financial management system, you will know not only how your business is doing financially, but why. And you will be able to use it to make decisions to improve the operation of your business.

> **tip** 
>
> How does your business measure up against others? Check out Annual Statement Studies, a massive and detailed comparison of financial data from the Risk Management Association's (RMA) member institutions. Find out more at RMA's website at rmahq.org (click on "Tools and Publications," then "Publications").

Why is financial management important? Because a good financial management system enables you to accomplish important big-picture and daily financial objectives. A good financial management system helps you become a better macromanager by enabling you to:

- Manage proactively rather than reactively
- Borrow money more easily; not only can you plan ahead for financing needs, but sharing your budget with your banker will help in the loan approval process
- Provide financial planning information for investors
- Make your operation more profitable and efficient
- Access a great decision-making tool for key financial considerations

Financial planning and control help you become a better micromanager by enabling you to:

- Avoid investing too much money in fixed assets
- Maintain short-term working-capital needs to support accounts receivable and inventory more efficiently
- Set sales goals; you need to be growth-oriented, not just an "order taker"
- Improve gross profit margin by pricing your services more effectively or by reducing supplier prices, direct labor, etc., that affect costs of goods sold
- Operate more efficiently by keeping selling and general and administrative expenses down more effectively
- Perform tax planning
- Plan ahead for employee benefits

- Perform sensitivity analysis with the different financial variables involved

Creating Financial Statements

The first step in developing a financial management system is the creation of financial statements. To manage proactively, you should plan to generate financial statements on a monthly basis. Your financial statements should include an income statement, a balance sheet, and a cash-flow statement (see pages 615, 618, and 623, respectively).

A good automated accounting software package will create monthly financial statements for you. If your bookkeeping system is manual, you can use an internal or external bookkeeper to provide you with monthly financial statements.

aha!

Many business owners make the mistake of preparing financial statements only at year-end when the IRS requires it. The consequence is reactive financial planning. If you want to be a proactive financial manager, generate monthly financial statements and use them to make the key financial decisions that affect the daily success of your business.

Income Statement

Simply put, the income statement measures all your revenue sources vs. business expenses for a given time period. Let's consider an apparel manufacturer as an example in outlining the major components of the income statement:

- *Sales*. This is the gross revenues generated from the sale of clothing less returns (cancellations) and allowances (reduction in price for discounts taken by customers).
- *Cost of goods sold*. This is the direct cost associated with manufacturing the clothing. These costs include materials used, direct labor, plant manager salaries, freight, and other costs associated with operating a plant (e.g., utilities, equipment repairs, etc.).
- *Gross profit*. The gross profit represents the amount of direct profit associated with the actual manufacturing of the clothing. It is calculated as sales less the cost of goods sold.

- *Operating expenses.* These are the selling and general and administrative expenses that are necessary to run the business. Examples include office salaries, insurance, advertising, sales commissions, and rent. (See the "Schedule of Operating Expenses" on page 616 for a more detailed list of operating expenses.)
- *Depreciation.* Depreciation expense is usually included in operating expenses and/or cost of goods sold, but it is worthy of special mention due to its unusual nature. Depreciation results when a company purchases a fixed asset and expenses it over the entire period of its planned use, not just in the year purchased. The IRS requires certain depreciation schedules to be followed for tax reasons. Depreciation is a noncash expense in that the cash flows out when the asset is purchased, but the cost is taken over a period of years depending on the type of asset.

  Whether depreciation is included in cost of goods sold or in operating expenses depends on the type of asset being depreciated. Depreciation is listed with cost of goods sold if the expense associated with the fixed asset is used in the direct production of inventory. Examples include the purchase of production equipment and machinery and a building that houses a production plant.

  Depreciation is listed with operating expenses if the cost is associated with fixed assets used for selling, general, and administrative purposes. Examples include vehicles for salespeople or an office computer and phone system.
- *Operating profit.* This is the amount of profit earned during the normal course of operations. It is computed by subtracting the operating expenses from the gross profit.
- *Other income and expenses.* Other income and expenses are those items that do not occur during the normal course of business operation. For instance, a clothing maker does not normally earn income from rental property or interest on investments, so these income sources are accounted for separately. Interest expense on

debt is also included in this category. A net figure is computed by subtracting other expenses from other income.

- *Net profit before taxes.* This figure represents the amount of income earned by the business before paying taxes. The number is computed by adding other income (or subtracting if other expenses exceed other income) to the operating profit.
- *Income taxes.* This is the total amount of state and federal income taxes paid.
- *Net profit after taxes.* This is the "bottom line" earnings of the business. It is computed by subtracting taxes paid from net income before taxes.

Income Statement

ABC Clothing Inc.

	Year 1	Year 2
Sales	$1,000,000	$1,500,000
Cost of Goods Sold	–750,000	–1,050,000
Gross Profit	250,000	450,000
Operating Expenses	–200,000	–275,000
Operating Profit	50,000	175,000
Other Income and Expenses	3,000	5,000
Net Profit Before Taxes	53,000	180,000
Income Taxes	–15,900	–54,000
Net Profit After Taxes	**$37,100**	**$126,000**

Figure 38.1. Income Statement

Schedule of Operating Expenses

ABC Clothing Inc.

	Year 1	Year 2
Advertising	$5,000	$15,000
Auto Expenses	3,000	7,500
Bank Charges	750	1,200
Depreciation	30,000	30,000
Dues & Subscriptions	500	750
Employee Benefits	5,000	10,000
Insurance	6,000	10,000
Interest	17,800	15,000
Office Expenses	2,500	4,000
Officers' Salaries	40,000	60,000
Payroll Taxes	6,000	9,000
Professional Fees	4,000	7,500
Rent	24,000	24,000
Repairs & Maintenance	2,000	2,500
Salaries & Wages	40,000	60,000
Security	2,250	2,250
Supplies	2,000	3,000
Taxes & Licenses	1,000	1,500
Telephone	4,800	6,000
Utilities	2,400	2,400
Other	1,000	3,400
Total Operating Expenses	**$200,000**	**$275,000**

Figure 38.2. Schedule of Operating Expenses

Balance Sheet

The balance sheet provides a snapshot of the business's assets, liabilities, and owner's equity for a given time. Again, using an apparel manufacturer as an example, here are the key components of the balance sheet:

- *Current assets.* These are the assets in a business that can be converted to cash in one year or less. They include cash, stocks, and other liquid investments, accounts receivable, inventory, and prepaid expenses. For a clothing manufacturer, the inventory would include raw materials (yarn, thread, etc.), work-in-progress (started but not finished), and finished goods (shirts and pants ready to sell to customers). Accounts receivable represents the amount of money owed to the business by customers who have purchased on credit.
- *Fixed assets.* These are the tangible assets of a business that will not be converted to cash within a year during the normal course of operation. Fixed assets are for long-term use and include land, buildings, leasehold improvements, equipment, machinery, and vehicles.
- *Intangible assets.* These are assets that you cannot touch or see but that have value. Intangible assets include franchise rights, goodwill, noncompete agreements, patents, and many other items.
- *Other assets.* There are many assets that can be classified as other assets, and most business balance sheets have an "other assets" category as a catchall. Some of the most common other assets include cash value of life insurance, long-term investment property, and compensation due from employees.
- *Current liabilities.* These are the obligations of the business that are due within one year. Current liabilities

> ***"Great companies are built by people who never stop thinking about ways to improve the business."***
>
> —J. Willard Marriott, founder of Marriott International Inc.

Balance Sheet

ABC Clothing Inc.

	Year 1	Year 2
Assets:		
Current Assets:		
Cash	$10,000	$20,000
Accounts Receivable	82,000	144,000
Inventory	185,000	230,000
Prepaid Expenses	5,000	5,000
Total Current Assets	282,000	399,000
Fixed Assets:		
Land	0	0
Buildings	0	0
Equipment	150,000	120,000
Accumulated Depreciation	–30,000	–30,000
Total Fixed Assets	120,000	90,000
Intangible Assets	0	0
Other Assets	10,000	11,000
Total Assets	**$532,000**	**$590,000**

Figure 38.3. Balance Sheet

include notes payable on lines of credit or other short-term loans, current maturities of long-term debt, accounts payable to trade creditors, accrued expenses and taxes (an accrual is an expense such as the payroll that is due to employees for hours worked but has not been paid), and amounts due to stockholders.

- *Long-term liabilities.* These are the obligations of the business that are not due for at least one year. Long-term liabilities typically consist of all bank debt or stockholder loans payable outside of the following 12-month period.

Balance Sheet

ABC Clothing Inc.

	Year 1	Year 2
Liabilities & Equity:		
Current Liabilities:		
Notes Payable—Short Term	60,000	42,400
Current Maturities of Long-Term Debt	30,000	30,000
Accounts Payable	82,000	86,000
Accrued Expenses	7,900	13,500
Taxes Payable	0	0
Stockholder Loans	0	0
Total Current Liabilities	179,900	171,900
Long-Term Liabilities	120,000	90,000
Total Liabilities	$299,900	$261,900
Owner's Equity:		
Common Stock	75,000	75,000
Paid-in-capital	0	0
Retained Earnings	37,100	163,100
Total Owner's Equity	112,100	238,100
Total Liabilities & Equity	**$412,000**	**$500,000**

Figure 38.3. Balance Sheet, continued

- *Owner's equity.* This figure represents the total amount invested by the stockholders plus the accumulated profit of the business. Components include common stock, paid-in-capital (amounts invested not involving a stock purchase), and retained earnings (cumulative earnings since inception of the business less dividends paid to stockholders).

>> By the Numbers

All new businesses should produce an annual year-end financial statement. This statement should be prepared by your CPA, who will offer you three basic choices of financial statement quality:

1. *Compilation*. This is the least expensive option. Here, the CPA takes management's information and compiles it into the proper financial statement format.
2. *Review*. In addition to putting management's information into the proper format, the CPA performs a limited review of the information.
3. *Audit*. This option is the most costly but offers the highest quality. Audited financial statements are prepared in accordance with generally accepted accounting principles and are the type preferred by most lenders and investors.

Cash-Flow Statement

The cash-flow statement is designed to convert the accrual basis of accounting used to prepare the income statement and balance sheet back to a cash basis. This may sound redundant, but it is necessary. The accrual basis of accounting generally is preferred for the income statement and balance sheet because it more accurately matches revenue sources to the expenses incurred generating those specific revenue sources. However, it also is important to analyze the actual level of cash flowing into and out of the business.

Like the income statement, the cash-flow statement measures financial activity over a period of time. The cash-flow statement also tracks the effects of changes in balance sheet accounts.

The cash-flow statement is one of the most useful financial management tools you will have to run your business. The cash-flow statement is divided into four categories:

1. *Net cash flow from operating activities*. Operating activities are the daily internal activities of a business that either require cash or generate it. They include cash collections from customers; cash paid to

>> Balance Boosters

A common problem for small-business owners is maintaining adequate cash-flow levels. And increasing sales is not always the answer. Here are some tips that enhance your bank balance regardless of whether or not sales are on the rise:

> *Practice good inventory management*. Don't try to be all things to all people, particularly if you are a wholesaler or retailer. Keeping slow-moving inventory in stock "just in case" costs money.

> *Concentrate on higher margin items*. Focus your efforts on selling those items that generate the most profit rather than on the items that sell the fastest.

> *Take full advantage of trade terms*. Wait until the day a bill or an invoice is due to pay it. Your cash flow will be enhanced, and your valued supplier relationships will not be harmed because you will still be paying on time.

> *Shop for lower priced suppliers*. Before you get started, check with a number of different suppliers to see which one offers the best price and terms.

> *Control operating expenses better*. Utilities expenses can be lowered by minimizing the use of electricity and by adjusting the thermostat upward or downward a few degrees during the summer and winter months. Insurance and telephone service providers should be comparison-shopped on a regular basis. Keep a close eye on employee downtime and overtime. And shop for the best lease rates.

> *Extend bank loans on longer terms*. Many banks are more than willing to extend the term on a loan to businesses in search of cash-flow relief. For instance, by extending the term on a $20,000 loan (at 9 percent interest) from two years to three, a business realizes annual cash-flow enhancement of $3,336.

suppliers and employees; cash paid for operating expenses, interest and taxes; and cash revenue from interest dividends.

2. *Net cash flow from investing activities.* Investing activities are discretionary investments made by management. These primarily consist of the purchase (or sale) of equipment.
3. *Net cash flow from financing activities.* Financing activities are those external sources and uses of cash that affect cash flow. These include sales of common stock, changes in short- or long-term loans, and dividends paid.
4. *Net change in cash and marketable securities.* The results of the first three calculations are used to determine the total change in cash and marketable securities caused by fluctuations in operating, investing, and financing cash flow. This number is then checked against the change in cash reflected on the balance sheet from period to period to verify that the calculation has been done correctly.

save

Many new business owners can't afford to seek paid professional advice. Here are three free resources for invaluable financial guidance:

1. *Your banker.* Even if you aren't borrowing money for startup, get to know a loan officer where you have your checking account. Meet periodically to discuss the financial direction of your venture.
2. *Other business owners.* Make the time to network with other small-business owners.
3. *SCORE.* This is a national volunteer organization set up for the sole purpose of helping new business owners succeed.

Cash-Flow Analysis

The cash-flow statement enables you to track cash as it flows in and out of your business and reveals to you the causes of cash-flow shortfalls and surpluses. The operating activities are the daily occurrences that are essential to any business operation. If these are positive, it indicates to the owner that the business is self-sufficient in funding its daily operational cash flow internally. If the number is negative, then it indicates that outside funds were needed to sustain the operation of the business.

Investing activities generally use cash because most businesses are more likely to acquire new equipment and machinery than to sell old fixed assets. When a company does

Cash-Flow Statement

ABC Clothing Inc.

	Year 1	Year 2
Net Cash Flow from Operating Activities:		
Cash received from customers	$918,000	$1,438,000
Interest received	3,000	5,000
Cash paid to suppliers for inventory	(853,000)	(1,091,000)
Cash paid to employees	(80,000)	(120,000)
Cash paid for other operating expenses	(69,300)	(104,400)
Interest paid	(17,800)	(15,000)
Taxes paid	(15,900)	(54,000)
Net cash provided (used) by operating activities	($115,000)	$58,600
Net Cash Flow from Investing Activities:		
Additions to property, plant, and equipment	(150,000)	0
Increase/decrease in other assets	(10,000)	(1,000)
Other investing activities	0	0
Net cash provided (used) by investing activities	($160,000)	($1,000)
Net Cash Flow From Financing Activities:		
Sales of common stock	75,000	0
Increase (decrease) in short-term loans (includes current maturities of long-term debt)	90,000	(17,600)
Additions to long-term loans	120,000	0
Reductions of long-term loans	0	(30,000)
Dividends paid	0	0
Net cash provided (used) by financing activities	$285,000	($47,600)
Net Increase (Decrease) In Cash	**$10,000**	**$10,000**

Figure 38.4. Cash-Flow Statement

need cash to fund investing activities in a given year, it must come from an internal operating cash-flow surplus, financing activity increases, or cash reserves built up in prior years.

Financing activities represent the external sources of funds available to the business. Financing activities typically will be a provider of funds when a company has shortfalls in operating or investing activities. The reverse is often true when operating activities are a source of excess cash flow, as the overflow often is used to reduce debt.

The net increase/decrease in cash figure at the bottom of the cash-flow statement represents the net result of operating, investing, and financing activities. If a business ever runs out of cash, it can't survive, so this is a key number.

Our hypothetical clothing business, ABC Clothing Inc., provides a good example. In Year 1, the growth in the business's accounts receivable and inventory required $115,000 in cash to fund operating activities. The purchase of $150,000 in equipment also drained cash flow. ABC funded these needs with the sale of common stock of $75,000 and loans totaling $210,000. The outcome was that the company increased its cash resources by $10,000.

Year 2 was a different story. Because the company had a net income of $126,000, there was a good deal more cash ($58,600) flowing in from customers than flowing out to suppliers, employees, other operating expenses, interest, and taxes. This enabled ABC to reduce its overall outside debt by $47,600 and increase its cash balance by $10,000.

When you start your business, you'll be able to use the cash-flow statement to analyze your sources and uses of cash not only from year to year, but also from month to month if you set up your accounting system to produce monthly statements. You will find the cash-flow statement to be an invaluable tool in understanding the hows and whys of cash flowing into and out of your business.

As a new business owner, you will need accurate and timely financial information to help you manage your business effectively. Your financial statements will also be critical budgeting tools as you seek to achieve financial milestones in your business.

> ***"Formula for success: Rise early, work hard, strike oil."***
>
> —J. Paul Getty, founder of The Getty Oil Company

CHAPTER

39

On the Money

Effectively Managing Your Finances

By J. Tol Broome Jr., Freelance Business Writer and Banker with 33 Years of Experience in Commercial Lending

Now that you have the framework for establishing a bookkeeping system and for creating financial statements, what's next? In this chapter, we will explore how to analyze the data that results from an effective financial management and control system. Additionally, we'll consider the key elements of a good budgeting system. The financial analysis tools we will discuss are: gross profit margin and markup, break-even, working capital, and financial ratio analyses. In the section on budgeting, we will look at when, what, and how to budget as well as how to perform a sensitivity analysis.

> ***"Success is the ability to go from one failure to another without the loss of enthusiasm."***
>
> —Winston Churchill

Gross Profit Margin and Markup

One of the most important financial concepts you will need to learn in running your new business is the computation of gross profit. And the tool that you use to maintain gross profit is markup.

The gross profit on a product sold is computed as:

Sales – Cost of Goods Sold = Gross Profit

To understand gross profit, it is important to know the distinction between variable and fixed costs. Variable costs are those that change based on the amount of product being made and are incurred as a direct result of producing the product. Variable costs include:

- Materials used
- Direct labor
- Packaging
- Freight
- Plant supervisor salaries
- Utilities for a plant or a warehouse
- Depreciation expense on production equipment and machinery

Fixed costs generally are more static in nature. They include:

- Office expenses such as supplies, utilities, a telephone for the office, etc.
- Salaries and wages of office staff, salespeople, officers, and owners
- Payroll taxes and employee benefits
- Advertising, promotional, and other sales expenses
- Insurance
- Auto expenses for salespeople
- Professional fees
- Rent

Variable expenses are recorded as cost of goods sold. Fixed expenses are counted as operating expenses (sometimes called selling and general and administrative expenses).

Gross Profit Margin

While the gross profit is a dollar amount, the gross profit margin is expressed as a percentage. It's equally important to track since it allows you to keep an eye on profitability trends. This is critical, because many businesses have gotten into financial trouble with an increasing gross profit that coincided with a declining gross profit margin. The gross profit margin is computed as follows:

Gross Profit ÷ Sales = Gross Profit Margin

There are two key ways for you to improve your gross profit margin. First, you can increase your prices. Second, you can decrease the costs to produce your goods. Of course, both are easier said than done.

An increase in prices can cause sales to drop. If sales drop too far, you may not generate enough gross profit dollars to cover operating expenses. Price increases require a very careful reading of inflation rates, competitive factors, and basic supply and demand for the product you are producing.

The second method of increasing gross profit margin is to lower the variable costs to produce your product. This can be accomplished by decreasing material costs or making the product more efficiently. Volume discounts are a good way to reduce material costs. The more material you buy from suppliers, the more likely they are to offer you discounts. Another way to reduce material costs is to find a less costly supplier. However, you might sacrifice quality if the goods purchased are not made as well.

Whether you are starting a manufacturing, wholesaling, retailing, or service business, you should always be on the lookout for ways to deliver your product or service more efficiently. However, you also must balance efficiency and quality issues to ensure that they do not get out of balance.

Let's look at the gross profit of ABC Clothing Inc. (see page 615) as an example of the computation of gross profit margin. In Year 1, the sales were $1 million and the gross profit was $250,000, resulting in a gross profit margin of 25 percent

tip

As you start your business, it will be important to track external financial trends to ensure you are headed in the right direction. It also will be critical to compare your company's performance to others in your industry. If you are a member of a trade association, the group should offer comparative industry data. Information may also be available from your CPA or banker.

($250,000/$1 million). In Year 2, sales were $1.5 million and the gross profit was $450,000, resulting in a gross profit margin of 30 percent ($450,000/$1.5 million).

It is apparent that ABC Clothing earned not only more gross profit dollars in Year 2, but also a higher gross profit margin. The company either raised prices, lowered variable material costs from suppliers, or found a way to produce its clothing more efficiently (which usually means fewer labor hours per product produced).

Computing Markup

ABC Clothing did a better job in Year 2 of managing its markup on the clothing products that they manufactured. Many business owners often get confused when relating markup to gross profit margin. They are first cousins in that both computations deal with the same variables. The difference is that gross profit margin is figured as a percentage of the selling price, while markup is figured as a percentage of the seller's cost.

Markup is computed as follows:

(Selling Price – Cost to Produce) ÷ Cost to Produce = Markup Percentage

Let's compute markup for ABC Clothing for Year 1:

($1 million – $750,000) ÷ $750,000 = 33.3%

Now, let's compute markup for ABC Clothing for Year 2:

($1.5 million – $1.05 million) ÷ $1.05 million = 42.9%

While computing markup for an entire year for a business is very simple, using this valuable markup tool daily to work up price quotes is more complicated. However, it is even more vital. Computing markup on last year's numbers helps you understand where you've been and gives you a benchmark for success. But computing markup on individual jobs will affect your business going forward and can often make the difference in running a profitable operation.

In bidding individual jobs, you must carefully estimate the variable costs associated with each job. And the calculation is different in that you typically seek a desired markup with a known cost to arrive at the price quote. Here is the computation to find a price quote using markup:

(Desired Markup x Total Variable Costs) + Total Variable Costs = Price Quote

Let's again use ABC Clothing as an example. ABC has been asked to quote on a job to produce 100 dozen shirts. Based on prior experience, the owner estimates that the job will require 100 labor hours of direct labor and five hours of supervision from the plant manager. The total material costs based on quotes from suppliers (fabric, sewing thread, buttons, etc.) will be $40 per dozen. If ABC Clothing seeks a markup of 42.9 percent on all orders in Year 2, it would use a markup table (like the one on page 630) to calculate the price quote.

aha!

When you set up your computerized bookkeeping system to create automatic monthly financial statements, make sure you also automate your business's financial ratios. There's no sense in having to compute them manually when the information is available on your PC. Reviewing financial ratios monthly will help you keep an eye on your business's financial trends.

What if you are a new business owner and don't have any experience to base an estimate on? Then you will need to research material costs by getting quotes from suppliers as well as study the labor rates in the area. You should also research industry manufacturing prices. Armed with this information, you will have a well-educated "guess" to base your job quote on.

How you use markup to set prices will depend on the type of business you are starting. If you are launching a manufacturing, wholesale, or retail operation, you will be able to compute markup using the aforementioned formulas to factor in all the variables in the cost of producing or generating the items you will be selling. Markup can also be used to bid one job or to set prices for an entire product line.

If you are starting a service business, however, markup is more difficult to calculate, particularly for new business owners. With most service businesses, the key variable cost associated with delivering the service to your customers will be you and your employees' time. In computing proper markup for a service business, you must pay close

Markup Computation for ABC Clothing

Price Quote

	Hours/ Dozen	Cost/ Hour	Cost/ Dozen	No. of Dozens	Total Cost
Labor	1.00	$7.00		100	$700.00
Supervision	0.05	$20.00		100	$100.00
Total Labor Cost					$800.00
Fabric		$35.00		100	$3,500.00
Sewing Thread		$2.50		100	$250.00
Buttons		$2.50		100	$250.00
Total Materials Cost		**$40.00**		**100**	**$4,000.00**
Total Labor & Materials Costs					**$4,800.00**
Desired Markup					0.429
Price Quote to Customer					**$6,859.20**

Figure 39.1. Markup Computation for ABC Clothing

attention to the time spent to provide the service to customers, as well as to market prices of the services provided. In starting a service business, you will need to research the going rate paid to employees and the market prices for the services you will be providing.

For instance, if you are starting a staffing service, you will need to know what rate is typically paid to employees in this industry as well as the market rate charged to your customers for temporary labor. This will

warning

You must include break-even analyses as part of your pricing policy to ensure you're making money on every unit you sell and that you're able to be profitable based on your costs and sales. If you're not profitable, you won't stay in business. It's as simple as that.

Price Quote Worksheet for a Service Business

	Hours/ Unit	Cost/ Hour	Cost/ Unit	No. of Units	Total Cost
Labor #1		$			$
Labor #2		$			$
Supervision		$			$
Total Labor Cost[1]					$
Other Variable Costs					$
Total Labor & Other Variable Costs[2]					$
Desired Markup[3]					%
Price Quote to Customer[4]					**$**

1. Depending on the type of service business, there may be many more labor contributions. All should be considered.
2. Derived by adding together Total Labor Cost & Other Variable Costs
3. Stated as a percentage markup on the costs to provide the service. In most service businesses, this will range from 25% (0.25) to 100% (1.0).
4. Price Quote computed as follows:

Total Labor Cost + Other Variable Costs +

([Total Labor Cost + Other Variable Costs] x Desired Markup)

Figure 39.2. Price Quote Worksheet for a Service Business

enable you to compute the proper markup in setting your price to ensure that you will be profitable.

(See the "Markup Computation" chart on page 630 for how the price quote was calculated for ABC Clothing, and use the worksheets above and on page 632 to come up with quotes for your own business.)

Price Quote Worksheet for a Nonservice Business

	Hours/ Unit	Cost/ Hour	Cost/ Unit	No. of Units	Total Cost
Labor #1		$			$
Supervision		$			$
Total Labor Cost[1]					$
Materials Item #1			$		$
Materials Item #2			$		$
Materials Item #3			$		$
Total Materials Cost[2]					$
Other Variable Production Costs					$
Total Labor, Materials, & Other Variable Production Costs[3]					$
Desired Markup[4]					%
Price Quote to Customer[5]					**$**

1. Depending on the type of company, there may be many more labor contributions. All should be considered.
2. Depending on the type of company, there may be many types of materials used to produce a product. All should be considered.
3. Derived by adding together Total Labor Cost, Total Materials Cost & Other Variable Production Costs
4. Stated as a percentage markup on production costs. In some businesses, this may be as low as 5% (.05); in others it might be 100% (1.0) or higher.
5. Price Quote computed as follows:

Total Labor Cost + Total Materials Costs + Other Variable Production Costs + ([Total Labor Cost + Total Materials Costs + Other Variable Production Costs] x Desired Markup)

Figure 39.3. Price Quote Worksheet for a Nonservice Business

Break-Even Analysis

One useful tool in tracking your business's cash flow will be the break-even analysis. It is a fairly simple calculation and can prove very helpful in deciding whether to make an equipment purchase or in knowing how close you are to your break-even level. Here are the variables needed to compute a break-even sales analysis:

- Gross profit margin
- Operating expenses (less depreciation)
- Total of monthly debt payments for the year (annual debt service)

Since we are dealing with cash flow, and depreciation is a noncash expense, it is subtracted from the operating expenses. The break-even calculation for sales is:

(Operating Expenses + Annual Debt Service) ÷
Gross Profit Margin = Break-Even Sales

Let's use ABC Clothing as an example and compute this company's break-even sales for Years 1 and 2:

	Year 1	Year 2
Gross Profit Margin	25.0%	30.0%
Operating Expenses (less depreciation)	$170,000	$245,000
Annual Current Maturities of Long-Term Debt*	$30,000	$30,000

*This represents the principal portion of annual debt service; the interest portion of annual debt service is already included in operating expenses.

Break-Even Sales for Year 1:

($170,000 + $30,000) ÷ .25 = $800,000

Break-Even Sales for Year 2:

($245,000 + $30,000) ÷ .30 = $916,667

It is apparent from these calculations that ABC Clothing was well ahead of break-even sales both in Year 1 ($1 million in sales) and Year 2 ($1.5 million).

Break-even analysis also can be used to calculate break-even sales needed for the other variables in the equation. Let's say the owner of ABC

Clothing was confident he or she could generate sales of $750,000, and the company's operating expenses are $170,000 with $30,000 in annual current maturities of long-term debt. The break-even gross margin needed would be calculated as follows:

($170,000 + $30,000) ÷ $750,000 = 26.7%

Now let's use ABC Clothing to determine the break-even operating expenses. If we know that the gross margin is 25 percent, the sales are $750,000, and the current maturities of long-term debt are $30,000, we can calculate the break-even operating expenses as follows:

(.25 x $750,000) – $30,000 = $157,500

Working Capital Analysis

Working capital is one of the most difficult financial concepts for the small-business owner to understand. In fact, the term means a lot of different things to a lot of different people. By definition, working capital is the amount by which current assets exceed current liabilities. However, if you simply run this calculation each period to try to analyze working capital, you won't accomplish much in figuring out what your working capital needs are and how to meet them.

A more useful tool for determining your working capital needs is the operating cycle. The operating cycle analyzes the accounts receivable, inventory, and accounts payable cycles in terms of days. In other words, accounts receivable are analyzed by the average number of days it takes to collect an account. Inventory is analyzed by the average number of days it takes to turn over the sale of a product (from the point it comes in your door to the point it is converted to cash or an account receivable). Accounts payable are analyzed by the average number of days it takes to pay a supplier invoice.

Most businesses cannot finance the operating cycle (accounts receivable days + inventory days) with accounts payable financing alone. Consequently, working capital financing is needed. This shortfall is typically covered by the net profits generated internally or by externally borrowed funds or by a combination of the two.

Most businesses need short-term working capital at some point in their operations. For instance, retailers must find working capital to fund seasonal inventory buildup between September and November for Christmas sales. But even a business that is not seasonal occasionally experiences peak months when orders are unusually high. This creates a need for working capital to fund the resulting inventory and accounts receivable buildup.

Some small businesses have enough cash reserves to fund seasonal working capital needs. However, this is very rare for a new business. If your new venture experiences a need for short-term working capital during its first few years of operation, you will have several potential sources of funding. The important thing is to plan ahead. If you get caught off guard, you might miss out on the one big order that could put your business over the hump.

Here are the five most common sources of short-term working capital financing:

1. *Equity.* If your business is in its first year of operation and has not yet become profitable, then you might have to rely on equity funds for short-term working capital needs. These funds might be injected from your own personal resources or from a family member, a friend, or a third-party investor.
2. *Trade creditors.* If you have a particularly good relationship established with your trade creditors, you might be able to solicit their help in providing short-term working capital. If you have paid on time in the past, a trade creditor may be willing to extend terms to enable you to meet a big order. For instance, if you receive a big order that you can fulfill, ship out, and collect in 60 days, you could obtain 60-day terms from your supplier if 30-day terms are normally given. The trade creditor will want proof of the order and may want to file a lien on it as security, but if it enables you to proceed, that should not be a problem.

tip

If you decide to hire a factoring company, you could Google "Factoring" to start your search, but a safer bet is to call your bank for a recommendation. You might also want to seek recommendations from your industry's trade associations or local business chamber of commerce.

3. *Factoring.* Factoring is another resource for short-term working capital financing. Once you have filled an order, a factoring company buys your account receivable and then handles the collection. This type of financing is more expensive than conventional bank financing but is often used by new businesses.
4. *Line of credit.* Lines of credit are not often given by banks to new businesses. However, if your new business is well-capitalized by equity and you have good collateral, your business might qualify for one. A line of credit allows you to borrow funds for short-term needs when they arise. The funds are repaid once you collect the accounts receivable that resulted from the short-term sales peak. Lines of credit typically are made for one year at a time and are expected to be paid off for 30 to 60 consecutive days sometime during the year to ensure that the funds are used for short-term needs only.
5. *Short-term loan.* While your new business may not qualify for a line of credit from a bank, you might have success in obtaining a one-time short-term loan (less than a year) to finance your temporary working capital needs. If you have established a good banking relationship with a banker, he or she might be willing to provide a short-term note for one order or for a seasonal inventory and/or accounts receivable buildup.

In addition to analyzing the average number of days it takes to make a product (inventory days) and collect on an account (accounts receivable days) vs. the number of days financed by accounts payable, the operating cycle analysis provides one other important analysis.

From the operating cycle, a computation can be made of the dollars required to support one day of accounts receivable and inventory, and the dollars provided by a day of accounts payable. Let's consider ABC Clothing's operating cycle (see page 637). Had the company maintained accounts receivable at Year 1 levels in Year 2, it would have freed up $20,550 in cash flow ($4,110 x 5 days). Likewise, the ten-day improvement in inventory management in Year 2 enhanced cash flow by $28,770 ($2,877 x 10 days).

You can see that working capital has a direct impact on cash flow in a business. Since cash flow is the name of the game for all business owners,

Operating Cycle

ABC Clothing Inc.

	Year 1	Year 2
Accounts Receivable Days	30	35
Inventory Days	90	80
Operating Cycle	120	115
Accounts Payable Days	–32	–29
Days to Be Financed	88	86
Purchases	$935,000	$1,095,000
$ Per Day Accounts Receivable	$2,740	$4,110
$ Per Day Inventory	$2,055	$2,877
$ Per Day Accounts Payable	$2,562	$3,000

Calculations are as follows:

Accounts Receivable Days = (Accounts Receivable x 365) ÷ Sales

Inventory Days = (Inventory x 365) ÷ Cost of Goods Sold

Accounts Payable Days = (Accounts Payable x 365) ÷ Purchases

Purchases = Cost of Goods Sold + Ending Inventory – Beginning Inventory

$ Per Day Accounts Receivable = 1 ÷ 365 x Sales

$ Per Day Inventory = 1 ÷ 365 x Cost of Goods Sold

$ Per Day Accounts Payable = 1 ÷ 365 x Purchases

Figure 39.4. Operating Cycle

a good understanding of working capital is imperative to making any venture successful.

Building a Financial Budget

For many small-business owners, the process of budgeting is limited to figuring out where to get the cash to meet next week's payroll. There are so many financial fires to put out in a given week that it's hard to find the time to do any short- or long-range financial planning. But failing to plan financially might mean that you are unknowingly planning to fail.

Business budgeting is one of the most powerful financial tools available to any small-business owner. Put simply, maintaining a good short- and long-range financial plan enables you to control your cash flow instead of having it control you.

Operating Cycle Worksheet

	Year 1	Year 2
Accounts Receivable Days		
Inventory Days		
Operating Cycle		
Accounts Payable Days		
Days to Be Financed		
Purchases	$	$
$ Per Day Accounts Receivable	$	$
$ Per Day Inventory	$	$
$ Per Day Accounts Payable	$	$

Calculations are as follows:

Accounts Receivable Days = (Accounts Receivable x 365) ÷ Sales

Inventory Days = (Inventory x 365) ÷ Cost of Goods Sold

Accounts Payable Days = (Accounts Payable x 365) ÷ Purchases

Purchases = Cost of Goods Sold + Ending Inventory – Beginning Inventory

$ Per Day Accounts Receivable = 1 ÷ 365 x Sales

$ Per Day Inventory = 1 ÷ 365 x Cost of Goods Sold

$ Per Day Accounts Payable = 1 ÷ 365 x Purchases

Figure 39.5. Operating Cycle Worksheet

The most effective financial budget includes both a short-range month-to-month plan for at least a calendar year and a long-range quarter-to-quarter plan you use for financial statement reporting. It should be prepared during the two months preceding the fiscal year-end to allow ample time for sufficient information-gathering.

tip

Everything's rosy, huh? Business owners tend to overestimate their income and underestimate expenses. So when preparing your budget, it's always a good idea to have an objective third party review your information to make sure you're being realistic.

The long-range plan should cover a period of at least three years (some go up to five years) on a quarterly basis, or even an annual basis. The long-term budget should be updated when the short-range plan is prepared.

While some owners prefer to leave the one-year budget unchanged for the year for which it provides projections, others adjust the budget during the year based on certain financial occurrences, such as an unplanned equipment purchase or a larger-than-expected upward sales trend. Using the budget as an ongoing planning tool during a given year certainly is recommended. However, here is a word to the wise: Financial budgeting is vital, but it is important to avoid getting so caught up in the budget process that you forget to keep doing business.

What Do You Budget?

Many financial budgets provide a plan only for the income statement; however, it is important to budget both the income statement and balance sheet. This enables you to consider potential cash-flow needs for your entire operation, not just as they pertain to income and expenses. For instance, if you had already been in business for a couple of years and were adding a new product line, you would need to consider the impact of inventory purchases on cash flow.

Budgeting only the income statement also doesn't allow a full analysis of the effect of potential capital expenditures on your financial picture. For instance, if you are planning to purchase real estate for your operation, you need to budget the effect the debt service will have on cash flow. In the future, a budget can also help you determine the potential effects of expanding your facilities and the resulting higher rent payments or debt service.

How Do You Budget?

In the startup phase, you will have to make reasonable assumptions about your business in establishing your budget. You will need to ask questions such as:

- How much can be sold in Year 1?
- How much will sales grow in the following years?
- How will the products and/or services you are selling be priced?
- How much will it cost to produce your product? How much inventory will you need?
- What will your operating expenses be?
- How many employees will you need? How much will you pay them? How much will you pay yourself? What benefits will you offer? What will your payroll and unemployment taxes be?
- What will the income tax rate be? Will your business be an S corporation or a C corporation?
- What will your facilities needs be? How much will it cost you in rent or debt service for these facilities?
- What equipment will be needed to start the business? How much will it cost? Will there be additional equipment needs in subsequent years?
- What payment terms will you offer customers if you sell on credit? What payment terms will your suppliers give you?
- How much will you need to borrow?
- What will the collateral be? What will the interest rate be?

> **tip** 
>
> Budgeting shouldn't be approached as something to do when you have time but instead as a priority and part of your overall business financial management plan. Breaking your budget into monthly increments eases the process, making it less overwhelming. Make some general financial goals for the year, then determine how you can achieve them through a monthly budget.

As for the actual preparation of the budget, you can create it manually or with the budgeting function that comes with most bookkeeping

>> How Do You Rate?

Ratio analysis is a financial management tool that enables you to compare the trends in your financial performance as well as provides some measurements to compare your performance against others in your industry. Comparing ratios from year to year highlights areas in which you are performing well and areas that need tweaking. Most industry trade groups can provide you with industry averages for key ratios that will provide a benchmark against which you can compare your company.

Financial ratios can be divided into four subcategories: profitability, liquidity, activity, and leverage. Here are 15 financial ratios that you can use to manage your new business. (See page 643 for sample financial ratios for ABC Clothing Inc.)

Profitability Ratios

Gross Profit ÷ Sales = Gross Profit Margin

Operating Profit ÷ Sales = Operating Profit Margin

Net Profit ÷ Sales = Net Profit Margin

Net Profit ÷ Owner's Equity = Return on Equity

Net Profit ÷ Total Assets = Return on Assets

Liquidity Ratios

Current Assets ÷ Current Liabilities = Current Ratio

(Current Assets – Inventory) ÷ Current Liabilities = Quick Ratio

Working Capital ÷ Sales = Working Capital Ratio

Activity Ratios

(Accounts Receivable x 365) ÷ Sales = Accounts Receivable Days

(Inventory x 365) ÷ Cost of Goods Sold = Inventory Days

>> How Do You Rate?, continued

(Accounts Payable x 365) ÷ Purchases = Accounts Payable Days

Sales ÷ Total Assets = Sales to Assets

Leverage Ratios

Total Liabilities ÷ Owner's Equity = Debt to Equity

Total Liabilities ÷ Total Assets = Debt Ratio

(Net Income + Depreciation) ÷ Current Maturities of Long-Term Debt = Debt Coverage Ratio

software packages. You can also purchase separate budgeting software such as Quicken or Microsoft Money. Yes, this seems like a lot of information to forecast. But it's not as cumbersome as it looks. (See page 647 for a financial budget and income statement worksheet; you should find a similar format in any budgeting software.)

The first step is to set up a plan for the following year on a month-to-month basis. Starting with the first month, establish specific budgeted dollar levels for each category of the budget. The sales numbers will be critical since they will be used to compute gross profit margin and will help determine operating expenses, as well as the accounts receivable and inventory levels necessary to support the business. In determining how much of your product or service you can sell, study the market in which you will operate, your competition, potential demand that you might already have seen, and economic conditions. For cost of goods sold, you will need to calculate the actual costs associated with producing each item on a percentage basis.

For your operating expenses, consider items such as advertising, auto, depreciation, insurance, etc. Then factor in a tax rate based on actual business tax rates that you can obtain from your accountant.

On the balance sheet, break down inventory by category. For instance, a clothing manufacturer has raw materials, work-in-progress, and finished goods. For inventory, accounts receivable, and accounts payable, you will

Comparative Financial Ratios

ABC Clothing Inc.

	Year 1	Year 2
Profitability Ratios:		
Gross Profit Margin	25.0%	30.0%
Operating Profit Margin	5.0%	11.7%
Net Profit Margin	3.7%	8.4%
Return on Equity	33.1%	52.9%
Return on Assets	9.0%	25.2%
Liquidity Ratios:		
Current Ratio	1.57	2.32
Quick Ratio	0.54	0.98
Working Capital Ratio	0.10	0.15
Activity Ratios:		
Accounts Receivable Days	30	35
Inventory Days	90	85
Accounts Payable Days	32	29
Sales to Assets	2.43	3.00
Leverage Ratios:		
Debt to Equity	2.68	1.10
Debt Ratio	0.73	0.52
Debt Coverage Ratio	2.24	5.20

Figure 39.6. Comparative Financial Ratios

>> Smarter to Barter?

Remember how pioneers would trade a deer skin for a musket? It was called bartering. Today, the concept is back in a big way—especially online. The companies are everywhere on the net: itex.com, bbubarter.com, u-exchange.com.

The barter industry is growing rapidly, with barter sales increasing from $40 million in 1991 to more than $20 billion in 2000. The International Reciprocal Trade Association reports that approximately $16 billion in transactions were conducted in North America in 2008, while the U.S. Department of Commerce estimates that 30 percent of worldwide commerce is bartered. Bartering can be an invaluable tool for a startup company.

Bartering can be good for your business in good times, but it can be even better in bad, and, let's face facts, most startups have their share of downtimes. The main advantage to going the barter route is that if you have unwanted inventory, you can use it to trade rather than spend money you don't have and pile more onto your already stretched-too-thin budget.

Here's how bartering works: Let's say a landscaper needs a root canal. The landscaper belongs to a bartering organization and learns that a local dentist is also part of the same organization. But it turns out the dentist doesn't need any landscaping done. OK, fine. So the landscaper instead does work for a small public relations firm and a restaurant management consultant. For that work, he has been banking "bartering dollars," enough to pay for other members' services, like a dentist, who will then use those bartering dollars to get something from another member. Meanwhile, to belong to a bartering organization, you're paying a monthly membership fee of $10 to $30.

Who determines what each service or product is worth? You pay the fair market value, which is determined by buyer and seller. But beware: There are some dishonest barterers out there who will charge higher prices to members or not give a service or product that was part of a deal. You need to keep track of bartering purchases and provide clients with Form 1099-B so you can file it on your taxes.

figure the total amounts based on a projected number of days on hand. (See page 638 for the calculations needed to compute these three key numbers for your budget.)

Consider each specific item in fixed assets broken out for real estate, equipment, investments, etc. If your new business requires a franchise fee or copyrights or patents, this will be reflected as an intangible asset.

On the liability side, break down each bank loan separately. Do the same for the stockholders' equity—common stock, preferred stock, paid-in-capital, treasury stock, and retained earnings.

Do this for each month for the first 12 months. Then prepare the quarter-to-quarter budgets for Years 2 and 3. For the first year's budget,

>> Where Credit Is Due

When you book a credit sale in your business, you must collect from the customer to realize your profit. Many a solid business has suffered a severe setback or even been put under by its failure to collect accounts receivable.

It is vital that you stay on top of your A/R if you sell on credit. Here are some tips that will help you maintain high-quality accounts receivable:

- *Check out references upfront.* Find out how your prospective customer has paid other suppliers before selling on credit. Ask for supplier and bank references and follow up on them.
- *Set credit limits, and monitor them.* Establish credit limits for each customer. Set up a system to regularly compare balances owed and credit limits.
- *Process invoices immediately.* Send out invoices as soon as goods are shipped. Falling behind on sending invoices will result in slower collection of accounts receivable, which costs you cash flow.
- *Don't resell to habitually slow-paying accounts.* If you find that a certain customer stays way behind in payment to you, stop selling to that company. Habitual slow pay is a sign of financial instability, and you can ill afford to write off an account.

you will want to consider seasonality factors. For example, most retailers experience heavy sales from October to December. If your business will be highly seasonal, you will have wide-ranging changes in cash-flow needs. For this reason, you will want to consider seasonality in the budget rather than take your annual projected Year 1 sales level and divide by 12.

As for the process, you need to prepare the income statement budgets first, then balance sheet, then cash flow. You will need to know the net income figure before you can prepare a pro forma balance sheet, because the profit number must be plugged into retained earnings. And for the cash-flow projection, you will need both income statement and balance sheet numbers.

Whether you budget manually or use software, it is advisable to seek input from your CPA in preparing your initial budget. His or her role will depend on the internal resources available to you and your background in finance. You may want to hire a CPA to prepare the financial plan for you, or you may simply involve him or her in an advisory role. Regardless of the level of involvement, your CPA's input will prove invaluable in providing an independent review of your short- and long-term financial plan.

In future years, your monthly financial statements and accountant-prepared year-end statements will be very useful in preparing a budget.

Sensitivity Analysis

One other major benefit of maintaining a financial budget is the ability to perform a sensitivity analysis. Once you have a plan in place, you can make adjustments to it to consider the potential effects of certain variables on your operation. All you have to do is plug in the change and see how it affects your company's financial performance.

Here's how it works: Let's say you've budgeted a 10 percent sales growth for the coming year. You can easily adjust the sales growth number to 5 percent or 15 percent in the budget to see how it affects your business's performance. You can perform a sensitivity analysis for any other financial variable as well. The most common items for which sensitivity analysis is done are:

Financial Budget and Income Statement Worksheet

	Month 1	Month 2	Month 3	Month 4	Month 5	Month 6	Month 7	Month 8	Month 9	Month 10	Month 11	Month 12	Total
Sales													
Cost of Goods Sold													
Gross Profit													
Operating Expenses:													
Advertising													
Amortization													
Auto Expenses													
Bank Charges													
Depreciation													
Dues & Subscriptions													
Employee Benefits													
Insurance													
Interest													
Office Expenses													
Officers' Salaries													
Payroll Taxes													
Professional Fees													
Rent													
Repairs & Maintenance													
Salaries & Wages													
Security													
Supplies													
Taxes & Licenses													
Telephone													
Utilities													
Other													
Total Operating Expenses													
Net Profit before Taxes													
Income Taxes													
Net Profit after Taxes													

Figure 39.7. Financial Budget and Income Statement Worksheet

Balance Sheet Worksheet

	Month 1	Month 2	Month 3	Month 4	Month 5	Month 6	Month 7	Month 8	Month 9	Month 10	Month 11	Month 12	Total Year 1
Assets:													
Cash													
Investments													
Accounts Receivable													
Inventory													
Prepaid Expenses													
Other Current Assets													
Land													
Buildings													
Equipment													
Less: Accumulated Depreciation													
Long-Term Investments													
Intangibles													
Other Assets													
Total Assets													
Liabilities & Equity:													
Notes Payable—Short Term													
Current Maturities of Long-Term Debt													
Accounts Payable													
Accrued Expenses													
Taxes Payable													
Stockholder Loans													
Other Current Liabilities													
Bonds Payable													
Long-Term Debt													
Common Stock													
Paid-in-capital													
Treasury Stock													
Retained Earnings													
Total Liabilities & Equity													

Figure 39.8. Balance Sheet Worksheet

Cash-Flow Worksheet

	Month 1	Month 2	Month 3	Month 4	Month 5	Month 6	Month 7	Month 8	Month 9	Month 10	Month 11	Month 12	Total Year 1
Cash Available:													
Net Income after Taxes													
Depreciation													
Amortization													
Decrease in A/R													
Decrease in Inventory													
Increase in Accounts Payable													
Increase in Notes Payable-ST													
Increase in Long-Term Debt													
Decrease in Other Assets													
Increase in Other Liabilities													
Total Cash Available													
Cash Disbursements:													
Owners' Draw/Dividends													
Increase in A/R													
Increase in Inventory													
Decrease in Accounts Payable													
Capital Expenditures													
Decrease in Notes Payable-ST													
Current Maturities of Long-Term Debt													
Increase in Other Assets													
Decrease in Other Liabilities													
Total Cash Disbursements													
Monthly Cash Flow													
Cumulative Cash Flow													

Figure 39.9. Cash Flow Worksheet

- Sales
- Cost of goods sold and gross profit
- Operating expenses
- Interest rates
- Accounts receivable days
- Inventory days
- Accounts payable days on hand
- Major fixed-asset purchases or reductions
- Acquisitions or closings

CHAPTER

40

Pay Day

How to Pay Yourself

It's your business and your budget—which means the size of your paycheck is entirely up to you. But while the freedom of setting your own salary sounds great in theory, in practice most business owners find it a tough call. Should you pay yourself what you need to cover expenses? What your business can afford? The salary you left behind to launch your business?

Your best bet is to factor in all three—and a whole lot more. Obviously, you want your business to succeed and may be willing to accept a temporary drop in income to make that happen. On the other hand, paying yourself far less than you're worth, or nothing at all, paints an unrealistic picture of the viability of your business for both you and any investors you hope to appeal to now or in the future.

What You Need

Your salary needs will depend on your living expenses, financial situation, and comfort level with drawing on personal savings. The first step in planning your pay is to put together a comprehensive list of your expenses. Be sure to include all annual, quarterly, and monthly expenses, including your rent or mortgage; car payments, car insurance and gasoline bills; credit cards with outstanding balances; gym membership; grocery bills; and everything else you'll spend money on in the coming year. Underestimating personal expenses is one of the biggest mistakes a new business owner can make. If you slip into the red, chances are your business will, too.

aha!

Talk to your accountant about whether a deferred salary— setting a salary but not collecting it until your company becomes profitable—is an option for your company. The salary becomes a liability for the company, offsetting taxable future profits, which you'll get back with interest when revenue comes in.

When you've computed your annual personal expenses, divide by 12 to come up with the monthly salary you'll need to receive to keep from dipping into your savings. Next, decide what portion of your savings you'll feel comfortable drawing on during the early stages of your company—these must be savings separate from the funds you'll use to launch your business. If you plan to keep your job, add your annual salary to the personal savings figure. Subtract this number from your total annual personal expenses, and divide by 12. This gives you the minimum monthly salary you'll need, even if you choose to supplement your startup salary with personal savings or employment income. Now you have a range that runs from the minimum salary needed to cover all your personal expenses to the bare minimum salary you can afford to take by supplementing your income—your minimum salary range.

There are two equally valid methods for computing your market worth:

1. *Open market value.* Given your experience and skills, what would you be paid by an employer in today's market? While this salary

>> Taxing Matters

Tax ramifications are another factor to keep in mind when deciding what to pay yourself and how to structure your compensation. Your tax situation was determined when you chose a business structure (see Chapter 9).

If you're a sole proprietor, for instance, the IRS considers you and your company to be a single entity. Profits from your business are funneled directly onto your tax return as taxable personal income, whether you draw them out as a salary or leave them in your business account as cash holdings. Similarly, partnership profits flow directly through to the partners, who report their share of the business's profits or losses on their tax returns—again, whether the profits are left in the business or drawn out as compensation. In both cases, profits retained in the business and later withdrawn by a sole proprietor or partner in subsequent tax years are not taxed again. However, sole proprietors and partners are liable for self-employment tax, which runs at more than 15 percent.

On the other hand, if you form a corporation, your business is a separate legal entity and must file its own return and pay taxes on any profits earned. On the plus side, since the IRS views you and any other owners of the business as employees, any salary you draw is considered a deductible expense.

Corporations also have the option of distributing profits in the form of dividends, typically as cash or company stock. But dividends distributed to shareholders are taxed twice—once as corporate profit and again as income for the recipient—so salaried compensation is a far more tax-efficient way of taking profits from your business. However, the IRS is all too aware of the incentive to distribute profits as salaries and requires that executive salaries be "reasonable." The IRS prohibits salary deductions it identifies as being "disguised dividends" and assesses hefty penalties for the transgression. Since the tax code doesn't provide a clear definition of reasonable compensation, it's wise to check with your tax advisor to ensure your salary is in line with the company's revenues and expenses or with those at comparative companies.

won't take into account the additional time you'll put into a start-up, the income you're sacrificing to start your business is a useful benchmark in setting your salary.

2. *Comparable companies.* What do the owners of similarly sized firms in the same industry and geographic region pay themselves? To get comparable salaries, check with trade associations, other entrepreneurs in your industry, or the local Small Business Development Center.

Neither of these methods takes into account the additional work you'll be taking on as an owner, nor the risk you're taking in starting a business. Some entrepreneurs boost market-worth-based salaries by 3 to 5 percent to offset the added responsibilities and risk. Others look at the potential long-term advantage of owning a successful business as compensation for these factors.

What Your Business Can Afford

Once you know the salary you need and the salary you deserve, it's time to balance those figures against your business's finances. You'll need to check the cash-flow projection in your business plan to ensure that you have enough money coming in to cover your own draw in addition to your other operating expenses. In an ideal scenario, your cash flow will have a surplus large enough to pay your market-worth salary, reinvest funds in the business, and leave a little margin for error. Unfortunately, that's unlikely. Since most startups initially operate at a loss—generally for at least six months and possibly for as long as two years—you should plan to start with compensation within the minimum salary range. You can ratchet up toward a market-worth salary as your business reaches a break-even point and continues to grow.

warning

Before you boost your compensation, check your balance sheet to ensure that the increase in the rest of your overhead hasn't outpaced the bump in revenue. A bump beyond inflation—such as an office rent hike or new hire—may require adjusting your plans for a salary boost.

> **tip** 
>
> Planning to take no salary and funnel your profits back into your business? Before you go that route, be sure to take retirement planning into account. The amount you can contribute to an IRA, Keogh, or other qualified retirement plan is based on a percentage of eligible compensation. Without earnings, you won't be able to fund your retirement with pretax dollars.

Because your business income may ebb and flow initially, a base salary with a bonus structure that kicks in when your business reaches the break-even point is usually the best way to handle owner's compensation in an early-stage company. You might, for example, decide that when your business moves into the black, you'll take a percentage of profits every fiscal quarter as a bonus. Bonus percentages range widely, depending on an owner's goals for the business, personal financial needs, and philosophy on reinvesting business earnings. But while your aim may be to reach your market-worth salary rapidly, it's a good idea to leave some profits in your business as a safety net and to fund future growth.

When the business reaches a point of consistent profitability, it's time to re-evaluate your salary. Typically, this means taking a salary increase equal in percentage to the business's annual growth rate, then reinvesting the remaining profit in your business. But as with your bonus structure, there is no silver bullet equation for determining the appropriate salary hike. You'll want to factor in the nature of your industry and your business goals. For example, if you're in a turbulent or cyclical industry, you may want to retain the quarterly bonus structure and the flexibility it affords. Or, if your business has the potential for rapid growth, you may want to forego the salary boost and use the extra capital to fund new products, expansion plans, or marketing initiatives.

Whatever you decide in the early phase of your business, plan to reassess your compensation every six months. As your business evolves, its cash-flow model and capital needs may change dramatically—as may your own. A regular assessment enables you to adjust accordingly.

Minimum Salary Range Worksheet

To determine your minimum salary range, you need to consider your annual living expenses, personal savings, and any income you'll have during the startup phase of your business. You may need to add additional expense categories, but the worksheet below offers a starting point.

	Annual Expenses
1. Rent/mortgage	
2. Health insurance	
3. Car payment	
4. Other transportation	
5. Car insurance	
6. Recreation activities (includes gym/club dues/ restaurants)	
7. Food	
8. Utilities	
9. Misc. living expenses	
10. Credit card payments	
11. Child care	
12. Entertainment	
13. Other expenses	
14. Total Annual Expenses	
15. Portion of personal savings allocated to startup costs	
16. Salary or other ongoing income	
17. Sum of lines 15 and 16	
18. Subtract line 17 from line 14 for Bare Minimum Annual Salary	
19. Divide line 18 by 12 for Bare Minimum Monthly Salary	
20. Total from line 14: Minimum Annual Salary	
21. Divide line 20 by 12: Minimum Monthly Salary	

Lines 19 and 21 represent your Minimum Monthly Salary Range

Figure 40.1. Minimum Salary Range Worksheet

>> Added Value

Salaries, bonuses, and dividends aside, here are some other ways to get value from your business:

- *Hire family members*. Hiring your spouse, son, or daughter to work for you can help you keep money in the family. The caveat? The family member must actually perform work for your company, not just collect a paycheck.
- *Pick up perks*. Country club memberships, company cars, travel, and other attractive perquisites are among tax-deductible expenses business owners can write off—provided they have a legitimate business purpose. If you're caught disguising personal expenses as business ones, you'll incur hefty IRS penalties, so check in with your accountant first.
- *Be a borrower*. You can take loans from your company, as long as it's documented in writing, includes interest at market rate, and is tied to a repayment schedule.

CHAPTER

41

Tax Talk

What You Need to Know About Your Taxes

By Joan Szabo, Freelance Writer on Tax Issues for More than 30 Years

When it comes to taxes, there's no way to get around the fact that you have to pay them regularly. Federal, state, and local taxes combined can take a big chunk out of your company's money, leaving you with less cash to operate your business.

That's why it's important to stay abreast of your business's tax situation and work with a qualified accountant to understand all that's required of you by federal and state governments. The task is by no means simple. New business owners face a host of tax requirements and ever-changing rules.

If you miss deadlines or fail to comply with specific rules, you may be hit with large penalties, and, in the worst-case scenario, be forced to close up shop. You'll also want to pay close attention to tax planning, which will help you find legitimate ways to trim your overall tax liability. Your goal is to take the deductions to which you're entitled and to defer taxes as long as you possibly can.

While a knowledgeable accountant specializing in small-business tax issues will keep you out of potential tax quagmires, you'll be on more solid footing if you spend time acquiring your own working knowledge and understanding of the tax laws.

e-fyi

Get the scoop on wage reporting for yourself and your employees at the Social Security website at ssa.gov.

First Things First

One of the first steps you will take as a business owner is to obtain a taxpayer identification number so the IRS can process your returns. There are two types of identification numbers: a Social Security number and an Employer Identification Number (EIN).

The EIN is a nine-digit number the IRS issues. It is used to identify the tax accounts of corporations, partnerships, and other entities. You need an EIN if you have employees, operate your business as a corporation or partnership, or have a Keogh plan. Be sure to include your EIN on all returns or other documents you send to the IRS.

You can apply for an EIN by phone, fax, mail, or online (as long as your business is an entity that is allowed to apply online). You can receive your EIN immediately by phone or by going online. To apply online, go to www.irs.gov/Businesses/Small-Businesses-&-Self-Employed/Apply-for-an-Employer-Identification-Number-(EIN)-Online. A completed fax request takes about four to five business days. An online application can be fulfilled in half that time. If you apply by mail, be sure to send in Form SS–4 (*Application for Employer Identification Number*) at least four or five weeks before you need the EIN to file a return or make a deposit.

Ins and Outs of Payroll Taxes

If you do any hiring, your employees must complete Form I-9 (*Employment Eligibility Verification*) and Form W–4 (*Employee's Withholding Allowance Certificate*). Form I–9 provides verification that each new employee is legally eligible to work in the United States. This form can be obtained from the U.S. Citizenship and Immigration Service (USCIS) by visiting uscis.gov; keep this form in your files in the event an IRS or USCIS inspector wants to see it. Your employees should also complete a state withholding certificate (similar to the W-4) if your state imposes personal income taxes.

Form W-4 indicates the employee's filing status and withholding allowances. These allowances are used to determine how much federal income tax to withhold from an employee's wages. To determine how much to withhold from each wage payment, use the employee's W-4 and the methods described in IRS Publications 15, *Employer's Tax Guide*, and 15-A, *Employer's Supplemental Tax Guide*. These publications are available online at irs.gov.

You must also withhold Social Security and Medicare taxes—these are known as FICA (Federal Insurance Contributions Act) taxes. The FICA tax actually consists of two taxes: a 6.2 percent Social Security tax and a 1.45 percent Medicare tax. To calculate the tax you need to withhold for each employee, multiply an employee's gross wages for a pay period by the tax rates. In addition, as an employer, you are required to pay a matching amount of FICA taxes on each of your employees.

Here's how it works: If an employee has gross wages of $1,000 every two weeks, you must withhold $62 ($1,000 x 0.062) in Social Security taxes and $14.50 ($1,000 x .0145) in Medicare taxes, or $76.50. As an employer, you owe a matching amount as well, so the total amount in FICA taxes to be paid is $153. In the 2014 tax year, the maximum amount of wages subject to Social Security tax is $117,000. The Medicare tax rate is 1.45 percent on the first $200,000 and 2.35 percent above $200,000. The IRS requires any business paying more than $200,000 annually in payroll taxes or other federal taxes to pay them

tip

Consider using a payroll tax service to take care of all payroll tax requirements. The fees charged by such services are relatively reasonable. In addition, these firms specialize in this area and know the ins and outs of all the rules and regulations. With a service, you don't have to worry about making mistakes or being tardy with payments.

through the Electronic Federal Tax Payment System (EFTPS). If you pay less than that amount, you can still deliver a check for payroll taxes owed to an authorized financial institution able to accept federal tax deposits. To enroll in EFTPS, call 1-800-945-8400 or 1-800-555-4477. You can obtain additional information on EFTPS requirements by accessing Publication 966 (www.irs.gov/pub/irs-pdf/p966.pdf). You can also register online and get more information from www.eftps.gov. You typically pay these taxes monthly, depending on the size of your business. Approximately five to six weeks after you receive your EIN, the IRS will send you the coupon book.

In addition to making your monthly payroll deposits, you are required to file quarterly Form 941 (*Employer's Quarterly Federal Tax Return*). This is a form that provides the government with information on the federal income taxes you withheld from your employees' pay as well as the FICA taxes you withheld and paid. It also tells the government when the taxes were withheld so the IRS can determine if the federal tax deposit was made on time.

Another tax you have to pay is FUTA (Federal Unemployment Tax Act) taxes, which are used to compensate workers who lose their jobs. You report and pay FUTA tax separately from FICA and withheld income taxes.

You pay FUTA tax on your payroll if during the current or prior calendar year you meet one of two tests: You paid total wages of $1,500 to your employees in any calendar quarter, or you have at least one employee working on any given day in each of 20 different calendar weeks.

The FUTA tax is figured on the first $7,000 in wages paid to each employee annually. The gross FUTA tax rate is 6 percent. However, you are given a credit of up to 5.4 percent for the state unemployment tax you pay, effectively reducing the tax rate. As an employer, you pay FUTA tax only from your own funds. Employees do not have this tax withheld from their pay. You generally deposit FUTA taxes quarterly. In addition, you must file an annual return for your FUTA taxes using Form 940 (*Employer's Annual Federal Unemployment Tax Return*), which must be filed by January 31 of the following year. Most small employers are eligible to use Form 940-EZ.

Federal payroll taxes are not your only concern. States and localities have their own taxes, which will most likely affect you. Forty-one states have a personal income tax on wages (nine do not), which means you are also required to withhold this tax from your employees' wages in those 41 states.

The same is true if you do business in a city or locality with an income tax.

When applying for an EIN from your state, which you will need to do business there, ask about the procedures and forms for withholding and depositing state income taxes. The place to start is with your state department of revenue.

warning

If you withhold taxes but don't deposit or pay them to the IRS, you face a penalty on the unpaid tax, plus interest. If you deposit the taxes late, you will also be hit with a penalty.

At the end of the tax year, you must furnish copies of Form W-2 (Wage and Tax Statement) to each employee who worked for you during the year. Be sure to give the forms to your employees by January 31 of the year after the calendar year covered by the form. Form W-2 provides information on how much money each employee earned and the amount of federal, state, and FICA taxes you withheld. You must send copies of W-2s to the Social Security Administration as well.

Declaration of Independents

You may decide your business can't afford to hire too many full-time employees, and you'd like to use the services of an independent contractor. With an independent contractor, you don't have to withhold and pay the person's income, Social Security, and Medicare taxes.

While independent contractors (ICs) do translate to lower payroll costs, be advised that the IRS scrutinizes the use of ICs very carefully. The IRS wants to make sure that your workers are properly classified and paying the government the necessary income and payroll taxes that are due.

To stay out of hot water with the IRS, be sure the workers you classify as ICs meet the IRS definition of an IC. The determining factors fall into three main categories: behavioral control, financial control, and relationship of the parties. The IRS uses 20 factors when deciding a worker's status. Here are some of the major ones:

- *Who has control*? A worker is an employee if the person for whom he works has the right to direct and control him concerning when and where to do the work. The employer need not actually exercise control; it is sufficient that he has the right to do so. An independent contractor also has freedom to set his or her own work hours.

- *Right to fire.* An employee can be fired by an employer. An IC cannot be fired so long as he or she produces a result that meets the specifications of the contract.
- *Training.* An employee may be trained to perform services in a particular manner. However, ICs ordinarily use their own methods and receive no training from the employer.
- *Expenses and payments.* Independent contractors are more likely to have unreimbursed expenses than employees do. And they're more likely to be paid a flat fee for a job or a limited scope of work if paid hourly.

>> It's a Plan

Employee benefits such as health insurance and pension plan contributions provide attractive tax deductions. With a qualified pension plan, you not only receive a tax deduction for the contributions you make on behalf of your employees, but the money you contribute to your own retirement account is also deductible and is allowed to grow tax-deferred until withdrawn. (A qualified plan meets the requirements of the Employee Retirement Income Security Act [ERISA] and the Internal Revenue Code.)

There are many different plans available, ranging from a Savings Incentive Match Plan for Employees (SIMPLE) to a traditional 401(k) plan (see Chapter 24). The pension design may be slightly different, but they all offer important tax benefits for business owners. So take the time to find out which plan will work best for you.

As far as health insurance is concerned, if your business is incorporated and you work for it as an employee, you can deduct all costs for your own insurance as well as for the coverage for your employees. Self-employed individuals can deduct 100 percent of the premiums paid for health insurance for themselves and their families, as long as the amount isn't more than the net earnings from the business.

- *Benefits.* Independent contractors do not generally get benefits like insurance, paid vacation, or sick days. And the relationship is not considered permanent—rather the relationship is defined by a specific project or period of time.

To stay on the right side of the IRS, it is best to document the relationship you have with any ICs in a written contract. This can be a simple agreement that spells out the duties of the IC. The agreement should state that the independent contractor, not the employer, is responsible for withholding any necessary taxes. In addition, have the IC submit invoices. It's a good idea to have a copy of the contractor's business license and certificate of insurance as well as his or her business card. Also, be sure you file Form 1099–MISC (*Miscellaneous Income*) at year-end, which is used to report payments made in the course of a transaction to another person or business that is not an employee. By law, you are required to file and give someone Form 1099 if you pay that person more than $600 a year. The form must be given to the IC by January 31 of the following year; Form 1099 with its transmittal Form 1096 must be filed with the IRS by February 28.

Whether an individual is determined to be an independent contractor or an employee, it is required that you obtain their complete name, Social Security number, and address before any money is paid. If this information is not obtained, you are required to withhold backup withholding taxes for federal income taxes.

If the IRS finds you have misclassified an employee as an independent contractor, you will pay a percentage of income taxes that should have been withheld on the employee's wages and be liable for your share of the FICA and unemployment taxes, plus penalties and interest. Even worse, if the IRS determines your misclassification was "willful," you could

warning

If you hire independent contractors, make sure you know whether they are covered under your state's workers' comp laws. If an independent contractor is injured on the job in a state where he's not covered by workers' comp, he's not limited in the type of civil action he can file against the employer. If he is covered by workers' comp laws, the contractor is limited to the remedies provided under those laws.

owe the IRS the full amount of income tax that should have been withheld (with an adjustment if the employee has paid or pays part of the tax), the full amount of both the employer's and employee's share of FICA taxes (possibly with an offset if the employee paid self-employment taxes), interest, and penalties.

Be advised that there is some relief being offered. If a business realizes it is in violation of the law regarding independent contractors, it can inform the IRS of the problem and then properly classify the workers without being hit with an IRS assessment for prior-year taxes. The newer Voluntary Classification Settlement Program allows you to receive partial relief from missed federal employment taxes while reclassifying workers for future tax periods. The program is voluntary and has some eligibility requirements. You can apply to participate by filing Form 8952 and eventually entering into an agreement with the IRS that typically involves paying 10 percent of the tax liability that would have been due, without penalties or interest.

Selecting Your Tax Year

When you launch your business, you'll have to decide what tax year to use. The tax year is the annual accounting period used to keep your records and report your income and expenses. There are two accounting periods: a calendar year and a fiscal year.

A calendar year is 12 consecutive months starting January 1 and ending December 31. Most sole proprietors, partnerships, limited liability companies, and S corporations use the calendar year as their tax year. If you operate a business as a sole proprietorship, the IRS says the tax year for your business is the same as your individual tax year.

A fiscal tax year is 12 consecutive months ending on the last day of any month other than December. For business owners who start a company during the year and have substantial expenses or losses, it may be smart to select a fiscal year (as long as

warning

Once you have selected to file on either a calendar- or fiscal-year basis, you have to get permission from the IRS to change it. To do so, you must file Form 1128, and you may have to pay a fee.

the IRS allows it) that goes beyond the end of the first calendar year. This way, as much income as possible is offset by startup expenses and losses.

Filing Your Tax Return

Your federal tax filing obligations and due dates generally are based on the legal structure you've selected for your business and whether you use a calendar or fiscal year.

- *Sole proprietorships.* If you are a sole proprietor, every year you must file Schedule C (*Profit or Loss From Business*) with your Form 1040 (*U.S. Individual Income Tax Return*) to report your business's net profit and loss. You also must file Schedule SE (*Self-Employment Tax*) with your 1040. If you are a calendar-year taxpayer, your tax filing date is April 15. Fiscal-year taxpayers must file their returns no later than the 15th day of the fourth month after the end of their tax year.

  In addition to your annual tax return, many self-employed individuals such as sole proprietors and partners make quarterly estimated tax payments to cover their income and Social Security tax liability. You must make estimated tax payments if you expect to owe at least $1,000 in federal tax for the year after subtracting your withholding and credits and your withholding will be less than the smaller of: 1) 90 percent of the tax to be shown on your current year tax return or 2) 100 percent of your previous year's tax liability. The federal government allows you to pay estimated taxes in four equal amounts throughout the year on the 15th of April, June, September, and January.
- *Partnerships and limited liability companies (LLCs).* Companies set up with these structures must file Form 1065 (*U.S. Return of Partnership Income*) that reports income and loss to the IRS. The partnership must furnish copies of Schedule K-1 (*Partner's Share of Income, Credits, Deductions*), which is part of Form 1065, to the partners or

> ***"Opportunities are usually disguised as hard work, so most people don't recognize them."***
>
> —Ann Landers

LLC members by the filing date for Form 1065. The due dates are the same as those for sole proprietors.

- *Corporations.* If your business is structured as a regular corporation, you must file Form 1120 (*U.S. Corporation Income Tax Return*). For calendar-year taxpayers, the due date for the return is March 15. For fiscal-year corporations, the return must be filed by the 15th day of the third month after the end of your corporation's tax year.
- *S corporations.* Owners of these companies must file Form 1120S (*U.S. Income Tax Return for an S Corporation*). Like partnerships, shareholders must receive a copy of Schedule K–1, which is part of Form 1120S. The due dates are the same as those for regular corporations.

Sales Taxes

Sales taxes vary by state and are imposed at the retail level. It's important to know the rules in the states and localities where you operate your business, because if you are a retailer, you must collect state sales tax on each sale you make.

While a number of states and localities exempt service businesses from sales taxes, some have changed their laws in this area and are applying the sales tax to some services. If you run a service business, contact your state revenue and/or local revenue offices for information on the laws in your area.

Before you open your doors, be sure to register to collect sales tax by applying for a sales permit for each separate place of business you have in the state. A license or permit is important because in some states it is a criminal offense to undertake sales without one. In addition, if you fail to collect sales tax, you can be held liable for the uncollected amount.

If you're an out-of-state retailer, such as a mail order seller who ships and sells goods in another state, be careful. In the past, many retailers have not collected sales taxes on the sales of these goods. Be sure you or your accountant knows the state sales tax requirements where you do business. Just because you don't have a physical location in a state doesn't always mean you don't have to collect the sales tax.

Many states require business owners to make an advance deposit against future taxes. Some states will accept a surety bond from your insurance company in lieu of the deposit.

It's possible for retailers to defer paying sales taxes on merchandise they purchase from suppliers. Once the merchandise is sold, however, the taxes are due. The retailer adds the sales taxes (where applicable) to the purchase. To defer sales taxes, you need a reseller permit or certificate. For more details on obtaining a permit, contact your state tax department.

Tax-Deductible Business Expenses

According to the IRS, the operating costs of running your business are deductible if they are "ordinary and necessary." The IRS defines "ordinary" as expenses that are common and accepted in your field of business. "Necessary expenses" are those that are appropriate and helpful for your business. Following are some of the business expenses you may be able to deduct.

Equipment Purchases

Under the Internal Revenue Code Section 179, expensing allowance, business owners can fully deduct from taxable income a limited amount of the cost of new business equipment in a year rather than depreciating the cost over several years. In 2014, the maximum federal allowance is $25,000. For more information, get a copy of IRS Publication 946, *How to Depreciate Property*, and read "Electing The Section 179 Deduction." You also can find a free Section 179 calculator at section179.org.

Business Expenses

Some common business expenses for which you can take a deduction include advertising expenses, employee benefit programs, insurance, legal and professional services, telephone and utilities costs, rent, office supplies, employee wages, membership dues to professional associations, and business publication subscriptions.

Auto Expenses

If you use your car for business purposes, the IRS allows you to either deduct your actual business-related expenses or claim the standard mileage rate, which is a specified amount of money you can deduct for each business mile you drive. The rate is generally adjusted each year by

>> Start Me Up

The expenses you incur when launching a new business can run into a lot of money. But how do you treat them when it comes time to do your taxes? If you start a business, you may deduct up to $5,000 of startup costs in the year you launch it and another $5,000 in organizational expenses, which include costs related to creating a corporation. These deductions are reduced if you have more than $50,000 of either type of expense. Keep in mind that startup costs that are not deductible in the year you started the business can be amortized over 15 years beginning in the month you launched your business.

Amortization is a method of recovering (or deducting) certain capital costs over a fixed period of time. Startup costs include advertising expenses and any wages you paid for training employees and fees paid to consultants.

If you spent time looking for a business but did not purchase one, the expenses you incurred during the search may be deductible.

the IRS. To calculate your deduction, multiply your business miles by the standard mileage rate for the year.

If you use the standard mileage rate, the IRS says you must use it in the first year the car is available for use in your business. Later, you can use either the standard mileage rate or actual expenses method. For tax purposes, be sure to keep a log of your business miles, as well as the costs of business-related parking fees and tolls, because you can deduct these expenses.

If you use five or more vehicles at the same time in your business, the IRS requires you to use the actual cost expenses method. With the actual cost method, the IRS allows you to deduct various expenses, including depreciation, gas, insurance, garage rent, leasing fees, oil, repairs, tolls, and parking fees. If you use this method, keep records of your car's costs during the year and multiply those expenses by the percentage of total car mileage driven for business purposes.

While using the standard mileage rate is easier for record-keeping, you may receive a larger deduction using the actual cost method. If you qualify to use both methods, the IRS recommends figuring your deduction both ways to see which gives you a larger deduction, as long as you have kept detailed records to substantiate the actual cost method. For more details on using a car for business, see IRS Publications 334 (*Tax Guide for Small Business*) and 463 (*Travel, Entertainment, Gift and Car Expenses*).

Meal and Entertainment Expenses

To earn a deduction for business entertainment, it must be either directly related to your business or associated with it. To be deductible, meals and entertainment must be "ordinary and necessary" and not "lavish" or "extravagant." The deduction is limited to 50 percent of the cost of qualifying meals and entertainment.

To prove expenses are directly related to your business, you must show there was more than a general expectation of gaining some business benefit other than goodwill, that you conducted business during the entertainment, and conducting business was your main purpose.

To meet the "associated" with your business test, the entertainment must directly precede or come after a substantial business discussion. In addition, you must have had a clear business purpose when you took on the expense.

Be sure to maintain receipts for any entertainment or meal that costs $75 or more, and record all your expenses in an account book. Record the business reason for the expense, amount spent, dates, location, type of entertainment, and the name, title, and occupation of the people you entertained.

save

To help you wade through all the tax laws and regulations, the IRS offers these free publications: *Tax Guide for Small Business* (Publication 334), *Business Expenses* (Publication 535), *Travel, Entertainment, Gift and Car Expenses* (Publication 463), *Circular E, Employer's Tax Guide* (Publication 15), and *Employer's Supplemental Tax Guide* (Publication 15-A). To obtain copies of these publications, you can download them from the IRS website at irs.gov.

Travel Expenses

You can deduct ordinary and necessary expenses you incur while traveling away from

> ## >> In the Red?
>
> If you find, after you've tallied up all your business deductions and subtracted them from your income, that you're in the red for the year, don't despair. There's something called the net operating loss deduction that will help. It allows you to offset one year's losses against another year's income.
>
> The IRS lets you carry this operating loss back two years and use it to offset the income of those previous two years. Doing so may result in a refund. If you still have some losses left after carrying them back, you can carry them forward for up to 20 years. If you don't want to use the two-year carryback period, you can elect to deduct the net operating loss over the next 20 years. However, once you make that election, you can't reverse it. Remember, if there is any unused loss after 20 years, you may no longer apply it to any income.

home on business. Your records should show the amount of each expense for items such as transportation, meals, and lodging. Be sure to record the date of departure and return for each trip, the number of days you spent on business, the name of the city, and the business reason for the travel or the business benefits you expect to achieve. Keep track of your cleaning and laundry expenses while traveling because these are deductible, as is the cost of telephone, fax, and modem usage.

Home Office

If you use a portion of your home exclusively and regularly for business, you may be able to claim the home office deduction on your annual tax return. This generally applies to sole proprietorships. To claim the deduction, the part of the home you use for your office must be your principal place of business, or you must use it to meet or deal with clients in the normal course of business. Keep in mind that you can't claim the deduction if you have an outside office as well.

Business owners who keep records, schedule appointments, and perform other administrative or management activities from their home offices qualify for a deduction as long as they don't have any other fixed place of business where they do a large amount of administrative or management work. This holds true even if they don't see clients or customers in their home offices. The IRS scrutinizes this deduction very carefully, so be sure to follow the rules and keep good records.

Tax Planning

As you operate your business, be on the lookout for ways to reduce your federal and state tax liability. Small-business owners typically have a lot of ups and downs from one year to the next. If you make a lot of money one year and have to pay taxes on all that profit, your business won't have the reserves needed to tide you over in some other year when business may not be as good.

That's why it's important to defer or reduce taxes whenever possible. This is a good way to cut business costs without affecting the quality of your product or service.

Throughout the year, periodically review your tax situation with the help of your accountant. If your income is increasing, look for deductions to help reduce your taxes. For example, if you are a cash-basis taxpayer, think about doing some needed business repairs or stocking up on office supplies and inventory before the end of the year. Cash-basis taxpayers can also defer income into the next year by waiting until the end of December to mail invoices.

For businesses using the accrual method, review your accounts receivable to see if anything is partially worthless. If it is, you can take a deduction for a portion of the amount of the uncollected debt. Check with your accountant to determine whether you meet IRS requirements to claim a bad-debt deduction.

Both cash and accrual taxpayers can make charitable donations before the end of the year and take deductions for them. Beware: If you donate $250 or more, you must obtain written substantiation of the contribution amount or a description of the property given from

e-fyi

Believe it or not, the IRS does publish understandable business tax information. Visit the Small Business and Self-Employed Tax Center on its website at irs.gov.

the charity, as well as a bank record, such as a canceled check or bank statement.

Tax planning is a year-long endeavor. Be sure you know what deductions are available to you, and keep good records to support them. This way, you can reap tax savings, which you can use to successfully operate and grow your business.

APPENDIX

Business and Government Resources

Accounting and Taxes

Associations

American Accounting Association
(941) 921-7747
aaahq.org

American Institute of Certified Public Accountants
aicpa.org

Association of Credit and Collection Professionals
(952) 926-6547
acainternational.org

CCH Inc.
(888) 224-7377
cch.com

PrimeGlobal
International association of independent accounting firms
accountants.org

Internet Resources

CPA Practice Advisor
http://www.cpapracticeadvisor.com/directory

American Express OPEN for Business
Resources, workshops, and articles related to small businesses, including financial management and marketing ideas
(800) 492-3344
openforum.com

Fiserv
Offers different types of business payment solutions, including the option of paying bills and receiving payments electronically
(262) 879-5000
fiserv.com

Advertising and Marketing

Associations

American Advertising Federation
(800) 999-2231
aaf.org

American Marketing Association
(800) AMA-1150, (312) 542-9000
ama.org

Direct Marketing Association
(212) 768-7277
thedma.org

Marketing Research Association
{202) 800.2545
marketingresearch.org/

Radio Advertising Bureau
(800) 232-3131
rab.com

Internet Resources

ICANN (Internet Corp. for Assigned Names & Numbers)
internet security information
(310) 823-9358
icann.org

24/7 Media
provides marketing solutions and products
(212) 231-7100
xaxis.com

Website Marketing Plan
Lots of informative articles, as well as sample business and marketing plans
websitemarketingplan.com

Credit Services

Dun & Bradstreet
Provides business credit-reporting services
(866) 203-3151
dnb.com

Equifax Credit Information Services Inc.
Provides credit-reporting services
(888) 202-4025
equifax.com

Experian
Provides credit-reporting services
(888) 397-3742
experian.com

First Data Corp.
Provides credit-processing services
firstdata.com

Telecheck
Provides check-guarantee services
telecheck.com

TransUnion
Provides credit-reporting services
(866) 922-2100
transunion.com

Microsoft Support
The latest news, support, and web solutions from America's premier software company
support.microsoft.com

More Business
Sample business forms, agreements and marketing plans, as well as informative articles and links
morebusiness.com

Web Site 101
Free online tutorials, surveys and articles related to ecommerce
website101.com

Business Planning and Development

Internet Resources

AllBusiness.com
Articles, business forms, contracts, news and advice
(415) 694-5000
allbusiness.com

BPlans.com
Free sample business plans, articles and online tools
(541) 683-6162
bplans.com

Center for Business Planning
Sample business plans and planning guidelines for business owners
(800) 423-1228
businessplans.org

Franchise and Business Opportunities

Association

International Franchise Association
(202) 628-8000
franchise.org

Internet Resource

***Entrepreneur* magazine's FranchiseZone**
Loads of information on buying and researching a franchise
entrepreneur.com/franchise

Federal Resources

Business.gov
The official business link to the U.S. government

Census Bureau
census.gov

Copyright Clearance Center
(978) 750-8400
copyright.com

Copyright Office
Library of Congress
(202) 707-3000
loc.gov/copyright

Department of Agriculture
(202) 720-2791
usda.gov

Department of Commerce
(202) 482-2000
doc.gov

Department of Energy
(202) 586-5000
energy.gov

Department of the Interior
(202) 208-3100
interior.gov

Department of Labor
(866) 487-2365
dol.gov

Department of Treasury
(202) 622-2000
treasury.gov

Equal Employment Opportunity Commission
eeoc.gov

Export-Import Bank of the United States
(800) 565-3946, (202) 565-3946
exim.gov

FCC
(888) 225-5322
fcc.gov

FTC
(202) 326-2222
ftc.gov

International Postage Price Calculator
ircalc.usps.gov

IRS
(800) 829-4933
irs.gov

Minority Business Development Agency
U.S. Department of Commerce
(888) 324-1551
mbda.gov

Occupational Safety and Health Administration
osha.gov

SBA
(800) 827-5722
sba.gov

Securities & Exchange Commission
(202) 942-8088
sec.gov

U.S. Consumer Product Safety Commission
(301) 504-7912
cpsc.gov

U.S. Food and Drug Administration
(888) 463-6332
fda.gov

U.S. Patent & Trademark Office
(800) 786-9199
uspto.gov

U.S. Postal Service
usps.com

U.S. Printing Office
(202) 512-1800
access.gpo.gov

USA.gov
Government information by topic

General Business Resources

Associations

American Express OPEN for Business
Resources, workshops, and articles related to small businesses, including financial management and marketing ideas
(800) 492-3344
openforum.com

American Management Association
(877) 566-9441
amanet.org

Equipment Leasing and Financing Association
(703) 527-8655
elfaonline.org

Ewing Marion Kauffman Foundation
For entrepreneurship and education
(816) 932-1000
kauffman.org

Independent Insurance Agents & Brokers of America
(800) 221-7917
independentagent.com

Insurance Information Institute
Provides information and tools on how to adequately insure your business
(212) 346-5500
iii.org

National Association of Women's Business Owners
Resources and networking opportunities for women-owned businesses
(800) 55-NAWBO
nawbo.org

National Association for the Self-Employed
(800) 649-6273
nase.org

National Association of Professional Employer Organizations
(703) 836-0466
napeo.org

National Minority Supplier Development Council
Links minority-owned businesses with corporations that want to purchase goods and services
(212) 944-2430
nmsdc.org

Internet Resources

BizBuySell
Useful website to find businesses for sale, as well as online tools and articles
(888) 777-9892
bizbuysell.com

Business.gov
Official business link to the U.S. Government, with business startup and other information
business.gov

Business Know-How
Ideas, advice, information, and resources for small and homebased businesses
(631) 467-8883
businessknowhow.com

Business Owners Idea Café
Lots of ideas, articles, and resources to start and run a business
businessownersideacafe.com

Business Town
Plenty of resources and links to start and run a small business
businesstown.com

Entrepreneur.com
Tons of resources, guides, tips, articles, and more at this informative website for startup businesses and growing companies
(949) 261-2325
entrepreneur.com

The Entrepreneurship Institute
Provides resources and networking opportunities for business owners
(614) 895-1153
tei.net

Smart Biz
Resources for small business, including email marketing campaigns, website creation, legal and business forms, and online tools and equipment
smartbiz.com

TradePub.com
Free trade publications and white papers for small-business owners
(800) 882-4670
tradepub.com

Homebased Business Resources

Associations

American Home Business Association
homebusinessworks.com

Mothers Home Business Network
homeworkingmom.com

National Association of Home Based Businesses
(410) 367-5308, (410) 367-5309
usahomebusiness.com

Internet Resource

Power Home Biz
Lots of resources that include tools, articles, and information on how to start, manage, and grow a home business
powerhomebiz.com

Inventors and Idea Protection

Associations

American Society of Inventors
(215) 546-6601
asoi.org

Innovation Assessment Center
Washington State University
(888) 585-5433
http://www.business.wsu.edu/organizations/iac/Pages/inventor.aspx

Invention Services International
Sponsors the Invention Convention Trade Show Administrative & Communications Center
(800) 458-5624, (323) 878-6951
inventionconvention.com

The Inventors Assistance League International Inc.
(877) IDEA-BIN
inventions.org

Inventory Management Software

AdvancePro
AdvanceWare Technologies
(888) 792-3826
advanceware.net

inFlow Inventory Software
(866) 923-4974
inflowinventory.com

Traker Systems
(800) 314-6863, (951) 693-1376
trakersystems.com

Laws, Regulations, and Employee Benefits

Internet Resources

Benefits Link
Informative website regarding employee benefits, laws, and regulations
(407) 644-4146
benefitslink.com

BizFilings
Information on incorporating and related services for business owners, including forms, advice, and tools needed
(800) 981-7183, (608) 827-5300
bizfilings.com

Employers of America
Information on writing job descriptions, HR manuals, safety tips, training resources, and more
(800) 728-3187
employerhelp.org

FindLaw
Links to regulatory agencies, sample forms and contracts, articles on all aspects of business development
(800) 455-4565
smallbusiness.findlaw.com

Small Business Advisor
Lots of articles and advice for startup businesses
isquare.com

Small Business Notes
Useful site that features a wide variety of business articles and resources, including legal issues and record-keeping
smallbusinessnotes.com

Startup Assistance

Associations

American Bankers Association
(800) BANKERS
aba.com

Association of Small Business Development Centers
(703) 764-9850
asbdc-us.org

Commercial Finance Association
(212) 792-9390
cfa.com

Independent Community Bankers of America
(202) 659-8111
icba.org

National Business Incubation Association
Provides incubator location assistance
(740) 593-4331
nbia.org

National Venture Capital Association
(703) 524-2549
nvca.org

SCORE
national office
(800) 634-0245
score.org

Small Business Investment Alliance
(202) 628-5055
sbia.org

Internet Resource

Business Finance
Thousands of business loan and capital sources
(800) 835-8857
businessfinance.com

Stats

Internet Resources

American FactFinder
Online source for population, housing, economic, and geographic data
(301) 763-INFO (4636),
(800) 923-8282
http://factfinder2.census.gov/faces/nav/jsf/pages/index.xhtml

BizStats
Quick online access to useful financial ratios, business statistics and benchmarks
(717) 909-6000
bizstats.com

Industry Research Desk
Provides online tools and links for researching businesses and industries
virtualpet.com/industry

ProQuest
Extensive online information retrieval system
proquest.com

Valuation Resources
Provides links to a wide variety of industry information resources
(812) 459-7742
valuationresources.com

Time Management

Personal Time Management Guide
A website with tips on goal setting, critical skills, teamwork, managing stress and more
time-management-guide.com

Project Management and Collaboration Basecamp
An online project management tool that increases communication among teams and clients
basecamphq.com

Glossary

4G: one of the newest generation of cellular phone networks that offers much faster speeds for sending and receiving all types of data

80-20 rule: principle of inventory control that says 80 percent of a business' sales typically come from 20 percent of its inventory; as a result, most attention should be focused on the 20 percent that generates the most profit

ABC method: method of inventory control that divides items into A, B, and C groups based on their importance to the business; most attention is then devoted to the A, or essential, items

Absolute net lease: a lease in which the tenant agrees to pay a basic rent and be responsible and separately pay for all maintenance, operating, and other expenses of the building or office

ACA (Affordable Care Act): a 2010 law that expanded Medicaid eligibility, established health insurance exchanges, and prohibited health insurers from denying coverage due to pre-existing conditions; people without health insurance are required to buy it, in most cases, with subsidies provided for lower-income individuals

Accounts payable: a company liability that represents amounts due for goods or services purchased on credit

Accounts receivable: money due to a business from clients and customers; outstanding invoices

Accrued expenses: expenses that have been accounted for on the income statement but that have not yet been paid

Affiliate: a company that sells another company's products or services on its site for a commission

Alternative dispute resolution (ADR): a way of resolving disputes without resorting to litigation

Amenities: any material goods, services, or intangible items that increase the comfort, attractiveness, desirability, and value of an office suite or building

Americans with Disabilities Act (ADA): law passed in 1990 that prohibits employers with 15 or more employees from refusing to hire people with disabilities if making "reasonable accommodations" would enable the person to perform the job

Angel, angel investor: describes a private individual who invests money in a business

Assemblage: the combining of two or more contiguous properties into one large property; an assemblage will often make the one large property more valuable than the separate parts

Assessment: the determination or setting of a tax or other charge based on a building's estimated value

Asset: tangible or intangible object of value to its owner

Asset acquisition: a method of buying a business in which the buyer purchases only those assets of the business he or she wants

Asset remarketers, asset remarketing companies: firms that work with equipment leasing companies to resell repossessed office equipment through a network of dealers and wholesalers as well as directly to business owners

Attornment: a lease provision that the tenant agrees, in advance, to accept and pay rent or other required payments to a new landlord or legal owner

B2B sales: marketing your products and services to other businesses, as opposed to individual consumers

Balance sheet: a "snapshot" of the assets, liabilities, and owner's equity of a business for a given period

Balloon payment: a large payment (the balloon) at the end of a lease

Base salary: fixed compensation for services, paid to a person on a regular basis

Batch counter: feature on a letter-folding machine that prevents the machine from folding too many sheets together

Binding arbitration: form of ADR in which the arbitrator's decision is legally binding

Binding letter of intent: a letter of intent would be upheld in a court of law as the actual leasing of space by the tenant from the landlord and by the landlord to the tenant regardless of whether an actual lease document was agreed to or signed

Bluetooth: a short-range wireless protocol for transferring voice and data among cell phones and computing devices; most smartphones can use it, some printers, laptops, and tablets also can connect via Bluetooth

Bonding: a guarantee of performance required either by law or consumer demand for many businesses, typically general contractors, temporary personnel agencies, janitorial companies, and businesses with government contracts

Bonus: a sum of money in addition to salary that's part of total compensation

Brand audit: examining your brand from every angle to see how well it's working

Brand equity: the dollar value your brand generates over decades in the demand it drives and the customer loyalty it creates; brand equity for a very large, well-known company like Nike translates into billions of dollars

Brand identity: the visual aspects of your brand that include your signs, packaging, and stationery; customer service also falls into this category

Branding: your company's reason for being; the synchronization of all aspects of your company that leads to consistency and creates value around your product or service

Brandmark: the illustration that distinguishes your company; in other words, your logo

Brand position: how your customers view your brand vis-à-vis the competition

Brand promise: how you tell customers about the most important benefit of your product or service, who in turn should be able to connect this benefit right back to your product

Brand strategy: a written plan for applying your brand strategically

Broadband modem: any device that connects your computer to the same cable that brings content to your TV, or to the T1, ATM fiber relay or DSL of the telephone companies

Broker: an insurance agent who represents many different insurance companies

Browser: software used for navigating the web

Building standard work letter: a list and/or detailed specifications of the construction items (both quantity and quality) that will be provided by the developer to be used in building out a tenant's office space

Business broker: a person who helps buy and sell businesses, similar to a real estate broker

Business interruption insurance: pays for the cost of repairing or rebuilding a business, as well as income lost, while the business is out of commission

Business opportunity: legal definitions vary; in its simplest terms, a business opportunity is a packaged business investment that allows the buyer to begin a business

Cable modem: modem that connects to your cable TV line to give you high-speed access to the internet

Cash-flow statement: the financial statement that reflects all inflows and outflows of cash resulting from operating, investing, and financing activities during a specific time period

Certified Development Companies (CDCs): nonprofit intermediaries that work with the SBA and banks to make 504 Loans available to entrepreneurs

Chadder: type of letter-opening machine that cuts one-eighth of an inch from the end of the envelope

Chargeback: when a customer purchases an item using a credit card and then returns it, this is called a chargeback

Chart of accounts: the list of accounts that are tracked within the general ledger

Chattel-mortgage contract: type of credit contract used for equipment purchase in which the equipment becomes the property of the purchaser on delivery, but the seller holds a mortgage claim against it until the contract amount is fully paid

Closed-end lease: type of equipment lease in which no money is owed when the lease period ends; the lessee simply turns in the equipment and walks away

Cohort marketing: marketing to people based on the groups or "cohorts" they were part of during their formative years

Collateral: anything of value that can be pledged against a loan, including stocks and bonds, equipment, home equity, inventory, and receivables; if you cannot repay the loan, the lender will look to your collateral as a backup source of repayment

Commissioned financial planner: financial planner who receives commissions on products he or she sells

Common stock: stock representing equity ownership in a company; it entitles the holder to elect corporate directors and collect dividends

Competitive analysis: section of a business plan that assesses the competition's strengths and weaknesses

Conditional sales contract: type of credit contract used for equipment purchase in which the purchaser does not receive title to the equipment until it is paid for

Consolidated Omnibus Budget Reconciliation Act (COBRA): law requiring employers to extend health insurance coverage to employees and dependents beyond the point at which such coverage traditionally ceases (such as the termination or death of the covered employee)

Consumer: an individual who purchases services or products from a business

Contiguous office space: office suites adjacent to each other or having a common demising wall

Cookie: a piece of data given to your browser by a web server when you visit a web page; the browser stores the cookie in a file and sends a message back to the server each time you revisit that web page

Corporation: a legal entity that's separate and distinct from its owners

Cost accounting: the process of allocating all direct and indirect expenses associated with the production and/or sale of a product

Cost of goods sold: the cost that a business incurs to produce a product for sale to its customers

Count cycle: the period at which you count your inventory; a four-week count cycle means you count inventory every four weeks

CPA (certified public accountant): an accountant who has passed a nationally standardized exam in accounting

CPM (cost per thousand): figure that tells you how much it costs to reach 1,000 potential customers with a given form of advertising

CPU: the central processing unit, or the brains of the computer, now commonly includes two separate processing engines bolstered by a lot of on-chip cache memory

Credit: the right-side entries in a double-entry accounting system

Cross-training: training employees to fill more than one position

Crowdfunding: The use of small amounts of capital from a large number of individuals to finance a new business venture

Cure provision: part of the default section of a promissory note, the cure provision allows you a certain amount of time (usually ten days) to remedy a default after you've been notified

Current maturities of long-term debt: the portion of long-term debt that is due in one year or less

Debit: the left-side entries in a double-entry accounting system

Debit card: a card that can be used to debit money directly from the customer's checking account

Debt financing: capital in the form of a loan, which must be paid back

Deductions: business and other expenses that reduce your income

Delivery cycle: the time it takes for inventory to be delivered; a ten-week delivery cycle means inventory takes ten weeks to arrive

Depreciation: allocation of the cost resulting from the purchase of a fixed asset over the entire period of its use

Design and development plan: section of a business plan that describes the product's design and charts its development within the context of production, marketing, and the company itself

Direct mail: any form of advertising material that's mailed directly to potential customers, including catalogs, brochures, letters, fliers, postcards, and newsletters

Direct writer: an insurance agent who represents one insurance company

Disability insurance: pays a fixed percentage of average earnings if the insured is unable to continue working due to disability

Discount rate: the actual percentage the merchant is charged per credit card transaction by the credit card company or bank; the discount rate is based on sales volume, risk, and other factors

Disguised dividend: total compensation in the form of salary, bonus, and perquisites that is judged to be excessive by the IRS

Distribution: means of getting product to the end user; describes entire process of moving product from factory to end user

Dividend: distribution of a portion of a company's earnings, determined by the board of directors, to a class of its shareholders

Dollar-control system: tracking system where sales receipts are compared with delivery receipts to determine the cost and gross profit margin on inventory items

Domain name: the words or phrases a user types into their browser to go to a website, such as www.[YourWebsiteName].com

Double-entry accounting: a system of accounting in which the total of all left-side entries is equal to and offset by the total of all right-side entries

Downline: the group of sales representatives that a given sales rep has recruited to join a multilevel marketing system; the rep receives a percentage of their sales

Due diligence: the process of investigating legal, financial, and other aspects of any business deal (such as buying a business) before the deal is completed

Easement: the right of an individual or entity to use the land of another individual or entity, usually for a specific purpose

Ecommerce: the process of conducting business on the internet and accepting credit cards or other forms of digital payments (using PayPal, for example)

Email auto responder: an automatic email response generated by the web server in response to a customer's email inquiry

Employee leasing company: company that administers personnel functions for clients and "leases" the client's employees back to them; also known as a professional employer organization (PEO)

Employee stock ownership plan: a plan that gives employees shares of stock in a company

Employment practices liability insurance: an optional part of workers' compensation coverage, this protects the corporation from being sued for acts of individual employees (such as in a sexual harassment case)

Empowerment zones/renewal communities: designated economically disadvantaged zones that offer state and/or federal tax breaks and other incentives to businesses that locate there

Engagement letter: letter of agreement between a lawyer or an accountant and his/her client that spells out the terms

Equity financing: capital received in exchange for part ownership of the company

Errors and omissions liability coverage: protects professionals, such as consultants or accountants, from damages resulting from an error or omission in their work

Escalator(s): term used to describe how a tenant's payment for rent or service shall increase

Ethernet: a packet-based wired transmission protocol primarily used in local area networking; Ethernet is the common name for the IEEE 802.3 industry specification that is often identified by its data transmission rate

Executive search firm: company that recruits executive, technical, or professional job candidates for client companies; also called recruitment firm or headhunter

Executive summary: the opening section of a business plan; describes the business, product, or service in brief

Expense: money spent for goods or services

Factors: companies that buy businesses' accounts receivable

Family and Medical Leave Act (FMLA): law requiring certain employers to give employees 12 weeks of unpaid leave for the birth or adoption of a baby or the serious illness of the employee or a close family member

FBML: Facebook Markup Language, a subset of HTML used to create or enhance a more personalized Facebook page and experience for the end user

Fee-for-service planner: financial planner who charges a fee for making recommendations on what you should do to achieve your financial goals

Financial budget: a projection of future financial performance

First in, first out (FIFO): method of inventory accounting that assumes items purchased first are sold first

Fixed assets: assets that are not bought and sold in the normal course of business but that are purchased for long-term use in the production or sales process

Flipcam: a handheld camera that's easy to use and fits in your pocket; it's affordable and starts up within seconds; to upload clips to a computer, simply flip out a USB connection and hook it up to your computer for video download

Focus group: type of primary market research where a group of potential customers (typically five to 12 of them) come together in an informal environment, under the guidance of a moderator, to discuss a product or service

Franchise disclosure document: a disclosure document franchisors are legally required to provide to prospective franchisees

Franchisee: the person who buys a system of doing business from a franchisor

Franchisor: a person or company that sells a system of doing business to franchisees and provides them with ongoing training and support

Friction feeder: feature on a letter-folding machine that pulls sheets through using a rubber wheel

Fulfillment: shipping and handling of sales orders

General ledger: the main records of the assets, liabilities, owner's equity, income, and expenses of an organization

General liability coverage: insures the business against accidents and injuries that happen on its premises as well as exposure to risk related to its products

Generational marketing: marketing to consumers based on social, economic, demographic, and psychological factors

Gross profit margin: the percentage of gross profit realized on goods sold after subtracting cost of goods sold from sales

Guarantee and surety agreement: for businesses with insufficient operating history or assets on which to base a loan, banks will require the loan to be guaranteed with your personal assets, such as the equity in your home, in a guarantee and surety agreement

Hard drive: one or more physical hard drives, each of which can be divided into several local hard drives, are the warehouses where you store multi-megabyte programs and gigabytes worth of data

Hold harmless and indemnify: a clause in a contract that protects one party to a business purchase from being held responsible for results of the other party's actions prior to the purchase

Holdover rent: an extremely high rent intended as a penalty to a tenant who continues to use or remain in possession of a leased premises beyond the lease term

House list: the mailing list a business develops in-house, comprised of names and addresses collected from current or potential customers

Income: money received for goods or services produced or as a return on investment

Income statement: a financial statement that charts revenues and expenses over a period of time

Independent sales organization: representatives from out-of-town banks that, for a commission, match businesses with banks that will grant them merchant status

Intangible asset: an asset of a business such as patents, franchise rights, and goodwill that does not physically exist but that has value to the business

Intellectual property: a nontangible property, such as a trade secret, patent, or trade name, to which one has legal rights

Internal control: a system that is designed to minimize the risk of financial loss due to incompetence or dishonesty of an employee or an outside bookkeeper

ISP: an acronym for internet service provider; see *online service*

Job description: an outline of how a job fits into the company, listing broad goals and basic responsibilities

Job specification: more detailed than a job description, this describes the job but also lists specific education, experience, skills, knowledge, or physical requirements for performing the job

Jogger: mechanism on a letter-opening machine that helps settle contents of envelopes so they don't get cut

Key person insurance: life insurance policy taken out on "key people" in the company, where the beneficiary is the company; proceeds are used to buy out the deceased's shares or ownership interest in the company

Laptop: portable devices that weigh between 3 and 8 pounds and typically offer all the computing power and functionality of a desktop computer, only they're portable and can run on battery

Last in, first out (LIFO): method of inventory accounting that assumes most recently purchased items are sold first; allows business owner to value inventory at the less expensive cost of the older inventory

Laundering: the practice of depositing one merchant's sales slips through another merchant's account; it is illegal in many states and prohibited by both Visa and MasterCard

LCD: liquid crystal displays have totally replaced CRT monitors; 17-inch LCDs are giving way to 19- to 27-inch screens for desktops, and up to 17-inch screens for laptops

Leasehold improvements: the construction, fixtures, attachments, and any and all physical changes and additions made to lease premises by the tenant (with or without the landlord's permission), or on the tenant's behalf by the landlord or a representative (e.g., subcontractor) of the tenant

Leasing agent: an individual who specializes in leasing commercial real estate, including office, retail, and industrial space; a leasing agent must work for a principal broker and be licensed

Letter of credit: a letter from a major customer showing that the customer has contracted to buy from you; can be used in establishing relationships with suppliers

Letter of intent: an agreement signed by both tenant and landlord prior to the lease, setting forth primary terms, conditions and considerations that are to form the basis of the lease

Liability: an obligation to another party

Liability of landlord provision: a lease clause severely limiting the landlord's liability for use of the building and office space by tenants, guests, employees, visitors, etc.

Life-stage marketing: marketing to consumers based on what they are doing at a given period in life, such as having children, buying a home, or retiring

Limited liability company (LLC): a hybrid business structure that combines tax advantages of a partnership with liability protection of a corporation

Link: a programming command that allows users to jump from one web page to another in one mouse click

LinkedIn: a social networking site that includes businesspeople from around the world, representing 300 million members in 200 countries, on which you can find, be introduced to, and collaborate with qualified people who can help you accomplish your business and professional goals

Liquidation preference: stockholders with liquidation preference are first in line to recover their investment if the company goes under

List broker: company that locates and arranges the rental of direct mail and email lists of potential customers to other businesses

List-rental company: company that rents mailing lists of consumer or business names and addresses

Loan agreement: written contract specifying terms of a loan

Long-term debt: the portion of external debt (usually from banks) that is due after one year

MacBook/MacBook Pro/MacBook Air: Apple's version of a laptop computer that runs the Mac operating system (and Windows as well)

Manual tag system: system of inventory tracking in which tags are removed from products at the time of the sale and then cross-checked against physical inventory later to figure out what was sold

Market rent: the current rental rates paid by tenants for like use (office space) in buildings of comparable size with similar qualities of construction and building amenities and comparable surrounding neighborhood characteristics and environment; term is often used in renewal clauses as the rent that will be paid if lease renewal occurs

Market research: research into the characteristics, spending habits, location, and needs of your business's target market, the industry as a whole, and the particular competitors you face

Market survey: the study of the spending characteristics and purchasing power of the consumers who are within your business's geographic area of operation

Markup: the percentage above the cost of producing a product that is charged to the customer

Merchant account: an account that allows a merchant to accept payment from customers via credit card; may be granted through banks or directly from a credit card company

MFD: multifunction devices are different combinations of printer, scanner, copier, and fax sharing the same color or black-and-white page description engine; usually based on laser or inkjet technology

Minority business enterprise (MBE): a business that is certified owned by a minority entrepreneur; certification can be obtained from a variety of organizations and is generally required for participation in government set-aside programs

Mission statement: a short written statement of your business goals and philosophies

Needs period: the sum of the count cycle, delivery cycle, and order cycle

Netbook: a scaled-down laptop computer that typically weighs less than three pounds and is used primarily for basic computing functions, such as word processing or surfing the net while on the go; cost is typically under $300, while a traditional laptop runs $500 to $1,500 or more

Network marketing: a system of doing business in which participants recruit other sales representatives as part of their "downline" and receive a commission based on sales of their downline as well as on their own sales

Nonbinding arbitration: form of ADR in which the arbitrator makes a recommendation that parties can accept or reject

Nonvoting stock: stock that pays a fixed dividend and is given preference ahead of common stockholders in the event of liquidation

Notes payable: short-term notes of less than one year either under lines of credit or with a stated repayment date

Occupational Safety and Health Administration (OSHA): federal agency that regulates workplace safety

Online service: a company that offers internet access, website hosting services, or an ecommerce turnkey solution, for example

Open-end lease: type of equipment lease in which if the value of the equipment at the end of the lease is less than the value established in the lease contract, the lessee must pay the difference

Open-to-buy: the amount budgeted for inventory purchases for a given period

Operating expenses: the day-to-day expenses incurred in running a business, such as sales and administration, as opposed to production

Operations and management plan: section of a business plan that describes how the business will function on a day-to-day basis

Optical drive: various combinations of CD, DVD, and Blue-ray optical drives come bundled with computers

Order cycle: the time it takes to process paperwork and place orders with your vendors for inventory

Outsourcing: practice of sending certain job functions outside a company instead of having an in-house department or employee handle them; functions can be outsourced to a company or an individual

Owner's equity: excess of total assets minus total liabilities

Package policy: insurance policy that combines several standard coverages, such as liability, burglary, and vehicle, in one package

Paid-in-capital: the additional amount paid for common stock over and above the value upon issuance

Paid search services: services that allow you to pay to have your website be part of the results of a user's query on a search engine site; there are three types: paid submission, pay-for-inclusion, and pay-for-placement

Partnership: a business that's unincorporated and organized by two or more individuals

Perquisites: a payment or profit received in addition to a regular wage or salary

Physiographics: the physical conditions related to aging, such as arthritis or nearsightedness

Pitch letter: an introductory letter sent to members of the media in an effort to get publicity for a business; sometimes this is a cover letter accompanying a press release

Plugins: consists of a computer program that interacts with a host application (a web browser or an email client, for example) to provide a certain, usually very specific, function "on demand"; also called add-in, add-on, snap-in, or extension

Point-of-sale (POS) software: software that records information about inventory, sales, and profits at the point of sale

Positioning statement: one- or two-sentence statement summarizing what differentiates your business from the competition

Preferred stock: stock that pays a fixed dividend and is given preference ahead of common stockholders in the event of liquidation

Premium: any free giveaway to customers (also called ad specialties); common premiums include key chains, caps, T-shirts, pens, and desk accessories

Prepaid legal plan: payment structure in which a client prepays a set monthly fee in return for a fixed amount of legal services per month (differs from monthly retainer in that services are more limited and relationship is not with one law firm, but with a prepaid legal service firm, which has relationships with many law firms)

Press kit: packet (typically a folder) containing a cover letter, a press release, photos, and additional information about a business; sent to members of the media to get publicity for the business

Press release: standard written notice sent to the media in an effort to get publicity for your business

Price comparison website: an online service that lets you compare multiple etailers and their product pricing; also displays consumer satisfaction scores or rankings so you can easily determine if an online company is reputable

Primary research: information you gain directly from the source, such as potential consumers

Private-label credit card: a credit card a merchant issues with his or her business's name on it

Promissory note: details the principal and interest owed on a loan and when they are due; it also outlines the events that would allow the bank to declare your loan in default

Property/casualty coverage: protects physical property and equipment of the business against loss from theft, fire or other perils; all-risk coverage covers against all risks; named-peril coverage covers only against specific perils named in the policy

Push email: an instant receipt capability for mobile workers that "pushes" email to an appropriate handheld device, such as a smartphone or tablet, as soon as a message lands on the server back at the office

Pyramid scheme: an illegal type of network marketing in which participants receive revenues primarily for recruiting others rather than for selling the company's products or services

Qualified retirement plan: a plan that meets requirements of the Internal Revenue Code and, as a result, is eligible to receive certain tax benefits

RAM: considerably slower and cheaper than cache, RAM is the bucket your computer's processor uses to hold vast amounts of data and program instructions while it works

Ratio analysis: the use of certain financial ratios to compare the performance of a business with years past and with industry peers

Replacement cost insurance: covers cost of replacing property at current prices

Rent abatement: a concession offered by a landlord as an inducement to tenants to lease office space; provides for a reduction of monthly rent by omitting a required payment for a specific number of months

Retained earnings: the cumulative amount of after-tax earnings less dividends paid that the owner draws over the life of a business

Safelist: a form of email marketing and advertising where the members have agreed to receive each other's messages

Sales: the gross amount of revenue generated by a business

S corporation: a type of corporation that provides its owners with tax treatment that is similar to a partnership

Script: hard copy of a website's contents that contains all text and graphics in sequential order, from the home page to the last page

Sealer: part of a postage meter's base that seals mail

Search engine: a navigational tool that lets web users type in a word or phrase to get multiple listings of sites containing that word or phrase

Secondary research: information that has already been gathered by other agencies or organizations and compiled into statistics, reports, or studies

Self-employment tax: tax paid by a self-employed person to help finance Social Security and Medicare

Sensitivity analysis: the process of changing financial variables in a financial budget to determine their potential impact on the company's future performance

Server: a host computer; see *web host*

Shopping cart program: software that allows the processing of online sales transactions

Slitter: type of letter-opening machine that slits the seam of the envelope

Smartphone: a handheld cell phone that integrates the functionality of a basic cell phone with that of a personal digital assistant (PDA) or other information device; used for voice calls as well as for wireless internet applications, such as surfing the web and email; can also handle applications, such as contact management and scheduling, budgeting, inventory, and more

Sole proprietorship: a business organization that is unincorporated and has only one owner

Social media: websites and applications that enable users to create and share content or to participate in social networking popular sites include Facebook, Twitter, LinkedIn, Pinterest

Stacker: part of a postage meter's base that stacks mail

Stock acquisition: a method of buying a business in which the buyer purchases the actual stock of the business

Tablet: a general-purpose computer contained in a touch-screen pane, including the iPad and Samsung Galaxy

Target market: the specific group of consumers or businesses you want to sell to

Temporary help company: company that recruits employees to work for client companies on a temporary basis

Tenant construction work letter: an addendum or attachment to the lease document that details the responsibilities of both the tenant and the landlord as they relate to the construction of the tenant's office space

Tenant improvements: the construction, fixtures, physical changes, and additions made to an office space for the benefit of the tenant by the tenant (usually with the landlord's permission) or on the tenant's behalf by the landlord or a representative (subcontractor)

Total counter: feature on a letter-folding machine that tells you how many sheets have been folded

Trade credit: billing a business for products with a grace period (typically 30 days) before payment is due

Trade-out: term used in the radio industry to refer to bartering products or services for airtime

Turnover: turning over your inventory means that 100 percent of original inventory has been sold

Twitter: a mini blog that streams people's posts in real-time; main focus of the site is it allows people to share and discover information that's happening now; your posts can spread across the globe to millions, immediately

Umbrella coverage: protects you for payments in excess of your existing coverage or for liabilities not covered in your other policies

Unique selling proposition: what differentiates your product or service from others of a similar type; what makes it unique

Unit-control system: system of inventory tracking in which bin tickets are kept with each product type, listing stock number, description, maximum and minimum quantities stocked, cost (in code) and selling price; these tickets correspond to office file cards that list a stock number, selling price, cost, number of items to a case, supply source, order dates, quantities, and delivery time

URL (universal resource locator): the accepted convention for specifying web addresses (domain names)

Vacuum feeder: feature on a letter-folding machine that pulls sheets through using air suction; good for coated and glossy paper stock

Venture capital: generally refers to institutional venture capital firms that invest other people's money and manage it for them; venture capitalists typically seek a high degree of involvement and expect a high rate of return in a short time; venture capitalists look for an idea that is well-formulated, well-documented, and well-protected

VoIP (voice over internet protocol): sends voice conversations over the internet using a packet-based outline as opposed to the analog circuit-switched technology used in PSTN (public-switched telephone network)

Voting stock: see *common stock*

Waiver: form that typically accompanies or is part of an employment application; when signed by applicant, it authorizes former employers or schools to release information about the applicant

Web host: any computer that's dedicated (always connected) to the internet and has access to the web

Widgets: a portable chunk of web code that can be installed and inserted into your website or blog, often taking the form of on-screen tools, such as clocks, event countdowns, stock market tickers, social site feeds, flight arrival information, daily weather, etc.

Workers' compensation insurance: covers medical and rehabilitation costs and lost wages for employees injured at work; required by law in all states

Index

A

B

O

P

T